SAN FRANCISCO MUSEUM OF MODERN ART: THE PAINTING AND SCULPTURE COLLECTION

SAN FRANCISCO MUSEUM OF MODERN ART: THE PAINTING AND SCULPTURE COLLECTION

SAN FRANCISCO MUSEUM OF MODERN ART

Introduction by Katherine Church Holland

Foreword by Henry T. Hopkins

HHH

THE PAINTING AND SCULPTURE COLLECTION

DIANA C. duPONT, KATHERINE CHURCH HOLLAND,

GARNA GARREN MULLER, AND LAURA L. SUEOKA

HUDSON HILLS PRESS, NEW YORK
in association with the San Francisco Museum of Modern Art

FIRST EDITION

© 1985 by the San Francisco Museum of Modern Art

Published in the United States by Hudson Hills Press, Inc., Suite 301, 220 Fifth Avenue, New York, NY 10001.

Distributed in the United States by Viking Penguin Inc.

Distributed in the United Kingdom, Eire, Europe, Israel, the Middle East, and South Africa by Phaidon Press Limited.

Editor and Publisher: Paul Anbinder

Copy-editor: Irene Gordon

Designer: Betty Binns Graphics/Betty Binns and Karen Kowles

Composition: U.S. Lithograph Inc.

Manufactured in Japan by Dai Nippon Printing Company

Library of Congress Cataloging in Publication Data
San Francisco Museum of Modern Art.
San Francisco Museum of Modern Art, the painting and sculpture collection.
Includes bibliographies and index.
1. Art—California—San Francisco—Catalogs. 2. San Francisco Museum of Modern Art—Catalogs. I. Du Pont, Diana, 1953–   . II. Title.
N740.5.A67   1985   709′.04′0074019461   84-11844
ISBN 0-933920-59-8

Contents

List of Colorplates   8

Foreword by Henry T. Hopkins   10

Acknowledgments   12

Introduction by Katherine Church Holland   14

Conservation of a Twentieth-Century Collection by James Bernstein   29
and Inge-Lise Eckmann

Highlights of the Collection   31
Essays and Colorplates   *32*
Documentation   *236*

Illustrated Checklist of the Collection   259

Index   394

Index of Donors   400

Photo Credits   402

Dedication

Elise Stern Haas has been guided throughout her life by the ideals of beauty, quality, and integrity. With these principles, which she drew from her mother, combined with the humor, spirit, and warmth that characterized her father, she has provided the San Francisco Museum of Modern Art, and many other important institutions, with leadership, energy, and vision.

It is singularly appropriate that this catalogue of the Museum's permanent collection of painting and sculpture be dedicated to Elise Haas, for it has been through her generosity in giving works of art to the Museum, and urging others to do so, that the collection has become so significant. She has enabled the San Francisco Museum of Modern Art to move to the front ranks of those museums whose collections have impact beyond their immediate geographic boundaries.

One of her special loves in the Museum is the Conservation Laboratory which she established in 1971. A result of her deep commitment to the care and preservation of treasured works of art, the conservation facility is not only vital to the Museum and its collections, it has also made the Museum far more valuable to the community it serves.

Beyond her energy and vision, however, it is her leadership that stands as Elise Stern Haas's permanent contribution to the Museum. After many active years on the Women's Board, she became a member of the Board of Trustees in 1955 and was subsequently elected president of the Board, serving in that capacity from 1964 to 1966. She established the Museum's first endowment fund, encouraged the continuing professionalism of the staff, and worked closely and effectively with both staff and trustees to ensure the growth and enrichment of the Museum. Her style of leadership, a combination of intelligence, graciousness, firmness, and elegance, is unparalleled, and it stands today as the hallmark of the Museum family.

In recognition of her many years of giving and leading, the San Francisco Museum of Modern Art dedicates this catalogue of the permanent collection of painting and sculpture, published at the time of the Museum's fiftieth anniversary, to Elise Stern Haas, with affection and gratitude.

HENRY T. HOPKINS

List of Colorplates

HENRI MATISSE
The Girl with Green Eyes (La Fille aux yeux verts), 1908   33
Portrait of Michael Stein, 1916   36
Portrait of Sarah Stein, 1916   37
The Slave (Le Serf), 1900–1903   39
Henriette, II (Grosse Tête; Henriette, deuxième état), 1927   41

KEES VAN DONGEN
The Black Chemise (La Chemise noire), ca. 1905–9   43

ANDRÉ DERAIN
Landscape, 1906   45

OTHON FRIESZ
Landscape (The Eagle's Beak, La Ciotat) (Paysage [Le Bec-de-l'Aigle, La Ciotat]), 1907   47

PABLO PICASSO
Street Scene (Scène de rue), 1900   49

JACQUES LIPCHITZ
Draped Woman, 1919   51

CONSTANTIN BRANCUSI
Blonde Negress (La Négresse blonde), 1926   53

GEORGES BRAQUE
The Gueridon (Le Guéridon), 1935   55
Vase, Palette, and Mandolin (Vase, palette, et mandoline), 1936   57

PABLO PICASSO
Jug of Flowers (La Cruche fleurie), 1937   59
Women of Algiers, E (Les Femmes d'Alger), 1955   61

JULIO GONZÁLEZ
Mask "My" (Masque "My"), ca. 1930   63
Small Sickle (Woman Standing) (Petite Faucille [Femme debout]), ca. 1937   63

AMÉDÉE OZENFANT
Still Life (Nature morte), 1920–21   65

MORGAN RUSSELL
Synchromy No. 3, ca. 1922–23   67

FRANZ MARC
Mountains (Rocky Way/Landscape) (Gebirge [Steiniger Weg/Landschaft]), 1911–12   69

MAX PECHSTEIN
Nelly, 1910   71

ALEXEJ JAWLENSKY
Woman's Head (Frauenkopf), 1913   74
Head: Red Light (Kopf: Rotes Licht), 1926   75

MAX BECKMANN
Landscape, Cannes (Landschaft, Cannes), 1934   77
Woman at Her Toilette, with Red and White Lilies (Frau bei der Toilette mit roten und weissen Lilien), 1938   79

PIET MONDRIAN
Church Façade/Church at Domburg, 1914   81

THEO VAN DOESBURG
Simultaneous Counter Composition (Contre composition simultanée), 1929   83

JOAQUIN TORRES-GARCIA
Constructivist Painting No. 8, 1938   85

LÁSZLÓ MOHOLY-NAGY
A IX, 1923   87

VASILY KANDINSKY
Brownish (Bräunlich), 1931   89

JOSEF ALBERS
Growing, 1940   91
Tenayuca, 1943   93
Study for Homage to the Square, 1972   95

GIORGIO DE CHIRICO
The Vexations of the Thinker; The Inconsistencies of the Thinker (Les Contrariétés du penseur), 1915   97

PAUL KLEE
Red Suburb (Rotes Villenquartier), 1920   99
Nearly Hit (Fast getroffen), 1928   101

JEAN (HANS) ARP
Head and Leaf; Head and Vase (Tête et feuille; Tête et vase), 1929   104
Objects Arranged According to the Laws of Chance III; Symmetrical Configuration (Objets placés selon les lois du hasard III; Configuration symétrique), 1931   105
Human Concretion without Oval Bowl (Concrétion humaine sans coupe), 1933   107

JOAN MIRÓ
Painting (Peinture), 1926   109
Dawn Perfumed by a Shower of Gold (L'Aube parfumée par la pluie d'or), 1954   111

SALVADOR DALI
Oedipus Complex, 1930   113

YVES TANGUY
Second Thoughts (Arrières-pensées), 1939   115

ALBERTO GIACOMETTI
Annette VII, 1962   117

JOSEPH CORNELL
Untitled (Pink Palace), ca. 1946–48   120
Untitled (Window Façade), ca. 1950–53   121

GEORGIA O'KEEFFE
Lake George, 1922   123
Black Place I, 1944   125

ARTHUR DOVE
Silver Ball No. 2, 1930   127

EDWARD HOPPER
Bridle Path, 1939   129

JOHN STORRS
Study in Form (Architectural Form), ca. 1923   131

JOSEPH STELLA
Bridge, 1936   133

CHARLES SHEELER
Aerial Gyrations, 1953   135

STUART DAVIS
Deuce, 1954   137

FRIDA (FRIEDA) KAHLO
Frieda and Diego Rivera, 1931   139

DIEGO RIVERA
The Flower Carrier, 1935   141

MORRIS GRAVES
Bird Maddened by the Sound of Machinery in the Air, 1944   143

MARK TOBEY
Written over the Plains, 1950   145

ARSHILE GORKY
Enigmatic Combat, 1936–37   147

JACKSON POLLOCK
Guardians of the Secret, 1943   149

CLYFFORD STILL
Untitled, 1945   151
Untitled, 1951–52   154
Untitled, 1960   155

ROBERT MOTHERWELL
Wall Painting No. 10, 1964   157

WILLEM DE KOONING
Woman, 1950   159

HANS HOFMANN
Table—Version II, 1949   161

MILTON AVERY
Clear Cut Landscape, 1951   163

MARK ROTHKO
Untitled, 1960   165

SAM FRANCIS
Red and Pink, 1951   167

PHILIP GUSTON
For M., 1955   169
Red Sea; The Swell; Blue Light, 1975   171–73
Back View, 1977   177

RICHARD DIEBENKORN
Berkeley #57, 1955   179
Cityscape I, 1963   181
Ocean Park #54, 1972   183

ELMER BISCHOFF
Orange Sweater, 1955   185

DAVID PARK
Man in a T-Shirt, 1958   187

NATHAN OLIVEIRA
Adolescent by the Bed, 1951   189

FRANK LOBDELL
March 1954, 1954   191

HASSEL SMITH
2 to the Moon, 1961   193

ROBERT RAUSCHENBERG
Collection, 1953–54   195

JASPER JOHNS
Land's End, 1963   197

CLAES OLDENBURG
Blue Legs, 1961   199

JAY DeFEO
Incision, 1958–61   201

BRUCE CONNER
Looking Glass, 1964   203

PETER VOULKOS
Sevillanas, 1959   205

JOHN MASON
Untitled *(Monolith)*, 1964   207

KENNETH PRICE
L. Red, 1963   209

LARRY BELL
Untitled, 1969   211

ROBERT IRWIN
Untitled, 1968   213

FRANK STELLA
Adelante, 1964   215
Khurasan Gate (Variation) I, 1969   217

ELLSWORTH KELLY
Red White, 1962   219

ROBERT MANGOLD
Red X within X, 1980   221

WILLIAM T. WILEY
Ship's Log, 1969   223

RICHARD SHAW
Melodious Double Stops, 1980   225

WAYNE THIEBAUD
Display Cakes, 1963   227

ROY DE FOREST
Country Dog Gentlemen, 1972   229

MANUEL NERI
Mary and Julia, 1980   231

ROBERT HUDSON
Out of the Blue, 1980–81   233

ROBERT ARNESON
California Artist, 1982   235

Foreword

THE AMERICAN ASSOCIATION OF MUSEUMS, an organization that includes members from every major history, science, and art museum in the United States, defines museums as "non-profit organizations dedicated to the collecting, preservation, study, display and educational use of objects." Clearly, museum professionals believe the permanent collections of their institutions to be the backbone that supports the flesh of other museum programs, including temporary exhibitions. It is therefore an extraordinary pleasure to bring this new, impressive catalogue of the painting and sculpture collection of the San Francisco Museum of Modern Art to our members and friends.

Since the publication of our first catalogue in 1970, the collection has undergone impressive growth in both quantity and quality. Important new works representing the Fauve, German Expressionist, Dada, Surrealist, and American Modernist schools, as well as almost every post-World War II movement have helped strengthen the historical continuity and visual flow of the museum's holdings. This does not signify that the collection is now comprehensive, but the number of gaps has narrowed and the acquisition of a few key works—a Vasily Kandinsky from the period 1908–16, a Piet Mondrian from the years 1921–44, a Pablo Picasso from the 1920s through the 1960s, a Jackson Pollock drip painting—would add immeasurable strength to the collection.

In addition to augmenting schools through works by different artists, we have also chosen to select a few artists for in-depth representation, such as Josef Albers, Joseph Cornell, and Clyfford Still, three major American artists of similar age but very different sensibilities. It is our belief that the study of works from different periods in the lives of individual artists will allow the observer to better understand the creative process and to develop sensitivity toward diversity of thought and execution.

While this publication focuses on painting and sculpture, other areas of the permanent collection have been expanding as well. Photography, our most comprehensive collection, has nearly doubled since the arrival of Van Deren Coke as head of the Photography Department in 1979. Because of their specialized nature, our holdings in photography will be documented in a separate catalogue. Works on paper, including drawings and prints,

have also seen steady growth, although at a slower pace than other areas. We have even acquired our first architecture and design objects, among them a pair of elevator doors from Louis Sullivan's Stock Exchange Building in Chicago, a Charles Eames plywood chair, and furniture designed by the California architect R. M. Schindler.

Acquisitions for the permanent collection follow closely the stated purpose of the museum, which is to collect, preserve, exhibit, and educate in the area of twentieth-century art in all its manifestations. Special emphasis is placed on works that were considered to be innovative at the time of their creation. For this reason, the gift or purchase of a European drawing from the early part of the twentieth century is as meaningful as the acquisition of a painting produced in America in the current decade, as long as each work contributes a new visual experience to the collection and its audience.

Works of art are acquired by the Museum through gift, purchase, or bequest. The director and curatorial staff present objects recommended for acquisition to the Accessions Committee, a standing committee of the Board of Trustees. After this body has considered and approved proposed acquisitions they are presented to the full board for final approval. Of the approximately three hundred thousand dollars available each year for the purchase of works of art, two-thirds are allocated for the purchase of painting and sculpture, one-quarter is earmarked for the purchase of photographs, and the balance is divided among all the other disciplines.

Gifts from donors have become the primary source of museum acquisitions, not only here but across the country. Favorable federal tax laws, ever-increasing values placed on works of art, and a significantly greater number of collectors combine to make the presentation of works of art from a private collection to a tax-exempt institution a desirable practice. Even before such beneficial laws were in place, a number of San Francisco collectors and groups supported the Museum through major donations of works of art or purchase funds. Many labels throughout the collection affirm the generosity of Albert M. Bender, W. W. Crocker, William L. Gerstle, Peggy Guggenheim, Mr. and Mrs. Walter A. Haas, Harriet Lane Levy, Charlotte Mack, Wilbur D. May, Jeanne Reynal, Mrs. Henry Potter Russell, Mrs. Ferdinand C. Smith, the T. B.

Walker Foundation, and the Women's Board (later the Modern Art Council) of the Museum. In more recent years, gifts from Mr. and Mrs. Harry W. Anderson, Rena Bransten, Mr. and Mrs. E. Morris Cox, Mrs. Walter A. Haas, Jr., the Hamilton-Wells Collection, Mr. and Mrs. William C. Janss, Clyfford Still, Mrs. Paul L. Wattis, and the Charles H. Land Family Foundation, as well as bequests from Joseph M. Bransten and Marian W. Sinton should be noted.

More than one hundred objects from the collection have been selected for special emphasis in this publication. Ranging from a Fauve painting by Henri Matisse to a wry self-portrait in clay by the California artist Robert Arneson, they represent not only the scope of our holdings, but also its unique pockets of strength in clusters of works by Josef Albers, Jean Arp, Richard Diebenkorn, Philip Guston, Clyfford Still, and others. The research and writing were accomplished by the Research/Collections Department of the Cowell Research Center, an ongoing department of the Museum that focuses on documenting and managing the permanent collection. Headed by Katherine Church Holland, Director, and Garna Garren Muller, Associ-

ate Director, the department staff includes Diana C. duPont, Marcy Reed, and Laura L. Sueoka. Heralding the opening of a landmark exhibition of the permanent collection which will fill our entire gallery spaces, the publication of this impressive catalogue is the first event in a year-long celebration of the fiftieth anniversary of the San Francisco Museum of Modern Art and is enduring evidence of our commitment to the permanent collection, its care, presentation, and continued growth.

This catalogue is dedicated to Elise Stern Haas, a significant patron of the museum. We greatly appreciate the generosity of Richard and Rhoda Goldman and the grandchildren of Elise Haas—Betsy and Roy Eisenhardt, Susan and Michael Gelman, Douglas Goldman, M.D., John Goldman, Richard W. Goldman, Michael S. Haas, Robert and Colleen Haas, Peter and Joanne Haas, Walter J. and Julie Haas, and Margaret Haas Jones—who provided the funding for this publication.

Henry T. Hopkins
Director

Acknowledgments

THIS PUBLICATION celebrating the painting and sculpture collections of the San Francisco Museum of Modern Art is the realization of a project that began in January 1979 with the formation of the Research/Collections Department, a separate entity within the Museum dedicated not only to the documentation of objects held by the institution, but also to the development of the collection. Throughout this undertaking we have experienced the encouragement, cooperation, and guidance of numerous individuals who shared our belief in the importance of the permanent collection. We wish here to express our gratitude.

Throughout every phase of this project we have enjoyed the warm support of Henry T. Hopkins, Director, who aided with suggestions and allowed us the freedom to accomplish our goals.

We are particularly indebted to Michael McCone, Associate Director for Administration, whose multiple talents and spirited enthusiasm helped us in innumerable ways, from raising funds to constructing the walls in our first office. We also extend our appreciation to Karen Tsujimoto, Curator, whose warmth, intelligence, and professionalism have served as a model for us all.

In 1981 the Research/Collections Department and the Registration Department were joined to form one large department with one long title, the Research/Collections and Registration Department. Since that time, the members of the staff have worked together in an atmosphere of mutual respect and affection. We gratefully acknowledge the invaluable contributions of Pamela Pack, Assistant Registrar, who coordinated the photography of the works in the collection; Carol Rosset, Associate Registrar/Permanent Collection, who aided in locating and measuring objects; Debra Neese, Associate Registrar/Exhibitions, who provided reinforcement whenever it was needed; and Marcy Reed, who supplied insight, advice, and extraordinary organizational skills.

The San Francisco Museum of Modern Art is fortunate in having a staff composed of creative, committed individuals. Of those not yet mentioned, many were particularly supportive during every stage of documentation and preparation for publication. The Conservation Laboratory, co-directed by James Bernstein and Inge-Lise Eckmann, contributed by helping us gain access to the versos of can-vases, deciphering indistinct inscriptions, and allowing us to utilize their records and photographs of objects treated in their facility. The installation crew, ably headed by Julius Wasserstein, helped immeasurably by moving and installing difficult objects. Eugenie Candau, Librarian, and her staff located myriad sources during our research.

We are especially indebted to Anne Munroe, Curatorial Assistant, for her calm, good-humored, and absolutely faultless direction of the publication process. Toby Kahn, Museum Bookshop Manger, provided cogent advice on the initial conception of the catalogue, and Suzanne Anderson, Graphic Designer, supplied valuable suggestions for its design. We are also grateful to Cecilia Franklin, Controller, for her support and astute budgetary advice.

During the final months of research and preparation we were fortunate to have the invaluable assistance of several individuals who gave freely of their time and talents. Maryse Posenaer and Rebecca Solnit, both of the graduate program of the University of California at Berkeley, and Sheila Van Every of the Center for Museum Studies, John F. Kennedy University, San Francisco, and Barbara Lee Williams executed much of the final research on the highlighted objects. Ms. Posenaer was also instrumental in translating titles and supplying foreign editing skills, while Ms. Solnit aided Diana duPont in initial editorial tasks. We also gratefully acknowledge the contribution of Judith McKinney, who assisted in the final compilation of material for publication.

Several individuals made particularly valuable additions to our documentation of the collection. Janice Parakilas undertook the foundation research of our Josef Albers holdings, Julie Berger Hochstrasser investigated paintings by Matisse, and Elizabeth Armstrong delved into the background of our works by German Expressionists. Steven High and Katherine Kleekamp contributed to various aspects of the project: facilitating the sculpture inventory, substantiating the artists' biographical data, and providing backup information for several highlighted works. Randi Fisher gathered key facts from New York galleries. Mark Ashworth and Paul Shank eased the photography of oversized or complex objects in the collection. Carolyn Birmingham, project director for the Cowell Research Center computer project, added immeasurably by introducing us to relevant data- and word-processing systems and by suggesting useful approaches to the organization of information.

The majority of the transparencies, and many of the black-and-white photographs of works in the collection, were taken by photographer Don Myer, who accomplished this monumental task with infinite patience and good humor.

The initial gathering of information, inventorying, and basic research were accomplished with the enthusiastic aid of numerous volunteers, interns, and work/study students. For their special contributions we acknowledge Anne Boreta Baxter, Sara Weinstein Beames, Melissa Broadus, duPont Coleman, Celeste Connor, Judith Eurich, Sharon Glick, Esin Gökner, Jeannette Hoorn, Ann Kasper, Judith Kays, Peggy Keeran, Deirdre Leber, Evie Lincoln, Andrea Liss, Beth McBride, Patricia Marra, Kerry O'Shea, Katherine Silbergh, Karna Slifer, Patrice Wagner, Denise Wakeman, Tessa Wilcox. We also gratefully recognize the help of Laura Adler, Martha Carleton, Carla Chammas, Michele De Alcuaz, Barbara De Cristofaro, Becky Ellis, Lou Grachos, Peter Hempel, Yvonne Jacques, Lee Kennedy, Mardi Leland, Dawn Morton, Mariette Muller, Mary Murray, Presh Pattee, Penny Pritzker, Susan Rieder, Shelley Schreiber, Ann Shumway, Lynn Baer Smith, Beau Takahara, Jane Wickware.

We are particularly grateful to staff members of institutions and libraries and to independent professionals who provided invaluable information and assistance. Special thanks go to Paula Baxter, Research Librarian, The Museum of Modern Art, New York; Noel S. Frackman; Marcel Giry, Université de Franche Comté, Besançon; Linda Roscoe Hartigan, Curator, Joseph Cornell Study Center, National Museum of American Art, Washington, D.C.; Janice Hellman, Fine Arts Museums of San Francisco, California Palace of the Legion of Honor; Lewis Kachur, The Solomon R. Guggenheim Museum, New York; Curt Klebaum, Castelli Feigen Corcoran, New York; Dr. Klaus Lankheit, Institut für Kunstgeschichte, Universität Karlsruhe; Michael Parke-Taylor, Curator of Exhibitions, Norman Mackenzie Art Gallery, University of Regina, Saskatchewan; Margit Rowell, Musée National d'Art Moderne, Centre Georges Pompidou, Paris; Roberta K. Tarbell; Nancy J. Troy, Northwestern University, Evanston, Illinois; Robert P. Welsh, University of Toronto.

Finally, we would like to express our profound gratitude to the sponsors of this project, who so generously provided the funds to accomplish the research reflected by this catalogue and for its publication. The research phase was supported by The National Endowment for the Arts, the Andrew W. Mellon Foundation, and the S. H. Cowell Foundation, which also funded our working facility and computer project. Publication funds were donated by Betsy and Roy Eisenhardt, Susan and Michael Gelman, Douglas Goldman, M.D., John Goldman, Richard and Rhoda Goldman, Richard W. Goldman, Michael S. Haas, Peter and Joanne Haas, Robert and Colleen Haas, Walter J. and Julie Haas, Margaret Haas Jones in honor of Elise Stern Haas.

Katherine Church Holland
Garna Garren Muller
Laura L. Sueoka
Diana C. duPont

Introduction

ON THE EVENING OF FRIDAY, January 18, 1935, four thousand enthusiastic art lovers, artists, patrons, and socialites converged on San Francisco's Civic Center to celebrate the opening of a new cultural institution, the San Francisco Museum of Art. Wined and dined in the vast sculpture rotunda that was the focal point of the galleries located on the fourth floor of the War Memorial Veterans' Building, the crowd was treated to a panoply of exhibitions ranging from contemporary art by Bay Region artists to Old Master drawings, from Gothic tapestries to Impressionist and Post-Impressionist paintings. Documented in the local newspapers, where it shared space with such timely topics as various matrimonial scandals and actress Grace Moore presiding over the annual automobile exposition, the inauguration of the Museum was viewed as a populist as well as a social event. One account headlined, "Galleries Stay Open Evenings/Art for All Is Purpose of New Showplace," while another emphasized the importance of the Museum to local artists by noting that of the fourteen new galleries, ten were devoted to the work of Californians.

The catalogue published on that occasion classified the institution as "The Museum of the San Francisco Art Association" and, in fact, its roots were inextricably linked to this artist organization. The Association, founded in 1871, had specified as its goals the "promotion and encouragement of art in the community."[1] To those ends it founded the School of Design in 1874. Armed with an impressive array of plaster casts, de rigueur for academic instruction in the nineteenth century, the school flourished, training both budding artists and teachers in such disciplines as mural painting, anatomy, and commercial design, in addition to the more traditional drawing, painting, and sculpture. In 1893, the former residence of railroad magnate Mark Hopkins located atop Nob Hill was deeded in trust by Edward F. Searles to the University of California for the Art Association. This signaled the founding of the Mark Hopkins Institute of Art, which encompassed both the School of Design and an exhibition space, the Mary Frances Searles Gallery. The Nob Hill facility was reduced to ruins in the earthquake of 1906, but within a year, a temporary building was erected on the site and the school and galleries were re-opened, under the name of the San Francisco Institute of Art.

The advent of the 1915 Panama-Pacific International Exposition distracted the populace of San Francisco from the grim realities of the war in Europe and fired the imagination and enthusiasm of the people who flocked to the "Rainbow City" by the bay. The Exposition's art extravaganza was housed in the Palace of Fine Arts, a Beaux-Arts composition featuring a towering rotunda flanked by a giant colonnade that curved along the edges of a reflecting lagoon. Designed by Bernard R. Maybeck, a San Francisco architect whose fame virtually derives from this project, the actual art gallery contained vast expanses of skylit open space within which rooms were constructed for exhibition purposes. Unlike the other buildings in the Exposition whose structures were composed of wood, the Palace of Fine Arts had an underlying steel network which was overlaid with lath and an ephemeral skin of nephilinic plaster.[2]

The far-reaching art display which, despite transportation difficulties brought on by wartime conditions, comprised both a national and a substantial international section, introduced to the Bay Area the work of the Italian Futurists—Giacomo Balla, Umberto Boccioni, and Carlo Carrà—as well as a few examples of the modern art of France in paintings by Pierre Bonnard, Edgar Degas, Claude Monet, and Edouard Vuillard. The United States section was the most comprehensive, with several American Impressionists represented including John Twachtman, Childe Hassam, and James McNeill Whistler. The success of this exhibition stimulated the Art Association to expand its facilities. The temporary building on Nob Hill was proving inadequate for both classroom and exhibition needs and a permanent new space was sought. Merging with the energetic San Francisco Society of Artists, the Association set about raising funds to achieve its goals. In its original constitution, dated 1871, the Association had asserted that "the object of this organization shall be to maintain a museum of fine arts and applied arts, and to provide for and conduct exhibitions."[3] In the years following the Panama-Pacific International Exposition the Association set out to do just that.

In 1916 the Art Association began mounting temporary exhibitions and annual juried shows of work by local artists in the Palace of

[1] John I. Walter, "The San Francisco Art Association," *Illustrated Catalogue of the Post-Exposition Exhibition in the Department of Fine Arts, Panama-Pacific International Exposition* (San Francisco: San Francisco Art Association, 1916), p. vii.

[2] Kenneth H. Cardwell, *Bernard Maybeck* (Santa Barbara and Salt Lake City: Peregrine Smith, 1977), p. 141.

[3] Constitution of the San Francisco Art Association as quoted in *San Francisco Art Association Bulletin*, vol. 1, no. 7 (November 1934), p. 2.

Fine Arts. The interest ignited by the initial Exposition exhibition continued, and by the end of the first fifteen months, total attendance reached 225,000. In 1921, the San Francisco Museum of Art was legally incorporated. Contained within its articles of incorporation was a statement of purpose in which the Museum trustees affirmed their intention to operate both as a fine arts museum and as an art gallery, and to act as representatives, in both fiduciary and proprietary matters, of the San Francisco Art Association. But it was obvious that the Maybeck-designed gallery would not suffice for long. Already the plaster exterior was deteriorating alarmingly, and the vast interior spaces were impossible to secure properly or to maintain financially. In 1925, beset by monetary and political problems, the Museum closed its doors.

In the meantime, shortly after the end of World War I, the Art Association and the Musical Association of San Francisco formulated plans to build both a symphony hall and an art museum. After raising over one and one-half million dollars, an insufficient amount to finance their construction scheme, the cultural groups joined with the politically powerful veterans organizations, but succeeded in raising only an additional $370,000. Aided by the influence of the veterans and local newspapers, the plan's backers were able to place a bond issue for the War Memorial complex on the June 1927 municipal ballot. With the passage of that bond issue, land was purchased and plans for the construction of two structures—a performing arts hall and a single edifice to house both the arts and veterans organizations—were solidified. Arthur Brown, Jr., an architect trained in the Beaux-Arts tradition, who had distinguished himself in earlier plans for San Francisco's City Hall and Civic Auditorium, was chosen to design both structures. Construction began in the summer of 1931, and by 1932 the twin granite structures were completed. It was not, however, until 1934 that the policies for the Museum were formulated and arrangements made to occupy the space.

Critical among these policies was the board's decision that the Museum establish as its primary goal the presentation of contemporary art and its sources in recent history. This constituted a radical shift in policy, for when the Art Association operated the San Francisco Museum of Art in the Palace of Fine Arts, it was the only art museum in the city. The M. H. de Young Memorial Museum was at that time a general institution, filled with natural history specimens and nineteenth-century armor, while the California Palace of the Legion of Honor was merely a twinkle in the eyes of Mr. and Mrs. Adolph Spreckels. By 1934, however, the de Young had completed three wings of its permanent building and had determined to focus on the work of masters of past centuries. The Legion, patterned after the Légion d'Honneur in Paris, had been built in Lincoln Park in 1924 and dedicated to the exhibition of the art of France. In light of these developments, the board determined to center programming in the new museum on temporary exhibitions featuring the work of artists of the region, pivotal figures in contemporary art of national and international reputation, and historical surveys which would provide context and promote understanding.

AND so the direction of the Museum was set. In November 1934, Grace L. McCann Morley was named to head the fledgling institution, which finally moved into its new quarters on the fourth floor of the Veterans' Building on January 2, 1935. The first two weeks of 1935 were hectic ones for the tiny staff. Morley, her assistant, Claudia Davis, and a bare-bones installation crew labored, sometimes around the clock, to prepare the galleries and write and edit the inaugural catalogue. Within a little over two weeks, six exhibitions were organized, assembled, and installed in the fourteen new galleries.

The group of inaugural shows reflects the diversity of subject matter that would characterize the Museum's exhibitions up to World War II. As a museum publication later reflected: "It was obvious that what San Francisco then needed was to catch up by means of a systematic exhibition program with all that had been developing in art since the 70's when Impressionism introduced a new manner of seeing and painting. . . . They endeavored to follow closely the growing edge of contemporary art, to stimulate the sympathetic interest and judgment of an informed public as a contribution to encouraging art development, locally and in general."[4] With a mighty swoop, the opening exhibitions covered huge swaths of historical ground, providing the individual museum-goer with

[4]"Exhibitions," *San Francisco Museum of Art Quarterly Bulletin*, Series 2, vol. 2, nos. 1–2 (1953), p. 5.

a broad spectrum of new visual experiences and historical data.

Foremost among these shows was the *Fifty-fifth Annual Exhibition of the San Francisco Art Association*. Continuing a tradition established by the Association in the 1870s, this juried annual not only reflected the scope of current trends in the area, but also, to a considerably lesser extent, gathered examples of work by artists across the country. While the preponderance of work was strongly conservative—portraits, landscapes, and still lifes, all quite realistically rendered—certain stylistic tendencies were evident. The impact of Diego Rivera's visit to San Francisco in 1930, when he executed murals at both the California School of Fine Arts (now the San Francisco Art Institute) and the San Francisco Stock Exchange, was reflected in the plethora of broadly defined, Giottesque figures, while vestiges of Cubism, particularly the brand brought by Hans Hofmann when he came to teach at the University of California at Berkeley in 1930, were also apparent, especially in work by artists living on the east side of San Francisco Bay.

In her quest to educate the Bay Area art community and the public at large, Grace Morley assembled a selection of work by French painters beginning with the Impressionists, drawn mainly from New York galleries, seasoned with a dollop of loans from local collections. Masterworks by Claude Monet, Camille Pissarro, Pierre-Auguste Renoir, Vincent van Gogh, Paul Gauguin, and Paul Cézanne provided an in-depth look at the contributions of these pioneering artists who, as Dr. Morley noted in her catalogue introduction, "have furnished a point of departure for so many leading artists of today."[5]

The balance of the exhibitions on view during those first months in the new facility offered the public additional facets of visual data. An exhibition featuring Chinese sculpture, bronzes, ceramic, jade, and textiles—originally conceived of as the impetus for a permanent display of Oriental art—surveyed the history of that country's art forms. A veritable inventory of master printers and printmaking techniques of the Western world was the subject of yet another show. Each period and process of the medium was presented and examined, from the tortured precision of Martin Schongauer, through the visionary linearity of Albrecht Dürer, the

romantic drama of Rembrandt, and the formal harmonies of Whistler's etchings of the late nineteenth century. A similar approach was taken in an exhibition of drawings from the collection of Mrs. W. H. Crocker which ranged from the Rococo *fêtes galantes* of Fragonard and Boucher to the Impressionist renderings of Edgar Degas and the sober work of Puvis de Chavannes. Finally, this incredibly rich mélange was topped off by a group of Gothic and Renaissance tapestries, also from the Crocker Collection, which were displayed on the sweeping walls of the great central hall.

Since the majority of the loans to these premiere exhibitions came from local collectors, a brief review of the offering illuminates the tenor of artistic taste prevalent at the time. Works created in past centuries were readily available, particularly those from eras popular with collectors at the turn of the century when wealthy San Franciscans filled their ornate Victorian residences with painted scenes of grazing sheep from the Barbizon School, rosy-cheeked goat girls by nineteenth-century Dutch and German artists, and Japanese and Chinese objects in every medium. There were a few daring collectors who ventured forth into more recent trends. Represented in the group of modern French paintings, for example, were significant works by Gauguin and van Gogh from the William W. Crocker Collection. Mr. Crocker, the first president of the Museum's Board of Trustees, and his sister, Mrs. Henry Potter Russell (Helen Crocker), the first president of the auxiliary Women's Board, had been instrumental in the founding of the Museum and were singularly active in the burst of growth that took place during its first decades. Two other San Franciscans, William L. Gerstle and Albert M. Bender, collected the work of local artists, as well as the graphic and easel work of the Mexican painters, particularly Diego Rivera. A few local individuals, such as Sarah and Michael Stein and Harriet Lane Levy, lived in Paris for a time and acquired the work of Henri Matisse and Pablo Picasso, among others, but they were exceptions to the rule. On the whole, regional holdings of works of quality relevant to the Museum's purposes were extremely limited.

It was on this base that Grace Morley and the Board of Trustees of the San Francisco Museum of Art began to build. Following the

[5] Grace L. McCann Morley, *Opening Exhibition* (San Francisco: San Francisco Museum of Art, 1935), p. 4.

16

opening shows was the presentation of the prestigious European section of the *1934/1935 Carnegie International*, organized by the Carnegie Institute of Pittsburgh, which included not only examples of contemporary European trends, but also a broad sampling of American developments.[6] In her introduction to the well-illustrated catalogue which the Museum published for the occasion, Dr. Morley stated: "Disagreements and discussions are healthful and it is well that in such an exhibition artists, critics and public should join in considering what is authentic and significant. San Francisco will find this showing of the Carnegie a vital experience, and one that is bound to be profitable and instructive."[7] Hardly controversial by present-day standards, the show did contain a sampling of comparatively recent works of the twentieth century: a lyrically classical painting by Picasso of the early twenties, a powerfully rendered allegory by Max Beckmann, and two figural paintings by Matisse dated around 1919. Surrealism was present in works by both Giorgio de Chirico and Salvador Dali, while Futurism was represented by Carlo Carrà and Gino Severini. The selections of work by such American artists as John Sloan and Reginald Marsh, Raphael Soyer and Peter Blume, Max Weber and Millard Sheets reflected the nationalism and eclecticism of the time as well as presenting their own individual visions of the American scene.

Subsequent exhibitions in 1935 explored further aspects of modern art and its derivations. The crucial contribution of African art to the development of Cubism in the first decade of the century was recognized in an extensive selection of objects drawn from that continent, while the impact of the Mexican muralists, particularly Diego Rivera, was acknowledged in a pair of exhibitions. Over sixty abstractions by Vasily Kandinsky were installed near mid-year, the first of many shows drawn from Galka Scheyer's extraordinary holdings of works by the Blue Four (Kandinsky, Lyonel Feininger, Alexej Jawlensky, Paul Klee). And, near year's end, early regional explorations of Surrealism were examined in a show comprising the work of the Post-Surrealists, a Los Angeles-based group of artists centered around Lorser Feitelson and Helen Lundeberg. By the close of December, seventy exhibitions had been mounted by the tiny professional staff and over 150,000

visitors had taken the facility's single elevator to its fourth-floor galleries.

FROM the inception of the Museum in its new space until the full impact of World War II was felt on the West Coast, the exhibition policy continued unmodified, in both pace and variety. The second year began with an exposition of paintings, sculpture, and graphics by Henri Matisse. Given the far-reaching scope of the Museum's programming, this in itself is not surprising; the fact that most of the works were borrowed from two prime local collections make it of unique significance. Of the thirty-five paintings and sculptures exhibited, twelve were owned by Sarah and Michael Stein, who in 1903 had left San Francisco for Paris, where they became interested in the work of Matisse and Picasso. Their historic, lifelong friendship with Matisse, whose work they subsequently collected almost exclusively, began in 1905. Harriet Lane Levy, a close friend of the Steins and owner of eight of the objects exhibited, had lived in Paris from 1907 to 1910 and, like her compatriots, had purchased the work of the progressive young artists of the day. Not only did this jewel-like exhibition of Matisse's work instill in the minds of the visiting public the joyous spirit of the artist's color and compositional harmonies, but it demonstrated as well the possibilities of private collecting. Happily for the Museum, many of the works exhibited eventually made their way into the permanent collection where they today form a critical nucleus of an exceptional Fauve collection.

A cluster of paintings by Yves Tanguy shown concurrently with those of Matisse reiterated the biomorphic strain of Surrealism introduced in a show of Joan Miró's work the previous year. These organic visions supplied the kernel that produced the interest and subsequent work in Abstract Surrealism by regional artists during the following decade. Nurturing this direction was another exhibition in 1936, *Cubism and Abstract Art*, organized by the Museum of Modern Art, New York, which traced abstraction through its various phases from Cubism to Rayonism, in painting, sculpture, graphics, furniture, architecture, and stage design.

By 1937 the annual number of exhibitions had climbed to over one hundred and national and international trends continued to balance local programming. While selections

[6]The American works were selections from the American section of the *1934/1935 Carnegie International*; this supplement was included only at the San Francisco Museum of Art showing of the exhibition tour.

[7]Grace L. McCann Morley, *1934/1935 Carnegie International: European Section* (San Francisco: San Francisco Museum of Art, 1935), n.p.

of paintings by Paul Klee and Alexej Jawlensky, both from Galka Scheyer, were shown early in the year, the highpoints of 1937 were two diverse choices. A landmark showing of the oils, watercolors, drawings, and prints of Paul Cézanne organized by the Museum drew over thirty thousand visitors to the galleries during its five-week run. Counterbalancing this quietly powerful show was an "adventure in a strange field of art," the Museum of Modern Art's survey *Fantastic Art, Dada, Surrealism*, which traced fantasy throughout the centuries, from the end of the Middle Ages to 1936. Meandering through the visions of Hieronymus Bosch and Albrecht Dürer, Francisco Goya and Honoré Daumier, the exhibition then brought the viewer into the modern versions of fantastic and irrational art, Dada and Surrealism, with examples of the work of Man Ray, Marcel Duchamp, Alberto Giacometti, and many others.

By the end of 1937, the impact of the three-year-old Museum was being felt by the populace. For city dwellers, the galleries were centrally located, in the heart of the Civic Center with convenient evening hours for the working person. The broad range of subject matter appealed to diverse groups, from those interested in Cézanne to those anxious to know the most recent trends in New York, from architects looking to the latest in building and landscape ideas to designers interested in innovations in furnishings and textiles. Even the art of children was exhibited regularly.

In addition to historical surveys and contemporary expositions, for the artists there were exhibitions of their peers, providing both a forum and a commercial outlet. A policy established at the outset stated that one-quarter to one-third of the exhibitions would be devoted to the work of local artists. This included the competitive annuals of the Art Association, intermittent shows of work by the members of other art organizations, single-person exhibitions, and selections of objects that reflected current local trends. In 1937, the Museum instituted the Art Association gallery, which featured an ongoing series of one-person shows of work by members of that organization.

A grant of $7,500 in March 1937 enabled the Museum to initiate an outreach program. Four series of six exhibitions each, centered around such themes as "The Language of

Art," "The Picture Making Process," and "Personalities of Modern Art," were produced, using graphics and reproductions of the "world's greatest paintings." Accompanied by relevant didactic material, the shows toured towns in rural areas of northern California. Paralleling this campaign to bring art to the people was a related program of bringing people to the art. Slide presentations, dance demonstrations, lectures, and hands-on workshops were organized at the Museum expressly to provide the public with a personal experience of all forms of art. These programs were only a part of an energetic program of education which has flourished throughout the five decades of the Museum's existence.

The energetic pace and broad scope of programming continued until late in 1939, when public attention was drawn away from the Museum and toward the buildings rising on a flat puddle of land in the midst of San Francisco Bay—Treasure Island, home of the Golden Gate International Exposition. In response to this diversion, Grace Morley scheduled only one "blockbuster" exhibition for 1940, the landmark *Picasso: Forty Years of His Art*, organized by the Museum of Modern Art, New York. A voluminous retrospective of painting, sculpture, drawings, and prints which traced Picasso's career from his early years in Barcelona, the exhibition culminated in *Guernica*, the artist's elegy for a Spanish tragedy. The enthusiastic public response was documented by the following item, which appeared in over fifty newspapers of the day: "ART VISITORS STAGE SIT-DOWN STRIKE. San Francisco: This city believes it can claim the honor of having staged the first art sit-down strike in history. When the 10 o'clock closing hour at the San Francisco Museum of Art, where an extensive collection of Picasso's paintings were being shown, arrived for the last day of the display, 1,300 visitors sat down and refused to leave till they had had their fill."[8] Offsetting the overwhelmingly positive critical response to the show was one lone critic, Alex Cordellis, who wrote in his column, "The Pulse of the Public": "Picasso's exhibit of monstrosities at the San Francisco Museum of Art is typical of the decay of European civilization. Nobody should miss it on that ground alone."[9] Grace Morley *had* said she wanted controversy and public participation!

[8] Quoted in *San Francisco Museum of Art Quarterly Bulletin*, vol. 1, no. 4 (Summer 1940), p. 20.
[9] *San Francisco News*, date unknown; quoted in *San Francisco Museum of Art Quarterly Bulletin*, loc. cit.

THE year 1940 marked the fifth anniversary of the Museum, and, in commemoration, Dr. Morley organized an exhibition consisting entirely of work held in private collections in San Francisco and its environs. In her foreword to the exhibition catalogue, Dr. Morley noted, "This exhibition emphasizes the Museum's constant preoccupation with art today in its full diversity, and the fact that all the Museum is and does is rooted intimately in the lives of the people of this community."[10] The makeup of the exhibition is interesting, for unlike the opening shows in which works drawn from private collections in the area were limited to objects created during the nineteenth century or very early in the twentieth century, the 1940 selection displayed the full range of modern art, from the early-nineteenth-century Romanticism of Eugène Delacroix to the atmospheric late work of Monet, and from turn-of-the-century paintings by Matisse to contemporary work of John Ferren, George Grosz, and Yves Tanguy.

When the Museum had opened in 1935, its collection had consisted of only a few paintings and a cluster of nineteenth- and early-twentieth-century prints. In fact, the organization's policy dictated that the energy of the institution should go into temporary exhibitions, rather than in the direction of collection enhancement. However, one magnanimous board member singlehandedly established the nucleus of a collection which multiplied both in number and stature for the succeeding fifty years. Albert M. Bender, the son of an Irish rabbi, had come to San Francisco before 1883 and had prospered in the insurance business. A congenial man generous to all with his time, energy, and financial resources, Bender collected and dispersed to worthy institutions great quantities of books and works of art, as well as sums of money which, though not extremely large, nonetheless were of great importance to the recipients, whether individuals or organizations. Not concerned with accumulation, he distributed his wealth equally to needy artists or shopkeepers and to a variety of cultural, educational, and philanthropic organizations. The San Francisco Public Library, the California Historical Society, libraries at Stanford University and Mills College and the California School of Fine Arts were but a few of the organizations that benefited from the generous spirit of Albert Bender.

For the San Francisco Museum of Art, the growth of the permanent collection that took place in its first five years was almost exclusively the result of Bender gifts. Not one to give a single object at a time, Bender's first gift consisted of thirty-six works, bestowed barely a week after the Museum opened. Bender donations of twelve lithographs by José Clemente Orozco and twenty drawings by Diego Rivera, joined by the donation of Rivera's masterful *The Flower Carrier*, provided the impetus not only for a far-reaching collection of Latin American works, but also for an aggressive program of exhibitions centered around the paintings and graphics of Rivera, Orozco, David Alfaro Siqueiros, and their contemporaries. Bender also contributed to the genesis of the Museum's photography collection with the gift of a penetrating portrait of Orozco by Ansel Adams, not only a strong example of Adams's incisive eye and technical skill, but a documentary enhancement of the growing holdings of Latin American work as well.

For Albert Bender art meant personal enjoyment as well as aesthetic appreciation, so most of his purchases and gifts were by artists from the immediate region or those he met on sojourns abroad. Frequently, too, he purchased objects from exhibitions held at the Museum. Capping the Museum's first year of operation was an exhibition of objects in the permanent collection, which consisted almost exclusively of the gifts of Albert Bender. For nineteen years thereafter, the closing exhibition of each year was dedicated to the works either given by him, purchased through the accessions fund he established, or bequeathed to the Museum when he died in 1941. In all, through his generosity, the permanent collection acquired over 1,100 objects, some of the most significant works in the collection.

The shadow of World War II reached the Museum in 1942, affecting it deeply. Because of the institution's location on the vulnerable West Coast, it was considered too dangerous to borrow or exhibit works of great historic or monetary value. Moreover, shipping space going across the country toward the Pacific theater was at a premium, thus forcing the curtailment of large exhibitions in favor of more compact ones. In September 1942, San Francisco began undergoing dimouts, which necessitated blackouts of some galleries and the evening closing of those which could not

[10] Grace L. McCann Morley, *Contemporary Art: Fifth Anniversary Exhibition* (San Francisco: San Francisco Museum of Art, 1940), p. 5.

be darkened; the public, concerned about possible occupation of the coast, was leery of venturing out on dark evenings. Adjusting its programming to those grim days, the Museum presented fewer serious lectures and classes in favor of lighter activities, particularly those affording direct experiences with art: workshops in printmaking and photography, classes in flower arranging, film series, and travel programs. The exhibition schedule, diminished because of wartime staff shortages, interspersed lighthearted fare, such as Douglas MacAgy's circus spectacle *Sawdust and Spangles* of 1942, with shows exploring artists' responses to the war and its effects.

At the close of the war, representatives of the Allied countries met in the War Memorial Veterans' Building to discuss the formation of the United Nations, and the Museum's galleries were taken over as office space for the conference delegates and the press. Within just a few days, the staff had relocated its activities and a few examples of the permanent collection to a location on Post Street in the downtown area, just off Union Square. Although drastically reduced in physical space, the temporary facility was easily accessible and, with its large display windows, gave the Museum great public visibility. Remaining there from March through July 1945, the Museum put on six exhibitions, including one-person showings of the work of Marsden Hartley and Lyonel Feininger. This foray into a new area of the city planted the seed idea of Museum branches, which was put into action in the following decade.

B Y 1946, the war years behind them, the Museum staff resumed programming in full force, and the public returned in great numbers. In 1935, the determination to bring the public up to date in its knowledge of historical and contemporary trends and movements had been stated as Museum policy. Now, eleven years later, it was felt that the groundwork had been laid. The public was well versed historically, and the pressure to educate, represented by over one hundred shows per year, was no longer necessary. Thus, in 1946, sixty-five exhibitions were hung; in 1947, there were sixty-seven; and by 1950, the count was down to fifty-eight. Emphasis was definitely on current art developments, a focus that had basically been in effect since the beginning of the decade. The policy of

devoting one-quarter to one-third of the exhibitions to local artists remained in force. With the San Francisco Art Association annuals continuing, broad cross-sections of regional tendencies were well represented, while the work of individual local artists was examined in a series of shows featuring the work of one person or small groups of artists. The Art Association gallery was discontinued in favor of integrating similar presentations into regular museum programming.

Most important to the exhibition program of the forties, however, was the predominance of shows that revealed the great strides being made by artists on the East Coast. From the 1941 show of Arshile Gorky's paintings to the exhibition of Jackson Pollock's gestural, mythic works in 1945, from Mark Rothko's biomorphic paintings shown in 1946 to Robert Motherwell's automatist abstractions exhibited the same year, each exhibition demonstrated to both the artists in the community and the public at large the dramatic breakthroughs being made in New York. The works spoke to a local artist population poised on the edge of change and anxious for new visual experience. Complementing the innovative programming of Jermayne MacAgy at the California Palace of the Legion of Honor and the spirited experimental attitude brought to the California School of Fine Arts by Douglas MacAgy in 1945, these shows contributed greatly to the burst of artistic creativity that occurred in San Francisco during the second half of the forties.

A similar emphasis was placed on exhibitions featuring the work of Latin American artists. Inspired by the influence of the Mexican muralists in the thirties, Grace Morley expanded this area of programming to include shows centered around individual artists or surveys of work produced in such countries as Peru, Argentina, Cuba, and elsewhere. This focus on the work of artists from countries to the south continued throughout Morley's tenure, accompanied by a like emphasis on acquiring works by these figures.

The forties also saw a great upswing in exhibitions featuring photography. Building upon the foundation established in 1935 when Peter Stackpole's dramatic photographs of the construction of the San Francisco Bay Bridge were exhibited, and continuing through subsequent shows of the achievements of Brett Weston and Edward Weston (1937), the Museum branched out into presentations of the work of Alma Lavenson (1942, 1948), Barbara Morgan (1945), Paul Strand (1946), Minor White (1948), and Julia Margaret Cameron (1949). These were interspersed, particularly early in the decade, with group presentations and two thematic exhibitions organized by the Museum of Modern Art, New York, *Masters of Photography* (1944) and *New Photographers* (1947), presenting the images of Harry Callahan, Aaron Siskind, and Frederick Sommer.

The swing toward the contemporary scene in exhibition programming during the forties was accompanied by a similar shift in direction in the growth of the collection. While Bender gifts continued to flow during 1940 and 1941, albeit in diminished numbers, they were joined by other key donations and modest purchases. Diego Rivera's eerily surreal *Landscape* was given by friends of the artist in 1940; in 1941, Gorky's *Enigmatic Combat*, which had been shown in the artist's one-man show, was presented by mosaicist Jeanne Reynal. After the death of Albert Bender in 1941, the Museum was the recipient of a significant group of objects from his estate, including twenty-six photographs by Ansel Adams, Brett and Edward Weston, Imogen Cunningham, and others. During the war, acquisitions slowed, although several pivotal works were acquired, Picasso's *Jug of Flowers* and Paul Klee's *Nearly Hit* purchased in 1944, and Jackson Pollock's *Guardians of the Secret* bought in 1945. Gifts from William L. Gerstle, longtime trustee and patron, of works by Bay Area artists were received through 1946, augmented by the key donation of Kandinsky's *Brownish* in 1944. Peggy Guggenheim, whose Art of This Century gallery was showing avant-garde work to an East Coast audience, strengthened West Coast holdings by the gift of Mark Rothko's seminal *Slow Swirl by the Edge of the Sea* in 1946, followed the next year by Untitled (*Self-Portrait*) by Clyfford Still and *The Numerous Family* by Max Ernst.

Museum activities in the forties were greatly enhanced by two new programs, Art in Cinema and the Rental Gallery, both initiated in 1946. Art in Cinema, founded by Frank Stauffacher, explored the film medium as an art form, both in programs which played to enthusiastic museum audiences and in an accompanying publication which contained articles on the art film and creative filmmaking. The Rental Gallery, organized by the Women's Board,

was the first of its kind in the country. By making art available to members on a rental basis, the Museum encouraged collecting by individuals and provided an additional commercial outlet for regional artists.

MOVING into the fifties, the Museum sported a recently renovated physical plant which included refurbished galleries, new classrooms, auditorium facilities in the sculpture court, and an enlarged bookshop; it also enjoyed a rapidly increasing membership and a director with an international reputation. In celebration of fifteen years of growth, an anniversary exhibition was organized which counterpoised work by Bay Area painters and sculptors with a selection of modern European art drawn from local collections. In a pair of articles written for the *San Francisco Chronicle*, Grace Morley reflected on the great changes that had occurred not only within the institution, but also in the entire direction of art, moving from the tightly representational approach evident in 1935 to the prevalence of abstraction, expressionism, and diversity in 1950. Posing the question of the Museum's part in this artistic evolution, Dr. Morley wrote, "It [the Museum] does believe its exhibitions have played their part for artists and public, and that its supplementary activities have helped to create an informed and interested public."[11] And in the *Quarterly Bulletin*, this attitude was reaffirmed: "The Museum deliberately endeavors to remain close to the growing edge of creative art of our time with the intention of bringing it to public attention while it is still news. It seeks to recognize quality while it is still only a promise and a prophecy."[12]

This attitude prevailed throughout the ensuing decades, but during the early years of the fifties more immediate concerns were pressing. Despite popular exhibitions such as *Henri Matisse*, organized by the Museum of Modern Art, New York, and exhibited in 1952, rising costs and limited income were making programming more and more difficult. Dr. Morley organized the United States representation at the *III Bienal* in São Paulo, Brazil (1955), which was then shown at the Museum in 1956, and retrospectives of Hans Hofmann and Stuart Davis, as well as a major show of Theodore Roszak's sculpture were presented in 1957.

While the exhibition program was being

[11] Grace L. McCann Morley, "The San Francisco Museum of Art Celebrates a Birthday," *San Francisco Chronicle, This World*, January 22, 1950.

[12] *San Francisco Museum of Art Quarterly Bulletin* (January 1950), p. lxxxi; also published in *Magazine of Art*, vol. 43, no. 1 (January 1950).

curtailed during the fifties, the permanent collection was thriving. The objects acquired by Harriet Lane Levy during her visits to Paris earlier in the century were gifted by bequest in 1950. Comprising forty-six works, the bequest included fifteen paintings, drawings, sculptures, and prints by Henri Matisse, seven graphic works and an early painting by Picasso, and one or two works each by Henri Manguin, Paul Cézanne, and Pierre-Auguste Renoir, among others. Significant for its historical value as well as for the outstanding quality of individual pieces, the Levy collection strengthened the Museum's holdings enormously, enabling visitors to experience not only the work of single artists in depth, but the breadth of a specific period in art history as well.

During the same year, the first gifts from Charlotte Mack were received, a pair of heads by Alexej Jawlensky, one painted in 1913, the other in 1926. In 1952 these were augmented by single works by Georgia O'Keeffe and Henry Moore, and in 1953 by significant watercolors by Paul Klee and John Marin. Mrs. Mack's generosity continued throughout the decade, culminating in the pivotal early painting by Josef Albers, *Growing*, given in 1959.

Other areas of the collection saw notable growth during this mid-century period. Sixty-eight photographs and photogravures spanning Alfred Stieglitz's entire career—from the early experimentation in Germany to an extraordinary set of his "equivalents," examples of his New York impressions, sensitive portraiture, and images of Lake George— were acquired by purchase and through gift of Georgia O'Keeffe in 1952. In 1955, the Women's Board began the first of what were to become nearly annual gifts with *Clear Cut Landscape*, by American poetic colorist Milton Avery. W. W. Crocker sustained his support of the Museum with periodic gifts: paintings by Matisse (1949) and Georges Rouault (1955), sculpture by Georges Braque and Henry Moore (1954, 1957), among others. The enthusiastic patronage of Mrs. Walter Haas began with the gift of two photographs by Edward Weston in 1938 and continued through the fifties, culminating in 1958 in the donation, with Agnes E. Meyer, of the great Brancusi bronze *Blonde Negress*. These acquisitions of national and international importance were supplemented in 1955 by a gift

from Jermayne MacAgy of a group of eleven drawings, paintings, and sculptures by Bay Region artists who had worked in various forms of Abstract Surrealism during the decade of the forties.

A unique era in the history of the San Francisco Museum of Art came to a close in August 1958 when Grace L. McCann Morley stepped down as director. Reflecting on her twenty-three-year tenure, Dr. Morley commented, "I tried to make the museum the intermediary between the artist and the public."[13] She left a public well versed in the art of the twentieth century and open to new trends and an artist community which had evolved from provincial conservatism to an internationally recognized position of dynamic leadership in contemporary expression. She had built up the permanent collection from a handful of paintings and prints to over three thousand objects which mirrored not only the goals of the Museum, but the tastes and interests of the Museum supporters as well. And she left an institution which closely involved its supporters, be it through its membership of well over four thousand subscribers, the Rental Gallery program, the schedule bursting with programs of poetry readings, dance presentations, lectures, films, and workshops, or its exhibitions which invited controversy and commitment.

GRACE MORLEY was succeeded as director by George D. Culler who had come to the Museum from the Art Institute of Chicago. Leading the institution through a difficult period of inadequate funding, Culler's program featured historical movements of the twentieth century. Retrospectives of Arthur Dove (1959), Vasily Kandinsky and Emil Nolde (1963), *The Precisionist View in American Art*, organized by the Walker Art Center (1961), and *Years of Ferment: The Birth of Twentieth Century Art 1886–1914*, from the UCLA Art Galleries (1965) were presented during his tenure. *The Art of Assemblage*, organized by the Museum of Modern Art, New York, which included the work of Bruce Conner, Jess (Collins), and Edward Kienholz, was shown in 1962. This exhibition put into historical context the underground group of California artists in both the northern and southern areas of the state who were creating compelling works of art from aggregates of urban detritus.

Both architectural design and the decora-

[13] Peter Hann, "Director of Museum Gives Inspiration to Modernists," *San Francisco Examiner*, February 10, 1950.

tive and functional arts were given an important place in Culler's exhibition schedule, while art of the region continued to be shown, although more sporadically. Two major surveys of local trends, *The Arts of San Francisco*, were presented in 1962 and in 1964. The first of the shows took the form of a summer-long, all-arts extravaganza featuring painting, sculpture, prints, graphic design, photography, architecture, crafts, dance, and theater. Reflected in both regional overviews was the shift away from both the abstract and the figurative toward a new individualism, the development of personal statements, idiosyncratic symbols, and new materials.

Funds for acquisitions were meager during the early sixties and the collection expanded almost exclusively through gifts, particularly those generated by members of the Board of Trustees. Most important was the group of seven major paintings gifted by Wilbur D. May in 1964. Included among these works, which remained in Mr. May's possession until his death in 1982, were the pivotal *The Black Chemise* by Kees van Dongen, Picasso's 1955 painting, *Women of Algiers, E,* and a 1937 painting by Klee, as well as works by Pierre Bonnard, Joan Miró, Marc Chagall, and André Derain. Crucial, too, were the works chosen by the Women's Board for the collection. Frank Lobdell's volatile *April 1959,* partnered with Niles Spencer's cerebral still life *The Desk* of 1948, entered the collection in 1959, while subsequent years saw the gifting of a strongly emotive painting by Theodore Stamos, followed by strong regional examples by David Park, Nathan Oliveira, Gordon Onslow Ford, Richard Faralla, James Weeks, William T. Wiley, Roy De Forest, and Arlo Acton. The establishment in 1961 of the T. B. Walker Foundation Fund, which in 1984 remains a vital source of moneys for acquisition, enabled single major purchases to be made annually beginning with Karel Appel's *Waiting for Us*, representative of the European expressionist group CoBrA, followed the next year by a collage by Corrado Marca-Relli, and, in 1963, Alexander Calder's delicately balanced mobile *Four Big Dots.*

The permanent collection of photography gained greatly by the addition in 1963 of the Henry Swift Collection, a group of eighty-five prints by original members of f/64: Ansel Adams, Imogen Cunningham, Willard Van Dyke, Brett Weston, Edward Weston, John Paul Edwards, and several other related photographers. This acquisition gave needed depth to a collection that had been growing by twos and threes since its inception in 1935.

I N 1965 George Culler resigned to take over the post of president of the Philadelphia College of Art, and Clifford R. Peterson, who had been serving as controller, assumed the title of acting director while a search was undertaken to find a new director. Late the following year, Gerald Nordland, who had been head of the Washington Gallery of Modern Art, arrived to assume the directorship.

Facing the challenges of limited funding, a timeworn physical plant, and a board accustomed to making operating as well as policy decisions, Nordland set about reinforcing ties with sister institutions, with whom the Museum could share major exhibitions, and increasing exhibitions organized in-house with accompanying publications. In 1967 the noteworthy Paul Klee retrospective, organized by the Solomon R. Guggenheim Museum, was presented, followed by two shows in 1969 from the Museum of Modern Art, New York, *The Sidney and Harriet Janis Collection* and the engrossing, eccentric *The Machine as Seen at the End of the Mechanical Age,* organized by K. G. Pontus Hulten. Nordland augmented these loan exhibitions with a program of one-person or group exhibitions of regional work. The curatorial staff organized retrospectives of Jeremy Anderson's sculpture, the paste-ups of Jess (Collins), the graphic work of Nathan Oliveira, and a three-person presentation of the sculpture of Jerrold Ballaine, Fletcher Benton, and Sam Richardson, as well as summer-long exhibition marathons centered around the theme of the arts in San Francisco. This interest in the art of the Bay Area was crowned by two related and extensive exhibitions developed by curator John Humphrey which traced the origins and development of northern California trends since World War II: *On Looking Back: Bay Area 1945–1960* (1968) and *Just Yesterday* (1969). Nordland initially organized exhibitions of East Coast artists Al Held, Gene Davis, and Leon Polk Smith in 1968, Edward Corbett and Robert Natkin in 1969. In 1970, he was joined by newly appointed curator Suzanne Foley who organized *Unitary Forms: Minimal Sculpture by Carl Andre, Don Judd, John McCracken, Tony Smith.*

By the late sixties Museum attendance was averaging well over two hundred thousand visitors per year and the galleries and public facilities were in dire need of refurbishing. After gaining possession of the third floor, the Museum embarked on an ambitious million-dollar project which restructured the fourth floor, turning a pre-existent members' room and adjacent classrooms into spacious galleries which added over thirty-five percent more space for exhibition; the galleries were outfitted with ceilings featuring flat skylights with custom glass filtering out rays detrimental to the works of art, new lighting systems, floors, and carpeting. Offices were relocated to the third floor and in their place a café, board room, and gallery for the exhibition of small-format works was constructed. A conservation laboratory, storage area for works on paper, and a new library were created on the third floor, while the bookshop, formerly nestled next to the elevator on the fourth floor, was expanded and moved to the ground floor. As culmination of Nordland's term as director and celebration of the expansion and renovation, four exhibitions were organized by the museum: *Peter Voulkos: Bronze Sculpture; Richard Diebenkorn: Paintings from the Ocean Park Series; Ansel Adams: Recollected Moments;* and *A Decade of Ceramic Art: 1962–1972, From the Collection of Professor and Mrs. R. Joseph Monsen,* each accompanied by an ambitious documentary catalogue.

While funding for accessions continued to be restricted during these years, the collection did experience some redefinition, not only through acquisitions, but also by exchanges and prudent trimming of works outside the collection's purview. The 1967 acquisition of Robert Motherwell's *Wall Painting No. 10* led to gifts of over twenty drawings from the artist's *Lyric Suite* in 1967 and two paintings from his Open Series in 1969. Maintaining its tradition of donating important works, the Women's Board expanded the collection in late 1966 with a vertically striped work by Washington colorist Gene Davis, a bronze floating figure by Gaston Lachaise in 1967, a stained canvas by Helen Frankenthaler in 1968, followed in 1969 by an expressive wooden sculpture by Alvin Light and a fiberglass wall relief by Tom Holland in 1970. The Museum's collection of ceramic sculpture by Californians was initiated in 1969 with a slab sculpture by James Melchert, quickly joined by works by Peter Voulkos, Robert Arneson, Richard Shaw, Robert Hudson, as well as a monolithic stoneware cross by John Mason, presented to the collection by the Women's Board in 1971. The major sources of accessions funding, the T. B. Walker Foundation Fund and the William L. Gerstle Fund, the latter restricted to the purchase of works by living American artists, provided the means to acquire seminal objects by Ellsworth Kelly, Nathan Oliveira, Ilya Bolotowsky, John Altoon, William T. Wiley, Philip Guston, and Manuel Neri, while the 1968 purchase of Frank Stella's *Adelante,* a silver shaped canvas dated 1964, marked the genesis for a pocket of works representing that one artist.

Curator John Humphrey increasingly turned his attention to the exhibiting and collecting of photographs. Between 1966 and 1973, he added to a foundation collection that consisted of photographs primarily by West Coast artists, representative selections of work by Aaron Siskind, Berenice Abbott, and Harry Callahan. Expanding the holdings of California photographers were newly acquired prints by Edmund Teske, Edward Weston, Vilem Kriz, Don Worth, and Ansel Adams, capped by a grouping of ninety-three prints spanning the entire career of Wynn Bullock.

At the end of 1972, Gerald Nordland resigned to assume the directorship of the Frederick S. Wight Gallery at the University of California, Los Angeles, and again the Museum conducted an extensive search for a new leader, leaving the daily operations and programming of the institution in the hands of deputy director Michael McCone and the curatorial staff. This interim period lasted one year, during which the collection saw expansion particularly in the sphere of work by Bay Area artists, such as Bruce Conner, Jess (Collins), James Melchert, and Wayne Thiebaud, and in objects by California ceramic sculptors David Gilhooly, Robert Hudson, and Richard Shaw. The rapidly developing interest in the area of ceramic sculpture was paralleled in the exhibition programming that featured a show, curated by Suzanne Foley, which chronicled the clay works produced during a year-long partnership between Hudson and Shaw.

IN January 1974, Henry T. Hopkins assumed the position of director. Formerly the head of the Fort Worth Art Museum,

Hopkins was not new to California; he had attended graduate school at the University of California, Los Angeles, and had been on the staff of the Los Angeles County Museum of Art for seven years. Hopkins quickly determined new directions for both the exhibition program and the status of the permanent collection and launched the Museum on a course of renewed activity, excitement, and expansion.

The exhibition schedule was strengthened not only by the quality of shows brought in from outside the institution, but also by the number of exhibitions organized by the Museum's staff. By 1976, plans were in place and the course of Hopkins's leadership became evident. Impressive exhibitions from outside institutions began with *Poets of the Cities: New York and San Francisco*, which examined the underground movement on both coasts during the fifties and early sixties; this was followed in short order by a Cy Twombly retrospective, the product of the Institute of Contemporary Art at the University of Pennsylvania, Pittsburgh.

The year of the country's bicentennial opened at the Museum with the remarkable exhibition celebrating Clyfford Still's gift of twenty-eight monumental paintings. In a liberally illustrated catalogue, Hopkins tracked the history of the gift and not only provided invaluable insights into the thought processes and concerns of the artist, but also examined the path by which a collection developed. The Museum of Modern Art's scholarly study of the brilliant colorists of the first decade of the twentieth century, *The "Wild Beasts": Fauvism and Its Affinities*, was the highlight of mid-year, while the opening of the fall season was heralded by the Museum's contribution to the Bicentennial, *Painting and Sculpture in California: The Modern Era*, which scrutinized the lines of creativity throughout the state since the advent of Modernism and documented the seminal figures and salient galleries, institutions, and collectors that contributed to the development of individual artistic expression on the West Coast of the United States. This tribute to the state was continued in *A View of California Architecture: 1960–1976*, a report on the trends and variety in contemporary building design.

Exhibitions continued to increase not only in scope, quality of documentation, and size, but in quantity as well. In 1975, gallery space was opened on the third floor, enabling the ongoing installation of small-scale works from the permanent collection. This construction project also included the renovation of the gallery for the Clyfford Still paintings and an enlarged bookstore facility. But growth was not limited to the public areas. A grant from the Irvine Foundation made possible the renovation and enlargement of storage and shop facilities, adding new spaces outfitted with sophisticated environmental controls for the housing of paintings and sculpture, as well as renovated receiving and carpentry areas.

The balance between exhibitions organized by sister institutions and in-house staff has continued throughout the ensuing years. While 1977 saw the "blockbuster" show of Robert Rauschenberg's work organized by the National Collection of Fine Arts (now the National Museum of American Art) of the Smithsonian Institution, and *America 1976*, the United States Department of the Interior's salute to the nation's parks, it also marked the continuation of presentations originated in the Museum in *Collectors, Collecting, Collection: American Abstract Art since 1945*, a survey of both private collections and the Museum's holdings. A survey of George Segal's evocative sculpture, organized by the Walker Art Center and exhibited in the spring of 1979, was followed by Judy Chicago's controversial *The Dinner Party*, which drew great numbers of new visitors to the Museum. The fall of that year featured a cross-section of European sculpture between the two world wars juxtaposed with *Space/Time/Sound—1970s: A Decade in the Bay Area*, curator Suzanne Foley's look at conceptual and performance art in the Bay Area.

The photography program, which had been steadily active throughout the seventies, took a leap forward with the appointment of Van Deren Coke early in 1979 as director of the Photography Department. Assuming responsibility for the exhibiting and collecting activities of the department, Coke immediately became active in both aspects. Beginning with *Fabricated to Be Photographed*, his look at images of manipulated situations, Coke went on to organize a multiplicity of exhibitions which offered fresh approaches not only to contemporary photography, but also to areas of historical interest, such as *Photography's Response to Constructivism* (1980), an investigation into the impact of Constructivism on the world of photography, and *Avant-Garde Photography in Germany: 1919–1939*, his landmark historical review, which opened in December 1980 and circulated throughout the country and to Europe during the following two years. These memorable shows were interspersed with other investigations of contemporary and historical photography with Dorothy Martinson's *Recent Color* (1982) and *The Nude in Photography* (1981), and Coke's *The Markers* of 1981 and *Weegee* of 1984, as well as *Beyond Color* (1980) and *Photography in California: 1945–1980* (1984), organized by Louise Katzman. In all, approximately one-third of all exhibitions installed annually have focused on photography under Mr. Coke's leadership.

The decade of the eighties opened with an even more intense schedule of exhibitions and related activities and with an ever-increasing number of internally generated presentations. Henry Hopkins's pivotal retrospective of Abstract and Figurative Expressionist Philip Guston opened to critical acclaim in January 1980, then circulated throughout the United States and internationally. Examining Guston's contribution to gestural abstraction and to the emerging concerns of expressive figuration, the show was of profound interest within the art world and to the public at large.

The following summer saw the initiation of the Museum's biennial survey of contemporary American attitudes, *Twenty American Artists*. Sponsored by Collectors Forum, a support group comprising individuals interested in developing private collections, this exhibition reported on the current work of photographers as well as painters and sculptors and presented the work of Christo, Jim Dine, Agnes Martin, and Lucas Samaras, among others, culminating in the magnificent Tony Smith sculpture *Tau*, which filled the newly restored sculpture court. This tradition was continued in the 1982 biennial, *20 American Artists: Sculpture 1982*, in which newly appointed associate director of art, George Neubert, reviewed the contemporaneous work of artists working in sculptural form, including a monumental Georgia O'Keeffe spiral piece and examples by Isamu Noguchi, Bruce Nauman, and others. The summer of 1984 saw the third in this series when Henry Hopkins and assistant curator Dorothy

Martinson examined expressive figuration in paintings, sculpture, drawings, prints, and photography in *The Human Condition: SFMMA Biennial III*.

Three major exhibitions marked the 1981 season. Co-organized by the San Francisco Museum of Modern Art and the Solomon R. Guggenheim Museum, *Expressionism: A German Intuition, 1905–1920* was an extensive, scholarly study of German Expressionism from its first stirrings to the aftermath of World War I. The quiet, contemplative still lifes of Italian painter Giorgio Morandi, assembled by the Des Moines Art Center, were exhibited in the fall, while the recent history of American art was dealt with in a retrospective of the work of Edward Hopper, circulated by the Whitney Museum of American Art.

While the Museum's close relationship with the Solomon R. Guggenheim Museum was sustained in 1982 with the showing of *Kandinsky in Munich: 1896–1914*, this was a year that truly highlighted the accomplishments of the Museum's own curatorial staff: of thirty-eight shows presented, twenty-nine were organized in-house. Particularly noteworthy were a thoroughly documented survey of the work of southern Californian Edward Ruscha, and a cluster of mini-retrospectives focused on ceramic sculptors in *Ceramic Sculpture: Six Artists*, co-organized with the Whitney Museum of American Art. The up-to-the-minute report of the summer's sculpture biennial was counterbalanced by a scholarly, historical overview of Precisionism, *Images of America: Precisionist Painting and Modern Photography,* curated and documented by Karen Tsujimoto.

The increased use of borrowed works in temporary exhibitions was paralleled in the expanded use of the permanent collection for exhibition purposes. Installations dealing with a range of aspects of twentieth-century art, drawn exclusively from permanent collection holdings, were mounted with increasing frequency. While in 1975 two exhibitions featuring works from the graphics collection were hung, in 1982 eleven shows were organized, ranging from the mural studies of Diego Rivera to works acquired during John Humphrey's twenty-five years as curator to the photographs of Ansel Adams. In 1981 Van Deren Coke introduced an ongoing series of installations from the photography collection under the umbrella title *Facets of the Collection*, which dealt at various times with such diverse themes as the world of illusion and fantasy, urban America, and Paul Strand, and presented as well periodic reports on recent acquisitions. In 1982, George Neubert initiated a sequence of shows drawn from the painting, sculpture, and graphics collections; titled *Resource/Reservoir*, they examined such topics as the gifts of Jermayne MacAgy, the holdings of collage and assemblage, and the paintings of Richard Diebenkorn. A related series, *Resource/Response*, commented upon new ideas and works of Bay Region, as well as national, artists.

THIS growing use of the permanent collection was made possible by the great explosion that took place in the Museum's pace of acquiring. During the year preceding the arrival of Henry Hopkins, seventy-seven works entered the collection through gift, purchase, or bequest; by 1983, well over six hundred were being acquired annually. This increase in quantity was fortunately coupled with a leap in quality. The acquisition of single key objects expanded the scope of the holdings, while periodic additions of groups of works by a single artist, or dealing with a specific theme, contributed to the collection's depth.

While the permanent collection that greeted Henry Hopkins upon his arrival in 1974 was one that had improved over the years, it was nonetheless a collection that reflected the donor community instead of being broadly representative. Determined to build on the collection's individualism and the unique qualities of the surrounding artistic community, and to strengthen as well the weak historical areas, Hopkins set out on a systematic reformation. His proposal to focus first on the acquisition of works by what he termed the "painterly painters" and related sculptors was approved enthusiastically by the Board of Trustees. In early 1974, Hopkins began a correspondence and a series of visits with Mr. and Mrs. Clyfford Still, lasting well over a year, which culminated in Still's gift to the Museum of twenty-eight extraordinary canvases ranging from a figurative work painted in 1934, while the artist was teaching at Washington State College in Pullman, to two monumental abstractions dated 1974. To house this historic group, the Museum renovated a gallery, outfitting it with movable walls which permitted the viewing of a great part of the collection in a single space, thereby creating an invaluable environment for scholars and students of Still's work.

The development of depth in the permanent collection was furthered in 1979 when seven paintings by Josef Albers were donated by Anni Albers and the Josef Albers Foundation. This gift, combined with the five paintings and numerous prints already in the collection, resulted in a mini-retrospective of the Bauhaus painter's contributions. Emphasizing Albers's explorations into color relationships by his use of an established format of squares within squares, the grouping includes ten examples from the Homage to the Square Series, as well as samplings of other serial investigations.

Other artists have been singled out for emphasis in the collection. In 1978, the purchase of a significant three-part painting by Philip Guston prompted a gift on the part of the artist of four works spanning the period from 1947 to 1977. These, added to the two paintings already in the Museum's possession, traced the evolution of the artist's concerns from figurative fantasy of the forties through the lyrically colored gestural canvases of Abstract Expressionism into his return to figuration in the seventies. Through single gifts and purchases the Museum also acquired holdings in depth of Richard Diebenkorn, represented by seven canvases, as well as numerous examples of his drawings and prints. Frank Stella, too, is well represented with five works in various mediums which exemplify five discrete series developed by the artist.

This collecting in depth was accompanied by the acquisition of single pivotal objects which enlarged the scope of the Museum's holdings of the art of the twentieth century. Throughout the seventies, the predominant gifts consisted of objects created during the preceding decade, thus strengthening significantly the representation of Color Field painting, shaped canvases, and second-generation Abstract Expressionism, as well as examples of both northern and southern California developments. Beginning in 1974, the collection received, through gift, important works by Larry Bell, Roy De Forest, Robert Irwin, Morris Louis, Agnes Martin, Joan Mitchell, Kenneth Noland, Ludwig

Sander, Hassel Smith, Andy Warhol, and William T. Wiley.

The tradition of giving established by the Women's Board in 1944 was maintained through the additions made to the collection by the board's successor, the Modern Art Council. Their 1977 choice of a multi-media drawing by Christo, which documented his Marin County project *Running Fence*, was followed by a monumental assemblage by Bruce Conner, an expressive figurative painting by Nathan Oliveira, and, in 1983, Robert Arneson's wryly humorous clay work *California Artist*.

The dependence of the collection on local donors declined during the seventies and was replaced by a national community of patronage. Significant groupings of works were received from Mr. and Mrs. William C. Janss of Sun Valley, Idaho, who gave pivotal examples of Abstract Expressionism by Hans Hofmann, Willem de Kooning, and Alfred Leslie, as well as multiple works by Jasper Johns, John Altoon, Jacques Villon, and a powerful outdoor sculpture by Isaac Witkin. In addition, gifts of single objects were received frequently from donors in New York, Texas, Los Angeles, and Seattle.

The expanding origin of gifts was paralleled in an increase in sources of funding. Private individuals and foundations, as well as the National Endowment for the Arts, and specified funds received from Museum activities greatly enhanced purchasing power. Funds bearing the names of valued supporters Doris and Donald Fisher, Evelyn and Walter Haas, Jr., Ruth and Moses Lasky, Madeleine Haas Russell, Mrs. Ferdinand Smith, and Mrs. Paul L. Wattis joined those of the Charles H. Land Family Foundation and the T. B. Walker Foundation, enabling the purchase of critical objects by both contemporary and historical figures: Jean Arp, Elmer Bischoff, Robert Mangold, Kenneth Price, George Segal, Paul Strand, and Paul Wonner. And, through the judicious pruning of redundant material from the collection, moneys were realized to acquire key works by Joseph Cornell, Julio González, Max Pechstein, John Storrs, and others.

While the collections of painting, sculpture, and graphics were growing arithmetically, the photography collection, under Van Deren Coke's direction, was increasing almost geometrically. Mirroring the policies in the other mediums, both single important prints and clusters of images related by artist or theme were acquired. As a result of the exhibition *Avant-Garde Photography in Germany*, which revealed new avenues of interest in photography, prints from this era were purchased or received by gift. To a collection replete with Adams, Bullock, and Weston were added the images of Kesting, Blumenfeld, and Umbo. Works by artists of more contemporary decades were added as well, the landscapes of Robert Adams, the searing investigations of the drug culture by Larry Clark, and the provocative figures of Robert Mapplethorpe. Donors enthusiastic about the statements of the photographic medium emerged to enhance the collection: Robert Shapazian donated prints by Man Ray, Maurice Tabard, and Ilse Bing, while Byron Meyer provided the means to acquire works by Tato, Joel-Peter Witkin, and Robert Frank. The number of photographs acquired between 1979 and the end of 1983 has amounted to well over 2,300.

The collections of the San Francisco Museum of Modern Art possess a unique character, which has been determined by its patrons and donors, its professional staff, and its boards of trustees. It reflects its proximity to a unique body of work by the independent artists of the area and its access to, yet distance from, the mainstream of national and international attitudes. Its areas of strength—the Fauves, German photography of the twenties and thirties, collage and assemblage objects, ceramic sculpture of California, the work of the "painterly" painters —provide thought-provoking experiences for the viewing public, while the broad spectrum of its holdings offers visitors a historical context and a wealth of varied visual experience. As the Museum embarks on its second fifty years, it looks forward to the continued development of the permanent collection.

Katherine Church Holland

Conservation of a Twentieth-Century Collection

WHY SHOULD RECENTLY CREATED ART need conservation or restoration treatment?

Working closely with modern art, we observe how quickly objects undergo changes after completion by the artist. Subtle metamorphoses take place, changes in appearance that inevitably alter the statement of the artist or the impact of the work. Environmental factors, handling, and inherent characteristics of the piece all contribute to the ephemeral nature of a work of art. Twentieth-century art is proving to be particularly susceptible to premature transmutation. Initially, permanence is influenced by the artist's materials and methods of fabrication. In this century, artists have had the benefit (and the bane) of a fantastic variety of readily available materials, many newly invented or not necessarily formulated for artists' use. Deviating from time-tested mediums and methods, contemporary artists have experimented with plastics, pigments, adhesives, and support materials, producing thereby an unending multiplicity of artistic inventions that defy standard definition. In the desire for immediate expression, an interest in permanence has often been put aside. On the other hand, a sizable contingent of artists continues to revel in fine craftsmanship and fabrication.

Whether casual or careful in construction, contemporary art is of unknown durability. Many of the materials of today's artists have not been in existence long enough for us to have a complete understanding of their physical and chemical stability. One area of critical concern is that of photographic materials, where the chemistry of the emulsions, coloring agents, and processing is the lifeline of the observed images. Some complex fabrications incorporate unrelated or incompatible materials, which predestines them to decay. There are many assemblages of this type in the San Francisco Museum of Modern Art collection, such as Robert Rauschenberg's *Collection* and Bruce Conner's *Looking Glass*. These creations, warmly nicknamed "conservator's nightmares," demand regular conservation attention and will continue to require treatment throughout their lifetime.

A variety of factors contribute to the vulnerability of contemporary collections. The irregular configuration, monumental scale, and considerable weight of many modern works of art make these mammoths tremendously difficult to handle. The nature of unprotected elements inherent in the designs also makes them susceptible to alteration. Open expanses of color, areas of exposed canvas, and unglazed ceramics are examples of materials and surfaces unable to withstand damages such as soiling, abrasions, burnish marks, or cracks. Any disfigurement to these surfaces will strongly detract from the artist's conception.

From the museum standpoint, art and artifacts are viewed as having a long life potential. Even informal art statements take on a significance in the long-range context of the ever-evolving history of art. The preservation of the artifacts of each era can only be achieved through research, study, and understanding of the works and the continuing care of the collections. Preventive care is the most important step toward the physical preservation of each object and maintaining the visual characteristics intended by the artist. A stable environment for exhibition and storage, and great care in transporting of works of art, are fundamental to this preservation.

When conservation treatment is required, minimal intervention is recommended. The materials used in repair must be compatible with and yet distinguishable from the original. Wherever possible, materials employed in conservation treatment should be reversible. Works that have survived from previous centuries have generally been restored numerous times, and the comparatively young art of our century will probably have to undergo repeated preservative treatments as well. Modern mediums often have properties that impose restrictions on cleaning, varnishing, or other conservation treatment. Continuing research and experimentation, which enables conservators to keep abreast of new art materials and formats, is essential to the constant development of new or modified conservation treatments to meet the demands of contemporary art. Conservation also extends beyond the Museum through frequent contacts with working artists, who consult with conservators on technical problems or questions about mediums and methods.

The behind-the-scenes conservation program of the San Francisco Museum of Modern Art consists of regular examination and inspection of the collections to determine structure, changes in condition, and damages in need of correction. Documentation of the works in written and photographic form provides an essential record for the care of each work of art. The conservation department works in close conjunction with the Curatorial, Research/Collections, and Registration departments to assemble a comprehensive dossier of information on each item in the permanent collection.

In the early decades of the Museum's history, the conservation program was modest, undertaken with the ad-hoc assistance of consulting conservators. Then, in the early seventies, the Museum expanded to the third floor of the Veterans' Building and the Elise S. Haas Conservation Laboratory was founded. Mrs. Haas had a special interest in conservation. For many years she shared a close association with the nationally recognized conservators and educators Sheldon and Caroline Keck. In honor of the Kecks, Mrs.

Haas generously funded the creation and operation of the facility. The laboratory rapidly established itself as a major conservation resource, developing the Museum's conservation programs and providing services to artists, other western museums, and the public as well. Originally, the facility was equipped to treat paintings and some objects. In 1975, through the assistance of the National Endowment for the Arts and additional gifts from Mrs. Haas, a site was outfitted for the conservation of works on paper. In 1982, the main laboratory was again up-dated, with substantial space and equipment improvements.

Conservation operations were begun by founding Chief Conservator Tony Rockwell and passed on to James Bernstein and Inge-Lise Eckmann, Co-directors since 1976. The diverse department includes four to six conservators, secretarial and technical support, and training positions for apprentices and interns pursuing studies in conservation.

The care of its permanent collection is the responsibility of every museum, but it is an obligation that is not always fulfilled. At the San Francisco Museum of Modern Art, we take great pride in our dedication to the permanent collection, which is maintained in excellent condition. This is demonstrated by the works of art themselves, which are fresh in appearance and impact. As the Museum grows and moves into the next century, so will our commitment to the preservation of the artifacts that constitute the art of the modern era.

James Bernstein and Inge-Lise Eckmann
Co-directors, Conservation

HIGHLIGHTS OF THE COLLECTION

Henri Matisse

FRENCH, 1869–1954

The Girl with Green Eyes

LA FILLE AUX YEUX VERTS
1908

oil on canvas
26 × 20″
66.0 × 50.8 cm

Bequest of Harriet Lane Levy
50.6086

IN 1904, THE YEAR FOLLOWING the completion of *The Slave* (page 39), Henri Matisse, spurred on by his close friends Paul Signac and Henri-Edmond Cross, began experimenting with the Pointillist technique of the Neo-Impressionists. The somber palette of his earlier paintings was replaced by increasingly high-keyed coloration. By the spring of 1905, when he exhibited *Luxe, calme, et volupté* at the Salon des Indépendants, Matisse's color had become intense, luminous, and completely arbitrary, free of the constrictions of natural depiction. His brush strokes, no longer subservient to structural definition, ranged from succinct daubings to sinuous linear arabesques.

In 1905, Matisse and his family spent the first of many summers at Collioure, a small fishing port on the southwestern coast of France. In the fall, two of the canvases he had executed there were hung at the Salon d'Automne together with work by André Derain (who had spent the summer with the Matisses), Henri Manguin, Albert Marquet, Maurice Vlaminck, and others. Violently colored with juxtaposed vermilions, persimmons, and ultramarines, freely and informally composed, intoxicating in feeling and seemingly lit from within, these works electrified public and critics alike, one of whom dubbed the artists as a group *les fauves*, the wild beasts.

By 1907, Matisse's predilection for the Fauvist freedom waned and his interest in the work of Cézanne was rekindled. A new concern for structure appeared in his canvases. In a series of portraits executed between 1907 and 1911 he painstakingly worked out compositional problems in which he experimented with various figure/background relationships. While in several paintings in this group the subject is presented against either a plain background, or a ground simply divided horizontally, thus effectively placing the focus on the sitter, in two of the portraits the background and the figure are visually almost equally weighted and the interplay between figure and ground is more complex. *The Girl with Green Eyes* is one of those compositions.

The figure and background compete for dominance, yet they are formally linked. The pendulous curve of the sitter's chin is repeated in the embroidery of her robe and the emphasized contour of the cast of Greek sculpture behind her. The brush handling, whether rendering patterns or broad, flat areas, is free and expressive. The planes are drawn closer by the repetitive rhythms of the arabesque-like strokes.

The freedom of the paint handling and coloration provides a foil for the static, frontal pose of the model, who has been positioned strictly vertically, though somewhat to the left of the central axis. Unlike the other portraits of this period, the head is not truncated by the top edge of the canvas. Here the horizontal yellow slash of the hat brim serves this purpose, cutting off the supposed curve of the hair and overlapping the sculpture behind it as well. The face, a chalky pink, pointed oval, gazes out with clear eyes, yet the personality is not revealed. The sitter is but one element in a many-faceted composition.

It is the joyous, audacious color of this portrait, however, which makes the initial impact. Matisse has taken his Fauve palette and made it richer, denser. Gone are the open areas of bare canvas which enlivened and informalized his landscapes and figures of 1905–6. Here, complementary colors are abutted and strident, closely hued areas are juxtaposed. The arcing black outlines, which in Matisse's later work will take on a life of their own, here intermittently delineate features and set off the brilliant pigments.   KCH

Henri Matisse

FRENCH, 1869–1954

Portrait of Michael Stein

1916

oil on canvas
26½ × 19⅞"
67.3 × 50.5 cm

Sarah and Michael Stein Memorial
Collection
Gift of Nathan Cummings
55.3546

Portrait of Sarah Stein

1916

oil on canvas
28½ × 22¼"
72.4 × 56.5 cm

Sarah and Michael Stein Memorial
Collection
Gift of Elise Stern Haas
54.1117

THE COLLECTING ACTIVITIES of the Stein family—Gertrude and Leo, Michael and his wife, Sarah—during the first decades of the twentieth century are well documented in the annals of art history. Their discovery of the avant-garde artists of the day, their collections, and their salons have been the subject of exhibitions and books alike. Emphasis in these chronicles is usually placed on Gertrude and Leo, for they were the initiators, the collectors with the wider range, and, generally speaking, the most colorful. But to the art community of the San Francisco Bay Area, it is Sarah and Michael who loom larger, for it was to this area that they returned after their years of living in France, it was here that much of their collection was dispersed, and it is in the museums of this region that many of the paintings by Henri Matisse which they purchased and cherished may be seen.

Michael, Leo, and Gertrude Stein were born in Allegheny, Pennsylvania, but the year Gertrude was born—when Leo was two and Michael, nine—their father dissolved his business partnership and took the family to Europe. When they returned some five years later they settled in Oakland, across the bay from San Francisco. Michael went East for his education, earning his degree from Johns Hopkins University, where he remained for an extra year of graduate work in biology, then returned to California to join his father's business. On the death of their father in 1891, Michael became his siblings' guardian and promptly moved them to San Francisco, where he himself had been living for a time. In 1893 he married Sarah Samuels, the daugther of a well-to-do San Francisco family, whose outgoing and affectionate nature was the perfect foil for her husband's quiet temperament.

In 1903, ostensibly discouraged by a labor dispute in which he sided with the workers, Michael retired from business. He, Sarah, and their young son soon settled in Paris near Leo and Gertrude, and they, too, became caught up in the younger pair's enthusiasm for recent art. Late in 1905, after participating in the family purchase of Matisse's Fauve canvas, Woman with Hat, exhibited at the Salon d'Automne, the Steins met the artist. From that point on the couple collected Matisse's work almost exclusively. The personal friendship between Matisse and the Steins developed rapidly, becoming one of mutual respect, affection, and support. Late in 1907, Sarah Stein, the sculptor

Hans Purrmann, and others founded the Académie Matisse, a school centered around Matisse's teaching. Matisse was a frequent visitor at the Steins' Saturday night gatherings, where he met many American collectors who, persuaded by Sarah's eloquent enthusiasm, acquired his work.

The portraits of Sarah and Michael Stein, painted by Matisse in 1916, are enduring evidence of this close friendship. Although nearly identical in size and similar in format, they differ greatly in approach and effect. The portrayal of Michael is by far the more traditional of the two. Like *The Girl with Green Eyes* (page 33), its direct, frontal pose is set slightly to the left, but here, in contrast to the earlier portrait, the palette is severely limited to ochers and browns with bold black outlines. The face is simply defined and broadly modeled, and the relationship between figure and background is seemingly straightforward, save for the fluid brushwork on the right side of the sitter's neck which momentarily links foreground and background, forcefully interjects the element of the will of the artist/creator, and visually frees the right side of the subject's head, essentially setting it adrift. Austerely presented, this portrait by Matisse nonetheless projects a feeling of warm affection and respect.

Fond as he was of Michael Stein, it was to Sarah that Matisse turned for advice, conversation, and approbation. He has been quoted as saying, "She knows more about my paintings than I do." In his portrait of her, this rapport is strongly in evidence. More adventurous than its companion and closer to Matisse's other work of 1916, it is also more insightful. In a preliminary charcoal study the artist determined the basic cuneate composition virtually filling the top half of the paper with the enlarged head and describing the facial features in abstract schematic shorthand. The painting retains this inverted-triangle composition, its left and right sides sliced by tapering black wedges which form a V that is echoed and reinforced by the throat of the sitter. This effectively frames the head and sets up the simple geometric structure of circle (head) within truncated triangle. Like many of Matisse's earlier portraits, the circular silhouette of the head is cut off along the top, thus moving the focus back to the face. Against this stark, flatly rendered backdrop, the visage emerges as a surprisingly sculptural form.   KCH

BORN IN 1869 IN NORTHERN FRANCE, in the town of Le Cateau-Cambrésis, Henri Matisse was initially trained to become a lawyer; it was not until he was twenty that he began to study art, drawing from plaster casts in a course taught by Professor Croisé in Saint-Quentin. Determined to receive formal training in Paris, Matisse moved to the capital in the winter of 1891/92. He studied briefly with the academician Adolphe Bouguereau at the Académie Julian and shortly afterward entered the studio of Gustave Moreau, where he remained until 1897. Moreau, a Symbolist and inveterate Romantic known for his jewel-like paintings of mysterious, Oriental themes, encouraged individualism in his students; his studio attracted the most talented of the young artists, among them Georges Rouault, Albert Marquet, and Henri Manguin.

While his early academic years entailed some study of the human body, Matisse's work throughout the Moreau years was dominated by landscapes, interiors, and still lifes. In 1899 he purchased a small painting of three bathers by Paul Cézanne. Moved by Cézanne's carefully studied approach to the human body, Matisse decided to re-examine the nude and he set out to do so in paintings, drawings, and sculpture.

Although he had briefly experimented with sculpture in 1894, executing a pair of bronze medallions depicting a woman's profile in shallow relief, it was not until he was thirty that he turned his full attention to the creation of three-dimensional objects. Determined to educate himself in the medium of sculpture, Matisse spent the evenings of the next two years at the Ecole Communale de la Ville de Paris thoroughly and painstakingly studying technique and anatomy. During this time he executed a free copy of Antoine-Louis Barye's 1852 sculpture of a jaguar devouring a hare, in which he concentrated on the visual dynamics of the attacking animal. In the winter of 1900 Matisse embarked on his first original sculpture, an examination of the male figure which he called *The Slave*.

On first inspection *The Slave* appears to be closely allied with the work of Auguste Rodin, and in truth, Matisse greatly admired the older master, whom he had met, possibly in 1898. But in the evolution of *The Slave*, a process that took three years, Matisse grappled with the work of both Rodin and Antoine Bourdelle, to whom he turned for technical advice, and painstakingly developed his own personal direction and statement. The model for *The Slave*, an Italian peasant named Bevilaqua, had in fact been the model for the legs of Rodin's *Walking Man* of 1875–78; but where the earlier sculpture had captured the figure in motion, alluding to the moment before and the moment after, Matisse stabilized his form, planting it heavily and solidly, and focused instead on the human essence. Eyes gravely cast downward, shoulders hunched forward, the figure turns upon itself, fixed and immobile. The emphasis is placed on the spirit of the subject, dignified, intense, introspective.

Matisse was acutely aware of the totality of the figure and it was to that end that he manipulated his surface. While basically true to the underlying anatomy, the energetic texturing, broken almost to the point of being pointillistic, takes on an aesthetic life of its own, sometimes serving to balance, sometimes to enliven. Working with his fingers to mold and model, Matisse also used the sculpture knife to pare and slice, cutting great swaths which he left unmodulated. The surface shimmers and pounds, reaching for the core.

Executed in the nascent years of the twentieth century, *The Slave* looks back to the studio-model sculpture of the preceding years and ahead to the rhythmic art to come, presaging the elements which Matisse and his contemporaries would develop and perfect.   KCH

38

Henri Matisse

FRENCH, 1869–1954

Henriette, II

GROSSE TÊTE; HENRIETTE,
DEUXIÈME ÉTAT
1927

bronze 6/10
13 × 9 × 12″
33.0 × 22.9 × 30.5 cm
Bequest of Harriet Lane Levy
50.6096

IN DECEMBER 1916, weary of the northern winters and constant pressures of metropolitan life, Matisse traveled to the city of Nice on the French Riviera. Finding both relaxation and inspiration there, Matisse gradually made this sunlit town his home base. The paintings executed in Nice during the subsequent years reflect not only the heightened colors of the environment—the sea, luxuriant foliage, exotic flowers—but also the area's proximity to the alluring lands of North Africa. Canvases depicting light-filled interiors crowded with richly patterned textiles, sensuous odalisques reclining on tufted chaises, or windowed scenes revealing the silky blue of the Mediterranean flowed from Matisse's hand. Midway through the following decade, perhaps in reaction to this decorative inclination, Matisse returned to the three-dimensional object, seeking to purify his forms and render them monumental. After completing a semi-reclining nude (*Seated Nude* in the Cone Collection, Baltimore Museum of Art), its pared surface and powerful silhouette speaking to the artist's new concerns, he commenced a series of three portrait heads of Henriette Darricarrère, a Nice model who had been posing for him since 1920.

The initial head in the series, executed in 1925, was rendered realistically, with a subtly animated surface and faithful adherence to the convex and concave nuances of the face. The following year Matisse began work on a second head. Reducing and purifying, stylizing and compacting, he achieved a classic ideal. Emphasis was on weightiness, underscored by the wide-set eyes, jowly, pear-shaped countenance, thickened neck, and downcast direction of eyebrows and mouth. Expunged of superfluous and even natural details, including ears, the smooth visage is volumetrically conceived, transmitting a sense of outwardly expanding pressure.

Albert Elsen has noted the presence of an African mask, perhaps of the Baules, in Matisse's studio during the time this sculpture was modeled.[1] The resemblance between the primitive and the modern is certainly visible in the serene, aloof aspect of the head, abstracted handling of the orbed, high forehead, and strictly controlled waves of the coiffure. The hair, in fact, nearly becomes a bas-relief applied to the basic ovoid. The final head, *Henriette, III*, executed in 1929, returns to a more personal expression, yet retains the austere aspect of its predecessor. Its surface is modeled and sliced, much of the facial definition is planar and angular, and the eyes are lidded. Although suggestive of an individual, it nonetheless shares with the rest of the series a sense of calm introspection.

The stylization found in the Henriette portraits was enhanced and made lyrical in Matisse's next series, the Tiaré, which marked the artist's return to the sensual aspects of feminine beauty in his sculptural oeuvre.   KCH

[1] Albert E. Elsen, *The Sculpture of Henri Matisse* (New York: Harry N. Abrams, 1972), pp. 166–67.

Kees van Dongen

FRENCH, BORN NETHER-
LANDS, 1877–1968

The Black Chemise

LA CHEMISE NOIRE
ca. 1905–9

oil on canvas with wood attachment
22¼ × 18¼″
56.5 × 46.4 cm

Gift of Wilbur D. May
64.59

THE LEGENDARY THIRTY YEARS of peace, prosperity, and social change in France that preceded World War I are nostalgically known as *la belle époque*. During this period Paris was the cultural capital of the world, a center for revolution in social mores, the arts, fashion, and the pleasures of life. Avant-garde artists flocked to this cultural mecca and as the old order clashed with the new, a bohemian underground was born. Montmartre, and particularly the *bateau-lavoir*, the building in which Picasso lived, were the center of this bohemian life and attracted many young artists and writers. Among them was the Dutch painter Kees van Dongen.

Settling in Paris in 1900, van Dongen experimented with Modernism by working first in an Impressionist style and then in a Neo-Impressionist vein. By 1905 he had arrived at a vibrantly colored, loose, impromptu style analogous to the Fauvism of Henri Matisse and his circle. Different from Fauvism, however, was van Dongen's penchant for depicting the nightlife of Montmartre. *La belle époque* was the era of the café and the cabaret, for in them artists found a new, free-form milieu in which to express their ideas. Café life fascinated van Dongen, as did the sinister and at times pathetic underworld of nighttime Paris. A general tendency toward the bizarre and a romantic taste for vice, poverty, and the lowlife—petty criminals, pimps, and prostitutes—shaped the attitudes of many intellectuals and artists in the early years of the century. Originating in French Realist literature, the theme of the prostitute in art was first extensively explored by Edgar Degas, in a series of monotypes made in 1879–80, and Henri de Toulouse-Lautrec during the 1890s. Influenced by Toulouse-Lautrec, Pablo Picasso's paintings of prostitutes of late 1900 and 1901 set an important precedent for the work of van Dongen, who lived at the *bateau-lavoir* from 1906 to 1907.

Dressed in black lace and black stockings, the demimondaine in van Dongen's *The Black Chemise* stands in an awkward pose, striving to appear feminine and alluring while being highly conscious of both the reality of the situation and her audience. Her large, deep, purple-black, nocturnal eyes stare wistfully into the distance. The soft, inviting atmosphere of the surrounding bedroom, loosely rendered in gentle pinks, lavenders, and whites, boldly contrasts with the stark figure in black. The disparity is underscored by the delicate, feminine bows on the bed and the bright floral-patterned rug stylized in the manner of Matisse.

While the overall coloration of *The Black Chemise* is subdued in comparison with other van Dongen works of the period, the use of non-naturalistic color, as seen in the green highlights and the purple shading of the face, is decidedly Fauvist.

Prostitution may have enabled some women to throw off the shackles of convention and experience the heady, exciting life of the cabarets and dance halls of *fin-de-siècle* Paris, but for many women, victims of increased urbanization and a changing family structure, prostitution was the only option and a harsh existence. Van Dongen sympathized with this sad woman of the night whose head is surrounded by an aura of melancholy purple. *The Black Chemise* is not an image of prurient voyeurism or wanton sensuality; rather it is a compassionate look at the underbelly of *la belle époque*. DCduP

42

André Derain
FRENCH, 1880–1954

Landscape
1906

oil on canvas mounted on board
20 × 25½″
50.8 × 64.8 cm

Bequest of Harriet Lane Levy
50.6075

THE CELEBRATED SALON D'AUTOMNE OF 1905 held at the Grand-Palais of the Champs-Elysées in Paris provoked a wave of virulent criticism that gave the name Fauvism to the first major aesthetic movement of the twentieth century. The essence of this hostile reaction to the vibrantly colored paintings of Henri Matisse, André Derain, Maurice Vlaminck, and their friends by provincial critics and a public weaned on academic art is captured by the words of Marcel Nicolle in his exhibition review for the *Journal de Rouen*: "We now come to the most stupefying gallery in this Salon so rich in astonishment. Here all description, all reporting as well as all criticism become equally impossible since what is presented to us here—apart from the materials employed—has nothing whatever to do with painting: some formless confusion of colors; blue, red, yellow, green; some splotches of pigment crudely juxtaposed; the barbaric and naïve sport of a child who plays with the box of colors he just got as a Christmas present."[1]

The three most important artists of the group, Matisse, Derain, and Vlaminck, were united by their friendship and by broadly similar aesthetic concerns, not by clearly defined ideological premises or a group manifesto, as were subsequent modern movements. As artists, they were all deeply committed to a belief in individual freedom and a desire to renew the instinctive directness and anti-theoretical nature of Impressionism, while also incorporating the exaggerated, heightened color and emotive possibilities of Post-Impressionist painting. The inviting, dazzling, idyllic images celebrating the pleasures of life that resulted seem today as far removed from the idea of *les fauves* (wild beasts) as possible, but to the public in 1905—who had not yet come to know or understand the work of Vincent van Gogh and the other Post-Impressionists—these paintings shattered their notion of the function of art and as a result appeared brutal and violent.

Fauvism emerged during the summer of 1905 when Matisse and Derain worked closely together at Collioure, a small Mediterranean seaport on the southwestern coast of France near the Spanish border. Even though Derain's *Landscape* was painted during the following summer when he was working at L'Estaque, also on the southern coast of France, it belongs to the height of the Fauvist movement. Daringly free in his paint application and rendering of natural appearances, Derain created a joyous, brilliantly colored image proclaiming the intensity and clarity of light of the warm, semi-tropical Mediterranean landscape. *Landscape* is the result of what has been characterized as "mixed-technique" Fauvism,[2] in which the broken brush strokes, ultimately derived from Neo-Impressionism, are combined with flat color planes which emphasize an absence of shadow. These flat divisions of color juxtaposed with the curvilinear rhythms of the tree trunks and their Fauvist color-breaks create a decorative mode indebted to the work of the Post-Impressionist Paul Gauguin. Through radiant, dissonant color, distorted drawing, and brisk, raw brushwork, Derain created a sensuous visual feast: a world of joy and pleasure removed from the anxieties of the dawning twentieth century.   DCduP

[1] Quoted in Alfred H. Barr, Jr., *Matisse: His Art and His Public* (New York: The Museum of Modern Art, 1951), p.55.

[2] John Elderfield, *"The Wild Beasts": Fauvism and Its Affinities* (New York: The Museum of Modern Art, 1976), p. 14.

44

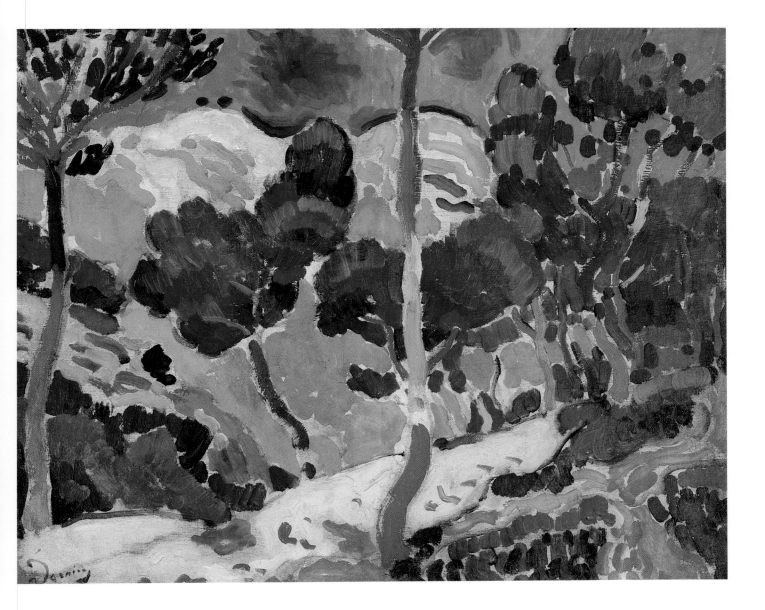

Othon Friesz

FRENCH, 1879–1949

Landscape (The Eagle's Beak, La Ciotat)

PAYSAGE (LE BEC-DE-L'AIGLE, LA CIOTAT)
1907

oil on canvas
25⅜ × 32″
64.5 × 81.2 cm

Bequest of Marion W. Sinton
81.52

[1]A term devised by Meyer Schapiro, quoted in John Elderfield, *The "Wild Beasts": Fauvism and Its Affinities* (New York: The Museum of Modern Art, 1976), p. 16.

[2]Marcel Giry, *Fauvism: Origins and Development* (New York: Alpine Fine Arts Collection, 1982), p. 240.

[3]See Elderfield, op. cit., pp. 97–139, for a discussion of this concept of the landscape.

LANDSCAPE WAS FAUVISM'S MOST CELEBRATED THEME. Stimulated by the "vacation culture"[1] subject matter and *plein air* tradition of the French Impressionists, the Fauvist painters exuberantly portrayed the pleasures of seashore and countryside. In the years between 1904 and 1907, many of them were drawn to the sun-drenched vistas and lush, semi-tropical vegetation of southern France.

Othon Friesz first visited this region during the summer of 1907. A latecomer to Fauvism, with Raoul Dufy and Georges Braque, he was among the last to gather around the Fauve circle, even though he had exhibited with Henri Matisse in 1904 and with *les fauves* (the wild beasts), as Matisse, André Derain, and their colleagues were called in the famous Salon d'Automne of 1905. While painting with Braque in Antwerp during the summer of 1906, he began to adopt a looser, more spontaneous drawing style and a bolder method of composition, although he remained fundamentally Impressionist in his use of spatial illusion and his concern for the nature of light at a given time of day or particular season. It was not until the fall of 1906 that Friesz began to intensify his color, for, like Braque, he appears to have been first influenced by Fauvist works exhibited at the Salon d'Automne that year rather than those of 1905.

Friesz's Fauvist style flourished during the summer of 1907 when he and Braque painted together in the south of France at La Ciotat. *Landscape*, a painting of Le Bec-de-l'Aigle, a well-known rock formation in the area, belongs to this productive period. Like Paul Cézanne's many studies of Mont Sainte-Victoire, this is one of a series of paintings in which Friesz features this unusual geological outcropping from varying viewpoints. He bathes Le Bec-de-l'Aigle and the surrounding landscape in a warm, golden sunlight, epitomizing the *joie de vivre* of the Fauvist landscape. He simplified his forms to an arrangement of colored areas and Art Nouveau-influenced arabesques that create a rhythmic, dynamic pattern. However flat this curvilinear design, it nonetheless appears placed over an illusion of spatial recession that suggests a lingering attachment to Impressionist tradition. The heightened Fauvist color, radiant and inviting, is primarily based on the harmonious warm tones of yellow, pink, and orange.

At the height of his Fauvist style, Friesz began a series of figure-in-landscape compositions that mark his transition to a more conservative mode influenced by Paul Cézanne. His spontaneous method of drawing and brilliant Fauvist color were replaced by a subdued palette and solidified, volumetric forms. "Color," he said, "ceased to be the master of the picture, and under volume and light the drawing was reborn; color remained a savoury adjunct."[2] In contrast to his image of Le Bec-de-l'Aigle, these works by Friesz speak of an alternative approach to the landscape that many of the Fauve painters explored concurrently. Besides celebrating the immediate joys of a dynamic, vital world of the present, some of the Fauvists also presented a serene, ideal, peopled landscape that nostalgically looks to a Golden Age, when man and nature peacefully co-existed.[3]   DCduP

46

Pablo Picasso

SPANISH, 1881–1973

Street Scene

SCÈNE DE RUE

1900

oil on canvas
18¾ × 26¼"
47.7 × 66.7 cm

Bequest of Harriet Lane Levy
50.6097

SPANNING THE FIRST THREE-QUARTERS of the twentieth century, the artistic achievements of Pablo Ruiz Picasso can be described, somewhat modestly, as extraordinary. Incessantly energetic and innovative, Picasso produced masterworks in nearly every medium—painting, sculpture, drawing, printmaking, ceramics—and participated in an impressive array of historic modern movements. From the psychological introspection of his turn-of-the-century canvases to the terrors conveyed by *Guernica*, from the cool objectivity of Analytic Cubism to the benign serenity of his classical figures, each new direction was explored fully, then discarded or assimilated, and later revived in another context.

Although the major portion of his work was done in France, Picasso was born, and remained throughout his life, a Spaniard. His fine arts studies were initiated when he was ten; his father, an artist, began instructing him in painting and drawing. By the age of sixteen he had received formal training at academies in both Barcelona and Madrid. During numerous trips to the Prado he enthusiastically viewed the work of the Spanish masters, most notably Velázquez and El Greco, whose attenuated forms would figure prominently in his future work. Steeped in the classical tradition, the drawings and canvases of these early years were somber in tone and academic in execution.

In 1899 Picasso began frequenting Els Quatre Gats, a Barcelona gathering place for artists and writers. There he designed menus and sketched the café habitués, his efforts exhibiting the heavy, quirky lines and caricature-like features of the posters of Henri de Toulouse-Lautrec and Théophile Steinlen which he had seen reproduced in Paris periodicals. In October of 1900, when he was just nineteen, Picasso made his first visit to Paris. Settling in Montmartre, he spent the following three months visiting galleries and exhibitions, and drawing and painting the cabaret life and inhabitants of the back streets of the city.

Street Scene, painted during that brief initial trip, reflects Picasso's ongoing sensitivity to the human condition. Marking a return to both the melancholy tone of his academic canvases and the subject of the poor, which he had explored in a series of portraits of beggars painted while he was still in school, it further foreshadows the mood of solitude and despair that pervades Picasso's work of the following five years, through both his "blue" and "rose" periods.

Set on a dingy urban road, the quiet scene is bathed in an impressionistic mist of gray, the shadowed hue of impending winter. The figures, psychologically isolated, are defined cursorily with emphasis placed on their bulky shapes rather than on any individual features. Reminiscent of Steinlen's canvases in its romantic, suffusive haze and containing traces of Daumier's influence in the expressive silhouettes of the unarticulated human figures, *Street Scene* looks back, rather than forward to Picasso's innovative work of the new century.   KCH

Jacques Lipchitz

FRENCH, BORN LITHUANIA
1891–1973

Draped Woman
1919

bronze 3/7
36¾ × 12⅝ × 13¼"
93.3 × 32.0 × 33.6 cm

Gift of Mr. and Mrs. Wellington S. Henderson
63.4

BORN IN LITHUANIA IN 1891, Jacques Lipchitz arrived in Paris in 1909, when Picasso and Braque were beginning the fragmentation of form that signaled the first stage of advanced Cubism. But Lipchitz continued his strictly academic training; after a brief stint at the Ecole des Beaux-Arts, he studied sculpture, anatomy, life drawing, and related subjects at the Académie Julian. His initial efforts at expressing the figure in three dimensions looked back to the previous century, bearing traces of Romanticism and the influence of Art Nouveau.

In 1913, Lipchitz's close friend Diego Rivera, then deep into Cubist experimentation, introduced the young artist to Picasso. A long affiliation with the audacious innovator started, and the application of Cubist principles to sculptural form began to preoccupy the young sculptor during these explorative years of his artistic career. Stylization and planar definition soon began appearing in Lipchitz's work. At first these took the form of surface application and did not resolve themselves into an integrated conception. But by 1915 Lipchitz had developed an approach which utilized the cutout planes of Synthetic Cubism in strictly vertical architectonic works that teetered on the edge of pure abstraction. Despite their formally conceived juxtaposition of opposing planes, streamlined rectilinearity, and rigidly disciplined syntax, they retained an implied humanity not only in the eyebrow lines, but also in the purposefully included eyes.

After 1916, Lipchitz re-emphasized figural references, this time breaking down the forms and reassembling them according to the tenets of Analytic Cubism, using faceted planes, multiplicity of views, and an increased emphasis on mass. Moving from a front-to-rear approach to a four-sided one, Lipchitz arranged the elements to initiate movement around the work. By 1917, interlocking planes cantilevering out from a spiral core directed the eye easily around the form. With its fractured surface, jutting and angular, the mass became more complex, setting up interplays of light and shadow which defined volume.

By 1919 Lipchitz had explored this direction to his satisfaction and he began to reintroduce curvilinear elements and to simplify planes once more. The cool objectivity of the analytical approach rubbed against his essentially humanistic nature, and he countered this by expressing individualism of personality in his figures. *Draped Woman* of 1919 stands at the crossroads of this change in direction. Although retaining the angularity and diagonal thrusts that defined rotating movement in the preceding works, this composition exhibits a softening of edges, hints of integrated curves, and a tendency toward frontality that denies the pivoting facets. While this figure can hardly be called representational, it does convey key components of personal particularism not only in its cascade of wavy hair, but also in the definition of eye and brow which project a sense of person and serve as stabilizing elements, reinforcing the frontality of the figure.

Moving away from an emphasis on form, yet always retaining vestiges of Cubism in his work, Lipchitz directed himself more and more toward Expressionism, transforming heroic themes into powerful statements of twentieth-century humanist concerns. KCH

50

Constantin Brancusi

FRENCH, BORN ROMANIA
1876–1957

Blonde Negress

LA NÉGRESSE BLONDE
1926

bronze (polished)
15⅛ × 4⅞ × 7⅜"
38.5 × 12.4 × 18.8 cm

Gift of Agnes E. Meyer and Elise
Stern Haas
58.4382

OF THOSE WHO FORGED THE REVOLUTION in modern sculpture, Constantin Brancusi gave new meaning to the classical pursuit of an ideal form. While never completely abandoning natural appearances, he increasingly simplified form with the aim of revealing the most basic, elemental organic shapes. With the few themes that he repeated and refined throughout his career, he explored the ideas of creation, birth, and the natural process of growth.

In Paris, where he settled in 1904, Brancusi worked among such avant-garde sculptors as Elie Nadelman, Alexander Archipenko, and Amedeo Modigliani and became a major influence in establishing the modern aesthetic of direct carving. Not interested in the traditional method of modeling, but preferring to carve directly into the material, he regained a sense of immediacy for modern sculpture. His wish was to return to fundamental sculptural values, a feeling encouraged by the example of non-Western and folk art.

At the same time, however, Brancusi continued to work with the established and sophisticated process of bronze casting, which illustrates the complex and at times contradictory aspect of his aesthetic. Cast from a carved original, Brancusi's calm and majestic *Blonde Negress* of 1926 is a highly simplified, schematic rendering of the human face, in which the head is reduced to a perfectly formed ellipse whose smooth, flowing surfaces reveal no trace of distinguishing features except for the large sensuous lips, top knot, and rear ornament. It is at once an allusion to the human countenance and an abstract arrangement of gracefully composed volumes. To Brancusi, the oval shape symbolized primordial beginnings. "The egg-skull," he is quoted as saying, is "elongated, full of angular, virtual, underlying structures, the mystery of creation."[1] While the upright thrust and extended proportions of the composition, as well as the staccato zigzag motif, are in the spirit of African sculpture, this influence has been generalized and thoroughly assimilated into a personal style.

His feeling for surfaces is revealed in the gleaming golden-yellow finish that was his modern invention. His polishing of the sculptural "skin," a technique antithetical to traditional bronze casting, initiates a dialogue with light and speaks of an involvement with the material that he aimed for as a direct carver.

As with his other major themes, *Blonde Negress* was executed as a series and presented in both marble (*White Negress*) and bronze (*Blonde Negress*). Furthermore, it was conceived in two versions: the double chignon type, of which there are four bronzes, including this work, and one marble of 1924; and a single chignon type, of which there are two bronzes and one marble of 1928.[2] Through subtle, reductive adjustments, Brancusi perfected each successive stage in the series. His pursuit of an ideal form and insistence on realizing simplification through constant refinement was classical in nature. Non-classical, however, was the radical simplification of form he achieved. This was decidedly modern, as was his choice of exotic subject matter, a theme favored by many other avant-garde artists who were likewise inspired by non-Western art and culture.

His concern with a hidden reality was also one shared by other early modernists. Like Vasily Kandinsky and Piet Mondrian, who were interested in mysticism, Brancusi, himself a Theosophist, emphasized the dichotomy between an inner and outer reality. "What is real," he said, "is not the external form, but the essence of things. . . . It is impossible for anyone to express anything essentially real by imitating its external surface."[3]   DCduP

[1] Athena Tacha Spear, "A Contribution to Brancusi Chronology," *Art Bulletin*, vol. 48, no. 1 (March 1966), p. 48.

[2] Loc. cit.

[3] Quoted in Peter Selz, *Art of Our Times: A Pictorial History 1890–1980* (New York: Harry N. Abrams, 1981), p. 272.

Georges Braque

FRENCH, 1882–1963

The Gueridon

LE GUÉRIDON
1935

oil and sand on canvas
71 × 29"
180.4 × 73.7 cm

Purchased with the aid of funds
from W. W. Crocker
46.3211

THE CAREER OF GEORGES BRAQUE spanned nearly sixty years, yet it is the work he created and the innovations he made during the initial decade of his mature output that have traditionally received the most attention. Arriving in Paris at the advent of the new century, Braque at first flirted with Impressionism, then in 1906 adopted the exhilarating, unfettered palette of the Fauves. An underlying concern for pictorial order led Braque, after meeting Picasso and viewing his revolutionary *Les Demoiselles d'Avignon* in the fall of 1907, to reassess his own work and, in a series of landscapes and still lifes painted during the summer of 1908, he began to explore the permanent, basic structure inherent in tangible reality. Building on the accomplishments of Cézanne, Braque developed, through angled and interlocking planes, the expression and definition of geometric volume and controlled space. Picasso, who independently had been moving in a similar direction, soon joined Braque in a historic partnership. These two divergent personalities, the mercurial temperament of Picasso and the thoughtful disposition of Braque, submerged individual concerns in their common goal, which resulted in the development of a new pictorial language, Cubism.

This pivotal coalition lasted from 1909 until 1914, through both the analytic and synthetic phases of Cubism. Braque's induction into the army in 1914 signaled the end of his close working relationship with Picasso. The following year he was wounded in combat, and upon recovery Braque embarked on a new direction in his painting, melding his Cubist discoveries with a heightened lyrical approach. Throughout the twenties, Braque investigated diverse new possibilities, experimenting with figurative themes, free-spirited linear tracings, and the representation of volume. By the beginning of the next decade, his sure sense of paint handling was enhanced by the introduction of illusory space, an increased use of both silhouetting and outlining, and a freely applied, ofttimes acidic palette. The addition of sand (which Braque had first introduced into his paint in 1912) resulted in a pebbled surface that emphasized the frontal picture plane and reinforced the reality of the painting itself.

In *The Gueridon*, Braque returned to a theme that had occupied him intermittently since 1911. The gueridon, a small occasional table, displays on its surface a still life composed of pieces of fruit and a glass. Despite its dry, dense, textured surface, the painting is lively and rhythmic. The zigzagging contrapuntal forces of the wallpaper pattern, the silhouetted grapes, and the edge of the tablecloth play off against a basically static horizontal/vertical underlying structure. Further enlivening the work is the twisting movement created by the curvilinear table legs and the strong diagonal thrust that bisects the tabletop. Vestiges of Cubism appear in the divergent viewpoints expressed simultaneously, the severely tilted tabletop, and the flattened and fractured fruit forms. The verticality of the table is accentuated not only by the elongated picture format, but by the background planes which extend above and below the still life, stretching it out and projecting it forward to the picture surface. Poised at the midpoint of the artist's career, *The Gueridon* looks forward to the lyricism and contemplative works of his later years.   KCH

Georges Braque

FRENCH, 1882–1963

Vase, Palette, and Mandolin

VASE, PALETTE, ET
MANDOLINE
1936

oil on canvas
32 × 39⅝"
81.3 × 100.7 cm

Purchased with the aid of funds
from W. W. Crocker
44.2641

THE STILL LIFE—a carefully arranged composition of everyday objects—preoccupied Braque during nearly his entire career. Returning again and again to these intimate tableaux of fruit, musical instruments, glasses, and jugs, he investigated and reinvestigated, arranged and rearranged, plumbing the myriad possible variations of color, patterning, line, and pictorial structure. It was by his use of this format that Braque developed the tightly woven planar faceting of Analytic Cubism. And it was to a still life that Braque attached the first fragments of patterned wallpaper, thereby introducing a new element of reality that complicated the intellectual and visual aspects of the idiom and led as well to increasingly flattened space, which resulted in the enrichment and expansion of Cubism in its second—Synthetic—stage. Throughout his life, Braque by turns endowed the still life with lyricism, monumentality, intensity, and sensuousness. Perfectly suited to his introspective nature, these compositions drawn from his immediate environment provided an appropriate vehicle for structural and formal potentialities.

In *Vase, Palette, and Mandolin*, painted the year following *The Gueridon*, Braque exhibits the diversity he achieved within the still-life theme. Here, within a horizontal, rather than attenuated vertical, format, the artist has isolated a tabletop arrangement of objects. Unlike the highly patterned backdrop of *The Gueridon*, a deep-toned matte background is employed, serving to concentrate the composition and project it out to the picture surface. The tabletop, severely tilted and expressed in jagged silhouette, confines the visual activity to a generally oval area, intensifying its visual interplay and setting up outward pressure. The objects, described through thinly washed planes of delicately hued color interwoven with opaque, textured or angularly patterned areas, set up contrapuntal rhythms. This use of the table surface as an important structural element providing visual concentration and spatial definition was a continuing thread in Braque's oeuvre.   KCH

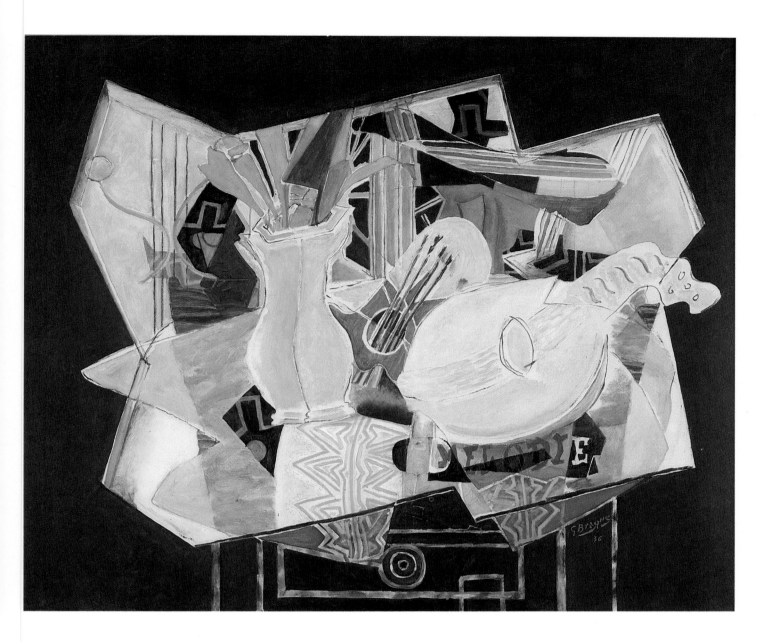

Pablo Picasso

SPANISH, 1881–1973

Jug of Flowers

LA CRUCHE FLEURIE
1937

oil on canvas
20 × 24¼″
50.8 × 61.6 cm

Purchased with the aid of funds
from W. W. Crocker
44.1499

WITH THE EXECUTION OF *Les Desmoiselles d'Avignon* in 1907, Picasso launched into a revolutionary visualization of pictorial space. Pioneering with his new friend Georges Braque, he began to fragment form into a series of planes that were then reassembled to create totally new structures. This new style of painting, Cubism, also utilized simultaneous shifting viewpoints within a single figure and, at least initially, a palette limited to browns and greens. Concentrating first on still lifes, then on the human figure, Picasso and Braque worked together to explore the possibilities and ramifications of their discoveries. In moving from the Analytic into the freer Synthetic Cubism, elements of collage were introduced, color was expanded, and line reassumed importance.

While continuing to investigate the implications of Cubism, Picasso experimented with a multitude of diverse approaches: realistic portraits, classically conceived sculptural figures, Surrealist visions. Early in the decade of the thirties he re-examined curvilinear Cubism and produced works in which his colors reached new levels of saturation, his line boldly stated in black.

In December 1936, six months before the Spanish town of Guernica was bombed by the German air force, Picasso embarked on a series of quiet still lifes that focus on two objects, a bowl of fruit and a pitcher. These small-scale studies, reflective and spontaneous, lighthearted in color and composition, form a pool of calm amid the violent minotauromachies and the terrifying frenzy of *Guernica* which emerged during the same months. Similar to the other canvases in the series, *Jug of Flowers*, painted on January 22, 1937, contains a double image, one of Picasso's favorite compositional formats in which the fruit compote on the left is juxtaposed with a pitcher on the right.

Divided vertically down the center, the painting plays with the concept of mirror image, although the two objects are in fact diametrically opposed. The fruit bowl, female in visualization, is set against a vaporous cloud of pink. Its form is transparent, the arbitrarily colored inner structure revealed through the outlined fruit forms. Lifted in part by looping horizontal curves, the bowl hovers above the steeply tilted tabletop, seemingly incorporeal. Its counterpart, the pitcher, is presented assertively, defined by curving shapes of chalky purple and black. Placed within a clearly comprehendible spatial context, it is planted securely on the table, a fact underlined by the presence of a simply stated, triangular shadow. An edgy tension is produced through the opposition of the two sides: dark/light, solid/transparent, enclosed/open, masculine/feminine.

The vestiges of fragmented interpenetrating planes and simultaneously stated diverse viewpoints reveal traces of Picasso's earlier Cubist work. Here, however, these principles are applied freely; loose definition and subjective coloration are expanded by the addition of volumetric concerns. Curvilinear elements prevail, repeated again and again in the tabletop, the forms of the objects, and the shapes of the fruit. Fragments of dark outlines and compartmentalized stained-glass color application hark back to the artist's landmark portraits painted earlier in the decade. The lyricism of this calm still life gives no hint of the torment of *Guernica*, Picasso's masterwork which followed within months.   KCH

Pablo Picasso

SPANISH, 1881–1973

Women of Algiers, E

LES FEMMES D'ALGER
1955

oil on canvas
18⅛ × 21⅝″
46.1 × 55.0 cm

Gift of Wilbur D. May
64.4

PICASSO'S EXTRAORDINARY IMAGINATION AND CREATIVITY often urged him to return to old themes, to mine the potential of already established compositional formats and favorite subjects. In 1954 he turned not to one of his own earlier themes, but to a work that had been painted over a century before, *The Women of Algiers* by Eugène Delacroix. Powerfully moved by the rich Oriental color and dazzling light he had experienced on a journey to Morocco in 1832, the French Romantic executed a series of works in which he recorded his impressions of this exotic land. Painted in 1834, *The Women of Algiers* is replete with dramatic color and sensuous curves. By juxtaposing complementary colors, Delacroix produced an animated, glowing surface that envelops the composition in unifying movement. Asymmetrically composed with a reclining figure in the lower left and three figures, seated and standing, at the right, a pattern of arcing rhythms and pervasive color reinforces a mood of sultry indolence.

Picasso, enthused by the voluptuousness and compositional complexities of Delacroix's work, painted not one, but fifteen free versions of this painting between December 13, 1954, and February 14, 1955. While the majority retain Delacroix's basic figural and environmental elements, all show drastic simplification of these forms. The first canvas displays traces of the volumetric modeling, flowing curves, and rich patterning of the prototype, but the variations soon diverge in their own directions. While the second version, close in composition to the first, is executed in grisaille, color returns quickly, not the saturated tones of Delacroix, but lighter, more spontaneous hues, suggesting the spirit of Matisse. In fact, it has been suggested that this series was motivated by the death of Matisse, just one month before Picasso began the first version.[1]

In *Women of Algiers, E,* the fifth variation, a recumbent nude, legs in the air, dominates the center foreground. A seated figure fills the entire left third of the canvas. The figure of the servant, who moves off to the right in the nineteenth-century version, is here relegated to the background, a sculpture-like streamlined silhouette of the original which nonetheless retains its characteristic gesture. Delacroix's deep Baroque space has been eliminated, the distant planes pulled forward, the wall patterning enlarged and gridded. A latticed doorway with rounded top that appears in preceding versions here becomes a nimbus behind the seated figure, further flattening the pictorial space. The figures, too, are flattened, realized simply with heavy black outlines and areas of flat color. Breast forms—circular linear shapes—are reiterated frequently, both as anatomical detailing and as decorative motif.

As the series progressed, the horizontal format metamorphosed into a vertically divided one reflecting the double mirror image and simultaneous subject juxtaposition of Picasso's prolonged artist/model theme. Seventy-three when he began this series, Picasso approached even traditional themes with new ideas and new pictorial solutions.   KCH

[1]Jane Fluegel, "Chronology," in William Rubin, ed., *Pablo Picasso: A Retrospective*, The Museum of Modern Art, New York, 1980, p. 416.

Julio González

SPANISH, 1876–1942

Mask "My"

MASQUE "MY"

ca. 1930

bronze 5/9
8 × 3½ × 3"
20.3 × 8.9 × 7.6 cm

Gift of E. Morris Cox from the
collection of Margaret Storke Cox
83.225

*Small Sickle
(Woman Standing)*

PETITE FAUCILLE
(FEMME DEBOUT)

ca. 1937

bronze 4/6
11½ × 4¾ × 3½"
29.2 × 12.1 × 8.9 cm

Gift of E. Morris Cox from the
collection of Margaret Storke Cox
83.224

[1] Quoted in Andrew Carnduff Ritchie, *Julio Gonzalez*, published as *The Museum of Modern Art Bulletin*, vol. 23, nos. 1–2 (1955–56), p. 42.

[2] Quoted in Josephine Withers, *Julio Gonzalez: Sculpture in Iron* (New York: New York University Press, 1978), p. 134.

[3] For a brief discussion of the issues relative to making cast bronzes from iron originals by González, see Rosalind Krauss, "This New Art: To Draw in Space," *Julio González: Sculpture & Drawings*, The Pace Gallery, New York, 1981; Gene Baro, "New York Letter," *Art International*, vol. 25, nos. 3–4 (March–April 1982), p. 100; and Sylvia Hochfield, "Problems in the Reproduction of Sculpture," *Art News*, vol. 73, no. 9 (November 1974), pp. 25–26.

[4] While González's primary medium was iron, *Small Sickle* was forged in bronze and illustrates how he also worked with other metals common to the metalsmith's trade, including brass, copper, and silver.

[5] In Withers, op. cit.

[6] Robert Hughes, "Misunderstood Master of Iron," *Time*, vol. 121, no. 15 (April 18, 1983), p. 92.

"THE AGE OF IRON BEGAN MANY CENTURIES AGO," Julio González wrote in 1932, "by producing very beautiful objects, unfortunately for a large part, arms. . . . It is time this metal ceased to be a murderer. . . . Today the door is wide open for this material to be, at last, forged and hammered by the peaceful hands of an artist."[1] And indeed, in the "peaceful hands" of González, along with those of Pablo Picasso and the American David Smith, forged and welded metal became a new medium of modern sculpture.

González grew up with iron. He was born to a Catalan family of craftsmen who had forged it for at least three generations, and in their tradition he was trained as a decorative metalworker. In 1928 Picasso called upon González's expertise to assist him in constructing in wire, rod, and sheet metal certain ideas he had been investigating on paper. Picasso's example encouraged González to channel his talents and, already past fifty years of age, he emerged from this celebrated collaboration wholeheartedly devoted to sculpture and with a liberated sense of the aesthetic possibilities of forged and welded iron.

While Picasso was one of the innovators of linear iron sculpture, González, in the brief ten years before his death in 1942, fully developed the idea. In embracing the radical concept of using space as a positive sculptural element, he replaced sculpture's traditional emphasis on mass with a focus on the void that is created by enclosing spatial volume with a linear metal framework. This new form of open sculpture—"to draw in space,"[2] as González termed it—evolved by applying the technique of forging and welding metal, particularly iron, to artistic purposes.

A bronze cast from an original iron, *Mask "My"* of circa 1930 is one of González's early sculptures, made during the period of his collaboration with Picasso.[3] The work, a highly simplified, schematic arrangement of planes that depicts the human face, is a technical tour de force, fashioned from a single sheet of metal out of which the features were cut with a jeweler's saw, the planes then pushed forward and back; crisp, straight lines and angled cuts contrast with curved contours. Despite the mask's formal rigor, its stylized wisp of hair (a motif synthesized from Picasso) and closed, meditative eyes suggest the poetic expressiveness that González fully explored during the 1930s.

If *Mask "My"* illustrates González's early planar idiom, *Small Sickle* of circa 1937[4] demonstrates his mature linear style. Here González transforms the human figure into an abstract hybrid form—part human, part plant, part object. Characteristic of González's open-form sculpture, this work is a linear configuration exemplifying the "union of real forms with imagined forms."[5] The curvilinear sickle is a cipher for the figure's head and the space it delineates suggests the full form.

The expressive body gesture that González had learned from modern dance and applied to his filiform dancers in 1934 is ever present in the taut, angular, oversized cactus-arm that is dramatically thrust downward. Both the cactus motif and the sickle in *Small Sickle* introduce a change in emotional tone. While the gentle, and at times fanciful, works of the early to mid-1930s are formal explorations, the harsh and anguished works of the late 1930s are political. The sickle is more than a sign for a human head, it is a symbol of the working class and of Communism—a weapon against Franco.[6] In *Small Sickle* González begins to express the horror and brutality of the Spanish Civil War as had his compatriot Picasso in 1937 in his great symbol of inhumanity, *Guernica*.   DCduP

62

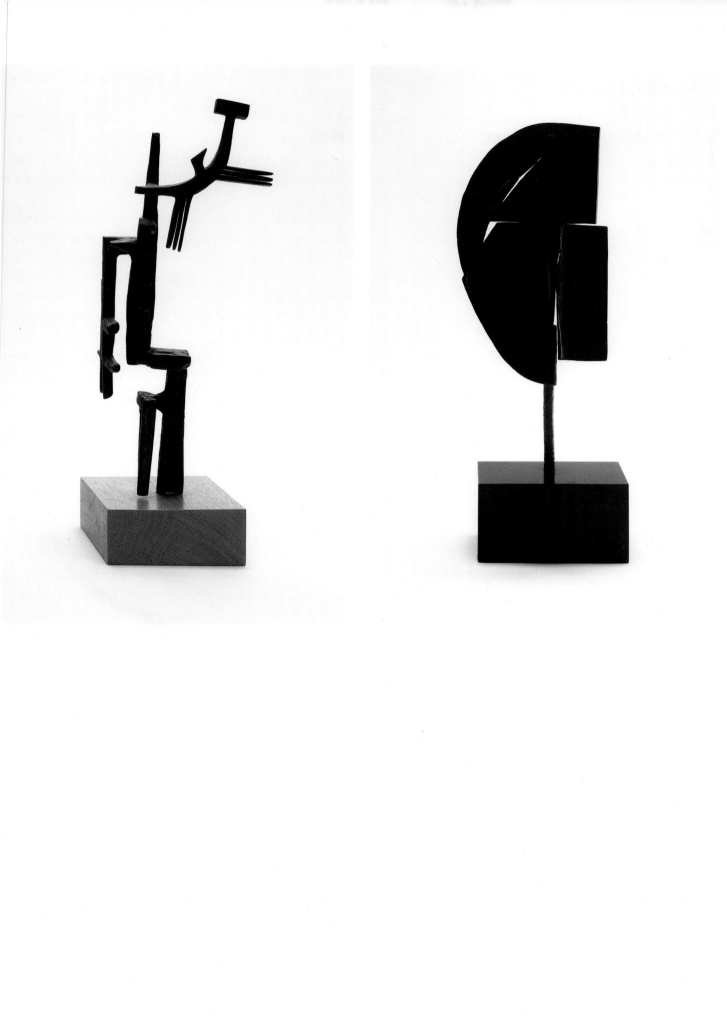

Amédée Ozenfant

FRENCH, 1886–1966

Still Life

NATURE MORTE
1920–21

oil on canvas
32 × 39⅝″
81.3 × 100.6 cm

Gift of Lucien Labaudt
37.2991

AT THE CLOSE OF WORLD WAR I, Amédée Ozenfant and Charles-Edouard Jeanneret (Le Corbusier), disillusioned with what they considered to be the decorative degeneration of Cubism, published a manifesto, *Après le cubisme*, in which they proposed a new art predicated on classical forms and an underlying geometric order. Intended to be a successor to Cubism yet inextricably linked to it, this new movement, termed Purism, called for an emphasis on universality realized through visual preconception, deletion of detail, and the use of objective subject matter.

Both the Ozenfant-Jeanneret partnership and the Purist style itself lasted from 1918 until 1925. Although during the formative years of the style the artists exhibited portraits and landscapes, the still life quickly emerged as the sole genre for Purist expression. Concentrating on a few classic objects—milk bottle, Bordeaux wine bottle, wine glass, fluted carafe, and guitar—set upon severely tilted tabletops and situated within interior spaces defined by simple architectural elements, the artists extracted and presented the stable essence with rigorous objectivity. Interwoven into these canvases is a spirit of modernism expressed not only through a palette that evokes the machine age—grays, steely blues, and subdued rusts—but also through the seemingly machine-made objects, each precisely turned and accurately grooved.

While Purism denounced what its exponents viewed as the excesses of Cubism, particularly the colorful, patterned embellishments that flourished during the Synthetic phase, it was nonetheless a direct offshoot of Cubism and, as such, retained several of its basic formal principles: simultaneity of perspectives, dislocated object components, and concurrent use of transparency and opacity. These precepts from Analytic Cubism joined the cutout silhouettes found in Cubism's later phase.

While both Jeanneret and Ozenfant had far-ranging interests within the world of art, Jeanneret was at heart an architect whose functional designs for living created in succeeding decades exploited his knowledge of Cubist space. Amédée Ozenfant's consuming concern was for painting. Born in 1886 in Saint-Quentin, northeast of Paris, he received his formal training there before moving to Paris in 1904 to study architecture and painting. Moved by the wide variety of styles visible in the capital, Ozenfant experimented eclectically, flirting not only with Impressionism and Fauvism, but with Cubism as well. His periodical, *L'Elan*, introduced in 1915, provided him an entrée to the most vital personages of the period, writers and poets, as well as artists. The formulation of Ozenfant's ideas regarding a pure form of art was hastened in 1918 when he and Jeanneret formed their historic cooperative partnership, which resulted in a body of canvases encompassing Purist precepts and a collection of publications that documented their viewpoint.

In 1920–21, at the height of his powers as a Purist painter, Ozenfant executed *Still Life* (*Nature morte*). Almost identical to a number of other works of the same subject, this austere arrangement of ordinary objects exemplifies Ozenfant's concern for purity and universality. Thoughtfully conceived with a fundamental geometric substructure and echoing curves and verticals, the flattened and silhouetted shapes are set into space defined by an architecturally described corner. The reductive, aloof sensibility is underscored by the smooth non-committal paint-handling as well as the cool, metallic tonality. Achieving a generality that approaches timelessness, this work epitomizes the thoughtful, static presence of Purism which, by 1925, had stagnated to the point of extinction.   KCH

Morgan Russell

AMERICAN, 1886–1953

Synchromy No. 3

ca. 1922–23

oil on canvas
23¾ × 16⅛"
60.4 × 40.9 cm

Purchase
72.1

THE LURE OF PARIS, traditionally a mecca for American art students, was never so strong as in the first decades of the twentieth century. While some stayed in the French capital just long enough to receive their academic training, many remained to play active roles in the revolutionary birth of modernism. Such was the case of Stanton Macdonald-Wright and Morgan Russell when in 1913 they presented their first exhibitions of Synchromism, a movement founded on the expressive utilization of the optical properties of color. This movement, thoroughly American yet grounded in the recent accomplishments of the French—Impressionism, Orphism, and the work of Paul Cézanne —was the result of the partnership of Macdonald-Wright and Russell, and its essential nature continued to be explored and developed throughout the following decade in the individual work of the two artists.

Morgan Russell had settled in Paris in 1909, fresh from his New York studies with Robert Henri and with James Earle Fraser at the Pennsylvania Academy of the Fine Arts. His initial interest was in sculpture, but he became fascinated with the work of Monet, whose affirmation of color as a product of the vagaries of light provided a spark for Russell's work. In 1910, Russell took up the study of Cézanne's paintings, provoked by his use of shapes, gradations, and juxtapositions of color to express volume, mass, and spatial relationships. A parallel investigation into the color theories of Michel Eugène Chevreul and Ogden Rood revealed the laws of harmony of analogous colors, the law of harmony of contrasts (both Chevreul), and the law of gradation (Rood), all of which figured prominently in his subsequent work.

In 1911, Morgan Russell and Stanton Macdonald-Wright met and began sharing their common interest in theories of color and light. They began extending their theoretical knowledge to pictorial form, at first tying it to subjects derived from the objective world—figures, landscapes, and still lifes. In the summer of 1913, Russell began painting abstract Synchromies, in which the fruition of their theories manifested itself. Reviving his longtime interest in sculpture, he first actually modeled these early abstractions, then expressed this structure on the painting surface by means of colored planes. Using the colors with the most light to define the frontal planes and the darker tones to express recession, the Synchromists also employed gradations of colors rather than modeling to define mass.

With the advent of World War I, the official affiliation of the two artists dissolved, Russell remaining in France and Macdonald-Wright returning to the United States. Both artists, however, continued to evolve, independently exploring the extensions and ramifications of Synchromism through their individual pictorial statements. Russell ceased painting his color-filled canvases in 1916, but after 1920 he resumed the Synchromies with renewed enthusiasm. *Synchromy No. 3*, painted around 1922–23, expresses the strength of these later works. Its density of pigment, impastoed surface, and use of graduated planes recall Russell's earlier sculptural considerations. Color triads, chords of three distinct hues, set up baroque rhythms across the surface, yet serve to define space and volume as well. The color tone, considerably deeper than in Russell's earlier work, provides a weightiness, underscored by the static division of the composition. Within the formalized scheme, however, the colors appear freer, more expressive than in the previous work.   KCH

66

Franz Marc

GERMAN, 1880–1916

Mountains (Rocky Way/Landscape)

GEBIRGE (STEINIGER WEG/
LANDSCHAFT)
1911–12

oil on canvas
51½ × 39¾″
130.8 × 101.0 cm

Gift of the Women's Board and
Friends of the Museum
51.4095

FRANZ MARC HAS BEEN APTLY DESCRIBED as a "shooting star" in the path of German Expressionism.[1] His artistic career spanned only eleven years, from 1903, the time he left the Munich Academy, to 1914, when he enlisted in the German Army at the outset of World War I. His rapid rise to a pivotal position among the Munich avant-garde was cut short by his tragic death in 1916 in the "war to end all wars."

Born in Munich in 1880, Marc studied theology as a student, but after a year of military service he decided to become an artist. Reacting against the skepticism and materialism of the time, he joined other artists and writers in a desire to return to spirituality. In his mature work, he selected the animal, particularly the horse, as a metaphor for purity, piety, and harmony with nature. He tried to render what, in 1908, he called the "organic rhythm" in nature by integrating curving animal masses with the rolling forms of the landscape.

Having developed the compositional means for capturing the continuum of the physical world, Marc sought a new approach to color. Influenced by the paintings he had seen by Henri Matisse, Vasily Kandinsky, and August Macke, he formulated his own color symbolism associated with the elemental forces of the universe. In December 1910 he wrote to August Macke: "Blue is the male principle, astringent and spiritual. Yellow [is] the female principle, gentle, gay and sensual. Red is matter, brutal and heavy. . . ."[2] Marc's sense of integrated composition and new-found color theory are synthesized in his masterful primary-color works of 1911. The vivid, non-naturalistic hues are complemented by a treatment of form more abstracted than previously seen in Marc's work.

In 1911, Marc and Kandinsky met and became friends and collaborators; together with Alfred Kubin and Gabriele Münter they founded the Blaue Reiter (Blue Rider) group. Marc originally completed *Mountains* in 1911 and exhibited it in the first Blaue Reiter exhibition in December of that year, under the title *Landschaft* (Landscape). Also included in this legendary exhibition were four paintings by the Orphist Robert Delaunay, whose concern with the issues of abstraction and brilliant color influenced members of the Blaue Reiter circle. In the autumn of 1912, Marc visited Delaunay in Paris and, upon his return, transformed *Landschaft*, which had become known as *Steiniger Weg* (Rocky Way), into an inventive fusion of Cubist, Orphist, and Futurist influences. Not only did he repaint the work at this time, he renamed it *Gebirge* (Mountains).

In this work, Marc adopted the Cubist fracturing of form to create an arrangement of faceted, triangular prisms which surge upward to suggest tall mountains at the sides and a rocky, zigzag path through the center. The planes of contrasting, spectral tonalities create a resplendent, near-abstract surface of colored light such as Delaunay realized in his most vibrant works of this period, the windows and disks series. This effect combined with the thrusting prismatic forms creates a dynamic, kaleidoscopic impression resembling the work of the Italian Futurists whom Marc defended in the pages of the periodical *Der Sturm* in 1912.

This unusual landscape, in which Marc's familiar animal subjects are absent, may reveal his Romantic, mystical inclinations and is perhaps a vehicle for the contemplation of the spiritual. The impellent triangular forms that point to the red sun at the summit seem to evoke a sense of striving toward another world. "The longing for indivisible Being," wrote Marc, "for liberation from the sense illusions of our ephemeral life, is the fundamental mood of all art."[3]   DCduP

[1] Mark Rosenthal, *Franz Marc: 1880–1916* (Berkeley: University of California, University Art Museum), 1979, p. 5.

[2] Ron Glowen, "The Spiritual, Empathetic and Abstract Animal," *Vanguard* (Summer 1980), p. 17.

[3] Klaus Lankheit, *Franz Marc: Sein Leben und seine Kunst* (Cologne: DuMont, 1976), frontispiece.

Max Pechstein

GERMAN, 1881–1955

Nelly
1910

oil on canvas
20⅜ × 20⅞″
51.8 × 53.1 cm
Purchase
84.9

DURING THE NINETEENTH CENTURY the stifling, straitlaced propriety of the European bourgeoisie induced some artists to seek what they viewed as the free-spirited, simplified, and natural way of life led by non-Westernized people in exotic lands. To painters and sculptors working in the early years of this century, the Post-Impressionist Paul Gauguin personified the simplifying artist par excellence. Turning his back on European culture a second time, Gauguin moved permanently to the South Seas in 1895 and pared his art to essentials in an attempt to break through convention and express a genuine reality. The German Expressionist artists who constituted the Brücke (Bridge), a group founded in Dresden in 1905 by Ernst Ludwig Kirchner, Erich Heckel, and Karl Schmidt-Rottluff, were inspired by Gauguin and looked to the art and life of primitive and exotic peoples as an ideal world in which fundamental values were respected and basic human emotions freely expressed.

The German Expressionist painter Max Pechstein, who became a member of the Brücke in 1906, was captivated by primitive art. "I visited the Ethnographic Museum in Dresden," he remembered, "and was spellbound by the South Sea carvings and African sculpture."[1] In *Nelly*, painted in Berlin in 1910, Pechstein reveals his romantic longing for the exotic well before his voyage to the South Seas in 1914. In coloring and facial structure, Nelly resembles a black African, but Pechstein has synthesized this exoticism with his native culture. Wearing blue bows in her hair, dangling earrings, and an electric-pink dress with black patterning, Nelly is perhaps a member of the cabaret scene, a common subject for Brücke artists. This vital, robust female with exaggerated, sensual lips suggests a frank sexuality that exhibits the German Expressionists' desire to overthrow the strictures of Victorianism. Concerned not with anatomical detail, but with a single dominating expression, Pechstein used broad areas of bold, glowing, Fauve-inspired color—pinks, reds, blues—and simplified form. Compositionally, he achieves a confrontational posture by placing his subject in a shallow, crowded space.

Like other Brücke artists, Pechstein coupled his reduction of form with a simplification in technique. He coarsened his paint application to create an expressive, agitated brushwork particularly evident in the background. A comparison of Pechstein's *Nelly* with portraits by the Viennese Expressionists Egon Schiele and Oskar Kokoschka demonstrates the range of Expressionist portraiture. *Nelly*, a vital, exuberant image of gaiety that flaunts an open sexuality, is far removed from the tortured, emaciated figures of Schiele and Kokoschka, whose exposed psyches symbolize the existential angst of modern experience.   DCduP

[1]Peter Selz, *German Expressionist Painting* (Berkeley and Los Angeles: University of California Press, 1957), p. 83.

Alexej Jawlensky

RUSSIAN, 1864–1941

Woman's Head

FRAUENKOPF
1913

oil on composition board
21¼ × 19½"
54.0 × 49.5 cm

Gift of Charlotte Mack
50.5518

Head: Red Light

KOPF: ROTES LICHT
1926

oil wax medium on cardboard
21 × 19"
53.4 × 48.3 cm

Gift of Charlotte Mack
50.5952

LIKE HIS COMPATRIOT Vasily Kandinsky, the Russian emigré Alexej Jawlensky developed a distinctive and mystical form of painting that was important in shaping German Expressionism. The dominant motif in his work throughout his career was the human face. "In the face," he wrote, "the whole universe becomes manifest."[1] Although closely associated with the Blaue Reiter (Blue Rider) group in Munich, which adopted the landscape as its primary theme, Jawlensky's intense focus on the human visage reveals an affinity with the contemporaneous Brücke (Bridge) artists of Dresden.

In the group of heads Jawlensky painted in Munich between 1911 and 1914, he assimilated the brilliant coloration and expressive paint-handling of Fauvism—with which he was well acquainted from his studies with Henri Matisse in Paris during 1907—into an individual style grounded in his Russian heritage. A deeply religious man, he was influenced by the stylized faces of Russo-Byzantine icons. Crowded close to the picture frame to heighten their intensity, most of his heads depict unusual, often Slavic-looking women with burning eyes rimmed with dark lines. They are rendered in bold, deeply saturated, sensual colors orchestrated to form a harmonious composition.

Woman's Head of 1913 belongs to this series of pre-World War I works. The generalized image of the woman bears a commanding presence achieved by simplifying the features into broad masses and tightly circumscribing the rounded head within a square format, creating tension at the picture's edge. The profound, dark contour lines contrast sharply with the light-colored background and white highlights of the face, while the vivid blue, red, green, and pink patches of facial paint recall such paintings by Matisse as his 1905 portrait of Madame Matisse known as *The Green Line*, in which vibrant, non-naturalistic color is used as a structural element. Jawlensky creates a rhythmic composition through the repetition of curved lines, from the shoulders, neckline, and eyes to the glowing halo-like rings emanating from the figure's head. His characteristic zigzag brush stroke accentuates this curvilinear movement and heightens the impact of the image.

The tragedy of World War I forced Jawlensky to flee to Switzerland and compelled him to re-evaluate the stylistic and philosophical basis of his art. "Then came the war," he wrote. "I tried to go on with my powerful, strongly colored paintings but I found I couldn't. My soul would not allow that sensuous painting . . . I felt I had to find another language, a more spiritual language."[2]

In 1921 Jawlensky returned to Germany and abandoned painting the abstract landscapes he had pursued during his exile to concentrate exclusively on the human face. He had been moving toward this direction in 1917; at that time he said: "I realized that great art should only be painted with religious feeling, and that was something I could bring only to the human face."[3] In the series called Constructivist Heads executed throughout the twenties, Jawlensky consistently explored the same subject in pursuit of deeper spiritual meaning. As he explained, "I am not so much searching for new forms but I want to go deeper, not to progress in breadth but in depth."[4]

During this time, Jawlensky was a member of the Blaue Vier (Blue Four), a group that included Vasily Kandinsky, Lyonel Feininger, and Paul Klee, who were all teachers at the Bauhaus, a major center of Constructivism. Influenced by Constructivist ideas, Jawlensky made these heads into extremely simplified schematic renderings in which the features are reduced to geometric forms and emphasis is given to the harmonious dynamics between broad, sharply defined areas of color and vertical, horizontal, and curvilinear lines. These heads, with their luminous, jewel-like color and quiet, introspective mood suggested by the closed eyes, radiate a mystical inner peace.

Head: Red Light of 1926 is part of the Constructivist Heads series. As in other paintings of this series, Jawlensky made only subtle adjustments in the main arrangement of geometric lines and planes. Color becomes the single most important variable within this highly repetitive format. *Head: Red Light* with its soft red and pink tones —which illustrate the principle of color harmony explored by Bauhaus artists—and contemplative expression glows with a transcendental aura. In abstracting the face to the point where it functions as a symbol, Jawlensky was striving toward the creation of a modern icon.   DCduP

[1]Clemens Weiler, *Jawlensky: Heads, Faces, Meditations* (New York: Praeger, 1971), caption for plate 18.
[2]Letter from Jawlensky to Father Willibrord Verkade, June 12, 1938; ibid., pp. 106, 108.
[3]Ibid., p. 11.
[4]Ibid., caption for plate 19.

Max Beckmann

GERMAN, 1884–1950

Landscape, Cannes

LANDSCHAFT, CANNES
1934

oil on canvas
27⅝ × 39½"
70.2 × 100.4 cm

Gift of Louise S. Ackerman
72.12

BITTER, INCISIVE PAINTINGS scrutinizing the shadowed side of man—man as predator, satyr, brute—these are the works for which Max Beckmann is best known. During the early years of the twenties, tormented by the horrors of World War I, Beckmann, in strident visual terms, lashed out at what he saw as human perversion, using his work as an ethical commentary on the state of man.

A native of Leipzig, Germany, where he was born in 1884, Max Beckmann spent the last years of the nineteenth century studying art at the conservative art academy in Weimar. After a brief visit to Paris in 1903, where he was struck by the work of van Gogh, the Impressionists, and, most significantly, the art of the Middle Ages, Beckmann settled in Berlin in 1904. Berlin at that time was a cosmopolitan capital, bursting with progressive ideas and energy, its artist community charged by the energies of Max Liebermann and Lovis.Corinth. Beckmann left Berlin in 1906 for a six-month sojourn in Florence, where he was captivated by Piero della Francesca's masterful space definition and the finely drafted musculature of Luca Signorelli. These influences, as well as that of Eugène Delacroix, determined Beckmann's pre-World War I work, which depicted mythological and biblical subjects in a romantic, muscular style, touched with an edge of cynicism that reflected the doomsday mood of Berlin in the days just preceding the war.

Beckmann volunteered for the army in 1914, but by 1915, spiritually wounded by the horrors he had witnessed as a medical orderly, he suffered a nervous breakdown and settled in Frankfurt to recuperate. The paintings and graphics he created during this period directly reflect his war-induced agony. Emotionally charged angular forms, vertically distorted to create strong upward movement, express allegorically the horrors of human conflict. Reflecting the economic chaos and severely fractured politics of contemporary Germany, the strongly political works exude tension and violence. While regarded as attacks directed against the established government, they were in fact more universal in scope: indictments against war, the cruelty of man, and the chasm between the poor and the wealthy.

By the mid twenties, Beckmann was enjoying acceptance by the social and cultural communities; as he became content with both his personal and professional life, his art mellowed. The strident, discordant colors of the earlier work became sensuous and lively; the flattened figures were replaced by sculpturally modeled forms; black outlines, much like those employed by Georges Rouault, appeared.

But in the early thirties, discord again surfaced. Modern art came under attack and Beckmann, dismissed from his prestigious teaching position, moved back to Berlin. *Landscape, Cannes*, painted in Berlin in 1934, reflects both the calm, positive spirit of the twenties and the ominous foreboding of the early thirties. It is a French scene viewed through Germanic eyes. The almost Matissean air of the picture with its cool Mediterranean coloration and clarity of atmosphere is countered by the aggressive composition, spiky forms, and heavy use of black. As in Beckmann's own personal environment, spreading shadows loom large over the countryside.   KCH

Max Beckmann

GERMAN, 1884–1950

Woman at Her Toilette, with Red and White Lilies

FRAU BEI DER TOILETTE MIT
ROTEN UND WEISSEN LILIEN
1938

oil on canvas
43½ × 25¾"
110.5 × 65.4 cm

Bequest of Marian W. Sinton
81.51

UNSETTLED TIMES CONTINUED for Beckmann throughout the years of World War II. Torn by attacks against his art by the Nazi government and the confiscation of his works from German collections, and stripped of his livelihood, he fled Berlin in the summer of 1937, taking up residence in Amsterdam. He had earlier expressed his feelings about leaving one's homeland in the monumental triptych *Departure* (1932–33), a deeply personal allegorical statement depicting a king and his family leaving a land filled with evil and tyranny for a future of freedom.

Woman at Her Toilette, with Red and White Lilies, painted in Amsterdam the year after his arrival, continues the sonorous use of color seen in *Landscape, Cannes* painted four years earlier. An awareness of the work of Matisse, with which Beckmann became well acquainted on his frequent extended trips to Paris, is also evident. The composition, with a strongly stated, vertically centered form positioned in the middle ground, overlaid with dominant elements spreading from the left foreground and balanced by a summarily described image in the upper right background, is one used often by Beckmann. Its major components were in fact utilized in *Landscape, Cannes*.

Distortion of the figure, prevalent in Beckmann's symbolic canvases, here underlines the verticality of the format. The exaggerated curvature of the shoulder line, the long, slender right arm ending in an oversized hand, and the plump, gently bowed left arm are reinforced by the elongated, splayed, and spiky forms of the lilies which fan out in front of the figure, setting up powerful upwardly expanding thrusts and multiple patterns of intersecting angles. The recurrent jagged forms which counter the smooth voluptuousness of the woman's body hark back to German Expressionist and medieval roots. The corseted figure, too, is reminiscent of Beckmann's earlier harsh comments on social decadence, but here the tone is softened and sophisticated, with only a faint overtone of conflict.   KCH

Piet Mondrian

DUTCH, 1872–1944

Church Façade/ Church at Domburg

formerly
CATHEDRAL
1914

charcoal on chipboard
28¼ × 19⅛"
71.8 × 48.6 cm

Purchase
70.43

[1]Piet Mondrian, *Toward the True Vision of Reality* (New York: Valentin Gallery, 1942).

[2]See Michel Seuphor, *Piet Mondrian: Life and Work* (New York: Harry N. Abrams, 1956), p. 379, no. 255; and *Mondrian: Drawings, Watercolors, New York Paintings*, Staatsgalerie, Stuttgart, 1980, p. 101.

[3]Seuphor, op. cit., pp. 260, 377, no. 232.

[4]Quoted in Seuphor, op. cit., p. 117.

[5]Quoted in Herschel B. Chipp, *Theories of Modern Art* (Berkeley: University of California Press, 1971), p. 315.

A MAZE-LIKE NETWORK of vertical, horizontal, and curved lines finely balanced to achieve a sense of harmony in asymmetry: such is the structure of *Church Façade/Church at Domburg* of 1914, one of a series of drawings by the Dutch modernist Piet Mondrian based on the village church at Domburg. In the course of creating this series—which culminated in the painting *Composition 1916* (The Solomon R. Guggenheim Museum, New York)—as well as the Pier and Ocean Series also of 1914, Mondrian began to formulate his personal philosophy of art and affirmed his path to abstraction, "toward" what he considered "the true vision of reality."[1]

In July 1914 Mondrian left Paris, where he had been living since late 1911, for a visit to his native Holland. The outbreak of World War I forced him to remain in the Netherlands and so he returned to Domburg, a village on the island of Walcheren off the southwestern coast, where he had spent almost every summer since 1908. In his drawings of the church at Domburg he carried further the implication of pure abstraction in Cubism, which he had pursued in Paris in his series of trees and building façades. Mondrian was a prolific draughtsman, and during his Cubist years (1913–16) drawing was essential to his developing abstraction. This 1914 charcoal is closest in style and technique to two other known drawings in the series[2] in its simplified, spare scaffolding of lines and in its elimination of architectural details, particularly the suppression of the "naturalistic" curves referring to the church's Gothic windows. The final painting, *Composition 1916*,[3] relies on a strictly horizontal-vertical format, a structure that derived from the theories of equilibrium Mondrian was studying at the time, which would evolve into the concept of integrating opposing elements—vertical and horizontal, masculine and feminine, negative and positive, subjective and universal—that guided Mondrian's art.

Like his European contemporaries Vasily Kandinsky, Franz Marc, and František Kupka, Mondrian's path to abstraction was intimately connected with a search for the spiritual. Both Mondrian and Kandinsky were inspired by the Theosophical movement. The text of two notebooks Mondrian apparently kept while at Domburg reveal the influence of Theosophist doctrine in his preference for spirituality over materiality: ". . . For our senses these are two different things—the spiritual and the material. To approach the spiritual in art, one will make as little use as possible of reality, because reality is opposed to the spiritual. Thus the use of elementary forms is logically accounted for. These forms being abstract, we find ourselves in the presence of an abstract art."[4]

The ideas contained in the church façade drawings and Mondrian's two notebooks of the same period form the basis of the important essays he later published in the magazine of the Dutch vanguard movement De Stijl. Founded in 1917 by Theo van Doesburg in association with Mondrian, Bart van der Leck, and other painters, sculptors, architects, and poets, De Stijl was the purest and the most idealistic of the European abstract movements. Neo-Plasticism, the theory of art developed by Mondrian, provided the most refined and absolute interpretation of De Stijl beliefs. Mondrian held that the fundamental relationships in art achieved by reducing pictorial form to its basic elements of line, color, and space, arranged in elemental compositions, were models for an ideal harmony both in the individual and in society. Mondrian and the other De Stijl artists possessed a vision of utopia in which art and life would form a perfect unity: "In the future," he wrote, "the tangible embodiment of pictorial values will supplant art. Then we shall no longer need paintings, for we shall live in the midst of realized art."[5] DCduP

Theo van Doesburg

DUTCH, 1883–1931

Simultaneous Counter Composition

CONTRE COMPOSITION
SIMULTANÉE
1929

oil on canvas
19¾ × 19¾"
50.2 × 50.2 cm

Gift of Peggy Guggenheim
51.3389

UPON FIRST GLANCE, it is clear that Theo van Doesburg's *Simultaneous Counter Composition* of 1929 possesses many of the characteristics of the mature painting of Piet Mondrian, with whom he launched the De Stijl group and its magazine in neutral Holland during World War I. The abstract, geometric vocabulary of grid lines and colored planes, the asymmetrical composition with the forms placed at the periphery, the fine, smooth facture, and the emphasis on the painting's edges are all extrapolations from Mondrian's Neo-Plasticism, the term he preferred to De Stijl. This revolutionary visual language of abstraction which reduced pictorial form to its fundamental elements—geometric shape; the primary colors, red, yellow and blue; and the non-colors, black, white, and gray—was principally the invention of Mondrian. Van Doesburg, however, was its primary spokesman and through his writing, lecturing, and publishing of the *De Stijl* magazine he spread the movement's ideas.

Yet, for all the similarities between van Doesburg's *Simultaneous Counter Composition* and Mondrian's work, there are key differences, such as the use of the diagonal.[1] By late 1924, in his new approach to Neo-Plasticism, which he termed Elementarism, van Doesburg rejected the strictly orthogonal compositions of Mondrian, on the grounds that their horizontal-vertical format was a remnant of naturalism since it paralleled the fundamental structural laws of the visible world, and that it was static and not reflective of the dynamic principle of modern life.[2] Van Doesburg introduced a diagonal element as a point of opposition by rotating his planes and grid lines to a forty-five-degree angle.

Van Doesburg's emphasis on the diagonal evolved from his architectural work of the early 1920s which proposed a new concept of space that would destroy the idea of architecture as an arrangement of horizontal-vertical masses defined by gravity. Instead, he hoped to create a space that was suspended and expressed space-time relationships through the use of diagonals and the interpenetration of planes. When translated into such Elementarist paintings as *Simultaneous Counter Composition*, the diagonal represents not only a challenge to Mondrian's horizontal-vertical format, but also to his conception of space as two-dimensional. "While the expressive possibilities of Neo-plasticism are limited to two dimensions (the plane)," van Doesburg wrote, "Elementarism realizes the possibility of plasticism in four dimensions, in the field of time-space."[3]

Van Doesburg's Elementarism and his use of the diagonal also challenged the idea of motion in Mondrian's Neo-Plasticism, for, like Constructivism and other movements of the 1920s, it reassessed this concept as explored in Cubism and Futurism. Van Doesburg asserted that Mondrian's "balanced" compositions, as he termed them, were static. For van Doesburg, movement found in opposition rather than equilibrium, and as expressed by the oblique, more effectively captured the complexity of the modern era. "Elementary (anti-static) counter-composition," he wrote, "adds to orthogonal, peripheral composition a new diagonal dimension . . . sloping planes, dissonant planes in opposition to gravity and static architectural structure."[4] As suggested by the title, in *Simultaneous Counter Composition*, van Doesburg contrasts the static and the dynamic by opposing both orthogonal and diagonal elements.

Even though van Doesburg sought to amend the principles of Neo-Plasticism, he retained the utopian idealism intrinsic to De Stijl thinking. He continued to look at the arts as a means for guiding and enlightening humanity. "Elementarism," he wrote, "is directed not only to art, architecture and objects of utility, but also to living man and society. It wishes to renew the life concept . . . to strengthen and arouse the spirit of opposition . . . and counts upon making possible . . . a real, inner renewal of our mentality."[5] DCduP

[1] Van Doesburg's color in this painting also differs from Mondrian's mature work in that he varies the scheme of primaries by using the red/green complementary pair. Van Doesburg emphasized the independence of color and looked at it "as energy, and also as dissonance, contrast and variant." See his "Painting and Sculpture: About Counter-composition and Counter-sculpture. Elementarism (Fragment of a Manifesto)," July 1926; in Hans L. C. Jaffe, *De Stijl* (New York: Harry N. Abrams, 1971), p. 211.

[2] It has commonly been assumed that Mondrian's split from De Stijl during the mid-1920s was due simply to Van Doesburg's introduction of the diagonal. This limited interpretation ignores the fact that Mondrian in his pre- and early-De Stijl work and in his diamond compositions experimented with the diagonal and belies the deeper differences between them.

[3] "Painting and Sculpture: Elementarism (Fragment of a Manifesto)," December 1925–April 1927; in Jaffe, op. cit, p. 214.

[4] "Painting and Sculpture: About Counter-composition . . . "; op. cit., p. 209.

[5] "Painting and Sculpture: Elementarism . . . "; op. cit., p. 215.

Joaquin Torres-Garcia

URUGUAYAN, 1874–1949

Constructivist Painting No. 8

1938

gouache on paperboard
31⅝ × 19½"
80.5 × 49.5 cm

Purchased through the aid of a gift of Willard Durham
50.3013

THE SYNTHESIS OF FORM AND IDEA, the fusion of abstract structure with images and symbols drawn from prehistoric, primitive, and autobiographical sources are the hallmarks of the work of Joaquin Torres-Garcia. Deeply impressed by the paintings and theories of Piet Mondrian and Theo van Doesburg, Torres-Garcia was an enthusiastic participant in abstractionist groups in Paris from 1929 to 1932. However, his particular brand of constructivism, which he called Universal Constructivism, eschewed purified abstraction and called instead for the inclusion of ideas relating to the objective world expressed through visual signs and pictographs.

Born in Montevideo, Uruguay, in 1874, Torres-Garcia moved with his family to Catalonia in 1891 and settled in Barcelona in 1892. After receiving his formal training at the Academia de Bellas Artes in Barcelona, he commenced his career by painting murals infused with the Neo-Classical spirit of Puvis de Chavannes in Catalan churches and government buildings. In 1926, Torres-Garcia moved to Paris where he quickly gravitated toward the abstractionist groups. In 1929, he and the Belgian artist and critic Michel Seuphor founded Cercle et Carré (Circle and Square) which pitted the constructivists against the then-dominant Surrealists. Although a short-lived organization, Cercle et Carré, which included among its members Mondrian, Arp, and George Vantongerloo, not only held a large-scale exhibition of geometric abstract art in 1930 at the Galerie 23, Paris, but also published a periodical that contained the writings of Le Corbusier (Charles-Edouard Jeanneret) and Mondrian as well as Seuphor.

The paintings of Torres-Garcia during these tumultuous years in Paris moved from formalized urban scenes, portraits, and still lifes, which exhibit a modicum of compartmentalization but remain tied to reality, to the austere abstractions of 1929, which clearly show the influence of van Doesburg in their aggressive use of diagonal elements. References to reality reappeared frequently, at first overlaid with a geometric grid, then fit within the discrete areas formed by the linear structure. The objects became more stylized and codified, with certain images appearing frequently: a clock, fish, sun, vase. Numbers and letters drawn from the Greek and Phoenician, as well as modern, alphabets became important motifs. The range of symbols grew and became more complex, stemming from a multitude of sources—events or objects of personal significance, pre-Columbian images, ancient alphabets.

In 1932 Torres-Garcia left Paris and returned, via Madrid, to his native city, Montevideo, where he resettled permanently. While his work for the most part continued to increase in complexity, he frequently returned to simpler formats reminiscent of the early abstract work (ca. 1918) of van Doesburg and Mondrian and suggestive of bas-relief walls. *Constructivist Painting No. 8*, painted four years after the artist's return to his homeland, stands in direct contrast to the intricate pictographs of the period. Utilizing a stark palette of white, black, and grays Torres-Garcia retains the compartmented structure of his pictographs, yet reduces the images to one, a truncated sphere, which is depicted bisecting the rectangular cells or resting precariously on structural elements. Introducing volume through cursory shadowing, the artist has also suggested shallow depth by overlapping compartments. Abstract, yet tied to objective reality, this work stands as a synthesis of these two seemingly opposing principles.   KCH

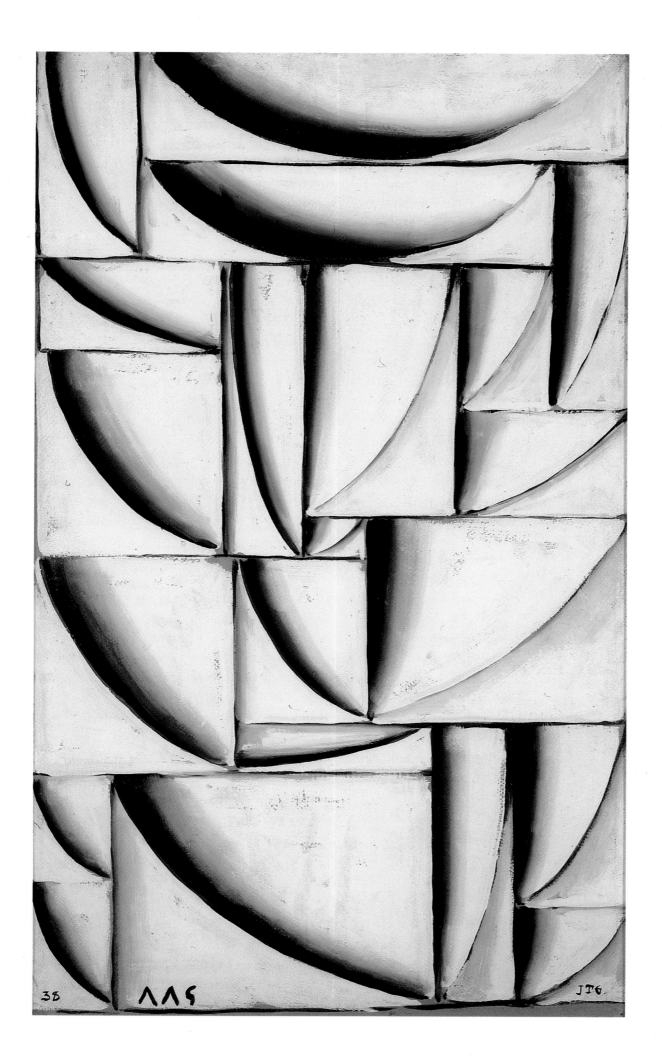

38 ΛΛς   JTG.

László Moholy-Nagy

AMERICAN, BORN HUNGARY,
1895–1946

A IX

1923

oil and pencil on canvas
50½ × 38¾"
128.3 × 98.4 cm

Gift of Sibyl Moholy-Nagy
51.3208

[1]Quoted in Sibyl Moholy-Nagy, *Moholy-Nagy: Experiment in Totality* (Cambridge: M.I.T. Press, 1969), p. 21.

[2]Loc. cit.

[3]Ibid., p. 17.

[4]Angelica Zander Rudenstine, *The Guggenheim Museum Collection: Paintings 1880–1945*, vol. 2 (New York: The Solomon R. Guggenheim Museum, 1976), p. 565.

[5]Quoted in Herbert Read, "A Great Teacher" [1947], in *Moholy-Nagy*, ed. Richard Kostelanetz (New York: Praeger, 1970), p. 205.

THROUGH HIS PIONEERING WORK as painter, photographer, designer, educator, and propagandist for abstract art, László Moholy-Nagy sought to extend the social revolutions that erupted in Europe in the late teens. "Constructivism is the socialism of vision," he wrote in 1922.[1] For Moholy-Nagy the aesthetic philosophy of Constructivism was based on a rejection of representational values in art for a universal form-language comprising basic abstract shapes and elemental colors, a vocabulary entirely objective and "accessible to all senses."[2] This universal language was intended to symbolize collective thought and a rationalized, functional society free of hierarchical values. Moholy-Nagy, who taught at the Bauhaus from 1923 to 1928, shared in the Utopian optimism that guided the various factions of the post-World War I avant-garde in Germany. He believed that art could elevate man's perceptions and thus lead to emotional fulfillment: "Constructive art is processual, forever open in all directions. It is a builder of man's ability to perceive, to react emotionally, and to reason logically."[3]

A IX, painted in 1923, the year Moholy-Nagy was invited by Walter Gropius to teach at the Bauhaus, is one of his early Constructivist works. His idea of a universal pictorial form is suggested by a composition of simple, geometric shapes suspended in space. The rectilinear lines that intersect in the circle recall the cross motif used by the Russian Suprematist Kasimir Malevich, an early influence on Moholy-Nagy. The unbroken areas of black, red, yellow, and white further emphasize visual fundamentals. With oil pigment, he here addresses the issues of overlapping forms and transparency which he explored in his collages and watercolors of the early 1920s. Painting on plastic, which he began in 1923, expanded this interest in transparency. His revolutionary experiments in photography also influenced his painting. The superimposition of planes, the emphasis on light, and the smooth, textureless surface are all photographic in nature.

Through the use of overlapping planes, transparency versus opaqueness, and contrasting color, Moholy-Nagy created what he called "space articulation." He transformed the two-dimensional paint surface into one of visual depth defined by advancing and receding planes, not by traditional means of perspective. This shifting of planes creates a kinetic composition, further emphasized by the crossing diagonal lines, in which he attempts to understand space in relation to time. Moholy-Nagy believed that this "vision in motion" satisfied the "specific need of our time" which called for relativity.[4] "The fixed viewpoint," he wrote, "the isolated handling of problems as a norm is rejected and replaced by a flexible approach, by seeing matters in a constantly changing, moving field of mutual relationships."[5]   DCduP

Vasily Kandinsky

FRENCH, BORN RUSSIA,
1866–1944

Brownish

BRÄUNLICH
1931

oil on cardboard
19⅜ × 27⅝″
49.2 × 70.2 cm

William L. Gerstle Collection
Gift of William L. Gerstle
45.100

DESPITE THE WORLD CRISES that marked his career—World War I, the German and Russian revolutions, the economic and political turmoil of the Weimar Republic, the rise of Nazism—Vasily Kandinsky remained an apolitical artist in the strictest sense. Yet, within a universal context, he felt a strong social responsibility. He repeatedly affirmed his belief that art was "not a mere purposeless creating of things that dissipate themselves in a void, but a power that has a purpose and must serve the development and refinement of the human soul."[1] To Kandinsky, abstraction, free from the ties of physical reality, possessed the greatest potential for developing a universal, cosmic sensibility in humanity.

The outbreak of World War I in 1914 forced Kandinsky to leave Munich, where he had been an active participant in the advanced art circles since his first arrival there in 1896, and to return to Russia. Back in Germany after the war, in 1922 he became a member of the Bauhaus faculty. *Brownish*, painted in 1931, during Kandinsky's last year at the Bauhaus, is characteristic of one of the varied pictorial modes he explored during this time. The painting is divided into broad, horizontal bands, a linear direction Kandinsky described as "cold" and "flat" in *Point and Line to Plane*,[2] his major theoretical treatise of the period, published in 1926 as part of the Bauhaus book series. Within this quiet, meditative space evocative of an inhabited, nocturnal landscape, he creates an arrangement of geometric shapes—circles, semi-circles, triangles, rectangles, and straight lines. In *Point and Line to Plane* he identified the circle, square, and triangle as the primary planar forms, with the circle and triangle being the most strongly contrasting pair.[3] Placed in the upper left, a location Kandinsky considered "heavenly," the largest circle is thus contrasted with the triangle in the lower right. In the lower left he has assembled a constellation of separate geometric forms—triangles, circles and semi-circles—which together suggest a four-legged creature and a rider's shield, perhaps a hieroglyphic reference to the St. George theme that figures so prominently in the paintings of Kandinsky's Munich years.[4]

The feeling of restraint created by the horizontal format is reinforced by the subdued color scheme: continuous gray for the lower third, solid black for the upper two-thirds. In *On the Spiritual in Art*, Kandinsky's pivotal theoretical statement of 1911, he described gray as "toneless and immobile" and black as having "an inner sound of nothingness bereft of possibilities,"[5] and characterized the subtle gradations of brown, which give the work its title, as "blunt, hard, and capable of little movement."[6]

For Kandinsky, more important than color gradation was the principle of contrast. He believed that a "strife of colors" more accurately represented the chaos and turbulence of his time. To create contradictory spatial illusions, which continued to fascinate him during his last years at the Bauhaus, he often used contrasting colors and varied textures for their advancing and retreating effects. In *Brownish* the stippled gray area sits firmly on the picture plane while the smooth, cool black above it recedes. This recession is halted, however, by the contrasting warm, bright red circle in the upper left, thus creating shifting spatial relationships. The relative size, location, and expressive color of this circle make it a central visual reference point in the work, but as Kandinsky's abstract cosmic symbol, it also becomes the focus of the painting's spiritual content. Even though Kandinsky's use of geometric form reflects the Bauhaus penchant for order and objectivity, it is this insistence on symbolic, expressive content that separates him from the prevailing attitudes at the school and establishes his personal, independent style.   DCduP

[1]Vasily Kandinsky, *On the Spiritual in Art*, vol. 1 of *Kandinsky: Complete Writings on Art*, eds. Kenneth C. Lindsay and Peter Vergo (Boston: G.K. Hall, 1982), p. 212.

[2]Vasily Kandinsky, *Point and Line to Plane*, vol. 2 of *Kandinsky: Complete Writings on Art*, op. cit., p. 574.

[3]Ibid., p. 600.

[4]In these works St. George symbolized the conquest of the spiritual over the material (represented by the dragon). For further discussion of this theme, see Peg Weiss, *Kandinsky in Munich 1896–1914*, The Solomon R. Guggenheim Museum, New York, 1982, p. 82.

[5]Kandinsky, *On the Spiritual in Art*, op. cit., p. 185.

[6]Ibid., p. 187.

Josef Albers

AMERICAN, BORN GERMANY
1888–1976

Growing

1940

oil on Masonite
24 × 26¾″
61.0 × 68.0 cm

Gift of Charlotte Mack
59.2668

THE MIND'S EYE was the province of Josef Albers. "The aim of art," he wrote, is the "revelation and evocation of vision."[1] Possessing the modernist faith in pure pictorial elements as the means for direct communication, Albers explored the qualities of human vision through the use of color and non-objective form, by means of which he developed an influential style of geometric abstraction. His concern with the nature of seeing began in Germany during the time he spent at the Bauhaus, where he enrolled as a student in 1920 and stayed on as a master teacher from 1923 to 1933. His colleagues there—Paul Klee, László Moholy-Nagy, Vasily Kandinsky—shared his interest in the complexities of visual perception, a subject that was also the focus of extensive investigation among Gestalt psychologists of the period.

After the Nazis forced the closing of the Bauhaus in 1933, Albers accepted an invitation to teach at the newly founded, experimental Black Mountain College in North Carolina. The color course that Albers formulated in the United States developed and refined the concepts that he and his fellow teachers had pursued at the Bauhaus. Through his teaching he originated numerous exercises that demonstrated the idea that became central to his work: "In visual perception a color is almost never seen as it really is. This fact makes color the most relative medium in art."[2] A collection of these exercises and his definitive statement on color theory were published in 1963 as *Interaction of Color.*

Painted in 1940 while Albers was teaching in North Carolina, *Growing* illustrates his early exploration of chromatic relativity. The composition is an arrangement of colored squares and rectangles repeated in varying sizes and positions whose mosaic-like patterning and variety of color recall the early glass pictures he executed at the Bauhaus. The blurred, irregular edges and emphasis on surface texture, however, suggest the improvisatory quality of a group of experimental paintings he called Free Studies that he made during the 1930s.

Interested in the idea that the shape of a given color and its quantity influence the way in which it is perceived, Albers presents the same color in different sizes and forms. By placing the same color adjacent to varying hues, Albers is also working with the concept that neighboring tonalities influence each other in terms of value, temperature, saturation, and brightness. Enclosed by pink, lavender, and orange, the gray-green rectangle in the center of the upper band, for example, appears lighter and closer to the surface than the one in the lower left, which seems to recede through its "interaction" with the surrounding rose, blue, and bright-green rectangles and the "cool" green background. Albers indicates the deceptive nature of color by showing how it can be modified by its context. The repetition of similar forms and the variation of tonal values, which suggest contrast between flatness and depth, create a dynamic, rhythmic composition. The elusive, delicate nuances of color expressed through geometric form as demonstrated in *Growing* were further explored and refined by Albers in his later work.   DCduP

[1] Eugen Gomringer, *Josef Albers* (New York: George Wittenborn, 1968), frontispiece.

[2] Josef Albers, *Interaction of Color* (New Haven: Yale University Press, 1963), p. 10.

Josef Albers

AMERICAN, BORN GERMANY
1888–1976

Tenayuca

1943

oil on Masonite
22½ × 43½"
57.2 × 110.5 cm

Purchased with the aid of funds
from Mr. and Mrs. Richard N.
Goldman and Madeleine Haas
Russell
84.1

AFTER HIS ARRIVAL at Black Mountain College in 1933, Albers underwent a period of experimentation during which he investigated divergent aesthetic directions. On the one hand there was the disciplined, systematic pursuit of a single motif and the variations possible through a limited color schema—the Treble Clef Series, for example—while on the other, there were the less rigidly geometric and more improvisational works—the Free Studies. Begun in 1936 in an ink study and finally realized as a painting in 1943, *Tenayuca* belongs at the end of Albers's exploratory years at Black Mountain. This work illustrates how, by the early 1940s, he returned to the more structured method of picture-making he had arrived at during his Bauhaus years.

The 1936 ink study, which presents the theme of *Tenayuca*, is among Albers's early isometric constructions dealing with the issue of contradictory spaces. In these constructions, he questions the nature of perception by contrasting two-dimensionality with the illusion of three-dimensionality. This investigation of space through rectilinear form is rooted in Cubism and Constructivism and may relate to concepts of non-Euclidean geometry that were important for early European modernism.[1]

Working from the construction defined in the ink study, Albers executed two versions of this painting: *Tenayuca Dark* in 1942 (Cincinnati Art Museum) and *Tenayuca* in 1943. In these works and the studies for them, Albers combined the linear articulation of space as used in the initial isometric drawing with a chromatic articulation of space. The process by which Albers achieved a solution for the depiction of space through color modulation is revealed by a comparison of *Tenayuca* and *Tenayuca Dark*. Both works contain two tones of red and two of gray. The overall coloration of *Tenayuca Dark* is subdued and more saturated, while in *Tenayuca* the reds are not only lighter, but distinctly different in hue. By distinguishing colors more clearly and emphasizing dark-light relationships, Albers suggests both plastic movement, as the varying colored planes appear to advance and recede, and the contrast between two-dimensionality and the illusion of three-dimensionality that was the subject of the early ink drawing.

In his later work Albers's demand for simplicity and economy of means led him to express the sensation of space through color and line separately. In his black-and-white graphic work, he concentrated on line, creating complex picture puzzles in which a multiplicity of spatial possibilities are presented. The phenomenon of color became the dominant theme in his painting, culminating in his renowned Homage to the Square Series. DCduP

[1]François Bucher, *Josef Albers: Despite Straight Lines* (Cambridge: MIT Press, 1977), p. 62.

92

Josef Albers

AMERICAN, BORN GERMANY
1888–1976

Study for Homage to the Square

1972

oil on Masonite
23⅞ × 23⅞"
60.6 × 60.6 cm

Gift of Anni Albers
and the Josef Albers Foundation
79.121

INTEREST IN THE SQUARE as a primary, universal shape was an important concern for such early pioneers of abstract painting as the Suprematist Kasimir Malevich, the De Stijl painter Piet Mondrian, and the Bauhaus artist Paul Klee. Albers first experimented with the square in his glass paintings of the Bauhaus period in which he combined the motif with rectangles of varying sizes. Working toward simplification and an economy of means, he ultimately arrived at the square as a neutral, fundamental shape through which to explore the autonomy of color. Albers began his extended Homage to the Square Series in the summer of 1949. Developed at Yale, where he assumed his third important teaching position as chairman of the Department of Design in 1950, this series absorbed Albers for the remainder of his career.

The first Homage paintings consisted of four squares; later paintings were based on three squares. To these formats, Albers added a narrow white border which acts as a fourth or fifth square. Each variation is governed by a set system of proportions; however, the actual size of the squares within each arrangement differs, as does the overall scale of the paintings in the series. Within a given format, Albers established an imaginary point of convergence common to all the squares, but to avoid what he referred to as "static fixation," he placed it below dead center. The focused vision and arresting impact of this single-motif composition resemble the meditative quality of mandala images.

Within this highly consistent framework, Albers set himself the challenge of creating ever-new color combinations. The problem was not thematic variety, but a deepening of the understanding of color and perception. Constructed with four squares and a white border, *Study for Homage to the Square* explores the chromatic relationships between tones of red and orange, colors which lend the painting a heated, yet not flaming atmosphere. By comparing related spectral hues that blend, such as red and orange, Albers suggests the color principle of harmony; he makes reference to the principle of gradation by using two tones of red and two of orange. Of primary importance to Albers was the psychological impact of color. He believed that the "origin of art" was "the discrepancy between physical fact and psychic effect."[1] In *Study for Homage to the Square,* and all the other Homage paintings, the colors are not mixed but are applied directly from the tube, and they are in contact only at the edges of the squares. The overlapping or intersecting of colors that appears is due to their visual "interaction," how they mutually influence each other. "Choice of the colors used," Albers wrote on his Homage to the Square Series, "as well as their order, is aimed at an interaction—influencing and changing each other forth and back."[2] Color alone creates movement in this painting as it changes from dark in the center to light at the edges, resulting in a tunnel-like recession.

The Homage to the Square Series is the culmination of a lifetime career devoted to the nature of seeing. This work, as well as Albers's contribution as a teacher and theoretician, had significant repercussions for art in America. In addition to influencing the general direction and acceptance of geometric abstraction in this country, Albers established the theoretical and visual basis for Hard Edge painting, Op Art, and Color Field painting that emerged in the 1960s.   DCduP

[1]Eugen Gomringer, *Josef Albers* (New York: George Wittenborn, 1968), frontispiece.

[2]Statement by the artist, "On My 'Homage to the Square,'" *Josef Albers* (New York: The International Council of the Museum of Modern Art, 1964), unpaginated.

94

Giorgio de Chirico

ITALIAN, BORN GREECE
1888–1978

The Vexations of the Thinker; The Inconsistencies of the Thinker

LES CONTRARIÉTÉS DU
PENSEUR
1915

oil on canvas
18¼ × 15″
46.4 × 38.1 cm

Templeton Crocker Fund Purchase
51.8

THE HUMAN FIGURE AS WE KNOW IT rarely traverses the desolate, melancholy piazzas of Giorgio de Chirico's early mature work, the *arte metafisica* of circa 1912 to circa 1919. Instead, eerie specters, sculptural monuments, and still-life objects inhabit the work of this period, the result of a progressive "de-personalization"[1] of man that grew out of his search for new symbols. Sometime prior to 1915 he wrote that one of "the aim[s] of future painting [will be] to suppress man as guide, or as a means to express symbol, sensation or thought, once and for all to free itself from the anthropomorphism that shackles sculpture: to see everything, even man, in its quality of *thing*."[2] For de Chirico, inanimate objects superseded the traditional human figure in their potential for expressiveness and the evocation of a hidden reality.

Through the irrational or incongruous juxtaposition of familiar objects, de Chirico made the commonplace both mysterious and disturbing. In *The Vexations of the Thinker* of 1915, a remote Italian side street is the unexpected setting for a medieval knight cum automaton. There is a sense of impending confrontation, as this part warrior-part mechanistic object faces a wall on which its ghostly doppelgänger appears to be drawn. Though held in suspension, this transformed being possesses the potential for action, underscoring an atmosphere of anticipation commonly expressed in de Chirico's painting of the *arte metafisica* period. Like the Italian Futurists, de Chirico was concerned with the inevitable process of change; in *The Vexations of the Thinker* there is the "collision of past and present"[3] in this synthesis of armored knight and modern machine which communicates a sense of lost heroism and the malaise of modern life. The element of nostalgia present here recurs in the artist's 1929 novel *Hebdomeros*: "'Gladiators! There's an enigma in that word,' said Hebdomeros. . . . And he thought of the music-halls whose brightly-lit ceilings conjure up visions of Dante's Paradise; he also thought of those afternoons in Rome, when the Games would be over for the day and the sun sinking lower in the sky. . . . Vision of Rome, when the world was young, Anguish at nightfall, a sailor's song."[4]

Despite its seeming affinity with Renaissance tradition in its classical architecture and thinly applied paint of fresco-like clarity, *The Vexations of the Thinker* demonstrates de Chirico's fluency in modernism.[5] During his Paris years (1911–15) he became well acquainted with both Cubist and Futurist theory. In this work, the compressed, vertiginous space and the multiple vanishing points generated by Cubism create a disconcerting mood that overturns the logic and order of fifteenth-century Italian painting. Also anti-classical are the broad areas of opaque color and bold contrasts of light and dark passages that emphasize flatness, in place of traditional modeled roundness. The gaping torso reveals de Chirico's exploration of Umberto Boccioni's Futurist concept of "open[ing] up the figure like a window" so as to merge object and environment.[6]

The sense of narrative in *The Vexations of the Thinker*, however vague and undefined, encourages the viewer to feel that he has stumbled upon a dream in progress. De Chirico wrote repeatedly of the dream, emphasizing how it revealed a higher, metaphysical reality. In both his ideas and his art, he anticipated the Surrealist painters who greatly admired his early mature work. They were captivated by his poetic imagery, his strange combinations of objects that mixed pictorial metaphors in new and startling ways. The clarity and precision of his technique influenced the verisimilitude of such later Surrealist painters as René Magritte, Salvador Dali, and Yves Tanguy. In *The Vexations of the Thinker* and his other metaphysical paintings, de Chirico "made the dream look real."[7]   DCduP

[1] For a discussion of the representation of man in de Chirico's work, see Marianne W. Martin, "Reflections on De Chirico and *Arte Metafisica*," *Art Bulletin*, vol. 60, no. 2 (June 1978), p. 348.

[2] Loc. cit.

[3] Ibid., p. 346.

[4] Giorgio de Chirico, *Hebdomeros* (New York: The Four Seasons Book Society, 1966), p. 25.

[5] William Rubin identifies and fully discusses the problematic assumption that de Chirico was a classicist in his essay "De Chirico and Modernism," *De Chirico*, The Museum of Modern Art, New York, 1982, pp. 55–79.

[6] Martin, op. cit., p. 349; for a discussion of de Chirico's relationship to Futurism, see pp. 346–53.

[7] Robert Hughes, *The Shock of the New* (New York: Alfred A. Knopf, 1981), p. 221.

J. de Chirico
1915

Paul Klee

SWISS, 1879–1940

Red Suburb

ROTES VILLENQUARTIER

1920

oil on cardboard
14⅜ × 12½"
36.5 × 31.8 cm

Purchase
51.3207

[1]Gert Schiff, "René Crevel as a Critic of Paul Klee," *Arts Magazine* (Special Issue), vol. 52, no. 1 (September 1977), p. 136.
[2]O. K. Werckmeister, "The Issue of Childhood in the Art of Paul Klee," ibid., p. 138.

"THE WORK OF KLEE is a complete museum of dreams,"[1] wrote the French Surrealist poet René Crevel in 1930. Indeed, throughout his career Paul Klee explored the realm of fantasy. Synthesizing elements from almost every major development in early modern painting, he created one of the most individual and fanciful forms of expression, an oeuvre varied in style and technique.

An important early association for Klee was the Munich artists group the Blaue Reiter (Blue Rider). It was during 1911 that he met its two principal leaders, Vasily Kandinsky and Franz Marc. Sympathetic to their anti-materialistic attitude and their emphasis on individualistic expression in search of "inner truth," Klee submitted seventeen works to the second Blaue Reiter exhibition (1912) and is represented by a drawing in the Blaue Reiter almanac, which features articles on music, theater, and the visual arts, as well as illustrations ranging from primitive art to contemporary painting.

The admiration of the Blaue Reiter group for non-Western and non-traditional art forms was shared by Klee, who particularly valued children's art, which he viewed as a form of "pure creation" that could offer insight into the fundamental nature of visual and symbolic thinking. In his review of the first Blaue Reiter exhibition (1911), he wrote: "For there are still primordial origins of art, as you would rather find them in the ethnographic museum or at home in the nursery (don't laugh, reader), children can do it too . . . there is positive wisdom in this fact. . . . In truth all this is to be taken much more seriously, *if* the art of today is to be reformed."[2] Throughout his oeuvre Klee referred to children's art, ingeniously combining the spontaneous, intuitive feeling of this work with advanced trends in modern painting.

Red Suburb, painted in 1920, is an imaginary landscape of flat boxlike houses and twisting roads that captures the naïve feeling of a fairy-tale vision. Disregarding modeling and correct optical proportion, Klee's schematic rendering of the houses, trees, and roadways is analogous to the work of children. His contours, which deliberately emphasize a lack of full linear control, possess a certain immediacy and freedom. The rough surface texture resembles children's crayon etchings, in which an initial layer of bright color is coated with a darker one that is then scratched into to reveal the vibrant hues underneath.

At the same time, Klee's sophisticated vision draws upon the Cubist plane to create an arrangement of flat rectangles reminiscent of the colored-square format of his Tunisian and Kairouan landscapes which he began to paint in 1914. Across the entire picture plane he repeats the tree and house motif and interconnects the houses by a series of pathways, creating a rhythmic, structural network. The nature of visual perception is questioned by his dynamic treatment of space which bends and contorts as the roadways and houses twist and turn. The delicate tonal variations—primarily reds, greens, and golds—are subtly blended and demonstrate his mastery of color. In this peopleless suburb, the bird and moon lend a mysterious atmosphere characteristic of the other rhythmic landscapes Klee executed around 1920.   DCduP

Paul Klee

SWISS, 1879–1940

Nearly Hit

FAST GETROFFEN
1928

oil on board
20 × 15½″
50.8 × 39.4 cm

Albert M. Bender Collection
Albert M. Bender Bequest Fund
Purchase
44.2640

[1] Will Grohmann, *Paul Klee* (New York: Harry N. Abrams, 1954), pp. 86–87.

[2] Ibid., p. 97.

[3] Mark Lawrence Rosenthal, "Paul Klee and the Arrow" (Ph.D. diss., University of Iowa, 1979), p. 79.

[4] Ibid., p. 74.

DURING THE 1920S, Klee's paintings combined the Constructivist tendencies of the Bauhaus, where he had begun to teach in 1920, with a poetic lyricism that resulted in a truly personal idiom, diverse in subject, style, and technique. The relationship between reason and instinct interested him, for he did not consider the formal Constructivist approach to be complete and insisted that "intuition still remains an important element."[1] Many works of this period have backgrounds composed of horizontal bands or grid patterns that utilize the color principle of tonal gradation taught at the Bauhaus. Yet within this rationalized, geometric space, Klee frequently presented playful, childlike narratives.

Klee felt a deep kinship with nature and, influenced by the developments in microbiological research and physics, believed that art should reveal the inner forces and structures behind appearances. "Art does not render the visible," he wrote, "rather, it makes visible."[2] Among his varied subjects of the 1920s are images of garden flora and underwater plant and fish life which reveal new and magical cosmogonies celebrating biological form and infinitesimal processes invisible to the naked eye. Teaching at the Bauhaus allowed Klee to refine and organize his aesthetic and philosophical ideas, resulting in the publication of "Wege des Naturstudiums" (Ways of Studying Nature) in 1923 and, in 1925, the *Pädagogisches Skizzenbuch (Pedagogical Sketchbook)*.

Composed with an economy of means, *Nearly Hit* was painted in 1928 while Klee was at the Bauhaus. In this work he emphasizes line and fundamental geometric shapes to form an image of an abstracted human head floating in a vortex of powerful, flamelike brush strokes of pink, orange, gray, and white.

Modern investigations into electromagnetic fields encouraged Klee's fascination with the notion of invisible cosmic forces, and perchance *Nearly Hit*, whose background is a mass of swirling tensions, is symbolic of a field of mental energy. Klee repeatedly used the arrow motif in his paintings as a metaphor for conflicting forces at work within the universe. *Nearly Hit* has been interpreted as an image of fright with the arrow symbolizing a threatening element.[3] Perhaps equally plausible is the suggestion that the work addresses the issue of reason versus intuition, linear thought versus sudden enlightenment, which concerned Klee throughout his career. Indeed, it may be a humorous comment on man's failed attempts at producing spontaneous revelation. In the *Pädagogisches Skizzenbuch* Klee wrote, "The father of the arrow is the thought,"[4] and, as a symbol, the arrow came to embody the notion of thought in many of Klee's works of the Bauhaus period. In *Nearly Hit* it points directly at the figure's cerebrum, but ultimately misses, as indicated by the witty title. The figure's startled expression perhaps suggests the incipient moment of illumination which swiftly fades away. DCduP

Jean (Hans) Arp

FRENCH, 1887–1966

Head and Leaf;
Head and Vase

TÊTE ET FEUILLE; TÊTE ET
VASE
1929

formerly
HEAD AND NAVEL, ca. 1926

string and oil on canvas mounted on
board
13½ × 10½″
34.3 × 26.7 cm

Evelyn and Walter Haas, Jr. Fund
Purchase
80.390

Objects Arranged
According to the
Laws of Chance III;
Symmetrical
Configuration

OBJETS PLACÉS SELON LES
LOIS DU HASARD III;
CONFIGURATION SYMÉTRIQUE
1931

oil on wood
10⅛ × 11⅜ × 2⅜″
25.7 × 28.9 × 6.1 cm

Purchase
84.5

A CONCERN WITH SPIRITUALITY and the desire to render visible what is invisible has been one of the fundamental aspirations of modern art. In Europe in the early decades of this century, Vasily Kandinsky, Constantin Brancusi, Paul Klee, Piet Mondrian, and Jean Arp all shared a mutual desire to express an inner vision. "Art should lead to spirituality, to reality—to mystical reality," Arp declared.[1] Prompted by a personality that combined a contemporary Romantic spirit influenced by Oriental philosophy and the mystical writings of the German poet and novelist Novalis, Arp sought to unveil the mysteries of nature. He envisioned nature as a dynamic, cyclic process, and in his collages, reliefs, and sculpture he created visual metaphors for birth, the process of growth, and man's relationship to the natural world. He sought the essence of nature's formative powers and attempted to express it in archetypal form. The writer Hugo Ball wrote of Arp: "If I understand him well, he is concerned less with richness than with simplification. . . . He strives to purify the imagination, and concentrates less on exploring its treasure of images than on discovering the basic pattern of these images."[2] Arp —who stated, "Art is a fruit that grows in man, like a fruit on a plant, or a child in its mother's womb"[3]—introduced into art an entirely new vocabulary of form: biomorphism. A type of abstraction based on organic, curvilinear shapes, biomorphism evolved from Art Nouveau and became the form-language for many of the Dadaist and Surrealist artists who found the geometric quality of Cubism antithetical to their expressive needs.

The organic, undulating line in this string relief of 1929, *Head and Leaf; Head and Vase,* is characteristic of Arp's morphology, which evokes plant and animal forms and alludes as well to anthropomorphic structure. The joining of two circles constructed of string and placed vertically suggests a whimsical human form, recalling the torso-vase motif that occurs early in his oeuvre and remains a dominant theme. In this work, one of a series of string reliefs begun in 1926, Arp employs chance as a primary aesthetic factor, as he had done in his earlier Dada collages. As a leading figure of the Dada movement, he had championed accident as a means of subverting conventional artistic practice and eliciting from the unconscious deeply felt experience. "Dada," he wrote, "was against the mechanization of the world. Our African evenings were simply a protest against the rationalization of man. My gouaches, reliefs, plastics were an attempt to teach man what he had forgotten—to dream with his eyes open."[4] In *Head and Leaf; Head and Vase,* loops of string were dropped onto the ground and the shapes formed by chance were then used as evocative points of departure. The carefully cut and placed twine demonstrates how the image was consciously rearranged based on the inspiration of accident. The simple form, materials, and method, however meticulously realized, suggest an improvisational, childlike quality and a gentle humor characteristic of much of Arp's oeuvre.

Arp, like Klee an artist-poet, often used titles as important adjuncts to his work, in many cases to suggest unusual juxtapositions. In providing two titles for this relief —*Head and Leaf; Head and Vase*—allusions are made to man and nature and to man and object. The parallelism of leaf and vase encourages ambiguity and the free, poetic association that Arp sought in his imagery. On the one hand, he links the human head with a leaf, perhaps in hope of a cosmic unity between man and nature, while on the other, he connects it with his familiar humanized amphora motif. Man, he felt, in adhering to the classical idea that he was the "measure of all things," had severed himself from nature. "Man, hidden away in his vanity," he wrote, "believes himself to be the summit of creation . . . [and] has broken from nature."[5] Since Arp believed man should exist in harmony with the natural world, *Head and Leaf* perhaps aims at a reunion.

One of Arp's many wood reliefs, *Objects Arranged According to the Laws of Chance III; Symmetrical Configuration* of 1931 is a metaphor for nature's processes of birth and evolution. A seeming genus of living biological specimens, this work is an arrangement of simple, organic forms. Its spirit of creation is captured by the number of similar but not identical parts and their range in size from large to small. New offspring have been generated and each in its own way will develop individually. Arp has endowed these organic forms with a vitalism, an inner tension that suggests evolution. He reinforces this sense of change by the irregular, undulating edges of the wood ground which appear continually to expand and contract.

This work is one of seven wood reliefs generically titled *According to the Laws of Chance* which Arp began in 1929. They continue the explorations he initiated during his Dada period in a series of collages of the same title in which he had dropped pieces of paper onto a ground and then worked from the random pattern that resulted, although now the forms are organic rather than geometric. Even though *Symmetrical Configuration* pursues the aesthetic and philosophic implications of chance, its carefully crafted machine-sawn shapes illustrate, as did the precise technique of the 1929 string relief, the presence of Arp's conscious hand. There is also a consistent disposition of parts throughout the series. The placement of the larger forms generally remains the same; however, the smallest circular unit in some works is freely turned at different angles. Color is also a subtle variant. *Symmetrical Configuration* is painted a smooth, steel gray, but other works in the series have a natural finish that exploits the quality of wood grain. This interest in material and smooth-finished surfaces, an influence from Brancusi, is fully explored by Arp in his three-dimensional sculpture.   DCduP

[1] Quoted in Carola Giedion-Welcker, *Jean Arp* (New York: Harry N. Abrams, 1957), p. XXXII.

[2] Ibid., p. XXXIV.

[3] Quoted in Robert Melville, "On Some of Arp's Reliefs, in *Arp* (New York: The Museum of Modern Art, 1965), p. 27.

[4] Jean Arp, "Looking," in *Arp*, ibid., p. 13.

[5] Quoted in Mark Levy, "Jean Arp: A Study of His Three-Dimensional Sculpture" (Ph.D. diss., Indiana University, 1977), p. 21.

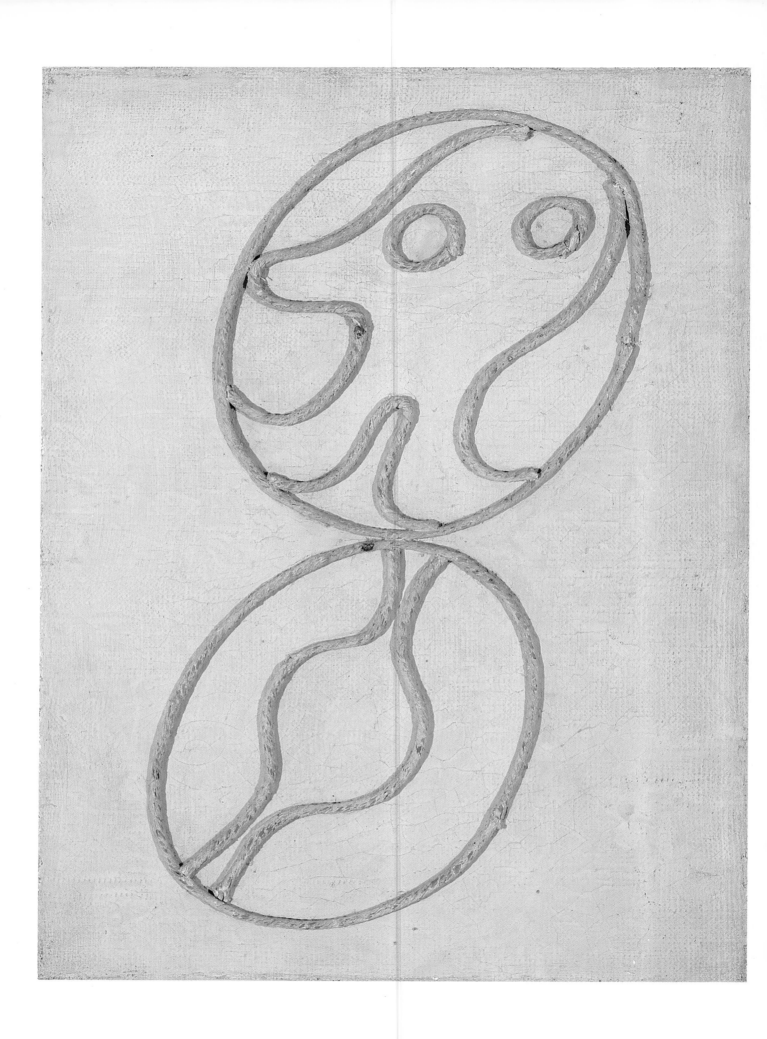

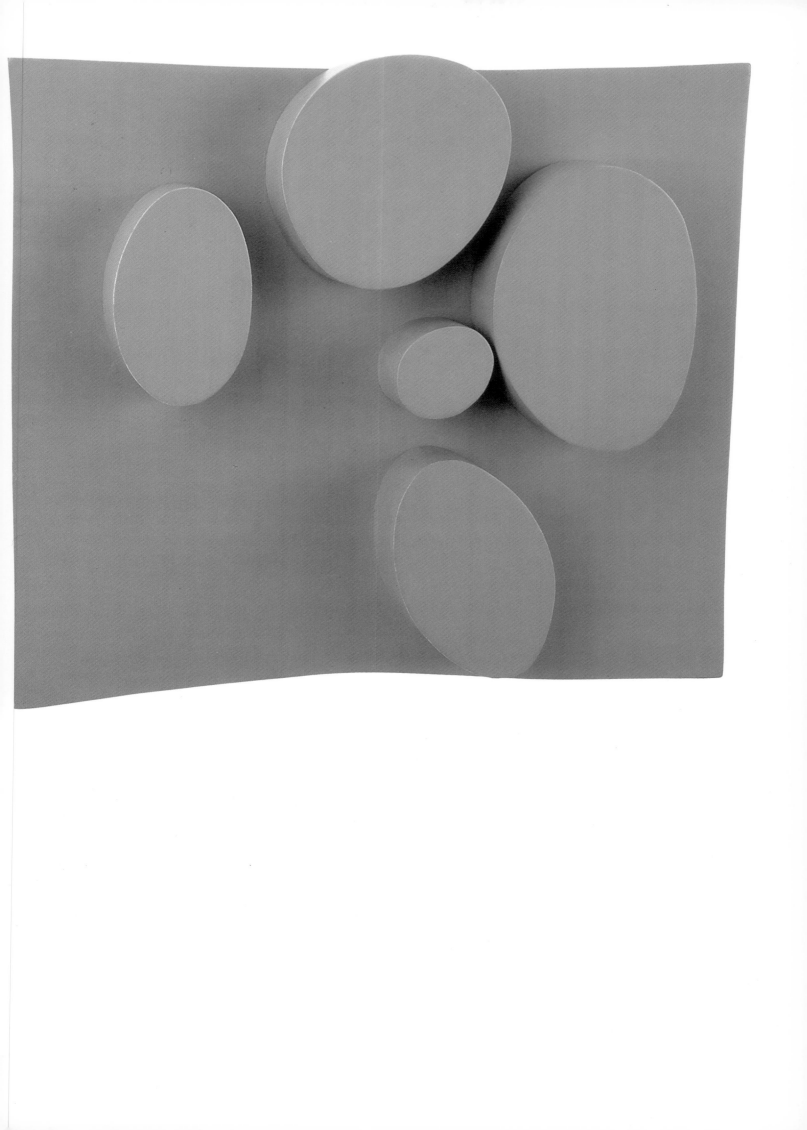

Jean (Hans) Arp

FRENCH, 1887–1966

Human Concretion without Oval Bowl

CONCRÉTION HUMAINE
SANS COUPE

1933

bronze (polished) 2/3
23 × 22⅝ × 15¾"
58.5 × 57.5 × 40.0 cm

William L. Gerstle Collection
William L. Gerstle Fund Purchase
62.3421

[1] Jean Arp, "Looking," *Arp* (New York, The Museum of Modern Art, 1958), pp. 14–15.

[2] William S. Rubin, *Dada, Surrealism, and Their Heritage* (New York, The Museum of Modern Art, 1968), p. 41.

[3] Jean Arp, *On My Way: Poetry and Essays 1912 . . . 1947* (New York: Wittenborn, Schultz, 1948), p. 70.

[4] Albert E. Elsen, *Modern European Sculpture 1918–1945: Unknown Beings and Other Realities* (New York: George Braziller, in association with the Albright-Knox Art Gallery, Buffalo, N.Y., 1979), p. 26.

BY 1930, in an attempt to break away from the plane of the wall, Arp detached the relief and placed it in free space. Soon the biomorphism he had poineered in his reliefs was fully translated into three dimensions. Turning to the traditional medium of plaster—which provided him with the ease of increasing the size and complexity of his work—between 1933 and 1935 Arp created his Human Concretions Series in which he advanced a new image of man. A new sculptural unity between the human and the natural is expressed in Arp's account of the Concretions:

"Suddenly my need for interpretation vanished, and the body, the form, the supremely perfected work became everything to me. . . . I engaged in sculpture and modeled in plaster. The first products were two torsos. Then came the 'Concretions.' Concretion signifies the natural process of condensation, hardening, coagulating, thickening, growing together. . . . Concretion designates solidification, the mass of the stone, the plant, the animal, the man . . . something that has grown. I wanted my work to find its humble, anonymous place in the woods, the mountains, in nature."[1]

Human Concretion without Oval Bowl of 1933, one of the first works in the series, is a configuration of two sensuous, undulant forms, the smaller seeming to have grown organically from the larger upon which it rests. It evokes at once vegetation, animal life, and the human form. Arp has been characterized as "always preferring the ambiguous form that suggests much but identifies nothing."[2] As in *Symmetrical Configuration,* the forms possess an internal dynamic which implies continual transformation and sexual potency.

The graceful integration of the forms reveals Arp's concern for equilibrium and placement. The young, placed in counterpoint, is delicately balanced upon its source. While his self-contained forms celebrate sculptural mass in the manner of his fellow modernist Brancusi, Arp opened up the sculpture and emphasized the interplay between negative and positive by creating air spaces between the two forms and along the bottom. The smooth, refined surface of this highly polished golden bronze—an attribute shared by much of Brancusi's sculpture—is characteristic of Arp's style throughout his career. This work and the entire series address the issue of the base-pedestal in modern sculpture, a concern Brancusi also explored. Many of the Concretions do not possess a base, nor—so as to avoid a fixed perspective—is there a specific front or back. These sculptures appear rooted in the earth and reaffirm Arp's ideal of the unity between man and nature. In reaction to man's "most dangerous folly: vanity," Arp sought anonymity. "The great works of concrete art," he wrote, "should not be signed by their creators . . . these sculptures, these objects, should remain anonymous in the great studio of nature."[3]

Although the more serious, sublimated tone of *Human Concretion without Oval Bowl* contrasts with the fanciful *Head and Leaf; Head and Vase,* both works speak of Arp's ideal of man's unity with nature and illustrate how these two divergent approaches ran a parallel course throughout his career. They embody a positive vision, a new humanism that inverts the classical Greek and Renaissance tradition by presenting a new image of man as living in symbiosis with nature. Shaped by the cataclysmic social and political upheaval of World War I, Arp wanted to create an art that would "simplify, beautify and transform life."

"I wanted to find another order, another value for man in nature. He was no longer to be the measure of all things, no longer to reduce everything to his own measure, but on the contrary, all things and man were to be like nature, without measure. I wanted to create new appearances, extract new forms from man."[4]   DCduP

106

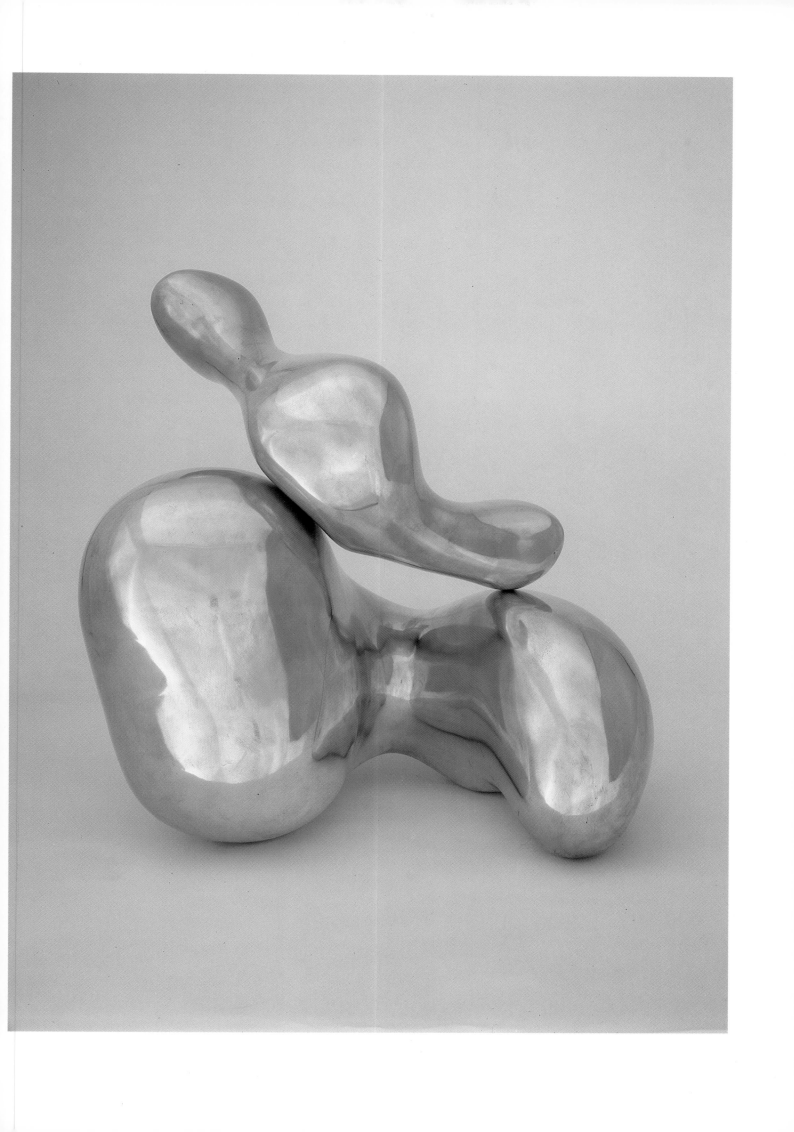

Joan Miró

SPANISH, 1893–1983

Painting

PEINTURE

formerly
DARK BROWN AND WHITE
OVAL
1926

oil on canvas
28⅞ × 36¼"
73.4 × 92.0 cm

Gift of Joseph M. Bransten in
memory of Ellen Hart Bransten
80.428

[1] Rosalind Krauss and Margit Rowell,
Joan Miró: Magnetic Fields, The
Solomon R. Guggenheim Museum,
New York, 1972.

JOAN MIRÓ WAS BORN IN BARCELONA in 1893, twelve years after the birth of his fellow Spaniard Pablo Picasso. His youth in Catalonia instilled in Miró a deep attachment to the heritage and landscape of the region, and his initial educational experience at the Escola de Bellas Artes, La Lonja, introduced him to Catalan primitive art with its stylized forms and vibrant coloration. Later, while studying at the Escola d'Arte de Gali in Barcelona, Miró encountered the work of the European mainstream—the Impressionists, Post-Impressionists, and Fauves. The saturated, discordant color of van Gogh and faceted planar structure of Cézanne particularly fascinated the young artist and he assimilated and utilized these formal elements in his paintings of 1917–18. In 1919 Miró made his initial visit to Paris where he met Picasso and savored the vitality and fervor of the artistic activity then swelling in the French capital. Although he settled in Paris the following year, Miró continued to make extended annual visits to his family's farm at Montroig, near Barcelona, for renewal and inspiration, frequently using the buildings and surrounding fields as subjects.

The years 1921 and 1922 saw Miró creating complex canvases teeming with isolated images rendered in painstaking detail which were then integrated into an abstractly conceived structure. The resulting conflict between ultra-realism and the stylized format, combined with a pronounced distortion of scale, lent an otherworldly quality to the works. In 1923 Miró's imagery moved into the fantastic. Tendrils sprouted, parts of the body ballooned, geometrical configurations took on biomorphic outlines.

For two years, from 1925 through 1927, Miró painted an extraordinary group of canvases, often called "magnetic fields,"[1] earmarked by spare monochromatic grounds inhabited by simple, often whimsical biomorphic shapes. By then aligned with the Surrealists, Miró left behind his tightly structured and detailed works related to Cubism and turned instead to the free "automatism" of the Surrealists, submerging conscious thought to evoke and express subconscious, dream-oriented images. Perhaps the result of a combination of a lack of food, mental strain, and an almost fanatic preoccupation with his art, these nearly hallucinatory canvases are among the most "surreal" of Miró's entire career.

The single image of *Painting*, executed midway through this prolific period, beams across the empty, hazy space of the picture. The ground, randomly clouded, brushed with thin washes, almost transparent, is an allover bister, which obliterates the distinction between earth and sky, reality and dream. The only apparent reference to spatial definition is provided by a dotted line which connects the picture edge with the smiling form and then extends upward. Yet, while working to interconnect earth, sky, and "personage," this intermittent thread serves to confuse space rather than define it. Spontaneous and intuitive, the isolated biomorph is tenuously tied to a rectangular base, its glazed grin lit by the half-shadowed moon. The dreamlike atmosphere casts a pall, imbuing the smiling, lonely figure with an impalpable eeriness.   KCH

108

Joan Miró

SPANISH, 1893–1983

Dawn Perfumed by a Shower of Gold

L'AUBE PARFUMÉE PAR LA
PLUIE D'OR
1954

watercolor and plaster on composition
board
42½ × 21⅝"
108.0 × 54.9 cm

Gift of Wilbur D. May
64.58

FOLLOWING THE SPARE APPARITIONS of the mid-twenties, Miró moved to develop a unique iconography of signs and pictograms drawn from his imagination, his environment, and his Catalan heritage. Closely linked historically to the Surrealists yet isolated from them by consummate individualism, he delved into the realm of dreams and fantasy, using images that evoked subconscious recognition and universal emotions. The compositions again became more complex, sometimes taking the form of a landscape in which disparate object-images are combined within a single arena, sometimes becoming ambiguous arenas where biomorphic forms float on amorphous backdrops. Miró fused poetry with pictorial concerns, alluding to the literary conjugation of beauty with lyrical titles that provide keys to the symbols depicted.

Miró's creation of a pictorial vocabulary reached its apex in 1940 when he executed a series of small gouaches entitled Constellations. Beginning with a few discrete images, Miró added more and more forms, constantly unbalancing then balancing until a veritable heaven of signs connected by a delicate linear webbing achieved a complex compositional equilibrium. Some of the myriad signs and symbols were familiar, some were new: anatomical parts, tendriled biomorphs, elemental stars and moons, as well as seemingly abstract hourglass shapes, and simple circles and ovoids. For Miró, new materials and textured surfaces were sources of ongoing inspiration, leading him in the late twenties to adhere bits of paper, rope, and small metal objects to the picture surface, and, shortly thereafter, to join seemingly unrelated objects into suggestive sculptural assemblages. During the forties, this same concern for the tactile provoked a renewed interest in ceramics. Working with his longtime collaborator, Joseph Llorens Artigas, Miró first experimented with surface manipulation and decoration, then, in subsequent trials, created new non-functional forms.

While Miró's attention was occupied with work in a variety of mediums in the early years of the fifties, he continued to produce a number of easel paintings. *Dawn Perfumed by a Shower of Gold*, executed in 1954, with its whimsical sexuality and gaily hued palette, characterizes the joyous nature of the output of the period. A strictly limited number of images, including the artist's hallmark star, fills the vertical picture plane, concentrating its focus and endowing it with an upward sense of elation. The central image, an elongated personage with sexually explicit appendages, is defined by linear arabesques, a weightless network grounded by a brightly checkered pedestal. The playing-off of line against flat, articulated shapes which change color at the overlapping of planes, sets up a playful rhythm, and together these elements extricate themselves from their airy, sunlit ambiance. The picture surface is pebbled and scumbled, suggesting the title's "shower of gold" and adding yet another element of visual activity. This work expresses the multifaceted nature of Miró's talent, one which combines joy with serious dedication, formal concerns with poetic ones, and reality with the world of fantasy.   KCH

110

Salvador Dali

SPANISH, BORN 1904

Oedipus Complex

1930

pastel on paper
24⅛ × 19¾"
61.3 × 50.2 cm

Purchase
51.3393

[1]Quoted in "First-Class Paranoiac," *Newsweek*, vol. 56, no. 8 (August 22, 1960), p. 86.

[2]Salvador Dali, *Declaration of the Independence of the Imagination and the Rights of Man to His Own Madness* (Privately published, 1939); part reprinted in "Dali Manifests," *Art Digest*, vol. 13, no. 19 (August 1, 1939), p. 9.

[3]Quoted in Dawn Ades, *Dali and Surrealism* (New York: Harper & Row, 1982), p. 74.

[4]Robert Descharnes, *Salvador Dali* (New York: Harry N. Abrams, 1976), colorplate 15.

TO SALVADOR DALI, THE ART OF SPECTACLE has been just as, if not more important than the art of painting. "My eccentricities are concentrated, deliberate acts," he once said. "They are no joke, but what counts most in my life."[1] His life has been a continuous performance by a brilliant showman whose "critical" writings and anarchic gestures have often been in the best tradition of Dada humor. After he joined the Surrealists in Paris in 1929, his flamboyant exhibitionism and outrageous effrontery, such as his delivery of a lecture at the 1936 *International Surrealist Exhibition* (London) in a diving suit, and, later, his *Declaration of the Independence of the Imagination and the Rights of Man to His Own Madness*,[2] provided this circle with constant amusement and controversy.

The outrageous in Dali's personal behavior was paralleled by the then-shocking subject matter of his painting. But if his gestures were full of humor, the canvases from his most creative Surrealist years, 1929–circa 1939, were truly disturbing for the iconography he created of abnormal human psychology. His themes of sexuality, death, and metamorphosis reveal an obsession with castration, putrefaction, impotence, masturbation, and voyeurism. Like the other Surrealists, Dali was influenced by Sigmund Freud's revolutionary studies of the mind. He said of Freud's *Interpretation of Dreams*, "This book presented itself to me as one of the capital discoveries in my life."[3] Like Freud, Dali turned to the dream as a mechanism for mining the unconscious. Using his "paranoiac-critical method," as he termed it, he claimed to have achieved a waking dream, a paranoia-induced state of delirium somewhere between true sleep and complete wakefulness which he then meticulously recorded in the Old Master style of illusionism for which he is renowned (see page 114).

Oedipus Complex, of 1930, deals with a classic Freudian subject. This pastel on paper is a variant of the oil painting *The Enigma of Desire: My Mother, My Mother, My Mother*[4] which Dali painted at the end of 1929. Much simpler than its prototype, this dreamscape presents a beach scene bathed in a glowing, ghostly light with eerie de Chirico-like shadows that make mystery of this allusion to the Mediterranean coast where Dali has lived a large part of his life. The view to the steep horizon features a lone, hollow-headed figure and a large biomorphic shape that recalls the rocks of Cape Creus, worn by the tide, the wind, and the passage of time. Dali has punctured this form with orifices, within each one of which he has written "ma mere." In *The Enigma of Desire*, where Dali pictured himself, the biomorphic shape expands from his head almost as a thought cloud. Although a self-contained entity in the *Oedipus Complex*, the form still suggests a thought cloud, and the repetition of the phrase "ma mere" underscores the notion of obsessive sexual desire. This eroticism is reinforced by the provocative object isolated in the foreground. As in other paintings of the period, the theme of sexual desire is coupled with a vision of horror, in this case, an infestation of ants which eat away at the biomorphic form and suggest rot and decay.

By the mid-1930s Dali's relationship with André Breton and the Surrealists began to deteriorate, and by 1939 he was estranged from most members of the group. His indifference to the cataclysmic world events of the decade outraged these artists, who were committed to political and social change. Moreover, they felt that his self-aggrandizement had become tiresome and that his increasing association with high society and commercialism was antithetical to their aims. Dali's late work has suffered from his tendency to repeat his manic vision so unique to the Surrealist revolt. Yet he has remained the poseur whose deliberate personal contradictions have encouraged the self-mystification at which he has always aimed.   DCduP

Yves Tanguy

FRENCH, 1900–1955

Second Thoughts

ARRIÈRES-PENSÉES
1939

oil on canvas
36⅛ × 29¼"
91.7 × 74.3 cm

William L. Gerstle Collection
William L. Gerstle Fund Purchase
52.4155

[1] Quoted in William S. Rubin, *Dada, Surrealism, and Their Heritage*, The Museum of Modern Art, New York, 1968, p. 64.

[2] In his essay "De Chirico and Modernism," *De Chirico*, The Museum of Modern Art, New York, 1982, pp. 62-63, William Rubin discusses how, in mistaking de Chirico's style as a revival of old-master illusionism, Tanguy, Dali, and Magritte based their painting on classical traditions. While Tanguy's work is modern in its use of abstract forms, its technique, unlike de Chirico's, is thoroughly academic.

[3] Salvador Dali, *Conquest of the Irrational*, trans. from the French by David Gascoyne (New York: Julien Levy, 1935), p. 12.

IN THE FIRST SURREALIST MANIFESTO OF 1924, André Breton, the founder of Surrealism, wrote: "I believe in the future resolution of the states of dream and reality, in appearance so contradictory, in a sort of absolute reality, or *surréalité*. . . . "[1] For those pioneer Surrealist painters—Yves Tanguy, Salvador Dali, and René Magritte—who pursued a style of academic illusionism as opposed to the "abstract" biomorphism of Joan Miró and André Masson, the landscape was where dream and reality met. From the Metaphysical painting of Giorgio de Chirico, their predecessor, the illusionist Surrealists learned the poetic possibilities of vast and desolate spaces; yet unlike de Chirico, their subject was the natural, not urban landscape. From de Chirico as well as early Max Ernst they also grasped the lyric potential of realistically portrayed fantasy. For Tanguy, Dali, and Magritte the landscape provided a familiar context in which to "fix" the dream image veristically. It endowed fantasy with credibility. Vast, open space, particularly in the work of Tanguy and Dali, acts as a stage for the unexpected and as a metaphor for the frontier of the unconscious. The landscape becomes a "mindscape."

In Tanguy's *Second Thoughts* of 1939 an expansive landscape is the setting for an eerie, dreamlike universe sparsely populated with mysterious biomorphic forms. Reviving the perspective techniques of fifteenth-century Italian painting, Tanguy creates the illusion of a deep, recessive space which the viewer perceives as a continuation of his own world.[2] The conventional horizon line, however, is not distinct but amorphous; it appears to melt into a misty haze. Also classical is Tanguy's smoothly graduated modeling and his painstaking, uninflected facture which contributes a kind of photographic realism.

If Tanguy's technique was classical, his subject and content were thoroughly modern, and particularly Surrealist. Scattered in foreground and middleground are fantastic bonelike forms interconnected by thin, delicate etched and painted lines. Tanguy's assembly of unknown beings recalls the enigmatic congregations of Hieronymus Bosch, whose work he greatly admired. Unlike the other illusionist Surrealists, Tanguy's poetic imagery is less specifically literary and his forms are not recognizable. While at times they may appear anthropomorphic, they are never rendered with human features or anatomical details.

Along with his personal morphology, Tanguy's soft, opalescent palette with its bright accents of yellow and red contributes to a sense of the bizarre. A stark, white, artificial light isolates each form and encourages the feeling of a heightened reality. The jet-black shadows cast by this light take on a life of their own, as the disembodied shadows in de Chirico's work. Also more dreamlike than real is the painting's quality of absolute silence and suspended time.

Second Thoughts is the reverse of corporeal reality. It is a vision of a mental universe that appears to exist concurrently with the phenomenal realm. Here Tanguy rendered the dream credible, made it "of the same consistency, of the same durability . . . and communicable thickness as that of the exterior world,"[3] and in doing so expressed the Surrealist belief in the validity of the unconscious.   DCduP

Alberto Giacometti

SWISS, 1901–1966

Annette VII

1962

bronze 2/6
18½ × 10¾ × 7½"
47.0 × 27.3 × 19.1 cm
Gift of Mr. and Mrs. Louis Honig
69.83

IN THE LATE 1940S AND EARLY 1950S, Alberto Giacometti emerged as one of the major sculptors of the post-war era in France. Searching for alternatives to his earlier Surrealist work, he began a series of standing and walking figures whose gaunt, attenuated frames, rough, craggy skin, and solitude in the vastness of space spoke to such Existentialist writers as Simone de Beauvoir and Jean-Paul Sartre, who saw Giacometti's sculpture as a visual metaphor for modern man. Worn by the spatial void that ravages their contours, these generalized figures, modeled from memory and not life, are non-portraits that symbolize universal man and woman. They illustrate Giacometti's primary concern with the figure in space and how space acts upon mass, rather than space being displaced by mass as in traditional sculpture. "Giacometti knows," wrote Sartre, who became a friend of the artist, "that there is nothing redundant in a living man, because everything there is functional; he knows that space is a cancer on being, and eats everything; to sculpt, for him, is to take the fat off space."[1]

This extreme dematerialization of the figure, however, is less severe in Giacometti's last works of the late 1950s and early 1960s. Although there remains a sense of space impinging upon the figure, there is greater sculptural solidity. In place of standing figures, Giacometti now concentrated on a group of portrait busts of his brother Diego and his wife, Annette, which were modeled from life and rendered, in some cases, with more descriptive sensibility than in his earlier work. Included in this group, the less-than-life-size bust *Annette VII* of 1962 possesses the lonely, self-contained, almost tragic expression that marks Giacometti's works. The eyes are a point of focus as they gaze intensely outward, not at the viewer but beyond him. The truncated arms and characteristically scabrous surface modeling, which exhibits how Giacometti incised and pushed and pulled the clay with his fingers, share in the legacy of Auguste Rodin's sculpture.

Viewed from the rear the head is not fully developed, for the bust is intended to be seen frontally. This emphasis on frontality relates to Giacometti's concern with the nature of seeing. His aim was not to sculpt what he "knew" from classical convention to be volume in space, but rather to sculpt exactly what he perceived; thus he distinguished between conceptual perception and visual perception. In an interview at the time he was executing the busts of Annette, Giacometti commented: "I wouldn't think of getting up and walking around you. If I didn't know that your skull had a certain depth, I couldn't guess it. Therefore, if I made a sculpture of you absolutely as I perceive you, I would make a rather flat, scarcely modulated, sculpture."[2]

Giacometti worked on the series of Annette busts from circa 1960 to 1964, and, of the various versions, *Annette VII* is the most realistic. The nature of this relationship to the other busts in the series may be clarified by considering Giacometti's technique in his other favored medium, painting. Eloquently discussed in *A Giacometti Portrait* by the American writer James Lord, who was painted by the artist in 1964, Giacometti's approach was one of constant revision that vacillated between a kind of realism and a generalized abstraction. During the painting of his portrait, Lord observed: "What really disturbs me is the way the painting seems to come and go, as though Alberto himself had no control over it. And sometimes it disappears altogether."[3] These extremes exist in the Annette Series and underscore the importance of process for Giacometti, for although he said "to render what the eye sees is impossible," he was perpetually motivated by the challenge of capturing his unique perceptions.[4] DCduP

[1] Jean-Paul Sartre, Introduction to *Alberto Giacometti: Exhibition of Sculptures, Paintings, Drawings*, Pierre Matisse Gallery, New York, 1948, p. 6.

[2] Alberto Giacometti, "An Interview with Giacometti by David Sylvester [Autumn 1964]," in *Giacometti: Sculptures, Paintings, Drawings*, Whitworth Art Gallery, Manchester, Eng., 1981, p.3.

[3] James Lord, *A Giacometti Portrait* (New York: The Museum of Modern Art, 1965), p. 28.

[4] Quoted in Roy McMullen, "To Render What the Eye Sees Is Impossible," *Horizon*, vol. 18, no. 1 (Winter 1976), p. 86.

Joseph Cornell

AMERICAN, 1903–1972

Untitled

PINK PALACE
ca. 1946–48

wooden box containing photostat
with ink wash, wood, mirror, plant
material, and artificial snow
8⅝ × 14¼ × 4⅜"
21.9 × 36.2 × 11.1 cm

Purchased through gifts of Mr. and
Mrs. William M. Roth and William
L. Gerstle
82.328

Untitled

WINDOW FAÇADE
ca. 1950–53

wooden box containing paint on
wood, nails, glass, and mirror
20 × 11 × 4¼"
50.8 × 27.9 × 10.8 cm

Albert M. Bender Collection
Purchased through a gift of Albert
M. Bender
82.329

"WHAT KIND OF MAN IS THIS," wrote Robert Motherwell in 1953, "who, from old brown cardboard photographs collected in secondhand bookstores, has reconstructed the nineteenth-century 'grand tour' of Europe for his mind's eye more vividly than those who took it. . . . Who found on Fourth Avenue [New York City] the only existing film of Loie Fuller's serpentine dance . . . [who] can incorporate this sense of the past in something that could only have been conceived of at present . . . what kind of man indeed?"[1] For Motherwell, this "kind of man" was Joseph Cornell.

Contrary to popular belief, Cornell was not an entirely reclusive artist, squirreled away in his modest wood-frame house in Flushing, New York. He was fascinated by Manhattan and haunted the bookstores and souvenir shops of Fourth Avenue, as well as its libraries, archives, galleries, museums, and theaters. New York provided Cornell, who neither attended college or art school, nor traveled to Europe, with an education in the arts, humanities, and sciences. Although he denied being an intellectual and a trained artist—"I can't draw, paint, sculpt, make lithographs"[2]—the rich complexity of his unique shadow-box constructions and collages reveals the learned man and consummate visual poet that he was.

Cornell was a cultural scavenger in search of fragments from the past which he would rescue from "complete oblivion"[3] and reanimate in his box constructions. Captivated by the heterogeneous, even schizophrenic, nature of American culture, he repeatedly combined Americana with found objects reminiscent of old-world Europe to create a "poetic theater of memory." "Where else but in America," wrote Cornell, "would you find a biography of the composer of Giselle wrapped around a piece of penny gum?"[4]

The idea of the found object as art has its roots in Dada. It was first addressed by Marcel Duchamp in his Readymades of the 1910s, and during the 1920s and 1930s this issue was further explored by the Surrealists. Although Cornell's early work was created in the context of American Surrealism as it developed in the milieu of the Julien Levy Gallery in New York, he never officially joined the group and, in fact, considered his approach to be different. "I do not share in the subconscious and dream theories of the surrealists," Cornell wrote.[5]

While Cornell's technique of assembling familiar objects in a poetic manner is indebted to the branch of Surrealism termed "illusionist" (see page 114), he did not emphasize its irrational or incongruous juxtaposition of commonplace objects. Rather, he stressed the subtle visual, verbal, and textural affinities, however vague and mysterious, in his combinations of the flotsam and jetsam of our daily lives.[6] Furthermore, his imagery possesses none of the Freudian themes, the deeply psychological, paranoid, and explicitly erotic subject matter characteristic of the Surrealist painting of René Magritte, Salvador Dali, and Yves Tanguy.

Untitled (*Pink Palace*), of circa 1946–48, with its stately European mansion bathed in rosy pink surrounded by palatial steps covered with snow and a deep, enchanted black forest, is one of Cornell's most bewitching shadow boxes. Within this sealed treasury Cornell demonstrates his collector's sensibility by gathering together a decorative frame covered with gleaming blue chips, a wooden cutout papered with a tinted photostat, mirrored windows, twigs, and a sheet of mirror in the background. The imagery of the Pink Palace illustrates Cornell's love of the European past and reflects the influence of the Surrealist Max Ernst, who pioneered the technique of collaging cutouts of existing images.

One of a series, Untitled (*Pink Palace*) is among Cornell's most overtly theatrical pieces. The nineteenth-century miniature theater, a souvenir item mass produced for assembly at home, fascinated him, as did the Victorian toy shadow box. In Untitled (*Pink Palace*) the sense of theater-in-miniature is captured by the sparkling blue proscenium through which one looks to the intimately scaled scene staged within. Through this window the fantasy world of castles, kings, queens, and fairy princesses is magically brought to life. Yet, the box is imbued with enigma and paradox, for although it evokes the realm of fairy tales and child's play, its hermetic space suggests an eerie stillness as well.

In Untitled (*Window Façade*), of circa 1950–53, the suggestion of narrative in Untitled (*Pink Palace*) is replaced by an emphasis on formal structure. This austere, rectilinear box construction, which again is part of a series, exhibits Cornell's increasing distillation of imagery from 1950 on. Fewer elements are employed, and those that are—wood, glass, and mirror—are more abstract, less objectively referential than the twigs, snow, and building façade of Untitled (*Pink Palace*). Within this sealed box, a sheet of glass is sandwiched between two white, wooden grids. Also painted white are the horizontal and vertical lines on the glass sheet which suggest window panes within each rectangle and complete the allusion to the geometrically patterned window facades of New York skyscrapers.

Cornell's love of New York included his fascination with windows, a logical extension for one obsessed with making shadow boxes. In his Window Façade Series, Cornell seems to suggest the idea that the window frames modern urban experience, whether it consists of riding in a car, a bus, the subway, or simply sitting at a desk. When Cornell worked at the Traphagen Commercial Textile Studio during the 1930s, he stared through his window at the windows in the building across from him. In an essay entitled "Discovery—New York City 1940," he wrote:

"All day long, week in-week out, I look across the street from my studio table at the monotonous grey facade. . . . Every night promptly at five uniformed guards appear simultaneously at each of the myriad windows drawing in the ponderous rivet-studded shutters for the night. But this summer evening? promptly on time, the ethereal form of Fanny Cerrito, breathless resplendent . . . appearing simultaneously in each casement. . . ."[7] The mystery and surprise behind the window, the notion of a larger reality behind the frame, intrigued him.

Cornell's related interest in Lewis Carroll's through-the-looking-glass idea led him, as in Untitled (*Pink Palace*), to use mirrors; in this case a sheet of mirror lines the rear of the box. In this shadow box, instead of looking into a distant, magical wonderland as in Untitled (*Pink Palace*), one looks through the façade of windows to see one's self and one's world reflected, but the vision is entirely fragmented. The dynamic interplay between the grid patterns and their reflections interwoven with the reflections of the viewer and his world creates a fractured, Cubistic space that captures the essence of the modern experience.

While Joseph Stella and Arthur Dove experimented with assemblage[8] during the 1920s, Cornell was the first American artist of this century to work extensively in the medium. His poetry of the commonplace set an important precedent for the younger American artists, who emerged during the late 1950s and early 1960s, such as Robert Rauschenberg and Jasper Johns on the East Coast and the Beat Generation artists, including Wallace Berman, Bruce Conner, and Edward Kienholz on the West Coast. DCduP

[1] Robert Motherwell, "Preface to a Joseph Cornell Exhibition," in *Joseph Cornell: Portfolio—Catalogue*, Leo Castelli Gallery, Richard L. Feigen and Company, and James Corcoran Gallery, New York and Los Angeles, 1976, n.p.

[2] Sandra Leonard Starr, *Joseph Cornell and the Ballet* (New York: Castelli Feigen Corcoran, 1983), p. 81 n. 6 (published on the occasion of an exhibition of the same title).

[3] Ibid., p. 12.

[4] Ibid., p. 2.

[5] Quoted in Dawn Ades, "The Transcendental Surrealism of Joseph Cornell," in *Joseph Cornell*, The Museum of Modern Art, New York, 1980, p. 19.

[6] For an in-depth discussion of Cornell's relationship to Surrealism, see Ades, ibid., pp. 15–39.

[7] Starr, *Joseph Cornell and the Ballet*, op. cit., p. 31.

[8] The term *assemblage* is used here in the generic sense, to mean all forms of composite art, whether two-dimensional or three-dimensional.

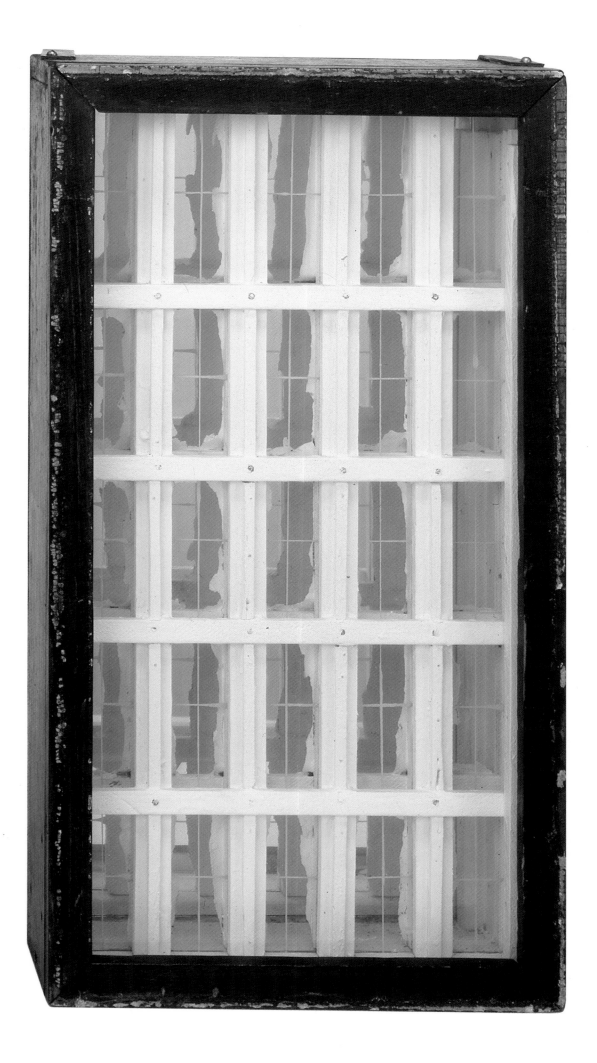

Georgia O'Keeffe

AMERICAN, BORN 1887

Lake George
formerly
REFLECTION SEASCAPE
1922

oil on canvas
16¼ × 22"
41.2 × 55.9 cm

Gift of Charlotte Mack
52.6714

IMAGERY DISTILLED FROM THE FLORA AND FAUNA of Lake George, the skyscrapers of New York City, and the New Mexican desert encompass the unique vision of Georgia O'Keeffe. A keen and intuitive observer of life, this pioneer of early American modernism has painted subject matter ranging from magnified views of flowers to abstractions of the intangible forces found in nature. Based primarily on natural imagery, the paintings of O'Keeffe utilize an innovative vocabulary of vivid color, rhythmic line, and essential form to render visible the artist's perceptions.

Born on a farm near Sun Prairie, Wisconsin, in 1887, O'Keeffe decided at a young age to become an artist. She initially studied at the Art Institute of Chicago and at the Art Students League in New York but soon became discouraged with academic training and stopped painting altogether. It was not until 1912 that her interest in fine art was rekindled when she enrolled in Alon Bement's art class at the University of Virginia in Charlottesville. Through Bement, O'Keeffe became familiar with the ideas of the art educator Arthur Wesley Dow. Influenced by Far Eastern art and the teachings of the Orientalist Ernest Fenollosa, Dow's methods employed strong outlines, patterns, and a harmonious balance of dark and light.

In the fall of 1915, while teaching in South Carolina, O'Keeffe began to draw and paint again. Influenced by Dow's emphasis on the beauty inherent in formal elements of composition, she created an original series of abstract charcoal drawings which explored the expressive qualities of line and shape and suggested natural imagery. Encouraged by the results, O'Keeffe sent the drawings to a friend who showed them to Alfred Stieglitz, proponent of modernism in America. Stieglitz exhibited the drawings in the spring of 1916 at his "291" gallery in New York and a year later presented the artist's first solo exhibition.

O'Keeffe continued to teach and to paint highly sensitive and emotionally direct responses to her environment. Some of the most powerful and personal statements of early American modernism were painted while she was living in Canyon, Texas, from 1916 to 1918. Deeply moved by the remote windswept landscape, she painted works alluding to natural phenomena—sunrises, clouds, and starlight—utilizing flat frontal abstract patterns. By 1918, O'Keeffe had accepted an invitation from Stieglitz, whom she would marry in 1924, to stay in New York and paint. For the next ten years, she lived in New York City, spending the summers in Lake George, New York, at the Stieglitz family estate.

Unlike many of her contemporaries, among them Marsden Hartley and Arthur Dove, O'Keeffe did not travel to Europe for artistic direction. She was well aware of avant-garde activities abroad through reading the theories of Kandinsky and Arthur Jerome Eddy's *Cubists and Post-Impressionism* (1914) and through exhibitions mounted by Stieglitz at 291. O'Keeffe chose, however, to create works that spoke of a spiritual relationship to nature, following the American traditions of landscape painting.

During the early 1920s, O'Keeffe began to focus on themes from her immediate environment, particularly the flowers, hills, and trees of the area surrounding Lake George. In the painting *Lake George* of 1922, O'Keeffe paints the lake at sunset—a magical time, when the light is most diffuse and luminous and the reflective properties of water are greatest. Streamlined, clear and crisp, the abstracted forms represent the elemental components of the landscape: sky, hills, shadows, water, and light on water. Evocative of a landscape of spaciousness and quiet grandeur, the composition can also be viewed as a poetic arrangement of subtle color variations, expressive line, and flattened planes composed of crystalline, smooth, even brush strokes.　LLS

Georgia O'Keeffe

AMERICAN, BORN 1887

Black Place I
1944

oil on canvas
26 × 30⅛″
66.0 × 76.6 cm

Gift of Charlotte Mack
54.3536

[1]Georgia O'Keeffe, *Georgia O'Keeffe* (New York: The Viking Press, 1976), n.p.

SINCE CHILDHOOD, Georgia O'Keeffe has been fascinated by the American Southwest. As a young woman living on the plains of Texas, she produced abstract drawings and watercolors that evoked the powerful forces of nature and the "wonderful emptiness" of the region. In the summer of 1929, O'Keeffe traveled to New Mexico to visit the collector Mabel Dodge Luhan in Taos. Captivated by the austere beauty of the desert landscape, she was drawn back every summer thereafter until Stieglitz's death in 1945 when she settled permanently in Abiquiu, a small village west of Taos.

The clarity and simplicity embodied in the hills, mesas, and sun-whitened bones found in the desert inspired the work of O'Keeffe after 1929. She painted animal skulls brought home as icons of the desert, infusing her canvases with a mystical and transcendental power. Placing the bare bleached bones against the wide open ranges, O'Keeffe portrayed the essence and spirit of the landscape through a detached yet emotionally intense representation.

In later paintings, skulls combined with desert flowers suggested the natural order and chain of life, death, and regeneration. By 1943, O'Keeffe magnified pelvis bones and placed them against a background of clear blue sky. The smooth, sculptural surfaces and holes which punctuated the bones intrigued the artist, resulting in an eloquent exploration of form. Utilizing both representation and abstraction, O'Keeffe cut through to the essential characteristics of her subjects, enabling texture, color, and shape to speak fully to the senses.

"I must have seen the Black Place driving past on a trip to the Navajo country and, having seen it, I had to go back to paint—even in the heat of midsummer. It became one of my favorite places to work. . . . The Black Place is about one hundred and fifty miles from Ghost Ranch and as you come over the hill it looks like a mile of elephants— grey hills all the same size with almost white sand at their feet."[1]

The Black Place, a remote hilly portion of the desert outside of Abiquiu, became a subject she painted repeatedly beginning in 1944. As in her earlier paintings, O'Keeffe explored this theme through both realistic and abstract means. In the painting *Black Place I* of 1944, a rolling sea of deeply furrowed gray hills is depicted with a softly eroded ravine traversing the center of the composition. The muted graduated colors of the desert—mauve, lavender, gray, and black—further accentuate the undulating contours and form a rhythmic cadence extending far back into space. In the vast badlands, small clumps of green vegetation appear in the crevices—testaments to the presence of life and the artist's acute awareness of existence around her.   LLS

Arthur Dove

AMERICAN, 1880–1946

Silver Ball No. 2

1930

oil and metallic paint on canvas
23¼ × 30"
59.1 × 76.2 cm

Rosalie M. Stern Bequest Fund
Purchase
59.2348

Yes I could paint a cyclone. . . .I would show the repetitions and convolutions of the rage of the tempest. I would paint the wind, not a landscape chastized by the cyclone.[1]

SNOWSTORMS, waterfalls, resonating foghorns and starry heavens were among the subjects envisioned in the paintings and assemblages of Arthur Dove. Inspired by the richness of sensory experience, Dove sought to evoke the essences found in nature through the abstract arrangement of color, line, and form. Paralleling Vasily Kandinsky, his contemporary in Europe, Dove was one of the first artists in America to supplant an external depiction with an internal one, rendering the spiritual forces inherent in an object or experience through non-objective means.

After a brief but successful tenure as an illustrator in New York, Arthur Dove abandoned his commercial career in 1908 to work in the thriving artistic climate of Paris. During a year's stay in France, he became aware of the modernist advances of the day represented in the work of Cézanne, Matisse, and his fellow Fauves. Deeply affected by the flattened forms of Cézanne and the high-pitched color of Matisse, Dove infused his paintings with a simplified compositional structure and a liberated sensual palette.

Returning to the United States in 1909, Dove became acquainted with Alfred Stieglitz, champion of modernism in America and founder of the pivotal New York gallery "291." Thereafter, Dove exhibited regularly in shows organized by Stieglitz, rapidly becoming a major figure in the Stieglitz circle, which included John Marin and Georgia O'Keeffe. Through a close association with this coterie, Dove was able to continue his absorption of vanguard ideas, particularly Cubism and Futurism, which were evolving on the Continent and taking root in America.

By the 1920s, the decade preceding *Silver Ball No. 2*, Dove had forged a personal mode of abstraction based primarily on natural motifs. A diverse body of work was completed during this decade in which he experimented with the expressive quality of line, flattened interlocking organic forms, and simplified geometric renderings based on industrial images. Although Dove's work was akin to Precisionism in subject matter and technique, the guiding principle underlying it was the subjective evocation of an object or experience.

In *Silver Ball No. 2*, dated 1930, the artist distilled landscape and extraterrestrial images to the simple abstract shapes of circles, ellipses, and undulating bands of color. In addition to the intuitive reduction of natural motifs to essential forms, Dove experimented with advanced compositional devices. Aware of the vanguard photographic methods of the day practiced by Stieglitz and Paul Strand, he utilized the techniques of the close-up, of enlarging images and cropping them. The seemingly immense shining orb is powerfully suggested through its partial representation, and through this great metallic globe Dove conjures up lunar and stellar images, bringing to mind the vastness of objects in space and the timeless movement of celestial bodies. The silver sphere may also represent the man-made entity of a looming water tower in a country landscape, thus relating to the industrial themes of the previous decade.

The search to uncover and record intrinsic truths embodied in natural phenomena was of paramount concern to Dove. Color, line, and shape became the tools with which he expressed a highly personal view of the vitality, harmony, and eternal order found in nature.   LLS

[1] Arthur Dove, as quoted in Barbara Haskell, *Arthur Dove*, San Francisco Museum of Art, 1974, p. 7.

Edward Hopper

AMERICAN, 1882–1967

Bridle Path

1939

oil on canvas
28⅜ × 42⅛"
72.1 × 107.0 cm

Anonymous gift
76.174

USING THE LANGUAGE OF LIGHT, Edward Hopper portrayed the pathos of loneliness and the drama of the American scene. Segregated by choice from the European trends toward abstraction, Hopper utilized realism as a vehicle to express his deeply felt vision and personal state of mind. Emotionally committed to his subjects, yet visually detached, Hopper assumed the role of concerned observer, whether depicting the granite outcroppings of the Maine coast, the bleakness of an all-night coffee shop, or the isolation of a lonely traveler.

Hopper began his formal training as a commercial illustrator, but his real love was for the fine arts, which led him to the New York School of Art where he studied painting with William Merritt Chase and Robert Henri. Chase's style, shot through with bravura and sophisticated elegance, had a limited impact on Hopper's work, but Henri's philosophy deeply touched the young artist. Emphasizing the expression of mood and depiction of surrounding environment, Henri further exhorted his students to experience Europe. Hopper followed this advice and in 1906 made his first trip to Paris, a journey he repeated in 1908 and again in 1910. While he did not study in the French capital, Hopper did spend his time sketching and painting the boulevards and cafés. Struck by the work of the Impressionists, he lightened and brightened his palette and developed an interest in the use of light as a means of conveying mood. Although he employed French subjects and considered this foreign experience to be important, his work evolved primarily internally and the subsequent years were spent experimenting with tonal changes, emotional tone, compositional configurations, and new subjects.

After exploring the mediums of etching and watercolor, Hopper returned with vigor to paint and canvas, and by the mid-twenties his mature style crystalized, not to alter appreciably for the remainder of his career. Using overtly American subjects as vehicles for expression, Hopper exploited light, the glaring rays of the noonday sun, or the oblique glow of dusk to impart drama or solitude. Using a limited number of compositional formats, he combined actual, gleaned-from-life sketches with images summoned from his fertile mind, synthesizing reality and the imaginary.

The cityscape of New York, façades and interiors, provided Edward Hopper with a rich source of subject matter. Extracting material from theaters and hotels, sidewalks and offices, he examined the theme of isolation within a populated environment. *Bridle Path*, inspired by Hopper's many visits to Central Park, transmits not an overt sense of human detachment, but a latent one, communicated through the averted faces of anonymous figures, the ominous overhang of the craggy rocks and gaping underpass, and the oppressively vacant façade of the building that looms overhead. This is not a tableau with a single dejected figure. Three humans engaged in physical activity are represented, yet through manipulation of light, Hopper has diverted attention from them, rendering them neutral and devoid of emotional interaction. The arched entrance to the tunnel provides a form often seen in Hopper's work—in bridges, theater arcades, railroad overpasses—but it is the severely cropped architectural façade which seems most Hopper-like. Windows shaded, surfaces flattened, the structure radiates emptiness but serves a rational function, compressing the composition and narrowing its focus. Hopper has transformed this glimpse of reality into a transcendent statement of timelessness.   KCH

John Storrs

AMERICAN, 1885–1956

Study in Form (Architectural Form)

ca. 1923

stone
19½ × 3⅛ × 3¼"
49.6 × 8.0 × 8.3 cm

Purchased through a gift of Julian and Jean Aberbach
81.3

BORN AND RAISED IN CHICAGO, birthplace of the American skyscraper, the sculptor John Storrs shared with contemporary architects a belief in a new building type that would emphasize verticality instead of the horizontal direction of classical architecture. An architecture student early in his career, he was well versed in architectural theory and personally knew some of the major figures who helped formulate the new skyscraper style —Louis Sullivan, John W. Root, and Edward H. Bennett. More than any other American sculptor, he advocated an interdependence between architecture and sculpture.

Storrs's series of works entitled Studies in Architectural Form and Forms in Space of the 1920s were influenced by the contemporary theory and practice of the skyscraper style. An expression of "growth toward the sun and sky,"[1] these sleek, streamlined forms echo Sullivan's vision of the modern office building that would be "every inch a proud and soaring thing, rising in sheer exultation."[2] Although several Europeans and the American Max Weber preceded Storrs in creating examples of purely abstract sculpture, with these skyscraper forms he was one of the earliest sculptors to create a large, mature body of non-representational works.

Storrs's awareness of abstraction was encouraged by his contact with European modernism. After studying sculpture in several of the Paris academies, he worked with Auguste Rodin until the outbreak of World War I. During the war years he remained in Paris and became well acquainted with sculpture by the Cubist Jacques Lipchitz and the Vorticist Henri Gaudier-Brzeska. In 1917 he created his first non-objective sculptures —three vertical, free-standing stone panels with inlays of black marble and mirror glass. The use of stone, marble, and glass within one piece suggests that Storrs knew of Umberto Boccioni's "Technical Manifesto of Futurist Sculpture" (1912), which advocated combining different materials.

Although he continued to live in France until 1927, Storrs found inspiration for his formal studies in the geometric skyline of the modern American cityscape. During this period he frequently visited Chicago, and occasionally New York, and in his sculpture he caught the spirit of the skyscraper form that was changing the face of the urban scene in America. Study in Form of circa 1923, one of the pieces comprising the Studies in Form Series, is an austere, streamlined monolith, perfectly symmetrical on all four sides. Its source is in one of Storrs's earlier tower forms of circa 1922, in which a squared column with pagoda-like top is surrounded by faceted planes.[3] In the interest of utter simplicity, the tower shape in this later work has been removed from any surrounding mass and appears powerfully self-contained in its isolation. The smooth, machine-precision surfaces suggest the pristine finish that Storrs later achieved in his metal skyscraper pieces. He opens up the structure and enlivens its surface with light-and-shadow contrasts by cutting such mechanistic motifs as repeated horizontal bars into the mass. Despite its intimate scale, this slender, unadorned structure possesses a sense of monumentality.

Indeed, Storrs's skyscraper forms are monuments to the modern technological society in America. Like the Precisionist painters Joseph Stella, Charles Sheeler, and Louis Lozowick, and the photographers Walker Evans, Berenice Abbott, and Margaret Bourke-White, he looked to the changing American cityscape for symbols to celebrate the new machine age. In his call for the interaction between fine art and industrial design, he revealed his belief in the strength and potential of industrial America, "Let the artists create for your public buildings and homes forms that will express that strength and will to power, that poise and simplicity that one begins to see in some of America's factories, rolling-mills, elevators and bridges."[4]   DCduP

[1] Ann Rosenthal, "John Storrs, Eclectic Modernist," in John Storrs & John Flannagan: Sculpture & Works on Paper, Sterling and Francine Clark Art Institute, Williamstown, Mass., 1980, p. 16.

[2] Loc. cit.

[3] Reproduced in Noel S. Frackman, "John Storrs and the Origins of Art Deco" (Master's thesis, New York University, Institute of Fine Arts, 1975), pl. 64.

[4] Quoted in Jeffrey Wechsler, "Machine Aesthetics and Art Deco," in Vanguard American Sculpture 1913–1939, Rutgers University Art Gallery, The State University of New Jersey, Rutgers, 1979, p. 95.

Joseph Stella

AMERICAN, BORN ITALY
1877–1946

Bridge

1936

oil on canvas
50⅛ × 30⅛"
127.3 × 76.5 cm

WPA Federal Arts Project Allocation
to the San Francisco Museum of Art
3760.43

THE BROOKLYN BRIDGE with its soaring towers and arcing cables was for many literary and visual artists of the early twentieth century *the* symbol of America, capturing the essence of this country, representing its energetic progress and advanced technology. For Joseph Stella, this structure provided more than just inspiration; it was, in his words, "an ever growing obsession,"[1] an image to which he returned with fervor again and again during his lifetime.

Stella was born in 1877 in Muro Lucano, Italy. At the age of nineteen he emigrated to the United States where he first studied medicine, which he quickly abandoned for study at the Art Students League in New York and later at the New York School of Art. In 1912, during an extended visit to Europe, Stella saw the work of the Italian Futurists in an exhibition at the Galerie Bernheim-Jeune in Paris and met Umberto Boccioni, Carlo Carrà, and Gino Severini. He returned to the United States deeply affected and in 1913 began to paint in a Futurist mode, executing canvases that displayed the faceted form, charged motion, and high-pitched coloration of the Italians.

In 1918, Joseph Stella began exploring a theme that had fascinated him since his first arrival in the United States—the Brooklyn Bridge. In preliminary studies and a canvas dated circa 1919, Stella moved away from Futurist pictorial concerns and focused instead on the triangular configuration of the man-made span, abstracting and fracturing the framework, capturing its dynamic forces, then reassembling the elements into a stable composition imbued with a mystical, nocturnal light.

From 1920 to 1922, Stella worked on a monumental five-canvas polyptych, a paean to New York entitled *New York Interpreted* in which, on one of the panels, he returned to the theme of the bridge. Here, the last vestiges of Futurism have been erased and the work focuses on the monumentality of the bridge's structure. The upward thrust of the cables emerges predominant, while the towers become Gothic arches framing the stained-glass vista of the city beyond. The lozenge-like forms, which for Stella represented subways and tubes, the veins and arteries of the city, are concentrated along the lower edge of the composition, forming a predella. The ultimate effect is that of an altarpiece, a deification of the majesty of urban engineering.

In 1935, Joseph Stella was hired by the Works Progress Administration (WPA). In March of the following year he wrote Holger Cahill, then director of the Federal Art Project, that he was working enthusiastically on a WPA commission for a painting of the Brooklyn Bridge. This 1936 canvas, allocated to the San Francisco Museum of Art in 1943, was based directly on the bridge panel of *New York Interpreted*. The later picture, however, exhibits an overall simplification in which the composition has been reduced to simple, aggressive forms arcing and forcing their way upward. The network of cables which had earlier defined a complex pictorial space moving back toward a depiction of the city now becomes evenly spaced ribs, positioned within the same plane, which reinforce the dominant vertical thrust. The bridge takes on the soaring qualities of a Gothic cathedral. The city, which in earlier works blazed in the background, has become indistinct; no longer is the bridge envisioned as a conduit to the metropolis; it has become a monument for its own sake. The palette has been simplified as well; the glowing yellows, formerly so prevalent, have been reduced to highlights along the lower border and the preponderance of the composition is rendered in electric blues, blacks, and the granite grays of an urban skyscraper.   KCH

[1] Quoted in John I. H. Baur, with Irma B. Jaffe, *Joseph Stella* (New York: Praeger, 1971), p. 34.

132

Charles Sheeler

AMERICAN, 1883–1965

Aerial Gyrations

1953

oil on canvas
23⅜ × 18⅝"
60.0 × 47.3 cm

Mrs. Manfred Bransten Special Fund
Purchase
74.78

CHARLES SHEELER'S STARK VISIONS of the American landscape, eloquent interpretations of city and countryside, stand as paradigms of Precisionism. Austere and monumental, purged of human presence and emotion, these images of blast furnaces and skyscrapers, clapboard barns and soaring stacks speak to the vitality and power of a rapidly developing nation. Using both photography and painting as means of expression, Sheeler revealed the geometric order and clarity of form which he found within engineered industrial facilities and finely crafted buildings.

A native of Philadelphia, Sheeler was initially trained in applied design, then spent three years studying with William Merritt Chase, whose stylish spontaneity and bravura brushwork were immediately adopted by the young artist. A trip to Europe in 1908–9 revealed to Sheeler the work of the Italian Renaissance and, in particular, that of Piero della Francesca, whose underlying architectonic structure appealed to him. In Paris he was introduced to the work of Cézanne and Matisse, as well as that of Picasso and Braque who were just formulating Cubism. This exposure, coupled with the experience of the Armory Show in 1913, profoundly affected Sheeler and he spent the next few years moving away from the Chase-inspired style and toward analysis and abstraction of form. Taking up photography as a means of financial support, Sheeler soon discovered its potential for artistic expression. Photographing first the interior of his own house, later the skyscrapers of New York, Sheeler not only achieved consummate syntheses of abstraction and reality, but also examined and experimented with compositional devices and themes which would subsequently appear in his paintings.

A move to New York in 1919 triggered Sheeler's fascination with urban themes. In his first paintings that can be labeled Precisionist, he eliminated all details and concentrated instead on flat, sleek planes which defined the shallow pictorial space of the Cubists. Thereafter moving back toward realism, Sheeler discovered the formal beauty of two seemingly opposite themes, the metallic geometry of industrial America, found at the Ford Motor Company's River Rouge plant, and the functional grace of the architecture of the Shaker community, which he explored through both camera and paint. Developing a process of previsualization, Sheeler analyzed and planned, often making multiple preliminary studies in photographic and graphic form before embarking on the final painting.

During the decade of the fifties, Sheeler returned to the simplified planes and severely limited space of thirty years earlier. His ongoing interest in photography had led him to the use of double exposures, color film, and transparency overlays. In *Aerial Gyrations*, painted in 1953, a complex interplay of forms is created through repetitive and shadowed images and a multiplicity of perspectives, the visual product of Sheeler's photographic experiments. The cool palette of blues, greens, browns, and blacks is non-imitative, yet it captures the steely surfaces of the industrial structures. Viewed as gleaming, looming cylinders, these blast furnaces are devoid of the transience of either worker or flames. Reductive and synthesized, controlled and rational, *Aerial Gyrations*, like all of Sheeler's work, stands as a dispassionate paean to functional design. KCH

Stuart Davis

AMERICAN, 1894–1964

Deuce

1954

oil on canvas
26 × 42¼"
66.0 × 107.3 cm

Gift of Mrs. E. S. Heller
55.4734

THE QUICKENING PULSE OF AMERICA in the twentieth century provided the inspiration for the work of Stuart Davis. Plucking images and rhythms from the honky-tonks, back streets, and industrial clutter of the city, Davis extracted and formalized, producing paintings that captured the tempo and spirit of the vigorous, expanding country.

Born to a family centered around art—his father was an art editor and his mother a sculptor—Davis began his formal training by studying with Robert Henri, who rejected academic traditions and opened Davis's eyes to the wealth of subject matter in his immediate surroundings. Confident that social realism was the fitting idiom for expressing his ideas, Davis was strongly jolted when the 1913 *International Exhibition of Modern Art*, known as the Armory Show, provided his first exposure to the avant-garde art of both Europe and the United States. Particularly struck by the work of Gauguin, van Gogh, and Matisse with their intuitive use of color and simplified forms, Davis took time to ponder these innovations and, beginning in 1915, started to experiment with both Post-Impressionist and Cubist techniques, applying color arbitrarily and expressively, reducing and flattening forms, and approaching the painting as an object rather than as a representation.

After integrating some of the principles of Synthetic Cubism—particularly its cutout shapes and overlapping planes—into his work, Davis concentrated on working through objective reality to arrive at independent formal elements in the Eggbeater Series of 1927-28. Thereafter settling on the urban scene as his predominant theme, Davis explored multiple compositional structures using, among others, angles and modular square units. He interjected words and signs, which acted as formal components as well as associative images. Emphasizing the picture plane with flat, eccentric shapes and poster-like colors, the paintings became increasingly complex, evolving into a staccato of fragmented forms, high-keyed color, and quirky lines, paralleling the driving, fractured rhythms of jazz. Ever tied to the city, the works evoked the rhythms of urban life more through their patterns of line, color, and plane than through specific images.

A shift toward consolidation occurred in the early fifties. The splintered shapes became larger and simpler and the palette adjusted accordingly, offering fewer, brighter colors. While Davis often dipped back and reworked earlier compositions, he did so within the parameters of this new perspective. *Deuce*, painted in 1954, looks back to a compositional device Davis first used in 1931. The horizontal picture format is divided into two distinct halves, suggesting frames in a film. Bordered by flat planes of dense red, black, white, and vibrant blue, the apposing units contain views that suggest the urban environment, expressed in skeletal delineations of black against white. Like bits of the world seen from a passing train, recognizable but not definable, the units are set out in fragmented form, one close up and simplified, the other distanced yet more intricate. Contrasting yet similar, the bisections set up a visual bounce that activates the composition and conversely achieves a balance. Upbeat and streamlined, energetic yet reasoned, this work, like all of Stuart Davis's oeuvre, encapsulates the modern beat of America.   KCH

Frida (Frieda) Kahlo

MEXICAN, 1910–1954

Frieda and Diego Rivera

1931

oil on canvas
39⅜ × 31″
100.0 × 78.7 cm

Albert M. Bender Collection
Gift of Albert M. Bender
36.6061

Here you see us, me, Frieda Kahlo, with my beloved husband Diego Rivera. I painted these portraits in the beautiful city of San Francisco California for our friend Mr. Albert Bender, and it was in the month of April of the year 1931.[1]

THE FAMILIAR SELF-PORTRAITS of Frida Kahlo, anguished, introspective, interwoven with suffering, provide a clear reflection of the life and sensibilities of this Mexican artist. Born of the physical pain she endured throughout her life, the tumult of her marriage to Diego Rivera, and the despair of not being able to bear a child, her autobiographical paintings convey each grief in visceral detail and visionary symbolism.

Born just outside Mexico City in the town of Coyoacan and an active participant in the cultural upheaval that swept Mexico following the revolution of 1910–20, Kahlo consciously looked to her heritage for inspiration and found a clear medium for expressing her inner emotions through the myths and often macabre symbols of the native culture. Private and self-searching, her small-scaled panels evoked the richness of the Mexican folk tradition, emanating most directly from the form of *retablos*, painted scenes of calamities in which Christ, Mary, or a saint intervenes, rescuing the victim from disaster. Offered in gratitude by the faithful, these realistically rendered, fantasy-laden images abound in the churches of the Mexican countryside. Like miniature stages that present tableaux of miracles, they exhibit the shallow space, simple presentation, and dramatic coloration that Kahlo used in her own work.

Frida Kahlo's outlook was shaped in large part by her physical frailty. At the age of fifteen she was involved in a streetcar/bus accident in which she was gravely injured, suffering multiple spinal fractures, a broken foot, and a shattered pelvis. In constant pain ever after, Kahlo endured numerous operations during her lifetime and lived with the specter of disability and helplessness. Much of her art is a product of introspection brought about by physical torment.

In 1929, Kahlo married Diego Rivera, already an established master. Each possessing a strong will, both confident in their own art, theirs was a marriage of passion and turbulence. Late in 1930 they traveled to San Francisco where Rivera had been commissioned to execute murals at both the California School of Fine Arts (now the San Francisco Art Institute) and the San Francisco Stock Exchange. The months spent in the bayside city were happy ones for Kahlo and the double portrait she painted there for their friend and longtime supporter, Albert M. Bender, reflects that contentment.

Taking the form of a traditional colonial wedding portrait, complete with a dove holding the banderole in its bill, the brightly colored painting is almost primitive in its directness. The figures, positioned frontally, gaze out impassively, Kahlo's head tilted deferentially toward her husband, her face displaying traces of the stoicism that was to reappear frequently in her subsequent work. Her diminutive figure clothed in a long-skirted native costume, her feet enclosed in tiny, decorated slippers, contrasts sharply with the bulky presence of her husband in his rumpled work clothes, palette in hand. The disparities in physical appearance in many ways exemplify the differences in their art, for while his was the art of the public monument, the grand gesture, the broad description, hers was miniature and detailed, chimerical and intensely personal. KCH

[1]Translation of the inscription that appears in the streamer above the figures.

138

Diego Rivera
MEXICAN, 1886–1957

The Flower Carrier
formerly
THE FLOWER VENDOR
1935

oil and tempera on Masonite
48 × 47¾"
121.9 × 121.3 cm

Albert M. Bender Collection
Gift of Albert M. Bender in memory
of Caroline Walter
35.4516

THE BUILDING OF A MODERN POLITICAL STATE in Mexico following the revolution of 1910–20 brought with it a cultural renaissance which rejected the stagnant academic art of the pre-war years and replaced it with an art considered to be relevant to the people. A lively revival of interest in the aesthetic contributions of the native population developed, and the government sponsored numerous projects for the decoration of public buildings by Mexican artists. These murals glorifying the revolution and ennobling Mexican workers and peasants began to emerge early in the twenties. Out of the brutality of the frescoes of José Clemente Orozco, the volatile turbulence of the paintings of David Alfaro Siqueiros, and the combination of history and social protest in the murals of Diego Rivera, a new nationalist style was forged which reflected indigenous forms and symbols, yet spoke to a political vitality.

Diego Rivera had arrived at his patriotism via a circuitous route. Born in the mountain town of Guanajuato in 1886, he received his formal training in Mexico City where, outside the classroom, he had been deeply affected by an engraver of popular broadsheets, José Guadalupe Posada, who fostered Rivera's populist philosophy and taught him to imbue his work with emotion. In 1907 Rivera left Mexico, traveling first to Spain, then to Paris where, save for a short visit to Mexico during the revolution in 1910, he remained until 1920. After immersing himself in the study of both old and modern masters, Rivera came under the influence of Picasso and in 1913 he began to paint in a Cubist style.

A sojourn in Italy in 1920–21, during which he viewed the work of the Florentines Giotto and Cimabue, prefaced Rivera's return to his homeland. In a series of governmental mural commissions he revived the Renaissance medium of fresco, which had impressed him in Italy, and executed grand-scale wall paintings depicting historical and revolutionary themes expressed in terms easily understood both subjectively and aesthetically by the common citizen. Exhibiting the shallow depth of Giotto, broadly described to carry clearly to the viewer, and initially starkly composed, these murals related closely to their architectural contexts.

Commissions to paint murals at the California School of Fine Arts (now the San Francisco Art Institute) and the San Francisco Stock Exchange brought Rivera and his wife, Frida Kahlo, to San Francisco in 1930. Utilizing a theme of California, its people and resources, Rivera executed the Stock Exchange fresco, then turned his attention to the school, where he illustrated the making of a fresco, in which he, as artist, is represented seated on the scaffold, his posterior to the viewer. The impact on the artists of the area was immediate, inciting them not only to experiment with the long-neglected technique of fresco, but to mine their immediate environment for subject material as well.

In March 1935, Albert Bender commissioned a painting from the artist for the San Francisco Museum of Art. In response, Rivera painted *The Flower Carrier*, which unites the simplicity and clarity of his drawings with the monumentality of his frescoes and stands as a masterwork in his oeuvre. Strongly reminiscent of Giotto's frescoes in its pared-down, tight composition, restricted depth, and use of compositional force-lines to underline emotional content, this painting conveys the surface and texture of fresco through the use of oil and tempera on gesso-covered panel. The figures are heavy and volumetric, the weight of the burden conveyed by the tightly bound basket sling, the curves of shoulders and back, the downcast heads, and spatulate hands. Expressed in colors of the earth, clay reds, reed tans, and chalky whites, Rivera ennobled the laboring class, recognized and elevated their struggle, and ultimately embedded in the composition a subtle exhortation to revolt.   KCH

140

Morris Graves

AMERICAN, BORN 1910

Bird Maddened by the Sound of Machinery in the Air

1944

watercolor on rice paper
32⅝ × 59⅜″
82.9 × 150.8 cm
Anonymous gift
51.1735

THE GENTLE QUIETUDE of the Pacific Northwest landscape has traditionally provided an ambiance conducive to inner-directed artistic development. During the decades immediately preceding and succeeding mid-century, the art of this region gained prominence nationally and internationally. Reflective and transcendental, the paintings and sculpture mirrored not only the cultural leanings of the area's people, but the fauna and foliage of the land as well.

Morris Graves's response to his natural surroundings provided allegorical form for his spiritual convictions which in turn grew out of his belief in the principles of Zen. A native of Oregon, Graves was born in 1910 and spent his early years in Seattle. He was first exposed to Eastern art and philosophy on a trip taken to the Orient when he was seventeen. This interest was nurtured and developed as Graves matured and was assimilated into his painting as well. In 1938, Graves, then living on the rocky shores of Puget Sound, met Mark Tobey and was greatly impressed with his pictorial device of "white writing." Comprehending that Tobey utilized this interwoven skein of light as a structural element in his work, Graves began incorporating into his paintings a similar line, not as a strictly formal component but as a means of creating an atmosphere or aura.

By the outset of the forties, Graves had determined his mature style. Thin washes of watercolor or corruscated fields of tempera or gouache were applied to the richly textured, highly porous surfaces of Japanese and Chinese papers. Animals, particularly birds, haunted these works, radiating powerful emotions as they reacted to the forces surrounding them.

Morris Graves's semi-reclusive, introspective life was shattered in 1942 when, despite having registered as a conscientious objector, he was inducted into the army. After a year of turmoil, during which he spent many months in a military stockade, he was finally released and returned to his isolated retreat on an island in Puget Sound. The works he produced over the following two years reflect the depth of his feelings about his military experiences. At first anguished and ominous, then progressively more spiritual, they deal with themes of devastation, transformation, and regeneration.

In *Bird Maddened by the Sound of Machinery in the Air*, one of a series of four similar works painted during the war, in the winter of 1943/44, Graves allegorically confronted the terrors of war. The mechanistic world, in its destructive state, has invaded the world of nature. Drenched in a mystical moonlight, the wild-eyed bird pauses, terror-stricken, clinging tenuously to a bit of rock, frantically contemplating the imminent, inevitable sweep of ruin. The muted earthen colors, delicately washed on fragile Oriental rice paper, are traversed by an assertive glide of white linear fibers, underscoring the exposed vulnerability of the land and its inhabitants. White writing, expressing this sweep, also gives form to the solitary spectral bird, its luminosity imparting an ethereal, lunar aura. In the distance, an angular, more intensely colored form approaches, intrusive and threatening. The portrayal of sound and its effects, a challenge that Graves later investigated in depth, is here implied visually, yet strongly sensed. Confronted by the encroachment of the machinery of war, man and nature are, ultimately, helpless.   KCH

Mark Tobey

AMERICAN, 1890–1976

Written over the Plains

1950

tempera on Masonite
30⅛ × 40″
76.5 × 101.7 cm

Gift of Mr. and Mrs. Ferdinand C. Smith
51.3169

A DELICATELY BRUSHED FILAMENT OF WHITE, alluding to the calligraphy of the East yet interpreting themes of Western man, characterizes the work of Mark Tobey. Utilizing "white writing," as he termed his linear networking, Tobey built a unified pictorial structure, set up a sense of space, and evoked aspects of subjective reality—patterns of light, the turmoil of a metropolis, the aura of a landscape.

Although Mark Tobey is generally regarded as the dean of Pacific Northwest painting, for he resided many years in the Seattle area, he was brought up in the Midwest, traveled extensively during his life, and spent most of his later years in Europe. Born in Wisconsin in 1890 and raised in a village on the Mississippi River, Tobey's vivid memories of his life on the flat plains later resurfaced frequently, finding their way into his paintings as subject matter. While following a career as a fashion illustrator, portraitist, and interior decorator, Tobey became a follower of the Baha'i World Faith, a decision that deeply affected both his art and personal life. Persian in origin, the Baha'i faith emphasizes the unity of mankind and the pre-eminence of man, separate from, and ruler of, the natural world.

While living in Seattle in 1923, Tobey was introduced to Oriental art and calligraphy and, after what he described as a "personal discovery of cubism,"[1] he developed a unique approach to space in which he fragmented form into cells, utilizing a different perspective within each discrete area. A journey to the Orient in 1934 enabled him to study calligraphy both in Shanghai and at a Zen monastery in Japan. The following year he began using a calligraphic line in his paintings, then fused the formal aspects of the line with his memories of parades in New York celebrating the armistice of World War I. Developing the formal tools of white writing and multiple space perspective, he investigated and interpreted images from both his immediate environment and his memory.

Written over the Plains, painted in 1950, alludes visually to the tangle and frenzy of the city while evoking visions of Tobey's rural youth. Following the Baha'i philosophy of unity, this work expresses the oneness of life—youth and maturity, rural and urban, corporeal and spiritual. The maze of intermeshed lines invites study and contemplation, reaching an equilibrium between surface and space. The linear web, which establishes ambiguous spatial fields, is superimposed layer upon layer, in the distance rendered as smoke-like tendrils, while in the frontal plane taking on assertive and conscious forms. The line itself is ever-varied: thread-thin then heavily brushed, tightly spiraled then thrown out and ricocheted. Gently attracted toward the center, forming a vaporous nebula, the skeins do not refer specifically to human activity but suggest it. Consciously separating line from color, the artist plays off the agitated strands against diffused, softly-keyed tones of gray and terra-cotta.   KCH

[1] William C. Seitz, *Mark Tobey*, The Museum of Modern Art, New York, 1962, p. 46.

Arshile Gorky

AMERICAN, BORN TURKISH
ARMENIA, 1904–1948

Enigmatic Combat

1936–37

oil on canvas
35¾ × 48″
90.8 × 121.9 cm

Gift of Jeanne Reynal
41.3763

THE ART OF ARSHILE GORKY, precariously poised at the edge of Abstract Expressionism, combines a knowledgeable awareness of the formal discoveries of the European avant-garde with a curiously eclectic mixture of images. Fragments summoned from the rich tapestry of his childhood heritage join forms drawn from the work of modern masters, yet made his own, to achieve a polyphonic, personal iconology. Emotionally charged, filled with conflicting signals of joy and anguish, rationality and intuition, nostalgia and fantasy, Gorky's paintings and drawings synthesize the structural principles of the Cubists with the ambiguous pictorial flow of the Surrealists, forging new ground and providing a crucial bridge between the twentieth-century innovations of the Europeans and the Americans.

Born Vosdanik Adoian, Gorky began his tumultuous life in Khorkom, an Armenian village in the province of Van. His early years, filled with joy and an acute sensitivity to place, were shattered by the Turkish persecution and massacre of the Armenians, which drove the artist's family from their homeland. After the tragic death of his mother, Adoian emigrated to the United States, arriving in 1920. He changed his name to Arshile Gorky and settled in New York City in 1924. After a brief formal training, he embarked on a personal study of the pivotal styles and artists of the early twentieth century. For inspiration and instruction Gorky turned not to the modernist styles of the Americans, but to European prototypes. Laboriously working through Cézanne's analytical approach to structure, Gorky then focused on the Synthetic Cubist work of Braque and Picasso, gaining understanding by faithfully re-creating their overlapping planes, stylized forms, and shallow space.

By the thirties, Surrealistic images and approaches became evident, and Gorky's style loosened. Beginning in 1931 he concentrated on a series of works, primarily black-and-white drawings, loosely centered around the theme of Nighttime, Enigma, and Nostalgia. In these, plastically rendered biomorphic forms, many endowed with symbols of fertility—seeds, sexual organs or orifices, fruit—inhabit ambiguously defined interior environments.

Enigmatic Combat, of 1936–37, integrates many of the images and develops a number of the pictorial concerns of the earlier series while further revealing the impact of Picasso on Gorky's work. Employing the heavy black lines and "cloisonné" color found in Picasso's canvases of the same decade, Gorky flattened the images, overlapped them, and set them afloat within a closely held, angularly sectioned space. While the high-intensity colors and generous use of white pigment lend an almost illuminated quality to the work, the dark-toned aperture at top center and the shadowed areas that form a punctuated swath across lower center suggest the presence of night. The curvilinear flow found in the Nighttime works is here fractured by angular elements, which activate the heavily impastoed surface.

Images drawn from the vocabulary of Picasso and the Surrealists join those alluding to Gorky's childhood in Van. A palette-shaped head in profile, obviously borrowed from Picasso, echoes the Surrealist reniform biomorph opposite, while striped passages are reminiscent of the skeletal ribs found in Picasso's "bone" works of the twenties and Synthetic Cubist combings. Scattered throughout are fragments summoned from gardens of his past—birds, fish, and fruit, bisected to expose the seeds of a new generation. Emotionally charged through its expressive brushstrokes, richly associative in imagery, this work reveals the lyrical power of Arshile Gorky.   KCH

Jackson Pollock

AMERICAN, 1912–1956

Guardians of the Secret

1943

oil on canvas
48⅜ × 75⅜"
122.9 × 191.5 cm

Albert M. Bender Collection
Albert M. Bender Bequest Fund
Purchase
45.1308

JUST PRIOR to the revolutionary "poured" paintings of 1947–50, Jackson Pollock reached a mature means of expression in a group of paintings that contained vestiges of recognizable subject matter. In these works featuring mythological creatures and enigmatic primitive signs, Pollock created a personal cosmos of primordial imagery verging on abstraction. *Guardians of the Secret*, completed in 1943, demonstrates the concerns of this particularly fertile period. A complex amalgam of vanguard artistic theories and historical traditions, this seminal work richly documents the influences that shaped Pollock's innovative style and prefaced his classic "drip" paintings.

Perhaps the most celebrated of the American painters among the first-generation Abstract Expressionists, Jackson Pollock was born in 1912 in Cody, Wyoming. After a youth spent in Arizona and California, he moved to New York City in 1930 to study art. For the next two years, he attended Thomas Hart Benton's class at the Art Students League and was influenced by the Regionalist's rhythmic, attenuated figures and his knowledge of Renaissance and Baroque art. Other influences during Pollock's formative years included the darkly Romantic paintings of Albert Pinkham Ryder and the powerful monumental figures and legendary subjects depicted by the Mexican muralists, José Clemente Orozco, Diego Rivera, and David Alfaro Siqueiros.

By the late thirties, Pollock's interest in the work of Benton and Renaissance models abated and he turned instead toward modernist tenets, particularly those of Pablo Picasso and Joan Miró. From the work of Picasso, Pollock absorbed the faceted planarity of Cubist space and the Spanish master's later vocabulary of mythic, fragmented forms embodied in works such as *Guernica*. In the Surrealist paintings of Miró, he found inspiration in the allover configuration of calligraphic line.

Surrealist concepts became familiar to Pollock through such exhibitions as *Fantastic Art, Dada, Surrealism*, held at the Museum of Modern Art in 1936, and through the work of the Surrealist émigrés Max Ernst, André Breton, and André Masson who exhibited at Peggy Guggenheim's Art of This Century gallery. Pollock's first one-man exhibition, which included *Guardians of the Secret*, was held in 1943 at this center of Surrealist activity. Like Mark Rothko, Clyfford Still, and Robert Motherwell, Pollock was drawn to the Surrealist technique of automatism and the wealth of biomorphic primordial images that rose from unconscious sources. During this time, the theories of Freud and Jung were well known in artistic circles, and Pollock's adoption of universal symbols may have been reinforced by his contact with Jungian analysts from 1939 to 1941.[1]

In *Guardians of the Secret*, a vast array of animal-like images, primitive script, and private symbols pervade the canvas suggesting ancient rites conceived in the deep recesses of the artist's psyche. Featured in the painting are two totemic figures and a reclining dog, which may be interpreted as "guardians" of the central panel containing the "secret," an indecipherable personal code of the artist. The predominantly geometric framework of horizontal and vertical planes suggests Cubist space, while the continuous field of improvisational imagery relates to the automatic writing of Surrealism.

Both figurative and abstract, *Guardians of the Secret* contains identifiable images which appear, then slip into labyrinthine webs of gestural brush strokes. Beginning with recognizable subjects, Pollock "chose to veil the imagery,"[2] translating the swirling forms into a complex allover pattern of rubbed and clotted pigment. The spontaneity and directness of this method would culminate in just a few years in the evocative "poured" paintings which changed the course of modern art.   LLS

[1] For a discussion of the influence of Jungian models in Pollock's work, see Judith Wolfe, "Jungian Aspects of Jackson Pollock's Imagery," *Artforum*, vol. 11, no. 3 (November 1972), pp. 65–83, and William Rubin, "Pollock as Jungian Illustrator: The Limits of Psychological Criticism," *Art in America*, vol. 67, no. 7 (November 1979), pp. 104–23; vol. 67, no. 8 (December 1979), pp. 72–91.

[2] Elizabeth Frank, *Jackson Pollock* (New York: Abbeville Press, 1983), p. 43.

Clyfford Still

AMERICAN, 1904–1980

Untitled

formerly
SELF-PORTRAIT
1945

oil on canvas
70⅞ × 42″
180.1 × 106.7 cm
(Ph-233)

Gift of Peggy Guggenheim
47.1238

I held it imperative to evolve an instrument of thought which would aid in cutting through all the cultural opiates, past and present, so that a direct, immediate, and truly free vision could be achieved, and an idea be revealed with clarity.[1]

WHILE MOST OF THE ARTISTS associated with Abstract Expressionism were assimilating the European traditions of Cubism and Surrealism during their developmental years in the late thirties and early forties, Clyfford Still was actively purging these influences from his work. Seeking a radically independent and personal means of expression, he created monumentally scaled abstractions of arresting power and vitality. As fellow artists Mark Rothko and Barnett Newman, Still would eventually utilize vast expanses of color to evoke the transcendental and sublime and establish the precedents for Color Field painting in America.

Born in 1904 in Grandin, North Dakota, Clyfford Still spent his formative years in Spokane, Washington, and in southern Alberta, Canada. After graduating from Spokane University in 1933, he held several positions teaching art at Washington State College, Pullman, and at the Richmond Professional Institute in Virginia. From 1941 to 1943, Still lived in San Francisco where he was employed in war industries, and although he had little time for painting, his first solo exhibition was held at the San Francisco Museum of Art (now the San Francisco Museum of Modern Art) in 1943. During that same year, he met Mark Rothko in Berkeley, who introduced him to the vanguard New York collector and gallery owner Peggy Guggenheim when Still moved to New York City in 1945. The following spring, Peggy Guggenheim offered him a one-man exhibition at her gallery, Art of This Century, and purchased the painting Untitled (formerly *Self-Portrait*). A year later, the painting entered the collection of the San Francisco Museum of Art as a gift of Peggy Guggenheim.

The presence of primeval forces and creative energies are suggested in the early paintings of Clyfford Still. Utilizing the automatist imagery favored by his contemporaries Jackson Pollock, Robert Motherwell, and Rothko, Still featured biomorphic organisms and primitive totemic shapes in landscape-like settings. A somber tenebrous ground became a dominant element; of this predilection, the artist stated: "Black was never a color of death or terror for me. I think of it as warm and generative."[2]

In this painting a streaking skeletal form springs forth from an atmosphere of dark fermentation. Juxtaposing a palette of primary colors with black and white, Still creates a dramatic arrangement of contrast and balance. The brilliant yellow rectangular shape in the lower right appears to contain rootlike images which parallel the germinative qualities of the white linear form. By the late forties, Still had dispelled practically all references to figurative or landscape images. Within pure abstraction, he communicated themes that suggested the creative and spiritual forces inherent in life processes.

Previously known as *Self-Portrait*, the painting's title was changed by the artist in 1979 to Untitled. Still abandoned the use of titles early in his career, as he felt they could influence the viewer's interpretation of the work. As a result, with the exception of a few early paintings, all of Still's works are either untitled or bear alphabetical and numerical designations.   LLS

[1] Letter from Clyfford Still to Gordon Smith; quoted in *Paintings by Clyfford Still* (Buffalo, N.Y.: The Buffalo Fine Arts Academy and Albright Art Gallery, 1959), p. 7.
[2] Quoted in *Clyfford Still: Thirty-Three Paintings in the Albright-Knox Art Gallery*, foreword by Katharine Kuh (Buffalo, N.Y.: The Buffalo Fine Arts Academy, 1966), p. 11.

Clyfford Still

AMERICAN, 1904–1980

Untitled

1951–52

oil on canvas
113⅜ × 156″
288.0 × 396.2 cm
(Ph-968)

Gift of the artist
75.30

Untitled

1960

oil on canvas
113⅛ × 155⅞″
287.3 × 395.9 cm
(Ph-174)

Gift of Mr. and Mrs. Harry W. Anderson
74.19

IN THE FALL OF 1946, following his exhibition at Art of This Century, Clyfford Still returned to San Francisco to teach at the California School of Fine Arts (now the San Francisco Art Institute). With the arrival of Still and under the direction of Douglas MacAgy, the California School of Fine Arts entered a "golden age" of progressive art education. Highly influential as an artist and teacher, Still established a direct and expressive form of abstraction in the Bay Area and provided his students with an exhilarating liberation from artistic conventions. During his four-year tenure at the school, Still spawned an outburst of creative activity and influenced the work of Frank Lobdell, Hassel Smith, and subsequent generations of Bay Area artists.

By the close of the forties, Still had obliterated recognizable imagery from his work and begun to formulate his mature style. On canvases of immense scale he created unified, vertically oriented fields of richly textured paint. The traditional figure-ground relationship was abandoned in favor of a continuous fusion of pictorial elements.

In both Untitled of 1951–52 and Untitled of 1960, Still utilizes this monumental format and features sinuous flame-like shapes and craggy forms that surge across the canvas. The dense jagged planes conjure up images of the grandeur and expansiveness found in the natural forms of cliffs, canyons, and stormy, lightning-filled skies. Although Still vigorously denied any direct associations with landscape imagery in his work—"I paint only myself, not nature"[1]—his work nonetheless evokes the elemental and transcendental power associated with vast terrain.

In Untitled of 1951–52 Still featured impacted, tightly drawn forms, the troweled pigment suggestive of volcanic flows. By the late fifties, however, he had simplified his shapes and orchestrated raw areas of canvas along with the monolithic forms, as seen in the more spacious, open format of Untitled, 1960. Stylistically, Still did not follow a direct line of development, but was engaged in a continual process of exploration and re-exploration throughout his life, often interjecting new meaning into former themes. Maintaining that each work was a fragment of a fuller, more complete experience, Still believed that his paintings should be viewed in a cumulative context so that the thread of continuity could be revealed and the artist's lifelong concerns apprehended.

In 1975, Clyfford Still presented a gift of twenty-eight paintings to the San Francisco Museum of Modern Art. The museum in turn established a permanent gallery in which a grouping of these paintings could be viewed by the public, students, and scholars. Untitled of 1951–52 is a part of this remarkable gift which was personally culled by Still to document his development from the formative years to his later achievements. Augmented by the important paintings, Untitled, 1945, from Peggy Guggenheim and Untitled, 1960, a gift of Mr. and Mrs. Harry W. Anderson, the collection allows the evolution of Clyfford Still's art to emerge clearly and his liberated vision to be grasped in its totality.   LLS

[1]Quoted in J. Benjamin Townsend, "An Interview with Clyfford Still," *Gallery Notes* (The Buffalo Fine Arts Academy, Albright-Knox Art Gallery), vol. 24, no. 2 (Summer 1961), p. 11.

Robert Motherwell

AMERICAN, BORN 1915

Wall Painting No. 10
1964

acrylic on canvas
69 × 92"
175.3 × 233.7 cm

Gift of the friends of Helen Crocker Russell
67.21

THE ASSOCIATIVE AND EXPRESSIVE POWER of simple abstract images and natural colors has been explored and exploited by Robert Motherwell throughout his career. Firmly tied to experiential reality yet couched in non-objective terms, his works possess the capacity to operate as formally perceived objects while simultaneously eliciting from the viewer a range of images and emotions—the sea, sun-washed clay, despotism, freedom. Deftly balancing subjective and objective, Motherwell combines the spontaneous outpourings of the subconscious with rational formalization, and raw power with an innately sophisticated, even elegant, sensibility.

Robert Motherwell was the youngest of the defiant American artists whose emotion-packed abstractions exploded the art world in the forties. Schooled in the philosophy of aesthetics, he arrived in New York in 1940 to study art history with Meyer Schapiro at Columbia University and shortly thereafter took up painting. Introduced by Schapiro to the European Surrealists then living in exile in New York, Motherwell was particularly struck by their use of automatism, the suspension of consciousness which allows the release of ideas and images from the subconscious. Organically tinged ovoids and biotic cells soon appeared in his work, together with angular linear tracery, all set within a geometrically configured structure.

Motherwell was a knowledgeable voice and active participant in the emergence of the Abstract Expressionist movement in New York, and during the forties his work became increasingly spontaneous and emotional. In 1949, sparked by an image made while illustrating a poem by Harold Rosenberg, Motherwell launched his series of Elegies, forceful canvases of black-and-white ovules held in place by vertical bars, metaphors of spirit and energy entrapped but not subdued, which commemorated the death struggles of the Spanish people during the Civil War.

Motherwell's concern for the integrity of the painting as a two-dimensional object in and of itself extended into the concept of the painting surface as a wall, the theme of a series which occupied him intermittently for two decades. An archetypal work, *Wall Painting with Stripes* executed in 1944, exhibited a progression of ocher and white vertical stripes interwoven with a single gray arc. Ten years later, Motherwell resumed the theme with *Wall Painting No. 1* in which elongated, dark, phallic shapes interspersed with amorphic forms are set against a horizontally oriented rectangular inset, limited and defined at the left edge and allowed to extend beyond the right. By 1964, the date of *Wall Painting No. 10*, the black forms had lengthened into sinuous arcing bands that reverberate across the canvas, punctuated by small organisms that formally reinforce the verticality of the background adobe-ocher striping. The left extremity, bounded by a static black rectangle, propels the visual forces back toward the right edge and beyond, suggesting a continuum.   KCH

Willem de Kooning

AMERICAN, BORN
NETHERLANDS 1904

Woman

1950

oil on paper mounted on Masonite
36⅝ × 24½"
93.1 × 62.3 cm

Purchase
68.69

WILLEM DE KOONING, together with Jackson Pollock and Hans Hofmann, catapulted American painting to the forefront of the international art scene through their complex, richly gestural abstract paintings. Spontaneously conceived and vigorously executed, de Kooning's work during the 1940s was widely acclaimed for capturing an unprecedented immediacy and expressiveness within pure abstraction. By 1950, however, figurative images of women began to appear in his paintings and drawings. Distorted and volatile, these frenzied females were greeted by a storm of controversy and outrage, for de Kooning had dared to resurrect the figure, place it in the same realm as his advanced abstractions, and infuse an age-old theme with contemporary meaning.

Willem de Kooning developed a deep reverence for the figure and the expressive power of drawing in his early training in fine and applied art. Despite a radical departure from his classical education, he remained firmly tied to art of the past: the figural tradition of Ingres, the Expressionism of Soutine, and the theories of Cubism and Surrealism. At the age of twenty-two, de Kooning left Rotterdam and made his way to America, settling in Hoboken, New Jersey. The following year he established a studio in Manhattan and became acquainted with Arshile Gorky. Sharing a close working relationship, the two artists incorporated in their early work the floating biomorphic images of Joan Miró and Jean Arp and the flattened fractured space employed by Picasso.

In addition to exploring non-objective forms in his early work, de Kooning experimented with figurative subject matter as well. The figure became inextricably linked to the development of his abstraction, exiting and returning again and again. During the late thirties, de Kooning depicted seated figures with bodily parts reduced to abstract linear forms, and by the forties he had created colorful abstractions composed of organic shapes resembling dislocated hips, buttocks, legs, and breasts. Around 1947, de Kooning began to realize his gestural style in a group of abstractions in which organic shapes covered the surface, obliterating illusionistic space.

The anatomical fragments in de Kooning's abstractions began to coalesce in 1950, forming recognizable female figures. Completed during that pivotal year, *Woman* is part of a series that culminated in such violent and demonic depictions as *Woman I*, 1950–52 (The Museum of Modern Art, New York). Compared to the frenetic, open brushwork of that painting, *Woman* is a quieter, more contained, and less distorted portrayal. Here the greater part of the figure is defined in Cubist planes and is differentiated from background forms, unlike the explosive fusion of parts seen in de Kooning's later figure paintings.

Presented in a monumental frontal manner, the figure fills up the pictorial space, powerfully engaging the viewer. Broad sweeps of chalky white and fleshy pink pigment suggest limbs and voluptuous breasts, while a network of lines and planes activates the facial features and wide-eyed gaze. The curve of a shoulder and the blond mane of hair are defined by viscous brush strokes of yellow color. Riveting and provocative, the arresting power of *Woman* lies not only in the disquieting image, but in the manner of execution whereby tension is created through the rubbed, scumbled, dripped, and splattered surfaces.

For de Kooning, the image of the woman represented the opportunity to express an ancient theme in contemporary terms. Fascinated by the banal in American advertising and intrigued by the universal images that inundated society, de Kooning responded with his creation of a twentieth-century goddess, not a softly rounded idol of fertility, but a garish, vulgar, and comic siren of the modern industrial age.   LLS

158

Hans Hofmann

AMERICAN, BORN GERMANY
1880–1966

Table—Version II

1949

oil on canvas
48 × 36″
122.0 × 91.4 cm

Gift of Mr. and Mrs. William C. Janss
78.203

THE CAREER OF HANS HOFMANN spanned well over half the twentieth century, from its genesis in Paris during the decade of Fauvism and Cubism to fruition in the heady days of American gestural abstraction around mid-century. Linking these two seminal moments in the history of Western art, he brought to Abstract Expressionism a thoroughly assimilated concept of the possibilities of Fauvist color and a belief in the applicability of the planar structure of Cézanne.

Hofmann's maturity as a painter came late in life. Born in Bavaria in 1880, he was educated in Munich, then spent ten years in Paris, from 1904 to 1914, where he not only experienced the nascent development of modern art, but established personal relationships with key figures of the revolutionary trends: Matisse, Robert Delaunay, Braque, and Picasso. Returning to Munich in 1915, he opened his own school and thus began an extended successful career as teacher and theoretician.

With the political situation in Germany darkening, Hofmann came to the United States, initially for brief teaching stints at the University of California, Berkeley (1930, 1931), and the Chouinard Art Institute, Los Angeles (1931). In 1932 he settled permanently in New York where he again opened a school. Preoccupied with teaching responsibilities, Hofmann temporarily abandoned painting and instead concentrated on drawing until 1935 when, returning to the easel, he began working through a series of landscapes and still lifes in which he confronted, absorbed, and translated the pictorial elements of the Fauves and Cubists, interjecting exuberant color, expressive brushwork, stacked or floating planes, and automatic drawing into increasingly abstract compositions.

Hofmann constructed his paintings with color, using this single element to establish space, energy, and animation. Juxtaposing parallel fields of primary colors, he created a lively sense of multiple, changing depths. He termed the resulting tension between opposing forces "push-pull," alluding to the instated shifting balance.

Table—Version II, painted in 1949, exhibits the dynamics of this counterpoise. In a bisected format the artist has set red against blue, effecting a dialogue between the halves of the canvas and establishing an indeterminate interior space. The objects in the still life—table with objects, mirror—are stated and restated in increasingly abstract Cubist terms: in the right panel clearly recognizable, in the left reduced to angular, articulated, suggestive forms and gestures. Pitting primary against primary, angular against curvilinear, object against abstract, gesture against gesture, the artist achieves a pulsing animation. This liveliness is underscored by the sheer corporeality of the color, dense and palpable, and the strongly manipulated brushwork. Ranging from rich passages of mosaic-like patches to wide swaths of chalked pigment or saturated hues, the color emanates light and powerfully promotes the underlying expressiveness of the composition.

Painted when Hofmann was nearly seventy, *Table—Version II* exemplifies not only the melding of Abstract Expressionism with early revolutionary trends, but also the extraordinary vigor of the artist whose career continued with ever-increasing strength and vision for over fifteen years thereafter.   KCH

Milton Avery
AMERICAN, 1893–1965

Clear Cut Landscape
1951

oil on canvas
32⅛ × 44"
81.6 × 111.8 cm

Gift of the Women's Board
55.4813

IN A MEMORIAL ADDRESS IN 1965, Mark Rothko paid tribute to Milton Avery: "His is the poetry of sheer loveliness, of sheer beauty. Thanks to him this kind of poetry has been able to survive in our time."[1] Throughout a long and vital career, Milton Avery pursued a personal and solitary vision. At a time when American art was steeped in academic realism and the socio-political themes of American Scene painting, Avery created highly poetic figurative and landscape compositions which often bordered on abstraction. In paintings, drawings, and prints Avery explored the possibilities of uniting the basic elements of color and form and helped pioneer the way for future experiments by such colorists as Rothko, Barnett Newman, and Adolph Gottlieb.

By 1911, Milton Avery had decided to pursue a career in art and enrolled in classes at the Connecticut League of Art Students in Hartford, where he studied academic realism and genre painting. Influenced by these traditions, Avery's early subject matter featured landscape motifs, portraits, and figural groups often imbued with a sense of humor and intimacy. After 1935, however, landscape themes of deep serenity and contemplation dominated his work. Although Avery began with a factual image, recording the visual truth was secondary to capturing the mood or essence of the subject. He abandoned a realistic representation in favor of an intuitive one featuring simplified, flattened shapes and non-associative color.

During the 1920s and 1930s, Avery combined the themes of American academic painting with the advanced techniques of European artists. In particular, he was deeply influenced by the sensitive color modulations of Pablo Picasso's Rose Period works and the flattened planes of arbitrary color employed by Henri Matisse. By 1944, Avery had fully adopted a non-naturalistic palette, and color became the primary expressive force in his work.

Avery's enigmatic fusion of color and form is exemplified in *Clear Cut Landscape* of 1951. Based on a naturalistic scene, probably near Woodstock, New York, Avery distilled elements of the landscape to essential, clearly defined planes of a single hue. Characteristic of his mature style, the simplified shapes of the painting function both as recognizable images and as beautifully orchestrated abstract forms. As in many paintings of the fifties, Avery represented the component parts of the landscape through horizontal bands of color. The depth and dimensionality of the pictorial space is communicated through the juxtaposition of colors—the aquamarine and midnight blues of the middleground adjacent to the lavender foreground and creamy mauve sky. Of this method, Avery stated: "The two-dimensional design is important, but not so important as the design in depth. I do not use linear perspective, but achieve depth by color—the function of one color with another."[2]

Color had been an important aspect of Avery's work beginning with the American Impressionist paintings he completed as an art student. The thick impastoed layers of closely related hues in these works eventually evolved into the thinly applied luminous chromatic fields found in later paintings such as *Clear Cut Landscape*. To further heighten his color harmonies, Avery often scraped pigment from his canvas, exposing traces of underlying color and creating an activated textural surface.

Through the simplification of forms and a highly inventive use of color, Milton Avery produced unparalleled poetic statements of a certain time or place and provided a deep source of inspiration to younger generations of artists who would further explore the expressive possibilities of color.   LLS

[1] Memorial address delivered at the New York Society for Ethical Culture, 2 West Sixty-fourth Street, on January 7, 1965.

[2] Quoted in *Milton Avery: Mexico*, with an introduction by Sally M. Avery and essay by Dore Ashton, Grace Borgenicht Gallery, New York, 1983, n.p.

Mark Rothko

AMERICAN, BORN RUSSIA
1903–1970

Untitled

1960

oil on canvas
69 × 50⅛"
175.3 × 127.3 cm

Acquired through a gift of Peggy
Guggenheim
62.3426

[1] Mark Rothko, lecture given at Pratt
Institute, 1958; quoted in *Mark
Rothko*, Newport Harbor Art Mu-
seum, Newport Beach, California,
1974, p. 18.
[2] Mark Rothko, "The Romantics Were
Prompted," *Possibilities I* (Winter
1947/48), p. 84; quoted in Irving
Sandler, "Mark Rothko (In Memory
of Robert Goldwater)," *Mark Rothko:
Paintings 1948–1969*, Pace Gallery,
New York, 1983.

*There are some artists who want to tell all, but I feel it is more shrewd to
tell little.*[1]

THE MATURE PAINTINGS OF MARK ROTHKO, expunged of image and symbol and reduced to geometrically configured banks of tinted cloud floating within opaque fields,
superficially tell little. Their power lies neither in the telling, nor in the representing
that has preoccupied artists throughout history, but in each work's ability to trigger
complex emotional responses within the viewer, responses which transcend the specific
and move into the realm of the mystic and the religious. Monumental in scale, the
works surround and envelop, providing an ambience that transports and removes,
inducing contemplation.

Key to the potency of Rothko's work is his expressive use of color. Glowing, even
hallucinatory, the hues range from electric pinks and blinding yellows to pathos-filled
grays and burgundies. Through their sheer resonance, the high-pitched colors elicit
not gaiety and sensuality but a disquieting shock, while the dusky tints are permeated
with overtones of tragedy, solitude and despair.

Like many of the artists working in New York in the forties, Rothko encountered the
exiled Surrealists, whose use of automatism struck a responsive chord. By 1942, mythic
creatures and hybrid organisms began appearing in Rothko's work, interwoven with
calligraphic tendrils and references to Greek tragedies. The imagery gradually became less specific and aqueous biomorphs became predominant, set on washed fields
which were bisected, then trisected into stacked veiled rectangles of thin pigment.

In 1947 Rothko wrote, "The familiar identity of things has to be pulverized in order
to destroy . . . finite associations."[2] Abandoning all images, he brought forth the vaporous fields, endowed them with ofttimes rectilinear shapes, and set them afloat to
levitate and bump, drip and converge within a vertically oriented format. Then,
dissatisfied with the flux and fluidity inherent in these works, Rothko further simplified,
setting one rectangular pillow atop another, apposing apparitions which hovered and
murmured in a kind of stasis.

In response to inner forebodings, Rothko's palette turned dark and brooding around
1957, exuding sensations of tragedy and death. With its leaden grays and blued blood-
red, Untitled, 1960, conveys this sense of apprehension and resignation, of life floating
into death. The three shadowed forms, blurred and ethereal, are suspended in a vast,
seemingly endless field of atmospheric dark. Delicate in its execution, heavily laden
with implications, this work clearly transmits the spiritual power of the artist.   KCH

Sam Francis

AMERICAN, BORN 1923

Red and Pink

1951

oil on canvas
81¾ × 65¾"
207.6 × 167.0 cm

Partial gift of Mrs. Wellington S. Henderson
69.111

Glory be to God for dappled things—
For skies of couple-color as a brindled cow

Gerard Manley Hopkins, *Pied Beauty*

THE COUPLE-COLORED SKIES of Sam Francis's early paintings, filled with luminosity, heavy with vapor, are manifestations of the artist's on-going preoccupation with light and water, dreams and levitation. Centered within delicately tinted or heavily saturated curdled atmospheres, these works of 1950 through 1955 envelop and suspend, speaking at once to a continuum of space and the pressures of confinement.

For Francis, the original impetus to become an artist was the result of a prolonged hospital stay. While he was a pilot in the Army Air Corps, an accident-induced injury developed into spinal tuberculosis. Immobilized at army hospitals first in Denver, then in San Francisco, Francis took up painting. While his initial efforts tended toward clichéd subjects—horses, rural scenes, and nudes—the paintings done in late 1945 and 1946 in the Bay Area, perhaps as a result of a friendship with David Park, exhibit strong tendencies toward the mechanistic geometric Surrealism then practiced by artists such as Clay Spohn and James McCray at the California School of Fine Arts (now the San Francisco Art Institute) where Park was a teacher. By 1947, Francis's work showed signs of the biomorphic forms of Mark Rothko and, to a lesser extent, the linear tracings of Arshile Gorky and rough-hewn pillars of Clyfford Still.

The visual impact of Rothko, who taught at the California School of Fine Arts during the summers of 1947 and 1949, continued to increase. The paintings produced after Francis entered the University of California at Berkeley in 1948 correspond closely to those of Rothko of the same years. Diaphonous washes of color create nebulous drifts of space within which float softly defined shapes, sometimes vaguely rectangular, sometimes undulant and organic. Gradually the shapes coalesced, filling each vertical canvas with a cloud of pulsating cells. Purged of overlaid forms which stagnated the oscillating space, the canvases were subsequently drained of color as well. Moving from the blood-red paintings of late 1949 and early 1950, in which evocations of corpuscles suspended in plasma are inevitable, the palette turned silvery, the brushwork diffuse. This swing, generally ascribed to Francis's move from California to the hazy environs of Paris, greatly altered the effect of the work. No longer corporeal but hinged to the life process, the paintings levitate, filled with light and buoyancy, reflecting transmuted hues.

Red and Pink, painted in 1951, marks a re-entry of color into Francis's work. The red, previously searing, is now subdued and nacreous, a tinted mist filling each cell. Like stippled light on a rosy pool, the surface shimmers, allowing penetration at points, reflection at others. The diluted medium is allowed to drip and run, denying the contours of each cellule, yet affirming them as well.

A living sense of expansion permeates the canvas. Free to move within the undefined space of the center, the cells solidify along the periphery, forming an intermittent, clotted barrier. Pulsing against this restraint, they emit a sense of pressure which reaffirms the edge. This opposition of forces, clustering inward, pressing outward, energizes the space, causing it to flicker and shift. Gleaming through the pigment, canvas light emerges. It was toward the liberation of this white space that Francis eventually moved, parting the cells, charging them with vibrant primaries, and setting them afloat on spacious fields.   KCH

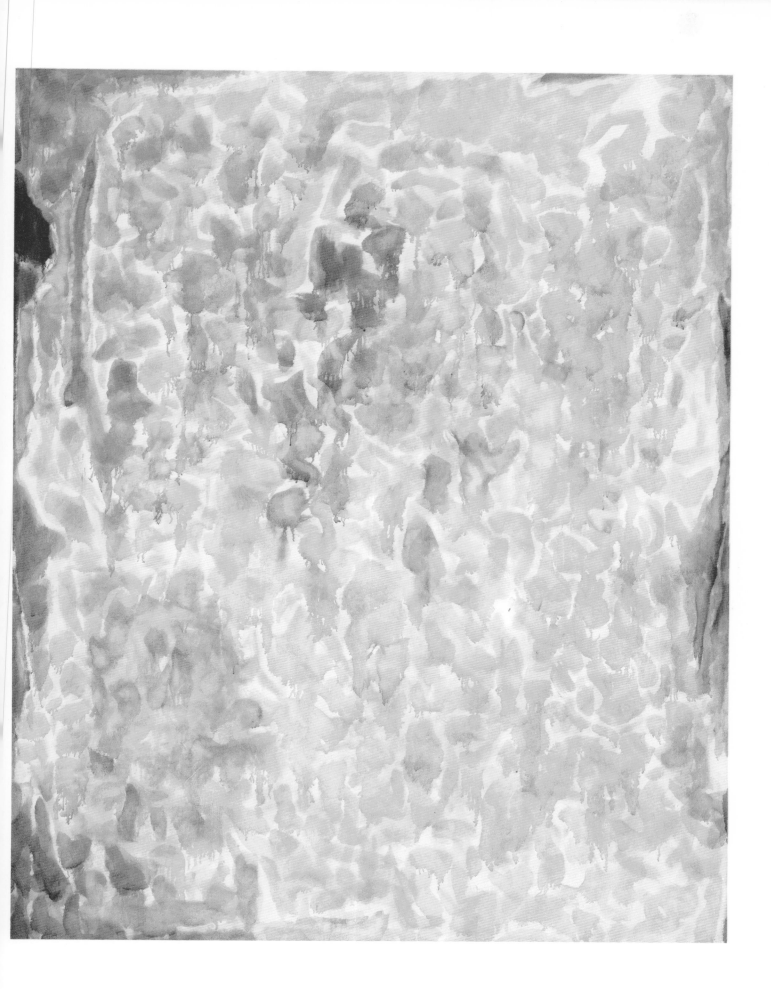

Philip Guston

AMERICAN, BORN CANADA
1913–1980

For M.

1955

oil on canvas
76⅜ × 72¼"
194.0 × 183.5 cm

Gift of Betty Freeman
72.21

KNOWN FOR HIS HIGHLY POETIC ABSTRACTIONS of delicately colored interwoven brush strokes, Philip Guston gained recognition as a leading figure of Abstract Expressionism during the 1950s. By the late 1960s, however, Guston's celebrated abstract style underwent a major metamorphosis recalling elements of his earlier representational paintings. Powerful and disturbing images of figures and everyday objects began to populate, then dominate his canvases of the subsequent decade. The roughly painted, darkly comic autobiographical nature of these late works paralleled the international re-emergence of figurative subject matter in the 1970s and reinforced the direction of artists seeking a vital means of expression through the image.

The son of Russian-Jewish immigrants, Philip Guston was born in 1913, in Montreal, Canada. When he was six, his family moved to California, seeking better fortune in Los Angeles. The developing culture of Los Angeles in the 1920s and early 1930s was fertile ground for the formative years of the artist. The film industry chronicled the dreams and frustrations of the American public and nurtured Guston's faculties for social commentary and caricature. While fascinated by popular culture, Guston was also profoundly influenced by art of the past, the paintings of the Italian masters Piero della Francesca and Andrea Mantegna, as well as the work of the present, of Pablo Picasso and Giorgio de Chirico.

In 1927, Guston enrolled in Manual Arts High School in Los Angeles, at which time his interest in art, literature, and leftist politics flourished. His enthusiasms were shared by classmate Jackson Pollock, whom Guston soon befriended. Eight years later, encouraged by Pollock, Guston moved to New York City, where he participated in the Federal Art Project of the Works Progress Administration (WPA) along with such artists as Willem de Kooning, Arshile Gorky, and James Brooks. He was awarded his first important commission in 1939 for the façade of the WPA building at the New York World's Fair.

After four years of involvement with the WPA mural project, in 1940 Guston shifted his attention to easel painting. Although recognizable themes of urban life were still present in his work, he abandoned the use of monumental figures in illusory space and adopted flattened, delineated forms with geometric qualities. By the end of the 1940s Guston began to question the legitimacy of representational subject matter, and in 1947 he produced his first completely abstract painting.

In 1950, Guston, like his contemporaries de Kooning, Franz Kline, and Mark Rothko, explored the possibilities of painting directly and spontaneously. During this period, he began to refine his abstract compositions, using gestural brush strokes of light luminescent colors concentrated in a central core. These abstractions allied him with the New York School and identified him as one of their ablest poets.

In the painting *For M.*, dedicated to his wife Musa, Guston fully explored abstraction with richly applied expressionistic brush strokes. Four years earlier in *White Painting I*, 1951, also in the Museum's collection (see Checklist), Guston first experimented with spontaneously applying paint for a period of time without stepping away to view the canvas. By the time he painted *For M.*, he had formulated a style that provided a central focus of abstract forms, unlike many other practitioners of Abstract Expressionism, who concentrated on an overall treatment of the canvas. Here Guston confines his shimmering brush strokes of rose, cream, and pearl gray to a tightly drawn whole and radiates them outward unto near disintegration along the perimeters. The dark calligraphic forms interwoven in the center provide a sense of depth and contrast. Forms such as these eventually gained in weight and importance and became a major element in Guston's work of the 1960s. LLS

Philip Guston

AMERICAN, BORN CANADA
1913–1980

*Red Sea; The Swell;
Blue Light*

1975

oil on canvas
left panel 73½ × 78¾"
             186.7 × 200.1 cm
center panel 73 × 78⅛"
             185.5 × 198.5 cm
right panel 73 × 80½"
             185.5 × 204.5 cm

Purchased through the Helen
Crocker Russell and William H.
and Ethel W. Crocker Family Funds,
the Mrs. Ferdinand C. Smith Fund,
and the Paul L. Wattis Special Fund
78.67 A–C

TOWARD THE CLOSE OF THE 1950S, the delicate, light-filled abstractions of Philip Guston, which many described as "Abstract Impressionism," gave way to forms of increasing mass and turbulence. Concurrently, Guston darkened his palette from hues of rose and cream of the previous decade to a dominance of black and gray. Given titles such as *Painter*, *Actor*, and *Traveller*, these works anticipated the artist's return to figurative subject matter in the late 1960s. After 1966, a period of transition and struggle ensued in which Guston equivocated between abstract drawings and drawings of everyday objects in his studio. By 1968, he began to feel comfortable with the representational drawings and began to paint again in this mode.

In 1970, Guston unleashed a wide and powerful spectrum of images: hooded figures alluding to the brutality and violence of the Ku Klux Klan, old shoes, mangled legs, empty bottles, cigarette butts. In his paintings of the next five years he often featured images from his studio—canvases, brushes, cigarettes, clocks—which were re-examined and used as props to express a variety of emotions: rage, pathos, anxiety, fear, humor. Although many considered these subjects to be an unexplained reversal of the artist's poetic evolution toward abstraction, these late paintings in fact reconciled many major themes found throughout his work.

The monumental triptych *Red Sea*; *The Swell*; *Blue Light* of 1975 illustrates the artist's return to figurative subject matter after 1970. A strong narrative sense present in the work recalls the Old Testament text on the persecution of the Jews, their flight from Egypt, and the destruction of the Egyptians in the Red Sea. Guston parallels his personal struggle and inner conflict through images of tangled legs, soles of shoes, and the ghostly apparition of the artist floating in agitated waters. Despite the cataclysmic theme, Guston's final message is a redemptive one. In the third panel, *Blue Light*, the flood waters recede and the artist and his canvases are bathed in a venerable blue light.

Among the themes to re-surface in late works such as this are a passion for caricature and social comment, the deep mystery and timelessness of Piero della Francesca, and the darkly subversive qualities of Giorgio de Chirico. In addition, the immediate and spontaneous brush strokes of Guston's celebrated Abstract Expressionist works are clearly recalled in the rich impastoed surfaces of blue, red, pink, and black pigment.   LLS

Philip Guston

Philip Guston

AMERICAN, BORN CANADA
1913–1980

Back View

1977

oil on canvas
69 × 94″
175.3 × 238.8 cm

Gift of the artist
82.33

DURING THE 1970S, Philip Guston had infused a repertory of everyday images with compelling power and significance. Through the examination of the commonplace, Guston charged objects such as the oversized coat and shoes of *Back View* with symbolic and mysterious meaning. Since 1966, the shoe had become a favorite image, appearing again and again as an element suggesting the mundane. In emulation of the Russian writer Gogol, whom Guston admired, he used the theme of the overcoat to cross the barriers between the animate and inanimate world, between real and surreal experience. The metaphysical realm of de Chirico is suggested through the hooded mannequin-like figure isolated in a vacant, enigmatic domain.

The richly painted surfaces composed of broad impastoed areas and shimmering swirls of pigment reveal Guston as a master of Abstract Expressionism. The hovering anticipatory quality of the brush strokes creates a tension and urgency reminiscent of his finely wrought abstractions of the fifties. As in his earlier paintings, the forms are drawn together in the center of the canvas while the activity dissipates along the edges.

Completed three years before his death, *Back View* reflects the universality Guston aspired to in his later paintings. The sardonic conspiratorial humor of the cartoon-like figures he featured in the early 1970s is supplanted by a somber vision of the tragic and absurd.   LLS

Richard Diebenkorn

AMERICAN, BORN 1922

Berkeley #57

1955

oil on canvas
58¾ × 58¾"
149.3 × 149.3 cm

Bequest of Joseph M. Bransten in
memory of Ellen Hart Bransten
80.423

THE WORK OF RICHARD DIEBENKORN is characterized by change and evolution, experiment and contemplation, reality and abstraction. Grounded in the land, space, and light of the West, it is charged as well with the traditions of twentieth-century art. Yet it is singularly individual, the product of introspection, reason, and intellect.

Diebenkorn's formative years were dedicated to the study of the work of others—Matisse, Cézanne, Miró especially—and drawing and painting on his own. Born in Portland, Oregon, in 1922, he determined early that he would be an artist. After studying at Stanford University and serving in the military, in 1946 Diebenkorn enrolled in the California School of Fine Arts (now the San Francisco Art Institute). The school at that time was simmering with activity. Douglas MacAgy had become director the previous summer and already his energy was making an impact. Provocative teachers were hired and the student body swelled with returning GI's eager to experiment and chart new territory. Diebenkorn, first as a student and after 1947 as a teacher, reacted strongly and positively to the liberated environment and lively teacher/student dialogue. His wholly abstract work, at first tightly linear and strongly predicated on Cubism, gradually loosened, the lines fluidly delineating painted areas, the colors growing warmer and more personal, the shapes increasingly biomorphic.

A move in 1950 to the arid land of the Southwest triggered a direct response in his paintings. Forms flattened and expanded, and lines were freed to act on their own, now looped, now dragged, often calligraphic. Elements of the landscape appeared, sometimes veiled, sometimes overt, interpreted with a palette dependent upon the sun-bleached tones of the desert clay. Diebenkorn's longtime predilection for Matisse was underscored in 1952 when, on his way to a teaching position at Urbana, Illinois, he saw a comprehensive Matisse retrospective. The paintings he made during his year in the Midwest reflect Matisse's color, vibrant and intense with acid greens and vivid blues.

In the fall of 1953, Diebenkorn returned to California, settled in Berkeley, and began to work on an open-ended suite of abstract canvases, the Berkeley Series. At first closely related to earlier works in tonality and maplike configuration, the paintings soon gained strong ties to the landscape, exhibiting dynamic horizontal striations and coloration reminiscent of the vegetation, sea, and sunlight of his immediate surroundings.

Exuberant and emotional, the spontaneity of the medium was nonetheless moderated by an underlying architecturally organized framework. *Berkeley #57*, one of the final works in this series, exhibits this architectonic structure. The square format is partitioned horizontally into six gently sloping, angularly bent, or triangular, divisions. The agitated surface, intermixing linear elements and semi-flat brushed areas, and sometimes strident color juxtapositions at first emit a sense of frenetic disarray. But quickly the work settles in and the eye concentrates on the focal area, an oblique swath positioned centrally and densely packed with closely related patches of color and looping linear traceries. The dominant tonality, a glowing gold, is electrified by adjacent fields of apple green, cobalt, and fleshy pinks.   KCH

Richard Diebenkorn

AMERICAN, BORN 1922

Cityscape I

formerly
LANDSCAPE I
1963

oil on canvas
60¼ × 50½″
153.1 × 128.3 cm

Purchased with funds from trustees
and friends in memory of Hector
Escobosa, Brayton Wilbur, and J. D.
Zellerbach
64.46

THE SAME YEAR that Diebenkorn painted *Berkeley #57* he shifted dramatically away from energetic abstractions and began to experiment with representation. As he stated in 1964, "I came right up against limitations that certain conceptions of abstract space impose. As I felt the urgency of particularizing more in my painting, I saw that this had become impossible within the abstract idiom."[1] Beginning with simple still lifes and later turning his attention to figures, landcapes, and cityscapes, he modulated and adapted his free, gestural handling of paint and expansive color to the depiction of objects. The high energy level of the non-objective paintings decreased, the mood of the works became quiet and contemplative. The geometric structure present in the abstract canvases became more overt, expressed at times by a knife consciously placed on a diagonal, the acute angle of a tilted table-edge, or the extended leg of a seated woman.

The motif of the landscape appears frequently in Diebenkorn's work; even his non-objective paintings of the fifties were often referred to as "abstract landscapes" because of their structural and tonal links to the environment. Early in the sixties Diebenkorn, then still living in Berkeley, painted a group of representational canvases featuring scenes of the land and the city. *Cityscape I* (originally titled *Landscape I*) combines a carefully reasoned relationship between color and space with a sensitivity to subject. Strong, oblique rays of late-afternoon sun sweep across a suburban hill, casting long metallic blue shadows and illuminating rooftops and verdant vacant lots. Hopper-like in effect, the light and shadows accentuate the absence of human presence, removing personal involvement. The canvas is approached intellectually, coolly, the focus on composition and palette.

The structure is forcefully stated by the aerial perspective and tilted planes of the hill. Shallow-angled lines appear but, unlike their horizontal direction in the abstract works, here they take the form of verticals, moving swiftly up and back into deep space. Horizontal layering, particularly apparent in the delft-blue band across the top, occurs as well, but is counterbalanced by nearly converging vertical thrusts. Asymmetrical, the composition counterposes a compact row of houses against open, geometrically divided fields, the two sides bisected by a street streaking uphill, alternately plunged into shadow or bathed in sunlight.

The emerald greens of the field, the lucid blue of the sky band, and steely grays of the shaded areas are snapped into place by the deftly positioned shapes of oyster white. Each color is built up, veil upon veil, revealing traces of pentimenti and underlying hues. Color and structure, taken together, point directly to Diebenkorn's abstract work to come.   KCH

[1]Quoted by Henry J. Seldis, "Diebenkorn: BMOC at Stanford," *Los Angeles Times*, February 2, 1964.

Richard Diebenkorn

AMERICAN, BORN 1922

Ocean Park #54

1972

oil on canvas
100 × 81″
254.0 × 205.7 cm

Gift of friends of Gerald Nordland
72.59

RICHARD DIEBENKORN'S WORK took yet another wide swing in 1967 when he returned to non-objective painting and began a series of monumental abstractions which blended linear geometric structure with fields of luminous color. In the fall of the previous year, having accepted the position of professor of art at the University of California at Los Angeles, Diebenkorn moved from Berkeley and established his studio in the Ocean Park section of Santa Monica near the shores of the Pacific Ocean. Responding in part to the palpable, hazy light of southern California, the flat openness of the land, and his close proximity to the sea, he began to paint the Ocean Park Series.

The large-scale vertical format of these canvases establishes a restricted focus within which is set up a geometric framework. What had been latent in the emotional abstractions of the fifties, then more obvious in the later figurative work, here becomes predominant. The scaffold, composed of vertical, horizontal, and angled linear elements, encloses fields of fluctuating depth, delicately balancing space and line. Spatial illusion is created by semi-transparent skins of pigment washed one upon another, concealing, revealing. Pentimenti, records of the artist's decisions made, changed, and remade are visible on the picture surface. Sometimes rubbed, often thinly veiled, they expose Diebenkorn's intuitive process of picture-making.

Ocean Park #54, painted in 1972, five years after the commencement of the series, is reminiscent of a window on the sea. The dominant hue is that of the ocean touched with a delicate light—tender and calm. The fervent gold of *Berkeley #57* has been lightened by the southern California sun and enriched with the addition of white to become a palpable cream. Shadowed diagonals emerge through the clouded films of pigment and even vestiges of curved fragments appear. Space is built up, layer upon layer, held in check by the overlying linear scaffolding. This architectural network reinforces the upright rectangular shape of the canvas through narrow bands skimming the left and right edges and horizontal fillets banding the upper border. The preponderance of structural complexity and color interest has been moved to the top of the composition, the lower two-thirds of the canvas open to expanses of blue and cream.   KCH

Elmer Bischoff

AMERICAN, BORN 1916

Orange Sweater

1955

oil on canvas
48½ × 57″
123.2 × 144.8 cm

Gift of Mr. and Mrs. Mark Schorer
63.20

IN 1957, PAUL MILLS, then curator of the Oakland Art Museum, organized an exhibition entitled *Contemporary Bay Area Figurative Painting*. Centered around the paintings of three artists from the San Francisco Bay Area, Elmer Bischoff, Richard Diebenkorn, and David Park, and augmented by the work of nine others, the exhibition focused on a return of the figure as subject in art. The three focal artists had all been active at the California School of Fine Arts (now the San Francisco Art Institute) during the last half of the 1940s and all had developed individual statements in Abstract Expressionism. But eventually, each found gestural abstraction to be too easy, too insubstantial, and beginning with David Park in 1950, they individually returned to the figure and landscape for subject matter.

In the introduction to the exhibition catalogue, Mills counseled the public not to view these artists as a group or movement, but despite his admonition, the national media responded immediately by categorizing the artists as "The Bay Area Figurative School." Opinions of this re-examination of representation were mixed: for some it was a progressive direction, utilizing the lessons learned in Abstract Expressionism for the realization of the object; for others, the interjection of realism was retrogressive, a retreat from the great strides made by American abstraction.

For Elmer Bischoff the return to painting the objective world was the culmination of a search for "more stimulus and provocation." Born in Berkeley in 1916, Bischoff attended the University of California there from 1934 until 1939, when he received his master's degree. The emphasis of the Berkeley art department during those years was on Cubism, and Bischoff emerged from his schooling with a style thoroughly grounded in the late Synthetic Cubism of Picasso. After serving in the military, in 1946 he returned to the Bay Area and began teaching at the California School of Fine Arts. Deeply involved in the well-known ferment that swept the school during the following years, Bischoff developed a highly charged active style. In 1952, dissatisfied with what he considered to be a lack of challenge in non-representational painting, he began painting objects and scenes which at first were quite specific and then, as he progressed, became more and more nebulous. In a one-man exhibition held in 1955 at the Paul Kantor Gallery in Beverly Hills and another at the beginning of 1956 at the California School of Fine Arts, Bischoff exhibited canvases which merged expressionistic paint-handling and brushwork with scenes of figures in environments.

Orange Sweater, painted in 1955 and exhibited in the landmark 1957 exhibition in Oakland, exemplifies Bischoff's comment of 1956, "What is most desired in the final outcome is a condition of form which dissolves all tangible facts into intangibles of feeling."[1] The scene is, perhaps, a library, the focal figure engrossed in reading. But the setting and the single figure, defined minimally, are enwrapped in a web of paint that surfaces, then submerges, in the expressive brush strokes. The figure, visually luminous yet psychologically neutral, takes its place as but one element of the whole, its violent persimmon exploding the opalescent and silvered colors. The surroundings are pared down and expressed as translucent layers, the right half of the bisected canvas bathed in nearly celestial light, the left in grayed green shadows. The writer Mark Schorer, who with his wife donated this painting to the Museum in 1963, had written of the work: "Screens of green, gray, pearl, white recede into what appears to be space without end, and still, while all luminous, all reaching on and on, it is all still perfectly contained within the limits of the canvas . . . all around the intent figure, the apocalyptic color and light and brightness. The small human figure is defined in daylight, and so, momentarily, am I."[2] KCH

[1] Elmer Bischoff, *Elmer Bischoff* (San Francisco: California School of Fine Arts, 1956), p. 3.
[2] Mark Schorer, *Recent Paintings/Elmer Bischoff*, Staempfli Gallery, New York, 1960.

David Park

AMERICAN, 1911–1960

Man in a T-Shirt

1958

oil on canvas
59¾ × 49¾"
151.8 × 126.4 cm

Gift of Mr. and Mrs. Harry W.
Anderson
76.26

DAVID PARK'S DETERMINATION to paint "troublesome" canvases led him in 1950 to shift abruptly from abstract work to figurative painting. Having just spent four years steeped in the frenetic energy of the California School of Fine Arts (now the San Francisco Art Institute), where he had temporarily abandoned objective art for freely gestured abstraction, Park was anxious to return to the object which, he felt, would set pictorial elements free to, as he put it, "evolve naturally."

A native of Boston, Park had had only one year of formal art training at the Otis Art Institute in Los Angeles when he arrived in San Francisco in the summer of 1929 to become an assistant to the sculptor Ralph Stackpole, in which capacity he cut stone for Stackpole's monumental figures at the San Francisco Stock Exchange. Park's paintings during this period exhibited the flattened space, undulating contours, and emphasis on negative as well as positive space which characterized Picasso's late Synthetic Cubist phase. While the works carried such titles as *Two Violinists* or *Woman in Red and White Robe* and were basically figural, depiction of the human form was of considerably less importance than the development of formal aspects.

After being hired by Douglas MacAgy to teach at the California School of Fine Arts in 1944, Park experimented with Abstract Expressionism, spurred on not so much by Clyfford Still and Mark Rothko, as by the combined energy and enthusiasm of the school's students and teachers, particularly Hassel Smith and Elmer Bischoff. Never completely satisfied with his abstract canvases, Park destroyed nearly all of them in 1949, but the few extant reproductions of these works show explorations in gesture which nonetheless contain conscious negative/positive space juxtapositions. The following year, Park introduced figures into his compositions. At first the paintings exhibited offbeat compositional approaches. Within a single canvas, perspectives changed dramatically from straight-on to bird's-eye view. Space was often divided vertically down a voided center or bisected diagonally, the resultant halves exhibiting completely disparate spatial relationships. The figures, distended or severely truncated, were flattened and pushed to the edge of the canvas or expanded to fill much of the foreground. Their faces, broadly conceived and summarily modeled, contained few hints of individuality.

By mid-decade, Park's work took on a more naturalistic, expansively energetic tone. The figures became more generalized; their visages, when at all visible, were pared of all unique characteristics. The heretofore tightly composed, specific environment unfolded and became diffused, enveloping the forms. Spontaneous and open brushwork took on a life of its own, creating an atmospheric ambience.

While nudes, expressed with a few forcefully stated strokes of the brush, dominated the canvases of this period, *Man in a T-Shirt*, painted in 1958, features a casually dressed male figure. Stolid, weighty, monumental, the form looms in the foreground, seemingly oblivious to the undefined deep space behind it. Foreground and background are identically described, richly colored, vigorously scrubbed. The form literally emerges from its palpable ambience. Powerfully illuminated from the left, the figure in large part is volumetrically defined by the highlights and shadows which punctuate its form. From the dragged brush strokes to the scattered paint drips, the presence of the artist's hand is unmistakable. The figure, stripped of its unique personal traits, implies universality.   KCH

186

Nathan Oliveira
AMERICAN, BORN 1928

Adolescent by the Bed
1959

oil on canvas
60¼ × 60⅛"
153.1 × 152.7 cm

William L. Gerstle Collection
William L. Gerstle Fund Purchase
67.48

THE SPECTRAL PAINTINGS of Nathan Oliveira made their appearance on the national scene just as Bay Area Figurative Painting was reaching its peak in public recognition and acclaim. Like the figurative triumvirate Elmer Bischoff, Richard Diebenkorn, and David Park, Oliveira explored the expression of human form by means of gestural painting, and he shared with the others a predilection for setting up ambiguous figure/environment relationships. But Oliveira's paintings, and the innumerable prints which he executed as well, were frankly romantic, more direct in attitude and dramatic in both execution and coloration. Concentrating predominantly on single human forms silhouetted against densely pigmented, positive backgrounds or submerged in veiled, generalized settings, Oliveira imbued his phantom figures with a primitive power evocative of shamans and fetishes.

Born in Oakland in 1928, Oliveira was educated there at the California College of Arts and Crafts where he received his Master of Fine Arts in 1952. Unlike the California School of Fine Arts (now the San Francisco Art Institute) across the bay which focused on abstraction, the faculty at CCAC stressed objective painting, with added emphasis on figuration. Oliveira's interest in the figure was further underscored by a summer spent studying with Max Beckmann at Mills College in 1950. Beckmann's approach to painting in which all superfluities were eliminated, thus revealing the essence, greatly impressed Oliveira who integrated this attitude into his own work. Influences from other sources were assimilated during this formative period: the paint handling of Willem de Kooning, the isolated figures of Edvard Munch, the attenuated verticality of Alberto Giacometti.

Oliveira experimented briefly with abstraction around 1956, but by the following year his absorption with figurative expression was firmly established. In the paintings of the late fifties, solitary vertical figures, often in profile, stand isolated before single-hued, palpable spaces, the distance relieved only by strongly stated or loosely implied horizon lines. Facial features obliterated, detailing of the torso effaced with exploding slashes of pigment, these simplified forms were allowed only seemingly arbitrary anatomical definition, an enlarged hand broadly expressed in flashy pink, or an extended upper leg picked out in thickly impastoed ultramarine. Layer upon layer of paint was applied, utilizing every technique in the artist's extensive vocabulary of brush strokes, the resultant surface, tactile and dramatic, displaying a richly nuanced coloration.

Oliveira has stated, "A process of elimination sets in and brings you back to some confrontation."[1] This elimination and confrontation are evident in the 1959 canvas, *Adolescent by the Bed*. A lone spectral female looms ominously, her hooded head reminiscent of the sphinx. Eyes shrouded, the nose, mouth, and chin emerge from the shadows to suggest individuality but stop short of definition. Haunting and powerful, the phantom-like figure emanates pathos and strongly awakening sexuality.

Unlike the majority of Oliveira's contemporary paintings, this work contains the image of an object, a bed, which lends specificity while reinforcing sexual implications. Working as a formal device, the bed divides the right side of the picture geometrically, introducing strong diagonals and angled forces reminiscent of Richard Diebenkorn, which play off against the verticality of the centrally positioned figure. Expressed in variations of gray, from vaporous pearl to ashen smoke, the painting exudes mysterious power, a tenebrous hallucination hovering between reality and the world of dreams. KCH

[1] Quoted in Frederick Wight, *Nathan Oliveira*, UCLA Art Galleries, University of California, Los Angeles, 1963, n.p.

Frank Lobdell

AMERICAN, BORN 1921

March 1954

1954

oil on canvas
69½ × 65½"
176.6 × 166.4 cm
Anonymous gift
76.197

THE ABSTRACT EXPRESSIONISM which emerged in the San Francisco Bay Area after the close of World War II and gathered steam in the first years of the fifties was raw and zealous, free and experiential. Responsible for catapulting the Bay Region to a position of national prominence, its impact was felt not only by artists on the eastern seaboard, but, through the Ferus Gallery, by southern California artists as well. The heroic pictorial statements of Hassel Smith, Frank Lobdell, Richard Diebenkorn, and Ernest Briggs, among many others, spoke to the open and highly charged artistic climate of the time, which allowed and encouraged diversity of inspiration and expression.

Frank Lobdell, born in Kansas City in 1921, was one of the mature and motivated World War II veterans who enrolled at the California School of Fine Arts (now the San Francisco Art Institute) during the era of Douglas MacAgy and Clyfford Still. During the three years he was a student there, from 1947 until 1950, Lobdell developed a profound dedication to expressive abstraction. By 1953 he had evolved a unique lexicon of personal symbols with mythic overtones which he reworked and reinterpreted throughout the decade. Using a drastically limited palette, Lobdell initially set his forms against thickly laid chalky grounds, allowing them to twist diagonally back into deep, undefined space. Later in the decade he shadowed his compositions, releasing dramatically lit, torquing images into roily, nocturnal fields. His forms hinted at the influence of Still's ragged stalactites, Gorky's biomorphic linearity, and Picasso's tormented imagery of the mid-thirties, but ultimately they came from within the artist. Anthropomorphisms, they struggled to consciousness bringing with them the pain and release of birth.

March 1954, painted during Lobdell's black-on-white period of the early fifties, gives strong evidence of the artist's relentless pictorial powers and deep sense of commitment. An organically conceived abstract form, bearing references to a splayed bestial figure, struggles diagonally upward. Torn from its rhizome-like base, it rises heavily, laden with impasto, then hesitates, barred from continuing by an ominous pillow of black and the confines of the canvas edge. The directional forces upward are underscored by thickly applied ragged or gently curving black outlines, the striping of the base, and the stippled surface of the tortured figure.

A densely gestured and scrubbed milky ground, simple in its coloration, yet activated by brushwork, establishes fathomless space against which the figure is set, typical of Lobdell's dedication to traditional figure/ground relationships. Not a spontaneous painting, *March 1954* rather illustrates the artist's thoughtful and serious methodology. Working slowly, redefining frequently, drawing from deep within himself for not only inspiration but strength as well, Lobdell's resolute sense of purpose has been sustained throughout his career.   KCH

Hassel Smith

AMERICAN, BORN 1915

2 to the Moon

1961

oil on canvas
67⅞ × 67⅞"
172.4 × 172.4 cm

Gift of Mr. and Mrs. William C.
Janss
78.206

THE INTELLECTUAL AND CREATIVE CLIMATE at the California School of Fine Arts in San Francisco (now the San Francisco Art Institute) during the last years of the decade of the forties exuded exhilaration and prodigious activity. Orchestrated by Douglas MacAgy, who headed the school from 1945 to 1950, the program at the hillside urban campus included a cast of audacious teachers anxious to break new artistic ground, an abundance of eager veterans complete with GI Bill tuitions, maturity, and a context within which to learn, and the presence of some stellar outside figures, catalysts, as it were, for the brew. Clyfford Still, then on the cusp of national acclaim and success, taught there from 1946 through 1950; during the summers of 1947 and 1949, Mark Rothko was in residence. At various times from 1945 to 1950, Elmer Bischoff, Richard Diebenkorn, David Park, Clay Spohn, and Hassel Smith were on the teaching staff, while students included Jeremy Anderson, Frank Lobdell, and Ernest Briggs, among others. The volatile teacher/student dialogues, liberal ambience, and sense of a new beginning led to an explosion of Abstract Expressionism involving a surprising number of extremely talented artists. The historical facts of this "golden age" have been thoroughly documented, but the sheer impact and energy of those times continues to amaze.

Hassel Smith had attended the school as a student a decade earlier, when its atmosphere was stifling and academic. Returning as a teacher in 1945, he experienced the tumultuous birth of expressive abstraction and, in fact, was profoundly swayed by Still's personality and work. Smith's representational paintings of the early forties, brushy, satirical, often figurative, gave way in 1947 to vigorous, ofttimes violent abstractions. At first closely allied visually to Still's large masses of impastoed color and adjoining rough-hewn planes, Smith gradually came into his own, interjecting linear elements, enlivening color, aerating forms and setting them afloat. Replacing Still's grandeur and weight with a spontaneous, "upbeat excitement," Smith drew upon his love of jazz and dancing for visual cadence and rhythm. Humor, too, was added, materializing in the titles or in unexpected calligraphic snippets.

From 1958 to 1962, confident, materially comfortable, convinced of the "rightness" of his work, Smith produced a body of paintings which epitomizes the California brand of Abstract Expressionism. *2 to the Moon*, painted at the height of this period, exhibits many of the elements of Smith's work. A field of chrome yellow, freely brushed, is bisected diagonally. The jagged division, sometimes open and specific, sometimes merely implied, draws together like pieces of a jigsaw puzzle the irregularly triangular parts of the stridently hued field, tempering spontaneity with stability and presence. The flowing yellow mass forces multicolored areas into the upper right where they are cut off, setting up tension at the edges of the canvas.

Despite its abstraction, figurative references, if not blatantly stated, are nonetheless implied. The fluent calligraphic line, looping or sharply angular, autonomous or directly linked to the color fields, vaguely describes anatomical forms or subtly suggests humanistic configurations. Using his broad vocabulary of paint application, Smith juxtaposes or overlaps the layers of paint, sometimes allowing them to dwindle to merely stained or bare canvas, at other times building passages of dense pigment. The unrestrained energy of expressionism is here contained and controlled through the intellect and formal geometric means which later became predominant in Hassel Smith's work.   KCH

2 to the moon
1961

Robert Rauschenberg

AMERICAN, BORN 1925

Collection

formerly
UNTITLED
1953–54

oil, paper, fabric, and metal on wood
80 × 96 × 3½″
203.2 × 243.9 × 8.9 cm

Gift of Mr. and Mrs. Harry W. Anderson
72.26

THE INTRODUCTION IN 1955 OF THE COMMON OBJECT into the realm of art shattered the accepted dominance of Abstract Expressionism, opened the way for a re-examination of the nature of art, and led directly to the rise of American Pop artists in the years following. In the work entitled *Bed* (1955), Robert Rauschenberg assembled a composite of his own bedclothes, applied to it a broad traverse of gesticulated, dripping pigment, and mounted the whole on a wooden support. Termed a "combine" by the artist, the work operated on two distinct and conflicting levels. The object, a bed, clearly retained its original identity, carrying with it a plethora of personal and experiential connotations. Yet this "object" was just as obviously a work of art, for its rumpled surface was clotted with paint consciously applied, and the rectangular format was framed and hung on a wall. The tension set up between these two seemingly distinct worlds, the world of reality and the world of art, elicited an active, open-ended response on the part of the viewer and suggested a middle ground in which a multiplicity of preconceptions and implications co-existed in a rich, questioning ambience.

Bed did not mark the first time that Rauschenberg had incorporated commonplace objects into his art, for collaged elements had frequently appeared in his previous work. In 1949, after spending a year studying with Josef and Anni Albers at Black Mountain College in North Carolina (where he met his later collaborators John Cage, David Tudor, and Merce Cunningham), Rauschenberg had settled in New York and enrolled at the Art Students League. Beginning in 1951 he concentrated on three series of paintings, each based on a single monochromatic tone. His initial series, the "white paintings," consisted of ensembles of rectangles whose undifferentiated fields were painted with flat white house paint; the next series, the "black paintings," incorporated crumpled bits of paper beneath layers of first glossy, then dull black paint. In 1953, Rauschenberg embarked on the "red paintings," in which collaged elements acting as discrete images rather than merely textural interest took on their own life and importance within the painting structure.

Near the end of 1953, Rauschenberg began *Collection*, a major work which in many ways presaged the combines of the coming years. Much as in the collages of Kurt Schwitters, whose work had a vital influence on Rauschenberg, the objects here have been plucked out of the artist's experience and hung on a geometric scaffold. Predominantly red, *Collection* is composed of three adjoining vertical panels traversed by the same number of distinct horizontal bands. A strip of repeated vertical patches marks the lower border, the rectangular shapes defined by swatches of fabric in opaque pinks and primaries. Directly above this is a densely collaged median layered with fragments of printed fabric, newspaper clippings, and reproductions of art objects sporadically overpainted with broad gestures, the liquid paint allowed to dribble freely. Across the top runs an irregularly bounded striation composed of lighter-hued, larger-scaled areas. The uppermost edge is broken by the addition of wooden objects which deny the rectangular format and extend its limits, tentatively moving it into the environment of the spectator.

Entitled *Collection* by the artist in 1976, long after it was completed, the painting is indeed a collection, an assemblage of personal mementos mirroring the facets of a life— the cerebral, the aesthetic, the recreational—expressed as we visually perceive our surroundings, in bits and snatches. Rauschenberg has choreographed these fragments, allowing them the freedom to exist as entities yet unifying them through an underlying geometric structure, a superstratum of pigment, and a consistent emotional tone.   KCH

Jasper Johns
AMERICAN, BORN 1930

Land's End
1963

oil on canvas with stick
67 × 48¼"
170.2 × 122.6 cm

Gift of Mr. and Mrs. Harry W. Anderson
72.23

SHORTLY AFTER ROBERT RAUSCHENBERG'S audacious combine paintings appeared in New York, exploding the accepted domination of Abstract Expressionism, Jasper Johns's work was introduced to a reeling public. Presenting images of mundane objects and utilizing the animated brushwork of the action painters yet maintaining an emotional detachment, Johns established a dynamic dialogue that questioned the role of the object versus that of the painting. Impassively removing the object from its customary context and isolating it in a painting format, Johns, like Rauschenberg, forced a reconsideration of the nature of art and its ambiguous relationship to life.

Johns, a close friend of Rauschenberg, concentrated on a narrow spectrum of images in his first paintings. American flags and then targets were impassively presented. Visually focused and objectively rendered, the images elicited a plethora of ambiguous and conflicting responses. Letters and numbers were added to the repertoire shortly thereafter. Not "objects" in the literal sense, these elements worked on a number of levels, as visual forms, as commonly accepted symbols for concrete ideas, and as perplexing, often contradictory elements within the context of the painting. As the decade drew to a close, Johns's work exhibited more physical brushwork and he began inserting words into the work. Maps soon joined the vocabulary and, around 1962, Johns started complicating his work by including several images and a multitude of ideas in a single canvas. Physical objects—yardsticks, brooms, balls—were attached to the surface or wedged into openings between adjoining segments. Images, isolated and interpreted in various mediums during the fifties, were reconfronted, restated. A single image might be executed in oil, encaustic, Conté crayon, charcoal, lithography, and, occasionally, cast in bronze or lead as well. Within a single image and medium combination, variations in texture, color, or arrangement occurred.

Several paintings of this period carry names relating to the sea: *By the Sea*, 1961, *Diver*, 1962, and *Periscope (Hart Crane)*, 1963, related, perhaps, to Johns's move to the coast of South Carolina. *Land's End*, 1963, belongs to this group and exhibits several images and attitudes which Johns examined and re-examined during the early years of the sixties. A tripartite format sectioned horizontally is covered with loosely applied, dripping, overlapping gray pigment. Centered on each of the segments is a word —Red, Yellow, Blue—first stenciled, then manipulated, mirrored, or repeated in different scales. These words, clearly defined in everyday experience, are displaced here, positioned over colors that negate their meaning and thus throw them open to question. The flatly applied letters mark the surface of the canvas, but that flatness is contradicted by the overlapping, scrubbed areas which suggest a spatial depth.

Other elements allude to process or imminent change. The handprint of the artist culminating the shadow of an outstretched arm, a directional arrow, drips and smears of paint, the—theoretically—interchangeable triple elements of the format and, most importantly, the compass-like "device" all suggest movement past or future. First used in his painting *Device Circle* in 1959 and closely related to targets of his earlier days, this configuration is formed by the radial circuit of a painted stick on wet pigment and implies the active part played by the artist in the creation of the work.   KCH

Claes Oldenburg

AMERICAN, BORN SWEDEN
1929

Blue Legs

1961

plaster and muslin with enamel
48 × 36 × 7⅛"
121.9 × 91.5 × 18.1 cm

Anonymous gift
64.65

THE TENSION BETWEEN ILLUSION AND REALITY, between art and life, which Robert Rauschenberg and Jasper Johns had confronted was expounded upon by a subsequent wave of artists who culled images and objects from American popular culture, divested them of their intended function, restated them by using mechanical or traditional techniques, and then placed them into new contexts. These responses to everyday environments took a variety of forms: clichéd comics (Roy Lichtenstein), hammer-appended paintings (Jim Dine), repetitive rows of soup cans (Andy Warhol), grand-scale canvases filled with fragmented images (James Rosenquist), and the soft, sewn hamburgers of Claes Oldenburg.

Swedish-born and Yale-educated, Oldenburg had determined near the end of the fifties that he wanted to make art that was reflective of life around him, with all its platitudes, vagaries, and ambiguities. Initially drawn to objects displayed in shop windows and later turning to articles found in the home, Oldenburg transformed these fragments of reality into super-reality, paradoxically restating hard objects in soft materials and small ones in monumental scale.

In December 1961, Oldenburg opened The Store, an actual storefront he had rented on the Lower East Side of New York City. The rear of the space was reserved for a studio, but the front half was filled with objects he had made "after the spirit and in the form of popular objects of merchandise."[1] Displayed in cases or hung from the walls and ceiling, pies and ice cream cones, hats and gym shoes, jelly doughnuts, and even a cash register were offered for sale. All fashioned of plaster-dipped muslin formed over chicken wire, the pieces were enameled in violent, spattered color. Each had been re-created on the artist's own terms, fragmented or presented in its entirety, sometimes larger than life, sometimes smaller, occasionally life-sized. Oldenburg described his intentions: "In showing them together, I have wanted to imitate my act of perceiving them, which is why they are shown as fragments (of the field of seeing), in different scale one to another, in a form surrounding me (and the spectator), and in accumulation rather than in some imposed design. And the effect is I have made my own Store."[2]

Recorded as number forty-four on the artist's inventory of the store's contents is *Blue Legs*, priced at $299.99.[3] Like a passing glimpse, this fragmented form retains a ragged bit of backdrop. The image/moment has been isolated and expanded, not just in scale but in volume, moving out into the third dimension. With its liberally pigmented surface and volumetric configuration, the work lies in the realm between painting and sculpture, containing both the illusion of space and its reality. The over-sized scale is reiterated by the glossy enamel: royal blue, angled legs set off by a background of equally high-pitched green, and the white-white of "uptown" shoes. The impact is direct and the object is meant to be read from a distance, for when viewed at close range it dissolves into drips and gloss, plaster and enamel. Flesh enclosed in tights is translated here into hard shininess and yet maintains a sense, albeit somewhat jaded, of life. In its blatant banality and frank eroticism, this glance-made-into-an-object prefigures Oldenburg's soft sculpture and colossal monuments of the following years.   KCH

[1] Claes Oldenburg and Emmett Williams, *Store Days* (New York: Something Else Press, 1967), p. 16.
[2] Ibid., p. 26.
[3] Ibid., p. 33.

Jay DeFeo

AMERICAN, BORN 1929

Incision

1958–61

oil and string on canvas mounted
on board
118 × 55⅝ × 9⅜″
299.7 × 141.3 × 23.9 cm

Purchased with the aid of funds
from the Society for the Encouragement of Contemporary Art
67.89

DURING THE DECADE FOLLOWING MID-CENTURY, the dominance of Abstract Expressionism in the San Francisco Bay Area was challenged by two related but distinct offshoots. One group of artists, weary of abstraction, turned to the human form for subject and developed a lyrical yet gestural figuration. The other expanded Abstract Expressionist painting, extending it into the realm of sculpture. Searching out materials drawn from everyday activities, these artists mixed and assembled, building aggregations that fused art and life. For some, such as Wallace Berman, Bruce Conner, Wally Hedrick, and George Herms, the resultant objects were sculptural assemblages of discrete elements, evocative and compelling.

Like these underground artists, Jay DeFeo drew inspiration from mysticism, jazz, and poetry, but her focus remained on the energy and material attributes of action painting, with the peripheral addition at times of some found objects—string, for instance, or stones.

In 1961 Jay DeFeo wrote: "Although [I am] a painter by definition, my work as it has emerged in the past two years could more accurately be described as a combination of painting and sculpture. I consider the aspects of each inseparable and interdependent. . . ."[1] *Incision*, completed during this year, exists in this hybrid area of painting-sculpture. DeFeo applied stratum upon stratum of oil paint to the support, boldly moving the volcanically textured surface out into the third dimension. Paint was added, then scraped or troweled in broad gestures, for to DeFeo the carving was as crucial as the building. Having taken on a life of its own, the medium needed to be controlled and refined. The process became all important, the outer face with its vestiges of building, scraping, gashing, and rebuilding reflecting the many layers beneath.

In *Incision*, as in the vast majority of her work, DeFeo's palette has been limited to gray, but within that limitation she has used the full range available, from deep charcoals to the pearly near-whites that highlight the arcing diagonal swaths. The play of light over the crags and crevasses underlines the sheer substance of the medium. Yet this is illusory, for despite its seeming mass, the painting is in fact vulnerable; nearly five hundred pounds of paint hang on a canvas support, as precariously as the strings that dangle from its surface.

The same year she began *Incision*, DeFeo embarked on what she considered to be her ultimate statement, an overwhelming painting-sculpture which at its completion in 1967 weighed over a ton. This work, whose title evolved from *The Deathrose* to *The White Rose* to simply *The Rose* (San Francisco Art Institute), is closely related to *Incision* in its palette, scale, myriad paint strata, and slashed, encrusted surface. But while *The Rose* is dominated by a single emblematic image, a central radiating form that has been carved into glowing smoothness, *Incision* retains an essentially sedimentary quality, the focus being the sweeping gestures of the artist which intensify the lava-like essence. These curving, upward-directed strokes reflect back to the Abstract Expressionist tradition and DeFeo's work of the mid-fifties, while *The Rose* looks ahead to the single-object focus of the artist's later work.   KCH

[1] In "New Talent USA," *Art in America*, vol. 49, no. 1 (1961), p. 30.

Bruce Conner

AMERICAN, BORN 1933

Looking Glass
1964

paper, cotton cloth, nylon, beads, metal, twine, glass, leather, plastic, and wood on Masonite
60½ × 48 × 14½"
153.7 × 121.9 × 36.8 cm

Gift of the Modern Art Council
78.69

FOR A HISTORIC MOMENT in the mid-fifties, the cultural scene in San Francisco was infused with a laid-back spirit of creativity which interwove its every facet—music, art, literature, dance, theater. Emanating from North Beach, then an enclave of coffee houses, jazz clubs, bookstores, and galleries, this underground movement spawned poetry tinged with drug imagery and Oriental philosophy and exhaled the cerebral rhythms of jazz. Alienated by choice from the middle-class establishment, outwardly apathetic yet consumed with inner conflict, the participants in the movement, the Beats, led existential lives, praising the moment and questioning, or denying, the future.

Bruce Conner entered this scene in 1957, arriving in San Francisco shortly after receiving his Bachelor of Fine Arts from the University of Nebraska and having attended both the Brooklyn Museum School of Art and the University of Colorado, Boulder. Finding kindred spirits in the nihilistic words of the Beat poets and the spontaneous, experimental attitudes of the artists, Conner initially produced scabrous paintings and collages which alluded to the verities of life, birth, and death. Moved to integrate the material fragments of existence into his art, Conner began combining disparate, discarded elements, forming compelling assemblages that at first remained wall oriented, then gradually expanded out into the realm of sculpture.

From the beginning, Conner chose materials that were intensely personal and evocative, conjuring demented images of dusty Victorian parlors. Bits of fringe and fur, fragments of jewelry and ribbons were combined with cracked glass or mirror, summoning forth nostalgic visions, while other images and objects swung the focus toward the erotic. Photographs of pin-ups and showgirls, some startlingly explicit, were frequently juxtaposed with symbols of decay, death, and suffering. Black wax covered figures and surfaces like a tactile, macabre skin. But most ubiquitous was the nylon stocking which ensnared entire works in its enticing web or assumed phallic or breastlike shapes when filled with feminine fabrics or pieces of jewelry.

The art of assemblage absorbed Conner until 1964 when he turned his attention to making films. Save for a single free-standing sculpture executed in 1966, *Looking Glass*, 1964, was his final statement in the assemblage medium. A grand-scaled homage to feminine vanity, the work plays off a dense two-dimensional collage of nude female figures against a richly associative sculptural panoply of once-elegant shoes, jewelry, and pendant lacy undergarments. A disquieting figure rests on the overhanging shelf which horizontally divides the carefully structured composition. Nestled among the disintegrating finery, with a head formed of stuffed stockings and mannequin arms ending in poised, polished nails, this memento mori presides over the whole, a poignant and enigmatic tribute to the temporality of beauty and the human body. KCH

Peter Voulkos
AMERICAN, BORN 1924

Sevillanas
1959

stoneware with iron slip and clear glaze
56¾ × 27¼ × 20″
144.1 × 69.2 × 50.8 cm

Albert M. Bender Collection
Albert M. Bender Bequest Fund Purchase
64.9

WITH AN INTENSE OUTPOURING OF ENERGY, Peter Voulkos and a small group of cohorts liberated ceramics from the "form follows function" tenets of its craft heritage and thrust it into the realm of sculpture. The first to sense the expressive potential of clay, they established it as a viable medium for the stylistic concerns of the day. Their intensive activity—with Voulkos as spiritual leader, generator, and catalyst of new ideas—brought forth a far-reaching revolution in the world of ceramics.

Voulkos studied painting at Montana State University in his native city of Bozeman and received a master of arts degree in ceramics and sculpture at the California College of Arts and Crafts in Oakland. Returning to Montana in 1952, he joined forces with Rudy Autio at the Archie Bray Foundation and together they experimented freely with conventional production pottery. Establishing a wide reputation, they drew visitors from as far away as Japan. One of the visitors, the folk potter Hamada, through his Zen-inspired "courting of the accidental" influenced Voulkos to depart from symmetrical wheel-thrown vessels and move toward rougher, irregular, and unpredictable shapes. Further influences came on a trip east to teach at Black Mountain College, where he was introduced to gestural abstraction in painting, jazz improvisation, and experiments in combined media.

Arriving in Los Angeles in 1954 to head the ceramics department at Otis Art Institute, Voulkos gathered around him a group of highly talented and inventive young artists: Billy Al Bengston, Michael Frimkess, John Mason, Kenneth Price, and Paul Soldner. Working their way through tons of clay, they participated in freewheeling experimentation that led them in diverse, independent, and often radical directions. Voulkos was using painting concepts on three-dimensional forms, taking inspiration from the painted ceramics of Picasso and Miró. Keenly aware of the developments in Abstract Expressionism occurring on both coasts, he saw the form and surface of clay as a vehicle for the contained spontaneous gesture.

In 1955 Voulkos's work began to break away from functional pottery. Inspired by Matisse's cutouts, he overlaid pattern-cut pieces of clay slab onto vessel forms, joining them with slip and painting them with bold color. Splashes of intensely hued glazes set up a tension between form and color that went beyond traditional surface decoration. Later, adding epoxy paints to the glazed surfaces, he prepared the way for the use of vibrant synthetic pigments on clay.

Intent on pushing his work to monumental proportion, Voulkos found the key in Fritz Wotruba's stacked and cantilevered stone sculptures. Throwing a large cylinder core with a thick base, Voulkos then attached basic vessel forms to it. Piled one over the other, they emerged at angles to the central core, bulging and jutting abruptly. Color areas of blue or black accentuated the edges of the joined planes and forms. Overcoming many technical difficulties, Voulkos was able to produce increasingly larger works which broke through the size barrier and pushed clay to a new stature. In 1958 and 1959, at a studio he shared with John Mason, Voulkos produced a series of massive sculptures made of clusters of stacked and balanced vessel forms cantilevered on a basic cylinder skeleton and painted iron-oxide black. In *Sevillanas*, as in pieces made later in 1959, Voulkos tore open the vessel forms so that both inside and outside are visible and skeleton and skin are one. The dark color unifies the form, enhancing the jagged, asymmetrical profile that activates the surface with light and shadow. Paddled, punched, and gouged, the forms turn and twist, emerging as one massive, earthbound volume, dark and brooding, charged with bestial energy. GGM

John Mason
AMERICAN, BORN 1927

Untitled
(Monolith)
1964

stoneware with glaze
66½ × 64 × 17″
168.9 × 162.6 × 43.2 cm

Gift of the Women's Board
71.68

THE BEGINNING OF THE 1960s marked a national trend toward reductionism in both painting and sculpture. Rejecting the emotional excesses of Abstract Expressionism, artists became interested in simplification and the distillation of forms. In responding to the impersonal, cool psychic spirit of the sixties, the work of John Mason evolved from an emphasis on surface manipulation to simplified shapes in which ambiguous references to nature were eliminated and shape and surface became unified. Bridging Expressionism and Minimalism, these massive cross forms and spear forms lead to Mason's later conceptual approach.

John Mason spent his early years in Nevada, where the vast desert terrain, with its sense of timelessness and awesome power, provided sources of inspiration for his later work. The opportunity to study at the Chouinard Art Institute brought him to Los Angeles in 1949. When he joined Peter Voulkos's class at Otis Art Institute in 1954 he was already an accomplished ceramicist. His association with the Voulkos circle opened for him new avenues of creative inquiry and experimentation, allowing him to break through the established conventions of craft. In a series of plaques produced during this period Mason departed radically from the wheel-thrown format. Dropping a slab of clay onto various objects, he subjected it to indentations, folds, tears, and stretches, making use of chance operations related to the experiments of John Cage. This abandonment of control was unheard-of in the pottery studio, where technical skill at the wheel had been the main objective.

In 1957 Mason and Voulkos began sharing a studio where they built a large kiln that enabled them to increase dramatically the scale of their work. Like Voulkos, Mason had worked in industry as a production potter, and their technical backgrounds enabled them to achieve the engineering innovations needed to produce works of monumental size. But while Voulkos's method was to assemble multi-part sculptures from wheel-thrown vessel forms, Mason, more interested in exploiting the plasticity of wet clay, built single-form structures by layering skins of clay over a handbuilt substructure.

Mason's move from vessel and plate forms to large-scale sculpture began with a series of large modular wall reliefs in which he used strips of clay as brush strokes, composing them as great gestural configurations over flat clay surfaces. During this same period he worked on a series of freestanding vertical pieces, assembling thick, rectilinear strips and chunks of clay around a central columnar support. Irregular in shape with jagged protrusions emanating from rough unglazed surfaces, these columns seem frozen in a moment of organic growth. Totemic, with surfaces left raw, they convey both a quality of rugged harshness, as though forged by the forces of nature, and a sense of mysterious ritual. As they evolved, these works became massive, the surfaces and shapes compacted into elemental images—crosses and arrows transformed into highly charged icons.

In Untitled (*Monolith*) of 1964, Mason condensed the powerful gesture, centralizing the source of energy to achieve an abstract symbolism. The thick, massive cruciform is dramatized by a central slit-like aperture. Viewed as a multi-armed totem, it has an imposing primeval presence, eliciting ritualistic associations without specific symbolic reference. Hard, angled edges are counterbalanced by the dark, richly textured surface in which the clay-layering process remains visible. Despite its crusty, almost painterly appearance, the surface is uniform in color and in textural consistency. The single-image, emblematic form has a sense of immediacy and impact which prefigures the brightly colored, surface-conscious geometric shapes that followed.   GGM

Kenneth Price

AMERICAN, BORN 1935

L. Red

1963

stoneware with lacquer and acrylic
10¼ × 8⅞ × 9¼"
26.1 × 22.6 × 23.5 cm

Evelyn and Walter Haas, Jr. Fund
Purchase
82.155

AT A TIME WHEN ARTISTS WERE PRODUCING heroic works of monumental dimensions, Kenneth Price created ceramic sculpture of intimate size, presenting a serious alternative to the macho bravado of Abstract Expressionism. His series of vividly colored ovoid forms coated with industrial lacquers and enamels have been placed among the earliest examples of a new style that brought a meticulous flair, the so-called L.A. Look or "finish fetish," to California art.

Price spent his formative years in Los Angeles and received his undergraduate degree at the University of Southern California. In 1956 he and his friend Billy Al Bengston joined the Peter Voulkos circle at the Otis Art Institute. At Otis, Price produced a body of ceramics much different from the abstractly expressive works of his colleagues. His vases, plates, and cups were more simplified, their shapes and surface designs related more to formal concerns. Intent on learning glaze technology, Price went to the acclaimed ceramics engineering school of the State University of New York at Alfred for a graduate degree. His goal was to produce forms that looked as if they were made of color. Returning to Los Angeles in 1959, Price produced a series of glazed, cone-shaped mounds which soon evolved into orbs of bright color. In order to fuse color with form Price needed to mask the physical characteristics of the clay. He avoided the unpredictability of glazes and used instead layers of burnished automobile lacquer, often overpainted with acrylic paint. This free use of materials defied craft tradition and was an important influence on the development of polychrome metal sculpture.

At the beginning of the 1960s Price developed podlike forms with smooth shells of intensely expressive colors, their seamless surfaces interrupted by crevices containing vermiform projections. Negating the traditional footed-pot form, they rested precariously on one point, as if weightless, or lay heavily on their sides. Painted surface designs of contrasting color served as a compositional device to resist or to exaggerate the ovoid's low center of gravity. To control the way in which his sculptures were viewed, Price designed carefully crafted wooden bases and pedestals which established the object's relation to ground and set the viewer's focus directly on the apertures. The prescribed installation of these works often imposed a set distance, promoting a sense of detachment or aloofness between object and viewer. Price's concern for the overall impact of his work led to conceptually based environmental sculptures that culminated in the Happy's Curios Series of 1972–77.

The polished surface of *L. Red* of 1963 is a brilliant red-orange, overlaid with purple amoeboid shapes outlining a small central orifice which reveals a dark, mysteriously soft interior. Two tentacles protruding from the aperture, tentatively emerging beyond the surface, provide slight evidence of the interior form concealed by the hard outer shell. The enigmatic egg shape with its sprouting germinal extrusions provokes strong allusions to organic metaphors indicative of Price's long interest in zoology, yet it also provides the vehicle for a unique expression of formalist aesthetic theory. The egg shape—archetypal of birth, origin, and creativity—and the tendrils—symbolic of growth whether organic or conceptual—are defined abstractly. Intense color, which denies organic references, takes on a three-dimensional presence and becomes the dominant expressive component. Price's sculpture provides powerful evocative effects contained in a rich variety of formal concepts.   GGM

Larry Bell
AMERICAN, BORN 1939

Untitled
1969

metallic compounds (vaporized)
on glass, chrome binding
18⅛ × 18⅛ × 18⅛"
46.0 × 46.0 × 46.0 cm

Anonymous gift through the
American Art Foundation
78.184

THE INTENSITY OF ARTISTIC ACTIVITY that erupted in Los Angeles at the close of the fifties precipitated the emergence of a loosely bound contemporary art movement predicated in part on the divergent dualities of light/space coupled with technology and the automobile. Emanating from the Ferus Gallery, the audacious hub of avant-gardism, artists such as John Altoon, Billy Al Bengston, Larry Bell, Robert Irwin, Craig Kauffman, Kenneth Price, and Ed Ruscha began breaking out of the Abstract Expressionist stronghold and conjugating new statements which related, at least tangentially, to various facets of the southern California environment. In fact, the works produced by these artists took on a multiplicity of forms, from the spontaneous eroticism of John Altoon's pastels and paintings to the high-pitched vacuum-formed reliefs of Craig Kauffman; from the glossy emblems of Billy Al Bengston to the ethereal visions of Robert Irwin. Like the aftermath of centrifugal action, the interests of the artists moved outward in disparate directions.

Larry Bell was introduced to the Ferus Gallery by Robert Irwin, whom he had met while attending the Chouinard Art Institute from 1957 to 1959. After a brief foray into heavily pigmented expressionist canvases, Bell began to paint simple monochromatic shapes, at first contained within a rectangular format. By 1962, the support had been shaped to conform to the image and volume began to intrude into the two-dimensional plane. Adding glass—black, white, mirrored, translucent, transparent—to interject spatial complications, Bell expanded his work first into shallow relief and then, by 1963, into three-dimensional boxes.

Initially the cubes carried geometric overlays on each face. Using reflective surfaces of varying degrees of transparency, Bell toyed with the illusion and reality of depth and space, visually tossing reflections back to the viewer or allowing the eye to pass through to fractured and fragmented shapes and space. The resulting perpetual motion of multiple images compounded and negated the cloistered volume of the cube.

By 1965 Bell had expunged all imagery from the faces of the cube and settled on a purified format consisting of a chrome-edged cube faced with optically coated, seemingly transparent, glass. He developed a process utilizing a vacuum chamber in which metallic compounds, heated until they vaporized, were deposited on the glass surface, thus—depending upon the density of the deposited compounds—either interfering with or aiding in the conduction of light rays. One of the last examples from this period, Untitled, 1969, represents this phase in its most refined state. Perceived initially as an object whose volume is defined by reflective edgings, upon close perusal it becomes a veritable light box, reflecting, transmitting, modulating almost imperceptibly a range of effects that extends from imaging the color spectrum of the room to announcing its own iridescent surface. Dematerialized yet tangible, the box operates on a number of levels, moving light within its bounds, yet opening it into the ambient space. Real, yet illusory, the pristine surfaces of the cube are evidence not only of the complex technology that produced them, but also of the sensitivity and commitment of the artist who conceived them. KCH

Robert Irwin

AMERICAN, BORN 1928

Untitled

1968

acrylic lacquer on Plexiglas
53¼ diam. × 24½"
135.5 × 62.3 cm
T. B. Walker Foundation Fund
Purchase
70.5 A–F

THE ART OF ROBERT IRWIN has been one of considered, progressive reduction. Proceeding from traditional object-grounded painting through non-objective painting into the realm of non-object creation, where perception takes over as the image-making force, Irwin has explored and exploited the ambiguities of the sensory processes of sight.

A native of southern California, Robert Irwin received his formal art training at the Otis Art Institute and the Jepson Institute, both in Los Angeles, then gravitated toward the Ferus Gallery, the center of creative activity in southern California in the late fifties. Introduced to the freewheeling West Coast brand of Abstract Expressionism by the coterie of artists then connected with the Ferus—Billy Al Bengston, John Altoon, Craig Kauffman, and others—Irwin began producing dynamically charged gestural canvases that exhibited a heady sense of color and a predilection for centripetal orientation.

After experimenting with a group of small-format, hand-held paintings in 1959, Irwin moved toward purging his compositions of any superfluous or image-evoking gestures. By 1960 he had arrived at the straight line as a neutral element for developing spatial illusion. On a canvas nearly square, Irwin applied layer upon layer of pigment, building up a fluid field on which he laid evenly spaced horizontal lines drawn out nearly to the picture edge. To the viewer, the canvases appeared to throb, pulsing gently within a shallow ambience.

Building on this developing interest in spatial illusion, Irwin continued to experiment with painting formats and images. After painting a series of canvases in which only two lines merged with then emerged from a ground of almost similar hue, Irwin began utilizing structural configurations that reinforced illusory effects. In his dot paintings, executed between 1964 and 1966, he stretched each canvas over a convexly bowed framework, then painted the surface with meticulously spaced dots which, when viewed, coalesced into center-oriented nebulae which advanced from the painting's surface.

In 1966, Irwin fused his concern for the center with an increasing interest in visual perception and began work on a series of disks fabricated of aluminum and sprayed with concentric clouds of closely hued nacreous pigment. Each disk was mounted on a concealed bracket which projected it two feet from the wall. Four light sources, two above and two below, were beamed on the disk, casting a roseate shadow. Edges dissolved in light and shadow and the disk, wall, and surrounding area were unified in space.

Untitled, 1968, belongs to Irwin's subsequent series of disks in which the supports were formed of Plexiglas. Spray-painted with varying densities of opalescent pigment, the shell is bisected by a three-inch-wide horizontal band which appears to be transparent, but is in fact sprayed lightly with opaque gray in the center fading out to transparency at the edges. As in the earlier works, the disk is cantilevered from the all and lit by a quartet of low-intensity spotlights. The total work is perceived both materially and immaterially. Experientially, the disk, bathed in light and shadow, dissolves into an elegant, ambient glow, while the axial band takes on a palpable substantiality, belying its actual nature. Using light as his medium, the artist has drawn the viewer into the creative process, manipulating perception to achieve a transient experience of sheer beauty.   KCH

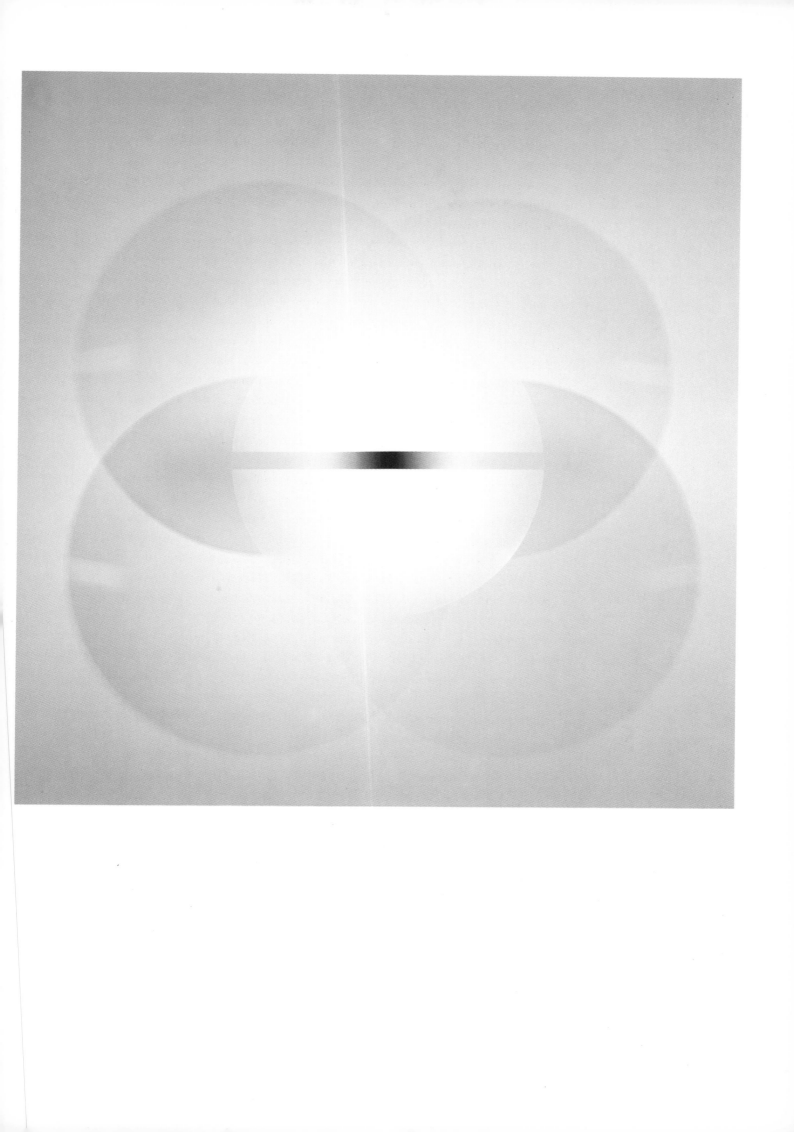

Frank Stella
AMERICAN, BORN 1936

Adelante
from the Running V Series
1964

metallic powder in polymer emulsion
on canvas
96¼ × 165½"
244.5 × 420.4 cm
T. B. Walker Foundation Fund
Purchase
68.53

[1]Lecture by Frank Stella delivered
at Pratt Institute, Brooklyn, N.Y.,
Winter 1959/60; for the text of this
lecture, see the appendix in Robert
Rosenblum, *Frank Stella*, Penguin
New Art, 1 (Baltimore: Penguin
Books, 1971), p. 57.

FRANK STELLA'S SHOCKINGLY SIMPLE, emotionally cool Black Paintings came into public view in 1959 in the Museum of Modern Art's *Sixteen Americans* exhibition. Composed of parallel black bands separated by thin strips of exposed canvas, these heraldic images challenged the accepted dominance of Abstract Expressionism. In contrast to the spontaneous gesture and spiritual fervor found in the works of such artists as Willem de Kooning, Jackson Pollock, and Hans Hofmann, these austere canvases with their repeated images and rational, premeditated working process announced the concerns of the sixties.

Born in Malden, Massachusetts, Stella pursued an interest in abstract art at Phillips Academy, Andover, and later at Princeton University where he studied with art historian William Seitz and painter Stephen Greene. Well versed in the tenets of Abstract Expressionism, Stella painted pictures inspired by Mark Rothko and Adolph Gottlieb, and during his last semester at Princeton he also became aware of the work of Jasper Johns and was greatly influenced by his aloof paintings of flags and targets.

After graduating from Princeton in 1958, Stella moved to New York City where he began his innovative series of Black Paintings. Attempting to eliminate illusionism and to assert a flat and even paint surface, he employed symmetry which, in his words, "forces illusionistic space out of painting at a constant rate by using a regulated pattern."[1] An arrangement of parallel bands of paint laid down with conventional housepainter's brushes emphasized an "allover-ness" and established an impenetrable surface which banished any hint of dimensionality from the work. The simplicity and unity of these compositions enabled the eye to comprehend the image immediately, a radical departure from the complex visual language of Abstract Expressionism.

In 1960, Stella became interested in the reflective surfaces achieved with commercial metallic paints and he began to use these at the same time that he developed the shaped canvas. In the Aluminum Series of 1960, portions of various sizes were removed from the edges or corners of the rectangular formats, by means of which Stella established a consonance between the shape of the canvas and the pattern inscribed on that field. In the Copper Series of 1960–61, the design again restated the contours of the field, but here references to a rectangular format were effectively obliterated by the cross-, T-, and U-shaped canvases Stella devised. In subsequent series Stella produced canvases of hexagons, polygons, and chevron-like shapes and also experimented with color in the Benjamin Moore Series, named after the flat alkyd wall paint which he used directly from the can.

In 1964, Stella returned to monochromatic metallic paint fields in the Running V Series. *Adelante*, which belongs to this series, illustrates the concerns pioneered by Stella: the shaped canvas and the parallel bands that echo its perimeters. Composed of horizontal bands interrupted by a symmetrically placed V shape, *Adelante* deviates from Stella's earlier works, which the eye could register in a single glance. Likened to multi-laned "pictorial highways" by art historian Robert Rosenblum, the softly glowing linear changes guide the eye in and out, creating a sense of dimensionality. Stella would further explore an increasing complexity in pattern, the manipulation of dimensionality, and the vibrant use of color in subsequent paintings based on the precedents established by works such as *Adelante*.   LLS

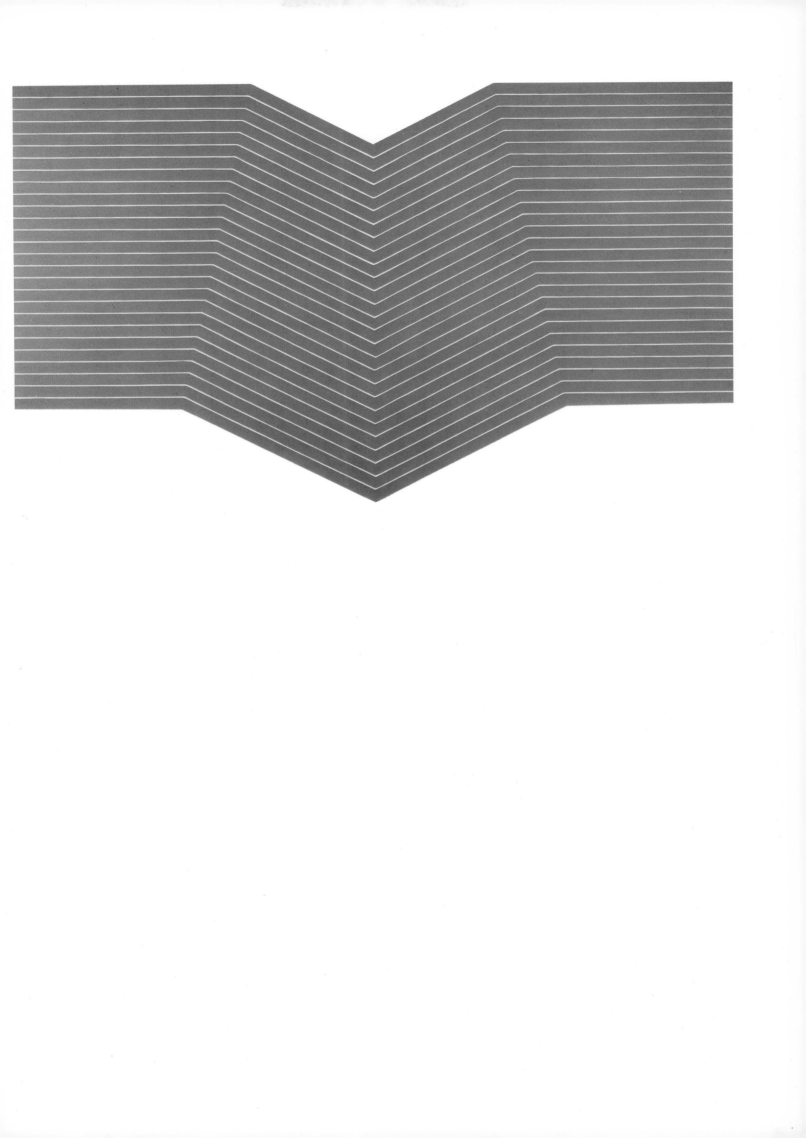

Frank Stella
AMERICAN, BORN 1936

Khurasan Gate (Variation) I
from the Protractor Series
1969

polymer and fluorescent polymer
on canvas
96¼ × 285½″
244.5 × 725.0 cm

Gift of Mr. and Mrs. Frederick R. Weisman
78.193

[1]William S. Rubin, *Frank Stella*, The Museum of Modern Art, New York, 1970, pp. 128–29.

DURING THE CLOSING YEARS OF THE SIXTIES, Frank Stella experimented with vivid fluorescent color and aspects of illusionism in the Protractor Series of 1967–69. Inspired by the ancient circular cities and gateways of the Middle East, Stella adopted the protractor shape as his basic design motif, creating rich decorative patterns on a monumental scale. *Khurasan Gate (Variation) I* of 1969 is part of this series, conceived by the artist to be executed in "thirty-one different canvas formats . . . to be realized in three different designs . . . 'interlaces,' 'rainbows,' and 'fans.'"[1]

At the time Stella was painting monochromatic metallic canvases, he was also exploring the effects of brilliant fluorescent Day-glo color in the Moroccan Series of 1964–65. Utilizing diagonal bands within a square format, he subtly created illusions of motion by alternating two contrasting colors, eventually achieving a kaleidoscope of multiple hues within a single canvas.

Prior to 1966, Stella's paintings were characterized by band-patterning which echoed the shape of the canvas. In the Irregular Polygon Series of 1966–67, he abandoned this theme and featured large, colored geometric forms intersected by and abutted to other geometric figures which did not necessarily relate to the framing edge. Elements of tension and dimensionality, which first began to appear in the Running V Series of three years earlier, were further developed while, simultaneously, a taut flat surface was asserted.

By 1967, Stella initiated paintings derived from the protractor shape and returned to wide bands of color, now in sweeping arcs which adhered to the semi-circular format. Instead of a regularized uniform repetition of bands, however, Stella constructed a complex interwoven arrangement of stripes. Overlapping and in turn overlapped, the bands of color set up a seemingly simple yet labyrinthine configuration. A sense of spatial depth was created as the bands appeared to advance and recede, but the illusionism was firmly held in check by the flat, even application of paint.

In *Khurasan Gate (Variation) I*, which belongs to the interlace format, a half circle intersects a reversed half circle. An audacious palette of highly saturated bands of tangerine orange, hot pink, radiant yellow, black, blue, and white and a complexity of pattern evoke an energy that is counterbalanced by the precise clarity and symmetrical realization of forms. Monumental in scale, the painting fills the viewer's immediate environment with immense arcs of joyous color. Influenced by the grand decorative painting of Henri Matisse and the chromatic harmonies of Robert Delaunay, Stella further extends this tradition within wholly abstract terms.   LLS

Ellsworth Kelly

AMERICAN, BORN 1923

Red White

1962

oil on canvas
80⅛ × 90″
203.5 × 228.6 cm
T. B. Walker Foundation Fund
Purchase
66.3

EXTRACTS FROM THE ARTIST'S ENVIRONMENT, past and present, abstracted and distilled into spare forms, are the basis of Ellsworth Kelly's painting and sculpture. Utilizing a drastically limited range of means—austere shapes, used alone or in simple combinations—and straightforward color juxtapositions—black/white, white/color, color/color, or color sequences—Kelly achieves a vast spectrum of nuance and evocative power.

Unlike the majority of American artists whose work came to the fore during the late fifties and early sixties, Kelly traced his roots not to a reaction against Abstract Expressionism, but to a combination of inner self-direction and an affirmation of European modern traditions. During the most formative years he worked not in New York, but in Paris. There, buoyed by the sheer size of the nineteenth-century paintings he saw in the Louvre, freed in line and approach by an introduction to automatic drawing, and touched by the work of Arp, which reaffirmed his pre-existent interest in collage and relief and suggested the use of the element of chance, Kelly developed an art based both on reality and abstraction.

An early preoccupation with the human figure quickly gave way to an almost obsessive concentration on the object. Taking quick glimpses of his surroundings, a window, the surface pattern of a wall, the shape of a roadside marker, he faithfully translated these into collage, relief, or painting, re-presenting the object by concentrating on its essential shape. The pieces of a drawing, cut or torn, then scattered at random on a surface, provided multiple formal suggestions, as did the structural arches of a bridge or shadows on a staircase.

By 1962, the year in which *Red White* was painted, Kelly had moved away from a complete dependence on observed sources for visual stimulation, yet the ties to the substantive world were still present. In *Red White*, a single monumental shape, painted a flat, intense red, is surrounded by a field of equally brilliant white. The form, at first understood clearly as abstract, begins to evoke connotations, tugging it toward reality. Not referentially specific, it nonetheless alludes to the tangible world.

Painted eight years after Kelly's return to New York, the work clearly displays the dualities which have continued to concern the artist; color versus non-color, dark versus light, curved versus angled, free versus restrained, all come into play, all carefully balanced. Unlike the paintings of the years just preceding, the shape is not truncated, but is contained completely within the picture surface. However, it is just barely contained, its angled points almost skimming the edges of the canvas. The extremity of the form, gently curved, obliquely angled, transmits pressure outward, pressing against the confines of the shape, rendering it volumetric. These counter pressures, which expand form and restrain picture periphery, create a tension which is accentuated by the slight asymmetry of the shape and its precarious positioning. Spatulate in configuration, it appears initially to be stable, but the longer one looks, the more vulnerable it becomes as it rests perilously on a single tip, ready to roll over in search of secure grounding. Yet all these tensions are held in check by the density and presence of the color which provides stability and support.   KCH

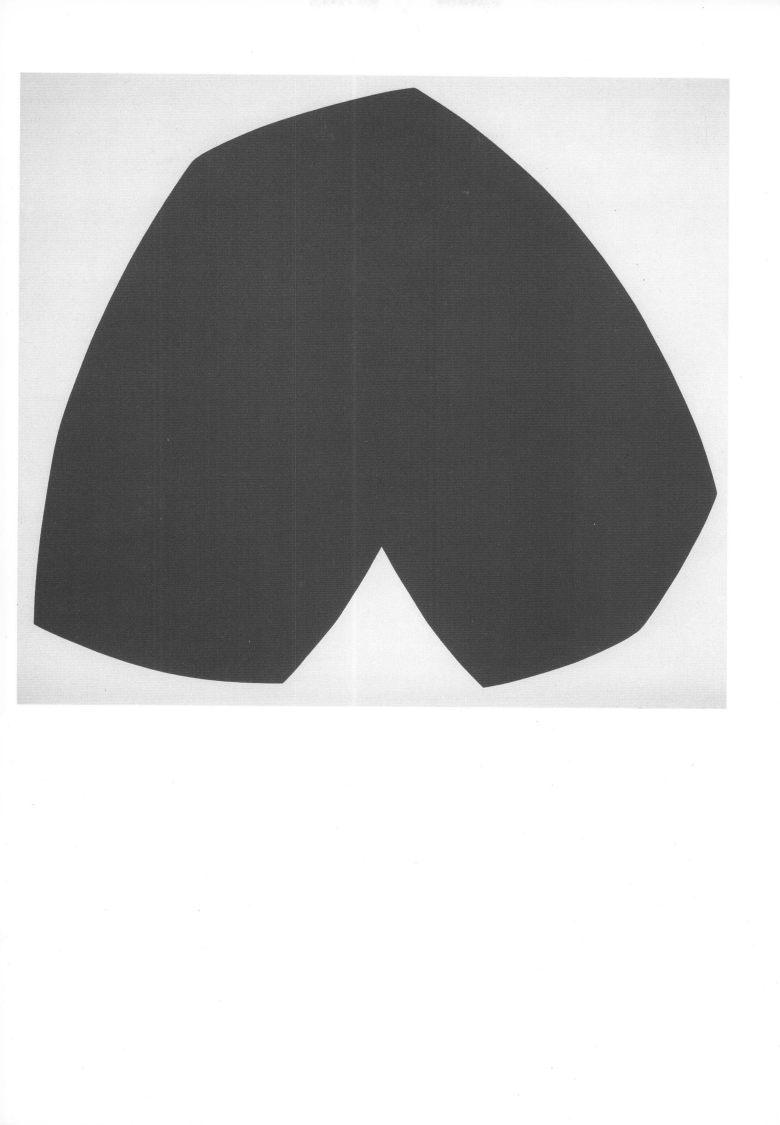

Robert Mangold

AMERICAN, BORN 1935

Red X within X

1980

acrylic and graphite on canvas
113½ × 113½"
288.3 × 288.3 cm

T. B. Walker Foundation Fund
Purchase
83.149 A–D

PROBING THE ESSENTIAL RELATIONSHIPS between color and form, surface pattern and framing edge, symmetry and distortion, Robert Mangold creates paintings of complexity and subtle nuance through the manipulation of simple geometric forms. Associated with the Minimalist movement that emerged in the early sixties, Mangold, like artists Donald Judd and Sol LeWitt, is concerned with purity of materials, uniformity of surface, and elimination of extraneous elements. Purged of illusionism or emotionalism, which might detract from the ability of the work to exist in its own right, free from associations or references, the paintings of Mangold represent a unified whole that can be comprehended immediately.

Born in 1935 in upstate New York, Mangold studied at the Cleveland Institute of Art and received a Master of Fine Arts degree from Yale University in 1963. Before graduating from Yale, he sought a fresh alternative to the well-worn tenets of Abstract Expressionism. Formative influences during this time included Jasper Johns's identification of the painting as an "object" and the flat repetitive bands found in the paintings of Frank Stella.

Mangold's early work was characterized by a cool, formal approach and an equal emphasis on color, line, and shape. Featuring large notched and shaped panels of Masonite in mono-tonal colors, he explored the interaction between the flat surface area and the external edges. Using standard commercial sheets of Masonite, which he either left intact or carefully shaped, the artist combined multiple panels into a single work—exploiting the resulting junction lines as compositional elements.

Aspects of subtle distortion figured prominently in both Mangold's early work and his subsequent paintings. By the juxtaposition of regular and irregular forms an elegant tension is created. Initially perceived as symmetrical, the shapes gradually assert their geometric irregularities. Through this device, Mangold establishes a multitude of dynamic relationships between surface images and grounds of slightly contorted circles, squares, trapezoids, and polygons.

The painting *Red X within X*, of 1980, is a large X-shaped canvas composed of sections with a drawn image situated asymmetrically on the surface. A careful balance is realized between the cropped resonating red canvas and the perfect black linear cross. Highly sensitive to the relationship of the internal surface and the framing edge, Mangold creates a complex interaction on a flat ground among the drawn black lines, the sectional edges, and the perimeter shape. Challenging the viewer's perceptions, Mangold presents a richly provocative arrangement of fundamental forms.   LLS

William T. Wiley

AMERICAN, BORN 1937

Ship's Log

1969

cotton webbing, latex rubber, salt
licks, leather, plastic, wood, canvas,
lead wire, nautical and assorted
hardware, and ink and watercolor on
paper
82 × 78 × 54″
208.3 × 198.1 × 137.2 cm

William L. Gerstle Collection
William L. Gerstle Fund Purchase
70.37 A–L

IDIOSYNCRATIC AND INTROSPECTIVE, sometimes humorous, always experimental, the work of William T. Wiley epitomizes much of the art produced in the San Francisco Bay Area during the decade spanning 1965 to 1975. Having grown up in the Pacific Northwest, Wiley came to San Francisco in 1956 and studied at the California School of Fine Arts (now the San Francisco Art Institute) where he learned not only from teachers, but from fellow students as well. The school, profoundly affected by the presence of Clyfford Still in the forties, had experienced a golden age of Abstract Expressionism, and the expressive attitude, later reinterpreted with the addition of figurative elements, was still prevalent when Wiley arrived. He quickly developed a unique style based on emotional abstraction but expanded by the addition of highly individual emblems, frequently repeated, which became a veritable lexicon.

By 1965, three years after Wiley received his Master of Fine Arts, the gestural aspects in his work receded and an attitude drawn from the Dada-Surrealist tradition took hold, which rapidly assumed importance. The personal symbols—pyramids, palettes, flags, triangles, infinity signs—appeared and flourished, occurring more and more frequently, singly or in combination, sometimes twisted, sometimes pierced, always recognizable. Favorite themes and formats were established, reworked and restated in a variety of mediums—painting, sculpture, watercolor, drawing, print, and film.

Ship's Log, executed in 1969, is an eclectic assortment of disparate elements assembled under a nautical theme, accompanied by an autobiographical journal which—using the metaphor of navigation—traces anecdotally and philosophically the process of making the work. The experimental nature of the artist's creative process is transmitted by the seemingly casual appearance of the piece—webbing loosely tied or allowed to wander across the floor, latex draped over crossbar—and is underscored by the attendant narrative which relates the past histories of many of the elements and images and testifies to the trials and errors that took place during creation. Some of the symbols used are familiar—the triangle, the infinity sign, the rectangular flag displaying an internal circle—all had been employed by the artist in earlier works. Additional objects, the floats and salt licks, for instance, had been collected for inclusion in other works and were added only as the piece evolved.

Wiley's use of the written word and visual/literary wordplays enters into this piece as well. The log, referred to in the title, reappears in the form of a triangle, the shape of a ship's "log," a device traditionally used to determine the speed of a ship; in the frontispiece illustration for the book, a watercolor rendering of a sailboat, its hull consisting of a tree trunk or "log"; and in the book itself, a "logbook" or "log." Physically placed in front of the sculpture, the logbook becomes an integral part of the sculptural totality; when read by the viewer, it serves to expand the scope of the piece well beyond the merely visual. KCH

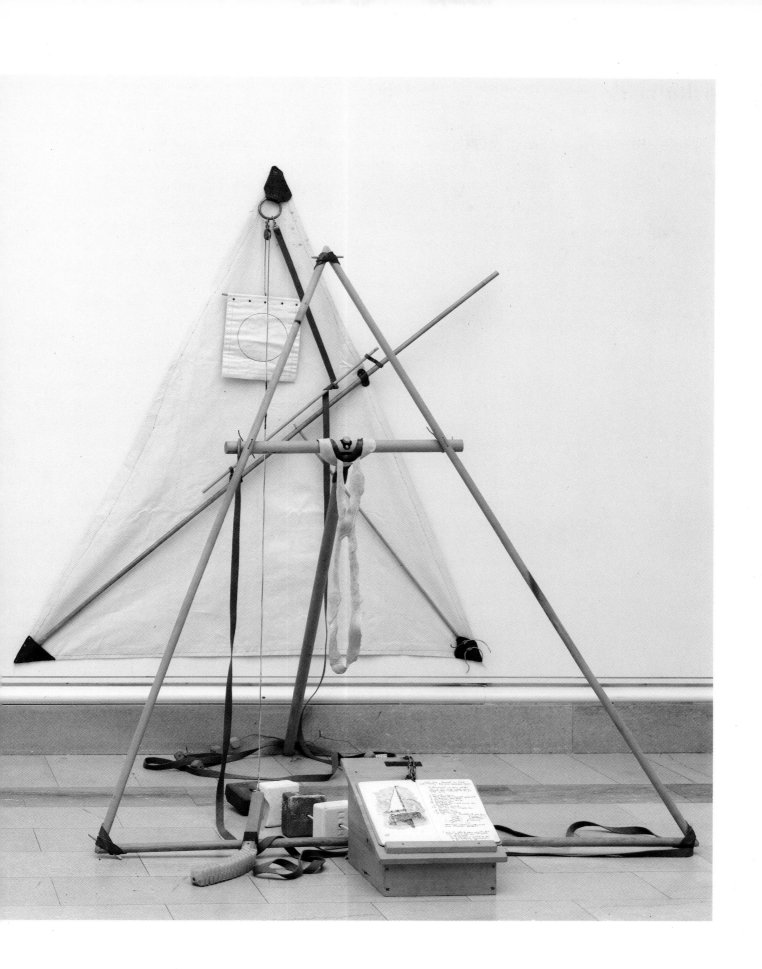

Richard Shaw

AMERICAN, BORN 1941

Melodious Double Stops

1980

porcelain with decal overglaze
38¾ × 12 × 14″
98.4 × 30.5 × 35.6 cm

Purchased with matching funds from the National Endowment for the Arts and Frank O. Hamilton, Byron Meyer, and Mrs. Peter Schlesinger
80.168

REPLICATING PRECISELY IN CERAMIC FORM the castoffs, debris, and souvenirs of every-day life, Richard Shaw transforms these elements through whimsical juxtaposition into humorous yet elegant still lifes and figures. His subject matter is based on a vocabulary of images drawn from the world of personal fantasy and myth, which operates in a foggy area between the surreal and the banal.

Shaw attributes his love of illusion and fantasy to his family background and to a childhood spent growing up in close proximity to Hollywood and the Walt Disney Studios. Both parents were artists, his father a cartoonist for Disney in 1941 when Shaw was born. After studying painting in junior college where he also experimented with traditional ceramics, Shaw made his first low-fire clay sculpture as a student at the San Francisco Art Institute. There he studied with Ron Nagle and Jim Melchert who at that time were using white earthenware in a delicate Oriental manner, a deviation from the funky earthenware objects of Robert Arneson and an alternative to the big, macho expressionist, stoneware pieces of Peter Voulkos and John Mason. At the University of California at Davis, where Shaw studied for his M.F.A. from 1966 to 1968 with Robert Arneson, a transition from coarse earthenware to low-fire whiteware had taken place. Inspired by an anti-art attitude brought about by the influence of Pop Art, ceramicists cultivated the slick look of dime-store knickknack pottery for which they needed the clear colors obtainable with low-fire ware. Shaw's work was of a hybrid genre—part sculpture, part painting—mysterious furniture and animal shapes painted with illusionistic decoration, such as a cruise ship sinking into an overstuffed sofa. This eclectic attitude and surreal juxtaposition of images were indebted to the neo-Dada assemblage tradition advanced by such California artists as George Herms and Bruce Conner.

In 1971, during an eighteen-month-long collaboration with Robert Hudson, Shaw developed a molding technique for porcelain which enabled him to duplicate surfaces and textures of fish, birds, leaves, and twigs with uncanny exactitude without sacrificing the sense that the forms were made of clay. These were combined with wheel-thrown and hand-formed elements resulting in teapots and containers resembling birds, ducks, and fish which were then painted and sprayed with eye-fooling imagery. Seeking the quiet feeling inspired by the nineteenth-century trompe l'oeil still lifes of William Harnett and John Peto, Shaw exploited the imitative abilities of porcelain and, beginning in 1974, devised a photo-silkscreen transferring method to duplicate labels, lettering, and patterning on ceramic surfaces.

Since 1978 Shaw has been concerned with figurative sculpture created by assembling porcelain casts of favorite studio paraphernalia. Found objects of a private and deliberately frivolous nature, all looking more real than real, are duplicated in a tour de force realism carried to a paradoxical dimension. In *Melodious Double Stops*, common objects are pieced together in a puzzle of implied meanings. An anthropomorphic still life with coffee-can belly, composition-book pelvis, pencil-stub fingers, this jaunty figure's frozen-action stance of anticipated animation relates to contemporary dance, perhaps as the personification of a halting musical rhythm.   GGM

Wayne Thiebaud

AMERICAN, BORN 1920

Display Cakes
1963

oil on canvas
28 × 38″
71.0 × 96.5 cm

Mrs. Manfred Bransten
Special Fund Purchase
73.52

REALISM, THE STRAIGHTFORWARD DEPICTION of actual objects and events, holds a singularly important, though universally underrated, position in the history of twentieth-century American art. In an era in which the abstracted forms of early Modernism and the emotionally charged gestures of the Abstract Expressionists appear to constitute the significant achievements of American artists, the solid contributions of such diverse realists as Edward Hopper and Philip Pearlstein, Alice Neel and Georgia O'Keeffe, Richard Diebenkorn and Wayne Thiebaud are only now being properly recognized and beginning to assert their importance and place in modern art.

For Wayne Thiebaud, "Reality is just a method of interpreting our perceptions."[1] The objects he has depicted throughout his career—creamy confections, human figures, urban and rural landscapes—are but extended vehicles for formal interpretation. He approaches each subject as an artistic challenge, an intellectual and perceptual problem to be grappled with and solved: how to convey the tactile quality of frosting; how to simulate the solidity of the human body. Isolating and scrutinizing, dissecting and distilling, he manipulates his seemingly simple subjects, extracting and exposing their formal essence. The use of primary compositional devices—frontal perspectives, symmetrical structure, serial placement—joins an ongoing fascination with the properties of light and the nature of color.

Wayne Thiebaud's early background was not in the area of painting and drawing but in the field of cartooning and commercial art. Drawn to the reductive nature of caricature and the formal aspects of graphic design, Thiebaud expanded these practical endeavors with the study of art history. Always utilizing objects as subject, his first ventures into painting, occurring in the late forties, contained Cubist elements combined with traces of the tortured romanticism of Los Angeles artist Rico Lebrun. The explosive brushwork of the Abstract Expressionists, especially Willem de Kooning, soon appeared in Thiebaud's work. With thick smears of pigment, he subjugated the underlying objective base. Near the end of the fifties, however, he reversed the relative importance of these two approaches, revived the object as his primary concern, and tamed his brushwork, using it to enhance his subjects rather than overwhelm them. By 1961 foodstuffs began to dominate his canvases. Rows of pie slices, platoons of suckers, single ice-cream cones—edible excerpts from a society consumed with consumption —were presented, employed in part for their social content, but, most importantly, for their formal possibilities.

In *Display Cakes*, 1963, Thiebaud's preoccupation with composition, involvement in the character of strong, theatrical light, and use of splintered color move to the fore. Three cakes, each iced with warmly hued pigment, are positioned symmetrically, their drumming, tripartite rhythm echoed by coolly colored attendant shadows. The underlying circular configurations, geometrically regular, are stated and restated, emphasis being achieved not only through this carefully orchestrated repetition, but also through accented edges in which attenuated strips of contrasting or complementary colors are juxtaposed or overlapped. The resulting visual bounce energizes the borders, enlivening and isolating the objects and moving them out toward the viewer. Although the focus is on the pastries, their variations, rather than the similarities, become clearly visible. KCH

1. Quoted in Henry Hopkins, *Fifty West Coast Artists: A Critical Selection of Painters and Sculptors Working in California* (San Francisco: Chronicle Books, 1981), p. 68.

226

Roy De Forest

AMERICAN, BORN 1930

Country Dog Gentlemen

1972

polymer on canvas
66¾ × 97″
169.6 × 246.4 cm

Gift of the Hamilton-Wells Collection
73.32

THE DEVELOPMENT OF PERSONAL ICONOLOGIES marked the work of several artists who matured in the Bay Area at the beginning of the sixties. Unique sets of highly individual symbols and motifs were invented by such artists as Robert Arneson, Roy De Forest, Robert Hudson, and William T. Wiley, who incorporated them into their work, sometimes as main subject, sometimes as visual vehicles for content. Roy De Forest's vocabulary of horses, ships, balloon-headed human figures, pointing hands, and dogs, dogs, and more dogs, populates his fantasy kingdom. Narrative and whimsical, his work invites the viewer to participate, to meander down stippled paths or ford patterned streams.

De Forest, born in Nebraska in 1930, spent his early years in central Washington where he attended two years of junior college before enrolling in San Francisco's California School of Fine Arts (now the San Francisco Art Institute) in 1950. Studying with such teachers as Elmer Bischoff, Edward Corbett, David Park, and Hassel Smith gave him a strong foundation not only in Abstract Expressionism, but in stylistic self-determination. Planning for a career in teaching, De Forest transferred to San Francisco State College where he received a bachelor of arts and in 1958, after a two-year stint in the military, a master's degree.

De Forest's work immediately following graduation utilized all-over patterning. Multiple small-scaled patches—some flatly colored, others speckled with dots or irregularly striped—were clustered tightly, overlaid with convoluted trails and seemingly random daubs of paint. But by the turn of the decade, the patches became larger, more defined, and varied in detailing. Soon specific images began to appear: the outstretched arm, the silhouetted human figure, profiles of horses and dogs, ships belching great schematized clouds of smoke. The paintings and painted wood constructions that De Forest was creating at the same time took on storytelling qualities, spinning tales of a magical world. Colorful and spontaneous, they resembled whimsically annotated maps.

After 1967 De Forest's work featured large flattened images which moved up to the picture plane. Establishing a foreground, they relegated the patterned "landscape" to a position of backdrop. This simply defined foreground/background relationship is employed in *Country Dog Gentlemen*. Bisected symmetrically and frontally oriented, the gaily colored, tropically foliaged composition is focused, the majority of activity occurring in the background, but even then held in place. Dogs viewed head-on menacingly guard the fantasy land, their eyes "as big as saucers," reminiscent of Hans Christian Andersen's fairy tale "The Tinder Box." Behind these sentries other canine species appear in three-quarter pose or profile, dotted sight lines streaming from their eyes, or organically rendered, empty word balloons emerging from their mouths. Sections of the stage scene are torn away, to reveal yet another layer of De Forest's "miniature cosmos."   KCH

228

Manuel Neri

AMERICAN, BORN 1930

Mary and Julia

1980

plaster with pigment
52 × 44 × 34½″
132.1 × 111.8 × 87.6 cm

Gift of Agnes Cowles Bourne
79.322.A–B

[1]Quoted in interview with Jan Butterfield, "Ancient Auras—Expressionist Angst: Sculpture by Manuel Neri," *Images and Issues* (Spring 1981), p. 43.

FOR MANUEL NERI THE HUMAN FORM is a vehicle for presenting his ideas about the source of the spiritual within mankind—the God-spirit. "I have always been intrigued with the spirit that the figure conveys. Not necessarily in Christian terms, but in relation, for example, to the Greek heroes with their dirty feet and curious morals —they were heroes just the same. It is this God-spirit that I think is the real God for us. It is this thing inside of us that I want to talk about in the figure."[1] Roughly hewn, partially painted, fragmented and crumbling, Neri's figurative sculptures evoke ancient Greek and Egyptian art, yet look disturbingly contemporary. The jarring, dissonant colors splashed, flung, and scratched into these nearly life-size figures upset their classical equilibrium and pull them into the present.

Neri's career has traversed and encompassed many facets in the recent development of Bay Area art. He attended classes at the California School of Fine Arts (now the San Francisco Art Institute) in 1949, at the time of Clyfford Still's influence on Bay Area Abstract Expressionism. With fellow student Peter Voulkos at the California College of Arts and Crafts, and at the Archie Bray Foundation summer session, Neri was involved in the initial stage of the ceramics revolution. At the San Francisco Art Institute from 1957 to 1959 he studied with Elmer Bischoff at the inception of the Bay Area figurative movement. He also participated in the free-flow exchange of ideas among jazz musicians, poets, filmmakers, and artists which took place in the cafés of North Beach and at The Six gallery, where he showed his work with Bruce Conner, Jay DeFeo, Wally Hedrick, and Joan Brown.

Neri began as a ceramicist and has worked with plaster, fiberglass, bronze, and marble; but plaster has been his predominant material for expressing a spontaneous gestural form of Action Sculpture. Working rapidly from the live model, he builds up the figure with handfuls of wet plaster over steel armatures padded with Styrofoam. After the plaster dries, he chops, carves, saws, and files the form, juxtaposing areas of rough texture with hand-smoothed ones. In his early work, Neri used color to break up the form; later, color accentuated the contours of the shape, heightening its impact.

A tour of Europe in 1961 precipitated a reworking of former concepts, while later trips to Mexico and South America awakened Neri to the spiritual quality in primitive art and its link to his own work. Subsequently, the figures were torn into, superfluous limbs whacked off, paint and plaster added and subtracted in a process of constant refinement and continuing change. This dialogue has absorbed Neri ever since. Left in a state of perpetual incompleteness, his works reflect a sense of abandonment and decay. Ravaged, fragmented body parts are often held together with baling wire, arms end in pawlike stubs, feet crumble. Rent to the core, they project a tough, mysterious inner beauty.

Mary and Julia represents two aspects of the same personality, that of Mary Julia Klimenko, a poet who was Neri's model for nearly nine years. Seated side by side, left arms crooked and resting on invisible supports, legs splayed, they are awkwardly erect, ungainly figures. Plaster skins are spectral white, one arm smeared with voltaic blue pigment. The aura projected by these enigmatic figures is ambiguous, fraught with a sense of anxiety and vulnerability, yet charged with fragile pride and tragic dignity. Abandoned at the very moment when the difference between creation and destruction is indiscernible, they are at one with man's historic past and ultimate future. GGM

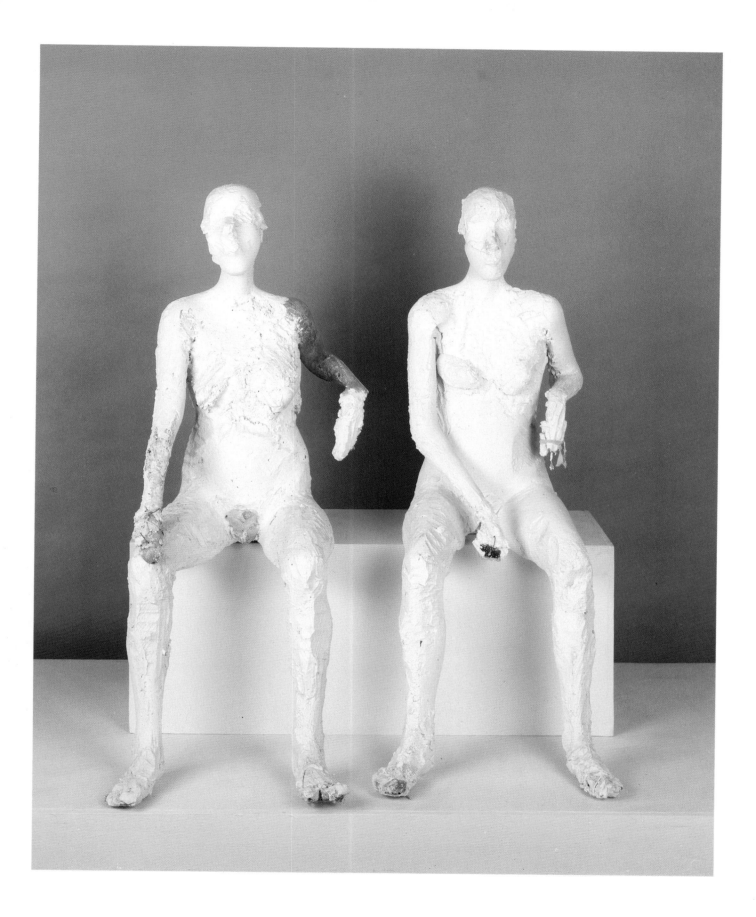

Robert Hudson

AMERICAN, BORN 1938

Out of the Blue

1980–81

acrylic on canvas with wooden chair,
plastic tree, wood, and steel tubing
96⅜ × 180⅞ × 27¾"
244.8 × 459.4 × 70.5 cm

Purchased with the aid of the
Byron Meyer Fund
81.57 A–D

THE DISTANCE SEPARATING San Francisco from New York is, when one talks about art, more than just geographical. Far removed from the intensely urban, highly pressured atmosphere of the eastern metropolis, the Bay Region, with its natural beauty and multitude of secluded living areas coupled with a convenient but not mandatory urban environment, has provided an environment favorable to the development of individual artistic expression. The resulting visual statements have been marked by a quirky sort of particularism which may take a variety of forms: a unique vocabulary of personal symbols, a fresh approach to materials, or a sense of freedom to pursue a multiplicity of mediums.

For Robert Hudson, this unrestrained climate has nurtured a desire to pursue personal concerns. Drawing from a reservoir of images, memories, ideas, and stories, he has developed a unique and ever-expanding language which he puts to use in a multitude of mediums. He continually adds new elements to this vocabulary as he works, reutilizing familiar favorites, reworking them, enhancing them, discovering new aspects of their characters.

Like several artists whose work came to public attention in San Francisco in the early sixties, Robert Hudson was raised in central Washington. At the age of twenty, he left for San Francisco where he entered the California School of Fine Arts (now the San Francisco Art Institute). Though still being taught at the school, Abstract Expressionism in its most vital form had faded, having been replaced in part by two idioms: a free-form figuration, and the aggregation of found objects, that is, assemblage.

Confronted by these possibilities, Hudson, like many of his peers, assimilated the key elements and commenced to develop audacious alternatives. His work of the sixties featured welded steel sculpture, polychromed with raucously colored automotive enamels and lacquers. Juxtaposing geometric configurations and organic biomorphs, he played with space: perspectively rendered geometric figures or windows with deep vistas beyond were drawn on flat surfaces, contradicting the two-dimensionality of the surface. Contrarily, adjoining angled planes were painted to read as one plane.

After a short period of producing restrained monochromatic sculpture completely purged of painterly passages, Hudson spent eighteen months, during 1971–73, with ceramicist Richard Shaw, creating small-scaled porcelain vessels which integrated snatches of nature—birds and horns, twigs and rocks—with brushy surfaces, subdued coloration and spatial play. In late 1973, Hudson turned to two-dimensional pictorial concerns and began applying vibrantly hued acrylic to grid-stitched cotton batting. A return to sculpture found illusory play complicated by the addition of real objects which were manipulated and colored to produce high-keyed assemblages.

The painting and construction *Out of the Blue* of 1980–81 displays numerous references to earlier phases of Hudson's work, yet emerges as a fresh statement. The canvas surface is covered with geometrically divided fields painted with flat, cartoon-like colors or filled with brightly tinted mists. Planes are parallel, tilted, stacked, or mitered, setting up contrapuntal spatial play. The sections of the canvas are bordered and separated by three vertical strips: the left one continuing the picture plane and horizontal bifurcation; the middle one, dripped and marbleized, acting as a narrow window to the vaporous atmosphere beyond, and the right strip, superficially echoing its neighbor to the left, yet achieving the opposite effect by extending out, physically, into the third dimension. An artificial tree and a scorched chair, affixed or related to the protruding strip, emphasize the sculptural nature of the right section and further serve to play off its tangibility against the illusory atmospheric depths of the remainder of the canvas. KCH

232

Robert Arneson

AMERICAN, BORN 1930

California Artist

1982

stoneware with glazes
68¼ × 27½ × 20¼"
173.4 × 69.9 × 51.5 cm

Gift of the Modern Art Council
82.108 A–B

DURING THE 1960S at the University of California, Davis, a group of maverick artist-teachers—including Robert Arneson, William T. Wiley, and Roy De Forest—and their students formulated an aesthetic complete with its own lexicon of private jokes, eccentric self-parodies, and satires of mainstream art. This regional expression, informed by the neo-Dada attitudes of the Beat generation and the banal subject matter of Pop Art, found its most effective voice in the highly personalized ceramic sculpture which evolved under the leadership of Robert Arneson. A widely influential educator, Arneson taught ceramics as art, dealing primarily with ideas and content rather than with the form and process of craft tradition.

Arneson's involvement in the ceramics revolution began in the summer of 1961. While manning an art-in-action booth at the California State Fair, he modeled a clay bottle cap and placed it atop a precisely formed, thin-necked bottle which he marked "No Return." This defiantly closed bottle, immediately transformed from functional container to aesthetic object, broke with ceramic convention and, for Arneson, transformed craft into art. Thus began Arneson's long-term concern with ceramics in which he has serially explored a wide range of themes.

Preoccupied with the concept of ideas manifested in concrete form, Arneson has presented the brick as the basic foundation of Western civilization, and plumbing fixtures as allusions to ceramic tradition without an art heritage. His anthropomorphized objects with raunchy sexual overtones created a major furor in the ceramics world, shocking the public and dismaying the critics.

During the mid-1960s Arneson's works drew upon Pop Art subject matter, which he presented with a wry sense of humor. But unlike the clean, impersonal character of Pop objects, Arneson's forms were rough and gestural, with Dadaesque overtones. Surprising juxtapositions of commonplace things evoked a sense of the ominous and surreal—eyes peering back from binoculars, fingers popping out of a toaster—at once macabre and amusing. Titles were often wordplays which transformed the object into a visual pun, such as *Call Girl*, 1967, an overtly sexual telephone. The pun has remained at the core of Arneson's expression of comic themes, satires of art movements, and commentaries on recent developments in art and politics.

At the end of the sixties, Arneson's work became more sculptural and more autobiographic, leading to a series of monumental self-portraits. Beginning with *Smorgy Bob*, 1971, a buffet tableau in illusionary perspective with Arneson as head chef, he has reinterpreted his image in myriad posturings in a manner not unlike conceptual body art. Although often preposterous caricatures, the portraits also deal with formal problems of painting and sculpture which demonstrate Arneson's mastery of complex glazing techniques and clay manipulation.

California Artist is a witty and biting self-portrait, the direct response to an attack by a New York art critic who cited the "impoverished sensibility of the provincial cultural life of California" and depicted Arneson's work as the "mark of a mind that is too easily pleased with his own jokes."[1] Thus, the artist's sunglasses frame gaping holes, where the eyes should be, through which one views the glazed blue lining of a hollow head, his arms are casually crossed in a gesture of defiant anti-intellectualism. The marijuana-embellished pedestal is littered with beer bottles and cigarette butts, epitomizing and mocking the decadent California life style. With characteristic wit, Arneson confronts the stereotype and turns it into an absurdity.   GGM

[1] Hilton Kramer, "Ceramic Sculpture and the Taste of California," *New York Times*, December 20, 1981.

234

Documentation for Colorplates

The paintings and sculptures highlighted by color reproductions in this catalogue range from the earliest years of the twentieth century to the most recent and represent some of the foremost artists of the modern world. As such they reflect the strengths, breadth, and depth of the permanent collection of the San Francisco Museum of Modern Art. This second section of the catalogue, arranged in the same sequence as the colorplates, offers more extensive documentation of these major works than is found in the checklist, where they are also listed.

In addition to the data concerning artist, title, medium, dimensions, and donor, these entries provide information on the history of the work. The presence of an inscription by the artist on either the front or back of a work is indicated, with location and content.

All previous owners, to the extent that they are known, are listed, the most recent preceding the earlier. The artist is listed as the earliest owner only in those cases where ownership of the work can be traced back to the artist without gaps.

Selected key exhibitions in which the work has been included are listed in chronological order, with notations regarding catalogue entries, references, and illustrations. Names of exhibiting institutions have been cited as they were at the time of exhibition or catalogue publication; if a present-day name differs substantially, the current name is given as well. In the citation of catalogue numbers and reference or illustration pages, if that information is not cited, it may be assumed by the reader that the catalogue was unnumbered and/or the publication unpaginated.

Substantive mentions, discussions, and illustrations that have appeared in newspapers, periodicals, general books, monographs, and catalogues raisonnés are also given in chronological order, with as complete information about each source as possible.

Where recent research, on the part of the Museum's staff or other scholars in the field, has uncovered new information regarding the genesis of a work, or proposes titles, dates, affinities, or interpretations, these are included under Remarks.

HENRI MATISSE
French, 1869–1954

The Girl with Green Eyes
(La Fille aux yeux verts), 1908
oil on canvas
26 × 20″
66.0 × 50.8 cm

Bequest of Harriet Lane Levy
50.6086

Inscribed
recto, lower right: *Henri-Matisse*

Provenance
Harriet Lane Levy, 1908
Galerie Bernheim-Jeune, Paris, 1908
Artist

Exhibitions
Galerie Bernheim-Jeune, Paris. *Henri Matisse*, February 14–March 5, 1910, cat. no. 60.
Grafton Galleries, London. *Manet and the Post-Impressionists*, November 8, 1910–January 15, 1911, cat. no. 111.
The Museum of Modern Art, New York. *Henri-Matisse*, November 3–December 6, 1931, cat. no. 19; ref. p. 18, ill. pl. 19.
California Palace of the Legion of Honor, San Francisco. *Exhibition of French Painting: From the Fifteenth Century to the Present Day*, June 8–July 8, 1934, cat. no. 203; ill. pl. 203.
San Francisco Museum of Art. *Henri-Matisse*, January 11–February 24, 1936, cat. no. 13; ill.
Colorado Springs Fine Arts Center, Colorado. *French Modern Paintings, Drawings and Prints*, January 2–31, 1942. Works from the Harriet Lane Levy Collection remained on loan to the Colorado Springs Fine Arts Center from December 15, 1941, to March 19, 1946.
California Palace of the Legion of Honor, San Francisco. *France—Comes to You*, November 5–21, 1948, cat.
The Museum of Modern Art, New York. *Henri Matisse*, November 13, 1951–January 13, 1952, cat. no. 22; ill. p. 18. Circulated to: The Cleveland Museum of Art, February 5–March 16, 1952; The Art Institute of Chicago, April 1–May 4, 1952; San Francisco Museum of Art, May 22–July 6, 1952; Los Angeles Municipal Art Department, July 24–August 17, 1952, cat. no. 13; ill. p. 14.
Fort Worth Art Center, Texas. *Inaugural Exhibition*, October 8–31, 1954, cat. no. 63; ill.
The Arts Club of Chicago. *Les Fauves*, January 10–February 15, 1956, cat. no. 18.
Musée National d'Art Moderne, Paris. *Henri Matisse: Exposition Rétrospective*, July 28–November 18, 1956, cat. no. 27; ill. pl. XI.
The Nelson Gallery and Atkins Museum (now The Nelson–Atkins Museum of Art), Kansas City, Missouri. *The Logic of Modern Art: An Exhibition Tracing the Evolution of Modern Painting from Cézanne to 1960*, January 19–February 26, 1961, cat. no. 3; ref. p. 6, ill. p. 14.
UCLA Art Galleries, University of California, Los Angeles. *Henri Matisse*, January 5–February 27, 1966, cat. no. 27; ref. p. 15, color ill. p. 56. Circulated to: The Art Institute of Chicago, March 11–April 24, 1966; Museum of Fine Arts, Boston, May 11–June 26, 1966.
The Solomon R. Guggenheim Museum, New York. *Gauguin and the Decorative Style*, June 23–October 23, 1966, cat.
Art Gallery of New South Wales, Sydney, Australia. *Modern Masters: Manet to Matisse*, April 10–May 11, 1975, cat. no. 66; ref. p. 90, ill. p. 91. Exhibition organized under the auspices of the International Council of the Museum of Modern Art, New York, circulated to: National Gallery of Victoria, Melbourne, May 28–June 22, 1975; The Museum of Modern Art, New York, August 4–September 1, 1975.
The National Museum of Modern Art, Tokyo. *Matisse*, March 20–May 17, 1981, cat. no. 25; ref. pp. 175, 176, color ill. p. 51. Circulated to: The National Museum of Modern Art, Kyoto, May 26–July 19, 1981.
Center for the Fine Arts, Miami. *In Quest of Excellence*, January 14–April 22, 1984, cat. no. 132; ref. p. 203, color ill. p. 198.
Kimbell Art Museum, Fort Worth, Texas. *Henri Matisse: Sculptor/Painter*, May 26–September 2, 1984, cat. no. 14; ref. pp. 68–69, color ill. p. 23.

Literature
P. G. Konody. In *Observer* (London), November 13, 1910.
"By Men Who Think the Impressionists too Naturalistic: The Manet and the Post-Impressionists Exhibition, at the Grafton Galleries." *Illustrated London News*, November 26, 1910, ill.
Roger Fry. In *Fortnightly Review*, May 1, 1911.
Alfred H. Barr, Jr. *Matisse: His Art and His Public*. New York: The Museum of Modern Art, 1951, ref. pp. 105, 111, 128, 130, 263, 559, ill. p. 352.
Raymond Escholier. *Matisse: A Portrait of the Artist and the Man*. Translated by Geraldine and H. M. Colvile. New York: Frederick A. Praeger, 1960, ill. pl. 11.
Ian Dunlop. *The Shock of the New: Seven Historic Exhibitions of Modern Art*. New York: American Heritage Press, 1972, ref. pp. 149, 151, 155, ill. pp. 140, 150.

Albert E. Elsen. *The Sculpture of Henri Matisse*. New York: Harry N. Abrams, 1972, ref. p. 105, ill. p. 104.
Frances Spalding. *Roger Fry: Art and Life*. London: Granada Publishing, 1980, ref. pp. 137–38, ill. p. 135.

Remarks
This painting has been dated 1909 in many references and in various exhibition catalogues. However, the original bill of sale, in the Museum's files, is clearly dated November 23, 1908, with a notation added February 4, 1909. Furthermore, the records of the Galerie Bernheim-Jeune list the date of sale as November 23, 1908. On the basis of these two documents the painting can be firmly dated as of 1908, that is, prior to the date previously cited.

Alfred Barr says that Miss Levy bought this painting in 1909 and that the Steins introduced Miss Levy to the work of Matisse. The original bill of sale from Bernheim-Jeune states, "Vendu à Mademoiselle Levy." However, the sales records of Bernheim-Jeune list the buyer of the painting as Michael Stein. Thus, it appears that Michael Stein acted as agent for Miss Levy's purchase of the painting.

La Fille aux yeux verts is the title given on the Galerie Bernheim-Jeune bill of sale of November 23, 1908. This work has been titled at various times *La Femme aux yeux verts*, *Jeune Femme aux yeux verts*, *La Femme aux yeux bleus*, *Lady with Green Eyes*, *Girl with Green Eyes*, and *The Girl with Green Eyes*.

Ian Dunlop gives an account of the exhibition at the Grafton Galleries in which this painting and others caused a furor. His reproduction from the *Illustrated London News* of November 26, 1910, which shows the most discussed paintings in the show, includes *The Girl with Green Eyes*. "Matisse outraged the critics even more than Van Gogh and Cézanne," writes Dunlop, and he quotes Konody as calling this painting "an intentionally childish daub."

Albert Elsen states that the sculpture in the left background of *The Girl with Green Eyes* is the fragment of the Parthenon pediment figure known as the Ilissus. This piece is also the central motif of Matisse's *Still Life with a Greek Torso*, painted in 1908.

HENRI MATISSE
French, 1869–1954

Portrait of Michael Stein, 1916
oil on canvas
26½ × 19⅞″
67.3 × 50.5 cm

Sarah and Michael Stein Memorial
Collection
Gift of Nathan Cummings
55.3546

Inscribed
recto, lower left: *Henri-Matisse 1916*

Provenance
Nathan Cummings, 1954
Estate of Sarah Stein, 1953
Michael and Sarah Stein, 1916
Artist

Exhibitions
San Francisco Museum of Art. *Henri-Matisse*, January 11–February 24, 1936, cat. no. 16, listed as *Portrait (Man)*, 1916.

Musée des Arts Décoratifs, Paris. *Collection Nathan Cummings d'Art Ancien du Pérou; Peintures Françaises XIXème–XXème Siècle, Collection Nathan Cummings*, March–May 1956, checklist no. 13.

San Francisco Museum of Art. *The Sarah and Michael Stein Collection*, March 13–April 22, 1962. Circulated to: Museum of Fine Arts, Houston, May 4–June 6, 1962.

Hayward Gallery, London. *Matisse: 1869–1954*, July 11–September 8, 1968, cat. no. 61; ill. p. 97. Exhibition organized by the Arts Council of Great Britain.

Grand-Palais, Paris. *Henri Matisse*, April–September 1970, cat. no. 136; ill. p. 207.

The Museum of Modern Art, New York. *Four Americans in Paris: The Collections of Gertrude Stein and Her Family*, December 19, 1970–March 1, 1971, cat. p. 163; ref. p. 44, ill. p. 34. Circulated to: Baltimore Museum of Art, April 4–June 13, 1971, cat. p. 17; San Francisco Museum of Art, September 15–October 31, 1971. Excerpted version at the National Gallery of Canada, Ottawa, under the title *Gertrude Stein & Picasso & Gris*, June 25–August 15, 1971.

The Art Institute of Chicago. *Major Works from the Collection of Nathan Cummings*, October 20–December 9, 1973, cat. no. 27; ref. p. 7, ill. p. 36.

The National Museum of Modern Art, Tokyo. *Matisse*, March 20–May 17, 1981, cat. no. 39; ill. p. 64. Circulated to: The National Museum of Modern Art, Kyoto, May 26–July 19, 1981.

Literature
Alfred H. Barr, Jr. *Matisse: His Art and His Public*. New York: The Museum of Modern Art, 1951, ref. pp. 181, 189, ill. p. 26.

George Wickes. *Americans in Paris*. New York: Doubleday, 1969, pl. 3.

James R. Mellow. *Charmed Circle: Gertrude Stein and Company*. New York: Praeger, 1974, ill. following p. 84.

Douglas Mannering. *The Art of Matisse*. London: The Hamlyn Publishing Group, 1982, color ill. p. 30.

HENRI MATISSE
French, 1869–1954

Portrait of Sarah Stein, 1916
oil on canvas
28½ × 22¼″
72.4 × 56.5 cm

Sarah and Michael Stein Memorial
Collection
Gift of Elise Stern Haas
54.1117

Inscribed
recto, lower right: *Henri Matisse*

Provenance
Mr. and Mrs. Walter A. Haas, 1954
Estate of Sarah Stein, 1953
Sarah and Michael Stein, 1916
Artist

Exhibitions
San Francisco Museum of Art. *Henri-Matisse*, January 11–February 24, 1936, cat. no. 17, listed as *Portrait (Woman)*, 1916.

Musée National d'Art Moderne, Paris. *Henri Matisse: Exposition Rétrospective*. July 28–November 18, 1956, cat. no. 46; ill. pl. XIX.

San Francisco Museum of Art. *The Sarah and Michael Stein Collection*, March 13–April 22, 1962. Circulated to: Museum of Fine Arts, Houston, May 4–June 6, 1962.

The Museum of Modern Art, New York. *Henri Matisse: Sixty-four Paintings*, July 18–September 25, 1966, cat. no. 34; ill. p. 38.

Hayward Gallery, London. *Matisse: 1869–1954*, July 11–September 8, 1968, cat. no. 60; ill. p. 96. Exhibition organized by the Arts Council of Great Britain.

Grand-Palais, Paris. *Henri Matisse*, April–September 1970, cat. no. 135; ill. p. 206.

The Museum of Modern Art, New York. *Four Americans in Paris: The Collections of Gertrude Stein and Her Family*, December 19, 1970–March 1, 1971, cat. p. 163; ref. p. 44, ill. p. 34. Circulated to: Baltimore Museum of Art, April 4–June 13, 1971, cat. p. 18; San Francisco Museum of Art, September 15–October 31, 1971. Excerpted version at the National Gallery of Canada, Ottawa, under the title *Gertrude Stein & Picasso & Gris*, June 25–August 15, 1971.

Literature
Alfred H. Barr, Jr. *Matisse: His Art and His Public*. New York: The Museum of Modern Art, 1951, ref. pp. 181, 189, ill. p. 404.

Gaston Diehl. *Henri Matisse*. Paris: Éditions Pierre Tisné, 1954, ill. pl. 69.

André Sauret. *Portraits par Henri Matisse*. Monte Carlo: Éditions du Livre, 1954, ill. p. 28.

Raymond Escholier. *Matisse: A Portrait of the Artist and the Man*. Translated by Geraldine and H. M. Colvile. New York: Frederick A. Praeger, 1960, ref. p. 151.

"Matisse's American Patrons." *Time*, vol. 79 (March 30, 1962), pp. 64–65.

Jean Guichard-Meili. *Matisse*. New York: Frederick A. Praeger, 1967, ref. pp. 54, 231, 251, ill. pl. 192.

James R. Mellow, *Charmed Circle: Gertrude Stein and Company*. New York: Praeger, 1974, ill. following p. 84.

HENRI MATISSE
French, 1869–1954

The Slave (Le Serf), 1900–1903
bronze 6/10
36⅛ × 14⅞ × 13″
91.8 × 37.8 × 33.0 cm

Bequest of Harriet Lane Levy
50.6095

Inscribed
left rear: *6/10 HM*
front center: *Le Serf*

Provenance
Harriet Lane Levy, 1930
Galerie Pierre, Paris
Artist

Exhibitions
San Francisco Museum of Art. *Henri-Matisse*, January 11–February 24, 1936, cat. no. 32, listed as *Serf*, 1902.

UCLA Art Galleries, University of California, Los Angeles. *Years of Ferment: The Birth of Twentieth Century Art 1886–1914*, January 24–March 7, 1965, cat. no. 32; ill. p. 33. Circulated to: San Francisco Museum of Art, March 28–May 16, 1965; The Cleveland Museum of Art, July 13–August 22, 1965.

Fresno Arts Center, California. *Masterworks of Modern Sculpture*, October 13–November 14, 1976, cat. no. 12; ill. pl. 12.

National Gallery of Art, Washington, D.C. *Rodin Rediscovered*, June 28, 1981–May 2, 1982, cat. no. 366.

Kimbell Art Museum, Fort Worth, Texas. *Henri Matisse: Sculptor/Painter*, May 26–September 2, 1984, cat. no. 1; ref. pp. 38-43, ill. pp. 38, 40.

Literature
References to this sculpture, although not necessarily to this particular cast, may be found in the following publications.

Alfred H. Barr, Jr. *Matisse: His Art and His Public*. New York: The Museum of Modern Art, 1951, ref. pp. 48, 52, 148, 179, ill. p. 305, listed as *The Slave*, 1900–03 (cast is 2/10, The Cone Collection, The Baltimore Museum of Art).

UCLA Art Galleries, University of California, Los Angeles. *Henri Matisse*. Catalogue of a retrospective exhibition shown January 5–February 27, 1966, with texts by Jean Leymarie, Herbert Read, William S. Lieberman, cat. no. 96, listed as *The Slave (Le Serf)*, 1900–03; ref. pp. 20, 21, ill. p. 124, pl. 96 (cast is 7/10, The Joseph H. Hirshhorn Collection, New York [now Hirshhorn Museum and Sculpture Garden, Smithsonian Institution, Washington, D.C.]).

Albert E. Elsen. "The Sculpture of Matisse, Part 1." *Artforum*, vol. 7, no.1 (September 1968), ref. pp. 21–29, ill. pp. 23, 24 (studio photograph with Matisse), 25–28 (cast is 2/10, The Cone Collection, The Baltimore Museum of Art).

Albert E. Elsen. *The Sculpture of Henri Matisse*. New York: Harry N. Abrams, 1972, ref. pp. 25–44, ill. pls. 26, 27, 40, 42, 44, 45, listed as *The Serf*, 1900–1903 (of various casts: 2/10, The Cone Collection, The Baltimore Museum of Art; 7/10, The Joseph H. Hirshhorn Collection, New York [now Hirshhorn Museum and Sculpture Garden, Smithsonian Institution, Washington, D.C.]; The Museum of Modern Art, New York [cast not marked]).

John Elderfield. *Matisse in the Collection of the Museum of Modern Art*. New York: The Museum of Modern Art, 1978, ref. pp. 28, 30, ill. p. 30, listed as *The Serf*, 1900–03.

HENRI MATISSE
French, 1869–1954

Henriette, II (Grosse Tête; Henriette, deuxième état), 1927
bronze 6/10
13 × 9 × 12″
33.0 × 22.9 × 30.5 cm

Bequest of Harriet Lane Levy
50.6096

Inscribed
back of neck, center: *6/10 HM*
back of neck, right: *CIRE/ VALSUANI/PERDUE*

Provenance
Harriet Lane Levy, 1930
Galerie Pierre, Paris
Artist

Exhibitions

San Francisco Museum of Art. *Henri-Matisse*, January 11–February 24, 1936, cat. no. 35, listed as *Classic Head*, 1930.

UCLA Art Galleries, University of California, Los Angeles. *Henri Matisse*, January 5–February 27, 1966, cat. no. 127, listed as *Henriette, Second State (Henriette, deuxième état)*, 1927; ref. p. 23, ill. p. 136. Circulated to: The Art Institute of Chicago, March 11–April 24, 1966; Museum of Fine Arts, Boston, May 11–June 26, 1966.

The Museum of Modern Art, New York. *The Sculpture of Matisse*, February 24–May 8, 1972, cat. no. 57; ref. p. 35, ill. p. 36. Circulated to: Walker Art Center, Minneapolis, June 20–August 6, 1972; University Art Museum, University of California, Berkeley, September 18–October 29, 1972.

Fresno Arts Center, California. *Masterworks of Modern Sculpture*, October 13–November 14, 1976, cat. no. 19; ill. no. 19.

Kimbell Art Museum, Fort Worth, Texas. *Henri Matisse: Sculptor/Painter*, May 26–September 2, 1984, cat. no. 42; ref. pp. 11, 121–22, ill. p. 121.

Literature

Alfred H. Barr, Jr. *Matisse: His Art and His Public*. New York: The Museum of Modern Art, 1951, ref. pp. 217, 559 Appendix G, ill. p. 456, listed as *Stout Head (Grosse tête)*, 1927.

Raymond Escholier. *Matisse: A Portrait of the Artist and the Man*. Translated by Geraldine and H. M. Colvile. New York: Frederick A. Praeger, 1960, ill. no. 46.

Albert E. Elsen. *The Sculpture of Henri Matisse*. New York: Harry N. Abrams, 1972, ref. pp. 160, 166, 170, ill. p. 164.

Henri Matisse: Paintings and Sculptures in Soviet Museums. Leningrad: Aurora Art Publishers, 1978, ref. pp. 190–91, ill. p. 190, listed as *Large Head*, 1927.

Remarks

The date reflects the year of completion; the sculpture was actually begun in 1926. In his book *The Sculpture of Henri Matisse* (New York: Harry N. Abrams, 1972), p. 166, Albert Elsen speaks of Matisse working on the sculpture in 1926 and reproduces a photograph from *Cahiers d'Art* of 1926 which shows Matisse at work on the sculpture.

Henriette Darricarrère, the subject of this sculpture, was one of Matisse's favorite models during the Nice period and posed for him from 1920 to 1927. In addition to this work, she was the model for a number of other important paintings,

sculptures, and graphic works of the period, including *Figure with a Scutari Tapestry* (1922) and *The Pink Blouse* (1922).

KEES VAN DONGEN
French, born Netherlands, 1877–1968

The Black Chemise
(La Chemise noire), ca. 1905–9
oil on canvas with wood attachment
22¼ × 18¼"
56.5 × 46.4 cm

Gift of Wilbur D. May
64.59

Inscribed

recto, lower right: *Van Dongen*

Provenance

Wilbur D. May, 1956
Marlborough Fine Art, Ltd., London

Exhibitions

[Galerie Bernheim-Jeune & Cie, Paris. *Exposition Van Dongen*, January 27–February 8, 1913, cat. no. 17.] See Remarks

James E. Church Fine Arts Building, University of Nevada, Reno. *Seventy Works by Fifty Modern Masters*, October 23–November 20, 1960, cat. no. 16; ill.

San Francisco Museum of Art. *Man, Glory, Jest, and Riddle: A Survey of the Human Form through the Ages*, November 10, 1964–January 3, 1965, cat. no. 247.

The University of Arizona Museum of Art, Tucson. *Cornelis Theodorus Marie Van Dongen 1877–1968*, February 14–March 14, 1971, cat. no. 57; ill. p. 71. Circulated to: Nelson Gallery and Atkins Museum of Fine Arts (now The Nelson–Atkins Museum of Art), Kansas City, Missouri, April 25–May 23, 1971.

Literature

La Renaissance [Paris], vol. 16 (October–November 1933), ill. p. 198, listed as *Femme à la chemise noire*, n.d.

The Architectural Review (London), vol. 117, no. 701 (May 1955), ill. p. 344.

"Chronique des arts." *Gazette des Beaux-Arts*, Supplément (February 1965), ill. p. 63.

Ian Dunlop. *The Shock of the New: Seven Historic Exhibitions of Modern Art*. New York: American Heritage Press, 1972, ill. p. 110.

Remarks

Donald E. Gordon, in *Modern Art Exhibitions 1900–1916* (Munich: Prestel-Verlag, 1974), vol. 1, p. 245; vol. 2, p. 663, notes that *La Chemise noire* was exhibited at the Galerie Bernheim-Jeune from January 27 to February 8, 1913, and was reproduced in the exhibition cata-

logue. However, in a letter from Galerie Bernheim-Jeune to the Museum, dated February 9, 1984, they state that the catalogue of that exhibition did not reproduce this work and therefore they could not be absolutely certain that this painting was included in that show.

ANDRÉ DERAIN
French, 1880–1954

Landscape, 1906
oil on canvas mounted on board
20 × 25½"
50.8 × 64.8 cm

Bequest of Harriet Lane Levy
50.6075

Inscribed

recto, lower left: *Derain*

Provenance

Harriet Lane Levy
Artist

Exhibitions

California Palace of the Legion of Honor, San Francisco. *Exhibition of French Painting from the Fifteenth Century to the Present Day*, June 8–July 8, 1934, cat. no. 183.

San Francisco Museum of Art. *Contemporary Art: Paintings, Watercolors and Sculpture Owned in the San Francisco Bay Region*, January 18–February 5, 1940, cat. no. 84.

Dallas Museum for Contemporary Arts. *Les Fauves*, January 29–March 16, 1959, cat. no. 10; ill.

Pasadena Art Museum (now Norton Simon Museum of Art at Pasadena), California. *A View of the Century*, November 24–December 19, 1964, cat. no. 5.

UCLA Art Galleries, University of California, Los Angeles. *Years of Ferment: The Birth of Twentieth-Century Art 1886–1914*, January 24–March 7, 1965, cat. no. 38; ill. p. 33. Circulated to: San Francisco Museum of Art, March 28–May 16, 1965; The Cleveland Museum of Art, July 13–August 22, 1965.

The Art Galleries, University of California, Santa Barbara. *Trends in Twentieth-Century Art: A Loan Exhibition from the San Francisco Museum of Art*, January 6–February 1, 1970, cat. no. 1; ill. pl. 1.

The Norman Mackenzie Art Gallery, University of Regina, Saskatchewan, Canada. *André Derain in North American Collections*, October 29–December 5, 1982, cat. no. 7; ref. p. 46, ill. p. 47. Circulated to: University Art Museum, University of California, Berkeley, January 12–March 13, 1983. Painting exhibited only at Berkeley.

Literature

"The Harriet Lane Levy Collection." *Magazine of Art* (San Francisco Mu-

seum of Art Edition), vol. 44, no. 3 (March 1951), ref. pp. cxxiii, cxxiv.

Nancy Marmer. "Los Angeles Letter." *Art International*, vol. 9, no. 4 (May 1965), ill. p. 44.

Remarks

Recent scholarship on André Derain indicates that *Landscape* was most likely painted in 1906 at L'Estaque. In his catalogue *André Derain in North American Collections* (The Norman Mackenzie Art Gallery, University of Regina, Canada, 1982, p. 46), Michael Parke-Taylor states: "There is some question whether this painting dates from 1905 at Collioure, or 1906 when Derain painted at L'Estaque. The latter date may be more correct based on stylistic affinities with *L'Estaque* 1906 [reproduced in John Elderfield, *The "Wild Beasts": Fauvism and Its Affinities* (New York: The Museum of Modern Art, 1976), p. 84]." Richard Stoppenbach, a British scholar working on a Derain catalogue raisonné, has written to the Museum in a letter of March 21, 1984, "In my opinion the date is 1906, and the location is L'Estaque."

OTHON FRIESZ
French, 1879–1949

Landscape (The Eagle's Beak, La Ciotat) (Paysage [Le Bec-de-l'Aigle, La Ciotat]), 1907
oil on canvas
25⅜ × 32"
64.5 × 81.2 cm

Bequest of Marian W. Sinton
81.52

Inscribed

recto, lower left: *Othon Friesz/07*

Provenance

Marian W. and Edgar S. Sinton, ca. 1960

Exhibition

M. H. de Young Memorial Museum, San Francisco. *The San Francisco Collector*, September 21–October 17, 1965, cat. no. 98; ill.

Remarks

Born Achille-Emile-Othon Friesz, the artist first signed his works Emile-Othon Friesz or E. Othon Friesz and later simplified this signature to Othon Friesz.

The identification of the subject as the landmark, Le Bec-de-l'Aigle (Eagle's Beak) in La Ciotat, is based on information and illustrations of a series of works by Friesz of the mountain presented in Marcel Giry, *Fauvism: Origins and Development* (New York: Alpine Fine Arts, 1982), p. 238, ill. nos. 97, 108. During the summer of 1907, while staying in La Ciotat with Georges Braque, Friesz made several paintings of this local landmark. Among these, the Museum's version is unique in its perspective, for it views the mountain from its western side rather than its eastern face as in the other five examples of the subject that have been identified to date. A letter to the Museum from Marcel Giry, March 16, 1984, identifies these as: Collection Werner E. Josten, New York; Musée d'Art Moderne de la Ville de Troyes; Musée des Beaux-Arts, Beziers; Private collection, Switzerland, reproduced in John Elderfield, *The "Wild Beasts": Fauvism and Its Affinities* (New York: The Museum of Modern Art, 1976, p. 92); Location unknown, reproduced in Maximilien Gauthier, *Othon Friesz* (Geneva: Pierre Cailler, 1957).

PABLO PICASSO
Spanish, 1881–1973

Street Scene (Scène de rue), 1900
oil on canvas
18¾ × 26¼"
47.7 × 66.7 cm

Bequest of Harriet Lane Levy
50.6097

Inscribed
recto, lower left: *P. R. Picasso*

Provenance
Harriet Lane Levy, 1930
Galerie Pierre, Paris
Artist

Exhibitions
The Museum of Modern Art, New York. *Picasso: Forty Years of His Art*, November 15, 1939–January 7, 1940, cat. no. 7, listed as *Paris Street*, 1900; ill. p. 25. Circulated to: The Art Institute of Chicago, February 1–March 3, 1940; Museum of Fine Arts, Boston, April 26–May 25, 1940; San Francisco Museum of Art, June 25–July 22, 1940.

San Francisco Museum of Art. *Picasso, Gris, Miró: The Spanish Masters of Twentieth Century Painting*, September 14–October 17, 1948, cat. no. 1, listed as *Street Scene, Paris*, 1900; ill. p. 55. Circulated to: Portland Art Museum, Oregon, October 26–November 28, 1948.

California Palace of the Legion of Honor, San Francisco. *France—Comes to You*, November 5–21, 1948, cat.

Santa Barbara Museum of Art, California. *Fiesta Exhibition 1953: Picasso, Gris, Miró, Dali*, August 4–30, 1953, cat. no. 1.

Santa Barbara Museum of Art. *The Private World of Pablo Picasso*, January 15–February 7, 1960.

The Art Gallery of Toronto. *Picasso and Man*, January 11–February 16, 1964, cat. no. 6; ref. pp. 8, 27, ill. p. 27. Circulated to: The Montreal Museum of Fine Arts, February 28–March 31, 1964.

Fort Worth Art Center Museum and Dallas Museum of Fine Arts. *Picasso: Two Concurrent Retrospective Exhibitions*, February 8–March 26, 1967, cat. no. 3, listed as *Street Scene, Paris*, 1900. Shown in Dallas.

Portland Art Museum, Oregon. *Picasso for Portland*, September 20–October 25, 1970, cat. no. 1; ref. p. 11, ill. p. 11.

Literature
Christian Zervos, *Pablo Picasso*. Paris: Editions Cahiers d'Art, 1954, vol. 6, cat. no. 302; ill. p. 37.

Pierre Daix and Georges Boudaille, with Joan Rosselet. *Picasso, The Blue and Rose Periods: A Catalogue Raisonné of the Paintings, 1900–1906*. Greenwich, Conn.: New York Graphic Society, 1967, cat. no. II.11, listed as *Street Scene*, 1900, with other titles given as well: *Paris Street, Old Man, Woman and Child in the Street*; ref. pp. 26, 30, ill. p. 122.

Josep Palau i Fabre. *Picasso, The Early Years: 1881-1907*. New York: Rizzoli International, 1981, cat. no. 503, listed as *Streets of Montmartre*, Autumn 1900; ref. p. 531, ill. p. 208.

JACQUES LIPCHITZ
French, born Lithuania, 1891–1973

Draped Woman, 1919
bronze 3/7
36¾ × 12⅝ × 13¼"
93.3 × 32.0 × 33.6 cm

Gift of Mr. and Mrs. Wellington S. Henderson
63.4

Inscribed
rear of base, top: *3/7 Lipchitz*
rear of base, top, left: [thumb print]

Provenance
Mr. and Mrs. Wellington S. Henderson
Otto Gerson Gallery, New York

Exhibitions
M. H. de Young Memorial Museum, San Francisco. *The San Francisco Collector*, September 21–October 17, 1965, cat. no. 92; ill. p. 92.

University Art Museum, University of California, Berkeley. *Excellence: Art from the University Community*, November 6, 1970–January 10, 1971, cat. no. 473.

Literature
A. M. Hammacher, *Jacques Lipchitz: His Sculpture*. New York: Harry N. Abrams, 1960, p. 35, pl. 27.

CONSTANTIN BRANCUSI
French, born Romania, 1876–1957

Blonde Negress
(La Négresse blonde), 1926
bronze (polished)
15⅛ × 4⅞ × 7⅜"
38.5 × 12.4 × 18.8 cm

Gift of Agnes E. Meyer and Elise Stern Haas
58.4382

Inscribed
stamped, middle of rear ornament: *Brancusi/Paris—1926*

Provenance
Elise Stern Haas
Mr. and Mrs. Eugene Meyer
Artist

Exhibitions
University Art Gallery, University of California, Berkeley. *Art from Ingres to Pollock: Painting and Sculpture since Neoclassicism*, March 6–April 3, 1960, cat. p. 56; ref. p. 28, ill.

San Francisco Museum of Art. *Modern Masters in West Coast Collections: An Exhibition Selected in Celebration of the Twenty-fifth Anniversary of the San Francisco Museum of Art, 1935–1960*, October 18–November 27, 1960, cat.

Literature
Ionel Jianou. *Brancusi*. Paris: Arted Editions d'Art, 1963, cat. p. 107, listed as *The White Negress*, 1924.

Athena Tacha Spear. "A Contribution to Brancusi Chronology." *Art Bulletin*, vol. 48, no. 1 (March 1966), ref. pp. 48–49, ill. no. 8.

Sidney Geist. *Brancusi: A Study of the Sculpture*. New York: Grossman, 1968, cat. no. 167b; ref. p. 98, ill. (cast unidentified) p. 98.

Sidney Geist. *Brancusi: The Sculpture and Drawings*. New York: Harry N. Abrams, 1975, cat. no. 179b.

Remarks
This sculpture is part of a series which has been subdivided into smaller groups by different scholars using varying criteria. Based on aesthetic considerations, Athena Tacha Spear differentiates between a group of sculptures "with double chignon" and another "with single chignon." The group with double chignon includes one marble of 1924 and four bronzes of 1926, one of which is the Museum's cast. The group with single chignon comprises one marble of 1928 and two bronzes of 1933.

Using medium and date as criteria, Sidney Geist divides the works into two groups, series I and II, which refer, respectively, to Spear's double- and single-chignon groupings. Series I comprises one marble of 1924 (*White Negress I*) and three bronzes of 1926 (*Blonde Negress I*), among

them this cast. (Geist does not list the "double chignon" bronze cast in the collection of the Museu de Arte Moderna, São Paulo, as identified by Spear.) Series II consists of one marble of 1928 (*White Negress II*) and two bronzes of 1933 (*Blonde Negress II*).

In "The Catalogue of Brancusi's Works," Ionel Jianou groups the entire series under the title of the first work in the series, *White Negress*, 1924.

The title *Blonde Negress* may have originated, as suggested by Spear, "in the poem by Georges Fourest, *La négresse blonde*, first published in Paris in 1909 but republished many times later."

GEORGES BRAQUE
French, 1882–1963

The Gueridon (Le Guéridon), 1935
oil and sand on canvas
71 × 29"
180.4 × 73.7 cm

Purchased with the aid of funds from W. W. Crocker
46.3211

Inscribed
recto, lower right: *G Braque/35*

Provenance
Paul Rosenberg, ca. 1936
Artist

Exhibitions
Palais des Beaux-Arts, Brussels. *Georges Braque*, November–December, 1936, cat. no. 79.

Liljevalchs Konsthall, Stockholm. *Matisse, Picasso, Braque, Laurens*, 1938, cat. no. 93, listed as *Frukt och Glas*, 1936. Circulated to: Kunstnernes Hus, Oslo; Statens Museum for Kunst, Copenhagen; Konsthallen, Göteborg, Sweden.

The Arts Club of Chicago. *Georges Braque: Retrospective Exhibition*, November 7–27, 1939, cat. no. 54. Circulated to: Phillips Memorial Gallery (now The Phillips Collection), Washington, D.C., December 6, 1939–January 6, 1940, cat. no. 51; San Francisco Museum of Art, February 5–March 6, 1940.

Palace of Fine Arts, Golden Gate International Exposition, San Francisco. *Art: Contemporary European Paintings*, 1940, cat. no. 625.

Portland Art Museum, Oregon, *Fiftieth Anniversary Exhibition 1892–1942*, December 2, 1942–January 3, 1943, cat. no. 99.

Paul Rosenberg & Co., New York. *Paintings by Braque and Picasso*, April 6–May 1, 1943, cat. no. 1.

Paul Rosenberg & Co., New York. *Paintings by Braque*, April 29–May 18, 1946, cat. no. 6.

California Palace of the Legion of Honor, San Francisco. *France—Comes to You*, November 5–21, 1948, cat.

San Francisco Museum of Art. *Fifteenth Anniversary Exhibitions*, January 11–February 5, 1950, cat.; ill.

Paul Rosenberg & Co., New York. *Masterpieces Recalled*, February 6–March 2, 1957, cat. no. 46, listed as *The Round Table*, 1936; ill. p. 38.

Museum of Fine Arts, Boston. *European Masters of Our Time*, October 10–November 17, 1957, cat. no. 23; ill. p. 99.

The Denver Art Museum. *Cubism in Retrospect: 1911–1929*, January 22–February 22, 1959, cat. no. 2; ill.

Fine Arts Pavilion, Seattle World's Fair. *Masterpieces of Art*, April 21–September 4, 1962, cat. no. 56; ill. p. 127.

The Contemporary Arts Center, Cincinnati. *Braque*, September 22–October 22, 1962, cat., listed as *The Table, Le guéridon (Le jou)*, 1936; ill. Circulated to: The Arts Club of Chicago, November 6–December 6, 1962; Walker Art Center, Minneapolis, December 20, 1962–January 20, 1963.

Paul Rosenberg and Co., New York. *Georges Braque, 1882–1963. An American Tribute: The Thirties*, April 7–May 2, 1964, cat. no. 25, listed as *Le Guéridon ("Le Jou . . .")*, 1935; ill. no. 25.

The Art Institute of Chicago. *Braque: The Great Years*, October 7–December 3, 1972, cat. no. 19; ref. pp. 69–71.

Art Gallery of New South Wales, Sydney, Australia. *Modern Masters: Manet to Matisse*, April 10–May 11, 1975, cat. no. 13; ref. p. 248, ill. p. 249. Exhibition organized under the auspices of the International Council of the Museum of Modern Art, New York, circulated to: National Gallery of Victoria, Melbourne, May 28–June 22, 1975; The Museum of Modern Art, New York, August 4–September 1, 1975.

Joslyn Art Museum, Omaha. *The Chosen Object: European and American Still Life*, April 23–June 5, 1977, cat. no. 45; ill. p. 24.

Literature
Nicole S. Mangin. *Catalogue de l'oeuvre de Georges Braque, Peintures 1936–1941*. Paris: Maeght Editeur, 1961, cat. no. 8, listed as *Le Guéridon (Le Jou)*, 1936; ill. no. 8.

Robert Hughes. "Objects as Poetics." *Time*, vol. 100 (October 9, 1972), ref. p. 69, ill. p. 67.

GEORGES BRAQUE
French, 1882–1963

Vase, Palette, and Mandolin
(Vase, palette, et mandoline), 1936
oil on canvas
32 × 39⅝″
81.3 × 100.7 cm

Purchased with the aid of funds from W. W. Crocker
44.2641

Inscribed
recto, lower right: *G. Braque/36*

Provenance
Paul Rosenberg, ca. 1936
Artist

Exhibitions
Galerie Paul Rosenberg, Paris. *Braque*, April 1937.

Liljevalchs Konsthall, Stockholm. *Matisse, Picasso, Braque, Laurens*, 1938, cat. no. 97, listed as *Vas, palett och mandolin*, 1936. Circulated to: Kunstnernes Hus, Oslo; Statens Museum for Kunst, Copenhagen; Konsthallen, Göteborg, Sweden.

Galerie Paul Rosenberg, Paris. *Braque*, November 1938, cat. no. 15.

Palais de la France, Section des Beaux-Arts, New York World's Fair, 1939. *L'Art Français Contemporain*, cat. no. 21; ill. no. 19, incorrectly captioned *Guitare, Partition, Pommes, Verre (Guitar, Score, Apples, Glass)*.

The Contemporary Arts Center, Cincinnati. *Braque*, September 22–October 22, 1962, cat.; ill. Circulated to: The Arts Club of Chicago, November 6–December 6, 1962; Walker Art Center, Minneapolis, December 20, 1962–January 20, 1963.

Paul Rosenberg and Co., New York. *Georges Braque, 1882–1963. An American Tribute: The Thirties*, April 7–May 2, 1964, cat. no. 23; ill. no. 23.

Galerie des Beaux-Arts, Bordeaux, France. *La Peinture Française: Collections Américaines*, May 13–September 15, 1966, cat. no. 86; ill. pl. 64.

Literature
Nicole S. Mangin. *Catalogue de l'oeuvre de Georges Braque: Peintures 1936–1941*. Paris: Maeght Editeur, 1961, cat. no. 12, listed as *Nature morte à la palette (Mélodie)*, 1936; ill. no. 12.

PABLO PICASSO
Spanish, 1881–1973

Jug of Flowers *(La Cruche fleurie)*
1937
oil on canvas
20 × 24¼″
50.8 × 61.6 cm

Purchased with the aid of funds from W. W. Crocker
44.1499

Inscribed
recto, lower right: *221.37./Picasso*
verso, upper right of stretcher:
22 Janvier   La Cruche   Fleurie   Picasso

Provenance
Paul Rosenberg Gallery, New York, 1937
Artist

Exhibitions
Galerie Paul Rosenberg, Paris. *Exposition Picasso*, January 1939, cat.

Thomas Welton Stanford Art Gallery, Stanford University, California. *French Modern Painting*, October 7–28, 1945, cat. Circulated to: Carmel Art Association, California, November 1945.

San Francisco Museum of Art. *Picasso, Gris, Miró: The Spanish Masters of Twentieth Century Painting*, September 14–October 17, 1948, cat. no. 13; ill. p. 60. Circulated to: Portland Art Museum, Oregon, October 26–November 28, 1948.

Santa Barbara Museum of Art. *The Private World of Pablo Picasso*, January 15–February 7, 1960.

The Art Galleries, University of California, Santa Barbara. *Trends in Twentieth-Century Art: A Loan Exhibition from the San Francisco Museum of Art*, January 6–February 1, 1970, cat. no. 12; ill.

Literature
Christian Zervos. *Pablo Picasso*. Paris: Editions Cahiers d'Art, 1957, vol. 8, cat. no. 326, listed as *Nature morte au pichet*, 20 [sic] *Janvier 1937*; ill. p. 152.

Ernest Raboff. *Pablo Picasso: Art for Children*. Garden City, N.Y.: Doubleday, 1968, ref., ill., listed as *Pitcher with Flowers*, 1937.

PABLO PICASSO
Spanish, 1881–1973

Women of Algiers, E *(Les Femmes d'Alger)*, 1955
oil on canvas
18⅛ × 21⅝″
46.1 × 55.0 cm

Gift of Wilbur D. May
64.4

Inscribed
recto, upper right: *Picasso*
verso, upper left: *16.1.55*

Provenance
Mr. and Mrs. Wilbur D. May, 1956
Saidenberg Gallery, New York
Mr. and Mrs. Victor Ganz, New York

Galerie Louise Leiris, Paris, 1955
Artist

Exhibitions
Musée des Arts Décoratifs, Paris. *Picasso: Peintures 1900–1955*, June–October 1955, cat. no. 127, listed as *Les Femmes d'Alger—E*, 16/1/1955; fig. no. 127 E. Circulated, with German translation of catalogue, to: Haus der Kunst, Munich, October 25–December 18, 1955; Rheinisches Museum, Köln-Deutz, December 30, 1955–February 29, 1956; Kunstverein in Hamburg, Kunsthalle-Altbau, March 10–April 29, 1956, cat. no. 121; ill. no. 121.

The Museum of Modern Art, New York. *Picasso: Seventy-fifth Anniversary Exhibition*, May 22–September 8, 1957, cat.; ref. pp. 108–9, ill. p. 108. Circulated to: The Art Institute of Chicago, October 29–December 8, 1957. Expanded version shown at Philadelphia Museum of Art, January 8–February 23, 1958, cat. no. 246; ill. no. 246.

Cordier-Warren Gallery, New York. *Picasso, An American Tribute: The Fifties*, April 25–May 12, 1962, cat. no. 10; ill. no. 10.

Literature
Daniel-Henry Kahnweiler. "Entretiens avec Picasso au sujet des Femmes d'Alger." *Aujourd'hui: Art et Architecture* (Paris), vol. 1, no. 4 (September 1955), ref. to the series pp. 12–13.

Christian Zervos. "Confrontations de Picasso avec des oeuvres d'art d'autrefois." *Cahiers d'Art*, vols. 33–35, no. 1 (1960), ref. to the series pp. 16, 26, 30, 41, ill. p. 48.

Christian Zervos. *Pablo Picasso*. Paris: Editions Cahiers d'Art, 1965, vol. 16, cat. no. 347; ill. pl. 126, fig. 347.

Leo Steinberg. *Other Criteria: Confrontations with Twentieth-Century Art*. New York: Oxford University Press, 1972, ref. pp. 135–36, ill. p. 135.

JULIO GONZÁLEZ
Spanish, 1876–1942

Mask "My" *(Masque "My")*
ca. 1930
bronze 5/9
8 × 3½ × 3″
20.3 × 8.9 × 7.6 cm

Gift of E. Morris Cox from the collection of Margaret Storke Cox
83.225

Inscribed
verso, lower right: *Gonzalez © 5/9*

Provenance
Mr. and Mrs. E. Morris Cox (Margaret Storke Cox)
Galerie Chalette, New York

Exhibitions

Galerie Chalette, New York. *Julio González*, October–November 1961, cat. no. 40, listed as *Mask*, 1935.

University Art Museum, University of California, Berkeley. *Excellence: Art from the University Community*, November 6, 1970–January 10, 1971, cat. no. 377, listed as *Mask*, 1935.

Literature

Vicente Aguilera Cerni. *Julio, Joan, Roberta González: Itinerario de una Dinastia*. Barcelona: Ediciones Polígrafa, 1973, cat. no. 152, iron original; ill. p. 212.

Josephine Withers. *Julio González: Sculpture in Iron*. New York: New York University Press, 1978, cat. no. 14, bronze original; ref. pp. 44, 157.

Margit Rowell. *Julio González: A Retrospective*. New York: The Solomon R. Guggenheim Museum, 1983, cat. no. 82, iron original; ref. pp. 24, 77, ill. p. 77.

Remarks

The original medium for this work is identified by Withers as bronze; however, Cerni and Rowell both reproduce an unsigned iron example of the work, with no edition number. In a letter to the Museum, dated June 4, 1984, Rowell has confirmed that the original *Mask "My"* is in iron, and that there is a bronze edition of nine or ten, as Withers states.

JULIO GONZÁLEZ
Spanish, 1876–1942

Small Sickle (Woman Standing) (Petite Faucille [Femme debout]) ca. 1937
bronze 4/6
11½ × 4¾ × 3½"
29.2 × 12.1 × 8.9 cm

Gift of E. Morris Cox from the collection of Margaret Storke Cox
83.224

Inscribed
bottom, side of leg: © *by Gonzalez 4/6*

Provenance
Mr. and Mrs. E. Morris Cox (Margaret Storke Cox)
Galerie Chalette, New York

Exhibitions

Galerie Chalette, New York. *Julio González*, October–November 1961, cat. no. 49, dated 1937; ill. p. 61.

University Art Museum, University of California, Berkeley. *Excellence: Art from the University Community*, November 6, 1970–January 10, 1971, cat. no. 378, dated 1937.

Literature

Josephine Withers. *Julio González: Sculpture in Iron*. New York: New

---

York University Press, 1978, cat. no. 114, forged bronze original, dated 1937; ref. pp. 82, 167, ill. p. 83.

Margit Rowell. *Julio González: A Retrospective*. New York: The Solomon R. Guggenheim Museum, 1983, cat. no. 204, forged bronze original; ref. pp. 26, 169, color ill. p. 169.

Remarks

The sickle is a frequent motif in both González's drawings and sculptures of the late 1930s; see, for example, Rowell, cat. nos. 137, 166, 201, 202, 203, 219. Of his sculptures in which the sickle is a major element, the *Small Sickle (Petite Faucille)* is most closely related to the *Large Sickle (Grande Faucille)* of the same date; Rowell, ill. no. 206. Both sculptures present the standing figure in a highly abstract form that synthesizes the curvilinear and the geometric to create a "sign" in space. In both works, the abstract, angular arms and legs are counterbalanced by the curved sickle-head. Albert E. Elsen, in *Modern European Sculpture 1918–1945: Unknown Beings and Other Realities* (New York: George Braziller, 1979), p. 38, notes, "*Grande Faucille* may have derived from memories of a Spanish peasant, and the sickle becomes the sign of the head as well as occupation of the subject."

AMÉDÉE OZENFANT
French, 1886–1966

Still Life (Nature morte), 1920–21
oil on canvas
32 × 39⅝"
81.3 × 100.6 cm

Gift of Lucien Labaudt
37.2991

Inscribed
recto, lower right: *Ozenfant*

Provenance
Lucien Labaudt
Artist

Remarks
Another version of *Still Life (Nature morte)* is in the collection of the Kunstmuseum, Basel.

MORGAN RUSSELL
American, 1886–1953

Synchromy No. 3, ca. 1922–23
oil on canvas
23¾ × 16⅛"
60.4 × 40.9 cm

Purchase
72.1

Inscribed
recto, upper left: *Russ*
verso, paper label with handwritten ink entries, upper left quadrant: *No. 3/Aigremont/Morga Ru[ ]ell /Aigremo[ ] par Pouilly*

Provenance
Stanton Macdonald-Wright, early 1920s
Artist

Remarks
By the inscription on the verso of the painting, it can be assumed that *Synchromy No. 3* was painted after Morgan Russell moved to the village of Aigremont in Burgundy, France, in 1921. According to Gail Levin, the artist continued to repaint versions of his earlier Synchromies at this time; *Synchromy No. 3* is a later version of the upper right panel of Russell's *Four-Part Synchromy, No. 7* of 1914–15 (Whitney Museum of American Art, New York).

FRANZ MARC
German, 1880–1916

Mountains (Rocky Way/Landscape) (Gebirge [Steiniger Weg/Landschaft]), 1911–12
oil on canvas
51½ × 39¾"
130.8 × 101.0 cm

Gift of the Women's Board and Friends of the Museum
51.4095

Inscribed
recto, lower right: *Marc*
verso, lower left: *Marc*

Provenance
Oscar and Elizabeth Gerson
Artist

Exhibitions

Moderne Galerie Thannhauser, Munich. *Die erste Austellung der Redaktion Der Blaue Reiter*, December 18–January 1, 1912, cat. no. 32, listed as *Landschaft*, n.d. Circulated to: Cologne, Berlin, Hagen, Frankfurt.

Der Sturm, Berlin. *Der Blaue Reiter, Franz Flaum, Oskar Kokoschka, Expressionisten*, March 12–(before April 12), 1912, cat. no. 94, listed as *Steiniger Weg*, n.d.

Münchner Neue Sezession, Munich. *Franz Marc: Gedächtnis-Ausstellung*, September 4–October 15, 1916, cat. no. 106, listed as *Gebirge*, 1912.

Der Sturm, Berlin. *Franz Marc: Gedächtnis-Ausstellung: Gemälde und Aquarelle/Holzschnitte*, November 1916, cat. no. 13, listed as *Gebirge*, n.d.

M. H. de Young Memorial Museum and California Palace of the Legion of Honor, San Francisco. *Seven Cen-*

---

turies of Painting: A Loan Exhibition of Old and Modern Masters, December 29, 1939–January 28, 1940, cat. no. Y-229, listed as *Mountains*, n.d. Shown at the de Young Museum.

The Denver Art Museum. *The Turn of the Century—Exhibition of Masterpieces, 1880–1920*, October 1–November 18, 1956, checklist no. 18, listed as *Mountain Landscape*, n.d.

Städtische Galerie im Lenbachhaus, Munich. *Franz Marc*, August 10–October 13, 1963, cat. no. 132, listed as *Gebirge (Steiniger Weg)*, 1912.

Kunstverein, Hamburg. *Franz Marc: Gemälde, Gouachen, Zeichnungen, Skulpturen*, November 9, 1963–January 5, 1964, cat. no. 45, listed as *Gebirge (Steiniger Weg)*, 1912 (begun 1911); ill. no. 45.

The Portland Art Museum, Oregon. *Seventy-five Masterworks*, December 12, 1967–January 21, 1968, cat. no. 63, listed as *Mountains*, 1912; ill. no. 63.

The Art Galleries, University of California, Santa Barbara. *Trends in Twentieth-Century Art: A Loan Exhibition from the San Francisco Museum of Art*, January 6–February 1, 1970, cat. no. 2, listed as *Mountains*, 1912; ill. no. 2.

Fine Arts Gallery of San Diego. *Color and Form: 1909–1914*, November 20, 1971–January 2, 1972, cat. no. 61, listed as *Stoney Road (Steiniger Weg)*, 1912; color ill. p. 82. Circulated to: The Oakland Museum, California, January 25–March 5, 1972; Seattle Art Museum, March 24–May 6, 1972.

Pasadena Museum of Modern Art (now Norton Simon Museum of Art at Pasadena), California. *German Expressionist Paintings and Sculpture from California Collections*, April 16–June 2, 1974, checklist no. 33, listed as *Steiniger Weg*, 1912.

Museum of Contemporary Art, Chicago. *German and Austrian Expressionism: Art in a Turbulent Era*, March 10–April 30, 1978, cat. p. 28, listed as *Stony Path*, 1912.

University Art Museum, University of California, Berkeley. *Franz Marc: Pioneer of Spiritual Abstraction*, December 5, 1979–February 3, 1980, cat. no. 16, listed as *Rocky Way (Mountains/Landscape)*, 1911–12; ref. pp. 21, 52, ill. p. 75. Circulated to: The Fort Worth Art Museum, February 23–April 13, 1980; Walker Art Center, Minneapolis, May 4–June 15, 1980.

Literature

Alois J. Schardt. *Franz Marc*. Berlin: Rembrandt-Verlag, 1936, cat. no. 36, listed as *Gebirge (Steiniger Weg)*, 1912.

Herschel B. Chipp. "Orphism and Color Theory." *Art Bulletin*, vol. 40, no. 1 (March 1958), ref. p. 62, listed as *Mountains*, 1912, ill. pl. 6.

Klaus Lankheit. *Franz Marc: Katalog der Werke*. Cologne: Verlag M. DuMont Schauberg, 1970, cat. no. 194, listed as *Steiniger Weg (Gebirge/ Landschaft)*, 1911, repainted November 1912; ref. p. 68, ill. p. 68.

Klaus Lankheit. *Franz Marc: Sein Leben und seine Kunst*. Cologne: DuMont Buchverlag, 1976, ref. p. 93, listed as *Landschaft (Steiniger Weg)*, color ill. p. 95.

Ron Glowen. "The Spiritual, Empathetic and Abstract Animal." *Vanguard* (Summer 1980), ref. p. 18, ill. p. 18, listed as *Rocky Way (Mountains/ Landscape)*, 1911–12.

Remarks

The painting was begun in 1911 and first exhibited under the title *Landschaft* (Landscape) in the first Blaue Reiter exhibition at the Moderne Galerie Thannhauser, Munich, during the winter of 1911/12. In the Blaue Reiter exhibition of March–April 1912 at the gallery Der Sturm in Berlin it was shown under a new title, *Steiniger Weg* (Rocky Way). In November 1912, after having visited Robert Delaunay in Paris earlier in the fall, Marc repainted the work, at which time he changed the title to *Gebirge* (Mountains). According to Klaus Lankheit (letter from Lankheit to Museum, September 12, 1983), Marc kept a record book of his paintings. On p. 26 the entry reads verbatim as follows:

~~Steiniger Weg~~-Gebirge-~~600~~
I. blaue Reiter Collektion
München-Cöln-~~Berlin~~-
Sturm-Hagen-Frankf.
nach Sindelsdorf zurück
umgemalt 1912 November
Titel *Gebirge 900* z.Coll. II Tannhauser I. 1913

München-Jena-Berlin-Hamburg Gebirge was the title listed in the catalogue of Marc's memorial exhibition in 1916 at the Münchner Neue Sezession and the gallery Der Sturm. Since then, this work has been identified variously by all three titles.

MAX PECHSTEIN
German, 1881–1955

Nelly, 1910
oil on canvas
20⅜ × 20⅞"
51.8 × 53.1 cm

Purchase
84.9

Inscribed
recto, upper right: *HMP/1910*

Provenance
Lafayette-Parke Gallery, San Francisco
Marlborough Gallery, Inc., New York

Marlborough Galerie, Zurich
Marlborough Fine Art, London
Roman Norbert Ketterer, 1969
Galerie Wilhelm Grosshennig, Düsseldorf, 1967

Exhibitions
Galerie Wilhelm Grosshennig, Düsseldorf. *Ausstellung deutscher und französischer Meisterwerke des 20. Jahrhunderts, Gemälde-Plastik*, November 15, 1966–February 15, 1967, cat.; ill. p. 16.

Marlborough Gallery, Inc., New York. *Masters of the Nineteenth and Twentieth Centuries*, May 7–June 11, 1983, cat. no. 37, listed as *Nelly (Bildnis einer Negerin)*, 1910; color ill.

ALEXEJ JAWLENSKY
Russian, 1864–1941

Woman's Head (Frauenkopf), 1913
oil on composition board
21¼ × 19½"
54.0 × 49.5 cm

Gift of Charlotte Mack
50.5518

Inscribed
recto, lower left: *a. jawlensky*
verso, upper center: *N Frauenkopf, 1913/N. 24./A.v. Jawlensky*

Provenance
Charlotte Mack

Exhibitions
Mills College, Oakland, California. *Modern Art: Eighty-fifth Anniversary Exhibition*, April–May, 1937, cat. no. 26, listed as *Head*, ca. 1919.

San Francisco Museum of Art. *Contemporary Art: Paintings, Watercolors and Sculpture Owned in the San Francisco Bay Region*, January 18–February 5, 1940, cat. no. 147, listed as *Head*, n.d.; ill. p. 50.

San Francisco Museum of Art. *Art of Our Time: Tenth Anniversary Exhibitions*, January 18–February 5, 1945, cat. no. 16, listed as *Head*, n.d.

Pasadena Art Museum (now Norton Simon Museum of Art at Pasadena), California. *Alexei Jawlensky: A Centennial Exhibition*, April 14–May 19, 1964, cat. no. 49. Circulated to: Rose Art Museum, Brandeis University, Waltham, Mass., November 9–December 13, 1964; University Art Gallery, University of California, Berkeley, March 2–31, 1965.

The Art Galleries, University of California, Santa Barbara. *Trends in Twentieth-Century Art: A Loan Exhibition from the San Francisco Museum of Art*, January 6–February 1, 1970, cat. no. 3, listed as *Head*, 1913; ill. no. 3.

Städtische Galerie im Lenbachhaus, Munich. *Alexej Jawlensky 1864–1941*,

February 23–April 17, 1983, cat. no. 119, listed as *Kopf*, 1913; ill. p. 222. Circulated to: Staatliche Kunsthalle, Baden-Baden, May 1–June 26, 1983.

Remarks
According to Clemens Weiler, *Jawlensky: Heads, Faces, Meditations* (New York: Praeger, 1971), p. 120, "It was Jawlensky's habit to number all his works." This may explain the presence of "N.24" on the verso of the work in the artist's handwriting.

ALEXEJ JAWLENSKY
Russian, 1864–1941

*Head: Red Light
(Kopf: Rotes Licht)*, 1926
oil wax medium on cardboard
21 × 19"
53.4 × 48.3 cm

Gift of Charlotte Mack
50.5952

Inscribed
recto, lower left: *A.J.*
verso, upper right: *Kopf: "Rotes Licht" i926/A.v. Jawlensky*

Provenance
Charlotte Mack

Exhibitions
San Francisco Museum of Art. *Contemporary Art: Paintings, Watercolors and Sculpture Owned in the San Francisco Bay Region*, January 18–February 5, 1940, cat. no. 146, listed as *Abstract Portrait*, n.d.

San Francisco Museum of Art. *Art of Our Time: Tenth Anniversary Exhibitions*, January 18–February 5, 1945, cat. no. 15, listed as *Abstract Portrait*, n.d.

Pasadena Art Museum (now Norton Simon Museum of Art at Pasadena), California. *Alexei Jawlensky: A Centennial Exhibition*, April 14–May 19, 1964, cat. no. 146. Circulated to: Rose Art Museum, Brandeis University, Waltham, Mass., November 9–December 13, 1964; University Art Gallery, University of California, Berkeley, March 2–31, 1965.

Städtische Galerie im Lenbachhaus, Munich. *Alexej Jawlensky 1864–1941*, February 23–April 17, 1983, cat. no. 173; ill. p. 272. Circulated to: Staatliche Kunsthalle, Baden-Baden, May 1–June 26, 1983.

MAX BECKMANN
German, 1884–1950

*Landscape, Cannes
(Landschaft, Cannes)*, 1934
oil on canvas
27⅝ × 39½"
70.2 × 100.4 cm

Gift of Louise S. Ackerman
72.12

Inscribed
recto, lower left: *Beckmann/(C) 1934*
verso, right vertical stretcher bar: *Landschaft xxxxx Cannes*

Provenance
Louise S. Ackerman, 1947
Stephan Lackner, 1937
Artist

Exhibitions
Kunsthalle, Bern. *Max Beckmann, Marguerite Frey-Surbek, Martin Christ, Fernand Riard*, February 19–March 20, 1938, cat. no. 22. Circulated to: Kunstverein, Winterthur, April 3–May 8, 1938; Galerie Aktuaryus, Zürich, June 2–22, 1938.

Buchholz Gallery, New York. *Max Beckmann: Recent Paintings*, February 21–March 18, 1939, cat. no. 3, listed as *Cannes*, 1934.

Buchholz Gallery, New York. *Max Beckmann: Paintings 1936–1939*, January 3–27, 1940, cat. no. 17, listed as *Park near Cannes (Southern France)*, 1939.

The Arts Club of Chicago. *Max Beckmann Exhibition*, January 2–27, 1942, cat. no. 16, listed as *Cannes*, 1934.

Hamline University, St. Paul, Minnesota. *Landscapes: Real and Imaginary*, October 29–November 19, 1946. Exhibition organized by the Museum of Modern Art, New York, circulated to: The Arts Club of Chicago, December 2–28, 1946; Grand Rapids Art Gallery, Michigan, January 7–28, 1947; Norton Gallery and School of Art, West Palm Beach, Florida, February 8–March 2, 1947; Cranbrook Art Museum, Bloomfield Hills, Michigan, March 16–April 6, 1947; Indiana University, Bloomington, April 22–May 13, 1947; San Francisco Museum of Art, June 3–24, 1947; Honolulu Academy of Arts, August 1–22, 1947.

The Mills College Art Gallery, Oakland, California. *Max Beckmann*, July–August 1950, cat. no. 16, listed as *Palmtrees, Nice*, n.d.

San Francisco Museum of Art. *Modern Masters in West Coast Collections*, October 18–November 27, 1960, cat., listed as *Cannes*, 1934.

University Art Museum, University of California, Berkeley. *Excellence: Art from the University Community*, November 6, 1970–January 10, 1971, cat. no. 326, listed as *Cannes*, 1934.

Josef-Haubrich-Kunsthalle, Cologne. *Max Beckmann*, April 19–June 24, 1984, cat. no. 26.

Literature
Fritz Nemitz. "Max Beckmann." In *Kunst: Malerei, Plastik, Graphik, Architektur, Wohnkultur*. Edited by Franz Roh. Munich: Münchner Verlag, 1948, vol. 1, ill. p. 88.

Lothar-Günther Buchheim. *Max*

Beckmann. Feldafing: Buchheim Verlag, 1949, ill. no. 88, listed as *Palmenlandschaft mit Meer, Süd-frankreich* (Seascape with Palm-trees, Southern France), 1934.

Benno Reifenberg and Wilhelm Hausenstein. *Max Beckmann.* Munich: R. Piper, 1949, cat. no. 365, listed as *Parkbild*, 1937; ill. no. 61.

Erhard Göpel. In *In Memoriam: Max Beckmann 12.2.1884– 27.12.1950.* Frankfurt am Main: K. G. Lohse, 1953, ref. p. 31, as *Palmenallee*, 1937.

Franz Roh. *Deutsche Maler der Ge-genwart.* Munich: Knorr & Hirth, 1957, ref. pp. 12–13, ill. no. 5.

Erhard Göpel and Barbara Göpel. *Max Beckmann: Katalog der Ge-mälde.* Bern: Kornfeld Verlag, 1976, vol. 1, ref. pp. 262, 263, 525; vol. 2, ill. p. 130, listed as *Landschaft bei Cannes*, 1934.

Remarks

The inscription on the recto of the painting can be read as 1934. How-ever, in Reifenberg–Hausenstein, an important early source, the paint-ing is titled and dated *Parkbild*, 1937. In her catalogue raisonné, Barbara Göpel questioned the title and the date of *Landschaft, Cannes* because of that early source. She has since concluded that the in-formation given in Reifenberg–Hau-senstein under no. 365 actually corresponds to another work, titled and dated *Blick auf den Tiergarten mit weissen Kugeln*, 1937, and that the painting under consideration can be dated as 1934.

In spite of the inscription "(C) 1934," Göpel maintains that the work was begun in Berlin and not in Cannes, arguing that Beckmann was not in Cannes around 1933 (when he began the work) nor in 1934 (when he finished it).

MAX BECKMANN
German, 1884–1950

Woman at Her Toilette, with Red and White Lilies (Frau bei der Toilette mit roten und weissen Lilien)
1938
oil on canvas
43½ × 25¾″
110.5 × 65.4 cm

Bequest of Marian W. Sinton
81.51

Inscribed
recto, lower left: *Beckmann/A 38*

Provenance
Mr. and Mrs. Edgar Sinton, ca. 1955
Susanne Bernfeld, ca. 1950
Stephan Lackner, 1939
Artist

Exhibitions
The Mills College Art Gallery, Oakland, California. *Max Beck-*

mann, July–August 1950, cat. no. 19, listed as *Woman Dressing*, n.d.

Thomas Welton Stanford Art Gallery, Stanford University, California. *The Proud Possessors*, April 16–May 6, 1962, brochure no. 8, listed as *Woman with Flowers*, n.d.

M. H. de Young Memorial Museum, San Francisco. *The San Francisco Collector*, September 21–October 17, 1965, cat. no. 97, listed as *Woman and Flowers*, 1938.

Musée National d'Art Moderne, Paris. *Max Beckmann*, September 25–October 28, 1968, cat. no. 70, listed as *Femme à sa toilette avec des lis rouges et blancs*, 1938. Circu-lated to: Haus der Kunst, Munich, November 9, 1968–January 6, 1969, cat. no. 68, listed as *Frau bei der Toilette mit roten und weissen Lilien*, 1938; ill.; Palais des Beaux-Arts, Brussels, January 16–March 2, 1969.

Literature
Benno Reifenberg and Wilhelm Hausenstein. *Max Beckmann.* Munich: R. Piper, 1949, ref. p. 75, as *Frau bei der Toilette mit roten und weissen Lilien*, 1938.

Erhard Göpel and Barbara Göpel. *Max Beckmann: Katalog der Gemälde.* Bern: Kornfeld, 1976, vol. 1, ref. pp. 315, 528; vol. 2, ill. p. 172.

PIET MONDRIAN
Dutch, 1872–1944

Church Façade/Church at Domburg (formerly *Cathedral*)
1914
charcoal on chipboard
28¼ × 19⅛″
71.8 × 48.6 cm

Purchase
70.43

Inscribed
recto, lower left: *P M*
recto, lower right: *1 4*

Provenance
Paul Kantor, 1968
Mr. and Mrs. Herbert Matter, 1943
Artist

Exhibitions
The Solomon R. Guggenheim Mu-seum, New York. *Piet Mondrian: The Earlier Years*, December 11, 1957–January 19, 1958, cat., listed as *Cathedral*. Circulated to: San Francisco Museum of Art, February 6–March 23, 1958.

San Francisco Museum of Art. *Mondrian and American Neo-Plasticism*, January 25–February 13, 1972.

Milwaukee Art Center. *Mondrian and His American Followers: Diller, Glarner and Von Wiegand*, Decem-ber 10, 1980–January 31, 1981.

THEO VAN DOESBURG
Dutch, 1883–1931

Simultaneous Counter Composi-tion (Contre composition simultanée)
1929
oil on canvas
19¾ × 19¾″
50.2 × 50.2 cm

Gift of Peggy Guggenheim
51.3389

Inscribed
recto, lower left: *T.H.D. '29*
verso, center right: *Theo van Doesburg 1929*

Provenance
Mrs. Theo van Doesburg, 1931
Artist

Exhibitions
Parc des Expositions, Porte de Versailles, Paris. *Exposition Rétro-spective Van Doesburg*, January 15–February 1, 1932, cat. no. 54.

Kunsthalle, Basel. *Konstruktivisten*, January 16–February 14, 1937, cat. no. 7.

Art of This Century, New York. *Theo van Doesburg: Retrospective Exhibi-tion*, April 29–May 31, 1947, cat. no. 32, dated 1930. Circulated to: Los Angeles County Museum of History, Science and Art, June 17–July 15, 1947; San Francisco Museum of Art, July 29–August 24, 1947.

University Art Gallery, University of California, Berkeley. *Linearity in Paintings and Drawings from the Collections of the San Francisco Museum of Art*, February 5–March 11, 1962, cat. no. 3.

The Fine Arts Patrons of Newport Harbor, The Pavilion Gallery, Balboa, California (now Newport Harbor Art Museum, Newport Beach). *Some Continuing Directions*, November 6–December 4, 1966, cat. no. 40; ill. no. 40.

Literature
Joost Baljeu. *Theo van Doesburg.* New York: Macmillan, 1974, ill. pp. 200, 201 (studio views).

Evert van Straaten, ed. *Theo van Doesburg 1883–1931. Een documen-taire op basis van materiaal uit de Schenking van Moorsel.* The Hague: Staatsuitgeverij, 1983, ill. p. 179 (installation view of 1932 retrospec-tive at Parc des Expositions, Paris).

JOAQUIN TORRES-GARCIA
Uruguayan, 1874–1949

Constructivist Painting No. 8
1938
gouache on paperboard
31⅝ × 19½″
80.5 × 49.5 cm

Purchased through the aid of a gift of Willard Durham
50.3013

Inscribed
recto, bottom edge:
38 M G JT G

Exhibitions
Sidney Janis Gallery, New York. *J. Torres-Garcia*, April 3–22, 1950, cat. no. 8. Circulated to: San Fran-cisco Museum of Art, June 19–July 2, 1950.

The Mexican Museum, San Fran-cisco. *Día de la Raza*, October 7–November 15, 1976.

LÁSZLÓ MOHOLY-NAGY
American, born Hungary, 1895–1946

A IX, 1923
oil and pencil on canvas
50½ × 38¾″
128.3 × 98.4 cm

Gift of Sibyl Moholy-Nagy
51.3208

Inscribed
verso, right side (prior to relining):
L. Moholy-Nagy/A IX, 1923

Provenance
Sibyl Moholy-Nagy
Artist

Exhibitions
Kunsthalle, Basel. *Konstruktivisten*, January 16–February 14, 1937, cat.

The Museum of Non-Objective Paint-ing (now The Solomon R. Guggen-heim Museum), New York. *In Memoriam László Moholy-Nagy*, May 15–July 10, 1947, cat.; ill. p. 37.

Fogg Art Museum, Harvard Univer-sity, Cambridge. *Works of Art by Moholy-Nagy*, February 6–27, 1950, cat. no. 31.

Colorado Springs Fine Arts Center. *Moholy-Nagy 1895–1946*, May 15–31, 1950, cat.

Kent State University, Kent, Ohio. *Moholy-Nagy*, February 17–March 9, 1964. Exhibition organized by the Museum of Modern Art, New York, circulated to: University of Manitoba, Winnipeg, March 25– April 15, 1964; North Dakota State University, Fargo, May 1–22, 1964; Northern Michigan University, Marquette, June 8–28, 1964; Ohio State University, Columbus, July 13–31, 1964; Endahl-Cloyd Union, University of North Carolina, Ra-leigh, September 3–24, 1964; Allen Memorial Art Museum, Oberlin College, Ohio, October 10–31, 1964; Allegheny College, Meadville, Penn-sylvania, November 16–December 7, 1964; University of North Carolina, Greensboro, January 4–25, 1965; State University College, Cortland, New York, February 9–March 2, 1965; Watson Art Gallery, Elmira College, New York, March 12–April 2, 1965; State University College, Geneseo, New York, April 23–May 11, 1965.

University Art Museum, University of California, Berkeley. *Moholy-Nagy*, October 7–November 2, 1969.

Hirshhorn Museum and Sculpture Garden, Smithsonian Institution, Washington, D.C. *Dreams and Nightmares: Utopian Visions in Modern Art*, December 8, 1983–February 12, 1984, cat. no. 51; ref. p. 87, color ill. p. 85.

Literature

"1. moholy-nagy." *Telehor*, Special Supplement (1936), ill. p. 73.

Peter Selz. *Art in Our Times: A Pictorial History 1890–1980*. New York: Harry N. Abrams, 1981, ref. p. 269, color ill. p. 268.

VASILY KANDINSKY

French, born Russia, 1866–1944

***Brownish** (Bräunlich)*, 1931
oil on cardboard
$19\frac{3}{8} \times 27\frac{5}{8}''$
49.2 × 70.2 cm

William L. Gerstle Collection
Gift of William L. Gerstle
45.100

Inscribed

recto, lower left:
verso, upper left: <K /*„Bräunlich."/ i93i/ 70 × 49*

Provenance

Nierendorf Gallery, New York
J. B. Neumann
The Mayor Gallery, London
Artist

Exhibitions

San Francisco Museum of Art. *Art of Our Time*, January 18–February 5, 1945, cat. no. 17.

Pomona College, Claremont, California. *German Expressionist Painting, 1900–1950*, October 25–November 23, 1957, cat. no. 18; ill. no. 18. Circulated to: University Art Gallery, University of California, Berkeley, December 2–18, 1957; Santa Barbara Museum of Art, California, January 7–February 9, 1958.

The Columbus Gallery of Fine Arts, Ohio. *German Expressionism*, February 10–March 9, 1961, cat. no. 28.

Pomona College Gallery, Claremont, California. *Wassily Kandinsky 1866–1944*, February 10–March 6, 1966.

M. Knoedler and Co., New York. *Space and Dream*, December 5–29, 1967, cat. p. 53; ill. p. 53.

The Art Galleries, University of California, Santa Barbara. *Trends in Twentieth-Century Art: A Loan Exhibition from the San Francisco Museum of Art*, January 6–February 1, 1970, cat. no. 8; ill. no. 8.

The Solomon R. Guggenheim Museum, New York. *Kandinsky: Russian and Bauhaus Years 1915–1933*, December 9, 1983–February 12, 1984, cat. no. 273; ref. p. 80, ill. p. 308. Circulated to: The High Museum of Art, Atlanta, March 15–April 29, 1984; Kunsthaus, Zurich, May 29–July 15, 1984; Bauhaus-Archiv, Berlin, August 9–September 23, 1984.

Literature

Will Grohmann. *Wassily Kandinsky: Life and Work*. New York: Harry N. Abrams, 1958, cat. no. 550; ill. p. 382.

Hans K. Roethel and Jean K. Benjamin. *Kandinsky: Catalogue Raisonné of the Oil-Paintings, Volume Two 1916–1944*. Ithaca, N.Y.: Cornell University Press, 1984, cat. no. 996; ref. p. 899, ill. p. 899.

Remarks

This work is no. 550 in Kandinsky's handwritten list of his works which he called his "Hauskatalog," a term which has been translated as "House catalogue"; it has also been referred to as "handlist."

JOSEF ALBERS

American, born Germany, 1888–1976

Growing, 1940
oil on Masonite
$24 \times 26\frac{3}{4}''$
61.0 × 68.0 cm

Gift of Charlotte Mack
59.2668

Inscribed

recto, lower right: *A40*
verso, upper right: *Growing/Albers 1940* . . . [inscription continues with specifics on medium]

Provenance

Charlotte Mack
Design Incorporated, Boston, ca. 1941
Artist

Exhibitions

Addison Gallery of American Art, Phillips Academy, Andover, Massachusetts. *European Artists Teaching in America*, September 1–November 9, 1941, cat. no. 3; ill. p. 11.

California Palace of the Legion of Honor, San Francisco. *Josef Albers*, August 24–September 24, 1947.

The Metropolitan Museum of Art, New York. *New York Painting and Sculpture: 1940–1970*, October 18, 1969–February 1, 1970, cat. no. 1; ill. p. 113.

The Art Gallery, State University of New York, Albany. *Constructivist Tendencies: From the Collection of Mr. and Mrs. George Rickey*, August 30–September 27, 1970. Exhibition organized by the Art Galleries, University of California, Santa Barbara, circulated nationally through April 1972.

The High Museum of Art, Atlanta. *Bauhaus Color*, January 31–March 14, 1976, cat. p. 65. Circulated to: Museum of Fine Arts, Houston, April 8–May 30, 1976; Fine Arts Gallery of San Diego, August 1–September 21, 1976 (exhibited only at the Fine Arts Gallery of San Diego).

Fresno Arts Center, California. *Two Hundred Years of American Painting*, November 20–December 30, 1977, cat. no. 64.

Literature

"Who Teaches Who? This Is What European Artists Have Been Doing in America." *Art News*, vol. 40, no. 13 (October 15–31, 1941), ref. p. 18, ill. p. 18.

George Rickey. *Constructivism: Origins and Evolution*. New York: Braziller, 1967, ref. p. 45, ill. p. 45.

Constructivist Tendencies: From the Collection of Mr. and Mrs. George Rickey. Santa Barbara, Calif.: Art Galleries, University of California, Santa Barbara, 1970, ref. p. 8.

Allan Temko. "Homage to the Square—A Classic Lesson in Color." *San Francisco Sunday Examiner and Chronicle, This World* (September 7, 1980), ref. pp. 34–35.

Remarks

There is an oil-on-paper study for this work now in the collection of the Neuberger Museum, State University of New York at Purchase, which was donated to that institution by George Rickey and his wife. In an inscription on the verso of this work, Albers states: "It is a study for 'Growing' which Mrs. Charlotte Mack of San Francisco bought from the Nierendorf Gallery in New York and gave it some years ago to the San Francisco Museum." It has not been confirmed if and when the Nierendorf Gallery ever actually owned the final version of *Growing*, or if they sold it on behalf of Design Incorporated or another party.

JOSEF ALBERS

American, born Germany, 1888–1976

Tenayuca, 1943
oil on Masonite
$22\frac{1}{2} \times 43\frac{1}{2}''$
57.2 × 110.5 cm

Purchased with the aid of funds from Mr. and Mrs. Richard N. Goldman and Madeleine Haas Russell
84.1

Inscribed

verso, upper right: *Tenayuca Albers '43*
verso, lower right: *panel: high 22⅝ wide 43⅝"/________/paintings "21" 42"/*

Provenance

Sewell Sillman, 1972
Artist

Remarks

Sewell Sillman, a friend of Albers and the former owner of *Tenayuca*, writes: "Tenayuca is a pre-Conquest site in the upper valley of Mexico. Albers spent many summers in Mexico and had a great respect for the art of the Indians before the conquest. The image is not a copy of an Indian motif, rather it parallels the visual relationships which can be found in the work." (Letter from Sewell Sillman to the Museum, January 16, 1984.)

The isometric ink drawing of 1936 on which this painting and *Tenayuca Dark* are based is in the Museum's collection, as are the ink-on-paper study for *Tenayuca Dark* and the oil-on-Masonite study for *Tenayuca*. The partially completed work on the verso of the oil-on-Masonite study makes use of black and gray, and is probably the first attempt to follow the isometric drawing. The oil-on-Masonite study and the study for *Tenayuca Dark* make use of two tones of gray, which were then used in the final versions of both *Tenayuca Dark* and *Tenayuca*.

JOSEF ALBERS

American, born Germany, 1888–1976

Study for Homage to the Square
1972
oil on Masonite
$23\frac{7}{8} \times 23\frac{7}{8}''$
60.6 × 60.6 cm

Gift of Anni Albers and the Josef Albers Foundation
79.121

Inscribed

recto, lower right: A72
verso, upper right: *Study for/Homage to the Square* . . . [inscription continues with specifics on medium]

Provenance

Anni Albers and the Josef Albers Foundation, 1976
Artist

Literature

Allan Temko. "Homage to the Square—A Classic Lesson in Color." *San Francisco Sunday Examiner and Chronicle, This World* (September 7, 1980), ref. pp. 34–35.

GIORGIO DE CHIRICO

Italian, born Greece, 1888–1978

***The Vexations of the Thinker; The Inconsistencies of the Thinker** (Les Contrariétés du penseur)*, 1915
oil on canvas
$18\frac{1}{4} \times 15''$
46.4 × 38.1 cm

Templeton Crocker Fund Purchase
51.8

Inscribed
recto, lower left: *G. de Chirico/1915*

Provenance
Gordon Onslow Ford, 1940
André Breton
Artist

Exhibitions
San Francisco Museum of Art. *Art in the Twentieth Century*, June 17–July 10, 1955, cat. p. 12, dated 1914.
Santa Barbara Museum of Art, California. *Harbingers of Surrealism*, February 26–March 27, 1966, cat. no. 13; ill. no. 13.
The Museum of Modern Art, New York. *De Chirico*, March 31–June 29, 1982, cat. no. 52; ill. p. 169. Circulated to: The Tate Gallery, London, August 4–October 3, 1982, cat., listed as for the Museum of Modern Art, New York; Haus der Kunst, Munich, *Giorgio de Chirico*, November 17, 1982–January 30, 1983, cat. (in German and French), no. 38, listed as *Die Zerstreutheit des Denkers, La Contrariété du Penseur*; ill. p. 170; Centre Georges Pompidou, Musée National d'Art Moderne, Paris, February 24–April 25, 1983, cat. as for Haus der Kunst.

Literature
James Thrall Soby. *The Early Chirico*. New York: Dodd, Mead, 1941, ref. p. 55, ill. pl. 45.

PAUL KLEE
Swiss, 1879–1940

Red Suburb (Rotes Villenquartier)
1920
oil on cardboard
14⅜ × 12½″
36.5 × 31.8 cm

Purchase
51.3207

Inscribed
recto, lower left: *Klee/1920.74*

Provenance
Gordon Onslow Ford, 1939
Zwemmer Gallery, London
Mr. Lockett, 1935
The Mayor Gallery, London
Dr. Bernatti

Exhibitions
Galerie Alfred Flechtheim, Berlin. *Paul Klee: Neue Bilder und Aquarelle*, October 20–November 15, 1929, cat.
Santa Barbara Museum of Art, California. *The Art of Paul Klee*, April 12–May 8, 1960, checklist in the SBMA *Calendar*, April 1960, listed as *Colony of Red Houses*, 1920.
University Art Gallery, University of California, Berkeley. *Linearity in Paintings and Drawings from the Collections of the San Francisco*

Museum of Art, February 5–March 11, 1962, cat. no. 17, listed as *Colony of Red Houses*, 1920.
Santa Barbara Museum of Art, California. *Harbingers of Surrealism*, February 26–March 27, 1966, cat. no. 35, listed as *Colony of Red Roses*, corrected to *Colony of Red Houses*, 1920.
Pasadena Art Museum (now Norton Simon Museum of Art at Pasadena), California. *Paul Klee 1879–1940: A Retrospective Exhibition*, February 21–April 2, 1967, cat. no. 31, listed as *Suburb of Red Houses (Rotes Villenquartier)*, 1920; ill. p. 34. Exhibition organized in collaboration with the Solomon R. Guggenheim Museum, New York, circulated to: San Francisco Museum of Art, April 13–May 14, 1967; Columbus Gallery of Fine Art, Ohio, May 25–June 25, 1967; The Cleveland Museum of Art, July 5–August 13, 1967; William Rockhill Nelson Gallery of Art (now The Nelson-Atkins Museum of Art), Kansas City, Missouri, September 1–30, 1967; Baltimore Museum of Art, October 24–November 19, 1967; Washington University Gallery of Art, Saint Louis, December 3, 1967–January 5, 1968; Philadelphia Museum of Art, January 15–February 15, 1968.
Kunsthalle, Cologne. *Paul Klee: Das Werk der Jahre 1919–1933. Gemälde, Handzeichnungen, Druckgraphik*, April 11–June 4, 1979, cat. no. 27; ill. p. 151.
Städtische Galerie im Lenbachhaus, Munich. *Paul Klee: Das Frühwerk 1883–1922*, December 12, 1979–March 2, 1980, cat. no. 417; ill. no. 417.

PAUL KLEE
Swiss, 1879–1940

Nearly Hit (Fast getroffen), 1928
oil on board
20 × 15½″
50.8 × 39.4 cm

Albert M. Bender Collection
Albert M. Bender Bequest Fund Purchase
44.2640

Inscribed
recto, lower left: *Klee/1928 E3*

Provenance
Nierendorf Gallery, New York

Exhibitions
University Gallery, University of Minnesota, Minneapolis. *German Expressionism in Art: Painting, Sculpture, Prints*, October 23–November 27, 1951, cat. no. 56.
Santa Barbara Museum of Art, California. *The Art of Paul Klee*, April 12–May 8, 1960, checklist in the SBMA *Calendar*, April 1960.
The Denver Art Museum. *Paul Klee*

in Review, April 7–May 7, 1963, brochure no. 28.
Pasadena Art Museum (now Norton Simon Museum of Art at Pasadena), California. *Paul Klee 1879–1940: A Retrospective Exhibition*, February 21–April 2, 1967, cat. no. 99; ill. p. 71. Exhibition organized in collaboration with the Solomon R. Guggenheim Museum, New York, circulated to: San Francisco Museum of Art, April 13–May 14, 1967; Columbus Gallery of Fine Art, Ohio, May 25–June 25, 1967; The Cleveland Museum of Art, July 5–August 13, 1967; William Rockhill Nelson Gallery of Art (now The Nelson-Atkins Museum of Art), Kansas City, Missouri, September 1–30, 1967; Baltimore Museum of Art, October 24–November 19, 1967; Washington University Gallery of Art, Saint Louis, December 3, 1967–January 5, 1968; Philadelphia Museum of Art, January 15–February 15, 1968.
Des Moines Art Center. *Paul Klee: Paintings and Watercolors from the Bauhaus Years, 1921–1931*, September 18–October 28, 1973, cat. no. 39; ill. no. 39.
The Taft Museum, Cincinnati. *Best of Fifty*, March 24–May 8, 1977, cat.; color ill.
Kunsthalle, Cologne. *Paul Klee: Das Werk der Jahre 1919–1933. Gemälde, Handzeichnungen, Druckgraphik*, April 11–June 4, 1979, cat. no. 239; ill. p. 293.

Literature
San Francisco Museum of Art Quarterly Bulletin, Series 2, vol. 1, nos. 3–4 (1952), ref. p. 35, ill. p. 36.
Walter Abell. *The Collective Dream in Art: A Psycho-Historical Theory of Culture Based on Relations between the Arts, Psychology, and the Social Sciences*. Cambridge: Harvard University Press, 1957, pl. 36, fig. 100.

JEAN (HANS) ARP
French, 1887–1966

Head and Leaf; Head and Vase (Tête et feuille; Tête et vase), (formerly *Head and Navel*, ca. 1926), 1929
string and oil on canvas mounted on board
13½ × 10½″
34.3 × 26.7 cm

Evelyn and Walter Haas, Jr. Fund Purchase
80.390

Provenance
Robert Miller Gallery, Inc., New York
Private collection, New York
Artist

Exhibitions
Galerie Goemans, Paris. Spring 1929.
San Francisco Museum of Modern

Art. *Resource/Reservoir: Collage and Assemblage*, July 30–September 26, 1982, cat. no. 1; ref., ill.

Literature
"Hans Arp. (Galerie Goemans)." *Cahiers d'Art*, no. 4 (May 1929), ill. p. 420.
Hans Arp. "Poèmes." *Bifur*, no. 5 (July 1930), ill. p. 73.
Willi Baumeister. *Das Unbekannte in der Kunst*. Stuttgart: Curt G. Schwab, 1947, ill. no. 124, listed as *Kopf und Blatt*, ca. 1924.
Bernd Rau. *Jean Arp: The Reliefs, Catalogue of Complete Works*. New York: Rizzoli, 1981, cat. no. 194, listed as *Tête et feuille; Tête et vase. Kopf und Blatt; Kopf und Vase*; ref. p. 97, ill. p. 97.

JEAN (HANS) ARP
French, 1887–1966

Objects Arranged According to the Laws of Chance III; Symmetrical Configuration (Objets placés selon les lois du hasard III; Configuration symétrique), 1931
oil on wood
10⅛ × 11⅜ × 2⅜″
25.7 × 28.9 × 6.1 cm

Purchase
84.5

Inscribed
verso, upper left: *Arp*
typed label, verso, lower left: *ARP 438/configuration symétrique/relief bois couleur a l'huile/meudon 1931*

Provenance
Sidney Janis Gallery, New York, 1967
Galerie d'Art Moderne, Basel
Artist

Exhibitions
Sidney Janis Gallery, New York. *An Exhibition of Sculpture by Jean Arp*, March 6–April 6, 1968, cat. no. 42.
Sidney Janis Gallery, New York. *Exhibition of Sculpture in Marble, Bronze, & Wood Relief by Jean Arp*, January 10–February 16, 1980, cat. no. 41; ill. no. 41.

Literature
Bernd Rau. *Jean Arp: The Reliefs, Catalogue of Complete Works*. New York: Rizzoli, 1981, cat. no. 225, listed as *Objets placés selon les lois du hasard III; Configuration symétrique. Gegenstände nach den Gesetzen des Zufalls geordnet III; Symmetrische Konfiguration*; ref. p. 110, ill. p. 110.

Remarks
This relief is one of a series of seven reliefs closely related in style and configuration; see Rau, cat. nos. 188, 222, 223, 224, 226, 227. There are subtle variations in the

disposition of shapes and differences in color; some are painted and some exploit the natural finish of the wood.

JEAN (HANS) ARP
French, 1887–1966

Human Concretion without Oval Bowl (*Concrétion humaine sans coupe*), 1933
bronze (polished) 2/3
23 × 22⅝ × 15¾″
58.5 × 57.5 × 40.0 cm

William L. Gerstle Collection
William L. Gerstle Fund Purchase
62.3421

Provenance
Galerie Chalette, New York, 1962
Artist

Exhibitions
The Art Galleries and the Art Affiliates, University of California, Santa Barbara. *Sculpture—Twenties and Thirties*, February 22–March 26, 1972, cat. no. 2.
Fresno Arts Center, California. *Masterworks of Modern Sculpture*, October 13–November 14, 1976, cat. no. 21; ill. no. 21, color ill. back cover.
Mary Porter Sesnon Art Gallery, University of California, Santa Cruz. *Modern Sculpture: European and American Works in West Coast Collections*, February 13–March 13, 1977, cat.

Literature
Carola Giedion-Welcker. *Jean Arp.* New York: Harry N. Abrams, 1957, ref. to the Human Concretion theme p. XXVII.
Jean Arp. "Looking." *Arp.* New York: The Museum of Modern Art, 1958, ref. to the Human Concretion theme pp. 14, 15.
"Reviews: San Francisco—New Accessions 1962–1963, San Francisco Museum of Art." *Artforum*, vol. 2, no. 3 (September 1963), ref. p. 49.
Ionel Jianou. *Jean Arp.* Paris: Arted, Editions d'Art, 1973, cat. no. 14; ref. to the Human Concretion theme pp. 12, 32–34, 37, 39, ill. of unidentified cast.
Mark Levy. "Jean Arp: A Study of His Three-Dimensional Sculpture." Ph.D. diss., Indiana University, 1977, ref. to the Human Concretion theme and other works in the series, pp. 8, 40–54, 55, 57–58.

JOAN MIRÓ
Spanish, 1893–1983

Painting (Peinture), (formerly **Dark Brown and White Oval**), 1926
oil on canvas
28⅞ × 36¼″
73.4 × 92.0 cm

Gift of Joseph M. Bransten in memory of Ellen Hart Bransten
80.428

Inscribed
recto, lower right center: *Miró/1926*
verso, upper right: *Joan Miró/1926*

Provenance
Mr. and Mrs. Joseph Bransten, 1950
Sidney Janis Gallery, New York
Mrs. Russell
Artist

Exhibitions
California Palace of the Legion of Honor, San Francisco. *Joan Miró*, August 4–September 9, 1951.
San Francisco Museum of Art. *Art in the Twentieth Century*, June 17–July 10, 1955, cat. p. 15.
San Francisco Museum of Art. *Modern Masters in West Coast Collections: An Exhibition Selected in Celebration of the Twenty-fifth Anniversary of the San Francisco Museum of Art, 1935–1960*, October 18–November 27, 1960, cat.

Literature
Jacques Dupin. *Joan Miró: Life and Work.* New York: Harry N. Abrams, 1962, cat. no. 170, listed as *Painting*, 1926, erroneously as belonging to Philadelphia Museum of Art, Gallatin Collection; ill. p. 514.

Remarks
According to Sidney Janis Gallery, New York, this painting was purchased from a Mrs. Russell of New York under the title *Dark Brown and White Oval*, and ever since the work was sold by this gallery to Mr. and Mrs. Joseph Bransten it has been known variously as *Dark Brown and White Oval* and *Brown and White Oval*. However, further research points to the incongruity of this title and strongly suggests that *Painting (Peinture)* is in fact the correct appellation.

JOAN MIRÓ
Spanish, 1893–1983

Dawn Perfumed by a Shower of Gold (*L'Aube parfumée par la pluie d'or*), 1954
watercolor and plaster on composition board
42½ × 21⅝″
108.0 × 54.9 cm

Gift of Wilbur D. May
64.58

Inscribed
recto, lower right: *Miró*
verso, upper center: *Miró/1954*
verso, upper left: *L'AUBE PAR-FUMÉE/PAR LA PLUIE D'OR*

Provenance
Wilbur D. May, 1956
Artist

Exhibitions
Pierre Matisse Gallery, New York. *Spring Exhibition: Painting & Sculpture*, May 11–28, 1955, cat. no. 4.
James E. Church Fine Arts Building, University of Nevada, Reno. *Seventy Works by Fifty Modern Masters*, October 23–November 20, 1960, cat. no. 39; ill.
Des Moines Art Center, Iowa. *Art in Western Europe: The Postwar Years 1945–1955*, September 19–October 29, 1978, cat. no. 42.

Literature
Jacques Dupin. *Joan Miró: Life and Work.* New York: Harry N. Abrams, 1962, cat. no. 848; ref. p. 439, ill. p. 564.

SALVADOR DALI
Spanish, born 1904

Oedipus Complex, 1930
pastel on paper
24⅛ × 19¾″
61.3 × 50.2 cm

Purchase
51.3393

Inscribed
recto, lower left: *S. Dali–30–*

Provenance
Gordon Onslow Ford, 1939
Zwemmer Gallery, London
Artist

Exhibitions
The Phoenix Art Museum, Arizona. *Aspects of the Desert*, November 14, 1959–February 1960, cat. no. 11; ill. no. 11.
Art Gallery, University of California, Irvine. *Twentieth-Century Works on Paper*, January 30–February 25, 1968, cat. no. 9; ill. p. 13. Circulated to: Memorial Union Art Gallery, University of California, Davis, March 26–April 20, 1968.

YVES TANGUY
French, 1900–1955

Second Thoughts (*Arrières-pensées*), 1939
oil on canvas
36⅛ × 29¼″
91.7 × 74.3 cm

William L. Gerstle Collection
William L. Gerstle Fund Purchase
52.4155

Inscribed
recto, lower right: *Yves Tanguy/ Chemillieu/1939*

Provenance
Gordon Onslow Ford, 1939
Artist

Exhibitions
Centre Georges Pompidou, Musée National d'Art Moderne, Paris. *Yves Tanguy: Rétrospective 1925–1955*, June 17–September 27, 1982, cat. no. 79; ref. p. 122, ill. no. 79. Circulated to: Staatliche Kunsthalle, Baden-Baden, October 17, 1982–January 2, 1983, cat. no. 76, listed as *Hintergedanken*; ref. p. 255, ill. p. 198; The Solomon R. Guggenheim Museum, New York, *Yves Tanguy: A Retrospective*, January 21–February 27, 1983, brochure no. 79, listed as *Hidden Thoughts*.

Literature
André Breton. "La Maison d'Yves Tanguy." *London Bulletin*, nos. 18–20 (June 1940), pp. 17–18, ill. p. 16.
James Thrall Soby. "Inland in the Subconscious: Yves Tanguy." *Magazine of Art*, vol. 42, no. 1 (January 1949), ill. p. 2.

Remarks
Letter from Gordon Onslow Ford to the San Francisco Museum of Art, July 22, 1968: "Yves Tanguy painted *Arrières Pensées* in 1939 at Chateau Chemillieu where the André Bretons, the Mattas, Yves Tanguy, Esteban Frances, myself, and others were staying for the summer. . . . Chateau Chemillieu was on an isolated hilltop above the Rhone in Aix. I saw *Arrières Pensées* in every stage as it was made, and bought it as soon as it was completed, before it was dry. It was at this time that Tanguy became engaged to Kay Sage who was then Princess de San Faustino. . . . *Arrières Pensées* was . . . accompanied by a poem *La Maison d'Yves Tanguy* by André Breton that was written at Chemillieu at the same time the painting was made."

ALBERTO GIACOMETTI
Swiss, 1901–1966

Annette VII, 1962
bronze 2/6
18½ × 10¾ × 7½″
47.0 × 27.3 × 19.1 cm

Gift of Mr. and Mrs. Louis Honig
69.83

Inscribed
left side of base, top: *2/6 Alberto Giacometti*

Provenance
Mr. and Mrs. Louis Honig
Saidenberg Gallery, New York
Galerie Maeght, Paris

Exhibitions

University Art Museum, University of California, Berkeley. *Excellence: Art from the University Community,* November 6, 1970–January 10, 1971, cat. no. 375, listed as *Bust of Annette.*

The Solomon R. Guggenheim Museum, New York. *Alberto Giacometti: A Retrospective Exhibition,* April 5–June 23, 1974, cat. no. 106, listed as *Bust of Annette VII (Buste d'Annette VII);* ref. p. 122, ill. p. 122.

Literature

Thomas B. Hess. "Wright's Wrong for Giacometti." *New York* (June 10, 1974), ill. p. 72.

Remarks

Giacometti met his wife, Annette Arm, between 1942 and 1945 in Geneva, where he lived for most of the duration of the Second World War. They were married in 1949 in Paris where the artist had, once again, set up his studio. Annette became a central subject for both his painting and his sculpture in the late 1950s and early 1960s. *Annette VII* is one of a group of portrait busts executed between 1960 and 1964. Six of these busts, including the Museum's cast, are reproduced in the catalogue of the 1974 retrospective exhibition at the Solomon R. Guggenheim Museum (cat. nos. 103–8).

JOSEPH CORNELL
American, 1903–1972

Untitled *(Pink Palace)*
ca. 1946–48
wooden box containing photostat with ink wash, wood, mirror, plant material, and artificial snow
8⅝ × 14¼ × 4⅜"
21.9 × 36.2 × 11.1 cm

Purchased through gifts of Mr. and Mrs. William M. Roth and William L. Gerstle
82.328

Inscribed

verso of box, on label, lower right: *Joseph Cornell*

Provenance

Castelli Feigen Corcoran, New York
The Estate of Joseph Cornell, New York, 1972
Artist

Exhibitions

William Rockhill Nelson Gallery and Atkins Museum of Fine Arts (now the Nelson-Atkins Museum of Art), Kansas City, Missouri. *Boxes by Joseph Cornell,* October 8–November 7, 1977.

Castelli Feigen Corcoran, New York. *Joseph Cornell: Nine Masterpieces,*

1935–1950, November 6–December 30, 1979.

Rheinhallen, Cologne. *Internationale Ausstellung Köln 1981: Westkunst/ Contemporary Art since 1939,* May 30–August 16, 1981.

Castelli Feigen Corcoran, New York. *Joseph Cornell: Fifteen Masterworks 1939–1953,* May 11–June 18, 1982. See Literature.

San Francisco Museum of Modern Art. *Joseph Cornell: New Acquisitions,* November 9, 1982–January 2, 1983.

Fundación Juan March, Madrid. *Exposicion Joseph Cornell,* April 13–May 27, 1984, cat. no. 30; ill. no. 30. Circulated to: Fundacio Joan Miró, Barcelona, June 5–July 15, 1984.

Literature

Sandra Leonard Starr. *Joseph Cornell: Art and Metaphysics.* New York: Castelli Feigen Corcoran, 1982, cat. no. 11, listed as ca. 1946–50; ref. pp. 65–66, color ill. p. 64. (Published in conjunction with exhibition *Joseph Cornell: Fifteen Masterworks 1939–1953.*)

Remarks

Sandra Leonard Starr gives an iconographical reading of Cornell's work based on the ontology of Christian Science. Cornell became a Christian Scientist around 1925 and Starr claims that this was "the single most important force not only in his life but in his work" (p. 1). She states, "There is evidence that the initial inspiration for the *Pink Palace* series was . . . Charles Perrault and his tale of 'The Sleeping Beauty'" as translated into the ballet (p. 65). She interprets this fairytale ballet as "a metaphor for resurrection, immortality, and eternal youth" and thus relates it to the beliefs of Christian Science. However, a direct connection between *The Sleeping Beauty* and the Pink Palace Series has yet to be proven. Moreover, such a strict interpretation suggests that Cornell's way of thinking was linear when it seems, more appropriately, to have been an intuitive process emphasizing an infinite complex of ideas and associations.

JOSEPH CORNELL
American, 1903–1972

Untitled *(Window Façade)*
ca. 1950–53
wooden box containing paint on wood, nails, glass, and mirror
20 × 11 × 4¼"
50.8 × 27.9 × 10.8 cm

Albert M. Bender Collection
Purchased through a gift of Albert M. Bender
82.329

Provenance

Etablissement Taglioni, Liechtenstein
Fernando Garcia Guereta

Exhibition

San Francisco Museum of Modern Art. *Joseph Cornell: New Acquisitions,* November 9, 1982–January 2, 1983.

Remarks

In *Joseph Cornell and the Ballet,* Castelli Feigen Corcoran, New York, 1983, Sandra Leonard Starr discusses the theme of the ballet in Joseph Cornell's work, a predominant motif by the mid-1940s. Cornell was fascinated by the Romantic ballet and the nineteenth-century ballerina was a frequent muse, particularly Fanny Cerrito, who performed as an ethereal sea nymph in the ballet *Ondine, ou la Naïade* (1843). However, a direct connection between Fanny Cerrito/Ondine and the Window Façade Series has yet to be clearly established; but, as Starr points out, Cornell's essay "Discovery—New York City 1940" (originally titled "Windows and Fanny Cerrito") presents Ondine as an apparition in a window, as she was in the ballet. Moreover, in other discussions of New York City, Cornell mentions Ondine's name in reference to windows (p. 32).

GEORGIA O'KEEFFE
American, born 1887

Lake George (formerly *Reflection Seascape*), 1922
oil on canvas
16¼ × 22"
41.2 × 55.9 cm

Gift of Charlotte Mack
52.6714

Provenance

Charlotte Mack
Mr. Kleiser (?)
Paul Rosenfeld
Artist

Exhibitions

Städtische Kunsthalle, Düsseldorf. *Zwei Jahrzehnte amerikanische Malerei 1920–1940,* June 10–August 12, 1979, cat. no. 84, listed as *Reflection, Sunrise,* 1922. Circulated to: Kunsthaus, Zurich, August 23–October 28, 1979; Palais des Beaux-Arts, Brussels, November 10–December 30, 1979.

Art Gallery of Ontario, Toronto. *The Mystic North: Symbolist Landscape Painting in Northern Europe and North America, 1890–1940,* January 13–March 11, 1984, checklist no. 93. Circulated to: Cincinnati Art Museum, March 31–May 13, 1984.

Literature

Roald Nasgaard. *The Mystic North: Symbolist Landscape Painting in*

Northern Europe and North America, 1890–1940. Toronto: Art Gallery of Ontario, 1984, ref. p. 226, ill. p. 221.

GEORGIA O'KEEFFE
American, born 1887

Black Place I, 1944
oil on canvas
26 × 30⅛"
66.0 × 76.6 cm

Gift of Charlotte Mack
54.3536

Provenance

Charlotte Mack
The Downtown Gallery, New York
An American Place, New York
Artist

Exhibitions

An American Place, New York. *Georgia O'Keeffe Paintings—1944,* January 22–March 22, 1945, checklist no. 7.

San Francisco Museum of Art. *Twentieth Anniversary Exhibitions: Selections from the Museum Collections,* January 18–February 13, 1955.

The Art Galleries, University of California, Santa Barbara. *Trends in Twentieth-Century Art: A Loan Exhibition from the San Francisco Museum of Art,* January 6–February 1, 1970, cat. no. 15; ill. pl. 15.

Literature

San Francisco Museum of Art Quarterly Bulletin, Series 2, vol. 3, no. 4 (1954), ref. p. 28, ill. p. 28.

Lloyd Goodrich and Doris Bry. *Georgia O'Keeffe: Retrospective Exhibition.* New York: Whitney Museum of American Art, 1970, ref. p. 23.

Remarks

Black Place I is one of four paintings from the Black Place Series.

ARTHUR DOVE
American, 1880–1946

Silver Ball No. 2, 1930
oil and metallic paint on canvas
23¼ × 30"
59.1 × 76.2 cm

Rosalie M. Stern Bequest Fund Purchase
59.2348

Inscribed

recto, lower right: *Dove*

Provenance

The Downtown Gallery, New York
Mrs. Charles J. Liebmann (?)
Artist

Exhibitions

An American Place, New York. *Arthur G. Dove: Twenty-seven New Paintings,* March 22–April 22, 1930, cat. no. 16, listed as *Reflections.*

The Newark Museum, New Jersey. *Abstract Art: 1910 to Today*, April 27–June 10, 1956, cat no. 20.

UCLA Art Galleries, University of California, Los Angeles. *Arthur G. Dove*, May 9–June 15, 1959, cat. no. 34. Circulated to: Whitney Museum of American Art, New York, October 1–November 16, 1958; Phillips Memorial Gallery (now The Phillips Collection), Washington, D.C., December 1, 1958–January 5, 1959; Museum of Fine Arts, Boston, January 25–February 28, 1959; Marion Koogler McNay Art Institute, San Antonio, Texas, March 18–April 18, 1959; La Jolla Art Center, California, June 20–July 30, 1959; San Francisco Museum of Art, August 15–September 30, 1959.

Milwaukee Art Center. *Ten Americans*, September 21–November 5, 1961, cat. no. 17.

Literature
Paul Rosenfeld. "The World of Arthur G. Dove." *Creative Art*, vol. 10 (June 1932), ill. p. 429, listed as *Abstraction*, n.d.

EDWARD HOPPER
American, 1882–1967

Bridle Path, 1939
oil on canvas
28⅜ × 42⅛″
72.1 × 107.0 cm

Anonymous gift
76.174

Inscribed
recto, lower right: *Edward Hopper*

Provenance
Private collection, 1958
Frank Rehn Gallery, New York
Artist

Exhibitions
Whitney Museum of American Art, New York. *Edward Hopper: A Retrospective Exhibition*, September 29–November 29, 1964, cat.

Hirschl & Adler Galleries, Inc., New York. *The Artist in the Park*, April 29–May 30, 1980, brochure no. 56.

Whitney Museum of American Art, New York. *Edward Hopper: The Art and the Artist*, September 16,1980–January 25, 1981, cat. no. 254; ref. p. 46, color ill. p. 196. Circulated to: Hayward Gallery, London, February 11–March 29, 1981; Stedelijk Museum, Amsterdam, April 22–June 17, 1981; Städtische Kunsthalle, Düsseldorf, July 10–September 6, 1981; The Art Institute of Chicago, October 3–November 29, 1981; San Francisco Museum of Modern Art, December 16, 1981–February 10, 1982.

Literature
Lloyd Goodrich. *Edward Hopper*. New York: Harry N. Abrams, 1971, ill. p. 244.

JOHN STORRS
American, 1885–1956

Study in Form (Architectural Form), ca. 1923
stone
19½ × 3⅛ × 3¼″
49.6 × 8.0 × 8.3 cm

Purchased through a gift of Julian and Jean Aberbach
81.3

Provenance
Robert Schoelkopf Gallery, Ltd., New York
Estate of the artist, 1956
Artist

Exhibitions
Galerie Briant-Robert, Paris. *Exposition de Six Peintres américains. Deux Sculpteurs américains*, January 19–February 19, 1925.

The Brooklyn Museum, New York. *International Exhibition of Modern Art Arranged by the Société Anonyme*, November 19, 1926–January 9, 1927, checklist. Circulated to: The Anderson Galleries, New York, January 25–February 5, 1927, checklist; The Albright Art Gallery (now the Albright-Knox Art Gallery), Buffalo, February 25–March 20, 1927, checklist; The Art Gallery of Toronto, April 1–24, 1927, checklist. *See* Remarks.

The Brummer Gallery, New York. *Storrs Exhibition*, February 1–25, 1928, checklist.

The Downtown Gallery, New York. *John Storrs*, March 23–April 17, 1965, cat. no. 9, listed as *Forms in Space*, 1923.

Robert Schoelkopf Gallery, New York. *John Storrs*, March 4–29, 1975.

Museum of Contemporary Art, Chicago. *John Storrs (1885–1956): A Retrospective Exhibition of Sculpture*, November 13, 1976–January 2, 1977, cat. p. 17, listed as *Architectural Form*, ca. 1923; ill. p. 12.

Literature
"Modern U.S. Art on View Here," *New York Herald* (European Edition), January 20, 1925, ref. p. 2, ill. p. 6.

Katherine S. Dreier. *Modern Art*. New York: Société Anonyme–Museum of Modern Art, 1926, ill. p. 97.

Noel S. Frackman. "John Storrs and the Origins of Art Deco." Master's thesis, New York University, Institute of Fine Arts, 1975, ref. pp. 44, 46, ill. pl. 75, listed as *Study in Form*, ca. 1924–25.

Ruth L. Bohan. *The Société Anonyme's Brooklyn Exhibition: Katherine Dreier and Modernism in America*. Ann Arbor, Mich.: UMI Research Press, 1982, ref. p. 157, listed as *Study in Form I or II*, n.d.

Remarks
The Société Anonyme's 1926–27 exhibition was held at four different locations—the Brooklyn Museum and the Anderson Galleries, New York; The Albright Art Gallery, Buffalo; The Art Gallery of Toronto—and each organization issued a separate checklist. In the checklist for the exhibition at the Brooklyn Museum, three works are listed as *Study in Form* (numbered I, II, III). The Anderson Galleries checklist records two *Study in Form* sculptures (numbered I, II). Ruth Bohan has compiled a list that includes every work known to have been included in the four exhibitions. She lists three *Study in Form* sculptures in all, with their respective measurements and provenances (p. 157). *Study in Form III*, which once belonged to William Bullitt of South Deerfield, Mass., has different measurements from the Museum's work. *Study in Form I* and *Study in Form II*, however, cannot be distinguished from one another. The Museum's piece may be either no. 288 or 289 in the Brooklyn Museum listing; no. 165 or 166 in the Anderson Galleries listing; or, no. 164 or 165 in both the Albright Art Gallery and Art Gallery of Toronto listings.

JOSEPH STELLA
American, born Italy, 1877–1946

Bridge, 1936
oil on canvas
50⅛ × 30⅛″
127.3 × 76.5 cm

WPA Federal Arts Project Allocation to the San Francisco Museum of Art
3760.43

Inscribed
recto, lower right: *Jos Stella*

Exhibitions
Phillips Memorial Gallery (now The Phillips Collection), Washington, D.C. *National Exhibition: Mural Sketches, Oil Paintings, Water Colors, and Graphic Arts*, June 16–July 5, 1936, unpublished checklist.

The Museum of Modern Art, New York. *New Horizons in American Art*, September 14–October 12, 1936, cat. no. 108. Circulated to: The Art Institute of Chicago, January 4–February 1, 1937; California Palace of the Legion of Honor, San Francisco, February 15–March 15, 1937; Portland Art Association, Oregon, March 24–April 21, 1937; Dallas Museum of Fine Arts, August 25–September

22, 1937; Milwaukee Art Institute, October 8–November 7, 1937; George William Vincent Smith Art Gallery, Springfield, Massachusetts, November 21–December 19, 1937; Rochester Memorial Art Gallery, New York, January 1–31, 1938; The Cleveland Museum of Art, February 10–March 13, 1938.

Art Center in La Jolla, California. *Twentieth Anniversary Loan Exhibition: American Paintings from Pacific Coast Museums*, April 13–May 7, 1961, cat. no. 26.

The Art Galleries, University of California at Santa Barbara. *Trends in Twentieth-Century Art: A Loan Exhibition from the San Francisco Museum of Art*, January 6–February 1, 1970, cat. no. 9; ref. p. 7, ill. no. 9.

San Jose Museum of Art, California. *America VII: America between the Wars*, October 19–November 28, 1976, checklist p. 3.

Städtische Kunsthalle, Düsseldorf. *Zwei Jahrzehnte amerikanische Malerei 1920–1940*, June 10–August 12, 1979, cat. no. 44; ref. p. 66, ill. p. 67. Circulated to: Kunsthaus, Zürich, August 23–October 28, 1979; Palais des Beaux-Arts, Brussels, November 10–December 30, 1979.

Neue Gesellschaft für Bildende Kunst, Berlin. *Amerika. Traum und Depression 1920/1940*, November 9–December 28, 1980, cat. no. 333; ref. pp. 98–99, ill. p. 98. Circulated to: Kunstverein, Hamburg, January 11–February 15, 1981.

Literature
Irma B. Jaffe. *Joseph Stella*. Cambridge: Harvard University Press, 1970, ref. pp. 119, 120, 203, ill. p. 101, listed as *Bridge*, ca. 1936.

Remarks
In a letter dated March 20, 1936, from Joseph Stella to Holger Cahill, director of the Works Progress Administration/Federal Arts Project, Stella wrote: "Mr. Rollins has given me lately a commission to do a 'Brooklyn Bridge' 30 × 50. I am working with enthusiasm."

CHARLES SHEELER
American, 1883–1965

Aerial Gyrations, 1953
oil on canvas
23⅝ × 18⅝″
60.0 × 47.3 cm

Mrs. Manfred Bransten Special Fund Purchase
74.78

Inscribed
recto, lower right: *Sheeler 1953*
verso, center: *Aerial Gyrations/ Charles Sheeler/1953*

Provenance
Kennedy Galleries, Inc., New York,
1974
Dr. Melvin and Helen W. Boigon,
1953
The Downtown Gallery, New York
Artist

Exhibitions
UCLA Art Galleries, University of
California, Los Angeles. *Charles
Sheeler: A Retrospective Exhibition*,
October 1954, cat. no. 42; ill. p.
41. Circulated nationally.
The Downtown Gallery, New York.
Charles Sheeler, March–April 1958.
Whitney Museum of American Art,
New York. *The Museum and Its
Friends: Eighteen Living American
Artists Selected by the Friends of the
Whitney Museum*, March 5–April
12, 1959, cat.; ill. p. 35.
Walker Art Center, Minneapolis.
*The Precisionist View in American
Art*, November 13–December 25,
1960, cat. p. 58. Circulated to:
Whitney Museum of American Art,
New York, January 24–March 5,
1961; Detroit Institute of Arts, March
26–May 7, 1961; Los Angeles
County Museum, May 14–June 18,
1961; San Francisco Museum of Art,
July 2–August 6, 1961.
University of Iowa Art Museum,
Iowa City. *The Quest of Charles
Sheeler: Eighty-three Works Honor-
ing his Eightieth Year*, March 17–
April 14, 1964, cat. no. 61.
The Downtown Gallery, New York.
Charles Sheeler, January 5–23, 1965,
cat. no. 3; ill.
National Collection of Fine Arts
(now National Museum of Ameri-
can Art), Smithsonian Institution,
Washington, D.C. *Charles Sheeler*,
October 10–November 24, 1968,
cat. no. 141; ref. p. 47, ill. p. 54.
Circulated to: Philadelphia Museum
of Art, January 10–February 16,
1969; Whitney Museum of American
Art, New York, March 11–April 27,
1969.
Museum of Art, Carnegie Institute,
Pittsburgh. *Forerunners of American
Abstraction*, November 18, 1971–
January 9, 1972, cat. no. 97.
San Francisco Museum of Modern
Art. *Images of America: Precisionist
Painting and Modern Photography*,
September 9–November 7, 1982,
cat. no. 110; ref. p. 83, color ill. p.
53. Circulated to: The Saint Louis
Art Museum, December 6, 1982–
January 30, 1983; Baltimore Mu-
seum of Art, February 28–April 25,
1983; Des Moines Art Center, May
23–July 17, 1983; The Cleveland
Museum of Art, August 15–October
9, 1983.

Literature
Martin Friedman. *Charles Sheeler*.
New York: Watson-Guptill, 1975,
ref. p. 169, color ill. p. 201.

STUART DAVIS
American, 1894–1964

Deuce, 1954
oil on canvas
26 × 42¼"
66.0 × 107.3 cm

Gift of Mrs. E. S. Heller
55.4734

Inscribed
recto, upper right: *Stuart Davis*

Provenance
Artist

Exhibitions
The Downtown Gallery, New York.
Recent Paintings by Stuart Davis,
March 1–27, 1954.
Walker Art Center, Minneapolis.
Stuart Davis, March 30–May 19,
1957, cat. no. 36; ill. p. 39. Circu-
lated to: Des Moines Art Center,
June 9–30, 1957; San Francisco
Museum of Art, August 6–Septem-
ber 8, 1957; Whitney Museum of
American Art, New York, Septem-
ber 25–November 17, 1957.
National Collection of Fine Arts
(now National Museum of American
Art), Smithsonian Institution, Wash-
ington, D.C. *Stuart Davis Memorial
Exhibition*, May 25–July 5, 1965,
cat. no. 93; ref. p. 42, ill. p. 79.
Circulated to: The Art Institute of
Chicago, July 30–August 29, 1965;
Whitney Museum of American Art,
New York, September 14–October
17, 1965; UCLA Art Galleries, Uni-
versity of California, Los Angeles,
October 31–November 28, 1965.
Circulated, under the sponsorship
of the United States Information
Agency, Washington, D.C., to:
Musée d'Art Moderne de la Ville de
Paris. *Stuart Davis*, February 1966,
cat. no. 32; color ill.; Amerika
Haus, Berlin. *Stuart Davis: 1894–
1964*, April 23–May 21, 1966, cat.
no. 32; American Embassy, London.
Stuart Davis: 1894–1964, June 7–24,
1966, cat. no. 32.
The Art Galleries, University of
California, Santa Barbara. *Trends in
Twentieth-Century Art: A Loan Exhi-
bition from the San Francisco Mu-
seum of Art*, January 6–February 1,
1970, cat. no. 21; color ill.
The Brooklyn Museum, New York.
Stuart Davis: Art and Art Theory,
January 21–March 19, 1978, cat.
no. 95; ref. p. 213, ill. p. 170.
Circulated to: Fogg Art Museum,
Harvard University, Cambridge,
April 15–May 28, 1978.

Literature
John Lucas. "The Fine Art Jive of
Stuart Davis." *Arts*, vol. 31, no. 10
(September 1957), pp. 32–37.
Robert M. Coates. "The Art Galler-
ies: Exhibitions at the Whitney."
The New Yorker (October 19, 1957),
p. 123.

E. C. Goossen. *Stuart Davis*. New
York: George Braziller, 1959.
Rudi Blesh. *Stuart Davis*. New York:
Grove Press, 1960, pl. 11.
Diane Kelder, ed. *Stuart Davis*.
New York: Frederick A. Praeger,
1971, p. 8, color ill. VIII.

Remarks
The title refers to Davis's notion of
balance, "the theory of Pairs"; Stuart
Davis Papers, Index, December
1953 (Stuart Davis Papers, Fogg Art
Museum, Harvard University, Cam-
bridge, Mass.); citation noted in
John R. Lane, *Stuart Davis: Art and
Art Theory* (New York: The Brook-
lyn Museum, 1978), p. 170.

FRIDA (FRIEDA) KAHLO
Mexican, 1910–1954

Frieda and Diego Rivera, 1931
oil on canvas
39⅜ × 31"
100.0 × 78.7 cm

Albert M. Bender Collection
Gift of Albert M. Bender
36.6061

Inscribed
recto, on banderole above the heads
of Frieda and Diego: *Aqui nos veis, a
mi Frieda Kahlo, junto con mi amado
esposo Diego Rivera,/pinté estos re-
tratos en la bella ciudad de San
Francisco California para/nuestro
amigo Mr. Albert Bender, y fué en el
mes de abril año 1931*. [Here you
see us, me, Frieda Kahlo, with my
beloved husband Diego Rivera,/I
painted these portraits in the beautiful city of San Francisco California
for/our friend Mr. Albert Bender,
and it was in the month of April in
the year 1931.]

Provenance
Albert M. Bender, 1931
Artist

Exhibitions
California Pacific International Exposition, The Palace of Fine Arts,
San Diego. *Official Art Exhibition*,
February 12–September 9, 1936,
cat. no. 62.
The Institute of Modern Art, Boston.
Modern Mexican Painters, November 18–December 20, 1941, cat. no.
15, listed as *Diego and I*, 1931; ill.
p. 32. Circulated to: The Phillips
Memorial Gallery (now The Phillips
Collection), Washington, D.C., January 11–February 1, 1942; The Cleveland Museum of Art, February
10–March 10, 1942; Portland Art
Museum, Oregon, April 1–30, 1942;
San Francisco Museum of Art, May
19–June 14, 1942; Santa Barbara
Museum of Art, California, July
1–31, 1942.
Contemporary Arts Museum, Houston. *Mexican Paintings and Draw-

ings*, September 13–29, 1953, cat.
no. 18.
Los Angeles County Museum of
Art. *Women Artists: 1550–1950*, December 21, 1976–March 13, 1977,
cat. no. 157; ref. pp. 336–37, ill. p.
337. Circulated to: University Art
Museum, The University of Texas at
Austin, April 12–June 12, 1977;
Museum of Art, Carnegie Institute,
Pittsburgh, July 14–September 4,
1977; The Brooklyn Museum, New
York, October 8–November 27, 1977.
Museum of Contemporary Art, Chicago. *Frida Kahlo*, January 13–
March 5, 1978, cat. p. 26; ref. p.
14, ill. p. 5. Circulated to: Mande-
ville Art Gallery, University of California, San Diego at La Jolla, April
7–May 17, 1978; Phoenix Art Mu-
seum, June 9–July 23, 1978; Univer-
sity Art Museum, The University of
Texas at Austin, August 13–October
1, 1978; The Sarah Campbell Blaffer
Gallery, University of Houston, October 14–November 19, 1978; Neuberger Museum, State University of
New York at Purchase, December
8, 1978–January 14, 1979.
Whitechapel Art Gallery, London.
Frida Kahlo and/und Tina Modotti,
March 26–May 2, 1982, cat.; ill.
Circulated to: Haus am Waldsee,
Berlin, May 14–July 11, 1982; Kunst-
verein, Hamburg, July 29–
September 12, 1982; Kunstverein,
Hannover, September 26–November
7, 1982; Grey Art Gallery, New
York University, New York, March
1–April 16, 1983.

Literature
Hayden Herrera. "Frida Kahlo: Her
Life, Her Art." *Artforum*, vol. 14,
no. 9 (May 1976), ref. p. 14, ill. p.
40.
Hayden Herrera. *Frida: a Biography of Frida Kahlo*. New York:
Harper & Row, 1983, ref. pp. 123–
24, 317, 361; ill. no. III.
Michael Newman. "The Ribbon
around the Bomb." *Art In America*,
vol. 71, no. 4 (April 1983), ref. p.
165, ill. p. 165.

Remarks
Because of her German heritage,
Kahlo changed the spelling of her
name from Frieda to Frida during
the rise of Nazism in Germany in
the 1930s.

DIEGO RIVERA
Mexican, 1886–1957

The Flower Carrier (formerly *The
Flower Vendor*), 1935
oil and tempera on Masonite
48 × 47¾"
121.9 × 121.3 cm

Albert M. Bender Collection
Gift of Albert M. Bender in memory
of Caroline Walter
35.4516

Inscribed
recto, lower left: *Diego Rivera. 1935*
verso, upper left: *Diego Rivera.*
"The Flower carrier/Mexico City.
Juin 1935

Provenance
Artist

Exhibitions
San Francisco Museum of Art. *An Analysis of a Rivera Painting*, May 15–August 1, 1938.

The Institute of Modern Art, Boston. *Modern Mexican Painters*, November 18–December 20, 1941, cat. no. 31; ill. p. 48. Circulated to: The Phillips Memorial Gallery (now The Phillips Collection), Washington, D.C., January 11–February 1, 1942; The Cleveland Museum of Art, February 10–March 10, 1942; Portland Art Museum, Oregon, April 1–31, 1942; San Francisco Museum of Art, May 19–June 14, 1942; Santa Barbara Museum of Art, California, July 1–31, 1942.

The Art Gallery of Toronto. *Loan Exhibition of Great Paintings in Aid of Allied Merchant Seamen*, February 4–March 5, 1944, cat. no. 59.

San Francisco Museum of Art. *Art of Our Time*, January 18–February 5, 1945, cat.

Instituto Nacional de Bellas Artes, Departamento de Artes Plasticas/ Museo Nacional de Artes Plasticas, Mexico City. *Diego Rivera: Cinquenta Años de Su Labor Artistica*, August–December, 1949, cat. no. 525; ill.

Venice. *XXV Biennale Internazionale d'Arte*, June 8–October 15, 1950, cat. no. 17.

Santa Barbara Museum of Art, California. *Fruits and Flowers in Painting*, August 12–September 14, 1958, cat. no. 87.

Los Angeles County Museum of Art. *Master Works of Mexican Art: From Pre-Columbian Times to the Present*, October 1963–January 1964, cat. no. 964.

Yale University Art Gallery, New Haven. *Art of Latin America since Independence*, January 27–March 13, 1966, cat. no. 308; color ill. no. 77. Circulated to: The University of Texas Art Museum, Austin, April 17–May 15, 1966; San Francisco Museum of Art, July 2–August 7, 1966; La Jolla Museum of Art, August 27–September 30, 1966; Issac Delgado Museum of Art, New Orleans, October 29–November 27, 1966; Fine Arts Palace, Mexico City, February 9–April 9, 1967.

Art Gallery of the University of Arizona, Tucson. *The Art of Ancient and Modern Latin America: Selections from Public and Private Collections in the United States*, November 27, 1966–January 5, 1967, cat. no. 319; ill. no. 319.

The Queens Museum, Flushing, New York. *José Clemente Orozco and Diego Rivera: Paintings, Drawings and Prints*, September 15–November 11, 1979, cat. no. 30; ill. no. 30.

Center for the Fine Arts, Miami. *In Quest of Excellence*, January 4–April 22, 1984, cat. no. 179; ref. pp. 204, 205, color ill. p. 205.

Literature
Bertram D. Wolfe. *Diego Rivera: His Life and Times*. New York: Alfred A. Knopf, 1939, ref. pp. 319, 320, listed as *Flower Carrier in Xochimilco*, n.d.

Alfred Werner. "The Contradictory Señor Rivera." *The Painter and Sculptor* (London), vol. 3, no. 1 (Spring 1960), ill. p. 23.

Eugenio Chang-Rodriguez. *Latino America: Su Civilizacion y Su Cultura*. Rowley, Mass.: Newbury House, 1983, ill. p. 313, listed as *El Florero*, also *Vendedor de Flores*, n.d.

Remarks
In 1983, the title of this painting was changed from *The Flower Vendor* to the more accurate title *The Flower Carrier*, in view of information drawn from the work itself. It should be assumed that until 1983 the painting was titled *The Flower Vendor* in exhibition and literature entries, unless otherwise noted.

Bertram Wolfe reports that Albert Bender sent a letter to Rivera on June 21, 1935, in which he informed the painter that he had donated $500 to the San Francisco Museum of Art for the purchase of a painting intended as a memorial in honor of Mrs. Caroline Walter. The work was sent directly by the artist to the San Francisco Museum of Art and was thus never in Bender's private collection.

MORRIS GRAVES
American, born 1910

Bird Maddened by the Sound of Machinery in the Air, 1944
watercolor on rice paper
32⅝ × 59⅜"
82.9 × 150.8 cm

Anonymous gift
51.1735

Provenance
Artist

Exhibitions
Museu de Arte Moderna de São Paulo, Brazil. *III Bienal*, July–October 1955, cat. no. 20.

San Francisco Museum of Art. *Pacific Coast Art: United States' Representation at the IIIrd Biennial of São Paulo*, May 15–July 15, 1956, cat. p. 15; ill. p. 21. Circulated to:

Cincinnati Art Museum; Colorado Springs Fine Arts Center; San Francisco Museum of Art; Walker Art Center, Minneapolis.

San Francisco Museum of Art. *Art in Asia and the West*, October 28–December 1, 1957, cat. no. 28b.

A Rationale for Modern Art. Circulated nationally, October 1959–October 1960, by the American Federation of Arts, New York.

Auckland City Art Gallery, New Zealand. *Painting from the Pacific: Japan, America, Australia, New Zealand*, 1961, cat. no. 50; ill.

The Fine Art Patrons of Newport Harbor, The Pavilion Gallery, Balboa, California (now Newport Harbor Art Museum, Newport Beach). *Morris Graves Retrospective*, March 1–31, 1963, cat. no. 25; ref.

Santa Barbara Museum of Art, California. *Morris Graves*, January 30–March 3, 1968, cat.

Denver Art Museum. *The First Western States Biennial Exhibition*, March 7–April 15, 1979, cat. p. 16. Circulated to: National Collection of Fine Arts (now National Museum of American Art), Smithsonian Institution, Washington, D.C., June 8–September 3, 1979; San Francisco Museum of Modern Art, October 26–December 9, 1979; Seattle Art Museum, May 29–July 13, 1980.

The Phillips Collection, Washington, D.C. *Morris Graves: Visions of the Inner Eye*, April 9–May 29, 1983, cat. no. 72; ref. p. 42, ill. no. 72. Circulated to: Greenville County Museum of Art, Greenville, S.C., July 1–August 28, 1983; Whitney Museum of American Art, New York, September 15–November 27, 1983; The Oakland Museum, California, January 18–March 25, 1984; Seattle Art Museum, April 19–July 8, 1984; San Diego Museum of Art, July 24–September 4, 1984.

Remarks
This painting is part of a series of four which also includes *Bird Maddened by the War; Bird Maddened by the War Following St. Elmo's Fire*, and one other.

MARK TOBEY
American, 1890–1976

Written over the Plains, 1950
tempera on Masonite
30⅛ × 40"
76.5 × 101.7 cm

Gift of Mr. and Mrs. Ferdinand C. Smith
51.3169

Inscribed
recto, lower left: *Tobey/50*

Provenance
Artist

Exhibitions
California Palace of the Legion of Honor, San Francisco. *Mark Tobey*, March 31–May 6, 1951, cat. no. 70. Circulated to: Henry Gallery, University of Washington, Seattle, May 20–June 27, 1951; Santa Barbara Museum of Art, California, August 16–September 9, 1951; Whitney Museum of American Art, New York, October 4–November 4, 1951.

San Francisco Museum of Art. *Pacific Coast Art: United States' Representation at the IIIrd Biennial of São Paulo*, May 15–July 15, 1956, cat. p. 17. Circulated to: Cincinnati Art Museum; Colorado Springs Fine Arts Center; San Francisco Museum of Art; Walker Art Center, Minneapolis.

Venice. *XXIX Biennale Internazionale d'Arte*, June 14–October 19, 1958, cat. no. 52.

The Museum of Modern Art, New York. *Mark Tobey*, September 12–November 4, 1962, cat. no. 63; ref. p. 31, ill. p. 71. Circulated to: The Cleveland Museum of Art, December 11, 1962–January 13, 1963; The Art Institute of Chicago, February 22–March 24, 1963.

Dallas Museum of Fine Arts. *Mark Tobey Retrospective*, March 20–April 21, 1968, cat. no. 51; ill. p. 51.

National Collection of Fine Arts (now National Museum of American Art), Smithsonian Institution, Washington, D.C. *Art of the Pacific Northwest: 1930's to the Present*, February 8–May 5, 1974, cat. no. 119. Circulated to: Seattle Art Museum, July 12–August 25, 1974; Portland Art Museum, Oregon, September 17–October 13, 1974.

National Gallery of Art, Washington, D.C. *Mark Tobey: City Paintings*, March 18–June 17, 1984, cat. no. 36; ref. p. 19, color ill. p. 12, ill. p. 19.

ARSHILE GORKY
American, born Turkish Armenia, 1904–1948

Enigmatic Combat, 1936–37
oil on canvas
35¾ × 48"
90.8 × 121.9 cm

Gift of Jeanne Reynal
41.3763

Provenance
Jeanne Reynal
Artist

Exhibitions
San Francisco Museum of Art. *Paintings by Arshile Gorky*, August 9–24, 1941.

Whitney Museum of American Art, New York. *Arshile Gorky Memorial Exhibition*, January 5–February 18, 1951, cat. no. 15; ill. p. 23. Circulated to: Walker Art

Center, Minneapolis, March 4–April 22, 1951; San Francisco Museum of Art, May 9–July 9, 1951.

National Arts Club, New York. *In Memoriam*, September 10–20, 1955, cat. Exhibition organized by the American Federation of Arts, circulated to: Watkins Institute, Nashville, Tennessee, October 1–20, 1955; Hunter Gallery, Chattanooga, Tennessee, November 10–30, 1955; Gates Gallery, Port Arthur, Texas, December 14, 1955–January 4, 1956; Dallas Museum of Fine Arts, January 18–February 8, 1956; University of Manitoba, Winnipeg, February 25–March 24, 1956; Atlanta Public Library, April 7–28, 1956; Des Moines Art Center, June 17–August 1, 1956.

University Art Gallery, University of California, Berkeley. *Linearity in Paintings and Drawings from the Collections of the San Francisco Museum of Art*, February 5–March 11, 1962, cat. no. 10.

Venice. *XXXI Biennale Internazionale d'Arte*, July 16–October 7, 1962, cat. no. 7.

The Museum of Modern Art, New York. *Arshile Gorky: Paintings, Drawings, Studies*, December 17, 1962–February 12, 1963, cat. no. 34. Circulated to: Washington Gallery of Modern Art, Washington, D.C., March 12–April 14, 1963.

The Tate Gallery, London. *Arshile Gorky: Paintings and Drawings*, April 2–May 2, 1965, cat. no. 32; ill. no. 32. Circulated to: Palais des Beaux-Arts, Brussels, May 22–June 27, 1965; Museum Boymans-van Beuningen, Rotterdam, July 9–August 15, 1965, cat. no. 42; ill. no. 42.

The Art Galleries, University of California, Santa Barbara. *Trends in Twentieth-Century Art: A Loan Exhibition from the San Francisco Museum of Art*, January 6–February 1, 1970, cat. no. 11; ill.

University Art Museum, The University of Texas at Austin. *Arshile Gorky: Drawings to Paintings*, October 12–November 23, 1975, cat. p. 103; ill. p. 68. Circulated to: San Francisco Museum of Modern Art, December 4, 1975–January 12, 1976; Neuberger Museum, State University of New York at Purchase, February 10–March 14, 1976; Museum of Art, Munson-Williams-Proctor Institute, Utica, New York, April 4–May 9, 1976.

San Francisco Museum of Modern Art. *Collecting, Collection, Collectors: American Abstract Art since 1945*, April 22–June 5, 1977, cat. no. 11.

The Solomon R. Guggenheim Museum, New York. *Arshile Gorky, 1904–1948: A Retrospective*, April 23–July 26, 1981, cat.; color ill. pl.

104. Circulated to: Dallas Museum of Fine Arts, September 11–November 8, 1981; Los Angeles County Museum of Art, December 3, 1981–February 28, 1982.

Museum of Art, Carnegie Institute, Pittsburgh. *Abstract Painting and Sculpture: 1927–1944*, October 29–December 31, 1983, cat. no. 59; ref. pp. 152, 156, color ill. p. 107. Circulated to: San Francisco Museum of Modern Art, January 26–March 25, 1984; Minneapolis Institute of Arts, April 15–June 3, 1984; Whitney Museum of American Art, New York, June 28–September 2, 1984.

Literature

Ethel K. Schwabacher. *Arshile Gorky*. New York: Macmillan, 1957, ref. p. 56, ill. p. 60.

Harold Rosenberg. *Arshile Gorky: The Man, the Time, the Era*. New York: Horizon Press, 1962, ill. p. 61.

William S. Rubin. "Arshile Gorky, Surrealism and the New American Painting." *Art International*, vol. 7, no. 2 (February 1963), ref. p. 28, ill. p. 29.

Julien Levy. *Arshile Gorky*. New York: Harry N. Abrams, 1966, ill. p. 72.

William S. Rubin. *Dada and Surrealist Art*. New York: Harry N. Abrams, 1968, ref. p. 396, ill. p. 443.

Irving Sandler. *The Triumph of American Painting: A History of Abstract Expressionism*. New York: Praeger, 1970, ref. p. 51, ill. p. 52.

William Fleming. *Art and Ideas*. New York: Holt, Rinehart and Winston, 1974, ill. no. 399.

Stewart Buettner. "Arshile Gorky and the Abstract-Surreal." *Arts Magazine*, vol. 50, no. 7 (March 1976), ref. p. 87.

Jim M. Jordan and Robert Goldwater. *The Paintings of Arshile Gorky: A Critical Catalogue*. New York: New York University Press, 1982, ref. pp. 73–74, ill. p. 322.

JACKSON POLLOCK
American, 1912–1956

Guardians of the Secret, 1943
oil on canvas
48⅜ × 75⅜"
122.9 × 191.5 cm

Albert M. Bender Collection
Albert M. Bender Bequest Fund Purchase
45.1308

Inscribed
recto, lower right: *Jackson Pollock/8-43*

Provenance
Art of This Century, New York
Artist

Exhibitions
Art of This Century, New York. *Jackson Pollock: Paintings and Drawings*, November 9–27, 1943, cat. no. 2.

San Francisco Museum of Art. *Abstract and Surrealist Art in the United States*, August 30–September 29, 1944, cat. no. 64; ill. p. 22. Circulated to: Cincinnati Art Museum, February 8–March 12, 1944; Denver Art Museum, March 26–April 23, 1944; Seattle Art Museum, May 7–June 10, 1944; Santa Barbara Museum of Art, California, June–July 1944.

The Arts Club of Chicago. *Jackson Pollock*, March 5–31, 1945, cat. no. 2. Circulated to: San Francisco Museum of Art, August 7–26, 1945.

The Museum of Modern Art, New York. *Jackson Pollock*, December 19, 1956–February 3, 1957, cat. no. 2; ill. p. 13.

Museu de Arte Moderna, São Paulo, Brazil. *IV Bienal. Jackson Pollock 1912–1956*, September 22–December 31, 1957, cat. no. 3. Circulated, under auspices of the International Council of the Museum of Modern Art, New York, to: Galleria Nazionale d'Arte Moderna, Rome, March 1–31, 1958, cat. (in German) no. 3, listed as *Die Hüter des Geheimnisses*, 1943; Kuntsthalle, Basel, April 19–May 26, 1958; Stedelijk Museum, Amsterdam, June 6–July 7, 1958; Kunstverein, Hamburg, July 19–August 21, 1958; Berlin Cultural Festival, East Germany, September 1–October 1, 1958; Whitechapel Gallery, London, November 4–December 4, 1958; Musée National d'Art Moderne, Paris, January 16–February 15, 1959.

Dallas Museum of Fine Arts. *Directions in Twentieth-Century American Painting*, October 7–November 12, 1961, cat. no. 48.

The Museum of Modern Art, New York. *Jackson Pollock*, April 3–June 4, 1967, cat. no. 11; ref. pp. 29, 31, 34, 36, ill. p. 88. Circulated to: Los Angeles County Museum of Art, July 19–September 3, 1967.

The Cleveland Museum of Art. *The Spirit of Surrealism*, October 3–November 25, 1979, cat. no. 93; ref. pp. 154, 159, color ill. p. 155.

Centre Georges Pompidou, Musée National d'Art Moderne, Paris. *Jackson Pollock*, January 21–April 19, 1982, cat.; ref. pp. 243–45, 325, 336, 337, 338, 347, 348, color ill. pp. 114–15. Circulated to: Städelsches Kunstinstitut und Städtische Galerie, Frankfurt, June 4–August 1, 1982.

Literature
Clement Greenberg. In *Nation* (November 27, 1943), ref. p. 621.

Frank O'Hara. *Jackson Pollock*. New York: George Braziller, 1959, ref. p. 18, ill. pl. 14.

Bryan Robertson. *Jackson Pollock*. New York: Harry N. Abrams, 1960, ref. pp. 44, 45, 66, 87, 138, ill. p. 103.

Irving Sandler. *The Triumph of American Painting: A History of Abstract Expressionism*. New York: Praeger, 1970, ref. p. 107, ill. p. 107.

David Freke. "Jackson Pollock: A Symbolic Self-Portrait." *Studio International*, vol. 184, no. 950 (December 1972), ref. p. 220, ill. p. 219.

Stephen C. Foster. "Turning Points in Pollock's Early Imagery." *The University of Iowa Museum of Art Bulletin*, vol. 1, no. 1 (Spring 1976), ref. p. 30, ill. p. 29.

Francis Valentine O'Connor and Eugene Victor Thaw, eds. *Jackson Pollock: A Catalogue Raisonné of Paintings, Drawings and Other Works*. New Haven: Yale University Press, 1978, vol. 1, cat. no. 99, ill. p. 91.

William Rubin. "Pollock as Jungian Illustrator: The Limits of Psychological Criticism." *Art in America*, vol. 67, no. 7 (November 1979), ref. pp. 109, 117, 120, color ill. pp. 106, 107; no. 8 (December 1979), ref. pp. 72, 87, 88, 90, color ill. p. 90.

Robert Hughes. *The Shock of the New*. New York: Alfred A. Knopf, 1981, ref. p. 262, color ill. pl. 181.

CLYFFORD STILL
American, 1904–1980

Untitled
(formerly *Self-Portrait*), 1945
oil on canvas
70⅞ × 42"
180.1 × 106.7 cm
(Ph-233)

Gift of Peggy Guggenheim
47.1238

Inscribed
recto, lower right: *Clyfford 45*

Provenance
Peggy Guggenheim
Artist

Exhibitions
Richmond Professional Institute, Virginia. 1945.

Art of This Century, New York. *Clyfford Still*, February 12–March 2 (extended through March 7), 1946, cat.

Colorado Springs Fine Arts Center, Colorado. *New Accessions USA*, July 12–September 5, 1948, cat. no. 44.

San Francisco Museum of Art. *Art*

in the Twentieth Century, June 16–July 18, 1955.

The Amon Carter Museum of Western Art, Fort Worth, Texas. *The Artist's Environment: West Coast,* November 6–December 23, 1962, cat. no. 42; ref. p. 104, ill. p. 104. Circulated to: UCLA Art Galleries, University of California, Los Angeles, January 7–February 10, 1963; The Oakland Art Museum, California, March 17–April 14, 1963.

The Minneapolis Institute of Arts. *Four Centuries of American Art,* November 27, 1963–January 19, 1964, cat.

San Francisco Museum of Modern Art. *Clyfford Still,* January 9–March 14, 1976, cat. no. 11; color ill.

The Museum of Fine Arts, Houston. *Miró in America,* April 21–June 27, 1982, cat.; ref. p. 25, ill. p. 24.

Center for the Fine Arts, Miami. *In Quest of Excellence,* January 14–April 22, 1984, cat., not listed.

Literature
Irving Sandler. *The Triumph of American Painting: A History of Abstract Expressionism.* New York: Harper & Row, 1970, ill. p. 159.

John P. O'Neill, ed. *Clyfford Still.* New York: The Metropolitan Museum of Art, 1979, ref. pp. 183–84, ill. pp. 20, 183, installation photo p. 22.

Karen Tsujimoto. *Mark Rothko 1949: A Year in Transition. Selections from the Mark Rothko Foundation.* San Francisco: San Francisco Museum of Modern Art, 1983, ref. p. 8, ill. p. 11.

Remarks
In a 1975 interview with Henry Hopkins, Director of the San Francisco Museum of Modern Art, Clyfford Still stated that the painting designated as *Self-Portrait* was mistitled and that the painting should be listed as Untitled.

The "Ph" number is the artist's photographic documentation number, assigned when the painting was photographed; it has no correspondence with the chronological sequence of the paintings.

CLYFFORD STILL
American, 1904–1980

Untitled, 1951–52
oil on canvas
113⅜ × 156"
288.0 × 396.2 cm
(Ph-968)

Gift of the artist
75.30

Inscribed
verso, lower left: *PH 968/Clyfford/ 1951–2*

Provenance
Artist

Exhibition
San Francisco Museum of Modern Art. *Clyfford Still,* January 9–March 14, 1976, cat. no. 19; color ill.

Literature
Stephen Polcari. "The Intellectual Roots of Abstract Expressionism: Clyfford Still." *Art International,* vol. 25, nos. 5–6 (May-June 1982), ref. p. 27, ill. p. 34.

Remarks
The "Ph" number is the artist's photographic documentation number, assigned when the painting was photographed; it has no correspondence with the chronological sequence of the paintings.

This work is one of twenty-eight paintings given to the San Francisco Museum of Modern Art by the artist in 1975.

CLYFFORD STILL
American, 1904–1980

Untitled, 1960
oil on canvas
113⅛ × 155⅞"
287.3 × 395.9 cm
(Ph-174)

Gift of Mr. and Mrs. Harry W. Anderson
74.19

Inscribed
verso, lower left: *1960/N.Y. Clyfford/1960/133 × 155/PH 174*

Provenance
Mr. and Mrs. Harry W. Anderson, 1972
Marlborough Gallery, Inc., New York
Artist

Exhibitions
Shown privately in studio at 128 West Twenty-third Street, New York, 1960.

Marlborough-Gerson Gallery, New York. *Clyfford Still,* October–November, 1969, cat. no. 35, listed as *1960,* 1960; color ill. p. 69.

Galerie Beyeler, Basel. *America,* June 22–August, 1971.

San Francisco Museum of Modern Art. *Clyfford Still,* January 9–March 14, 1976, cat. no. 28; color ill.

Literature
Peter Selz. "Between Friends: Still and the Bay Area." *Art in America,* vol. 63, no. 6 (November–December 1975), ref. p. 70.

Remarks
The "Ph" number is the artist's photographic documentation number, assigned when the painting was photographed; it has no correspondence with the chronological sequence of the paintings.

ROBERT MOTHERWELL
American, born 1915

Wall Painting No. 10, 1964
acrylic on canvas
69 × 92"
175.3 × 233.7 cm

Gift of the friends of Helen Crocker Russell
67.21

Inscribed
recto, upper left: *R M*

Provenance
Artist

Exhibitions
Stedelijk Museum, Amsterdam. *Robert Motherwell,* January 7–February 20, 1966, cat. no. 75; ill. Exhibition sponsored by the International Council of the Museum of Modern Art, New York, circulated to: Stedelijk Museum; Whitechapel Gallery, London, March 18–April 17, 1966; Palais des Beaux-Arts, Brussels, May 5–June 5, 1966; Folkwang Museum, Essen, July 2–August 14, 1966; Museo Civico d'Arte Moderna, Turin, September 27–October 29, 1966.

San Francisco Museum of Art. *Robert Motherwell,* February 22–March 19, 1967. Among works installed to augment exhibition *Robert Motherwell: Works on Paper,* organized by The Museum of Modern Art, New York.

The Art Galleries, University of California, Santa Barbara. *Trends in Twentieth-Century Art: A Loan Exhibition from the San Francisco Museum of Art,* January 6–February 1, 1970, cat. no. 35; ill. no. 35.

San Francisco Museum of Modern Art. *Collectors, Collecting, Collection: American Abstract Art since 1945,* April 22–June 5, 1977, cat. no. 36.

Indianapolis Museum of Art. *Perceptions of the Spirit in Twentieth-Century American Art,* September 20–November 27, 1977, cat. no. 85; ref. pp. 27, 119. Circulated to: University Art Museum, University of California, Berkeley, December 20, 1977–February 12, 1978; Marion Koogler McNay Art Institute, San Antonio, March 5–April 16, 1978; Columbus Gallery of Fine Arts, Ohio, May 10–June 19, 1978.

Literature
Frank O'Hara. "The Grand Manner of Motherwell." *Vogue,* vol. 146, no. 6 (October 1965), pp. 206–7.

WILLEM DE KOONING
American, born Netherlands 1904

Woman, 1950
oil on paper mounted on Masonite
36⅝ × 24½"
93.1 × 62.3 cm

Purchase
68.69

Inscribed
recto, lower left: *de Kooning*
verso, upper right: *1950/de Kooning*

Provenance
Paul Kantor Gallery, New York
William Inge
Artist

Exhibitions
Sidney Janis Gallery, New York. *Two Generations: Picasso to Pollock,* January 3–27, 1967, cat., not listed.

University Art Museum, University of California, Berkeley. *Willem de Kooning: The Recent Work,* August 12–September 14, 1969.

The Art Galleries, University of California, Santa Barbara. *Trends in Twentieth-Century Art: A Loan Exhibition from the San Francisco Museum of Art,* January 6–February 1, 1970, cat. no. 19; ill. no. 19.

Boise Gallery of Art, Idaho. *Form and Figure,* January 12–February 17, 1980, checklist no. 3; ill. Exhibition organized under the auspices of the Western Association of Art Museums (now Art Museum Association of America), circulated to: Art Galleries, University of Minnesota, Minneapolis, March 17–April 13, 1980; Block Gallery, Northwestern University, Evanston, Illinois, May 1–30, 1980; Washington State University, Pullman, September 15–October 15, 1980.

San Francisco Museum of Modern Art. *The Human Condition: SFMMA Biennial III,* June 28–August 26, 1984, cat.

HANS HOFMANN
American, born Germany, 1880–1966

Table—Version II, 1949
oil on canvas
48 × 36"
122.0 × 91.4 cm

Gift of Mr. and Mrs. William C. Janss
78.203

Inscribed
recto, lower right: *49/hans/hofmann*
verso, top stretcher bar, center: *Table—Version II 36 × 48*

Provenance
Mr. and Mrs. William C. Janss, 1963
Harold Diamond
Donald Peters

Exhibitions

Kootz Gallery, New York. *Hans Hofmann*, November 15–December 5, 1949.

San Francisco Museum of Modern Art. *Collectors, Collecting, Collection: American Abstract Art since 1945*, April 22–June 5, 1977, cat. no. 19.

MILTON AVERY
American, 1893–1965

Clear Cut Landscape, 1951
oil on canvas
32⅛ × 44″
81.6 × 111.8 cm

Gift of the Women's Board
55.4813

Inscribed

recto, lower right: *Milton Avery 1951*
verso, upper left center: *Clear Cut Landscape 1951 Milton Avery*

Provenance

Grace Borgenicht Gallery, New York
Artist

Exhibitions

Department of Fine Arts, Carnegie Institute, Pittsburgh. *The 1952 Pittsburgh International Exhibition of Contemporary Painting*, October 16–December 14, 1952, cat. no. 10. Circulated to: California Palace of the Legion of Honor, San Francisco, January 30–March 1, 1953.
Whitney Museum of American Art, New York. *Milton Avery*, February 2–March 13, 1960, cat. no. 16; ill. Exhibition organized by the American Federation of Arts, New York, circulated to: Bennington College, Vermont, March 28–April 17, 1960; Bradford Junior College, Massachusetts, May 1–22, 1960; Heckscher Museum, Huntington, Long Island, New York, June 5–26, 1960; Everhart Museum, Scranton, Pennsylvania, July 11–31, 1960; Crapo Gallery, Swain School of Design, New Bedford, Massachusetts, August 14–September 5, 1960; Museum of Fine Arts, Bowdoin College, Brunswick, Maine, September 18–October 16, 1960; Lyman Allyn Museum, New London, Connecticut, November 6–27, 1960; Art Department, State College, Indiana, Pennsylvania, December 11, 1960–January 16, 1961; Baltimore Museum of Art, February 6–26, 1961; Art Department, University of Kentucky, Lexington, March 12–April 3, 1961; Art Gallery, University of Minnesota, Minneapolis, April 16–May 8, 1961; Krannert Art Museum, University of Illinois, Urbana, June 25–July 16, 1961; Flint Institute of Arts, Michigan, July 30–September 24, 1961; University Galleries, Southern Illinois University, Carbondale, October 8–29,

1961; Department of Art and Art Education, University of Wisconsin, Madison, November 12–December 3, 1961; Oklahoma Art Center, Oklahoma City, December 18, 1961–January 7, 1962; Santa Barbara Museum of Art, California, January 30–February 25, 1962.
National Collection of Fine Arts (now National Museum of American Art), Smithsonian Institution, Washington, D.C. *Milton Avery*, December 12, 1969–January 25, 1970, cat. no. 56; ill. Circulated to: The Brooklyn Museum, New York, February 17–March 29, 1970; The Columbus Gallery of Fine Arts, Ohio, April 24–May 31, 1970.

Literature

Bonnie Lee Grad. *Milton Avery*. Royal Oak, Mich.: Strathcona Publishing Company, 1981, ref. p. 7.

MARK ROTHKO
American, born Russia, 1903–1970

Untitled, 1960
oil on canvas
69 × 50⅛″
175.3 × 127.3 cm

Acquired through a gift of Peggy Guggenheim
62.3426

Inscribed

verso, upper right: *Mark Rothko/1960*

Provenance

Artist

Exhibitions

The Art Galleries, University of California, Santa Barbara. *Trends in Twentieth-Century Art: A Loan Exhibition from the San Francisco Museum of Art*, January 6–February 1, 1970, cat. no. 30; ill. no. 30.
Newport Harbor Art Museum, Newport Beach, California. *Mark Rothko: Ten Major Works*, January 30–March 10, 1974, cat. no. 5; color ill. p. 17.
Baltimore Museum of Art. *Two Hundred Years of American Painting*, January 16–February 6, 1977, cat. no. 44. Circulated to: Rheinisches Landesmuseum, Bonn, June 30–July 28, 1976; Museum of Modern Art, Belgrade, August 14–September 11, 1976; Galleria Nazionale d'Arte Moderna, Rome, September 28–October 26, 1976; National Museum of Poland, Warsaw, November 12–December 10, 1976.
San Francisco Museum of Modern Art. *Collectors, Collecting, Collection: American Abstract Art since 1945*, April 22–June 5, 1977, cat. no. 4.
San Jose Museum of Art, California. *America VIII: Post War Modernism*, November 4–December 31, 1977, cat.

Remarks

This painting was acquired in 1962 by exchange with the artist of *Slow Swirl at the Edge of the Sea*, 1944, which had been given to the Museum by Peggy Guggenheim in 1946.

SAM FRANCIS
American, born 1923

Red and Pink, 1951
oil on canvas
81¾ × 65¾″
207.6 × 167.0 cm

Partial gift of Mrs. Wellington S. Henderson
69.111

Provenance

Mrs. Wellington S. Henderson, 1968
Artist

Exhibitions

Palazzo Grassi, Venice. *Arte e Contemplazione*, July 15–October 1, 1961.
The Museum of Fine Arts, Houston. *Sam Francis*, October 1–November 19, 1967, cat. no. 1; ref. p. 15, ill. p. 29. Circulated to: University Art Museum, University of California, Berkeley, January 15–February 18, 1968.
Albright-Knox Art Gallery, Buffalo. *Sam Francis: Paintings 1947–1972*, September 11–October 15, 1972, cat. no. 12; ref. p. 17, ill. p. 43. Circulated to: Corcoran Gallery of Art, Washington, D.C., November 1–30, 1972; Whitney Museum of American Art, New York, December 10, 1972–January 14, 1973; Dallas Museum of Fine Arts, February 7–March 18, 1973.
De Saisset Art Gallery, University of Santa Clara, California. *Sam Francis*, September 22–October 30, 1973.
San Francisco Museum of Modern Art. *Collectors, Collecting, Collection: American Abstract Art since 1945*, April 22–June 5, 1977, cat. no. 7.

Literature

Peter Selz. *Sam Francis*. New York: Harry N. Abrams, 1975, ref. p. 34, color ill. p. 138.

PHILIP GUSTON
American, born Canada, 1913–1980

For M., 1955
oil on canvas
76⅜ × 72¼″
194.0 × 183.5 cm

Gift of Betty Freeman
72.21

Inscribed

recto, lower left center: *Philip Guston*
verso, upper left: *Philip Guston/"For M." 1955/72″ × 76″*

Provenance

Betty Freeman, 1959
David Herbert Gallery, New York
Sander L. Feldman
Sidney Janis Gallery, New York
Artist

Exhibitions

The Museum of Modern Art, New York. *Twelve Americans*, May 30–September 9, 1956, cat. p. 94.
Sidney Janis Gallery, New York. *Philip Guston*, January 1958.
Kassel, Germany. *II. Documenta. Kunst nach 1945*, July 11–October 11, 1959, cat. no. 1; p. 30.
The Solomon R. Guggenheim Museum, New York. *Philip Guston*, May 2–July 1, 1962, cat. no. 28; ill. p. 64. Circulated to: Stedelijk Museum, Amsterdam, September 21–October 15, 1962; Whitechapel Art Gallery, London, January 1–February 15, 1963; Palais des Beaux-Arts, Brussels, March 1–31, 1963; Los Angeles County Museum of Art, May 15–June 23, 1963.
The Metropolitan Museum of Art, New York. *New York Painting and Sculpture: 1940–1970*, October 18, 1969–February 10, 1970, cat. no. 114; ill. p. 172.
San Francisco Museum of Modern Art. *Philip Guston*, May 16–June 29, 1980, cat. no. 26; ill. p. 64. Circulated to: Corcoran Gallery of Art, Washington, D.C., July 20–September 9, 1980; Museum of Contemporary Art, Chicago, November 12, 1980–January 11, 1981; The Denver Art Museum, February 25–April 26, 1981; Whitney Museum of American Art, New York, June 24–September 13, 1981.

Literature

Dore Ashton. *Yes, but . . . A Critical Study of Philip Guston*. New York: Viking Press, 1976, ref. p. 108, ill. p. 109.

PHILIP GUSTON
American, born Canada, 1913–1980

Red Sea; The Swell; Blue Light
1975
oil on canvas
left panel 73½ × 78¾″
186.7 × 200.1 cm
center panel 73 × 78⅛″
185.5 × 198.5 cm
right panel 73 × 80½″
185.5 × 204.5 cm

Purchased through the Helen Crocker Russell and William H. and Ethel W. Crocker Family Funds, the Mrs. Ferdinand C. Smith Fund, and the Paul L. Wattis Special Fund
78.67 A–C

Inscribed

Red Sea, verso, upper left: *Philip Guston/"Red Sea" 1975/oil— 73½ × 78¾″*

The Swell, recto, lower right: *Philip Guston*
verso, upper left: *Philip Guston/ "The Swell" 1975/oil—73 × 78"*

Blue Light, recto, lower center: *Philip Guston*
verso, upper left: *Philip Guston/ "Blue Light" 1975/oil—73 × 80½"*

Provenance
Artist

Exhibitions
David McKee Gallery, New York. *Philip Guston: Paintings 1975*, March 6–April 10, 1976, cat. no. 1; ill.

San Francisco Museum of Modern Art. *Philip Guston*, May 16–June 29, 1980, cat. no. 61; color ill. pp. 92, 93, 94. Circulated to: Corcoran Gallery of Art, Washington, D.C., July 20–September 9, 1980; Museum of Contemporary Art, Chicago, November 12, 1980–January 11, 1981; The Denver Art Museum, February 25–April 26, 1981; Whitney Museum of American Art, New York, June 24–September 13, 1981.

Whitechapel Art Gallery, London. *Philip Guston: Paintings 1969–1980*, October 13–December 12, 1982, cat. no. 13; ill. p. 65, color ill. *Blue Light*. Circulated to: Stedelijk Museum, Amsterdam, January 13–February 27, 1983; Kunsthalle, Basel, May 8–June 19, 1983.

Literature
Roberta Smith. "The New Gustons." *Art in America*, vol. 66, no. 1 (January–February 1978), ref. p. 104, color ill. *Blue Light* p. 102.

PHILIP GUSTON
American, born Canada, 1913–1980

Back View, 1977
oil on canvas
69 × 94"
175.3 × 238.8 cm

Gift of the artist
82.33

Inscribed
recto, lower right: *Philip Guston*
verso, upper left: *Philip Guston/ "Back View" 1977/Oil on Canvas 69 × 94*

Provenance
Artist

Exhibitions
San Francisco Museum of Modern Art. *Philip Guston*, May 16–June 29, 1980, cat. no. 76; ref. pp. 29–30, color ill. p. 106. Circulated to: Corcoran Gallery of Art, Washington, D.C., July 20–September 9, 1980; Museum of Contemporary Art, Chicago, November 12, 1980–January 11, 1981; The Denver Art Museum, February 25–April 26, 1981; Whitney Museum of Ameri-

can Art, New York, June 24–September 13, 1981.

Museu de Arte Moderna, São Paulo, Brazil. *XVI Bienal. Philip Guston, Sus Ultimos Años*, October 16–December 20, 1981, cat. no. 10; ill. p. 19. Organized by the San Francisco Museum of Modern Art, circulated to: Museo de Arte Moderno, Mexico City, February–March 1982; Centro de Arte Moderno, Guadalajara, Mexico, April–May 1982; Museo de Arte Moderno, Bogotá, Colombia, July–August 1982.

Whitechapel Art Gallery, London. *Philip Guston: Paintings 1969–1980*, October 13–December 12, 1982, cat. no. 21; color ill. Circulated to: Stedelijk Museum, Amsterdam, January 13–February 27, 1983; Kunsthalle, Basel, May 8–June 19, 1983.

San Francisco Museum of Modern Art. *The Human Condition: SFMMA Biennial III*, June 28–August 26, 1984, cat.; ill. p. 18.

RICHARD DIEBENKORN
American, born 1922

Berkeley #57, 1955
oil on canvas
58¾ × 58¾"
149.3 × 149.3 cm

Bequest of Joseph M. Bransten in memory of Ellen Hart Bransten
80.423

Inscribed
recto, lower left: *RD 55*
verso, upper right: *Top/ R. Diebenkorn/Berkeley #57/1955*

Provenance
Mr. and Mrs. Joseph M. Bransten
Artist

Exhibitions
Poindexter Gallery, New York. *Richard Diebenkorn*, February 28–March 24, 1956.

San Francisco Museum of Art. *On Looking Back: Painting and Sculpture in the Bay Area 1945–1962*, August 8–September 8, 1968.

San Francisco Museum of Modern Art. *Resource/Response/Reservoir. Richard Diebenkorn: Paintings 1948–1983*, May 13–July 17, 1983, cat. no. 5.

RICHARD DIEBENKORN
American, born 1922

Cityscape I
(formerly *Landscape I*), 1963
oil on canvas
60¼ × 50½"
153.1 × 128.3 cm

Purchased with funds from trustees and friends in memory of Hector

Escobosa, Brayton Wilbur, and J. D. Zellerbach
64.46

Inscribed
verso, upper right: *10-31-63/ R. Diebenkorn/Landscape #1—1963*

Provenance
Artist

Exhibitions
San Francisco Museum of Art, *Eighty-third Annual Exhibition of the San Francisco Art Institute*, April 17–May 17, 1964, cat.

Washington Gallery of Modern Art, Washington, D.C. *Richard Diebenkorn*, November 6–December 31, 1964, cat. no. 47; ill. p. 55. Circulated to: The Jewish Museum, New York, January 13–February 21, 1965; Pavilion Gallery, Balboa, California (now Newport Harbor Art Museum, Newport Beach), March 14–April 15, 1965.

National Gallery of Art, Washington, D.C. *White House Festival of the Arts*, June 18–July 11, 1965, unpublished checklist no. 9.

The Art Museum of the University of Texas at Austin. *Painting as Painting*, February 18–April 1, 1968, cat. no. 22.

Pushkin Museum, Moscow. *Representations of America*, December 15, 1977–February 15, 1978. Organized by the Metropolitan Museum of Art, New York, circulated to: Hermitage Museum, Leningrad, March 15–May 15, 1978; The Palace of Art, Minsk, July 15–August 15, 1978.

San Francisco Museum of Modern Art. *Painting and Sculpture in California: The Modern Era*, September 3–November 21, 1976, cat. no. 111; ill. p. 128. Circulated to: National Collection of Fine Arts (now National Museum of American Art), Smithsonian Institution, Washington, D.C., May 20–September 11, 1977.

San Francisco Museum of Modern Art. *Resource/Response/Reservoir. Richard Diebenkorn: Paintings 1948–1983*, May 13–July 17, 1983, cat. no. 17; color ill. cover.

Literature
Daniel M. Mendelowitz. *A History of American Art*. 2d ed. New York: Holt, Rinehart and Winston, 1970, ref. p. 424, ill. p. 424.

Abraham A. Davidson. *The Story of American Painting*. New York: Harry N. Abrams, 1974, ref. p. 165, ill. p. 165.

Gerald Nordland. "The Figurative Works of Richard Diebenkorn." *Richard Diebenkorn: Paintings and Drawings, 1943–1976*. Buffalo: Albright-Knox Art Gallery, 1976, ref. p. 36.

Jan Butterfield. "Diebenkorn, A

Painter's Pentimento." *United Airlines Magazine* (June 1983), color ill. p. 112.

Remarks
The painting was formerly known as *Landscape I*, but the artist prefers the title *Cityscape I*.

RICHARD DIEBENKORN
American, born 1922

Ocean Park #54, 1972
oil on canvas
100 × 81"
254.0 × 205.7 cm

Gift of friends of Gerald Nordland
72.59

Inscribed
recto, lower left: *RD 72*
verso: *R. Diebenkorn/Ocean Park #54/1972*

Provenance
Artist

Exhibitions
San Francisco Museum of Art. *Richard Diebenkorn: Paintings from the Ocean Park Series*, October 14, 1972–January 14, 1973, cat., not listed.

Marlborough Fine Arts Ltd., London. *Richard Diebenkorn: The Ocean Park Series: Recent Work*, December 12, 1973–January 4, 1974, cat. no. 5; color ill. p. 31. Circulated to: Marlborough Galerie, Zürich, February–March 1974.

Albright-Knox Art Gallery, Buffalo. *Richard Diebenkorn: Paintings and Drawings, 1943–1976*, November 12, 1976–January 9, 1977, cat. no. 77; ref. p. 48, ill. p. 85. Circulated to: Cincinnati Art Museum, January 31–March 20, 1977; Corcoran Gallery of Art, Washington, D.C., April 15–May 23, 1977; Whitney Museum of American Art, New York, June 9–July 17, 1977; Los Angeles County Museum of Art, August 9–September 25, 1977; The Oakland Museum, California, October 15–November 27, 1977.

San Francisco Museum of Modern Art. *Resource/Response/Reservoir. Richard Diebenkorn: Paintings 1948–1983*, May 13–July 17, 1983, cat. no. 25; ill. no. 25.

ELMER BISCHOFF
American, born 1916

Orange Sweater, 1955
oil on canvas
48½ × 57"
123.2 × 144.8 cm

Gift of Mr. and Mrs. Mark Schorer
63.20

Inscribed
verso, upper left: *Orange Sweater*
verso, upper right: *Elmer Bischoff*

Provenance
Mr. and Mrs. Mark Schorer
Artist

Exhibitions
The Oakland Art Museum, California. *Contemporary Bay Area Figurative Painting*, September 1957, cat. p. 23; ill. Circulated to: Los Angeles County Museum, November 13–December 22, 1957.
Auckland City Art Gallery, New Zealand. *Painting from the Pacific: Japan, America, Australia, New Zealand*, 1961, cat. no. 36, listed as *Figure at a Table*, 1958.

DAVID PARK
American, 1911–1960

Man in a T-Shirt, 1958
oil on canvas
59¾ × 49¾"
151.8 × 126.4 cm

Gift of Mr. and Mrs. Harry W. Anderson
76.26

Inscribed
recto, lower left: *Park 58*

Provenance
Mr. and Mrs. Harry W. Anderson, 1969
Martha Jackson Gallery, New York, 1969
Staempfli Gallery, New York
Artist

Exhibitions
Staempfli Gallery, New York. *David Park: Recent Paintings*, September 30–October 17, 1959, cat. no. 12; ill. no. 12.
Staempfli Gallery, New York. *David Park 1911–1960: Retrospective Exhibition*, December 5–30, 1961, cat. no. 43; color ill. no. 43.
The J. L. Hudson Gallery, Detroit. *Four California Painters: David Park, Elmer Bischoff, Roland Petersen, Joan Brown*, February 9–March 2, 1966, brochure; ill.
Maxwell Galleries, Ltd., San Francisco. *David Park: A Retrospective Exhibition*, August 14–September 26, 1970, cat. no. 73.
Stanford University Museum of Art, Stanford, California. *A Decade in the West: Painting, Sculpture and Graphics from the Anderson Collection*, June 12–August 22, 1971, cat. no. 38. Circulated to: Santa Barbara Museum of Art, California, September 10–October 10, 1971.

Literature
Sidney Tillim. "New York Exhibitions: Month in Review." *Arts*

Magazine, vol. 36, no. 6 (March 1962), pp. 36–40, ill. p. 40.

NATHAN OLIVEIRA
American, born 1928

Adolescent by the Bed, 1959
oil on canvas
60¼ × 60⅛"
153.1 × 152.7 cm

William L. Gerstle Collection
William L. Gerstle Fund Purchase
67.48

Inscribed
recto, lower right: *Oliveira 59*

Provenance
David Stuart Galleries, Los Angeles
Mr. and Mrs. Melvin Hirsch
Artist

Exhibitions
Paul Kantor Gallery, Beverly Hills. *Nathan Oliveira*, December 7, 1959–January 2, 1960, cat. no. 5; ill. no. 5.
UCLA Art Galleries, University of California, Los Angeles. *Nathan Oliveira*, September 15–October 26, 1963, cat. no. 10; ill. pl. 10. Circulated to: San Francisco Museum of Art, November 8–December 8, 1963; Fort Worth Art Center, Texas, January 1964; Colorado Springs Fine Arts Center, March 1964.
Portland Center for the Visual Arts, Oregon. *Nathan Oliveira*, February 14–March 17, 1974.
The Boise Gallery of Art, Idaho. *American Abstracts, 1948–1965*, September 17–October 24, 1976.
Sesnon Gallery, College Five, University of California, Santa Cruz. *Nathan Oliveira: Paintings, Monotypes*, October 31–December 4, 1976, brochure.
U.S. International Communication Agency, Stockholm. The Art in Embassies Program. *Art in the Residence of the American Ambassador to Sweden*, 1979, checklist; ill.

FRANK LOBDELL
American, born 1921

March 1954, 1954
oil on canvas
69½ × 65½"
176.6 × 166.4 cm

Anonymous gift
76.197

Inscribed
verso, upper center: *Lobdell/March 1954*

Provenance
Private collection
Artist

Exhibitions
Pasadena Art Museum (now Norton Simon Museum of Art at Pasadena), California. *Frank Lobdell: Paintings and Graphics from 1948 to 1965*, March 15–April 10, 1966, cat. no. 14, listed as *March 1954 (2)*, 1954; ill. no. 14. Circulated to: Stanford Museum, Stanford University, California, May 1–31, 1966.
San Francisco Museum of Modern Art. *Painting and Sculpture in California: The Modern Era*, September 3–November 21, 1976, cat. no. 122; ill. p. 130. Circulated to: National Collection of Fine Arts (now National Museum of American Art), Smithsonian Institution, Washington, D.C., May 20–September 11, 1977.
San Francisco Museum of Modern Art. *Frank Lobdell: Paintings and Monotypes*, January 20–March 27, 1983, cat. no. 1; ref. p. 14, ill. p. 15.

HASSEL SMITH
American, born 1915

2 to the Moon, 1961
oil on canvas
67⅞ × 67⅞"
172.4 × 172.4 cm

Gift of Mr. and Mrs. William C. Janss
78.206

Inscribed
recto, lower edge center: *HWS 2 to the Moon/1961*
verso, upper right quadrant: *Hassel Smith/1961, /#40, 61*
verso, upper edge, left: *"2 to the Moon"*

Provenance
Mr. and Mrs. William C. Janss, 1962
Ferus Gallery, Los Angeles
Artist

Exhibition
San Francisco Museum of Modern Art. *Collectors, Collecting, Collection: American Abstract Art since 1945*, April 22–June 5, 1977, cat. no. 50.

ROBERT RAUSCHENBERG
American, born 1925

Collection (formerly **Untitled**)
1953–54
oil, paper, fabric, and metal on wood
80 × 96 × 3½"
203.2 × 243.9 × 8.9 cm

Gift of Mr. and Mrs. Harry W. Anderson
72.26

Provenance
Ileana Sonnabend, ca. 1959–60
David Meyers
Artist

Exhibitions
Museum Haus Lange, Krefeld, West Germany. *Robert Rauschenberg*, September 12–October 18, 1964, cat. no. 1; ill. no. 1.
Stedelijk Museum, Amsterdam. *Robert Rauschenberg*, February 23–April 7, 1968, cat. no. 2; ill. p. 18. Circulated to: Kölnischer Kunstverein, Cologne, April 19–May 26, 1968; Musée d'Art Moderne de la Ville de Paris, June 7–July 14, 1968.
Kunsthalle, Nuremberg. *II. Biennale Nürnberg. "Was die Schönheit sei, das weiss ich nicht." Künstler —Theorie—Werk*. April 30–August 1, 1971, cat. no. 325, listed as *Red Untitled*, 1953; color ill. p. 130.
National Collection of Fine Arts (now National Museum of American Art), Smithsonian Institution, Washington, D.C. *Robert Rauschenberg*, October 30, 1976–January 2, 1977, cat. no. 28; ref. pp. 5, 8, 77, ill. pp. 11, 77, color ill. p. 10. Circulated to: The Museum of Modern Art, New York, March 25–May 17, 1977; San Francisco Museum of Modern Art, June 24–August 21, 1977; Albright-Knox Art Gallery, Buffalo, September 23–October 30, 1977; The Art Institute of Chicago, December 3, 1977–January 15, 1978.

Literature
Andrew Forge. *Rauschenberg*. New York: Harry N. Abrams, 1969, color ill. p. 175.
Andrew Forge. *Rauschenberg*. New York: Harry N. Abrams, 1972, color ill. no. 4, listed as *Untitled, 1953–54*.
"The Most Living Artist." *Time*, vol. 108, no. 22 (November 29, 1976), ref. pp. 54, 60, color ill.
Jeff Perrone, "Robert Rauschenberg," *Artforum*, vol. 15, no. 6 (February 1977), ref. p. 24.
Maxime de la Falaise. "Rauschenberg à Washington et à New York." *XXe Siècle*, New Series, no. 49 (December 1977), ref. p. 29.

Remarks
Robert Rauschenberg titled the work *Collection* in 1976.

JASPER JOHNS
American, born 1930

Land's End, 1963
oil on canvas with stick
67 × 48¼"
170.2 × 122.6 cm

Gift of Mr. and Mrs. Harry W. Anderson
72.23

Inscribed
verso, upper right: *"Land's End"/J.Johns/1963/J Johns/1963*

255

Provenance
Private collection, Turin, Italy, 1970
Edwin Janss, 1963
Artist

Exhibitions
San Francisco Museum of Art. *Directions—American Painting*, September 20–October 20, 1963, unpublished checklist no. 19.
Pasadena Art Museum (now Norton Simon Museum of Art at Pasadena), California. *Jasper Johns*, January 26–February 28, 1965.
Pasadena Art Museum (now Norton Simon Museum of Art at Pasadena), California. *Painting in New York: 1944 to 1969*, November 24, 1969–January 11, 1970, cat. no. 5; ill. p. 24.
Dallas Museum of Fine Arts and Southern Methodist University, Dallas. *Poets of the Cities: New York and San Francisco 1950–1965*, November 20–December 29, 1974, cat. no. 29; ill. p. 133. Circulated to: San Francisco Museum of Art, January 31–March 23, 1975; Wadsworth Atheneum, Hartford, Connecticut, April 23–June 1, 1975.
Whitney Museum of American Art, New York. *Jasper Johns*, October 17, 1977–January 22, 1978, cat. no. 103; ref. pp. 49, 50, 92, ill. pl. 100. Circulated to: Museum Ludwig, Cologne, February 11–March 27, 1978; Centre Georges Pompidou, Musée National d'Art Moderne, Paris, April 19–June 4, 1978; Hayward Gallery, London, June 23–July 30, 1978, cat. no. 88; The Seibu Museum of Art, Tokyo, August 19–September 26, 1978; San Francisco Museum of Modern Art, October 20–December 10, 1978, cat. no. 77.

Literature
Alan R. Solomon. *Jasper Johns*. New York: The Jewish Museum, 1964, ref. p. 16.
Harold Rosenberg. *The Anxious Object: Art Today and Its Audience*. New York: Horizon Press, 1964, ref. p. 184.

CLAES OLDENBURG
American, born Sweden 1929

Blue Legs, 1961
plaster and muslin with enamel
48 × 36 × 7⅛"
121.9 × 91.5 × 18.1 cm

Anonymous gift
64.65

Inscribed
verso, upper right: *C.O. 1961*

Provenance
Private collection
Artist

Exhibitions
Ray-Gun Mfg. Co. and The Green Gallery, New York. *The Store*, December 1–31, 1961, checklist no. 44.
San Francisco Museum of Art. *Six Artists from New York*, April 15–May 22, 1966.

Literature
Claes Oldenburg and Emmett Williams. *Store Days*. New York: Something Else Press, 1967, ref. p. 33.

JAY DeFEO
American, born 1929

Incision, 1958–61
oil and string on canvas mounted on board
118 × 55⅝ × 9⅜"
299.7 × 141.3 × 23.9 cm

Purchased with the aid of funds from the Society for the Encouragement of Contemporary Art
67.89

Provenance
Artist

Exhibition
Civic Arts Gallery, Walnut Creek, California. *"Remember: It's Only Art,"* February 5–March 28, 1981, cat.

Literature
"New Talent USA," *Art in America*, vol. 49, no. 1 (1961), ref. p. 30, ill. p. 30, listed as *The Incision*, n.d.

Remarks
Incision is the left panel of what was originally intended to be a triptych. These panels were begun in 1958, at the same time the artist started *The Rose*. DeFeo worked on the panels for an initial period of six months; a few years later she resumed work on the left segment for another six months. She recalls that she completed this work on her birthday, March 31, 1961.
The title *Incision* refers to the plan for the triptych, in which a broad V would have extended across all three panels, reaching bottom at the center. A green heart was to be painted across the central and right panels. The right panel was never completed, and the center panel was lost or destroyed in the early eighties when DeFeo changed her residence.

BRUCE CONNER
American, born 1933

Looking Glass, 1964
paper, cotton cloth, nylon, beads, metal, twine, glass, leather, plastic, and wood on Masonite
60½ × 48 × 14½"
153.7 × 121.9 × 36.8 cm

Gift of the Modern Art Council
78.69

Provenance
Institute for Policy Studies, Washington, D.C.
Dennis Hopper
Artist

Exhibitions
Hyman Swetzoff Gallery, Boston. *Bruce Conner*, 1964.
The Alan Gallery, New York. *Bruce Conner: Assemblages 1954–1964 and New Drawings*, May 10–28, 1965, brochure no. 13.
The Rose Art Museum, Brandeis University, Waltham, Massachusetts. *Bruce Conner*, September 20–October 24, 1965, cat. no. 39; ref., ill.
Los Angeles County Museum of Art. *American Sculpture of the Sixties*, April 28–June 25, 1967, cat. no. 28; color ill. p. 104. Circulated to: Philadelphia Museum of Art, September 15–October 29, 1967.
Institute of Contemporary Art, University of Pennsylvania, Philadelphia. *Bruce Conner*, November 29–December 31, 1967, cat. no. 55.

Literature
Merril Greene. *Art as a Muscular Principle*. South Hadley, Mass.: Mount Holyoke College, 1975, ref. p. 39.

PETER VOULKOS
American, born 1924

Sevillanas, 1959
stoneware with iron slip and clear glaze
56¾ × 27¼ × 20"
144.1 × 69.2 × 50.8 cm

Albert M. Bender Collection
Albert M. Bender Bequest Fund Purchase
64.9

Inscribed
incised, left side, along base:
59/Voulkos

Provenance
Art Unlimited Gallery, San Francisco
Felix Landau Gallery, Los Angeles
Artist

Exhibitions
The Museum of Modern Art, New York. *Sculpture and Painting by Peter Voulkos/New Talent in the Penthouse*, February 1–March 13, 1960, brochure no. 5

The Oakland Art Museum, installed at Kaiser Center Roof Garden, Oakland, California. *Contemporary California Sculpture*, August 5–September 15, 1963.
San Francisco Museum of Modern Art. *Peter Voulkos: A Retrospective 1948–1978*, February 17–April 2, 1978, cat. no. 63; ill. Circulated to: Contemporary Arts Museum, Houston, June 3–July 30, 1978; Museum of Contemporary Crafts, New York, October 6–December 31, 1978; Milwaukee Art Center, February 23–April 15, 1979.
Whitney Museum of American Art, New York. *Ceramic Sculpture: Six Artists*, December 9, 1981–February 7, 1982, cat. p. 137; ill. p. 46. Shown at co-organizing institution, San Francisco Museum of Modern Art, April 8–June 27, 1982.

Literature
Anita Ventura. "Field Day for Sculptors." *Arts Magazine*, vol. 28, no. 1 (October 1963), pp. 62–65, ill. p. 63.
Rose Slivka, *Peter Voulkos: A Dialogue with Clay*. Boston: New York Graphic Society, 1978, p. 50, fig. 31.

JOHN MASON
American, born 1927

Untitled (Monolith), 1964
stoneware with glaze
66½ × 64 × 17"
168.9 × 162.6 × 43.2 cm

Gift of the Women's Board
71.68

Inscribed
Incised, right side, near base:
Mason 64

Provenance
Artist

Exhibitions
Los Angeles County Museum of Art. *John Mason: Sculpture*, November 16, 1966–February 1, 1967, cat. no. 9; ill. pl. 9.
Whitney Museum of American Art, New York. *Ceramic Sculpture: Six Artists*, December 9, 1981–February 7, 1982, cat. p. 137; ill. p. 64. Shown at co-organizing institution, San Francisco Museum of Modern Art, April 8–June 27, 1982.

KENNETH PRICE
American, born 1935

L. Red, 1963
stoneware with lacquer and acrylic
10¼ × 8⅞ × 9¼"
26.1 × 22.6 × 23.5 cm

Evelyn and Walter Haas, Jr. Fund Purchase
82.155

Provenance
Quay Gallery, San Francisco, 1982
Mr. and Mrs. Robert Lauter, 1963
Ferus Gallery, Los Angeles, 1963
Artist

Exhibitions
University Art Museum, University of California, Berkeley. *Funk*, April 18–May 29, 1967, cat. no. 50, listed as Untitled, 1965; ill. p. 42.
Whitney Museum of American Art, New York. *Ceramic Sculpture: Six Artists*, December 9, 1981–February 7, 1982, cat. p. 138, listed as Untitled, 1963. Shown at co-organizing institution, San Francisco Museum of Modern Art, April 8–June 27, 1982.

Literature
Dore Ashton. *Modern American Sculpture*. New York: Harry N. Abrams, 1968, ref. p. 46, color ill. pl. XXIX, listed as *B. G. Red*, 1963.

LARRY BELL
American, born 1939

Untitled, 1969
metallic compounds (vaporized) on glass, chrome binding
18⅛ × 18⅛ × 18⅛"
46.0 × 46.0 × 46.0 cm

Anonymous gift through the American Art Foundation
78.184

Provenance
Private collection, 1969
Artist

Exhibition
National Museum of American Art, Smithsonian Institution, Washington, D.C. *Art from the Vice President's House*, March 15, 1980–January 19, 1981.

ROBERT IRWIN
American, born 1928

Untitled, 1968
acrylic lacquer on Plexiglas
53¼ diam. × 24½"
135.5 × 62.3 cm

T. B. Walker Foundation Fund Purchase
70.5 A–F

Provenance
Artist

Exhibitions
San Francisco Museum of Art. *Museum Collections: Recent Acquisitions in Painting and Sculpture*, May 29–July 5, 1970.
San Francisco Museum of Modern Art. *Painting and Sculpture in California: The Modern Era*, September 3–November 21, 1976, cat.

no. 286. Circulated to: National Collection of Fine Arts (now National Museum of American Art), Smithsonian Institution, Washington, D.C., May 20–September 11, 1977.
National Museum of American Art, Smithsonian Institution, Washington, D.C. *Art from the Vice President's House*, February 20–May 5, 1981.
The Oakland Museum, California. *One Hundred Years of California Sculpture*, August 7–October 17, 1982, cat. p. 43.

FRANK STELLA
American, born 1936

Adelante, 1964
from the Running V Series
metallic powder in polymer emulsion on canvas
96¼ × 165½"
244.5 × 420.4 cm

T. B. Walker Foundation Fund Purchase
68.53

Provenance
André Emmerich Gallery, New York
Robert Rowan, 1967
Kasmin Ltd., London
Artist

Exhibitions
Kasmin Ltd., London. *Frank Stella: Recent Paintings*, September 29–October 24, 1964.
University of California, Irvine. *A Selection of Paintings and Sculptures from the Collections of Mr. and Mrs. Robert Rowan*, May 2–21, 1967, cat. no. 130. Circulated to: San Francisco Museum of Art, June 2–July 2, 1967. Painting exhibited only in San Francisco.
The Museum of Modern Art, New York. *Frank Stella*, March 26–May 31, 1970, checklist no. 24. Circulated to: Hayward Gallery, London, July 25–August 31, 1970; Stedelijk Museum, Amsterdam, October 2–November 22, 1970; Pasadena Art Museum (now Norton Simon Museum of Art at Pasadena), California, January 19–February 28, 1971; Art Gallery of Ontario, Toronto, April 9–May 9, 1971. Painting exhibited only in New York.
The Fine Arts Gallery of San Diego, California. *Monumental Paintings of the Sixties*, April 19–June 16, 1974, cat.; ill.
San Francisco Museum of Modern Art. *Collectors, Collecting, Collection: American Abstract Art since 1945*, April 22–June 5, 1977, cat. no. 22.
San Francisco Museum of Modern Art. *Resource/Response/Reservoir. Stella Survey: 1959–1982*, March 10–May 1, 1983, cat. no. 4; ill. no. 9.

Literature
William S. Rubin. *Frank Stella*. New York: The Museum of Modern Art, 1970, ref. pp. 101–2, ill. p. 103.

FRANK STELLA
American, born 1936

Khurasan Gate (Variation) I
1969
from the Protractor Series
polymer and fluorescent polymer on canvas
96¼ × 285½"
244.5 × 725.0 cm

Gift of Mr. and Mrs. Frederick R. Weisman
78.193

Inscribed
verso, upper center: *Khurasan Gate (Variation) I 96" × 288"/For L. Rubin*
verso, upper left: *F. Stella '69*

Provenance
Mr. and Mrs. Frederick R. Weisman, 1970
Artist

Exhibitions
The Museum of Modern Art, New York. *Frank Stella*, March 26–May 31, 1970, checklist no. 42. Circulated to: Hayward Gallery, London, July 25–August 31, 1970, checklist no. 37; ill.; Stedelijk Museum, Amsterdam, October 2–November 22, 1970; Pasadena Art Museum (now Norton Simon Museum of Art at Pasadena), California, January 19–February 28, 1971; Art Gallery of Ontario, Toronto, April 9–May 9, 1971. Painting exhibited only in New York and London.
San Francisco Museum of Modern Art. *Resource/Response/Reservoir. Stella Survey: 1959–1982*, March 10–May 1, 1983, cat. no. 8; ref., ill.

ELLSWORTH KELLY
American, born 1923

Red White, 1962
oil on canvas
80⅛ × 90"
203.5 × 228.6 cm

T. B. Walker Foundation Fund Purchase
66.3

Inscribed
verso, lower right: *EK 62*
verso, stretcher bar, right center: *Kelly 62*

Provenance
Sidney Janis Gallery, New York, 1964
Artist

Exhibitions
Washington Gallery of Modern Art, Washington, D.C. *Paintings, Sculp-*

---

ture and Drawings by Ellsworth Kelly, December 11, 1963–January 26, 1964. Circulated to: Institute of Contemporary Art, Boston, February 1–March 8, 1964.
Sidney Janis Gallery, New York. *An Exhibition of Recent Paintings by Ellsworth Kelly*, April 6–May 1, 1965, cat. no. 3; ill. p. 3.
Venice. *XXXIII Biennale Internazionale d'Arte*, June 18–October 16, 1966, cat. no. 7; ref. p. 29, ill. p. 31.
San Francisco Museum of Modern Art. *Collectors, Collecting, Collection: American Abstract Art since 1945*, April 22–June 5, 1977, cat. no. 14.

Literature
Henry Geldzahler. "Frankenthaler, Kelly, Lichtenstein, Olitski: A Preview of the American Selection at the 1966 Venice Biennale." *Artforum*, vol. 4, no. 10 (June 1966), ill. p. 38.
John Coplans. *Ellsworth Kelly*. New York: Harry N. Abrams, 1971, ref. p. 74, color ill. pl. 128.

ROBERT MANGOLD
American, born 1935

Red X within X, 1980
acrylic and graphite on canvas
113½ × 113½"
288.3 × 288.3 cm

T. B. Walker Foundation Fund Purchase
83.149 A–D

Inscribed
verso: *Red X Within X/ R. Mangold 1980*

Provenance
Artist

Exhibitions
Lisson Gallery, London. *Robert Mangold: Paintings*, April 29–May 30, 1981.
Kassel, Germany. *Documenta 7*, June 19–September 29, 1982, cat. p. 214; ill. p. 215.
Konrad Fisher Gallery, Düsseldorf. *Robert Mangold: Paintings*, October–November 1982.
Daniel Weinberg Gallery, Los Angeles. *Robert Mangold: Recent Paintings*, October 15–November 19, 1983.
University Art Museum, University of California, Berkeley. *Robert Mangold: Matrix/Berkeley 68*, December 19, 1983–mid-January, 1984, cat.

WILLIAM T. WILEY
American, born 1937

Ship's Log, 1969
cotton webbing, latex rubber, salt
licks, leather, plastic, wood, canvas,
lead wire, nautical and assorted
hardware, and ink and watercolor
on paper
82 × 78 × 54″
208.3 × 198.1 × 137.2 cm

William L. Gerstle Collection
William L. Gerstle Fund Purchase
70.37 A–L

Inscribed
Work includes handwritten "log"
book with extensive writing; signature and date on last page.

Provenance
Artist

Exhibitions
Hansen Fuller Gallery, San Fran-
cisco. *William T. Wiley*, November
1969, cat., not listed.
Hansen Fuller Gallery, San Fran-
cisco. Exhibition in conjunction
with the Zephyrus Image publication
of *Ships Log*, April 28–30, 1975.
Portland Center for the Visual Arts,
Oregon. *William Wiley*, December 4,
1975–January 4, 1976.
Whitney Museum of American Art,
New York. *Two Hundred Years of
American Sculpture*, March 16–Sep-
tember 26, 1976, cat. no. 334; ref.
p. 196, ill. p. 196.
Walker Art Center, Minneapolis.
Wiley Territory, December 9, 1979–
January 27, 1980, cat.; ref. pp. 36,
38, ill. p. 37; separate checklist no.
91. Circulated to: Dallas Museum of
Fine Arts, May 14–June 22, 1980;
The Denver Art Museum, July 19–
August 31, 1980; Des Moines Art
Center, September 29–November 9,
1980; San Francisco Museum of
Modern Art, December 11, 1980–
January 25, 1981.
Civic Arts Gallery, Walnut Creek,
California. *"Remember: It's Only Art,"*
February 5–March 28, 1981, cat.;
ref., ill. pl. 7.
De Saisset Museum, University of
Santa Clara, California. *Northern
California Art of the Sixties*, October
12–December 12, 1982, cat. no. 81.

Literature
William T. Wiley. Eindhoven,
Netherlands: Van Abbemuseum, 1973,
ill. p. 16.
William T. Wiley. Ships Log. San
Francisco: Zephyrus Image, 1975.
Unpaginated printed text of journal
which is part of the sculpture *Ship's
Log*; includes illustrations and a
photograph of assembled work.

RICHARD SHAW
American, born 1941

Melodious Double Stops, 1980
porcelain with decal overglaze
38¾ × 12 × 14″
98.4 × 30.5 × 35.6 cm

Purchased with matching funds from
the National Endowment for the
Arts and Frank O. Hamilton, Byron
Meyer, and Mrs. Peter Schlesinger
80.168

Inscribed
on book edges: *Rick Shaw*

Provenance
Artist

Exhibition
Whitney Museum of American Art,
New York. *Ceramic Sculpture: Six
Artists*, December 9, 1981–February
7, 1982, cat. p. 141; ill. p. 134.
Shown at co-organizing institution,
San Francisco Museum of Modern
Art, April 8–June 27, 1982.

Literature
*American Porcelain: New Expres-
sions in an Ancient Art*. Washington,
D.C.: Renwick Gallery, Smithsonian
Institution, 1980, ref., dated incor-
rectly as 1950; ill.

WAYNE THIEBAUD
American, born 1920

Display Cakes, 1963
oil on canvas
28 × 38″
71.0 × 96.5 cm

Mrs. Manfred Bransten Special Fund
Purchase
73.52

Inscribed
recto, upper right: *Thiebaud 1963*
upper horizontal stretcher bar, center: *Thiebaud 1963 "Display Cakes"*

Provenance
John Berggruen Gallery, San Fran-
cisco
Malcolm and Judy Weintraub
Artist

Exhibitions
Jerrold Morris International Gallery,
Toronto. *The Art of Things*, October
19–November 6, 1963.
The Albuquerque Museum, New
Mexico. *Reflections of Realism*, No-
vember 4, 1979–January 27, 1980,
cat.

ROY DE FOREST
American, born 1930

Country Dog Gentlemen, 1972
polymer on canvas
66¾ × 97″
169.6 × 246.4 cm

Gift of the Hamilton-Wells Collection
73.32

Inscribed
verso: *Roy De Forest/1972/Country
Dog/Gentlemen*

Provenance
Artist

Exhibitions
Hansen Fuller Gallery, San Fran-
cisco. *Roy De Forest*, March 5–31,
1973.
The Art Institute of Chicago. *Seventy-
first American Exhibition*, June 15–
August 11, 1974, cat. no. 13; ill.
p. 12.
Crocker Art Museum, Sacramento.
*Roy De Forest: Recent Paintings,
Drawings and Constructions*, Novem-
ber 8–December 28, 1980, cat. no.
1; ill.
Transamerica Center, Los Angeles.
Pets and Beasts, April 26–June 4,
1982, brochure; ref. Exhibition or-
ganized by Art Programs, Inc., San
Francisco and Los Angeles.
San Francisco Museum of Modern
Art. *The Human Condition: SFMMA
Biennial III*, June 28–August 26,
1984, cat.; ill. p.16.

MANUEL NERI
American, born 1930

Mary and Julia, 1980
plaster with pigment
52″ × 44″ × 34½″
132.1 × 111.8 × 87.6 cm

Gift of Agnes Cowles Bourne
79.322 A–B

Provenance
Artist

Exhibition
San Francisco Museum of Modern
Art. *Twenty American Artists*, July
24–September 7, 1980, cat. no. 4;
ill. p. 35.

Literature
Thomas Albright. "A Wide-Ranging
Modern Art Exhibition." *San Francisco Chronicle, This World*, August
3, 1980, ref. p. 35, ill. p. 35.

ROBERT HUDSON
American, born 1938

Out of the Blue, 1980–81
acrylic on canvas with wooden chair,
plastic tree, wood, and steel tubing
96⅜ × 180⅞ × 27¾″
244.8 × 459.4 × 70.5 cm

Purchased with the aid of the Byron
Meyer Fund
81.57 A–D

Provenance
Artist

Exhibition
Allan Frumkin Gallery, New York.
Robert Hudson, February 28–March
26, 1981, color ill. gallery
announcement.

ROBERT ARNESON
American, born 1930

California Artist, 1982
stoneware with glazes
68¼ × 27½ × 20¼″
173.4 × 69.9 × 51.5 cm

Gift of the Modern Art Council
83.108 A–B

Inscribed
impressed into back of jacket,
center: *California/Artist*
impressed into right rear tab and
button of jacket: *82 Arneson*

Provenance
Artist

Exhibition
Allan Frumkin Gallery, New York.
*War Heads and Others/Robert Arne-
son*, May 1983, cat. no. 1; ref., ill.

ILLUSTRATED CHECKLIST
OF THE COLLECTION

Note

This checklist records the paintings, sculpture, assemblages, and constructions in the permanent collection of the San Francisco Museum of Modern Art as of January 1984. The artists are arranged in alphabetical order. Where an artist is represented by more than one work, they are given in chronological order, with undated works last; within any single year, works are in alphabetical order by title.

Each entry contains the artist's name, and variant in cases in which the artist has worked under another name; nationality, and place of birth if different; and basic biographical dates. Western and Japanese artists appear with given names preceding family names; Chinese and Korean artists are listed with family name preceding given name. Where names are incomplete or biographical data are lacking, it is because this information has not been available.

Titles of works are given in English; where the artist has written the title on the work, it is rendered exactly as inscribed. Alternative titles by which the work may be known as well as those by which it has been previously recorded are given in parentheses, as are the titles in foreign languages where they were so assigned by the artist. All untitled works, whether given no title or designated "Untitled" by the artist, are set in Roman typeface; italicized phrases in parentheses following the untitled designation are descriptive phrases which have been published in connection with the work.

Date refers to date of execution; when two dates are separated by a slash, the second date is the casting or publication date.

In the case of multiple works, the citation "ed. 6," for example, indicates that an edition of six works was produced, but it is not known exactly which of the six this particular one is; the citation "2 / 3" indicates that the work is the second in an edition of three; "h.c." (hors commerce) indicates a work which was published outside the edition and was intended to be unavailable for purchase; "A / P G" indicates that a work was the seventh in a series of artist's proofs.

Dimensions are given in inches, followed by centimeters, and are listed in the sequence of height preceding width preceding depth. Where a work consists of more than one part, overall measurements are given unless otherwise noted.

Each entry concludes with an accessions or registration number. The first two digits indicate the year of acquisition; for works acquired after 1962, the remaining digits indicate the sequence within the year. Letters following these numbers indicate that the work consists of more than one part; in cases in which the accessions number is followed by a decimal point and further numbers, these digits reflect that the work consists of more than one part, and one or more of these parts may be shown individually. For works included in the WPA allocation, the first four digits reflect the chronological order in which they were received within a given year; the final two digits indicate the year of allocation.

ARLO ACTON
American, born 1933

Untitled, ca. 1956
stoneware
11⅜ × 8⅜ × 3⅛"
29.6 × 21.3 × 8.0 cm

Gift of Sally Lilienthal
71.45

ARLO ACTON
American, born 1933

Come One, Come Two
ca. 1963–64
wood
87 × 56¼ × 42½"
221.0 × 142.9 × 108.0 cm

Gift of the Women's Board
64.35 A–B

LUIS ALBERTO ACUÑA
Colombian, born 1904

***A Boy, a Horse, and a Somber
Landscape,*** 1939
oil on canvas
28¾ × 35¼"
73.1 × 89.6 cm

Purchase
44.3349

JANKEL ADLER
Polish, 1895–1949

Untitled, n.d.
oil, sand, and plaster on panel
22¾ × 31⅛"
57.8 × 79.1 cm

Gift of Mr. and Mrs.
Alfred Jaretzki, Jr.
62.3424

VIRGINIA ADMIRAL

***Abstraction No. 1 (Astrazione
No. 1),*** 1941
oil on canvas
34½ × 28"
87.7 × 71.1 cm

Gift of Peggy Guggenheim
66.11

THOMAS AKAWIE
American, born 1935

Imiut, 1980
acrylic on Masonite
18¼" diam.
46.5 cm

Purchased with the aid of funds
from Gene Alon
82.288

JOSEF ALBERS
American, born Germany,
1888–1976

Growing, 1940
oil on Masonite
24 × 26¾"
61.0 × 68.0 cm

Gift of Charlotte Mack
59.2668

See colorplate, p. 91

JOSEF ALBERS
American, born Germany,
1888–1976

***Study for "Tenayuca":
Two-Sided Painting,*** 1941–42
oil on Masonite
8½ × 15½"
21.6 × 39.4 cm

Purchased with the aid of funds from
Doris and Donald Fisher
84.3

JOSEF ALBERS
American, born Germany,
1888–1976

Tenayuca, 1943
oil on Masonite
22½ × 43½"
57.2 × 110.5 cm

Purchased with the aid of funds
from Mr. and Mrs. Richard N.
Goldman and Madeleine Haas
Russell
84.1

See colorplate, p. 93

JOSEF ALBERS
American, born Germany,
1888–1976

*Homage to the Square:
"Secluded,"* 1951
oil on Masonite
20⅞ × 20⅝"
53.0 × 52.4 cm

Gift of Anni Albers and the
Josef Albers Foundation
79.120

JOSEF ALBERS
American, born Germany,
1888–1976

*Homage to the Square:
"Confident,"* 1954
oil on Masonite
24 × 24"
60.9 × 60.9 cm

Gift of Anni Albers and the
Josef Albers Foundation
79.123

JOSEF ALBERS
American, born Germany,
1888–1976

*Adobe: Greens against
Blue,* 1958
oil on Masonite
22 × 25⅞"
55.8 × 65.7 cm

Gift of Anni Albers and the
Josef Albers Foundation
79.119

JOSEF ALBERS
American, born Germany,
1888–1976

*Study to Homage to the Square:
"In May,"* 1960
oil on Masonite
23⅞ × 24"
60.7 × 60.9 cm

Gift of Mr. and Mrs. William C.
Janss
78.210

JOSEF ALBERS
American, born Germany,
1888–1976

*Study for Homage to the Square:
"Dimmed Sound,"* 1961
oil on Masonite
16 × 16"
40.6 × 40.6 cm

Anonymous gift
69.75

JOSEF ALBERS
American, born Germany,
1888–1976

*Study for Homage to the Square:
"Shaded Green,"* 1961
oil on Masonite
16 × 16"
40.6 × 40.6 cm

Anonymous gift
69.76

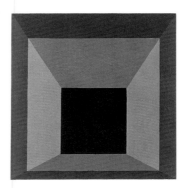

JOSEF ALBERS
American, born Germany,
1888–1976

Homage to the Square, 1962
oil on Masonite
23¾ × 23⅞"
60.3 × 60.6 cm

Gift of Anni Albers and the
Josef Albers Foundation
79.125

JOSEF ALBERS
American, born Germany,
1888–1976

Homage to the Square, 1967
oil on Masonite
23⅞ × 23⅞″
60.6 × 60.6 cm

Gift of Anni Albers and the
Josef Albers Foundation
79.122

JOSEF ALBERS
American, born Germany,
1888–1976

*Homage to the Square:
"Starting,"* 1968
oil on Masonite
48 × 48″
121.9 × 121.9 cm

Partial gift of Mr. and Mrs. Harry W.
Anderson and the William L.
Gerstle Fund, the Lucie Stern Trust
Fund, the Members' Accessions
Fund, and the Arthur W. Barney
Bequest Fund
76.22

JOSEF ALBERS
American, born Germany,
1888–1976

Homage to the Square, 1969
oil on Masonite
24 × 24″
60.9 × 60.9 cm

Gift of Anni Albers and the
Josef Albers Foundation
79.124

JOSEF ALBERS
American, born Germany,
1888–1976

*Study for Homage to
the Square*, 1972
oil on Masonite
23⅞ × 23⅞″
60.6 × 60.6 cm

Gift of Anni Albers and the
Josef Albers Foundation
79.121

See colorplate, p. 95

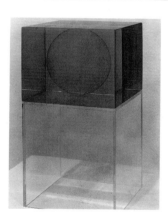

PETER ALEXANDER
American, born 1939

Untitled, 1967
polyester resin
3½ × 4½ × 4⅝″
8.9 × 11.5 × 11.8 cm

Gift of Daniel Weinberg
76.255

ZMIRA ALFI
Israeli, born Iraq

The Way to Jerusalem, 1975
oil on canvas
39¼ × 28⅞″
99.7 × 73.3 cm

Gift of the artist
83.41

WILLIAM ALLAN
American, born 1936

Book Life, 1966
wood and glass box, with glass jar,
metal lid, dictionary in water, glass
eyedroppers, book press and book,
and printed label
13⅛ × 22½ × 9⅝″
33.4 × 57.2 × 24.4 cm

Gift of Mr. and Mrs. Stephen D.
Paine
76.208 A–D

WILLIAM ALLAN
American, born 1936

The Architect's Nature, 1968
wooden box with tweezers, chalk,
sponge, and watercolor on paper
16¾ × 24 × 8⅞″
42.6 × 61.0 × 22.6 cm

Anonymous gift
70.44

WILLIAM ALLAN
American, born 1936

Traveling in Strange Circles, 1973
acrylic on canvas
76 × 88″
193.0 × 223.5 cm

Gift of the Women's Board
74.1

WILLIAM ALLAN
American, born 1936

Deception Pass. IV., 1974
acrylic on canvas
64¼ × 84¼″
163.2 × 214.0 cm

In memory of Pearl Joseph Walen
79.311

WILLIAM ALLAN
American, born 1936

Sea of Cortez #5, 1978
synthetic polymer on canvas
49⅛ × 58⅛″
124.8 × 147.6 cm

Gift of Rena Bransten
78.37

JOHN ALTOON
American, 1925–1969

Ocean Park Series #11, 1962
oil and acrylic on canvas
81½ × 84¼″
207.0 × 214.0 cm

Acquired through the aid of the
T. B. Walker Foundation Fund
70.29

DAVID ANDERSON
American, born 1946

Outer Star II, 1973
mild steel
66 × 96 × 46″
167.6 × 243.8 × 116.8 cm

Gift of Kristin Moore
81.197

DAVID ANDERSON
American, born 1946

Lantern/Paper #1, 1981
mild steel
66 × 16 × 17″
167.6 × 40.8 × 43.2 cm

Gift of Miriam Honig
81.224

JEREMY ANDERSON
American, 1921–1982

Undercurrents, 1953
redwood
7 × 30⅝ × 6¼″
17.8 × 77.8 × 15.9 cm

Gift of Robert B. Howard
79.317

JEREMY ANDERSON
American, 1921–1982

Doxie, 1960
redwood with bristles and paint
35½ × 71 × 13½″
90.2 × 180.4 × 34.3 cm

Anonymous gift through the
American Federation of Arts
61.4485

JEREMY ANDERSON
American, 1921–1982

Ancestor Worship, 1962
redwood and bronze
24⅛ × 25 × 5¼″
61.2 × 63.5 × 13.3 cm

Gift of Richard Faralla
71.1

RAOUL ANGUIANO
Mexican, born 1915

Marihuanos, 1938
oil on burlap
38½ × 29″
97.8 × 73.7 cm

Gift of Mrs. E. D. Lederman
52.5136

KAREL APPEL
Dutch, born 1921

Waiting for Us
(En attendant nous), 1959
oil on canvas
63¾ × 51″
161.9 × 129.6 cm

T. B. Walker Foundation Fund
Purchase
61.4100

KAREL APPEL
Dutch, born 1921

Jumping Fox with
Green Virgin, 1976
acrylic on wood, h.c.
19⅜ × 24⅜ × 2¾″
49.2 × 61.9 × 7.0 cm

Gift of Wil and Marilyn Fountain
79.130

KAREL APPEL
Dutch, born 1921

Flying Fish, 1977
wood with acrylic, h.c.
20 × 32 × 7¾″
50.8 × 81.3 × 19.7 cm

Gift of Wil and Marilyn Fountain
79.129

ALEXANDER ARCHIPENKO
American, born Russia, 1887–1964

Floating Torso, 1935–36
terra-cotta
6⅜ × 20¼ × 3⅜″
16.2 × 51.5 × 8.6 cm

Gift of Mrs. Drew Chidester
61.4517

RUTH ARMER
American, 1896–1977

Abstraction (Waterfall)
ca. 1940–46
oil on canvas
23¾ × 17¾″
60.4 × 45.1 cm

Gift of Mrs. Ansley K. Salz
46.4962

RUTH ARMER
American, 1896–1977

#328, 1958
oil on canvas
41⅞ × 28″
106.4 × 71.1 cm

Anonymous gift
58.2334

RUTH ARMER
American, 1896–1977

California Autumn, n.d.
oil on canvas
30⅛ × 38⅛″
76.5 × 96.8 cm

Albert M. Bender Collection
Gift of Albert M. Bender
36.694

ROBERT ARNESON
American, born 1930

Study for a Gargoyle, 1963
stoneware with glaze
34 × 16½ × 13″
86.4 × 42.0 × 33.1 cm

William L. Gerstle Collection
William L. Gerstle Fund Purchase
69.105

ROBERT ARNESON
American, born 1930

*Watch out that Indifference
Doesn't Get between
You and Progress*, 1970
porcelain with celadon glaze
8½ × 8¼ × 7⅛″
21.6 × 21.0 × 18.1 cm

Gift of Mrs. Edgar Sinton
70.46

ROBERT ARNESON
American, born 1930

Smorgi-Bob, the Cook, 1971
white earthenware with glaze, vinyl
tablecloth, and wood table
73 × 66 × 53″
185.4 × 167.7 × 134.6 cm

Purchase
72.38 A–CC

ROBERT ARNESON
American, born 1930

California Artist, 1982
stoneware with glazes
68¼ × 27½ × 20¼″
173.4 × 69.9 × 51.5 cm

Gift of the Modern Art Council
83.108 A–B

See colorplate, p. 235

CHARLES ARNOLDI
American, born 1946

Homer, 1973
lead on wood
49 × 25¾ × ⅞″
124.5 × 65.4 × 2.3 cm

Gift of Mrs. Philip Gersh
74.55

CHARLES ARNOLDI
American, born 1946

Sawbuck, 1973
tree branches with acrylic
95½ × 78¾ × 5″
242.6 × 200.1 × 12.7 cm

Gift of Mr. and Mrs. C. David
Robinson
75.185

JEAN (HANS) ARP
French, 1887–1966

Head and Leaf; Head and Vase
(*Tête et feuille; Tête et vase*)
(formerly *Head and Navel*,
ca. 1926), 1929
string and oil on canvas mounted on
board
13½ × 10½″
34.3 × 26.7 cm

Evelyn and Walter Haas, Jr. Fund
Purchase
80.390

See colorplate, p. 104

266

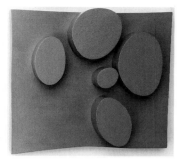

JEAN (HANS) ARP
French, 1887–1966

*Objects Arranged According to
the Laws of Chance III;
Symmetrical Configuration*
*(Objets placés selon les lois du
hasard III; Configuration
symétrique)*, 1931
oil on wood
10⅛ × 11⅜ × 2⅜"
25.7 × 28.9 × 6.1 cm

Purchase
84.5

See colorplate, p. 105

JEAN (HANS) ARP
French, 1887–1966

*Human Concretion without Oval
Bowl (Concrétion humaine sans
coupe)*, 1933
bronze (polished) 2/3
23 × 22⅝ × 15¾"
58.5 × 57.5 × 40.0 cm

William L. Gerstle Collection
William L. Gerstle Fund Purchase
62.3421

See colorplate, p. 107

JEAN (HANS) ARP
French, 1887–1966

Collage No. 1, ca. 1964–65
glass
19¾ × 13¾ × ⅜"
50.2 × 35.0 × 1.0 cm

Gift of Peggy Guggenheim
65.13

JEAN (HANS) ARP
French, 1887–1966

Dachshund Doll
(Poupée-Basset), 1965
bronze ed. 3
19⅝ × 5⅝ × 5⅞"
49.7 × 14.3 × 15.0 cm

Gift of Cyril Magnin
74.89

RICHARD ARTSCHWAGER
American, born 1924

Untitled (formerly *Box*), 1971
wood, Formica, hair, mirrored glass,
glass, and metal
11⅝ × 14¾ × 13"
29.6 × 37.5 × 33.1 cm

Purchase
72.39

RUTH ASAWA
American, born 1926

Untitled, n.d.
brass wire
19⅝ × 10 × 10"
49.8 × 25.4 × 25.4 cm

Gift of Robert B. Howard
75.43

GEORGE C. AULT
American, 1891–1948

*The Hudson from Riverside
Drive*, 1920–21
oil on linen
24 × 30"
61.0 × 76.2 cm

Gift of Rena Bransten
80.340

MILTON AVERY
American, 1893–1965

Three Figures and a Dog, 1943
oil on canvas
32½ × 44"
82.6 × 111.8 cm

Gift of Mr. and Mrs. Roy R.
Neuberger
55.6896

MILTON AVERY
American, 1893–1965

Clear Cut Landscape, 1951
oil on canvas
32⅛ × 44"
81.6 × 111.8 cm

Gift of the Women's Board
55.4813

See colorplate, p. 163

ALICE BABER
American, 1928–1982

Seven Green Leagues, 1967
acrylic on canvas
38 × 64"
96.5 × 162.6 cm

Gift of David Kluger
76.4

ALICE BABER
American, 1928–1982

*Lavender Ladder to
the Sun*, 1976
acrylic on canvas
71⅞ × 102¾"
182.6 × 261.0 cm

Gift of Dr. William C. Sawyer
76.211

JO BAER
American, born 1929

Untitled, 1964–72
oil on canvas
48 × 48"
121.9 × 121.9 cm

Gift of Rena Bransten
78.38

CLAYTON BAILEY
American, born 1939

ROY DE FOREST
American, born 1930

Dog Lamp, ca. 1970
earthenware with slip-stain and
glaze, and electrical apparatus
17½ × 11⅝ × 9¾"
44.4 × 29.4 × 25.1 cm

Gift of Raymond Holas
74.9

RUSSELL BALDWIN
American, born 1933

*Praxiteles Was Really
a Painter*, 1971
gabbro stone and canvas
38¾ × 38¾"
98.5 × 98.5 cm

Gift of the artist
82.48

JERROLD BALLAINE
American, born 1934

B-34 Double-Fold Bronze, 1969
plastic (vacuum-formed) with
Murano paint
45⅞ × 45⅛ × 10"
116.6 × 114.6 × 25.4 cm

Members' Accessions Fund
Purchase
69.31

ELLEN BANKS
American, born 1938

Midnight Sail, 1969
from the series Black and
White Plus
acrylic on Masonite
59⅝ × 17⅜"
151.5 × 44.1 cm

Gift of Channing J. Woodsum and
Judith L. Woodsum
83.111

WALTER DARBY BANNARD
American, born 1934

Green Valentine #6, 1965
alkyd resin on canvas
66⅝ × 62¾"
169.2 × 159.4 cm

Gift of John Berggruen
74.90

WALTER DARBY BANNARD
American, born 1934

Coral Sea #1, 1968
acrylic on canvas
66 × 99½"
167.7 × 252.8 cm

Gift of Mr. and Mrs. C. David
Robinson
79.312

PATROCINIO BARELA
American, 1908–1964

Heavy Thinker, n.d.
wood
15⅜ × 3¼ × 2½"
39.1 × 7.9 × 6.4 cm

WPA Federal Arts Project Allocation
to the San Francisco Museum of Art
3769.43

JOEL BARLETTA
American, born 1924

Blue Landscape, 1961
oil on canvas
66 × 56⅜"
167.6 × 143.2 cm

Gift of the Hamilton-Wells
Collection
69.78

JOEL BARLETTA
American, born 1924

BD/Series 1975 #2, 1975
acrylic on canvas
36 × 36"
91.4 × 91.4 cm

Gift of Joseph M. Bransten
in memory of Ruth Armer
80.49

MATTHEW BARNES
American, born Scotland,
1880–1951

Night Scene, 1932
oil on canvas
36½ × 42"
92.7 × 106.7 cm

Albert M. Bender Collection
Albert M. Bender Memorial Fund
Purchase
44.4334

MATTHEW BARNES
American, born Scotland,
1880–1951

The Appointment, 1939–43
oil on canvas
19⅝ × 23⅝"
49.9 × 60.0 cm

Gift of the Matthew Barnes Trust
51.1734

MATTHEW BARNES
American, born Scotland,
1880–1951

Landscape with Boat, n.d.
oil on canvas
19⅛ × 24"
48.5 × 61.0 cm

Gift of William Gaskin
52.101

CARL BARTH
German, born 1896

Two Frogs in the Night, 1954
oil on canvas
20¼ × 40¼″
51.5 × 102.3 cm

Gift of Dr. Henry Schaefer-Simmern
57.3334

JACK BARTH
American, born 1946

Xenia #2, 1971
paper and reflective paint on board
40⅜ × 72¾″
102.7 × 184.8 cm

Gift of Rena Bransten
75.99

JOHN BAXTER
American, 1912–1966

Cloud One and Two, 1956
stone
A: 7⅞ × 5½ × 4⅝″
20.0 × 13.9 × 11.8 cm
B: 2⅞ × 6¾ × 5¼″
7.3 × 17.2 × 13.3 cm

Gift of Mary Birdsall Van Liew in
memory of Donna B. Dreifus
68.20 A–B

JOHN BAXTER
American, 1912–1966

Metaphor II, 1961
wood
47¼ × 19⅜ × 12½″
120.1 × 49.3 × 31.8 cm

Gift of Mrs. F. K. Baxter and Frances
Baxter
67.50

JOHN BAXTER
American, 1912–1966

Harpy Listening, 1962
stone and wood
25 × 13⅞ × 12¼″
63.5 × 35.0 × 31.1 cm

Gift of Mr. and Mrs. Charles
Dreifus, Jr.
62.3428

JOHN BAXTER
American, 1912–1966

Sebastian, 1964
wood with carnelians
15¾ × 7¼ × 3½″
40.0 × 18.4 × 8.9 cm

Anonymous gift
82.29

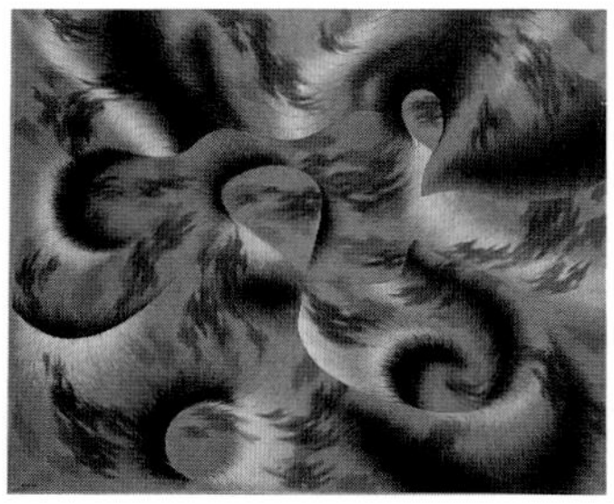

HERBERT BAYER
American, born Austria, 1900

Blue Movement, 1945
oil on canvas
40 × 50″
101.6 × 127.0 cm

Anonymous gift
49.6480

HERBERT BAYER
American, born Austria, 1900

The Bridge, 1958
from the series Architectural
oil on canvas
32 × 40″
81.3 × 101.6 cm

Gift of Joseph Bransten in memory
of Ellen Hart Bransten
67.22

270

ROBERT BECHTLE
American, born 1932

Alameda Gran Torino, 1974
oil on canvas
48 × 69″
121.9 × 175.3 cm

T. B. Walker Foundation Fund
Purchase in honor of John
Humphrey
74.87

BECK & JUNG

HOLGER BÄCKSTRÖM
Swedish, born 1939

BO LJUNGBERG
Swedish, born 1939

Game Chefrens, 1977
cotton rope and acrylic on canvas
45⅜ × 38⅝″
115.3 × 98.1 cm

Gift of Jan T. Paag
77.87

MAX BECKMANN
German, 1884–1950

*Landscape, Cannes
(Landschaft, Cannes)*, 1934
oil on canvas
27⅝ × 39½″
70.2 × 100.4 cm

Gift of Louise S. Ackerman
72.12

See colorplate, p. 77

MAX BECKMANN
German, 1884–1950

*Woman at Her Toilette, with Red
and White Lilies (Frau bei der
Toilette mit roten und
weissen Lilien)*, 1938
oil on canvas
43½ × 25¾″
110.5 × 65.4 cm

Bequest of Marian W. Sinton
81.51

See colorplate, p. 79

LARRY BELL
American, born 1939

Untitled, 1969
metallic compounds (vaporized) on
glass, chrome binding
18⅛ × 18⅛ × 18⅛″
46.0 × 46.0 × 46.0 cm

Anonymous gift through the
American Art Foundation
78.184

See colorplate, p. 211

LARRY BELL
American, born 1939

Untitled, 1970
metallic compounds (vaporized) on
glass
⅜ × 114 × 2″
1.0 × 289.5 × 5.1 cm

Gift of Anna Neilsen
75.175

LYNDA BENGLIS
American, born 1941

Lambda, 1972–73
aluminum screen, cloth, plaster,
paint, and sparkles
29½ × 25 × 8¼″
75.0 × 63.5 × 21.0 cm

Gift of Mr. and Mrs. Alfred H.
Daniels
79.51

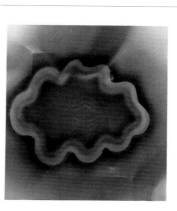

BILLY AL BENGSTON
American, born 1934

Untitled JWS, 1967
aluminum with lacquer and
polyester resin
11¼ × 12 × 1¾″
28.6 × 30.5 × 4.5 cm

Anonymous gift
83.86

BILLY AL BENGSTON
American, born 1934

Untitled, 1971
aluminum
49¾ × 47⅞ × 3¼″
126.4 × 121.6 × 8.3 cm

Gift of Marcia Weisman
83.42

KARL BENJAMIN
American, born 1925

I.F. Black, Gray,
Umber, Red, 1958
oil on canvas
62⅛ × 42¼″
157.5 × 107.3 cm

Gift of Ned C. Pearlstein
60.8568

FLETCHER BENTON
American, born 1931

144 Squares, 1965
aluminum, Plexiglas, wood, and
electrical apparatus
11¾ × 10 × 6″
29.8 × 25.4 × 15.2 cm

Gift of Dean Barnlund
81.225

FLETCHER BENTON
American, born 1931

Synchronetic C-3300 Series, 1966
aluminum, acrylic on Plexiglas,
and electrical apparatus
20⅛ × 24½ × 4⅝″
51.1 × 62.2 × 11.6 cm

Gift of Mr. and Mrs. William C.
Janss
78.204 A–B

FLETCHER BENTON
American, born 1931

Synchronetic C-2213-S, 1967
aluminum, Plexiglas, and electrical
apparatus
60⅜ × 51 × 8⅛″
153.4 × 129.5 × 20.6 cm

Gift of the Frederick Weisman
Company
81.114 A–C

FLETCHER BENTON
American, born 1931

Rolling Discs, 1969
aluminum, acrylic on Plexiglas,
and electrical apparatus
58 × 65 × 8″
147.3 × 165.1 × 20.3 cm

Gift of Rita and Toby Schreiber
81.226 A–B

FLETCHER BENTON
American, born 1931

Synchronetic C-2500-S, 1969
aluminum, Plexiglas, and electrical
apparatus
63⅝ × 71⅜ × 6¾″
161.6 × 181.3 × 17.2 cm

Gift of Mr. and Mrs. Harry W.
Anderson
77.244 A–B

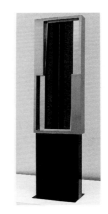

FLETCHER BENTON
American, born 1931

Synchronetic C-340-S, 1970
stainless steel, acrylic on Plexiglas,
wood, and electrical apparatus
73⅝ × 20½ × 12¼″
187.1 × 52.1 × 31.2 cm

Members' Accessions Fund
Purchase
71.23

FLETCHER BENTON
American, born 1931

Purple, Purple, 1974
stainless steel, acrylic on Plexiglas,
wood, and electrical apparatus
59¾ × 71⅝ × 12¼"
151.8 × 182.0 × 31.2 cm

Gift of the Modern Art Council
76.35 A–B

FLETCHER BENTON
American, born 1931

Dynamic Rhythms Orange, 1975
bronze
13¼ × 17⅞ × 13⅞"
33.6 × 45.4 × 35.3 cm

Gift of Mr. and Mrs. Peter
Schlesinger
76.249

FLETCHER BENTON
American, born 1931

Folded Square Alphabet O, 1979
from the series The Folded Square
Cor-ten steel
97 × 78 × 99"
246.4 × 198.2 × 251.5 cm

Gift of the Hamilton-Wells Collection
80.167 A–B

FLETCHER BENTON
American, born 1931

Balanced-Unbalanced T, 1981
from the series
Balanced-Unbalanced
mild steel with enamel
161¼ × 130 × 134"
409.6 × 330.2 × 340.4 cm

Gift of William S. Picher and Wally
Goodman
81.147 A–C

JANE BERLANDINA
American, born France, 1898–1970

*Still Life with
Potted Plant*, 1935
oil on canvas
32 × 23½"
81.3 × 59.7 cm

Albert M. Bender Collection
Gift of Albert M. Bender
38.2

EUGENE BERMAN
American, born Russia, 1899–1972

*Old Women among the Rocks
(Vieilles femmes dans
les rochers)*, 1933
oil on canvas
18⅛ × 23⅞"
46.1 × 60.6 cm

Albert M. Bender Collection
Acquired through a gift of
Albert M. Bender
69.109

WALLACE BERMAN
American, 1926–1976

Untitled (400.300.50), 1974
acrylic on rock with chain
5¾ × 7⅝ × 7⅝"
14.6 × 19.4 × 19.4 cm

Purchase
83.150

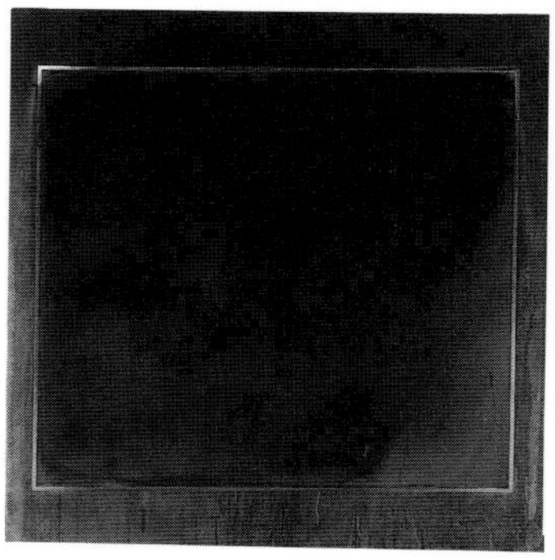

JAKE BERTHOT
American, born 1939

Scramble, 1970
acrylic on canvas
72 × 72⅛"
182.9 × 183.2 cm

Gift of John Berggruen
77.270

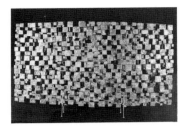

HARRY BERTOIA
American, born Italy, 1915

Untitled (formerly *Sculpture No. 1*)
ca. 1955
copper (brazed) and brazing rods
37¾ × 64 × 8″
95.9 × 162.6 × 20.3 cm

Gift of the Women's Board
56.3049

DAVID BEST
American, born 1945

Untitled, 1977
porcelain with feathers, dead mice
and birds, plastic lizard, shells, toy
cars, glass bottle, and pearl-like
necklace
A: 34½ × 14½ × 13½″
87.7 × 36.9 × 34.3 cm
B: 27 × 17 × 8″
68.6 × 43.2 × 20.3 cm

Gift in memory of Floyd Douglas
Conkey and Evelyn Blunt Conkey
78.12 A–B

LEO BIGENWALD
German, born 1904

Austere Form, 1957
Carrara marble and bronze
23⅞ × 11½ × 14⅜″
60.7 × 29.3 × 36.6 cm

Anonymous gift
59.1612

ELMER BISCHOFF
American, born 1916

Orange Sweater, 1955
oil on canvas
48½ × 57″
123.2 × 144.8 cm

Gift of Mr. and Mrs. Mark Schorer
63.20

See colorplate, p. 185

ELMER BISCHOFF
American, born 1916

Girl Reclining, 1960
oil on canvas
67¾ × 67⅝″
172.1 × 171.8 cm

T. B. Walker Foundation Fund
Purchase
83.23

ELMER BISCHOFF
American, born 1916

Yellow Sky, 1967
oil on canvas
79⅝ × 92⅛″
202.3 × 234.0 cm

Paul L. Wattis Special Fund
Purchase
76.36

JAMES BISHOP
American, born 1927

Farm, 1966
oil on canvas
68¾ × 68¾″
174.6 × 174.6 cm

Gift of Donald Droll
68.56

ED BLACKBURN
American, born 1947

Man Kneeling, 1979
white earthenware with china paint
and underglazes
34⅜ × 11¾ × 21¾″
88.0 × 29.8 × 55.2 cm

Purchased with the aid of funds
from the National Endowment for the
Arts and the Soap Box Derby Fund
79.244

RALPH BLAKELOCK
American, 1847–1919

Landscape, n.d.
oil on canvas
5½ × 11″
14.0 × 28.0 cm

Albert M. Bender Collection
Gift of Albert M. Bender
40.7261

PETER BLUME
American, born Russia, 1906

Hyacinth, 1920
oil on canvas
16 × 14″
40.7 × 35.6 cm

T. B. Walker Foundation Fund
Purchase
76.23

J. B. BLUNK
American, born 1926

Compote, 1954
Bizen ware
7⅛ × 16¼″ diam.
18.1 × 41.3 cm

Anonymous gift
59.1678

J. B. BLUNK
American, born 1926

Invisible Presence, 1962
cypress
58½ × 24¾ × 36¾″
148.6 × 62.9 × 93.4 cm

Anonymous gift
71.2

ROGER BOLOMEY
American, born 1918

FY 39, 1981
bronze
47⅝ × 20¾ × 20¾″
121.0 × 52.7 × 52.7 cm

Gift of Dr. and Mrs. Ralph Victor
81.227

ILYA BOLOTOWSKY
American, born Russia, 1907–1981

Vertical Yellow Plane, 1967–68
oil on canvas
72⅛ × 24¼″
183.2 × 61.6 cm

William L. Gerstle Collection
William L. Gerstle Fund Purchase
68.39

CAMILLE BOMBOIS
French, 1883–1970

Landscape, ca. 1932
oil on panel
5¾ × 7⅞″
14.7 × 20.0 cm

Gift of Mr. and Mrs. C. George Ross
74.91

PIERRE BONNARD
French, 1867–1947

Woman with White Stockings
(Femme aux bas blancs), ca. 1923
oil on canvas
18⅛ × 15⅜″
46.0 × 39.0 cm

Gift of Wilbur D. May
64.56

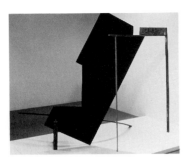

DAVID BOTTINI
American, born 1945

Other Thoughts, 1979
stainless steel with enamel and oil
pastel
72⅝ × 89 × 44½"
184.5 × 226.1 × 113.1 cm

Gift of Larry J. Silva
82.372

DAVID BOTTINI
American, born 1945

Shutter Doors, 1981
steel and stainless steel with enamel
and oil pastel
93 × 92 × 21¾"
236.2 × 233.7 × 55.2 cm

Gift of Agnes C. and William C.
Bourne
81.228

JEAN BOUCHER, attributed to
French, 1870–1939

Portrait of Ernest Renan, n.d.
bronze
8¾ × 10 × 8"
22.3 × 25.4 × 20.3 cm

Gift of Mr. and Mrs. William C.
Janss
81.236

CHERYL O. BOWERS
American, born 1938

Red Fence, 1978–79
oil on canvas and oil on linen
73¼ × 265"
185.7 × 673.2 cm

Gift of Cheryl O. Bowers and Seyburn
Zorthian
82.373 A–C

GEOFFREY BOWMAN
American, born 1928

Moira, 1961
oil and collage on canvas
66⅝ × 48¼"
169.3 × 122.6 cm

William L. Gerstle Collection
William L. Gerstle Fund Purchase
62.20

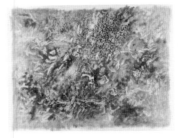

RICHARD BOWMAN
American, born 1918

Kinetogenics 77, 1963
oil on canvas
62½ × 81½"
158.8 × 207.0 cm

Gift of Derek M. Fairman
64.48

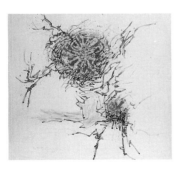

RICHARD BOWMAN
American, born 1918

Kinetogenics 91, 1965
oil on canvas
72½ × 79"
184.2 × 200.7 cm

Gift of Dr. Robert C. Dickenman
80.350

KEITH BOYLE
American, born 1930

Dewey Square, 1964
acrylic on canvas
74 × 73⅞"
188.0 × 187.6 cm

Acquired with the aid of a gift of
Dr. Ralph Speigl
64.50

ROBERT BRADY
American, born 1946

Untitled, 1974
from the series Step
earthenware and wire mesh
24½ × 16¾ × 22¾"
62.3 × 42.6 × 57.8 cm

Gift of Louis A. Hermes
82.374

ROBERT BRADY
American, born 1946

Wall Piece, Grid, 1975
earthenware with glazes
overall 97 × 96⅜ × 10½"
246.4 × 244.8 × 26.7 cm

Paul L. Wattis Special Fund
Purchase
76.129 A–Y

CONSTANTIN BRANCUSI
French, born Romania, 1876–1957

Blonde Negress
(La Négresse blonde), 1926
bronze (polished)
15⅛ × 4⅞ × 7⅜"
38.5 × 12.4 × 18.8 cm

Gift of Agnes E. Meyer and Elise
Stern Haas
58.4382

See colorplate, p. 53

GEORGES BRAQUE
French, 1882–1963

Still Life
(Nature morte), 1930–33
oil on canvas
17¾ × 21¾"
45.1 × 55.3 cm

Gift of Mr. and Mrs. Joseph M.
Bransten
61.566

GEORGES BRAQUE
French, 1882–1963

The Gueridon (Le Guéridon), 1935
oil and sand on canvas
71 × 29"
180.4 × 73.7 cm

Purchased with the aid of funds
from W. W. Crocker
46.3211

See colorplate, p. 55

GEORGES BRAQUE
French, 1882–1963

Vase, Palette, and Mandolin
(Vase, palette, et mandoline), 1936
oil on canvas
32 × 39⅝"
81.3 × 100.7 cm

Purchased with the aid of funds
from W. W. Crocker
44.2641

See colorplate, p. 57

GEORGES BRAQUE
French, 1882–1963

Small Head of a Horse
(Petite Tête de cheval), 1941/1956
bronze 1/6
5¾ × 3⅜ × 6"
14.6 × 8.6 × 15.3 cm

Purchased through a gift of W. W.
Crocker
56.3047

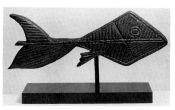

GEORGES BRAQUE
French, 1882–1963

Small Fish (Petit Poisson), 1942
bronze ed. 6
4⅞ × 14⅛ × ½"
12.4 × 35.8 × 1.3 cm

Gift of W. W. Crocker
54.3282

ANNE BREMER
American, 1872–1923

Landscape, 1923
oil on canvas
24⅜ × 29″
61.9 × 73.7 cm

Albert M. Bender Collection
Gift of Albert M. Bender
36.5391

ANNE BREMER
American, 1872–1923

The Highlands, n.d.
oil on canvas
30 × 36¼″
76.2 × 92.1 cm

Albert M. Bender Collection
Gift of Albert M. Bender
36.5392

ANNE BREMER
American, 1872–1923

Sentinels, n.d.
oil on canvas
40 × 35¼″
101.6 × 89.5 cm

Albert M. Bender Collection
Gift of Albert M. Bender
36.5390

ANNE BREMER
American, 1872–1923

Still Life, n.d.
oil on canvas
26 × 34¼″
66.1 × 87.0 cm

Albert M. Bender Collection
Gift of Albert M. Bender
35.1875

KAREN BRESCHI
American, born 1941

Mother Monument, 1973
clay, paint, glitter, glass, moss, and
false eyelashes
27⅞ × 46½ × 34¼″
70.8 × 118.2 × 87.0 cm

Gift of the artist
75.149

KAREN BRESCHI
American, born 1941

Vulture, 1979
clay, acrylic, rope, cloth, and resin
36 × 21 × 12″
91.4 × 53.4 × 30.5 cm

Gift of Allan Frumkin
83.170

NICK BRIGANTE
American, born Italy 1895

Mitosis of Sea Plankton, 1956
oil on canvas
60 × 36⅛″
152.4 × 91.8 cm

Gift of the artist
77.97

ERNEST BRIGGS
American, 1923–1984

Totem Figure, 1949
magnesite
44½ × 8¾ × 8¼″
113.1 × 22.3 × 21.0 cm

Gift of Jermayne MacAgy
55.6937

278

ERNEST BRIGGS
American, 1923–1984

Untitled, 1951
oil on canvas
68 × 77″
172.7 × 195.6 cm

Gift of Mr. and Mrs. Moses Lasky
64.7

ERNEST BRIGGS
American, 1923–1984

Deep Yellow, 1961
oil on canvas
105¼ × 140⅛″
267.3 × 355.9 cm

William L. Gerstle Collection
William L. Gerstle Fund Purchase
63.29

ALEXANDER BROOK
American, 1898–1980

Gloria, 1937
oil on canvas
20 × 16″
50.8 × 40.6 cm

Gift of Robert B. Howard
61.4525

JOAN BROWN
American, born 1938

The Vanity, 1975
enamel on canvas
84 × 72⅛″
213.4 × 183.2 cm

Paul L. Wattis Special Fund
Purchase
76.37

ERNEST BRIGGS
American, 1923–1984

Untitled, 1960
oil on cotton
117¼ × 92¾″
297.8 × 235.6 cm

Gift of Robert E. McCann
76.100

MORRIS BRODERSON
American, born 1928

The Death of Christ, 1960
oil on canvas
78 × 132″
198.1 × 335.3 cm

Gift of William Estler
61.1905

JOAN BROWN
American, born 1938

The Dancers in a City #2, 1972
enamel and fabric on canvas
81 × 72″
205.8 × 182.9 cm

Gift of Alfred E. Heller
80.407

JOAN BROWN
American, born 1938

Sacred Rocks on Nanda Devi
1979
from Nanda Devi Series #5
enamel on canvas
96 × 78″
243.9 × 198.2 cm

William L. Gerstle Collection
William L. Gerstle Fund Purchase
80.80

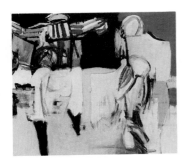

THEOPHILUS BROWN
American, born 1919

The Referee, 1956
oil on canvas
58 × 69″
147.3 × 175.3 cm

Gift of Mrs. Lloyd S. Ackerman
57.1240

THEOPHILUS BROWN
American, born 1919

Swimming Pool, 1963
oil on canvas
46 × 48″
116.8 × 121.9 cm

Gift of the Hamilton-Wells
Collection
72.42

EDWARD BRUCE
American, 1879–1937

A Lane in Huisseau, n.d.
oil on canvas
24 × 16½″
61.0 × 41.9 cm

William L. Gerstle Collection
Gift of William L. Gerstle
46.742

JOHN BUCK
American, born 1946

In the Eyes of the Beholder, 1979
wood with enamel
119½ × 126 × 21½″
303.6 × 320.1 × 54.7 cm

Gift of Roy and Gloria De Forest
79.128 A–Y

BENIAMINO BUFANO
American, born Italy, 1886–1970

Mother and Children, ca. 1925
plaster with metallic paint
51 × 17½ × 10″
129.5 × 44.5 × 25.4 cm

Albert M. Bender Collection
Bequest of Albert M. Bender
41.2982

BENIAMINO BUFANO
American, born Italy, 1886–1970

Bear, n.d.
lead, fiberglass, and stainless steel
76 × 32¼ × 70″
193.2 × 81.9 × 177.8 cm

Gift of Victor Bergeron
70.50

BENIAMINO BUFANO
American, born Italy, 1886–1970

Child Portrait, n.d.
stoneware with glaze
13¼ × 11¾ × 5½″
33.6 × 29.8 × 13.9 cm

Albert M. Bender Collection
Bequest of Albert M. Bender
41.2969

BENIAMINO BUFANO
American, born Italy, 1886–1970

Chinese Girl, n.d.
stoneware with glaze
19¾ × 13⅞ × 7½″
50.2 × 35.2 × 19.1 cm

Gift of Marian Bufano
36.4934

BENIAMINO BUFANO
American, born Italy, 1886–1970

Crucifixion of Youth, n.d.
stoneware with glaze and wood with
gold leaf
101 × 66¾ × 8½"
256.5 × 169.6 × 21.6 cm

Gift of Mr. and Mrs. Forrest
Engelhart in memory of Lisbeth
Backer Schley and Grant Barney
Schley
38.24

BENIAMINO BUFANO
American, born Italy, 1886–1970

Girl's Head, n.d.
stoneware with glaze
6⅛ × 7 × 3¼"
15.6 × 17.8 × 8.3 cm

Albert M. Bender Collection
Gift of Albert M. Bender
37.3093

BENIAMINO BUFANO
American, born Italy, 1886–1970

Head, n.d.
plaster with metallic paint
13½ × 8⅜ × 1"
34.3 × 21.3 × 2.5 cm

Albert M. Bender Collection
Gift of Albert M. Bender
37.3092

BENIAMINO BUFANO
American, born Italy, 1886–1970

Head of Albert M. Bender, n.d.
bronze
10⅛ × 7⅜ × 8⅝"
25.7 × 18.8 × 21.9 cm

Gift of Mrs. Walter A. Haas
44.30

BENIAMINO BUFANO
American, born Italy, 1886–1970

Man of Sorrows, n.d.
stoneware with glaze
22⅝ × 6⅛ × 4½"
57.5 × 15.5 × 11.5 cm

Albert M. Bender Collection
Bequest of Albert M. Bender
41.2983

BENIAMINO BUFANO
American, born Italy, 1886–1970

Mother of the Artist, n.d.
stoneware with glaze
15 × 15 × 8¾"
38.1 × 38.1 × 22.2 cm

Albert M. Bender Collection
Gift of Albert M. Bender
36.6345

BENIAMINO BUFANO
American, born Italy, 1886–1970

Portrait of a Baby, n.d.
stoneware with glaze
13 × 11⅛ × 7¼"
33.1 × 28.3 × 18.5 cm

Albert M. Bender Collection
Bequest of Albert M. Bender
41.2972

BENIAMINO BUFANO
American, born Italy, 1886–1970

Portrait of a Chinese, n.d.
stoneware with glaze
11⅞ × 13⅛ × 4¾"
30.2 × 33.4 × 12.1 cm

Albert M. Bender Collection
Bequest of Albert M. Bender
41.2973

BENIAMINO BUFANO
American, born Italy, 1886–1970

Portrait of a Girl, n.d.
stoneware with glaze
21³⁄₈ × 13 × 1³⁄₄″
54.3 × 33.1 × 4.5 cm

Albert M. Bender Collection
Bequest of Albert M. Bender
41.2974

BENIAMINO BUFANO
American, born Italy, 1886–1970

Portrait of a Girl, n.d.
stoneware with glaze
14³⁄₈ × 16 × 8³⁄₈″
36.6 × 40.7 × 21.3 cm

Albert M. Bender Collection
Bequest of Albert M. Bender
41.2975

BENIAMINO BUFANO
American, born Italy, 1886–1970

Portrait of a Little Girl, n.d.
stoneware with glaze
8⁷⁄₈ × 10¹⁄₄ × 8″
22.6 × 26.1 × 20.4 cm

Albert M. Bender Collection
Bequest of Albert M. Bender
41.2980

BENIAMINO BUFANO
American, born Italy, 1886–1970

Portrait of a Mandarin, n.d.
bronze
19³⁄₄ × 17¹⁄₄ × 6⁷⁄₈″
50.2 × 43.8 × 17.5 cm

Albert M. Bender Collection
Gift of Albert M. Bender
39.107

BENIAMINO BUFANO
American, born Italy, 1886–1970

Two Friends (also known as
Chinese Friends), n.d.
stoneware with glaze
16¹⁄₂ × 17¹⁄₄ × 7¹⁄₄″
42.0 × 43.8 × 18.5 cm

Albert M. Bender Collection
Gift of Albert M. Bender
36.4479

ALBERTO BURRI
Italian, born 1915

White (Bianco), 1952
oil, paper, and muslin on muslin
39¹⁄₂ × 33⁷⁄₈″
100.3 × 86.0 cm

Gift of Mr. and Mrs. Nathaniel
Owings
69.22

DEBORAH BUTTERFIELD
American, born 1949

*D.B. 10-78-V
(Reclining Horse)*, 1978
mud, sticks, and straw
35¹⁄₈ × 83¹⁄₄ × 53″
89.2 × 211.5 × 134.6 cm

Purchase
79.206

LAWRENCE CALCAGNO
American, born 1913

Nightsong for Orpheus, 1962
oil on canvas
108³⁄₈ × 108¹⁄₄″
275.3 × 275.0 cm

Gift of Mr. and Mrs. Meredith Long
72.13

ALEXANDER CALDER
American, 1898–1976

Woman on Cord, 1944
bronze and nylon cord
21¾ × 13¼ × 27⅛"
55.3 × 33.7 × 68.9 cm

Gift of Mr. and Mrs. William C.
Janss
83.216

ALEXANDER CALDER
American, 1898–1976

Spiral and Propeller, 1956
oil on canvas
17⅞ × 26⅛"
45.4 × 66.3 cm

Gift of Harry Turko
72.2

ALEXANDER CALDER
American, 1898–1976

Four Big Dots, 1963
sheet metal and steel wire with
enamel
29 × 113 × 113"
73.7 × 287.0 × 287.0 cm

T. B. Walker Foundation Fund
Purchase
63.28

KENNETH CALLAHAN
American, born 1906

March of the Blind, n.d.
oil on canvas
14¼ × 18"
36.2 × 45.8 cm

Anonymous gift
41.3322

MARY CALLERY
American, 1903–1977

Study for "Pyramid," 1949
bronze ed. 5
26 × 18 × 15¾"
66.0 × 45.7 × 40.0 cm

Gift of W. W. Crocker
52.3093

MARY CALLERY
American, 1903–1977

*Study for "Tomorrow Is a
Mystery,"* 1949
bronze 2/2
7¾ × 7½ × 3¼"
19.7 × 19.1 × 8.3 cm

Purchased through a gift of
W. W. Crocker
57.1827

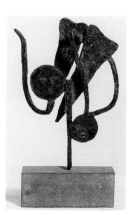

MARY CALLERY
American, 1903–1977

Study for "Orpheus," 1951
bronze 2/4
13 × 9¼ × 2¼"
33.0 × 23.5 × 5.7 cm

Purchased through a gift of
W. W. Crocker
57.1826

CRISTIANO CAMACHO
American, born 1946

Dogpatch Moonlight, 1974
wood
97 × 107⅛ × 18"
246.4 × 272.1 × 45.7 cm

Purchased with the aid of funds
from the National Endowment for
the Arts, the Soap Box Derby Fund,
and the New Future Fund Drive
77.79 A–D

SQUEAK CARNWATH
American, born 1947

Water Is Any Form, 1982
acrylic on canvas
29¾ × 22¾"
75.5 × 57.8 cm

Gift of the artist and Fuller Goldeen
Gallery, San Francisco
82.375

ANTHONY CARO
British, born 1924

Pavane, 1971
steel
34 × 114 × 111"
86.4 × 289.6 × 282.0 cm

Gift of Mr. and Mrs. C. David
Robinson
74.17 A–D

JON CARSMAN
American, born 1944

Leaving Lumberville, 1974
acrylic on canvas
50½ × 61"
128.3 × 155.0 cm

Gift of Dr. William Bernell
75.126

JON CARSMAN
American, born 1944

Winter's Vengeance, 1974
acrylic on canvas
69⅞ × 49⅞"
177.5 × 126.7 cm

Gift of Anton Bruehl
82.156

ALDO JOHN CASANOVA
American, born 1929

Great Owl II, 1961
bronze
21⅜ × 18 × 16"
54.3 × 45.7 × 40.6 cm

Gertrude Hopkins Crocker Memorial
Fund Purchase
62.17

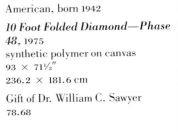

GUY JOHN CAVALLI
American, born 1942

*10 Foot Folded Diamond—Phase
48*, 1975
synthetic polymer on canvas
93 × 71½"
236.2 × 181.6 cm

Gift of Dr. William C. Sawyer
78.68

MARC CHAGALL
French, born Russia 1887

Lovers in the Red Sky
(Les Amants au ciel rouge), 1950
oil on canvas
25⅜ × 26⅛"
65.1 × 66.4 cm

Gift of Wilbur D. May
64.6

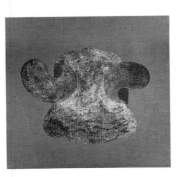

WESLEY CHAMBERLIN
American, born 1932

Council of Trent, 1967
oil on canvas
21¾ × 23⅝"
55.2 × 60.0 cm

Anonymous gift
69.120

RONALD CHASE
American, born 1934

The Wedding Party, 1968
wood, photographs, mirrors, paint,
manuscript, and electrical apparatus
67 × 50 × 10″
170.2 × 127.0 × 25.4 cm

Gift of Mrs. V. J. Gianelloni
71.3

WARREN CHENEY
American, born France 1907

Heavenly Love (Amor Caelestis)
1934
plaster with paint
44 × 11¼ × 15½″
111.8 × 28.6 × 39.4 cm

Albert M. Bender Collection
Gift of Albert M. Bender
36.1498

JUDY CHICAGO (née GEROWITZ)
American, born 1939

*Untitled (Gameboard and
Components #1)*, 1966
wood, brass, and latex
4 × 18¼ × 18¼″
10.2 × 46.4 × 46.4 cm

Gift of Diana Zlotnick
79.318 A–M

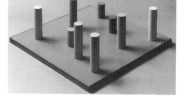

JUDY CHICAGO (née GEROWITZ)
American, born 1939

*Untitled (Gameboard and
Components #2)*, 1966
wood, brass, and latex
4 × 12½ × 12½″
10.2 × 31.8 × 31.8 cm

Gift of Diana Zlotnick
79.319 A–J

JUDY CHICAGO (née GEROWITZ)
American, born 1939

Georgia O'Keeffe Plate #1, 1979
whiteware with china paint
14⅞ × 14⅞ × 4¾″
37.8 × 37.2 × 12.1 cm

Gift of the artist
82.293

GIORGIO DE CHIRICO
Italian, born Greece, 1888–1978

*The Vexations of the Thinker;
The Inconsistencies of the
Thinker (Les Contrariétés du
penseur)*, 1915
oil on canvas
18¼ × 15″
46.4 × 38.1 cm

Templeton Crocker Fund Purchase
51.8

See colorplate, p. 97

CHRYSSA
American, born Greece 1933

Island House, 1976
oil on canvas
91¼ × 64¼″
231.8 × 163.2 cm

Gift of Guido Saveri and Richard
Saveri
80.422

CHRYSSA
American, born Greece 1933

Silence, 1978
oil on canvas
92¾ × 64″
235.6 × 162.6 cm

Gift of Guido Saveri and Richard
Saveri
80.421

ANTONI CLAVÉ
Spanish, born 1913

Little Girl with a Doll
(Fillette à la poupée), 1946
oil on canvas
29 × 23⅜"
73.7 × 60.0 cm

Gift of Mrs. Jaquelin H. Hume
82.30

ARNALDO COEN
Mexican, born 1940

Joins the Earth
(Se Junto en la tierra), 1967
oil on canvas
59 × 43¼"
149.7 × 109.9 cm

Gift of Dr. William C. Sawyer
69.2

GEORGE M. COHEN
American, born 1919

Red Maenad, 1959
oil on canvas
72 × 60"
182.9 × 152.4 cm

Anonymous gift through the
American Federation of Arts
65.20

ARDATH COLDWELL
American, born 1913

Two Sisters, ca. 1938–39
terra-cotta
23⅞ × 7¼ × 13¼"
60.6 × 18.4 × 33.6 cm

WPA Federal Arts Project Allocation
to the San Francisco Museum of Art
1042.43

ROBERT COLESCOTT
American, born 1925

End of the Trail, 1976
acrylic on canvas
74¾ × 96¼"
189.8 × 244.5 cm

Purchased with the aid of funds
from the National Endowment for
the Arts, the Soap Box Derby Fund,
and the New Future Fund Drive
77.78

JESS (COLLINS)
American, born 1923

Fig. 4—Far And Few . . .
(Translation #15), 1965
oil on canvas mounted on wood
18 × 26"
45.7 × 66.1 cm

Mrs. Manfred Bransten Special
Fund Purchase
73.36

BRUCE CONNER
American, born 1933

Dark Brown, 1959
oil, jewelry, metallic paint, and fur
on canvas
44½ × 44½"
113.0 × 113.0 cm

Gift of Harold Zellerbach
61.4102

BRUCE CONNER
American, born 1933

After Peyote, 1959–60
cardboard, nylon, glass, plastic,
feathers, metal, rubber, and twine
on book cover
43 × 7¾ × 3½"
109.3 × 19.8 × 9.0 cm

Gift of Nell Sinton
74.20

BRUCE CONNER
American, born 1933

The Heart Worm Mirror, 1960
wax, mirror, and metal on Masonite
19 × 17¾ × 4½"
48.3 × 45.1 × 11.5 cm

Gift of Mr. and Mrs. Bagley Wright
82.317

BRUCE CONNER
American, born 1933

March 17, 1960, 1960
lace, beads, paper, glass, hairpins,
playing cards, linoleum, metal, and
wood on cardboard book cover
9¾ × 7 × ¾"
24.9 × 17.8 × 2.0 cm

Gift of Robert B. Howard
79.320

BRUCE CONNER
American, born 1933

Music, 1960
film strip, wax, string, paint, Band-
Aid, postage stamps, tape, string
tags, and ink on music sheet paper
on cardboard with black velvet
21⅝ × 11 × ½"
55.0 × 27.9 × 1.3 cm

Gift of Mary Heath Keesling
82.376

BRUCE CONNER
American, born 1933

*St. Valentine's Day Massacre/
Homage to Errol Flynn*, 1960
feathers, nylon, glass, and paper on
wood
19 × 14½ × 3½"
48.3 × 36.9 × 8.9 cm

Gift of Dr. and Mrs. W. William
Gardner
64.61

BRUCE CONNER
American, born 1933

Homage to Chessman, 1961
wax, oil, plastic, wood, wire, and
light switch on wooden panel
41¾ × 18 × 6½"
106.1 × 45.8 × 16.5 cm

Gift of Irving Blum
73.37

BRUCE CONNER
American, born 1933

Ray Charles/Snakeskin, 1961
plastic, nylon, metal, paper, wood,
paint, and snakeskin tissue on
Masonite
25¾ × 18¾"
65.4 × 47.6 cm

Gift of the Women's Board
64.34

BRUCE CONNER
American, born 1933

Looking Glass, 1964
paper, cotton cloth, nylon, beads,
metal, twine, glass, leather, plastic,
and wood on Masonite
60½ × 48 × 14½"
153.7 × 121.9 × 36.8 cm

Gift of the Modern Art Council
78.69

See colorplate, p. 203

EDWARD CORBETT
American, 1919–1971

Untitled, ca. 1945
oil on canvas
27 × 31¾"
68.6 × 80.7 cm

Gift of Robert B. Howard
63.12

EDWARD CORBETT
American, 1919–1971

Untitled #3, 1950
oil and enamel on canvas
46 × $43\frac{7}{8}$″
116.8 × 111.4 cm

Purchased with the aid of funds from Peter Haas, Jr.
69.32

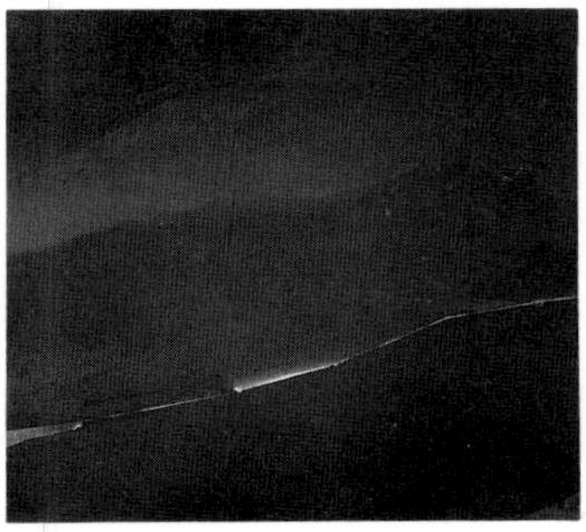

EDWARD CORBETT
American, 1919–1971

Washington, D.C., January #1
1964
oil on canvas
50 × $57\frac{3}{8}$″
127.0 × 145.7 cm

Gift of Rosamond Walling Corbett, Turhan W. Tirana, and Bardyl Rifat Tirana
69.23

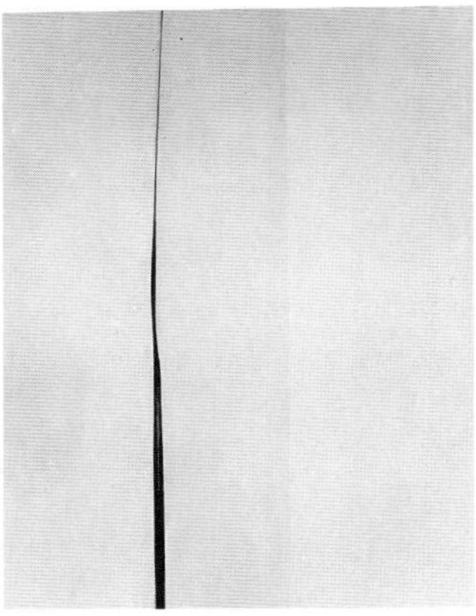

EDWARD CORBETT
American, 1919–1971

Washington, D.C., #1 January
1969
oil on canvas
$50\frac{1}{8}$ × 40″
127.3 × 101.6 cm

Gift of Rosamond Walling Corbett, Turhan W. Tirana, and Bardyl Rifat Tirana
69.24

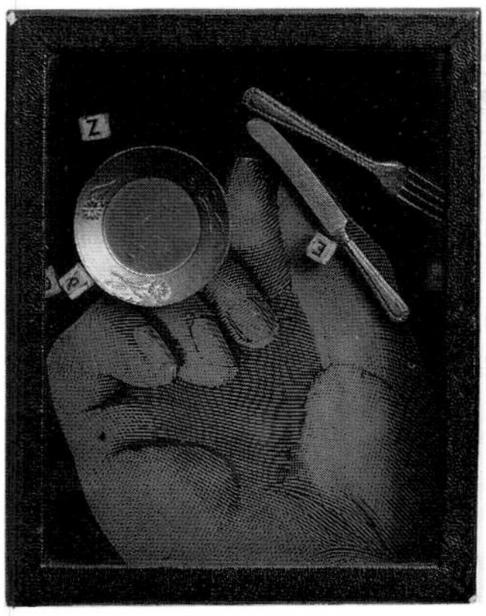

JOSEPH CORNELL
American, 1903–1972

Untitled *(Object)*, 1933
cardboard box containing glass, wood, paper, engraving, and metal
$5\frac{1}{4}$ × $4\frac{1}{4}$ × $\frac{7}{8}$″
13.3 × 10.8 × 2.2 cm

Gift of Leo Castelli, Richard L. Feigen, and James Corcoran
82.347

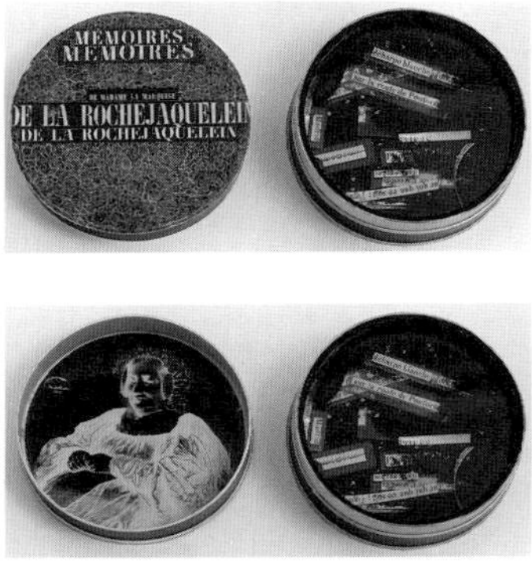

JOSEPH CORNELL
American, 1903–1972

Memories of Madame la Marquise de la Rochejaquelein *(Memoires de Madame la Marquise de la Rochejaquelein)*, 1943
cardboard box containing glass, sand, beads, printed text, ribbons, and gelatin silver print (negative image)
$1\frac{7}{8}$ × $4\frac{1}{4}$″ diam.
4.8 × 10.8 cm

Gift of Leo Castelli, Richard L. Feigen, and James Corcoran
82.346

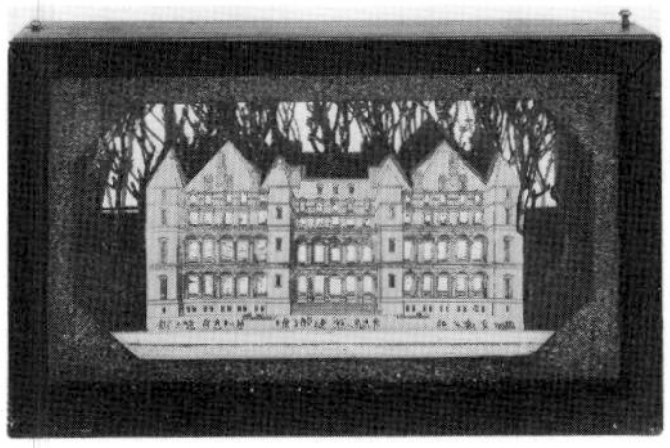

JOSEPH CORNELL
American, 1903–1972

Untitled *(Pink Palace)*
ca. 1946–48
wooden box containing photostat with ink wash, wood, mirror, plant material, and artificial snow
$8\frac{5}{8}$ × $14\frac{1}{4}$ × $4\frac{3}{8}$″
21.9 × 36.2 × 11.1 cm

Purchased through gifts of Mr. and Mrs. William M. Roth and William L. Gerstle
82.328

See colorplate, p. 120

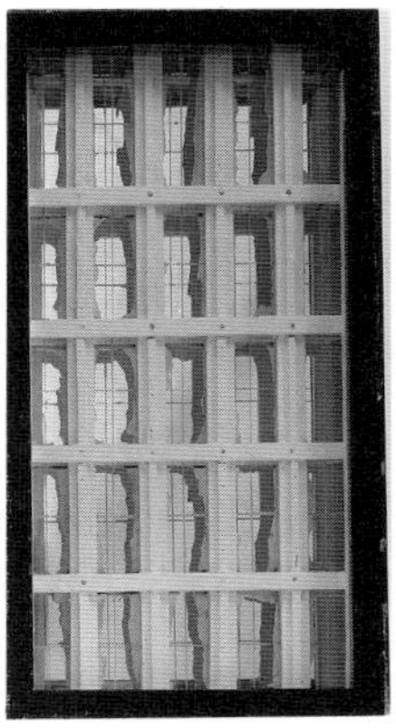

JOSEPH CORNELL
American, 1903–1972

Untitled *(Window Façade)*
ca. 1950–53
wooden box containing paint on wood, nails, glass, and mirror
20 × 11 × $4\frac{1}{4}$″
50.8 × 27.9 × 10.8 cm

Albert M. Bender Collection
Purchased through a gift of Albert M. Bender
82.329

See colorplate, p. 121

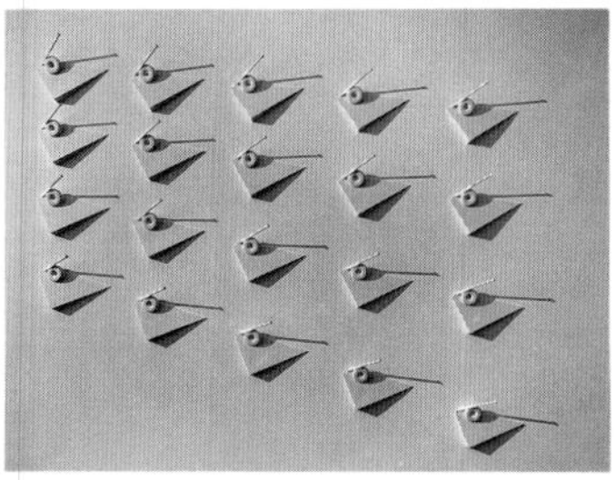

TONY COSTANZO
American, born 1948

Birds, 1975
earthenware
$81\frac{3}{4}$ × 104 × $5\frac{5}{8}$″
207.7 × 264.2 × 14.3 cm

Purchased with the aid of funds from the National Endowment for the Arts, the Soap Box Derby Fund, and the New Future Fund Drive
77.77 A–X

RUTH CRAVATH
American, born 1902

Portrait of a Woman, 1932
terra-cotta
14½ × 10½ × 1⅛″
36.9 × 26.7 × 2.9 cm

Albert M. Bender Collection
Bequest of Albert M. Bender
41.2970

RUTH CRAVATH
American, born 1902

Head of E. Spencer Macky
ca. 1934
marble
16⅜ × 9⅝ × 9½″
41.6 × 24.5 × 24.1 cm

Albert M. Bender Collection
Gift of Albert M. Bender
35.3394

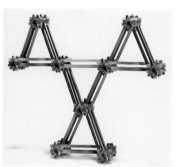

ALLAN CRAWFORD
American

#3, 1978
wood
13¾ × 12¼ × 2¾″
35.0 × 31.1 × 7.0 cm

Gift of Dr. A. G. B. Lowell
81.148

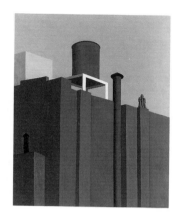

RALSTON CRAWFORD
American, born Canada, 1906–1978

Vertical Building, 1934
oil on canvas
40⅛ × 34⅛″
101.9 × 86.7 cm

Arthur W. Barney Bequest Fund
Purchase
75.7

CARLOS CRUZ-DIEZ
Venezuelan, born 1923

Physichromie No. 209, 1965
plastic over acrylic on paper mounted
on plywood
23½ × 23⅝″
59.7 × 60.0 cm

Gift of Benbow and Jean Bullock
79.313

RINALDO CUNEO
American, 1877–1939

Landscape, n.d.
oil on canvas
22 × 24¾″
55.9 × 62.9 cm

Albert M. Bender Collection
Gift of Albert M. Bender
35.1890

FRANK CYRSKY
American, born 1948

Masai Bride, 1973
oil on canvas
73 × 73″
185.4 × 185.4 cm

Gift of Dr. Cyril Ramer and
Dr. Barry Ramer
74.92

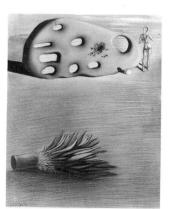

SALVADOR DALI
Spanish, born 1904

Oedipus Complex, 1930
pastel on paper
24⅛ × 19¾″
61.3 × 50.2 cm

Purchase
51.3393

See colorplate, p. 113

ANDREW MICHAEL DASBURG
American, 1887–1979

November in New Mexico, 1926
oil on canvas
18⅛ × 24⅛"
46.0 × 61.3 cm

Albert M. Bender Collection
Gift of Albert M. Bender
38.225

ALAN DAVIE
British, born 1920

Painting, 1951
oil on Masonite
23⅝ × 29⅞"
60.1 × 75.9 cm

Gift of Mr. and Mrs. William M.
Roth
78.144

ALAN DAVIE
British, born 1920

Strip for Fast Fishes, 1959
oil on paper mounted on Masonite
8⅜ × 35¾"
21.3 × 90.8 cm

Gift of Joseph M. Bransten in
memory of Ellen Hart Bransten
67.23

ALAN DAVIE
British, born 1920

The Milkmaid Always Says Yes
1963
oil on Masonite
60 × 96"
152.4 × 243.8 cm

William L. Gerstle Collection
William L. Gerstle Fund Purchase
65.18

GENE DAVIS
American, born 1920

Cool Buzz Saw, 1964
acrylic on canvas
113¾ × 115"
289.0 × 292.1 cm

Gift of the Women's Board
66.12

JERROLD DAVIS
American, born 1926

Tryst, 1957
oil on canvas
72 × 58"
182.9 × 147.3 cm

Gift of the Hamilton-Wells Collection
72.45

RONALD DAVIS
American, born 1937

Silver Top, 1968–69
fiberglass with pigmented polyester
resin
56⅝ × 135⅞ × 2⅛"
143.9 × 345.2 × 5.4 cm

Anonymous gift in honor of John
Humphrey
69.79

RONALD DAVIS
American, born 1937

U Shapes, 1969
polyester resin and fiberglass
33⅛ × 46¼ × 1⅛"
84.1 × 117.5 × 2.9 cm

Gift of John Berggruen
77.269

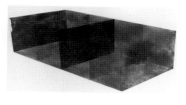

RONALD DAVIS
American, born 1937

Red Four Box, 1974
acrylic on fiberglass
58½ × 140½ × 1½″
148.6 × 356.9 × 3.8 cm

Gift of Thomas W. Weisel
83.112

RONALD DAVIS
American, born 1937

Arch Duo and Vented Star, 1976
acrylic on canvas
114 × 174¾″
289.6 × 443.9 cm

Purchased with the aid of funds
from the National Endowment for the
Arts and the New Future Fund Drive
77.70

STUART DAVIS
American, 1894–1964

Deuce, 1954
oil on canvas
26 × 42¼″
66.0 × 107.3 cm

Gift of Mrs. E. S. Heller
55.4734

See colorplate, p. 137

NAT DEAN
American, born 1956

Black Book, 1975
acrylic, graphite, ink, chalk on
paper, tissue, rhoplex, with book
cloth
open 2 × 11¾ × 8¾″
5.1 × 29.9 × 22.3 cm

Soap Box Derby Fund Purchase
80.177

GEORGE DEEM
American, born 1932

Working Painting (Manet), 1964
oil on canvas
42¼ × 36″
107.3 × 91.4 cm

Gift of Mr. and Mrs. William C.
Janss
78.208

JAY DeFEO
American, born 1929

Easter Lily, 1956
oil on canvas
59⅝ × 73⅜″
151.5 × 187.0 cm

Gift of Nell Sinton
72.46

JAY DeFEO
American, born 1929

The Veronica, 1957
oil on canvas
132 × 42⅜″
335.3 × 107.7 cm

Gift of Irving Blum
73.38

JAY DeFEO
American, born 1929

Incision, 1958–61
oil and string on canvas mounted on
board
118 × 55⅝ × 9⅜″
299.7 × 141.3 × 23.9 cm

Purchased with the aid of funds
from the Society for the
Encouragement of Contemporary Art
67.89

See colorplate, p. 201

291

ROY DE FOREST
American, born 1930

Brothers under the Feathers, 1962
wood with acrylic
32 × 23½ × 5¾"
81.3 × 59.7 × 14.6 cm

Gift of Robert B. Howard
79.321

ROY DE FOREST
American, born 1930

Autobiography of a Sunflower Merchant, 1962–63
oil and acrylic on canvas
67¼ × 67"
170.8 × 170.2 cm

Gift of the Women's Board
64.36

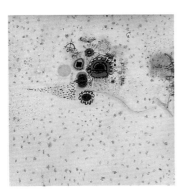

ROY DE FOREST
American, born 1930

Frère Jacques, 1963
oil on canvas
68½ × 64¼"
174.0 × 163.2 cm

Gift of the Hamilton-Wells Collection
69.80

ROY DE FOREST
American, born 1930

Country Dog Gentlemen, 1972
polymer on canvas
66¾ × 97"
169.6 × 246.4 cm

Gift of the Hamilton-Wells Collection
73.32

See colorplate, p. 229

ROY DE FOREST and
CLAYTON BAILEY

Dog Lamp
see entry under Clayton Bailey

WILLEM DE KOONING
American, born Netherlands 1904

The Springs, 1950
oil and masking tape on paper
mounted on board
21⅞ × 24⅜"
55.5 × 61.9 cm

Gift of Edwin Janss
78.141

WILLEM DE KOONING
American, born Netherlands 1904

Woman, 1950
oil on paper mounted on Masonite
36⅝ × 24½"
93.1 × 62.3 cm

Purchase
68.69

See colorplate, p. 159

WILLEM DE KOONING
American, born Netherlands 1904

Reclining Figure, 1962
oil on paper mounted on Masonite
22½ × 28⅜"
54.6 × 72.7 cm

Gift of Mr. and Mrs. William C. Janss
78.202

292

TONY DeLAP
American, born 1927

The Specialist, 1965
canvas, stainless steel, and lacquer
on board
48 × 48 × 4¼"
122.0 × 122.0 × 10.8 cm

Gift of the Women's Board
65.10

ANDRÉ DERAIN
French, 1880–1954

Landscape, 1906
oil on canvas mounted on board
20 × 25½"
50.8 × 64.8 cm

Bequest of Harriet Lane Levy
50.6075

See colorplate, p. 45

ANDRÉ DERAIN
French, 1880–1954

Biblical Group, ca. 1906
oil on canvas
10⅝ × 13¾"
27.0 × 34.9 cm

Gift of Wilbur D. May
64.57

ANDRÉ DERAIN
French, 1880–1954

Head of a Woman, ca. 1923–25
oil on canvas
20¼ × 18¼"
51.4 × 46.4 cm

Gift of Mrs. Joseph M. Bransten
54.1114

CHARLES DESPIAU
French, 1874–1946

Mademoiselle B., 1929
bronze 1/10
15 × 8½ × 10"
38.1 × 21.6 × 25.4 cm

Gift of the Women's Board and
Mrs. E. S. Heller in memory of
Mrs. Sigmund Stern
56.905

BORIS DEUTSCH
American, born Lithuania,
1892–1978

Abstraction, 1923
oil on cardboard
15⅝ × 15⅝"
39.7 × 39.7 cm

Albert M. Bender Collection
Gift of Albert M. Bender
36.5398

BORIS DEUTSCH
American, born Lithuania,
1892–1978

Three Heads, n.d.
oil on canvas
29¾ × 24½"
75.6 × 62.3 cm

Gift of Charlotte Mack
50.5515

DAVID DIAO
American, born China 1943

Scarface, 1969
acrylic on canvas
79 × 126½"
200.7 × 321.2 cm

Purchased with the aid of a gift of
the artist
69.106

RICHARD DIEBENKORN
American, born 1922

Untitled, 1946
oil on canvas
38 × 28¼"
96.5 × 71.8 cm

Gift of Jermayne MacAgy
55.6936

RICHARD DIEBENKORN
American, born 1922

#3, 1948
oil on canvas
27 × 38"
68.6 × 96.5 cm

Gift of Charles Ross
69.110

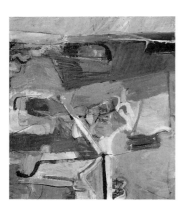

RICHARD DIEBENKORN
American, born 1922

Berkeley #23, 1955
oil on canvas
62 × 54¾"
157.5 × 139.1 cm

Gift of the Women's Board
58.1729

RICHARD DIEBENKORN
American, born 1922

Berkeley #57, 1955
oil on canvas
58¾ × 58¾"
149.3 × 149.3 cm

Bequest of Joseph M. Bransten in
memory of Ellen Hart Bransten
80.423

See colorplate, p. 179

RICHARD DIEBENKORN
American, born 1922

Cityscape I
(formerly *Landscape I*), 1963
oil on canvas
60¼ × 50½"
153.1 × 128.3 cm

Purchased with funds from trustees
and friends in memory of Hector
Escobosa, Brayton Wilbur, and
J. D. Zellerbach
64.46

See colorplate, p. 181

RICHARD DIEBENKORN
American, born 1922

Ocean Park #54, 1972
oil on canvas
100 × 81"
254.0 × 205.7 cm

Gift of friends of Gerald Nordland
72.59

See colorplate, p. 183

RICHARD DIEBENKORN
American, born 1922

Ocean Park #122, 1980
oil and charcoal on canvas
100 × 81"
254.0 × 205.7 cm

Charles H. Land Family Foundation
Fund Purchase
80.389

LADDIE JOHN DILL
American, born 1943

Untitled, 1980
glass on acrylic-polymer emulsion
in cement on wood
24 × 48 × 1¾"
60.9 × 121.9 × 4.5 cm

Gift of Kathryn and Michael Todd
82.378

JIM DINE
American, born 1935

Hammer Noises, 1962
oil on canvas with hammer
84 × 24⅛ × 2½"
213.4 × 61.3 × 6.4 cm

Anonymous gift
64.66

MARK DI SUVERO
American, born China 1933

Ferro, 1978–82
steel
123 × 162 × 162"
312.4 × 411.5 × 411.5 cm

Margaret K. Walker Memorial Fund
Purchase with the aid of funds from
the National Endowment for the
Arts
82.330

ROBERT DIX
American, born 1953

Iceberg, 1982
stoneware with latex and glaze
19½ × 13½ × 4"
49.6 × 34.3 × 10.2 cm

Gift of Dr. Austin Conkey
83.220

THEO VAN DOESBURG
Dutch, 1883–1931

*Simultaneous Counter
Composition*
*(Contre composition
simultanée)*, 1929
oil on canvas
19¾ × 19¾"
50.2 × 50.2 cm

Gift of Peggy Guggenheim
51.3389

See colorplate, p. 83

KEES VAN DONGEN
French, born Netherlands, 1877–1968

The Black Chemise
(La Chemise noire), ca. 1905–9
oil on canvas with wood attachment
22¼ × 18¼"
56.5 × 46.4 cm

Gift of Wilbur D. May
64.59

See colorplate, p. 43

ARTHUR DOVE
American, 1880–1946

Silver Ball No. 2, 1930
oil and metallic paint on canvas
23¼ × 30"
59.1 × 76.2 cm

Rosalie M. Stern Bequest Fund
Purchase
59.2348

See colorplate, p. 127

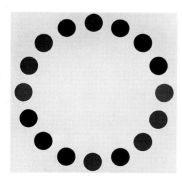

THOMAS DOWNING
American, born 1928

Ring Four, 1969
acrylic on canvas
110 × 109¼"
279.4 × 277.5 cm

Gift of Vincent Melzac
70.61

RALPH DU CASSE
American, born 1916

The Rapier, 1955
oil on canvas
60⅜ × 44⅜"
153.4 × 112.7 cm

Gift of the Women's Board
55.6955

RALPH DU CASSE
American, born 1916

Landscape #9, 1958
oil on canvas
68 × 52″
172.7 × 132.1 cm

Gift of Mrs. Walter A. Haas
61.4524

RALPH DU CASSE
American, born 1916

Landscape #10, 1958
oil on canvas
68⅛ × 52⅛″
173.0 × 132.4 cm

Gift of Win Ng
81.239

RALPH DU CASSE
American, born 1916

Land of Noo, ca. 1960
oil on canvas
68¼ × 96″
173.4 × 243.8 cm

Gift of the Hamilton-Wells Collection
73.35

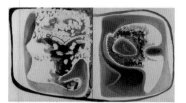

RALPH DU CASSE
American, born 1916

Reflections, ca. 1965–66
oil on canvas
68 × 120″
172.7 × 304.8 cm

Gift of Mary Heath Keesling
70.3 A–B

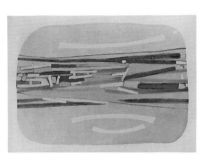

MARCEL DUCHAMP
French, 1887–1968

*The Box in a Suitcase
(La Boîte-en-valise)*, 1938–42
photographic reproductions, cel-
luloid, plaster, porcelain, vinyl,
paper, wood, and Masonite
closed 2⅞ × 13¾ × 15⅛″
7.3 × 35.0 × 38.4 cm

Purchase and gift of Richard B.
Freeman
81.40

DONALD DUDLEY
American, born 1930

Rainbow Series, 1964
acrylic on canvas
68 × 95¾″
172.7 × 243.2 cm

Gift of Sharon Dudley
71.72

ALFRED DUNN
British, born 1937

Quiet Noises, 1967
mild steel with
electrical apparatus
37 × 36¾ × 12¼″
94.0 × 93.4 × 31.1 cm

Gift of Mrs. Wellington S. Henderson
69.81

WALTER DUSENBERY
American, born 1939

Porta Rossa, 1978–79
red travertine
101 × 59 × 15¾″
256.5 × 149.7 × 40.0 cm

Gift of Peter Walker
82.294 A–Q

296

DUAN (SUSAN) DZAMONJA
Yugoslavian, born 1928

#24, No. 6, 1961
wood, metal nails with solder
14¾ × 11½ × 9⅝"
37.5 × 29.2 × 23.8 cm

Gift of Martha Jackson Gallery,
New York
69.3

FRIEDEL DZUBAS
American, born Germany 1915

Eastern, 1966
Magna on canvas
56⅝ × 192½"
143.8 × 489.0 cm

Gift of Mr. and Mrs. Moses Lasky
67.24

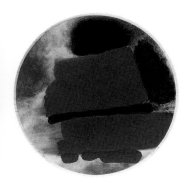

FRIEDEL DZUBAS
American, born Germany 1915

Procession, 1971
acrylic on canvas
23¾" diam.
60.4 cm

Gift of Dr. and Mrs. Robert Fenton
78.186

STEPHEN EDLICH
American, born 1944

Untitled, 1977
acrylic, paper, jute, and charcoal
on cotton
84⅛ × 60"
213.7 × 152.4 cm

Gift of Martin J. Rabinowitz
83.221

WILLIAM EDMONDSON
American, ca. 1870–1951

Untitled, ca. 1934–41
limestone
7¼ × 7½ × 4¾"
18.4 × 19.1 × 12.1 cm

Albert M. Bender Collection
Bequest of Albert M. Bender
41.2971

DAVID EDSTROM
American, born Sweden, 1873–1941

Portrait of Miss Levy, ca. 1907–8
terra-cotta
10⅛ × 9¾ × 8¼"
25.7 × 24.8 × 21.0 cm

Bequest of Harriet Lane Levy
50.6076

LOUIS MICHEL EILSHEMIUS
American, 1864–1941

Late-Afternoon Bathers, 1915–20
oil on board
19¾ × 14¼"
50.2 × 36.2 cm

Gift of James N. Rosenberg
53.1142

REDD EKKS
(ROBERT RASMUSSEN)
American, born Norway 1937

Rhinophore II, 1973
earthenware with glazes
56½ × 11¾ × 11¾"
143.5 × 29.8 × 29.8 cm

Gift of Mr. and Mrs. John Lowell
Jones
77.88 A–B

ELIN ELISOFON
American, born 1952

Anonymous Sacrifice #4, 1976
plaster, reeds, bird, wire, shoelace, thread, gauze, wax, and pencil
4⅜ × 11⅜ × 7⅞″
11.1 × 28.7 × 19.8 cm

Paul L. Wattis Special Fund Purchase
76.128 A–E

ELIN ELISOFON
American, born 1952

Untitled, 1978
balsa wood, bird, wax, cloth, thread, cactus, blood, bone, feathers, and wood shavings
closed 1⅞ × 8⅛ × 3⅜″
4.5 × 20.6 × 8.3 cm

Gift of the artist through the Society for the Encouragement of Contemporary Art
79.52 A–B

IRMA ENGEL
American, born Germany 1910

Spring Flowers, 1946
oil on canvas
30 × 24¼″
76.2 × 61.7 cm

Gift of Mrs. Walter A. Haas in memory of Albert M. Bender
46.2765

JACOB EPSTEIN
British, 1880–1959

Portrait of Mrs. Epstein, 1916
bronze
9½ × 8 × 7″
24.1 × 20.3 × 17.8 cm

Albert M. Bender Collection
Bequest of Albert M. Bender
41.2968

JIMMY ERNST
American, born Germany, 1920–1984

Recognition, 1960
oil on canvas
45⅛ × 50⅛″
114.6 × 127.3 cm

Gift of Mr. and Mrs. Moses Lasky
82.379

MAX ERNST
French, born Germany, 1891–1976

The Numerous Family
(La Famille nombreuse), 1926
oil on canvas
32⅛ × 25⅝″
81.6 × 65.1 cm

Gift of Peggy Guggenheim
47.1240

MAX ERNST
French, born Germany, 1891–1976

Head with Horns
(Tête à cornes), 1959
gold on wood
10⅞ × 7⅝ × 1″
27.7 × 19.4 × 2.6 cm

Bequest of Maurine Church Coburn
64.54

MAX ERNST
French, born Germany, 1891–1976

Bauta, 1964
glass
19⅝ × 9⅞ × 11″
49.9 × 25.1 × 27.9 cm

Gift of Peggy Guggenheim
67.52 A–B

CLAIRE FALKENSTEIN
American, born 1908

Moon II, 1958
mild steel and glass
20⅞ × 20½ × 17⅜″
53.0 × 52.1 × 44.1 cm

Gift of Charlotte Mack
61.1908

AMINTORE FANFANI
Italian, born 1908

*Entrance to the Harbor
(Bocca di porto)*, 1979
oil on panel
24⅞ × 38⅞″
63.0 × 98.5 cm

Gift of Mr. and Mrs. Amintore
Fanfani
81.149

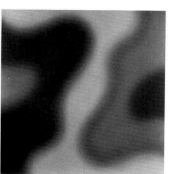

WOJCJECH FANGOR
American, born Poland 1922

M 63, 1969
oil on canvas
56⅛ × 56¼″
142.6 × 142.9 cm

Gift of Mr. and Mrs. Leonard S.
Field
77.98

RICHARD FARALLA
American, born 1916

Relief XIII, 1960
wood with latex
80 × 30 × 2⅝″
203.2 × 76.2 × 6.7 cm

Gift of Mr. and Mrs. William M.
Roth
74.58

RICHARD FARALLA
American, born 1916

Oval, 1961
from the Metric Series
wood with latex
48¾ × 71¾ × 7½″
123.8 × 182.3 × 19.1 cm

Gift of the Women's Board
62.3429

RICHARD FARALLA
American, born 1916

Relief '63, 1963
wood with latex
20¼ × 10½ × 3¾″
51.4 × 26.7 × 9.5 cm

Anonymous gift
81.200

RICHARD FARALLA
American, born 1916

*Relief I:
Homage to John Baxter*, 1966
paper egg cartons on wood with
latex and sand
11⅞ × 10⅝ × 1½″
30.2 × 27.0 × 3.8 cm

Gift of the artist in memory of John
Baxter
67.7

RICHARD FARALLA
American, born 1916

Untitled, 1970
wood with latex, nails, and mirror
open 8¾ × 12⅛ × 1½″
22.2 × 30.8 × 3.8 cm

Anonymous gift
81.95

RICHARD FARALLA
American, born 1916

Homage à J. H., 1976
wood with latex
6 × 11 × 1¾"
15.2 × 27.9 × 4.5 cm

Anonymous gift
81.96

AL FARROW
American, born 1943

Plié in Second on Pointe, 1979
from the series Dancer
bronze and steel with enamel
12½ × 23⅞ × 14⅞"
31.7 × 60.6 × 37.8 cm

Gift of Mr. and Mrs. Rene di Rosa
80.388

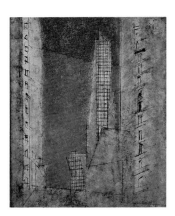

LYONEL FEININGER
American, 1871–1956

Manhattan, the Tower, 1944
oil on canvas
31¾ × 39½"
80.7 × 100.4 cm

Gift of Mrs. Drew Chidester
60.8569

LORSER FEITELSON
American, 1898–1978

Genesis, First Version, 1934
oil on Celotex
24 × 30"
60.9 × 76.2 cm

Gift of Helen Klokke
37.2978

LORSER FEITELSON
American, 1898–1978

Magical Forms, 1948
from the series Magical Forms
oil on canvas
36 × 30"
91.4 × 76.2 cm

Gift of the Lorser Feitelson and
Helen Lundeberg Feitelson Arts
Foundation, Los Angeles
81.196

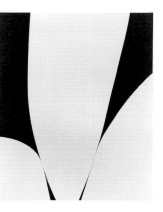

LORSER FEITELSON
American, 1898–1978

Magical Space Forms, 1963
from the series Magical Space Forms
enamel on canvas
72 × 60"
182.9 × 152.5 cm

Gift of the Lorser Feitelson and
Helen Lundeberg Feitelson Arts
Foundation, Los Angeles
82.161

JOHN C. FERNIE
American, born 1945

Untitled, 1970
wood with plaster, brass, aluminum,
nails, and plastic
48½ × 120 × 60"
123.4 × 304.8 × 152.4 cm

Anonymous gift
73.39

JOHN FERREN
American, 1905–1970

Abstraction, 1937
plaster with tempera and
engraving inks
10 × 4¾ × 1"
25.4 × 12.1 × 2.6 cm

Gift of Mr. and Mrs. Forrest
Engelhart
38.160

JOHN FERREN
American, 1905–1970

#8 (Paris), 1937
plaster with tempera and
engraving inks
11¾ × 9⅝ × 1″
29.8 × 24.4 × 2.6 cm

Gift of Mr. and Mrs. Forrest
Engelhart
38.161

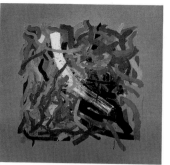

JOHN FERREN
American, 1905–1970

Untitled, 1962
oil on canvas
54 × 54″
137.1 × 137.1 cm

Gift of Roy Ferren
68.57

HELENE FESENMAIER
American, born 1937

Sinbad, 1974
wood with acrylic and acrylic on
canvas
84 × 39 × 20″
213.4 × 99.0 × 50.8 cm

Gift of Mr. and Mrs. Hamilton
Robinson, Jr.
77.249 A–D

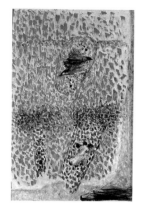

AMY FLEMMING
American

*Flowers, Birds, Children
in the Field*, 1963
oil on canvas
50 × 32⅛″
127.0 × 81.3 cm

Gift of Dr. Barbara de Wolf
71.18

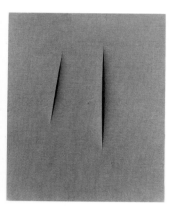

LUCIO FONTANA
Italian, born Argentina, 1899–1968

Spatial Concept: Waiting
(Concetto spaziale, Attese), 1961
glue size on linen
28⅞ × 23¾″
73.3 × 60.3 cm

Anonymous gift
74.115

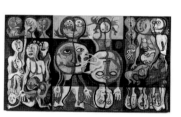

RAQUEL FORNER
Argentine, born 1902

Mutation in Space-Time
(Mutacion en espacio-tiempo), 1971
oil on canvas
63¾ × 110⅜″
161.9 × 280.4 cm

Gift of the Argentine Republic
74.18 A–C

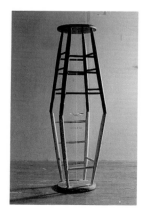

TERRY FOX
American, born 1943

A Metaphor, 1976
wood stools, magazine text, string,
and paper
56 × 16¾ × 16″
142.2 × 42.5 × 40.6 cm

Purchased with the aid of funds
from the National Endowment for
the Arts, the Soap Box Derby Fund,
and the New Future Fund Drive
77.76 A–D

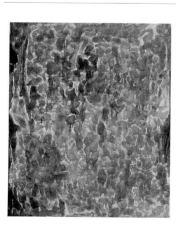

SAM FRANCIS
American, born 1923

Red and Pink, 1951
oil on canvas
81¾ × 65¾″
207.6 × 167.0 cm

Partial gift of Mrs. Wellington S.
Henderson
69.111

See colorplate, p. 167

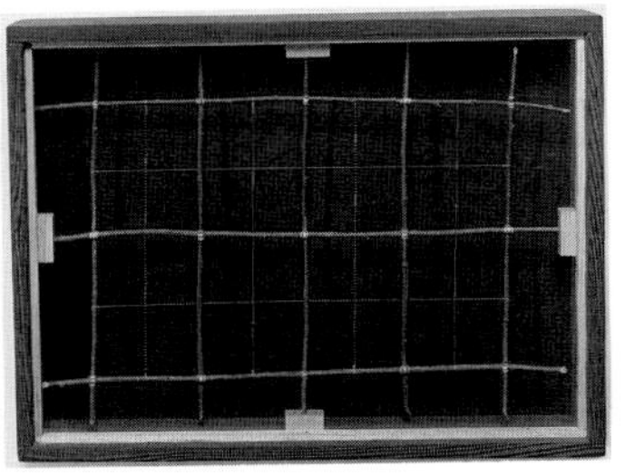

RICHARD FRANCISCO
American, born 1942

***Urban Compass*, 1972**
wood, glass, string, thread, and twigs
15 × 19⅞ × 2⅛″
38.1 × 50.5 × 5.4 cm

Helen Crocker Russell Memorial Fund Purchase
74.47

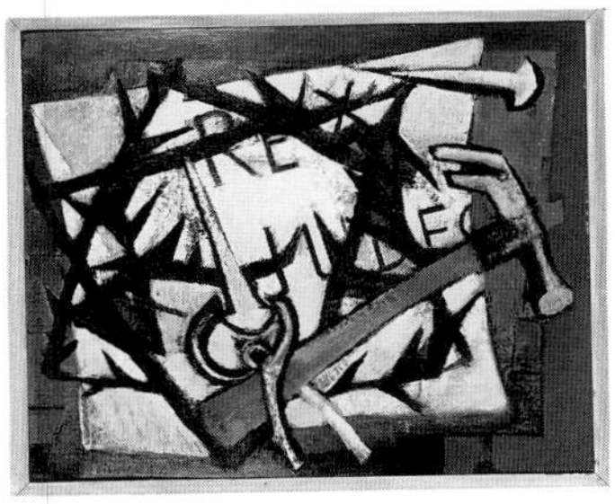

FREDERICK FRANCK
American, born Netherlands 1909

***Passion Still Life*, 1952**
oil and aluminum on Masonite
26 × 32″
66.0 × 81.3 cm

Gift of J. D. van Karnebeek
52.4260

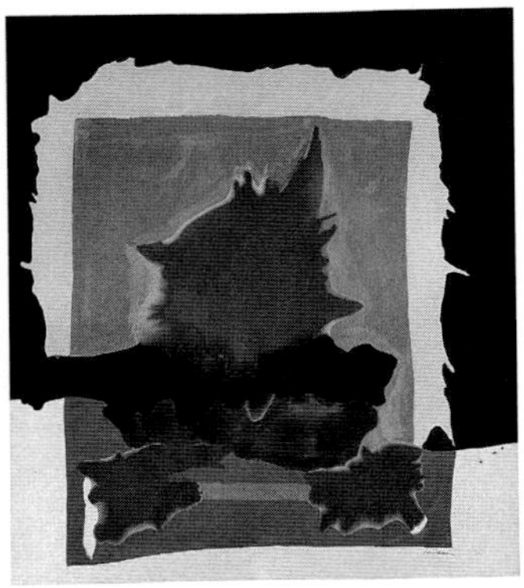

HELEN FRANKENTHALER
American, born 1928

***Interior Landscape*, 1964**
acrylic on canvas
104⅞ × 92⅝″
266.4 × 235.3 cm

Gift of the Women's Board
68.52

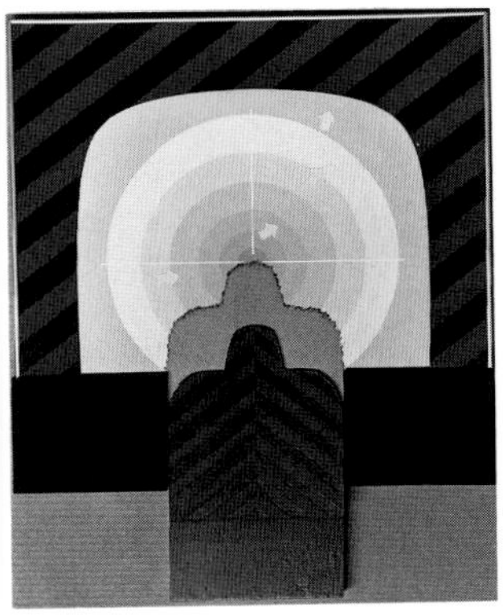

STEPHEN FRENCH
American, born 1934

***Release*, 1964**
acrylic on paper and wood
24 × 19″
61.0 × 48.3 cm

Gift of the Ford Foundation
65.2

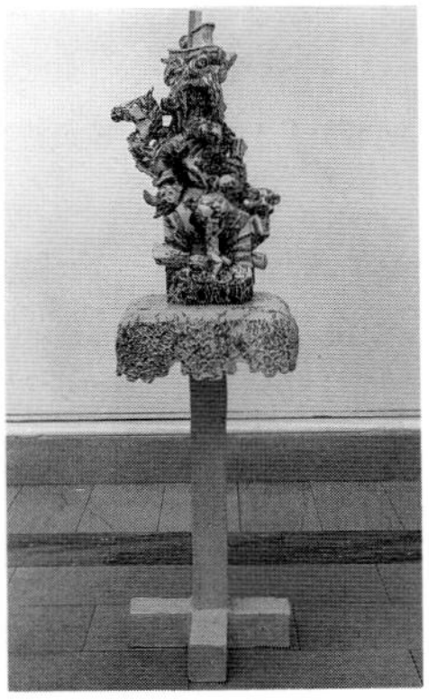

VIOLA FREY
American, born 1933

***Junkman, Bricoleur*, 1977**
whiteware, glaze, and china paint
71⅜ × 17⅞ × 18¾″
181.3 × 45.4 × 47.6 cm

Purchased with matching funds from the National Endowment for the Arts and the Soap Box Derby Fund
80.169 A–C

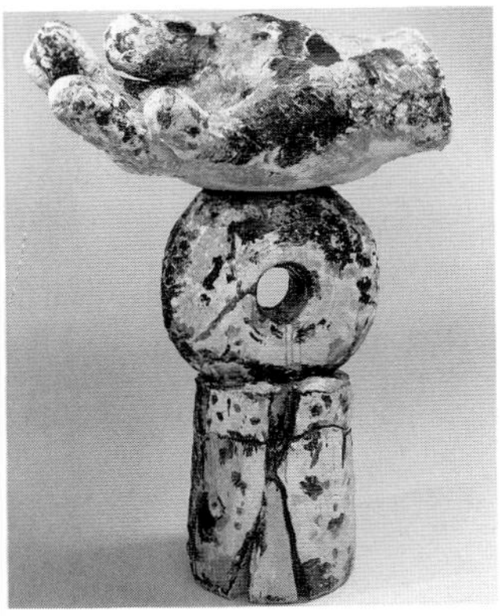

VIOLA FREY
American, born 1933

***Fortune's Glove*, 1977–80**
whiteware with china paint
59½ × 38 × 31″
151.1 × 96.5 × 78.7 cm

Gift of Win Ng
80.430 A–C

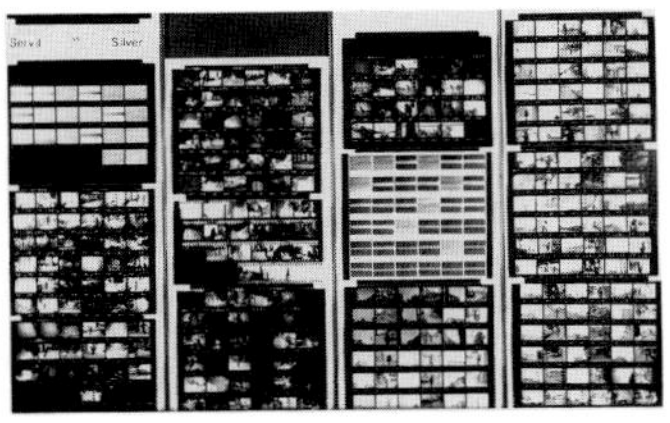

HOWARD FRIED
American, born 1946

***Long John Servil vs. Long John Silver*, 1972**
gelatin silver prints mounted on four panels
each 49⅝ × 19⅝″
126.0 × 49.9 cm

Purchased with the aid of funds from Rene di Rosa and the Soap Box Derby Fund
81.98 A–D

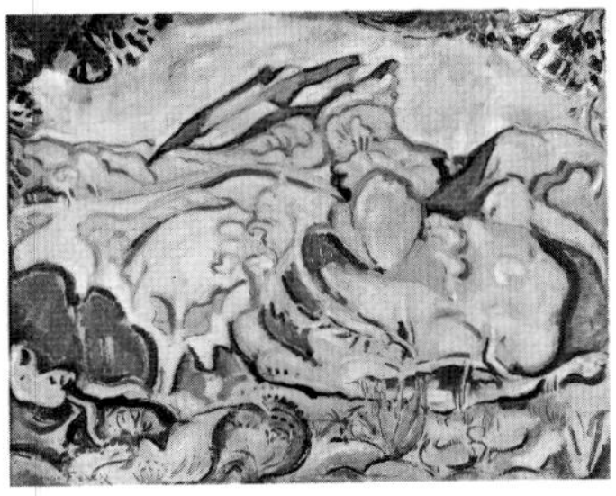

OTHON FRIESZ
French, 1879–1949

Landscape (The Eagle's Beak, La Ciotat) *(Paysage [Le Bec-de-l'Aigle, La Ciotat])*, 1907
oil on canvas
25⅜ × 32″
64.5 × 81.2 cm

Bequest of Marian W. Sinton
81.52

See colorplate, p. 47

DENNIS GALLAGHER
American, born 1952

Untitled, 1982
stoneware
91½ × 15¾ × 19¾″
232.4 × 40.0 × 50.2 cm

Gift of Win Ng
83.43 A–E

ALBERT EUGENE GALLATIN
American, 1881–1952

Parallel Forms II, 1941
oil on canvas
40 × 20⅛″
101.6 × 51.1 cm

Gift of Mrs. W. Floyd Nichols and
Mrs. B. Langdon Tyler
52.6713

GARBELL

Abstraction, n.d.
oil on Masonite
8¾ × 13″
22.2 × 33.0 cm

Gift of Dr. and Mrs. Allan Roos
62.9

WILLIAM A. GAW
American, 1895–1973

Still Life, ca. 1929
oil on canvas
30¼ × 36″
76.8 × 91.4 cm

Albert M. Bender Collection
Gift of Albert M. Bender
39.26

WILLIAM A. GAW
American, 1895–1973

African Marigolds, 1933
oil on canvas
27 × 21¼″
68.6 × 54.0 cm

Albert M. Bender Collection
Gift of Albert M. Bender
36.5988

WILLIAM A. GAW
American, 1895–1973

Gile's Porch, 1936
oil on canvas
32⅛ × 38¼″
81.6 × 97.1 cm

San Francisco Museum of Art
Purchase Prize, *Fifty-seventh Annual
Exhibition of the San Francisco Art
Association*
37.2063

WILLIAM A. GAW
American, 1895–1973

White Flowers, 1937
oil on canvas
40 × 34″
101.6 × 86.4 cm

Albert M. Bender Collection
Gift of Albert M. Bender
38.1

WILLIAM A. GAW
American, 1895–1973

The Vesper Hour, 1938
oil on canvas
34⅛ × 40⅛″
86.7 × 101.9 cm

San Francisco Museum of Art
Purchase Prize, *Fifty-eighth Annual
Exhibition of the San Francisco Art
Association*
38.118

WILLIAM A. GAW
American, 1895–1973

Summer in Marin County, n.d.
oil on canvas
21 × 27⅛"
53.3 × 68.9 cm

Albert M. Bender Collection
Gift of Albert M. Bender
39.24

WILLIAM A. GAW
American, 1895–1973

The Wine Glass, n.d.
oil on canvas
10¾ × 14½"
27.3 × 36.9 cm

Albert M. Bender Collection
Gift of Albert M. Bender
35.2216

SONIA GECHTOFF
American, born 1926

Mystery of the Hunt, 1956
oil on canvas
45¼ × 106"
114.9 × 269.2 cm

Gift of Irving Blum
73.40

SONIA GECHTOFF
American, born 1926

Painting IV, 1956
oil on canvas
96 × 48¼"
243.8 × 122.6 cm

Gift of William M. Roth
73.19

SONIA GECHTOFF
American, born 1926

Homage to Hieronymus, 1957
oil on canvas
104¼ × 64½"
264.8 × 163.8 cm

Gift of Mr. and Mrs. Moses Lasky
61.4512

SONIA GECHTOFF
American, born 1926

The Sheik, 1958
oil on canvas
69 × 68¼"
175.3 × 173.4 cm

Gift of Mrs. Ferdinand C. Smith
58.4380

WILLIAM GEIS
American, born 1940

A Token of My Appreciation
1973
wood, plaster, metal, glass,
and wire
6⅛ × 28⅞ × 30⅜"
15.5 × 73.3 × 77.9 cm

Gift of John Berggruen Gallery,
San Francisco
73.71

WILLIAM GEIS
American, born 1940

Green Smoke (For Lucas), 1977
fiberglass and plaster on wood with
paint, paper, and metal
73¼ × 92½ × 68⅜"
186.0 × 234.6 × 174.9 cm

Purchased with the aid of funds
from the National Endowment for
the Arts, the Soap Box Derby Fund,
and the New Future Fund Drive
77.75

NANCY GENN
American, born 1929

Pulsating Sphere, 1964
bronze
14 × 14 × 12″
35.5 × 35.5 × 30.5 cm

Gift of the Margery Hoffman Smith
Trust
82.49

ALBERTO GIACOMETTI
Swiss, 1901–1966

Seated Woman, 1947
oil on canvas
27⅜ × 14⅜″
69.6 × 37.2 cm

Gift of Jean Stein vanden Heuvel
in memory of Edith Sedgwick
76.198

ALBERTO GIACOMETTI
Swiss, 1901–1966

Lamp with Two Figures
(Lampe avec deux figures), 1949–50
bronze ed. 20
13⅜ × 14⅝ × 7¼″
34.0 × 37.2 × 18.4 cm

Gift of the Carl Djerassi and Norma
Djerassi Art Trust in memory of
Pamela Djerassi Bush
82.381

ALBERTO GIACOMETTI
Swiss, 1901–1966

Annette VII, 1962
bronze 2/6
18½ × 10¾ × 7½″
47.0 × 27.3 × 19.1 cm

Gift of Mr. and Mrs. Louis Honig
69.83

See colorplate, p. 117

H. PHELAN GIBB
British, 1870–1948

Notre-Dame, n.d.
oil on canvas
13 × 16⅛″
33.0 × 41.0 cm

Bequest of Harriet Lane Levy
50.6079

MATHEW GIL
American, born 1956

Cat #4, 1980
steel with enamel
69½ × 31½ × 15¼″
176.5 × 80.0 × 38.7 cm

Anonymous gift
82.382

DAVID GILHOOLY
American, born 1943

The Honey Sisters Do a
Garden Blessing, 1972
earthenware with glazes
19⅜ × 26⅜ × 33″
49.2 × 67.0 × 83.8 cm

William L. Gerstle Collection
William L. Gerstle Fund Purchase
73.50 A–G

MAX GIMBLETT
American, born New Zealand 1935

Buddha, 1977
acrylic on canvas
70 × 60⅛″
177.8 × 152.8 cm

Gift of Don Albert Grisanti
83.223

305

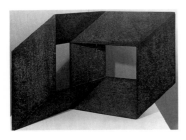

CHARLES GINNEVER
American, born 1931

Troika, 1976
Cor-ten steel 1/3
32 × 47¼ × 15″
81.3 × 120.0 × 38.1 cm

Gift of Mr. and Mrs. Robert D.
Haas, Mr. and Mrs. Walter J. Haas,
and Roy and Elizabeth Eisenhardt
80.172

JUDITH GODWIN
American, born 1930

Red Cross, 1975
oil on canvas
42 × 40″
106.7 × 101.6 cm

Gift of William E. Hague
77.3

RALPH GOINGS
American, born 1928

Untitled, 1957
oil on canvas
28¼ × 27⅞″
71.8 × 70.8 cm

Gift of Bill Bass
75.179

RALPH GOINGS
American, born 1928

Earth Movement, 1961
oil on canvas
31⅜ × 48¾″
80.3 × 123.8 cm

Gift of Bill Bass
75.178

RALPH GOINGS
American, born 1928

Body Reflection, 1962
oil and pencil on canvas
12¼ × 12⅛″
31.1 × 30.8 cm

Gift of Bill Bass
75.181

RALPH GOINGS
American, born 1928

Every Girl's Dream, 1962
oil on canvas
49½ × 45″
125.7 × 114.3 cm

Gift of Bill Bass
75.176

RALPH GOINGS
American, born 1928

Head Study, 1962
oil on canvas
12⅛ × 12¼″
30.8 × 31.1 cm

Gift of Bill Bass
75.180

RALPH GOINGS
American, born 1928

Woman in Girdle, 1962
oil on canvas
32 × 22⅛″
81.3 × 56.2 cm

Gift of Bill Bass
75.177

JULIO GONZÁLEZ
Spanish, 1876–1942
Mask "My" (Masque "My")
ca. 1930
bronze 5/9
8 × 3½ × 3"
20.3 × 8.9 × 7.6 cm

Gift of E. Morris Cox from the
collection of Margaret Storke Cox
83.225

See colorplate, p. 63

JULIO GONZÁLEZ
Spanish, 1876–1942
Head on Long Stem
(Tête longue tige), 1932/after 1942
bronze 2/8
27 × 8¾ × 5⅝"
68.6 × 22.3 × 14.3 cm

Purchase
82.1

JULIO GONZÁLEZ
Spanish, 1876–1942
Small Sickle (Woman Standing)
(Petite Faucille [Femme debout])
ca. 1937
bronze 4/6
11½ × 4¾ × 3½"
29.2 × 12.1 × 8.9 cm

Gift of E. Morris Cox from the
collection of Margaret Storke Cox
83.224

See colorplate, p. 63

JULIO GONZÁLEZ
Spanish, 1876–1942
The Monk, 1940–41
bronze 3/9
6 × 6¼ × 2"
15.3 × 15.9 × 5.1 cm

Gift of E. Morris Cox from the
collection of Margaret Storke Cox
84.33

ROBERT GOODNOUGH
American, born 1917
Light Movement, 1970
acrylic on canvas
92½ × 219"
235.0 × 556.3 cm

Gift of Robert A. Rowan
77.1

ROBERT GOODNOUGH
American, born 1917
White on White, 1970–71
acrylic on canvas
102⅜ × 102⅜"
260.1 × 260.1 cm

Gift of Mr. and Mrs. C. David
Robinson
79.314

CLAYTON GORDER
American, born 1936
Speeding Paralleloform—
Speeding Mouth, 1970
acrylic on canvas
54⅜ × 197 × 6¼"
138.1 × 500.4 × 15.9 cm

Gift of Dr. William C. Sawyer
71.74 A–C

SIDNEY GORDIN
American, born Russia 1918
75.61, 1961
steel
28⅜ × 16 × 8"
72.1 × 40.6 × 20.3 cm

Gift of the Hamilton-Wells Collection
72.43

ARSHILE GORKY
American, born Turkish Armenia,
1904–1948

Tracking down Guiltless Doves
1936
oil on composition board
12 × 16″
30.5 × 40.7 cm

Gift of Robert B. Howard
64.64

ARSHILE GORKY
American, born Turkish Armenia,
1904–1948

Enigmatic Combat, 1936–37
oil on canvas
35¾ × 48″
90.8 × 121.9 cm

Gift of Jeanne Reynal
41.3763

See colorplate, p. 147

ARSHILE GORKY
American, born Turkish Armenia,
1904–1948

Flowers in a Pitcher, ca. 1938–39
oil on canvas
28⅛ × 20⅛″
71.4 × 51.1 cm

Gift of Mr. and Mrs. David
McCulloch
82.296

ADOLPH GOTTLIEB
American, 1903–1974

Demon of the Night, 1946
oil on canvas
36⅜ × 48⅜″
92.4 × 122.9 cm

Purchase
69.57

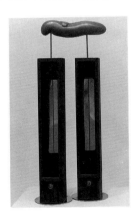

ROBERT GRAHAM
American, born Mexico 1938

The World's Fastest, 1963
wood, metal, and glass
19 × 8 × 4″
48.2 × 20.3 × 10.1 cm

Gift of Dr. and Mrs. William R.
Fielder
74.111

ROBERT GRAHAM
American, born Mexico 1938

Lise Dance Figure II, 1979
bronze with silk and oil colors 4/9
figure 32½ × 15 × 7″
82.6 × 38.1 × 17.8 cm
with base 92¾ × 20¼″ diam.
235.6 × 51.5 cm

T. B. Walker Foundation Fund
Purchase
81.1

ART GRANT
American, born 1927

Opalescent, 1962
mylar and plastic
20¼ × 23½″
51.4 × 59.7 cm

Gift of the artist
65.21

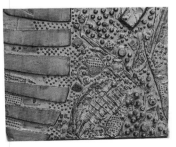

JAMES GRANT
American, born 1924

Rough Red, 1966
polyester resin on panel
42¾ × 53¾ × 3⅞″
108.6 × 136.5 × 9.8 cm

Gift of Charles Boone in memory of
Elizabeth Sharpe Boone
67.15

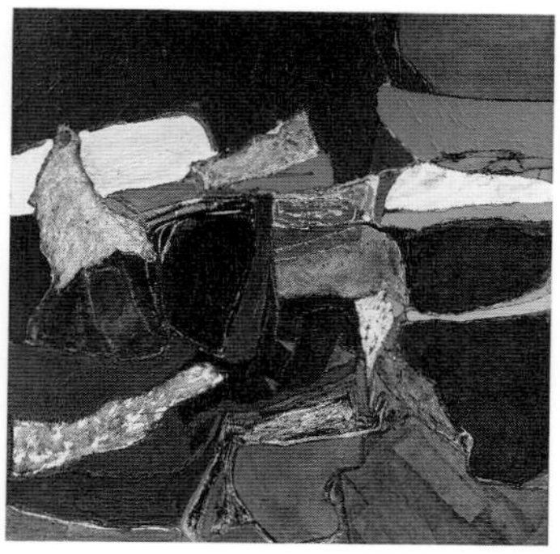

JAMES GRANT
American, born 1924
Square Collage with Bright Blue
n.d.
oil on canvas
79⅛ × 79⅛″
201.0 × 201.0 cm
Gift of Mr. and Mrs. Jay J. Levine
75.96

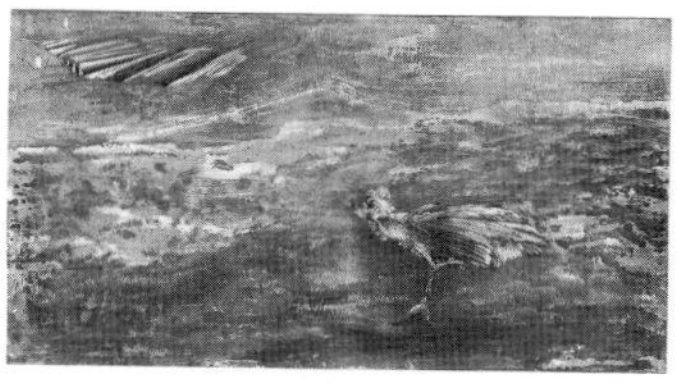

MORRIS GRAVES
American, born 1910
Bird Maddened by the Sound of Machinery in the Air, 1944
watercolor on rice paper
32⅝ × 59⅜″
82.9 × 150.8 cm
Anonymous gift
51.1735

See colorplate, p. 143

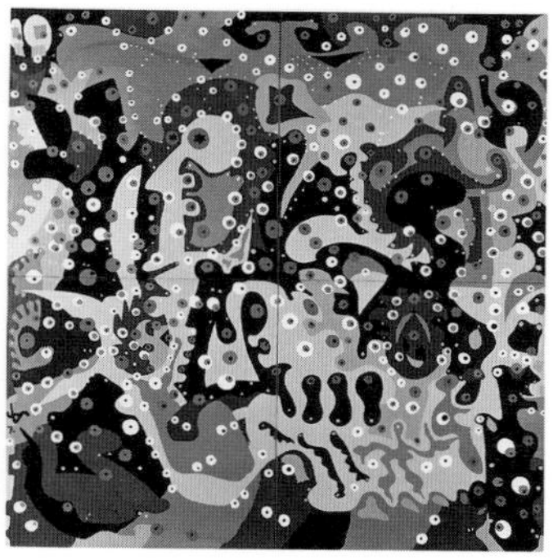

CHARLES GREELEY
American, born 1941
Reflections of the Omniliquent
1970
acrylic on canvas
96¼ × 96¼″
244.5 × 244.5 cm
Gift of George Sarkis
77.250 A–D

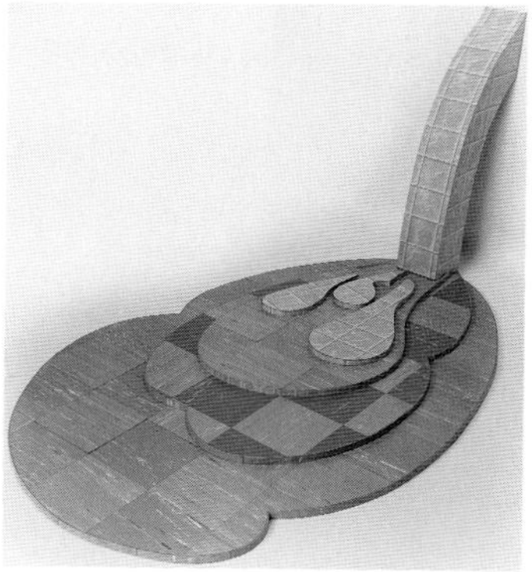

GEORGE GREEN
American, born 1943
Drip, 1971
linoleum tile on wood
32⅛ × 77¾ × 45″
81.6 × 197.5 × 114.3 cm
Gift of Dr. and Mrs. Robert Fenton
77.240

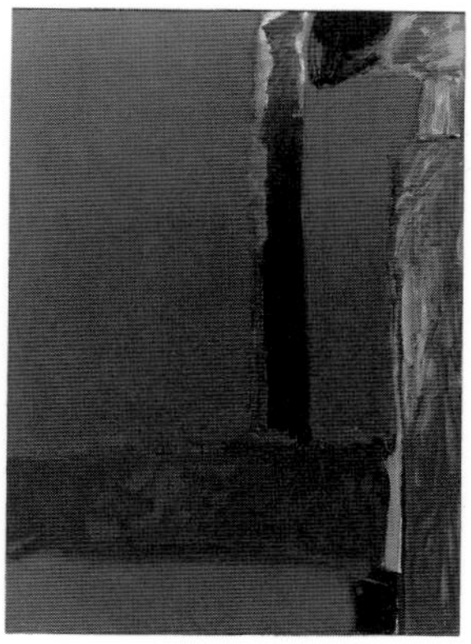

STEPHEN GREENE
American, born 1918
Nightwatch, 1960
oil on canvas
80 × 58″
203.2 × 147.3 cm
Gift of the Staempfli Gallery, New York
76.28

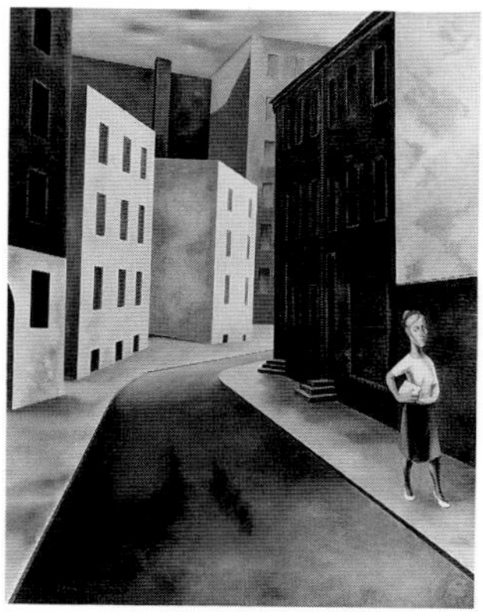

O. LOUIS GUGLIELMI
American, born Italy, 1906–1956
Street, 1939
oil on Masonite
30 × 24″
76.2 × 61.0 cm
WPA Federal Arts Project Allocation to the San Francisco Museum of Art
3747.43

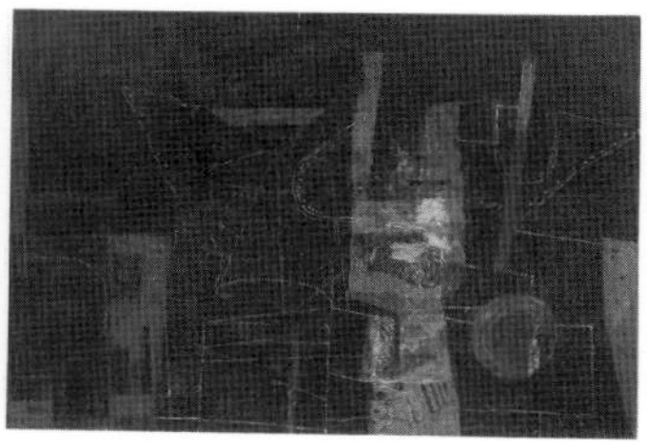

PHILIP GUSTON
American, born Canada, 1913–1980
The Tormentors, 1947–48
oil on canvas
40⅞ × 60½″
103.9 × 153.7 cm
Gift of the artist
82.34

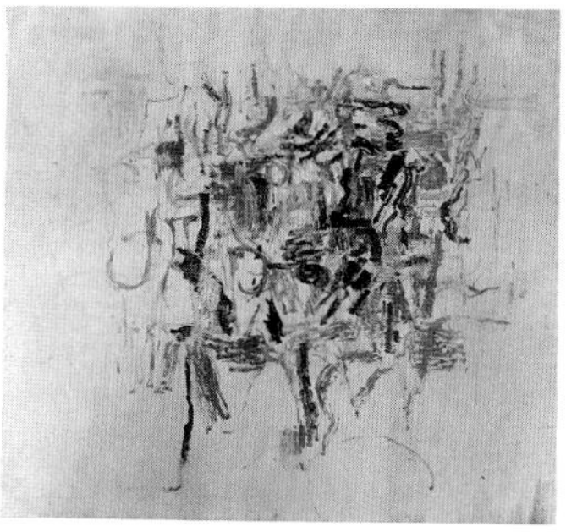

PHILIP GUSTON
American, born Canada, 1913–1980
White Painting I, 1951
oil on canvas
57⅞ × 61⅞″
147.0 × 157.2 cm
T. B. Walker Foundation Fund Purchase
71.43

PHILIP GUSTON
American, born Canada, 1913–1980

For M., 1955
oil on canvas
76⅜ × 72¼"
194.0 × 183.5 cm

Gift of Betty Freeman
72.21

See colorplate, p. 169

PHILIP GUSTON
American, born Canada, 1913–1980

New Place, 1964
oil on canvas
76 × 80"
193.1 × 203.2 cm

Gift of the artist
82.32

PHILIP GUSTON
American, born Canada, 1913–1980

Evidence, 1970
oil on canvas
75¼ × 114¼"
191.2 × 290.2 cm

Gift of the artist
82.31

PHILIP GUSTON
American, born Canada, 1913–1980

Blue Light, 1975
oil on canvas
73 × 80½"
185.5 × 204.5 cm

Purchased through the Helen
Crocker Russell and William H.
and Ethel W. Crocker Family
Funds, the Mrs. Ferdinand C.
Smith Fund, and the Paul L.
Wattis Special Fund
78.67 A

See colorplate, p. 173

PHILIP GUSTON
American, born Canada, 1913–1980

Red Sea, 1975
oil on canvas
73½ × 78¾"
186.7 × 200.1 cm

Purchased through the Helen
Crocker Russell and William H.
and Ethel W. Crocker Family
Funds, the Mrs. Ferdinand C.
Smith Fund, and the Paul L.
Wattis Special Fund
78.67 C

See colorplate, p. 171

PHILIP GUSTON
American, born Canada, 1913–1980

The Swell, 1975
oil on canvas
73 × 78⅛"
185.5 × 198.5 cm

Purchased through the Helen
Crocker Russell and William H.
and Ethel W. Crocker Family
Funds, the Mrs. Ferdinand C.
Smith Fund, and the Paul L.
Wattis Special Fund
78.67 B

See colorplate, p. 172

PHILIP GUSTON
American, born Canada, 1913–1980

Back View, 1977
oil on canvas
69 × 94"
175.3 × 238.8 cm

Gift of the artist
82.33

See colorplate, p. 177

HOWARD HACK
American, born 1932

Window #5, Grocery Store, 1963
oil on canvas
64½ × 61"
163.8 × 155.0 cm

Gift of Mr. and Mrs. Paul W. Hack
79.2

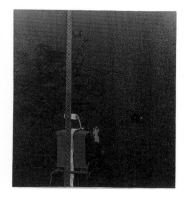

HOWARD HACK
American, born 1932

Window #6,
Calculating Machine, 1964
oil on canvas
64½ × 59⅞″
163.8 × 152.1 cm

Gift of Mr. and Mrs. Paul W. Hack
79.3

HOWARD HACK
American, born 1932

Window #7,
Gibson's Tailor Shop, 1967
oil on canvas
60 × 50″
152.4 × 127.0 cm

Gift of Robert G. Schwartz
77.89

HOWARD HACK
American, born 1932

Window #21,
F. Uri Meat Company, 1967
oil on canvas
85⅛ × 109″
216.2 × 276.9 cm

Gift of Mr. and Mrs. Harry W.
Anderson
76.99

HOWARD HACK
American, born 1932

Window #28, Wiki-Wiki, 1969
oil on canvas
72⅛ × 60″
183.2 × 152.4 cm

Gift of Mr. and Mrs. Paul W. Hack
79.4

RAOUL HAGUE
American, born Turkey 1905

Walnut Mink Hollow, 1961
walnut
57 × 37 × 22″
144.8 × 94.0 × 55.9 cm

Purchased with the aid of funds
from the National Endowment for
the Arts
70.20

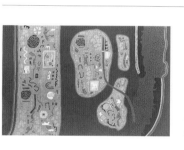

FRANK HAMILTON
American, born 1923

Orovada, 1965
acrylic on canvas
65⅛ × 96″
165.4 × 243.8 cm

Gift of Win Ng
81.240

FRANK HAMILTON
American, born 1923

Liverdun, 1966
acrylic on canvas
67⅛ × 84¼″
170.5 × 214.0 cm

Anonymous gift
68.46

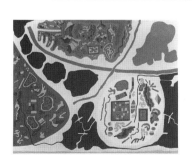

FRANK HAMILTON
American, born 1923

Edessa, 1967
acrylic on canvas
70⅜ × 125⅛″
178.8 × 319.7 cm

Anonymous gift
68.45

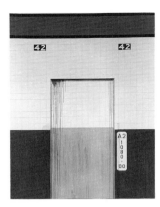

HISAO HANAFUSA
Japanese, born 1937

42nd Street (8th Ave.), 1974
acrylic on canvas
97 × 74⅛"
246.3 × 188.2 cm

Gift of Denise Wilstein
78.145

JO HANSON
American

There Are Many Manshions, 1974
from the series Crab Orchard
Cemetery
photo-silkscreen on styrofoam, plastic flowers, and ribbon
58 × 20¼ × 20¼"
147.3 × 51.4 × 51.4 cm

Gift of Priscilla Birge
77.277 A–C

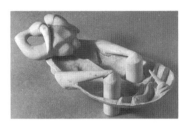

DAVID HARE
American, born 1917

Dead Elephant, 1945
Sorel cement
4⅜ × 11⅜ × 6¼"
11.1 × 28.9 × 15.9 cm

Gift of Jeanne Reynal
46.3154

DAVID HARE
American, born 1917

Trap for a Gorilla, 1945
Sorel cement with piano wire
25⅛ × 15⅝ × 14"
63.8 × 39.7 × 35.6 cm

Gift of Jermayne MacAgy
55.6935

PAUL HARRIS
American, born 1925

Man Wailing, 1972
bronze
23¼ × 13 × 4½"
59.1 × 33.0 × 11.4 cm

Partial gift of Dorothy and Paul
Schmidt
75.42

MARSDEN HARTLEY
American, 1877–1943

Jetty Seen through a Window
1936
oil on board
24 × 18"
61.0 × 45.7 cm

Gift of W. W. Crocker
53.5789

STANLEY WILLIAM HAYTER
British, born 1901

Marionette, 1950
oil on canvas
39¼ × 28⅞"
99.7 × 73.3 cm

Gift of Mr. and Mrs. Archibald
Taylor
64.68

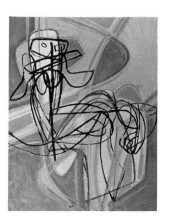

STANLEY WILLIAM HAYTER
British, born 1901

One-Man Band, 1950
oil on canvas
35 × 27⅛"
88.9 × 68.9 cm

Gift of Mr. and Mrs. Archibald
Taylor
64.67

312

STANLEY WILLIAM HAYTER
British, born 1901

Untitled, 1960
oil on canvas
35¾ × 45⅜"
90.8 × 115.3 cm

Anonymous gift
69.20

WALLY HEDRICK
American, born 1928

Orb of Power, 1962
oil on canvas
83⅛ × 57½"
211.2 × 146.1 cm

Gift of Rena Bransten
78.70

WALLY HEDRICK
American, born 1928

Here's Art for 'em, 1963
oil on canvas
131¼ × 43½"
333.4 × 110.5 cm

Purchased with the aid of funds
from the National Endowment for
the Arts, the Soap Box Derby Fund,
and the New Future Fund Drive
77.16

AL HELD
American, born 1928

House of Cards, 1960
acrylic on canvas
114¼ × 253¼"
290.2 × 643.3 cm

Gift of Mrs. George Poindexter
69.87 A–C

JEAN HÉLION
French, born 1904

Figure in Space
(Figure d'espace), 1937
oil on canvas
52 × 38"
132.0 × 96.5 cm

Albert M. Bender Collection
Albert M. Bender Bequest Fund
Purchase
45.1633

GILBERT HENDERSON
American, born 1925

Machine World #1, 1949
oil on canvas
49 × 64"
124.5 × 162.6 cm

Gift of Mr. and Mrs. Herbert Rushing
69.25

MEL HENDERSON
American, born 1922

Untitled, 1960
wood
38⅛ × 19½ × 17¾"
96.8 × 49.5 × 45.1 cm

Gift of the Hamilton-Wells Collection
69.88

RICHARD HENNESSY
American, born 1941

Untitled, 1975
oil on canvas
31 × 30"
78.7 × 76.2 cm

Gift of Dr. and Mrs. Harold Joseph
76.201

GEORGE HERMS
American, born 1935

Michelangelo Box, 1964
wooden box with printed book-
binding, feather, razor blade, thread,
hair, paint, printed material, and
rope
open 1⅛ × 12¼ × 18″
2.9 × 31.1 × 45.7 cm

Gift of Dr. and Mrs. William R.
Fielder
76.103

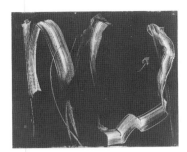

NANKOKU HIDAI
Japanese, born 1912

#57-3, 1957
oil on Masonite
20¾ × 25⅝″
52.7 × 65.1 cm

Gift of the artist
60.7419

CHARLES HILGER
American, born 1938

Aspect: Gesture, 1980
paper (vacuum formed) mounted on
board
68 × 52 × 4″
172.7 × 132.1 × 10.4 cm

Gift of Smith Andersen Gallery and
the artist in memory of Margaret K.
Walker
81.260

RANDAL HINZ
American, born 1944

Eclipse #7, 1971
acrylic on linen with Plexiglas
31¾ × 24¾″
80.6 × 62.9 cm

Gift of Mr. and Mrs. David Devine
78.2

JOSEPH HIRSCH
American, born 1910

Applause, n.d.
oil on canvas
27 × 30″
68.6 × 76.3 cm

WPA Federal Arts Project Allocation
to the San Francisco Museum of Art
3749.43

KARL HOFER
German, 1878–1955

Cardplayers, 1936
oil on canvas
28¾ × 35½″
73.1 × 90.2 cm

Albert M. Bender Collection
Gift of Albert M. Bender
37.2993

KARL HOFER
German, 1878–1955

Figure in the Night, 1950
oil on canvas
28 × 22⅛″
71.1 × 56.2 cm

Gift of Mrs. Walter A. Haas
56.211

HANS HOFMANN
American, born Germany, 1880–1966

Figure, 1949
gouache on matboard
17 × 14″
43.2 × 35.5 cm

Gift of the Hamilton-Wells Collection
76.189

HANS HOFMANN
American, born Germany, 1880–1966

Table—Version II, 1949
oil on canvas
48 × 36"
122.0 × 91.4 cm

Gift of Mr. and Mrs. William C.
Janss
78.203

See colorplate, p. 161

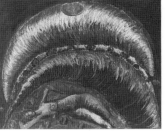

TOM HOLLAND
American, born 1936

Luv, 1963
oil on canvas
67⅜ × 54⅜"
171.1 × 138.8 cm

Gift of Dr. and Mrs. William R.
Fielder
76.184

TOM HOLLAND
American, born 1936

Leaf Place, 1964
oil on canvas
69 × 41⅜"
175.3 × 105.1 cm

Gift of Dr. and Mrs. William R.
Fielder
76.185

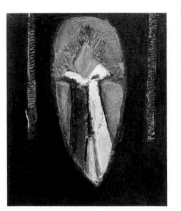

TOM HOLLAND
American, born 1936

Point Place, 1964
oil on canvas
31⅞ × 26½"
81.0 × 67.3 cm

Gift of Dr. and Mrs. William R.
Fielder
76.186

TOM HOLLAND
American, born 1936

Berkeley Series, 1969
epoxy on fiberglass
89¾ × 133½ × 3½"
228.0 × 339.1 × 8.9 cm

Gift of Dr. and Mrs. William R.
Fielder
76.183

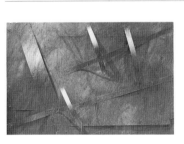

TOM HOLLAND
American, born 1936

Berkeley Series #108, 1970
epoxy on fiberglass
62¼ × 89¾ × 5¾"
158.1 × 228.0 × 14.6 cm

Gift of the Women's Board
70.57

TOM HOLLAND
American, born 1936

Lagle, 1973
epoxy on fiberglass
84½ × 132"
214.7 × 335.3 cm

Gift of Steven L. Robinson
73.41

ARTHUR HOLMAN
American, born 1926

Reflection, 1958
wax emulsion on canvas
66 × 66"
167.6 × 167.6 cm

Anonymous gift
77.195

315

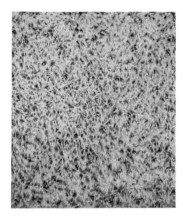

ARTHUR HOLMAN
American, born 1926

Summer, 1961
oil on canvas
78⅛ × 66″
198.4 × 167.6 cm

Gift of Mr. and Mrs. Moses Lasky
61.4513

BUDD HOPKINS
American, born 1931

Norbeck Yellow Vertical, 1969
oil on canvas
84 × 52″
213.4 × 132.1 cm

Gift of Leonard Bocour
69.48

CHARLES BENJAMIN HOPKINS
American, born 1882

Moonlight, n.d.
oil on canvas
28 × 39½″
71.1 × 100.4 cm

Gift of Templeton Crocker
43.5357

EDWARD HOPPER
American, 1882–1967

Bridle Path, 1939
oil on canvas
28⅜ × 42⅛″
72.1 × 107.0 cm

Anonymous gift
76.174

See colorplate, p. 129

DONAL HORD
American, 1902–1966

Seated Indian Woman, 1941
stone
14½ × 8½ × 9″
36.8 × 21.6 × 22.9 cm

WPA Federal Arts Project
Allocation to the San Francisco
Museum of Art
3771.43

PAUL HORIUCHI
American, born Japan 1906

Nobilities of Time, 1967
casein and rice paper on canvas
41½ × 34″
105.4 × 86.4 cm

Gift of Marjorie Gianelloni
69.112

CHARLES HOWARD
American, 1899–1978

First War Winter, 1939–40
oil on canvas
24¼ × 34″
61.7 × 86.4 cm

Purchase
40.5313

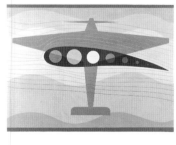

CHARLES HOWARD
American, 1899–1978

Abstraction in Flight, 1942
oil on canvas
72 × 96″
182.9 × 243.9 cm

WPA Federal Arts Project
Allocation to the San Francisco
Museum of Art
1034.43

ROBERT B. HOWARD
American, 1896–1983

Untitled, 1936
oil on panel
15¼ × 26¼"
38.7 × 66.7 cm

Albert M. Bender Collection
Gift of Albert M. Bender
36.6068

ROBERT B. HOWARD
American, 1896–1983

Semaphore, 1947
pear wood
44⅜ × 10⅛ × 13⅛"
112.7 × 25.7 × 33.3 cm

Gift of Mr. and Mrs. Brooks Walker
78.40

ROBERT B. HOWARD
American, 1896–1983

Multiple Compass, 1950
balsa, linen gauze, pigmented
adhesive, acrylic polymer, stainless
steel, and lead
70 × 81 × 81"
177.8 × 205.7 × 205.7 cm

Gift of Robert B. Howard
77.14

ROBERT B. HOWARD
American, 1896–1983

Ram, 1963
wood and plastic foam with glass
fibers and resin
80½ × 117½ × 41"
204.7 × 298.5 × 104.2 cm

Gift of Robert B. Howard
70.41 A–B

T. A. HOYER
American, born Denmark,
1872–1949

The Forest, ca. 1937
oil on canvas
29½ × 23¼"
74.9 × 59.1 cm

WPA Federal Arts Project
Allocation to the San Francisco
Museum of Art
3750.43

ROBERT HUDSON
American, born 1938

Untitled, ca. 1962
steel
22 × 12 × 7¾"
55.9 × 30.5 × 19.7 cm

Gift of Dr. Samuel A. West
64.2

ROBERT HUDSON
American, born 1938

Blue Peen Hammer, 1964
steel with enamel and lacquer
62½ × 55⅛ × 44"
158.7 × 140.3 × 111.8 cm

Gift of the Women's Board
64.69 A–B

ROBERT HUDSON
American, born 1938

Teapot, 1973
porcelain with underglazes and
china paint
8½ × 13¾ × 5⅜"
21.6 × 34.9 × 13.7 cm

William L. Gerstle Collection
William L. Gerstle Fund Purchase
73.49

ROBERT HUDSON
American, born 1938

Out of the Blue, 1980–81
acrylic on canvas with wooden
chair, plastic tree, wood, and steel
tubing
96⅜ × 180⅞ × 27¾"
244.8 × 459.4 × 70.5 cm

Purchased with the aid of the Byron
Meyer Fund
81.57 A–D

See colorplate, p. 233

ROBERT HUDSON
American, born 1938

Hot Water, 1982
steel with enamel, acrylic, and
metal teapot
91 × 36 × 53"
231.1 × 91.4 × 134.6 cm

Purchased with the aid of funds
from Rene di Rosa and an
anonymous donor
83.24 A–E

RALPH HUMPHREY
American, born 1932

Untitled, 1972
acrylic on canvas
60 × 60"
152.4 × 152.4 cm

Gift of Arthur A. Goldberg
77.2

BRYAN HUNT
American, born 1947

Daphne II, 1979
bronze
121 × 24 × 22"
307.3 × 61.0 × 55.9 cm

Purchased through a gift of Julian
and Jean Aberbach
81.2

PETER HUTTON
American

Untitled, 1969
Plexiglas box, stainless steel with
enamel, and polyvinyl chloride with
metal grommets
20¼ × 12 × 5½"
51.4 × 30.3 × 14.0 cm

Gift of Dr. and Mrs. William R.
Fielder
75.169 A–B

ROBERT INDIANA
American, born 1928

The Fair Rebecca, 1961
oil on canvas
41 × 39"
104.2 × 99.1 cm

Purchase
69.56

GENICHIRO INOKUMA
Japanese, born 1902

Wall Street, 1964
oil on canvas
80¼ × 70⅛"
203.8 × 178.1 cm

Gift of Madeleine Haas Russell
65.16

DAVID IRELAND
American, born 1930

South China Chairs, 1979
oil on Pelembang cane
43 × 50 × 45½"
109.2 × 127.0 × 115.6 cm

Gift of Agnes C. and William C.
Bourne
82.383.1–2

ROBERT IRWIN
American, born 1928

The Four Blues, 1961
oil on canvas
65⅜ × 65⅛"
166.7 × 165.4 cm

Purchased with the aid of a gift of
Rena Bransten
83.141

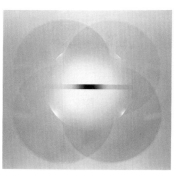

ROBERT IRWIN
American, born 1928

Untitled, 1968
acrylic lacquer on Plexiglas
53¼ diam. × 24½"
135.5 × 62.3 cm

T. B. Walker Foundation Fund
Purchase
70.5 A–F

See colorplate, p. 213

DAVID IZU
American, born 1951

Beacon, 1983
from the Ash not to Ash Series
acrylic, monofilament, and charcoal on canvas
76 × 52"
193.0 × 132.1 cm

Gift of Dr. William C. Sawyer
83.231

OLIVER JACKSON
American, born 1935

Untitled No. 7, 1978
oil enamel on canvas
81½ × 108¼"
207.0 × 275.0 cm

William L. Gerstle Collection
William L. Gerstle Fund Purchase
83.1

RODGER JACOBSEN
American, born 1939

Untitled, 1964
steel
68⅛ × 149½ × 36½"
173.0 × 379.7 × 92.7 cm

Gift of the Women's Board
66.1 A–B

SHIRLEY JAFFE
American, born 1923

Untitled, 1970
acrylic on canvas
63¾ × 51⅛"
161.9 × 129.9 cm

Gift of Sam Francis
75.143

ALEXEJ JAWLENSKY
Russian, 1864–1941

Woman's Head (Frauenkopf), 1913
oil on composition board
21¼ × 19½"
54.0 × 49.5 cm

Gift of Charlotte Mack
50.5518

See colorplate, p. 74

ALEXEJ JAWLENSKY
Russian, 1864–1941

*Head: Red Light
(Kopf: Rotes Licht)*, 1926
oil wax medium on cardboard
21 × 19"
53.4 × 48.3 cm

Gift of Charlotte Mack
50.5952

See colorplate, p. 75

319

JACK JEFFERSON
American, born 1921

Untitled, 1952
oil on canvas
48⅛ × 38⅛″
122.2 × 96.8 cm

Gift of Angela and Robin Kinkead
76.101

JACK JEFFERSON
American, born 1921

Embarcadero #3, 1963
oil on canvas
63⅞ × 72⅝″
162.2 × 184.3 cm

Gift of David B. Devine and Charles
Strong
81.198

PAUL JENKINS
American, born 1923

Untitled, 1960
acrylic on canvas
76¾ × 51½″
195.0 × 130.8 cm

Gift of Sam Francis
75.142

PAUL JENKINS
American, born 1923

*Phenomenon with Inviolate
Cadmium Red*, 1965
oil on canvas
40 × 50⅛″
101.6 × 127.3 cm

Gift of Joseph M. Bransten
68.1

ALFRED JENSEN
American, 1903–1981

Expulsion from Eden, 1958
oil on canvas
75½ × 40″
191.8 × 101.6 cm

Purchased with the aid of funds
from the National Endowment for
the Arts, Friends of the Museum,
and the Helen Crocker Russell
Memorial Fund
74.14

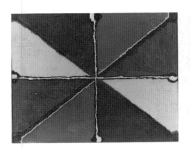

ALFRED JENSEN
American, 1903–1981

Emblematic Coloration, 1959
oil on canvas
36¼ × 46¼″
92.0 × 117.5 cm

Gift of Sam Francis
75.144

ALFRED JENSEN
American, 1903–1981

*Coordinative Thinking on the
Square and Rectangle; Per, IV.*
1974
oil and felt-tip pen ink on board
30 × 22″
76.2 × 55.9 cm

Gift of Sam Francis
78.187

JASPER JOHNS
American, born 1930

Flag, 1960–69
lead 47/60
16⅞ × 23 × 1¼″
42.8 × 58.4 × 3.1 cm

Gift of Mr. and Mrs. William
C. Janss
78.198

JASPER JOHNS
American, born 1930

Land's End, 1963
oil on canvas with stick
67 × 48¼"
170.2 × 122.6 cm

Gift of Mr. and Mrs. Harry W.
Anderson
72.23

See colorplate, p. 197

JASPER JOHNS
American, born 1930

The Critic Smiles, 1969
lead with gold and tin 46/60
22⅞ × 16¾ × 1¼"
58.1 × 42.5 × 3.1 cm

Gift of Mr. and Mrs. William C.
Janss `
81.229

JASPER JOHNS
American, born 1930

Light Bulb, 1969
lead 3/60
38⅞ × 17 × 1¼"
98.9 × 43.2 × 3.1 cm

Gift of Mr. and Mrs. William C.
Janss
78.199

BUFFIE JOHNSON
American, born 1912

Ritual Dance, 1958
oil on canvas
34 × 29⅞"
86.4 × 75.9 cm

Gift of Jacob Zeitlin
82.158

DANIEL LA RUE JOHNSON
American, born 1938

Untitled, 1961
wood with doll's head and enamel
8 × 6½ × 3¼"
20.3 × 16.5 × 8.3 cm

Gift of Diana Zlotnick
81.230

DANIEL LA RUE JOHNSON
American, born 1938

Untitled, 1961
wood and clay with enamel
7¼ × 5½ × 6"
18.4 × 14.0 × 15.2 cm

Gift of Diana Zlotnick
81.231

SARGENT JOHNSON
American, 1888–1967

Elizabeth Gee, 1927
stoneware with glaze
13⅛ × 10¾ × 7½"
33.3 × 27.3 × 19.1 cm

Albert M. Bender Collection
Gift of Albert M. Bender
37.3093

SARGENT JOHNSON
American, 1888–1967

Chester, 1931
terra-cotta
10⅞ × 6¾ × 6⅜"
27.6 × 17.1 × 16.2 cm

Albert M. Bender Collection
Bequest of Albert M. Bender
41.2978

SARGENT JOHNSON
American, 1888–1967

Forever Free, 1933
wood with lacquer on cloth
36 × 11½ × 9½"
91.5 × 29.2 × 24.2 cm

Gift of Mrs. E.D. Lederman
52.4695

SARGENT JOHNSON
American, 1888–1967

Mask, 1933
copper
10⅞ × 7⅞ × 2⅜"
27.6 × 20.0 × 6.0 cm

Albert M. Bender Collection
Gift of Albert M. Bender
35.3436

SARGENT JOHNSON
American, 1888–1967

Negro Woman, 1933
terra-cotta
9¼ × 5 × 6"
23.5 × 12.7 × 15.2 cm

Albert M. Bender Collection
Bequest of Albert M. Bender
41.2979

SARGENT JOHNSON
American, 1888–1967

Head of a Negro Woman
ca. 1935
terra-cotta
7⅜ × 4½ × 5¼"
18.8 × 11.4 × 13.3 cm

Albert M. Bender Collection
Gift of Albert M. Bender
35.3439

SARGENT JOHNSON
American, 1888–1967

Negro Woman, n.d.
wood with lacquer on cloth
32 × 13½ × 11¾"
81.3 × 34.3 × 29.8 cm

Albert M. Bender Collection
Gift of Albert M. Bender
36.6207

SARGENT JOHNSON
American, 1888–1967

Woman's Head, n.d.
stone
14½ × 7½ × 10⅛"
36.8 × 19.1 × 25.7 cm

Albert M. Bender Collection
Bequest of Albert M. Bender
41.2981

DAVID JONES
American, born 1948

Untitled, 1974
latex and cheese cloth
96 × 192"
243.8 × 487.7 cm

Acquired through an anonymous
gift and the Members' Accessions
Fund
74.79

RAYMOND JONSON
American, 1891–1982

Growth Variant No. VII, 1931
oil on canvas
34⅛ × 30⅝"
86.7 × 77.8 cm

Purchase
79.293

RICHARD JOSEPH
American, born 1939

Drawing Table, 1968
oil on canvas
60⅛ × 60⅛″
152.7 × 152.7 cm

Gift of Dr. and Mrs. Francis
L'Esperance
76.257

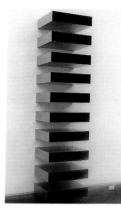

DONALD JUDD
American, born 1928

Untitled, 1973
stainless steel with oil enamel on
Plexiglas
114 × 27 × 24″
289.6 × 68.6 × 61.0 cm

Purchased with the aid of funds
from the National Endowment for
the Arts and Friends of the Museum
74.15 A–J

FRIDA (FRIEDA) KAHLO
Mexican, 1910–1954

Frieda and Diego Rivera, 1931
oil on canvas
39⅜ × 31″
100.0 × 78.7 cm

Albert M. Bender Collection
Gift of Albert M. Bender
36.6061

See colorplate, p. 139

EDITH KALLMAN
American

And On and On #5, 1977
ink on canvas
72 × 71¾″
182.9 × 182.3 cm

Gift of the artist
80.189

STEVEN KALTENBACH
American, born 1940

Untitled, ca. 1965
stoneware with glaze
6 × 4⅞ × 3½″
15.2 × 12.4 × 8.9 cm

Gift of Dr. and Mrs. William R.
Fielder
75.172

STEVEN KALTENBACH
American, born 1940

Untitled, ca. 1965
stoneware with glaze
6 × 5 × 3⅝″
15.2 × 12.7 × 9.2 cm

Gift of Dr. and Mrs. William R.
Fielder
75.173

STEVEN KALTENBACH
American, born 1940

Untitled, ca. 1965
earthenware with glaze
5 × 3⅞ × 3″
12.7 × 9.8 × 7.6 cm

Gift of Dr. and Mrs. William R.
Fielder
75.171

STEVEN KALTENBACH
American, born 1940

Untitled, ca. 1965
earthenware with glaze
9½ × 4 × 4″
24.1 × 10.2 × 10.2 cm

Gift of Dr. and Mrs. William R.
Fielder
75.170

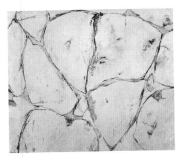

VASILY KANDINSKY
French, born Russia, 1866–1944

Brownish (Bräunlich), 1931
oil on cardboard
19⅜ × 27⅝"
49.2 × 70.2 cm

William L. Gerstle Collection
Gift of William L. Gerstle
45.100

See colorplate, p. 89

MATSUMI KANEMITSU
American, born 1922

White Spider, 1960
oil on canvas
72 × 84"
182.9 × 213.4 cm

Gift of Jules Horelick
70.18

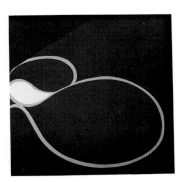

MATSUMI KANEMITSU
American, born 1922

Queen of the Bay, 1966
liquitex on canvas
66 × 66"
167.6 × 167.6 cm

Gift of Shizumi Patia Kanemitsu
67.18

MARC KATANO
American, born 1952

Sleeper, 1982
oil on canvas
56 × 79"
142.3 × 200.7 cm

Gift of Dr. William A. Henkin
83.142

CRAIG KAUFFMAN
American, born 1932

Untitled, 1960
oil on linen mounted on board
19⅛ × 24"
48.6 × 61.0 cm

Gift of Mr. and Mrs. L. James
Newman
72.61

CRAIG KAUFFMAN
American, born 1932

Untitled, 1968–69
acrylic lacquer on Plexiglas
45 × 88½ × 15½"
114.3 × 224.8 × 39.4 cm

Purchased with the aid of a gift of
Rena Bransten and the Doris and
Donald Fisher Purchase Fund
83.25

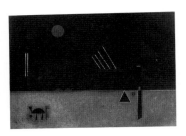

CRAIG KAUFFMAN
American, born 1932

Amarillo #4, 1979
acrylic and rag paper on silk
88 × 54¾"
223.5 × 139.1 cm

Clinton Walker Fund Purchase
80.165

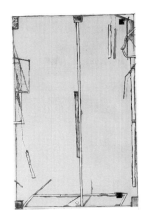

DONALD KAUFMAN
American, born 1935

Town Line, 1969
acrylic on canvas
115½ × 91"
293.4 × 231.1 cm

Purchase
70.39

DONALD KAUFMAN
American, born 1935

Sixth, 1970
acrylic on canvas
55 × 65⅛″
139.7 × 165.4 cm

Gift of Mr. and Mrs. Richard L.
Feigen
74.71

ELLSWORTH KELLY
American, born 1923

Red White, 1962
oil on canvas
80⅛ × 90″
203.5 × 228.6 cm

T. B. Walker Foundation Fund
Purchase
66.3

See colorplate, p. 219

JAMES KELLY
American, born 1913

Untitled, 1951
oil and tacks on canvas
31 × 25⅞″
78.7 × 65.7 cm

Gift of Mr. and Mrs. William M.
Roth
73.20

JAMES KELLY
American, born 1913

Assault on K-2, 1956
oil on canvas
84 × 66″
213.4 × 167.6 cm

Gift of Gump's, Inc.
58.1914

ADALINE KENT
American, 1900–1957

Figure Composition, 1925
plaster
19⅝ × 8⅞ × 7⅞″
49.8 × 22.5 × 20.0 cm

William L. Gerstle Collection
Gift of William L. Gerstle
46.4225

ADALINE KENT
American, 1900–1957

Dark Mountain, 1945
hydrocal
33¾ × 12½ × 8″
85.9 × 31.8 × 20.3 cm

Purchase
45.2109

ADALINE KENT
American, 1900–1957

Presence, 1947
magnesite
42¾ × 17¾ × 7¼″
108.6 × 45.0 × 18.4 cm

Gift of the Women's Board and the
Membership Activities Board
57.3736

ADALINE KENT
American, 1900–1957

Figment, 1953
bronze
64½ × 9½″ diam.
163.9 × 24.1 cm

Gift of Robert B. Howard
in honor of Grace L. McCann Morley
67.10

ADALINE KENT
American, 1900–1957

Muse, n.d.
bronze
9⅞ × 3⅝ × 4⅜″
25.0 × 9.2 × 11.1 cm

Gift of Raymond Larsson
37.3020

ADALINE KENT
American, 1900–1957

Young Woman, n.d.
bronze
27⅜ × 11⅜ × 6⅞″
69.5 × 28.9 × 17.5 cm

Albert M. Bender Collection
Gift of Albert M. Bender
36.6069

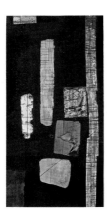

GYORGY KEPES
American, born 1906

The City, 1949–50
oil, sand, and paper on canvas
72 × 36⅛″
182.9 × 91.8 cm

Anonymous gift
59.1679

EARL KERKAM
American, 1891–1965

*Composition with Forms of
the Head*, 1960–61
oil on canvasboard
26 × 19″
66.0 × 48.3 cm

Gift of E. Bruce Kirk
69.90

LESLIE KERR
American, born 1934

Talisman II, 1961
oil on canvas
84⅛ × 68⅛″
213.7 × 173.0 cm

William L. Gerstle Collection
William L. Gerstle Fund Purchase
64.51

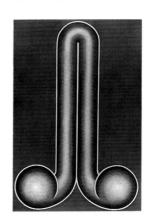

LESLIE KERR
American, born 1934

Pretty Baby, 1963
oil on canvas
50 × 33″
127.0 × 83.8 cm

Gift of John Bransten
81.241

EDWARD KIENHOLZ
American, born 1927

*The Bluebird of Happiness
Returns as a Bleached Blonde*
1957
oil, metal, and fiber on wood
24⅞ × 48 × 1¾″
63.2 × 121.9 × 4.5 cm

Gift of Peter Voulkos
83.232

EDWARD KIENHOLZ
American, born 1927

*Tomorrow's Leaders Are Busy
Tonight*, 1961
wooden box containing doll, skull,
glass, paint, wood, tape, fabric,
and paper; pedestal: wood with
paint and staples, pencil, tape,
and nails
65⅜ × 10¾ × 10″
166.1 × 27.3 × 25.4 cm

Gift of Betty and Monte Factor
81.232

EDWARD KIENHOLZ
American, born 1927

The Billionaire Deluxe, 1977
aluminum can with Fresnel lens
system, light bulb, and electronic
second counter 33/56
10⅜ × 15¼ × 14⅝"
26.4 × 38.7 × 37.1 cm

Purchase
77.187

KIM WHANKI
Korean, 1913–1974

26-I-70, 1970
oil on canvas
70¼ × 49⅞"
178.4 × 126.7 cm

Gift of Mrs. Whanki Kim
79.127

ERNST LUDWIG KIRCHNER
German, 1880–1938

Winter in Davos, ca. 1921–23
oil on canvas
31½ × 35½"
80.0 × 90.2 cm

Gift of Milton T. Pflueger and
friends in memory of Timothy L.
Pflueger
57.4405

JEROME KIRK
American, born 1923

Broken Circle, 1972
aluminum and stainless steel with
synthetic resin and enamel
56½ × 34 × 10¼"
143.5 × 86.4 × 26.0 cm

Gift of Mr. and Mrs. William C.
Janss
78.209

PAUL KLEE
Swiss, 1879–1940

Red Suburb
(Rotes Villenquartier), 1920
oil on cardboard
14⅜ × 12½"
36.5 × 31.8 cm

Purchase
51.3207

See colorplate, p. 99

PAUL KLEE
Swiss, 1879–1940

Nearly Hit (Fast getroffen), 1928
oil on board
20 × 15½"
50.8 × 39.4 cm

Albert M. Bender Collection
Albert M. Bender Bequest Fund
Purchase
44.2640

See colorplate, p. 101

PAUL KLEE
Swiss, 1879–1940

Fragments (Fragmente), 1937
oil on canvas
21¾ × 28"
55.2 × 71.1 cm

Gift of Wilbur D. May
64.5

FRANZ KLINE
American, 1910–1962

Untitled, ca. 1955
oil and gouache on board
30¼ × 17¼"
76.8 × 43.8 cm

Gift of Mr. and Mrs. L. James
Newman
72.64

FRANZ KLINE
American, 1910–1962

Study for "Andrus," 1961
paper and paint on paper
7⅝ × 12⅝"
19.4 × 32.1 cm

Anonymous gift through the
American Art Foundation
78.285

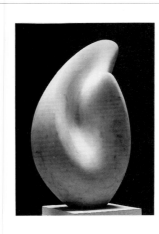

GUITOU KNOOP
French, born Russia 1909

Méditerranée No. 1, ca. 1950
marble
35½ × 25⅝ × 15⅞"
90.2 × 65.1 × 40.3 cm

Gift of Mr. and Mrs. H. G. Doll and
Pierre David-Weill
52.4168

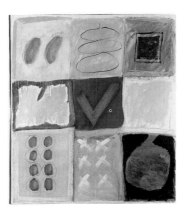

IDA KOHLMEYER
American, born 1912

Circus Series #2, 1978
acrylic, crayon, and canvas on canvas
73½ × 63¼"
186.7 × 160.7 cm

Gift of Dr. William C. Sawyer
80.424

PAUL KOS
American, born 1942

MARLENE KOS
American, born 1942

Tokyo Rose, 1975–76
aluminum screen and framing, tele-
vision monitor, and video tape
120 × 124 × 304"
304.8 × 315.0 × 772.2 cm

Purchased with the aid of the
T. B. Walker Foundation Fund
76.45 A–CCC

HARRY KRAMER
German, born 1925

Treestump Q 6, 1966
wood, wire, enamel, light bulb,
metal hook, and light reflector
31½ × 15½ × 10"
80.0 × 39.4 × 25.4 cm

Gift of Alfred E. Heller
75.1

PETER KRASNOW
American, born Russia, 1890–1979

Atlantis, ca. 1927
bronze
16½ × 3⅞ × 4¼"
41.9 × 9.8 × 10.8 cm

Albert M. Bender Collection
Gift of Albert M. Bender
36.4460

PETER KRASNOW
American, born Russia, 1890–1979

Untitled, 1940–45
walnut
81 × 16 × 20½"
205.7 × 40.6 × 52.1 cm

Gift of the artist
77.92 A–G

PETER KRASNOW
American, born Russia, 1890–1979

K-1, 1944
oil on board
48 × 36"
121.9 × 91.5 cm

Gift of the artist
77.93

328

PETER KRASNOW
American, born Russia, 1890–1979

K-3, 1953–62
oil on board
47¾ × 67″
121.3 × 170.2 cm

Gift of the artist
77.94

LEON KROLL
American, 1884–1974

Study for "Summer, New York"
n.d.
oil on canvas mounted on board
20¼ × 24¾″
51.4 × 62.9 cm

Albert M. Bender Collection
Gift of Albert M. Bender
38.218

LUCIAN KRUKOWSKI
American, born 1929

Wednesday Afternoon, 1959
oil on canvas
73⅝ × 73¾″
187.0 × 187.4 cm

Gift of the Staempfli Gallery,
New York
76.27

WALTER KUHLMAN
American, born 1918

No. 5-1955, 1955
oil on canvas
60 × 42½″
152.4 × 108.0 cm

Gift of the Women's Board
56.901

LUCIEN LABAUDT
American, born France, 1880–1943

Composition, 1927
oil on cardboard
34 × 42¾″
86.4 × 108.6 cm

Gift of the artist
35.1154

LUCIEN LABAUDT
American, born France, 1880–1943

Still Life, 1927
oil on cardboard
16¼ × 21¾″
41.3 × 55.3 cm

Albert M. Bender Collection
Gift of Albert M. Bender
36.5394

LUCIEN LABAUDT
American, born France, 1880–1943

On the Road to Half Moon Bay
1931
oil on panel
26¼ × 32¼″
66.6 × 81.9 cm

William L. Gerstle Collection
Gift of William L. Gerstle
41.3099

LUCIEN LABAUDT
American, born France, 1880–1943

After the Swim, 1932
oil on canvas
38 × 14⅛″
96.5 × 35.9 cm

Albert M. Bender Collection
Gift of Albert M. Bender
37.1908

LUCIEN LABAUDT
American, born France, 1880–1943

Sister of Mercy, 1932
oil on cardboard
16 × 12⅛"
40.6 × 30.8 cm

Albert M. Bender Collection
Gift of Albert M. Bender
40.7258

LUCIEN LABAUDT
American, born France, 1880–1943

At the Creek, 1933
oil on canvas
25⅛ × 20¼"
63.8 × 51.4 cm

Albert M. Bender Collection
Gift of Albert M. Bender
35.5263

LUCIEN LABAUDT
American, born France, 1880–1943

Wading, 1935
oil on canvas
30⅛ × 23⅝"
76.5 × 60.0 cm

Gift of Mr. and Mrs. Ansley K. Salz
52.5070

LUCIEN LABAUDT
American, born France, 1880–1943

Nude, n.d.
oil on Masonite
25 × 35"
63.5 × 88.9 cm

Albert M. Bender Collection
Gift of Albert M. Bender
37.2980

GASTON LACHAISE
American, born France, 1882–1935

Floating Nude Figure, 1924
bronze 5/6
12¾ × 17¾ × 6½"
32.4 × 45.1 × 16.5 cm

Gift of the Women's Board in honor
of its founding president, Helen
Crocker Russell
67.49

PETER LANYON
British, 1918–1964

Bird Wind, 1955
oil on canvasboard
43¾ × 36⅝"
111.1 × 93.1 cm

Gift of Mr. and Mrs. William M. Roth
80.425

BERTO LARDERA
Italian, born 1911

Archangel II
(formerly *Fallen Angel*), 1953–54
copper and iron with enamel
30 × 22 × 20½"
76.2 × 55.9 × 52.1 cm

Purchase
56.3046

HENRI LAURENS
French, 1885–1954

Undines, 1932
bronze 4/6
7½ × 15½ × 4¾"
19.0 × 39.3 × 12.0 cm

W. W. Crocker Memorial Fund
Purchase
65.23

CARLA LAVATELLI
American, born Italy 1929

Stele for a Prayer, 1971–72
slate and marble
82⅝ × 6¾ × 4⅛"
209.8 × 17.1 × 10.5 cm

Gift of Carlo Herrmann
81.115

FERNAND LÉGER
French, 1881–1955

Still Life (Nature morte), 1943
oil on canvasboard
24 × 19¾"
61.0 × 50.2 cm

Albert M. Bender Collection
Albert M. Bender Bequest Fund
Purchase
46.5174

FERNAND LÉGER
French, 1881–1955

Two Women, 1950–52
bronze 1/8
17⅞ × 14¼ × 2⅞"
45.4 × 36.1 × 7.2 cm

Gift of Mr. and Mrs. William C.
Janss
78.207

LEMMY
Malaysian, born 1940

Auras Gamma X S, 1970
polyester resin on acrylic
32¾ × 37½"
83.2 × 95.3 cm

Gift of Mrs. Edgar Sinton
71.17

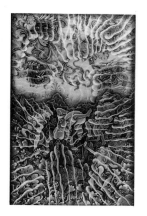

S. DEWA NJOMAN LEPER
Balinese

*Karna, Scenes from Barata
Juda*, n.d.
gouache on canvas
43⅛ × 27⅝"
109.6 × 70.2 cm

Gift of Mr. and Mrs. Leon Russell
57.4406

ALFRED LESLIE
American, born 1927

The Blue Rectangle, 1959–61
oil on canvas
60¼ × 66⅛"
153.1 × 168.0 cm

Gift of Mr. and Mrs. William C.
Janss
78.197

JACK LEVINE
American, born 1915

Nighttown Scene, 1936
oil on panel
48 × 24"
121.9 × 61.0 cm

WPA Federal Arts Project Allocation
to the San Francisco Museum of Art
3752.43

MARILYN LEVINE
Canadian, born 1935

Black Briefcase, 1980
stoneware, epoxy, nylon, oil, and
aluminum
13¼ × 16¾ × 6¾"
33.7 × 42.5 × 17.1 cm

Purchased with the aid of funds
from the National Endowment for the
Arts and the Soap Box Derby Fund
80.173

ISADORE LEVY
American, born 1899

Painting #1, 1969
oil on canvas
28⅜ × 39½"
72.1 × 100.3 cm

Anonymous gift
69.113

EDMUND LEWANDOWSKI
American, born 1914

The Silo, n.d.
oil on canvas
25⅛ × 20⅛"
63.8 × 51.1 cm

Helen Crocker Russell Memorial
Fund Purchase
75.108

TOM E. LEWIS
American, born 1909

Delphiniums, 1937
oil on canvas
30⅛ × 25⅛"
76.5 × 63.8 cm

William L. Gerstle Collection
Gift of William L. Gerstle
41.3100

TOM E. LEWIS
American, born 1909

Reclamation, ca. 1938
oil on canvas
30 × 36"
76.2 × 91.4 cm

San Francisco Museum of Art
Purchase Prize, *Fifty-ninth Annual
Exhibition of the San Francisco Art
Association*
39.45

SOL LeWITT
American, born 1928

Steel Structure
(formerly **Untitled**), 1975/1976
aluminum tubing with baking
enamel
120 × 120 × 120"
304.8 × 304.8 × 304.8 cm

T. B. Walker Foundation Fund
Purchase
76.21 A–Y

ANDRÉ LHOTE
French, 1885–1962

*Port of Bordeaux
(Port de Bordeaux)*, n.d.
oil on canvas
20⅛ × 30"
51.1 × 76.2 cm

Gift
37.2989

TOM LIEBER
American, born 1949

Spats, 1981
acrylic on canvas
76½ × 87¾"
194.3 × 222.9 cm

Gift of Kirk deGooyer
83.113

ALVIN LIGHT
American, 1931–1980

November 1964, 1964
wood with pigmented epoxy
98⅜ × 59 × 61⅛"
249.8 × 149.8 × 155.2 cm

Gift of the Women's Board
69.107

332

JUDITH LINHARES
American, born 1940

Swan Song, 1970
plywood, resin, Plexiglas, fluorescent light fixture, satin, velvet, rayon, feathers, rhinestones, and wax
30 × 17⅛ × 17″
76.2 × 43.5 × 43.2 cm

Purchased with the aid of funds from the National Endowment for the Arts, the Soap Box Derby Fund, and the New Future Fund Drive
77.84

JUDITH LINHARES
American, born 1940

Cat, 1978
oil on canvas
70 × 70″
177.8 × 177.8 cm

Gift of Philip Anglim
81.242

JACQUES LIPCHITZ
French, born Lithuania, 1891–1973

Draped Woman, 1919
bronze 3/7
36¾ × 12⅝ × 13¼″
93.3 × 32.0 × 33.6 cm

Gift of Mr. and Mrs. Wellington S. Henderson
63.4

See colorplate, p. 51

MARVIN LIPOFSKY
American, born 1938

Blue Glass/Lacquered/Sandblasted/Wooden Frame/Formica, 1966
glass with lacquer
17¾ × 11 × 4⅛″
45.1 × 27.9 × 10.5 cm

Gift of Madeleine Haas Russell
68.68

PAT LIPSKY
American, born 1941

Orange Top, 1970
acrylic on canvas
96⅛ × 113⅝″
244.3 × 288.6 cm

Gift of Anne and Peter Bienstock
74.95

FRANK LOBDELL
American, born 1921

March 1954, 1954
oil on canvas
69½ × 65½″
176.6 × 166.4 cm

Anonymous gift
76.197

See colorplate, p. 191

FRANK LOBDELL
American, born 1921

April 1959, 1959
oil on canvas
70⅞ × 74¼″
180.0 × 188.6 cm

Gift of the Women's Board
59.2670

FRANK LOBDELL
American, born 1921

Summer 1965, 1965
oil on canvas
83⅜ × 69″
211.8 × 175.3 cm

Partial gift of Mary and Frank Keesling in honor of John Humphrey
79.427

FRANK LOBDELL
American, born 1921

Fall 1968, Dedicated to the Memory of Martha Jackson, 1968
oil on canvas
79⅝ × 121″
202.3 × 307.3 cm

Gift of the Hamilton-Wells Collection
83.104

ROBERT LOBERG
American, born 1927

The Smasher, 1962
oil and paper on panel
72⅛ × 89⅝″
183.2 × 227.7 cm

Gift of David Stuart
69.39

SEYMOUR LOCKS
American, born 1919

Vertigo Landscape, ca. 1957–58
wood, copper, brass, iron nails, tin, aluminum, paint, wire, and plaster
58 × 13¾ × 8¼″
147.3 × 35.0 × 21.0 cm

Anonymous gift through the American Federation of Arts
61.4486

WARD LOCKWOOD
American, 1894–1963

Scintillation, 1959
acrylic on canvas
45 × 65″
114.3 × 165.1 cm

Bequest of Clyde Bonebrake Lockwood
71.55

ERLE LORAN
American, born 1903

Mountain Village, 1945
oil on board
19⅝ × 28″
49.8 × 71.1 cm

Lloyd S. Ackerman, Jr. Memorial Fund Purchase
46.98

HARRY LOUIE
American, born 1947

No. 2-1980, 1980
oil on canvas
37⅝ × 100″
93.0 × 254.0 cm

Gift of Lenore M. Louie
81.243

MORRIS LOUIS
American, 1912–1962

Ambi I (2-22), 1959–60
acrylic on canvas
94⅞ × 137¾″
241.0 × 349.9 cm

Gift of Sally Lilienthal
74.21

BORIS LOVET-LORSKI
American, born Lithuania, 1894–1973

Adolescence, 1929
brass 1/1
36¼ × 13 × 11″
92.1 × 33.0 × 28.0 cm

Gift of Maud Hill Schroll
67.60

334

HELEN LUNDEBERG
American, born 1908

Artist, Flowers, and Hemispheres, 1934
oil on Celotex
24 × 30″
61.0 × 76.2 cm

Gift of Helen Klokke
37.89

LOREN MacIVER
American, born 1909

Four O'Clock, New York
ca. 1936–38
oil on canvas
35⅝ × 23½″
90.5 × 59.7 cm

WPA Federal Arts Project
Allocation to the San Francisco
Museum of Art
3754.43

ROBERT McCHESNEY
American, born 1913

Arena #75, 1962
from the Arena Series
enamel, sisal, and sand on canvas
72¼ × 99″
183.5 × 251.5 cm

Gift of Suzanne and Neil Russack
78.137

JOHN McCRACKEN
American, born 1934

Right Down, 1967
fiberglass and polyester resin
on wood
84 × 46¼ × 2¾″
213.4 × 117.3 × 7.0 cm

Anonymous gift
74.114

JOHN McCRADY
American, 1911–1968

Returning Home, ca. 1937
oil on canvas
22 × 43⅞″
56.0 × 111.5 cm

WPA Federal Arts Project
Allocation to the San Francisco
Museum of Art
3755.43

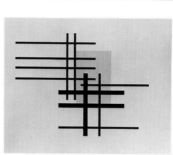

JOHN McLAUGHLIN
American, 1898–1976

Untitled, 1951
oil on Masonite
31⅞ × 38″
81.0 × 96.5 cm

T. B. Walker Foundation Fund
Purchase
77.71

JOHN McLAUGHLIN
American, 1898–1976

#6, 1959
oil on canvas
43⅞ × 60¼″
111.4 × 153.0 cm

T. B. Walker Foundation Fund
Purchase
77.72

JERRY McMILLAN
American, born 1936

Untitled Chrome Bag, 1970
chrome on copper foil
8⅛ × 4⅛ × 2⅝″
20.6 × 10.5 × 6.7 cm

Purchase
71.40

ARISTIDE MAILLOL
French, 1861–1944

Kneeling Girl without Arms
(La Jeune Fille agenouillée
sans bras), 1900
bronze 1/2
33⅜ × 16½ × 21⅞″
84.7 × 41.9 × 55.5 cm

Gift of Hans G. M. de Schulthess
and Amalia Loew de Schulthess in
memory of Alexandre Rabow
65.7

ARISTIDE MAILLOL
French, 1861–1944

Pomona Clothed
(Pomona vêtue), 1921
bronze
35 × 11⅛ × 6⅝″
88.9 × 28.3 × 16.8 cm

Gift of Mr. and Mrs. William C.
Janss
78.205

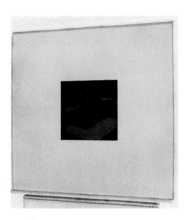

RONALD MALLORY
American, born 1935

Untitled, 1965
Plexiglas, mercury, and electrical
apparatus
14⅝ × 14⅝ × 4¾″
37.2 × 37.2 × 12.1 cm

Gift of Paul Jenkins
69.40

RONALD MALLORY
American, born 1935

Untitled, 1966
Plexiglas, mercury, and electrical
apparatus
12¾ × 12¾ × 5⅝″
32.4 × 32.4 × 14.3 cm

Gift of Paul Jenkins
69.41

RONALD MALLORY
American, born 1935

Mercury Sphere, 1969
acrylic resin and mercury
9⅛″ diam.
23.2 cm

Gift of Mr. and Mrs. Louis Honig
76.192

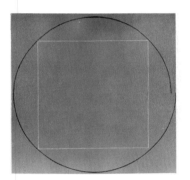

ROBERT MANGOLD
American, born 1935

Untitled, 1974
acrylic on canvas
24¼ × 24¼″
61.7 × 61.7 cm

Gift of Joy E. Feinberg, Berkeley
81.107

ROBERT MANGOLD
American, born 1935

Red X within X, 1980
acrylic and graphite on canvas
113½ × 113½″
288.3 × 288.3 cm

T. B. Walker Foundation Fund
Purchase
83.149 A–D

See colorplate, p. 221

HENRI MANGUIN
French, 1874–1949

Nude beneath the Trees
(Nu sous les arbres) (study), 1905
oil on canvasboard
12¾ × 16″
32.4 × 40.7 cm

Bequest of Harriet Lane Levy
50.6082

GIACOMO MANZÙ
Italian, born 1908

David, n.d.
bronze
15¼ × 16 × 15¼"
38.7 × 40.7 × 38.7 cm

Anonymous gift
73.34

FRANZ MARC
German, 1880–1916

*Mountains (Rocky Way/
Landscape) (Gebirge [Steiniger
Weg/Landschaft])*, 1911–12
oil on canvas
51½ × 39¾"
130.8 × 101.0 cm

Gift of the Women's Board and
Friends of the Museum
51.4095

See colorplate, p. 69

CORRADO MARCA-RELLI
American, born 1913

Seated Figure, 1955–56
oil and canvas on Masonite
25½ × 19"
64.8 × 48.3 cm

Gift of Mr. and Mrs. William M.
Roth
79.126

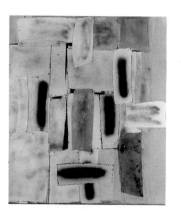

CORRADO MARCA-RELLI
American, born 1913

December 27, 1959
oil and canvas on canvas
71¾ × 60"
182.3 × 152.4 cm

T. B. Walker Foundation Fund
Purchase
62.21

MARCEL MARIEN
Belgian, born 1920

*The Painter's Hope
(L'Espoir du peintre)*, 1975
twigs and feathers on paper
14⅛ × 10⅝"
35.9 × 27.0 cm

Members' Accessions Fund
Purchase
83.66

HERMAN MARIL
American, born 1908

White Sand, 1969
oil on canvas
36¼ × 48⅛"
92.2 × 122.2 cm

Gift of Jules Horelick
70.19

JOHN MARIN
American, 1870–1953

The Sea—Cape Split, Maine
1938
oil on canvas
23¼ × 30¼"
59.1 × 76.8 cm

Gift of Mrs. Henry Potter Russell
55.5192

MARINO MARINI
Italian, 1901–1980

Head of Stravinsky, 1950
bronze
9 × 7 × 8¾"
22.8 × 17.7 × 22.3 cm

Gift of Mr. and Mrs. Walter A.
Haas
52.1682

AGNES MARTIN
American, born Canada 1912

Falling Blue, 1963
oil and pencil on canvas
71⅞ × 72″
182.6 × 182.9 cm

Gift of Mr. and Mrs. Moses Lasky
74.96

FRED MARTIN
American, born 1927

A Crown of Wild Angels, 1969
acrylic on canvas
66½ × 84½″
168.9 × 214.6 cm

Members' Accessions Fund
Purchase
70.21

FRED MARTIN
American, born 1927

Shells, Morning, 1971
oil on Masonite
18 × 18″
45.7 × 45.7 cm

Gift of Byron Meyer
80.426

MARIA MARTINS
Brazilian, 1900–1973

Macumba, 1943–44
bronze
31⅝ × 36 × 22½″
80.3 × 91.4 × 57.2 cm

Anonymous gift
44.2483

MARCELLO MASCHERINI
Italian, born 1906

Orpheus, 1954
bronze
57½ × 19¾ × 14½″
146.1 × 50.2 × 36.8 cm

Anonymous gift
74.69

ALDEN MASON
American, born 1919

Pink Blusher, 1974
oil on canvas
70 × 85″
177.8 × 215.9 cm

Gift of Mr. and Mrs. William C.
Janss
78.39

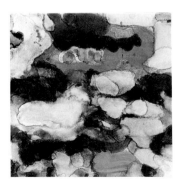

ALDEN MASON
American, born 1919

Lucky Orange, 1975
oil on canvas
18 × 18″
45.7 × 45.7 cm

Gift of Dr. and Mrs. Robert Seymour
in memory of Margaret K. Walker
81.150

JOHN MASON
American, born 1927

Untitled (*Monolith*), 1964
stoneware with glaze
66½ × 64 × 17″
168.9 × 162.6 × 43.2 cm

Gift of the Women's Board
71.68

See colorplate, p. 207

ANDRÉ MASSON
French, born 1896

The Pursuit
(La Poursuite), 1931
oil on canvas
27½ × 44″
69.8 × 111.7 cm

Gift of Mr. and Mrs. Hervey Parke
Clark
82.349

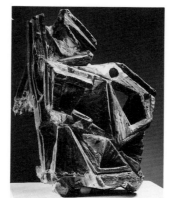

UMBERTO MASTROIANNI
Italian, born 1910

Composition, 1957
bronze
9⅝ × 14¼ × 7¾″
24.5 × 36.2 × 19.7 cm

Gift of Dr. and Mrs. Arthur Lejwa
66.13

HENRI MATISSE
French, 1869–1954

Corsican Landscape, 1899
oil on canvas
15⅛ × 18¼″
38.4 × 46.4 cm

Bequest of Harriet Lane Levy
50.6083

HENRI MATISSE
French, 1869–1954

Café Table
(La Table au café), ca. 1899
oil on canvas
16 × 12⅞″
40.7 × 32.7 cm

Bequest of Harriet Lane Levy
50.6089

HENRI MATISSE
French, 1869–1954

The Slave
(Le Serf), 1900–1903
bronze 6/10
36⅛ × 14⅞ × 13″
91.8 × 37.8 × 33.0 cm

Bequest of Harriet Lane Levy
50.6095

See colorplate, p. 39

HENRI MATISSE
French, 1869–1954

Madeleine, I, 1901
bronze 5/10
21½ × 7⅝ × 6¾″
54.6 × 19.4 × 17.2 cm

Bequest of Harriet Lane Levy
50.6094

HENRI MATISSE
French, 1869–1954

Fruit Dish
(Assiette de fruits), ca. 1902–3
oil on canvas
10⅝ × 13⅞″
27.0 × 35.3 cm

Bequest of Harriet Lane Levy
50.6085

HENRI MATISSE
French, 1869–1954

Still Life
(Nature morte), ca. 1902–3
oil on cardboard
9½ × 13¾″
24.2 × 34.9 cm

Bequest of Harriet Lane Levy
50.6092

HENRI MATISSE
French, 1869–1954

Flowers, ca. 1903
oil on cardboard
13⅜ × 10¼"
34.0 × 26.1 cm

Bequest of Harriet Lane Levy
50.6084

HENRI MATISSE
French, 1869–1954

*Landscape
(Paysage)*, ca. 1903
oil on panel
9½ × 14⅛"
24.2 × 36.2 cm

Bequest of Mrs. Henry Potter
Russell
74.8

HENRI MATISSE
French, 1869–1954

*Seascape (Beside the Sea)
(Marine [Bord de mer])*, ca. 1905–6
oil on cardboard mounted on panel
9⅝ × 12¾"
24.5 × 32.4 cm

Bequest of Mildred B. Bliss
69.67

HENRI MATISSE
French, 1869–1954

*Seascape (Marine
[La Moulade])*, ca. 1905–6
oil on cardboard mounted on panel
10¼ × 13¼"
26.1 × 33.7 cm

Bequest of Mildred B. Bliss
69.66

HENRI MATISSE
French, 1869–1954

*The Girl with Green Eyes
(La Fille aux yeux verts)*, 1908
oil on canvas
26 × 20"
66.0 × 50.8 cm

Bequest of Harriet Lane Levy
50.6086

See colorplate, p. 33

HENRI MATISSE
French, 1869–1954

Portrait of Michael Stein, 1916
oil on canvas
26½ × 19⅞"
67.3 × 50.5 cm

Sarah and Michael Stein Memorial
Collection
Gift of Nathan Cummings
55.3546

See colorplate, p. 36

HENRI MATISSE
French, 1869–1954

Portrait of Sarah Stein, 1916
oil on canvas
28½ × 22¼"
72.4 × 56.5 cm

Sarah and Michael Stein Memorial
Collection
Gift of Elise Stern Haas
54.1117

See colorplate, p. 37

HENRI MATISSE
French, 1869–1954

Vase of Anemones, 1918
oil on canvas
24⅛ × 18½"
61.3 × 47.0 cm

Gift of W. W. Crocker
49.3146

HENRI MATISSE
French, 1869–1954

Henriette, II (Grosse Tête;
Henriette, deuxième état), 1927
bronze 6/10
13 × 9 × 12″
33.0 × 22.9 × 30.5 cm

Bequest of Harriet Lane Levy
50.6096

See colorplate, p. 41

MATTA (ROBERTO SEBASTIAN
ANTONIO MATTA ECHAURREN)
Chilean, born 1911

Invasion of the Night, 1941
oil on canvas
38 × 60⅛″
96.5 × 152.7 cm

Bequest of Jacqueline Marie Onslow
Ford
82.50

CHARLES MATTOX
American, born 1910

Untitled, 1962
wood, linen, and electrical
apparatus
14 × 17¼ × 4⅝″
35.6 × 43.8 × 11.8 cm

Gift of Mr. and Mrs. John Bransten
67.20

CHARLES MATTOX
American, born 1910

Small Twist, ca. 1963
steel, string, wood, paint, wire,
and dry-cell-operated apparatus
27 × 4¼ × 10¼″
68.6 × 10.8 × 26.0 cm

Gift of Dr. William R. Fielder
69.116

CHARLES MATTOX
American, born 1910

Untitled, n.d.
brass with enamel and electrical
apparatus
42⅜ × 13¾ × 16¼″
108.6 × 34.9 × 41.3 cm

Gift of Dr. William R. Fielder
69.115

DAVID MAXIM
American, born 1945

Sun Shower, 1981
acrylic, bamboo, muslin, rhoplex,
string and pulley on canvas
57 × 43 × 16″
144.8 × 109.2 × 40.6 cm

Gift of Foster Goldstrom Fine Arts
in memory of Harlan J. Knechtges
81.233

BERNARD MEADOWS
British, born 1915

Very Important Person
(Personnage très important), 1962
bronze 2/6
23⅛ × 14 × 14¼″
58.7 × 35.6 × 36.2 cm

Gift of the Society for the
Encouragement of Contemporary Art
63.3

HOWARD MEHRING
American, born 1934

Red over Blue, 1968
acrylic on canvas
81 × 117″
205.7 × 297.2 cm

Anonymous gift
69.94

JAMES MELCHERT
American, born 1930

Door F, 1962
earthenware, wood, and lead
76 × 36 × 10½″
193.1 × 91.5 × 26.7 cm

Anonymous gift
69.5 A–B

JAMES MELCHERT
American, born 1930

Game in Layers #2, 1969
Plexiglas and whiteware with China
paint
23⅞ × 24 × 24″
60.6 × 61.0 × 61.0 cm

Purchase
73.27 A–K

JAMES MELCHERT
American, born 1930

Changing Walls, 1971
images produced by projected
35-mm slides
84 × 54″
213.4 × 137.2 cm

Purchase
73.28 A–DDD

CARLOS MÉRIDA
Guatemalan, born 1893

Study in Curves, 1925
oil on canvas
24 × 20″
61.0 × 50.8 cm

Albert M. Bender Collection
Gift of Albert M. Bender
35.4512

CARLOS MÉRIDA
Guatemalan, born 1893

Pisces and Cancer, 1944
oil on canvas
25 × 31⅜″
63.5 × 79.7 cm

Gift of Mrs. Leon Sloss,
Lloyd Stuart Ackerman Memorial
45.1000

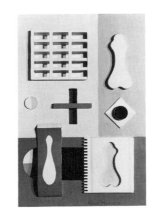

KNUD MERRILD
American, born Denmark,
1894–1954

Equilibrium, 1938
wood and cardboard with enamel
and steel
21⅝ × 14⅞ × 1¾″
55.0 × 37.8 × 4.5 cm

Gift of Mr. and Mrs. Walter C.
Arensberg
51.1160

ARNOLD MESCHES
American, born 1923

Bank of America, 1969
ink and acrylic on canvas
40⅛ × 60⅛″
101.9 × 152.7 cm

Gift of the San Francisco Women
Artists
69.73

JEAN METZINGER
French, 1883–1956

Seated Woman
(Femme assise), 1919
oil on canvas
36½ × 25¾″
92.7 × 65.4 cm

Gift of Sally Hellyer in memory of
Arthur J. Cohen, Jr.
68.3

GUILLERMO MEZA
Mexican, born 1917

Orpheus (Orfeo), 1940
oil on canvas
31⅝ × 23⅝"
80.3 × 60.1 cm

William L. Gerstle Collection
William L. Gerstle Fund Purchase
52.6789

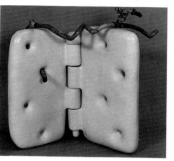

DAVID MIDDLEBROOK
American, born 1944

The Swing, 1979
whiteware (burnished)
27 × 29 × 10"
68.6 × 73.7 × 25.4 cm

Soap Box Derby Fund Purchase
80.391 A–E

JOAN MIRÓ
Spanish, 1893–1983

Painting (Peinture), (formerly
*Dark Brown and White
Oval*), 1926
oil on canvas
28⅞ × 36¼"
73.4 × 92.0 cm

Gift of Joseph M. Bransten in
memory of Ellen Hart Bransten
80.428

See colorplate, p. 109

JOAN MIRÓ
Spanish, 1893–1983

*Dawn Perfumed by a Shower of
Gold (L'Aube parfumée par la pluie
d'or)*, 1954
watercolor and plaster on composition board
42½ × 21⅝"
108.0 × 54.9 cm

Gift of Wilbur D. May
64.58

See colorplate, p. 111

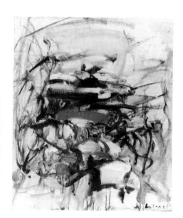

JOAN MITCHELL
American, born 1926

Untitled, ca. 1960
oil on canvas
24 × 19⅝"
61.0 × 49.8 cm

Gift of Sam Francis
75.146

JOAN MITCHELL
American, born 1926

Untitled, ca. 1960
oil on canvas
82⅜ × 74½"
209.2 × 189.3 cm

Gift of Sam Francis
79.440

GEORGE MIYASAKI
American, born 1935

Big Medicine, 1982
from the Rocky Mountain Series
acrylic and paper on canvas
96 × 72⅛"
243.8 × 183.2 cm

Gift of Stephen and Connie Wirtz
83.47

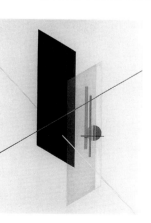

LÁSZLÓ MOHOLY-NAGY
American, born Hungary, 1895–1946

A IX, 1923
oil and pencil on canvas
50½ × 38¾"
128.3 × 98.4 cm

Gift of Sibyl Moholy-Nagy
51.3208

See colorplate, p. 87

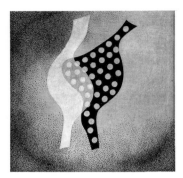

LÁSZLÓ MOHOLY-NAGY
American, born Hungary, 1895–1946

CH Space V, 1941
oil and pencil on burlap
47¼ × 47″
120.0 × 119.4 cm

Gift of S. I. Hayakawa
74.70

PIET MONDRIAN
Dutch, 1872–1944

*Church Façade/Church at
Domburg* (formerly *Cathedral*)
1914
charcoal on chipboard
28¼ × 19⅛″
71.8 × 48.6 cm

Purchase
70.43

See colorplate, p. 81

CLAUDE MONET
French, 1840–1926

*The Seine at Argenteuil
(La Seine à Argenteuil),* 1875
oil on canvas
23½ × 32″
59.7 × 81.3 cm

Bequest of Mrs. Henry Potter
Russell
74.4

KEITH MONROE
American, born 1917

Landscape, n.d.
bronze
19¼ × 21½ × 7″
48.9 × 54.6 × 17.8 cm

Gift of Charlotte Mack
68.42

ROBERTO MONTENEGRO
Mexican, born 1885

Still Life, 1936
oil on panel
12 × 15⅛″
30.5 × 38.4 cm

Albert M. Bender Collection
Gift of Albert M. Bender
37.1866

HENRY MOORE
British, born 1898

Reclining Figure, 1945
bronze ed. 7
7⅛ × 17 × 5¼″
18.1 × 43.2 × 13.3 cm

Gift of Charlotte Mack
52.6715

HENRY MOORE
British, born 1898

*Study for Time-Life
Building Screen,* 1952
bronze ed. 9
16½ × 42 × 6⅜″
41.9 × 106.7 × 16.2 cm

Gift of Charlotte Mack
58.4383

HENRY MOORE
British, born 1898

Maquette for "Seated Woman"
1956
bronze ed. 9
6⅜ × 6⅛ × 4⅜″
16.2 × 15.6 × 11.1 cm

Gift of W. W. Crocker
57.4408

WILLIAM MOREHOUSE
American, born 1929

Site of the Tower of Babel, 1963
oil on canvas
48 × 59¾"
121.9 × 151.8 cm

Gift of David Cole
81.244

CARL MORRIS
American, born 1911

Machine No. 2, 1951
oil on canvas
34⅛ × 38⅛"
86.7 × 96.8 cm

Gift of Mrs. Ferdinand C. Smith
51.4133

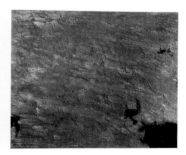

CARL MORRIS
American, born 1911

Sound and Sand, 1955
oil on canvas
39½ × 47⅞"
100.3 × 121.6 cm

Gift of the Women's Board
56.3048

CARL MORRIS
American, born 1911

Red Floe, 1961
oil on canvas
46 × 72"
116.8 × 182.9 cm

Purchase
61.4103

CARL MORRIS
American, born 1911

Ebb Tide, 1973
acrylic on canvas
63 × 75⅜"
160.2 × 191.5 cm

Gift of Mrs. Ferdinand C. Smith
74.88

ED MOSES
American, born 1926

Wedge, 1971
acrylic on canvas, fiberglass,
and resin
94 × 108"
238.8 × 274.3 cm

Gift of Edwin Janss
80.427

ED MOSES
American, born 1926

Big Wedge, 1972
acrylic on canvas, fiberglass,
and resin
90 × 103"
228.6 × 261.6 cm

Gift of the Women's Board
73.14

ROBERT MOTHERWELL
American, born 1915

Wall Painting No. 10, 1964
acrylic on canvas
69 × 92"
175.3 × 233.7 cm

Gift of the friends of Helen Crocker
Russell
67.21

See colorplate, p. 157

345

ROBERT MOTHERWELL
American, born 1915

Open No. 11 (in Raw Sienna with Gray), 1968
acrylic and charcoal on canvas
87 × 211⅜″
221.0 × 536.9 cm

Anonymous gift in honor of
Margaret H. Rosener
69.118

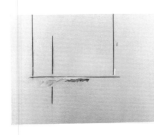

ROBERT MOTHERWELL
American, born 1915

Open No. 124, 1969
charcoal and acrylic on canvas
88¼ × 122″
224.2 × 309.8 cm

Anonymous gift
69.117

ROBERT MOTHERWELL
American, born 1915

Untitled *(Ultramarine)*, 1974
acrylic on canvas
72½ × 84½″
184.2 × 214.6 cm

Gift of Mr. and Mrs. George G.
Walker
77.266

LEE MULLICAN
American, born 1919

Garden Four O'Clock, 1947
oil on canvas
29⅞ × 42⅛″
75.9 × 107.0 cm

Gift of Herman Flax
48.252

LEE MULLICAN
American, born 1919

Untitled, ca. 1947–48
oil on canvas
34 × 17″
86.4 × 43.2 cm

Gift of Charles Campbell
68.37

LEE MULLICAN
American, born 1919

Tendril World, 1962
oil on canvas
60¼ × 50⅛″
153.0 × 127.0 cm

Gift of Mr. and Mrs. Louis Honig
65.1

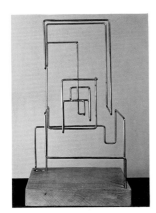

ERNEST MUNDT
American, born Germany 1905

Internal Dialogue, 1946
copper wire
9¼ × 5⅜ × 5⅝″
23.5 × 14.3 × 14.3 cm

Purchase
50.5937

SCOTT MUNDT
American, born 1954

Coracoidal Metamorphosis, 1980
stoneware
70¼ × 28 × 29″
178.4 × 71.1 × 73.7 cm

Gift of the artist
80.191 A–C

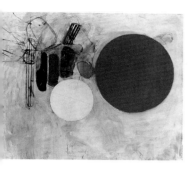

HENRY MUNDY
British, born 1919

Blue and White Disc, 1961
oil on Masonite
62⅞ × 77¾"
149.6 × 197.5 cm

Purchase
63.2

JUSTIN MURRAY
American, born 1911

Inequities #2 (formerly *Some
People Enjoying Themselves*)
1937–38
oil glazes on panel
9¾ × 11⅝"
25.0 × 29.7 cm

WPA Federal Arts Project Allocation
to the San Francisco Museum of Art
1033.43

JUSTIN MURRAY
American, born 1911

May Day, 1937–38
oil glazes on panel
9¾ × 11¾"
24.7 × 29.8 cm

WPA Federal Arts Project Allocation
to the San Francisco Museum of Art
1032.43

MASAYUKI NAGARE
Japanese, born 1923

Mind to Mind, 1965
granite
11½ × 28¾ × 15¼"
29.2 × 73.0 × 38.7 cm

Gift of Mrs. Walter A. Haas
73.11

MASAYUKI NAGARE
Japanese, born 1923

Study for "Transcendence," 1967
granite
13¾ × 26⅝ × 18"
35.2 × 67.6 × 45.7 cm

Gift of Bank of America
70.24

RON NAGLE
American, born 1939

Untitled, 1974
earthenware with glazes, wood, and
glass
4 × 3⅝ × 3½"
10.2 × 9.2 × 8.9 cm

Helen Crocker Russell Memorial
Fund Purchase
74.49

RON NAGLE
American, born 1939

Untitled, 1981
earthenware with glazes
4½ × 2⅞ × 2½"
11.4 × 7.3 × 6.4 cm

Ruth Nash Fund Purchase
81.183

ROBERT NATKIN
American, born 1930

Untitled, 1963
oil on canvas
25 × 23"
63.5 × 58.4 cm

Gift of Mr. and Mrs. Louis Honig
65.8

ROBERT NATKIN
American, born 1930

Apollo with Blue Center, 1969
acrylic on canvas
88 × 78"
223.5 × 198.2 cm

Gift of Mr. and Mrs. George
Poindexter
69.52

ROBERT NATKIN
American, born 1930

Untitled, 1969
oil on canvas
9¼ × 14½"
23.5 × 36.8 cm

Gift of Dr. Paul Ekman
80.429

BRUCE NAUMAN
American, born 1941
Untitled (*Wheels and Suspended
Double Pyramid 3B*), 1978
Cor-ten steel 2/3
109 × 107⅜ × 109"
276.9 × 272.7 × 276.9 cm

Mrs. Ferdinand C. Smith Fund
Purchase
79.310

ART NELSON
American, born 1942

Caged Sea Scrolls, 1980
talc clay and Egyptian paste clay
with glazes on steel wire
35¾ × 15 × 15"
90.8 × 38.1 × 38.1 cm

Gift of Dr. and Mrs. Richard
Gardner
80.408

ALEXANDER NEPOTE
American, born 1913

Secluded, 1948
oil on canvas
42⅛ × 34¼"
107.0 × 87.0 cm

Gift of Mr. and Mrs. Ansley K. Salz
50.39

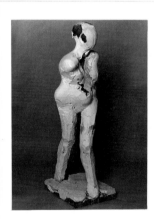

MANUEL NERI
American, born 1930

Chula, ca. 1958–60
plaster and pigment
46 × 14 × 16½"
116.8 × 35.6 × 41.9 cm

Partial gift of Mary Heath Keesling
81.234

MANUEL NERI
American, born 1930

Untitled, 1959
plaster with enamel
60 × 22 × 13½"
152.4 × 56.0 × 34.3 cm

William L. Gerstle Collection
William L. Gerstle Fund Purchase
72.40

MANUEL NERI
American, born 1930

Untitled, ca. 1974
plaster
58½ × 15½ × 13"
148.6 × 39.4 × 33.0 cm

Gift of Roland Petersen
81.201 A–B

MANUEL NERI
American, born 1930

Carrara Figure No. 1, 1979–80
marble with pigment
68 × 23 × 14"
172.7 × 58.4 × 35.6 cm

Gift of the Hamilton-Wells Collection
81.38

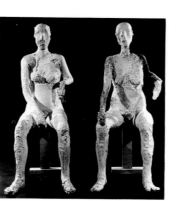

MANUEL NERI
American, born 1930

Mary and Julia, 1980
plaster with pigment
52 × 44 × 34½"
132.1 × 111.8 × 87.6 cm

Gift of Agnes Cowles Bourne
79.322 A–B

See colorplate, p. 231

MANUEL NERI
American, born 1930

Untitled, n.d.
plaster with gouache and graphite
14⅜ × 10¾ × 6½"
37.3 × 27.5 × 16.5 cm

Gift of Robert B. Howard
80.53

BEN NICHOLSON
British, 1894–1982

Nov 21-49 (Bird), 1949
oil and pencil on canvas
22 × 27"
55.9 × 68.0 cm

William L. Gerstle Collection
William L. Gerstle Fund Purchase
55.4718

ISAMU NOGUCHI
American, born 1904

Head of Orozco, 1931
terra-cotta
12½ × 7¾ × 10"
31.7 × 19.6 × 25.4 cm

Albert M. Bender Collection
Gift of Albert M. Bender
40.7259

ISAMU NOGUCHI
American, born 1904

Tiger, 1952
terra-cotta
10⅛ × 14¾ × 5⅜"
25.7 × 37.5 × 13.7 cm

Mrs. Leon Sloss Fund Purchase
58.4381

KENNETH NOLAND
American, born 1924

No Toll, 1970
acrylic on canvas
73 × 126⅛"
185.4 × 320.4 cm

Gift of Thomas W. Weisel
78.189

B. J. O. NORDFELDT
Swedish, 1878–1955

Untitled, ca. 1925
oil on canvas
25 × 30⅛"
63.5 × 76.2 cm

Gift of Mr. and Mrs. Charles Elkus
56.1393

349

EMILE NORMAN
American, born 1918

Horse, 1960
brass 12/12
16½ × 16⅞ × 9″
41.9 × 42.9 × 22.9 cm

Gift of A. A. Ehresmann
64.52

EMILE NORMAN
American, born 1918

Mountain Sheep, 1960
bronze 9/12
10½ × 13 × 4⅞″
26.7 × 33.0 × 12.4 cm

Gift of A. A. Ehresmann
64.53

IRVING NORMAN
American, born Poland 1910

The Circus, 1963–64
oil on canvas
98¾ × 74″
250.8 × 188.0 cm

William L. Gerstle Collection
William L. Gerstle Fund Purchase
82.10

THEODORE ODZA
American, born 1915

Arboc, 1977
steel
25⅞ × 11⅞ × 10¼″
65.8 × 30.2 × 26.1 cm

Gift of Michael Furay
81.235

RICHARD O'HANLON
American, born 1906

Andalusian Games, 1957
bronze
28 × 24 × 17⅜″
71.1 × 61.0 × 44.1 cm

Gift of the Membership Activities
Board
59.1679

KENZO OKADA
American, born Japan, 1902–1982

Flavor, 1956
oil on canvas
52 × 46″
132.1 × 114.3 cm

Gift of Mr. and Mrs. William M.
Roth
76.29

KENZO OKADA
American, born Japan, 1902–1982

Quality, 1956
oil on canvas
70 × 76″
177.8 × 193.0 cm

Gift of the Women's Board
57.3771

ARTHUR OKAMURA
American, born 1932

Returnings in a Cold Spring
1959
oil on canvas
55 × 50″
139.7 × 127.0 cm

Gift of J. Patrick Lannan
59.2107

GEORGIA O'KEEFFE
American, born 1887

Lake George
(formerly *Reflection Seascape*)
1922
oil on canvas
16¼ × 22″
41.2 × 55.9 cm

Gift of Charlotte Mack
52.6714

See colorplate, p. 123

GEORGIA O'KEEFFE
American, born 1887

Katchina, 1936
oil on canvas
7 × 7″
17.8 × 17.8 cm

Gift of the Hamilton-Wells Collection
76.188

GEORGIA O'KEEFFE
American, born 1887

Black Place I, 1944
oil on canvas
26 × 30⅛″
66.0 × 76.6 cm

Gift of Charlotte Mack
54.3536

See colorplate, p. 125

CLAES OLDENBURG
American, born Sweden 1929

Blue Legs, 1961
plaster and muslin with enamel
48 × 36 × 7⅛″
121.9 × 91.5 × 18.1 cm

Anonymous gift
64.65

See colorplate, p. 199

CLAES OLDENBURG
American, born Sweden 1929

Wedding Souvenir, 1966
plaster of Paris
each 6 × 6⅝ × 2½″
15.2 × 16.8 × 6.4 cm

Anonymous gift
82.393.1–.2

CLAES OLDENBURG
American, born Sweden 1929

Wedding Souvenir, 1966
plaster of Paris with metallic paint
6⅝ × 5⅞ × 2¼″
16.8 × 15.0 × 5.7 cm

Anonymous gift
83.239

JULES OLITSKI
American, born Russia 1922

Susie Wiles, 1965
acrylic on canvas
123⅛ × 92⅛″
312.7 × 234.0 cm

Purchased with the aid of funds
from the National Endowment for
the Arts
70.59

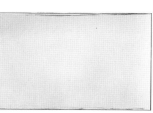

JULES OLITSKI
American, born Russia 1922

Darkness Spread-8, 1973
acrylic on canvas
89 × 151″
226.1 × 383.6 cm

Gift of Lawrence Rubin
82.35

NATHAN OLIVEIRA
American, born 1928

Adolescent by the Bed, 1959
oil on canvas
60¼ × 60⅛″
153.1 × 152.7 cm

William L. Gerstle Collection
William L. Gerstle Fund Purchase
67.48

See colorplate, p. 189

NATHAN OLIVEIRA
American, born 1928

Nude in Environment II, 1962
oil on canvas
72½ × 75⅜″
184.2 × 191.5 cm

Gift of Mr. and Mrs. Bagley Wright
72.50

NATHAN OLIVEIRA
American, born 1928

Shaman Woman, 1978
oil on canvas
96 × 78″
243.8 × 198.1 cm

Gift of the Modern Art Council
80.50

MICHAEL OLODORT
American, born 1942

Homage to Those Who Let Their Heads Go to Their Mouths and Vice Versa, 1970
wood, metal, plastic, paint, and cloth
28 × 21 × 6½″
71.1 × 53.4 × 16.5 cm

Gift of Diana Zlotnick
83.240

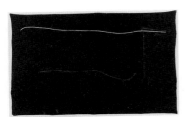

MARY LOVELACE O'NEAL
American

Untitled, 1977–78
lampblack, charcoal, glitter, masking tape, and pastel on canvas
84 × 144″
213.4 × 365.8 cm

Purchased with the aid of funds from the National Endowment for the Arts
79.245

GORDON ONSLOW FORD
American, born England 1912

Seductions of the Day, 1943
oil on canvas
31¾ × 43½″
80.6 × 110.5 cm

Bequest of Jacqueline Marie Onslow Ford
82.51

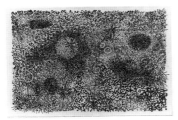

GORDON ONSLOW FORD
American, born England 1912

Constellations in Hand, 1961
Parle's paint on canvas
72 × 108″
182.9 × 274.2 cm

Acquired through gifts of the Women's Board, Victor Honig, and Mr. and Mrs. E. Morris Cox
72.76

DENNIS OPPENHEIM
American, born 1938

Final Stroke—Project for a Glass Factory, 1980
steel, glass, pulleys, springs, cable, rubber straps, gasoline-powered heater, vacuum cleaner, copper sulfate, electrical insulators, metal, coal, and wire mesh
16′ × 35′ × 60′
4.87 × 10.66 × 18.28 m

Gift of Warner Communications Inc.
83.502

MERET OPPENHEIM
Swiss, born Germany 1913

Miss Gardenia, 1962
plaster in metal frame with metallic
paint
10⅝ × 6 × 4¼"
27.0 × 15.2 × 10.8 cm

Helen Crocker Russell Memorial
Fund Purchase
80.45

JOSÉ CLEMENTE OROZCO
Mexican, 1883–1949

Sleeping, ca. 1930
oil on canvas
23⅛ × 31⅛"
58.7 × 79.1 cm

Albert M. Bender Collection
Bequest of Albert M. Bender
41.2927

AMÉDÉE OZENFANT
French, 1886–1966

Still Life (Nature morte), 1920–21
oil on canvas
32 × 39⅝"
81.3 × 100.6 cm

Gift of Lucien Labaudt
37.2991

See colorplate, p. 65

WOLFGANG PAALEN
American, born Austria, 1905–1959

Planetary Face, 1947
oil on canvas
59 × 55¼"
149.9 × 140.3 cm

Purchase
73.13

HAROLD PARIS
American, 1925–1979

Moment in D, 1963
bronze
7 × 12⅛ × 15¼"
17.8 × 30.8 × 38.7 cm

Gift of Mrs. Edgar Sinton
69.28

HAROLD PARIS
American, 1925–1979

Patois II, 1963
bronze
10¾ × 21¼ × 21⅝"
27.3 × 53.9 × 54.9 cm

Gift of Mr. and Mrs. Edgar Sinton
64.33

HAROLD PARIS
American, 1925–1979

Chai Series Triptych, 1969
plastic (vacuum formed) over wood
1/1
45 × 58½ × 25½"
114.3 × 148.6 × 64.8 cm

Gift of the Baredor Foundation
70.22

DAVID PARK
American, 1911–1960

Bathers, 1954
oil on canvas
42 × 54¼"
106.7 × 137.8 cm

Gift of the Women's Board
60.7412

DAVID PARK
American, 1911–1960

Man in a T-Shirt, 1958
oil on canvas
59¾ × 49¾"
151.8 × 126.4 cm

Gift of Mr. and Mrs. Harry W.
Anderson
76.26

See colorplate, p. 187

DAVID PARK
American, 1911–1960

Torso, 1959
oil on canvas
36⅜ × 27¾"
92.4 × 70.5 cm

Gift of the Women's Board
60.7426

RAYMOND PARKER
American, born 1922

Invention, 1950
oil on Masonite
48⅛ × 71⅞"
122.2 × 182.6 cm

Gift of Paul Kantor
67.85

RAYMOND PARKER
American, born 1922

Untitled, 1957
oil on canvas
28⅛ × 25⅛"
71.4 × 63.8 cm

Gift of Arthur L. Caplan
74.63

RAYMOND PARKER
American, born 1922

Untitled P-47, 1960
oil on canvas
72 × 68"
182.9 × 172.7 cm

Acquired through a gift of the
Women's Board
68.71

VERNON PATRICK
American, born 1943

Overextended Arch, 1977
earthenware with glaze
25½ × 27½ × 22¾"
64.8 × 69.9 × 57.8 cm

Gift of the Quay Ceramics Gallery,
San Francisco
77.267

ABBOTT PATTISON
American, born 1916

Job, 1959
bronze
48 × 11 × 10"
121.9 × 27.9 × 25.4 cm

Gift of Mr. and Mrs. Robert S.
Lauter
65.19

PHILLIP PAVIA
American, born 1912

African Nightfall, 1964
African marbles
48⅛ × 20½ × 23"
122.2 × 52.1 × 58.4 cm

Purchased with the aid of the Mrs.
Ferdinand C. Smith Fund
67.46

JOHN PEARSON
American, born England 1940

Head, 1963
bronze
13⅞ × 7⅝ × 9⅜"
35.3 × 19.5 × 23.9 cm

Gift of Mr. and Mrs. Edgar Sinton
64.32

MAX PECHSTEIN
German, 1881–1955

Nelly, 1910
oil on canvas
20⅜ × 20⅞"
51.8 × 53.1 cm

Purchase
84.9

See colorplate, p. 71

JAMES PENNUTO
American, born 1936

Call & Answer, 1973
35-mm color slides, magnetic tape
cassette, ink on paper, color photographs, in box with buckram binding A/P G
box 2⅛ × 8⅝ × 10⅝"
5.4 × 21.9 × 27.0 cm

Gift of Phoenix Gallery/Editions,
San Francisco
74.64 A–0000

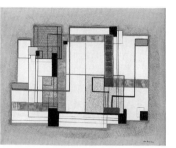

IRENE RICE PEREIRA
American, born 1905

Abstraction, 1940
oil on canvas
29⅞ × 36"
75.9 × 91.4 cm

Gift of Peggy Guggenheim
47.1239

VINCENT PEREZ
American, born 1938

***The Marriage of Vincent Perez
and Bette Crispens,*** 1966
acrylic on polyester mounted
on board
47⅞ × 36"
121.6 × 91.4 cm

Gift of Mrs. Edgar Sinton
70.51

MICHAEL PETERS
American, born 1943

Steeple Chase, 1969
from the series Coney Island
oil on canvas
82 × 100"
208.3 × 254.0 cm

Gift of Paul Trousdale
70.10

ROLAND PETERSEN
American, born Denmark 1926

Flag Festival, 1966
oil on canvas
60 × 68⅛"
152.4 × 173.0 cm

Gift of the artist
81.112

ROLAND PETERSEN
American, born Denmark 1926

Rain Picnic, 1981
acrylic on canvas
82¼ × 109¾"
208.9 × 278.8 cm

Gift of the artist
81.113

MARGARET PETERSON
American, born 1902

Man's Child, 1946
oil on panel
43⅛ × 46¾″
109.5 × 118.8 cm

Gift of Charlotte Mack and Mrs.
Ansley K. Salz
52.5077

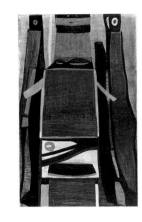

MARGARET PETERSON
American, born 1902

Spirit of Welcome, 1954
oil on Masonite
39⅜ × 24⅛″
100.0 × 61.3 cm

Gift of Charlotte Mack
55.5338

MARGARET PETERSON
American, born 1902

Ellen, n.d.
tempera on board
24 × 20″
61.0 × 50.8 cm

Gift of Samuel Yabroff
44.4312

RICHARD PETTIBONE
American, born 1938

Bridget and the King of the Crossing, 1963
oil on glass
12½ × 81½″
31.7 × 207.0 cm

Gift of Diana Zlotnick
83.241

EMILIO PETTORUTI
Argentine, 1892–1971

Coparmonica, 1937
oil on canvas
28⅞ × 39⅜″
73.3 × 100.0 cm

Purchase
43.5092

HELEN PHILLIPS
American, born 1913

Young Woman, ca. 1935
stone
28 × 13¾ × 19″
71.1 × 34.9 × 48.3 cm

San Francisco Museum of Art
Purchase Prize, *Fifty-sixth Annual
Exhibition of the San Francisco Art
Association*
36.641

HELEN PHILLIPS
American, born 1913

Leg Games (Jeux de jambes), n.d.
bronze
17 × 11¼ × 11¼″
43.2 × 28.5 × 28.5 cm

Gift of Charlotte Mack
68.41

GOTTARDO F. P. PIAZZONI
American, born Switzerland,
1872–1945

Decoration for Overmantel
ca. 1926
oil on canvas
30⅜ × 46¼″
77.1 × 117.5 cm

Albert M. Bender Collection
Gift of Albert M. Bender
36.5989

GOTTARDO F. P. PIAZZONI
American, born Switzerland,
1872–1945

Landscape, ca. 1926
oil on cardboard
8⅜ × 10⅝"
21.3 × 27.0 cm

Albert M. Bender Collection
Gift of Albert M. Bender
36.5998

PABLO PICASSO
Spanish, 1881–1973

Street Scene (Scène de rue), 1900
oil on canvas
18¾ × 26¼"
47.7 × 66.7 cm

Bequest of Harriet Lane Levy
50.6097

See colorplate, p. 49

PABLO PICASSO
Spanish, 1881–1973

Untitled (Still Life), 1921
oil on canvas
9 × 18"
22.9 × 45.7 cm

Gift of Gardner Dailey
50.5455

PABLO PICASSO
Spanish, 1881–1973

Jug of Flowers
(La Cruche fleurie), 1937
oil on canvas
20 × 24¼"
50.8 × 61.6 cm

Purchased with the aid of funds
from W. W. Crocker
44.1499

See colorplate, p. 59

PABLO PICASSO
Spanish, 1881–1973

Standing Figure
(Femme debout), 1947
bronze with gold wash   1/10
7⅞ × 3¼ × 2⅞"
20.0 × 8.2 × 7.3 cm

Gift of W. W. Crocker
54.3281

PABLO PICASSO
Spanish, 1881–1973

Women of Algiers, E (Les Femmes
d'Alger), 1955
oil on canvas
18⅛ × 21⅝"
46.1 × 55.0 cm

Gift of Wilbur D. May
64.4

See colorplate, p. 61

PABLO PICASSO
Spanish, 1881–1973

Centaur, ca. 1965
glass with pigment
12¼ × 3⅞ × 11½"
31.1 × 9.8 × 29.2 cm

Gift of Peggy Guggenheim
65.14

MICHELANGELO PISTOLETTO
Italian, born 1933

Features of People (Particolari di
persone), 1962
paper on stainless steel
49 × 48½"
124.4 × 123.2 cm

Gift of Edwin Janss
78.143

357

JACKSON POLLOCK
American, 1912–1956

Guardians of the Secret, 1943
oil on canvas
48⅜ × 75⅜"
122.9 × 191.5 cm

Albert M. Bender Collection
Albert M. Bender Bequest Fund
Purchase
45.1308

See colorplate, p. 149

THEODORE C. POLOS
American, born Greece 1902

Mexican Village, ca. 1940
oil on canvas
24⅛ × 32⅛"
61.3 × 81.6 cm

San Francisco Museum of Art
Purchase Prize, *Sixty-first Annual
Exhibition of the San Francisco Art
Association*
41.4250

LUCIAN OCTAVIUS POMPILI
American, born 1942

*Skepticism and the Life of
Emile Zola*, 1975
porcelain with glaze, lead, glass,
and wood
22¼ × 21⅛ × 21⅛"
56.5 × 53.6 × 53.6 cm

Gift of Roy and Helga Curry
76.182

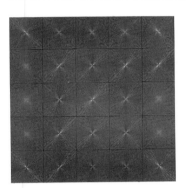

ERNEST POSEY
American, born 1937

#174-70, 1970
acrylic on canvas
59¾ × 59⅞"
151.8 × 152.1 cm

Gift of Zora Gross
70.4

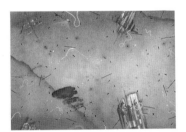

ERNEST POSEY
American, born 1937

Cipher, 1977
synthetic polymer on canvas
54 × 72⅛"
137.2 × 183.2 cm

Gift of Alvin H. Baum, Jr.
78.64

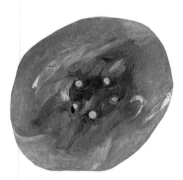

DON POTTS
American, born 1936

Five Pegged One, 1963
oil on canvas with wood
45¼ × 47⅝ × 5⅜"
114.9 × 121.0 × 13.7 cm

Gift of James Lucas
76.200

DON POTTS
American, born 1936

*A Made Blade Loses a Cut
Strut Winner*, 1965
wood, leather, automobile hood,
and fiberglass
77 × 60 × 25¼"
195.5 × 152.4 × 64.1 cm

Gift of Sally Lilienthal
71.21

PAUL PRATCHENKO
American, born 1944

*No Fretting When You Play
the Harp*, 1976
oil and egg tempera on canvas
25¼ × 26⅞"
64.1 × 68.3 cm

Gift of Michele and Mercury Bell
82.396

JAMES PRESTINI
American, born 1908

#159, 1967
structural steel with nickel plating
41⅜ × 18¼ × 7¾″
105.1 × 46.4 × 19.7 cm

Anonymous gift
69.43

GREGORIO PRESTOPINO
American, born 1907

American Landscape, 1936
oil on gesso board
24 × 18″
61.0 × 45.7 cm

WPA Federal Arts Project Allocation
to the San Francisco Museum of Art
3756.43

KENNETH PRICE
American, born 1935

L. Red, 1963
stoneware with lacquer and acrylic
10¼ × 8⅞ × 9¼″
26.1 × 22.6 × 23.5 cm

Evelyn and Walter Haas, Jr. Fund
Purchase
82.155

See colorplate, p. 209

KENNETH PRICE
American, born 1935

M.R. Green, 1970
earthenware with lacquer
1 × 5⅜ × 5⅝″
2.6 × 13.7 × 14.3 cm

Gift of Virginia Shirley
79.323

KENNETH PRICE
American, born 1935

Untitled, 1972–78
stoneware with acrylic
9⅛ × 12⅜ × 9⅝″
23.2 × 31.4 × 24.6 cm

Gift of Virginia Shirley
79.324

KENNETH PRICE
American, born 1935

Untitled *(Cup)*, 1979
earthenware with glaze
3⅛ × 3⅝ × 2⅞″
8.0 × 9.2 × 7.3 cm

Gift of Virginia Shirley
79.325

KENNETH PRICE
American, born 1935

Untitled *(Cup)*, 1979
earthenware with glaze
3 × 3¼ × 2⅝″
7.6 × 8.3 × 6.8 cm

Gift of Virginia Shirley
79.326

KENNETH PRICE
American, born 1935

Untitled *(Cup)*, 1979
earthenware with glaze
3⅛ × 3⅝ × 2⅞″
8.0 × 9.2 × 7.3 cm

Gift of Virginia Shirley
79.327

KENNETH PRICE
American, born 1935

Untitled *(Cup)*, 1979
earthenware with glaze
2¾ × 3⅝ × 3″
7.0 × 9.2 × 7.8 cm

Gift of Virginia Shirley
79.328

KENNETH PRICE
American, born 1935

Untitled *(Cup)*, 1979
earthenware with glaze
2¾ × 3½ × 2¾″
7.0 × 8.9 × 7.0 cm

Gift of Virginia Shirley
79.329

SAM PROVENZANO
American; born 1923

Black Wedge, 1967
from the Wedge Series
acrylic on canvas
67¾ × 53¾″
172.0 × 136.6 cm

Gift of Betty and Glen Slaughter
83.114

WALTER QUIRT
American, 1902–1968

Obeisance to Poverty, ca. 1938
oil on canvas
24 × 32″
61.0 × 81.4 cm

WPA Federal Arts Project Allocation
to the San Francisco Museum of Art
3757.43

CHERIE RACITI
American, born 1942

Suzanne's Green Overlap, 1977
rhoplex on tyvek
48 × 504″
121.9 × 1,280.2 cm

Purchased with the aid of funds
from the National Endowment for
the Arts, the Soap Box Derby
Fund, and the New Future Fund
Drive
77.83

JOSEPH RAFFAEL
American, born 1933

Man with Birds, 1969
oil on canvas on wood
78½ × 72″
199.4 × 182.9 cm

Helen Crocker Russell Memorial
Fund Purchase
72.37

MEL RAMOS
American, born 1935

Miss Grapefruit Festival, 1964
oil on canvas
40 × 34″
101.6 × 86.4 cm

Anonymous gift
70.31

ALFREDO RAMOS-MARTINEZ
Mexican, 1875–1946

Mexican Soldiers, n.d.
oil on canvas
50¼ × 40″
127.6 × 101.6 cm

Albert M. Bender Collection
Gift of Albert M. Bender
35.3073

JOSEPH RAPHAEL
American, 1869–1950

Cannero, 1938
oil on canvas
33 × 42″
83.8 × 106.7 cm

Albert M. Bender Collection
Gift of Albert M. Bender
39.35

JOSEPH RAPHAEL
American, 1869–1950

Portrait, n.d.
oil on canvas
17 × 13″
43.2 × 33.0 cm

Albert M. Bender Collection
Bequest of Albert M. Bender
41.2904

ROBERT RASMUSSEN
see REDD EKKS

FRITZ RAUH
American, born Germany 1920

Untitled, 1976
acrylic on canvas
57⅞ × 45½″
147.0 × 115.6 cm

Gift of David Cole
81.245

ROBERT RAUSCHENBERG
American, born 1925

Collection (formerly **Untitled**)
1953–54
oil, paper, fabric, and metal on wood
80 × 96 × 3½″
203.2 × 243.9 × 8.9 cm

Gift of Mr. and Mrs. Harry W.
Anderson
72.26

See colorplate, p. 195

ROBERT RAUSCHENBERG
American, born 1925

Untitled, 1973
pencil and oil on paper bags and
envelopes on paper
72 × 60″
182.9 × 152.4 cm

Gift of the Frederick Weisman
Company
81.151

ODILON REDON
French, 1840–1916

The Small Green Vase
(Le Petit Vase vert), ca. 1900–1904
oil on canvas
16⅛ × 10¾″
41.0 × 27.3 cm

Bequest of Mrs. Henry Potter
Russell
74.3

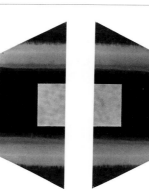

PAUL REED
American, born 1919

Gilport V, 1971
acrylic on canvas
58 × 55½″
147.4 × 141.0 cm

Anonymous gift
72.69 A–B

DON REICH
American, born 1932

Landscape with Green Sky, 1961
oil on canvas
48 × 45⅛″
121.9 × 114.6 cm

William L. Gerstle Collection
William L. Gerstle Fund Purchase
62.19

FRED REICHMAN
American, born 1925

The Earth Greens for Spring
1962
oil on canvas
68¼ × 51¼″
173.4 × 130.2 cm

Gift of Derek Fairman
64.49

FRED REICHMAN
American, born 1925

Summer at Fallen Leaf, 1970
oil on canvas
73⅞ × 53½″
187.6 × 135.9 cm

Gift of Rose Rabow in memory of
Alexandre Rabow
72.75

DOROTHY REID
American, born 1944

Carving, 1975
wood
125½ × 7½ × 1½″
318.8 × 19.1 × 3.8 cm

Purchased with the aid of funds
from the National Endowment for
the Arts, the Soap Box Derby Fund,
and the New Future Fund Drive
77.82

JAMES REINEKING
American, born 1937

Fall, 1970
fiberglass, mesh, aluminum, and
wood with enamel and electrical
sound device
36 × 76¾ × 5½″
91.4 × 195.0 × 14.0 cm

Anonymous gift
71.22

AD REINHARDT
American, 1913–1967

#12-1955–56, 1955–56
oil on canvas
106½ × 38¼″
270.5 × 97.2 cm

Gift of Morris Stulsaft
61.4408

DEBORAH REMINGTON
American, born 1930

Statement, 1963
oil on canvas
76⅝ × 70″
194.6 × 177.8 cm

Gift of the First Savings and Loan
Association, San Francisco
64.44

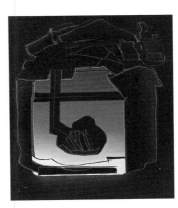

DEBORAH REMINGTON
American, born 1930

Untitled, 1966
oil on canvas
22 × 20¼″
55.9 × 51.4 cm

Gift of Robert B. Howard
79.315

GREGG RENFROW
American, born 1948

Untitled, 1976
rhoplex on fiber mesh
69 × 124″
175.3 × 315.0 cm

Gift of Dr. Arthur Fromowitz
76.187 A–C

MILTON RESNICK
American, born 1917

Untitled, 1957
oil on paper mounted on board
19⅝ × 19″
49.9 × 48.3 cm

Gift of Mr. and Mrs. L. James
Newman
72.70

SAM RICHARDSON
American, born 1934

*That Guy's Acre Has a Cloud
over It All the Time*, 1968
polyurethane foam, fiberglass, and
wood with nitro-cellulose lacquer
26⅛ × 11¾ × 11¾″
66.3 × 29.8 × 29.8 cm

Gift of Sally Lilienthal
71.59

SAM RICHARDSON
American, born 1934

*The Island Rises out of Incredibly
Deep Water*, 1969
polyester resin and polyurethane
foam, fiberglass, and wood with
nitro-cellulose lacquer
6¼ × 10¼ × 10¼″
15.9 × 26.0 × 26.0 cm

Gift of Byron Meyer
79.330

GERMAINE RICHIER
French, 1904–1959

*Don Quixote at the Windmill
(Don Quichotte au moulin à vent)*
1949/1957
bronze (gilt)
20¾ × 13¼ × 11⅝″
52.7 × 33.7 × 29.5 cm

Gift of the Women's Board
58.1881

GEORGE RICKEY
American, born 1907

Five Triangles Variation 1, 1966
stainless steel and lead 3/15
10⅜ × 12¼ × 3″
26.4 × 31.2 × 7.6 cm

Gift of Mr. and Mrs. Louis Honig
76.195 A–B

GEORGE RICKEY
American, born 1907

Two Lines up—Contrapuntal
1967
stainless steel on wood
36 × 2 × 3″
91.4 × 5.0 × 7.6 cm

Gift of Mr. and Mrs. Louis Honig
76.196

TOM RIPPON
American, born 1954

Rip's Table, 1979
lusterware
46½ × 30⅛ × 25″
118.1 × 76.5 × 63.5 cm

Purchased with the aid of funds
from the National Endowment for
the Arts and the Soap Box Derby
Fund
80.46 A–E

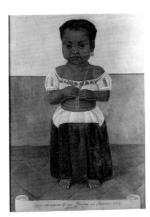

DIEGO RIVERA
Mexican, 1886–1957

***Indian Girl with Coral
Necklace***, 1926
oil on canvas
37⅛ × 27″
94.3 × 68.6 cm

Albert M. Bender Collection
Albert M. Bender Bequest Fund
Purchase
45.3004

DIEGO RIVERA
Mexican, 1886–1957

The Flower Carrier (formerly
The Flower Vendor)
1935
oil and tempera on Masonite
48 × 47¾″
121.9 × 121.3 cm

Albert M. Bender Collection
Gift of Albert M. Bender in memory
of Caroline Walter
35.4516

See colorplate, p. 141

DIEGO RIVERA
Mexican, 1886–1957

Symbolic Landscape, 1940
oil on canvas
47⅞ × 60⅛″
121.6 × 152.7 cm

Gift of friends of Diego Rivera
40.6551

JOSÉ DE RIVERA
American, born 1904

Copper Construction, 1949
copper
28⅛ × 21 × 20¾″
71.5 × 53.4 × 52.7 cm

Gift of Mrs. Henry Potter Russell
60.8570

HUGO ROBUS
American, 1885–1964

Modeling Hands (also known as
Sculptor's Hands), 1920–22
bronze 1/2
16½ × 14½ × 9½″
41.9 × 36.9 × 24.2 cm

Evelyn and Walter Haas, Jr. Fund
Purchase
81.97

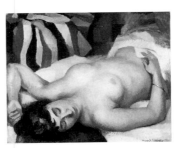

MARCEL ROCHE
French, 1890–1959

Nu, n.d.
oil on canvas
25¾ × 31¾″
65.4 × 80.6 cm

Gift
37.2990

HERBERT ROCKERE
Austrian, born 1941

***The 11th Investigation on the
Strategy of Liar's Dice***, 1976
ink and pencil on canvas
23¾ × 130″
60.3 × 330.2 cm

Gift of the artist
78.71

PHILIP ROEBER
American, born 1913

Untitled, 1961
oil and paper on canvas
83¾ × 66″
212.7 × 167.6 cm

Gift of William M. Roth
73.22

EMY ROEDER
German, 1890–1972

Portrait of Hans Purrmann
1950–51
bronze
10½ × 8¼ × 8¾"
27.7 × 21.0 × 22.3 cm

Purchased with the aid of funds
from Henry Schaefer-Simmern's
students
60.8571

JOHN ROLOFF
American, born 1947

#2 Exile Group, 1975
porcelain, Plexiglas, and wood
3¼ × 22¼ × 18⅜"
8.3 × 56.5 × 46.7 cm

Purchase
75.111

JAMES ROSEN
American, born 1933

Durham I, 1982
oil on canvas
99 × 78"
251.5 × 198.1 cm

Gift of Eva Gelfman
82.400

MARK ROTHKO
American, born Russia, 1903–1970

Untitled, 1960
oil on canvas
69 × 50⅛"
175.3 × 127.3 cm

Acquired through a gift of Peggy
Guggenheim
62.3426

See colorplate, p. 165

MARK ROTHKO
American, born Russia, 1903–1970

Untitled, 1969
oil on paper on canvas
38¾ × 25¼"
98.4 × 64.1 cm

Anonymous gift through the
American Art Foundation
78.190

GEORGES ROUAULT
French, 1871–1958

Head of a Clown, 1930
oil and pastel on cardboard
11 × 8¾"
27.9 × 22.2 cm

Albert M. Bender Collection
Albert M. Bender Fund Purchase
39.161

GEORGES ROUAULT
French, 1871–1958

Sea of Galilee, ca. 1937–38
oil on paper mounted on canvas
19 × 27⅜"
48.3 × 69.6 cm

Gift of W. W. Crocker
55.3547

HENRI ROUSSEAU, attributed to
French, 1844–1910

*Palace Hotel and the Rock of the
Blessed Virgin, Biarritz (Hôtel du
Palais et Rocher de la Vierge,
Biarritz)*, ca. 1885
oil on panel
10½ × 13¾"
26.6 × 34.9 cm

Bequest of Mrs. Henry Potter Russell
74.7

HENRI ROUSSEAU, attributed to
French, 1844–1910

View of Biarritz (Vue de la ville de Biarritz), ca. 1885
oil on panel
10½ × 13¾"
26.6 × 33.0 cm

Bequest of Mrs. Henry Potter Russell
74.6

RICHARDS RUBEN
American, born 1925

Double Portrait, 1957
oil on canvas
46 × 68⅛"
116.8 × 173.1 cm

Gift of Peter Selz and Dion Cheronis
81.246

RICHARDS RUBEN
American, born 1925

Genocide, 1958
oil on canvas
92½ × 140¾"
235.0 × 357.5 cm

Gift of Peter Voulkos
83.243 A–C

RICHARDS RUBEN
American, born 1925

Claremont 39, 1960
oil on canvas
79⅞ × 111"
202.9 × 282.0 cm

Gift of the artist
67.14

RICHARDS RUBEN
American, born 1925

Claremont 47, 1965
oil on canvas
107⅜ × 77¾"
272.7 × 197.5 cm

Gift of Irving Blum
73.43

ERIC RUDD
American

Night Fairy, 1974
acrylic and lacquer on polyurethane
84 × 80 × 6"
213.4 × 203.2 × 15.2 cm

Gift of Irving G. Rudd
76.210

MORGAN RUSSELL
American, 1886–1953

Synchromy, ca. 1914
oil on canvas
23¾ × 17¾"
60.4 × 45.1 cm

Purchased through a gift of Dr. and Mrs. Allan Roos
81.39

MORGAN RUSSELL
American, 1886–1953

Synchromy No. 3, ca. 1922–23
oil on canvas
23¾ × 16⅛"
60.4 × 40.9 cm

Purchase
72.1

See colorplate, p. 67

BETYE SAAR
American, born 1926

The Time Inbetween, 1974
wooden box containing photos, magazine illustration, paint, envelope, metal findings, glass beads, fan, glove, tape measure, lace, buttons, coin purse, velvet ribbon, cloth, feathers, bones, and photocopy of artist's hand
closed 3⅜ × 8½ × 11⅝″
8.6 × 21.6 × 29.6 cm

Purchase
78.19

JOHN SACCARO
American, born 1913

Tender Dislocations No. 3, 1955
oil on canvas
32 × 38″
81.3 × 96.5 cm

Gift of Mr. and Mrs. Ansley K. Salz
56.827

JOHN SAFER
American, born 1922

Cube on Cube, 1970
Plexiglas
15¾ × 10¼ × 10¼″
40.0 × 26.0 × 26.0 cm

Anonymous gift
70.53

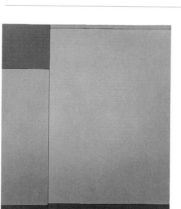

LUCAS SAMARAS
American, born Greece 1936

Chickenwire Box #40, 1972
acrylic on wire
25½ × 24 × 33½″
64.8 × 61.0 × 85.1 cm

Gift of Sally Lilienthal
73.12

FRED SANDBACK
American, born 1943

Untitled, 1977
wool fiber
ceiling height × 48 × 360″
ceiling height × 121.9 × 914.4 cm

Gift of the Security Pacific National Bank
80.56 A–B

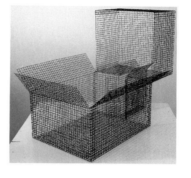

LUDWIG SANDER
American, born 1906

Monongohela IV, 1971
oil on canvas
60½ × 54¾″
153.6 × 139.1 cm

Gift of Mr. and Mrs. Edmond Nouri
72.5

DARRYL SAPIEN
American, born 1950

Cenotaph, 1976
latex, plaster, and acrylic
28 × 18 × ½″
71.1 × 45.7 × 1.3 cm

Gift of Richard Lorenz
81.237

JOHN SINGER SARGENT
American, born Italy, 1856–1925

Study for a Portrait of a Gentleman, n.d.
oil on canvas
26¼ × 17⅞″
66.4 × 45.4 cm

Gift of Mr. and Mrs. Jerd Sullivan
66.9

PAUL SARKISIAN
American, born 1928

Untitled *(Waynesboro, Pa.)*, 1969
acrylic on canvas
115⅞ × 148⅝"
294.4 × 377.5 cm

Gift of Mr. and Mrs. Harry W.
Anderson
78.191

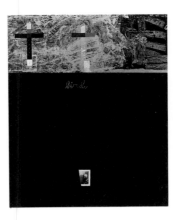

RAYMOND SAUNDERS
American, born 1934

Charlie Parker
(formerly **Bird**), 1977
enamel, masking tape, newsprint,
paper, and ink on canvas
96⅛ × 82⅜"
244.2 × 209.2 cm

Gift of Mr. and Mrs. Robert Krasnow
78.192

MORTEZA SAZEGAR
American, born Iran 1933

C12-68 No. 1, 1968
acrylic on canvas
80⅜ × 55¾"
204.2 × 141.6 cm

Gift of Mr. and Mrs. George
Poindexter
70.34

EMILIO SCANAVINO
Italian, born 1922

The Push 1959 (L'Urto 1959), 1959
oil on canvas
39½ × 32"
100.3 × 81.3 cm

Gift of Jaquelin H. Hume
63.10

JACQUES SCHNIER
American, born Romania 1898

Buzzy Perry 10 Years, 1937
bronze
11⅜ × 6⅞ × 8"
28.9 × 17.5 × 20.3 cm

Albert M. Bender Collection
Gift of Albert M. Bender
40.1096

JACQUES SCHNIER
American, born Romania 1898

Double-Horned Kite, 1971
acrylic resin
15¼ × 12½ × 11"
38.7 × 31.8 × 27.9 cm

Gift of Elise S. Haas
74.98

JACQUES SCHNIER
American, born Romania 1898

Pak Kwai Mau, n.d.
terra-cotta
16¼ × 5½ × 7½"
41.3 × 14.0 × 19.1 cm

Albert M. Bender Collection
Gift of Albert M. Bender
38.239

EMILE SCHUMACHER
German, born 1912

Official Person (Hohe Figur), 1960
oil on panel
68⅛ × 29⅞"
173.0 × 75.9 cm

Gift of Mr. and Mrs. Arthur A.
Goldberg
71.78

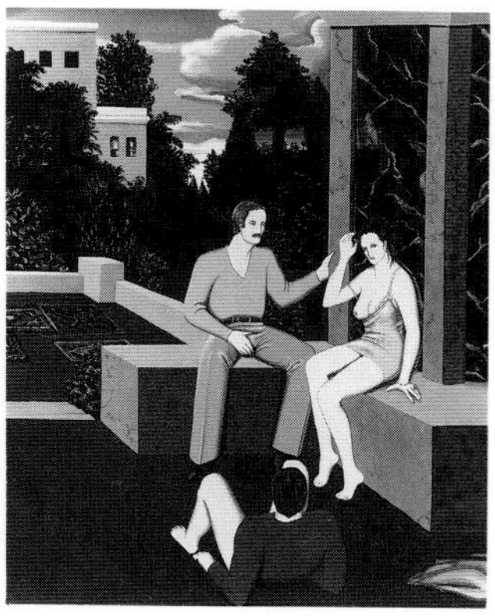

ROBERT SCHWARTZ
American, born 1947

Untitled, 1973
gouache on board
10 × 8″
25.4 × 20.3 cm

Gift of Win Ng
81.271

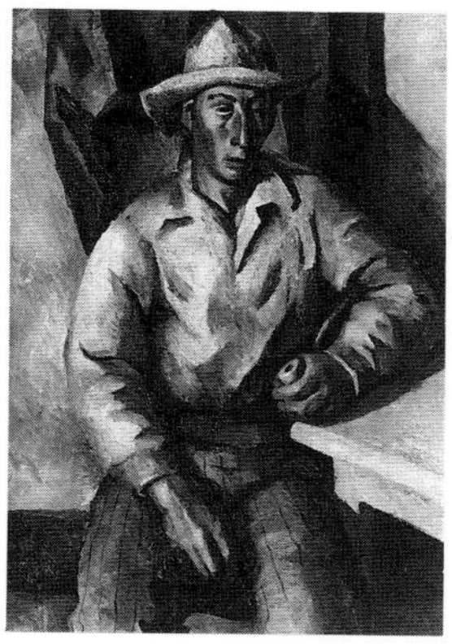

ERNESTO SCOTTI
Argentine

Portrait of a Farmer, 1938
oil on board
43⅛ × 30″
109.4 × 76.2 cm

Purchase
42.78

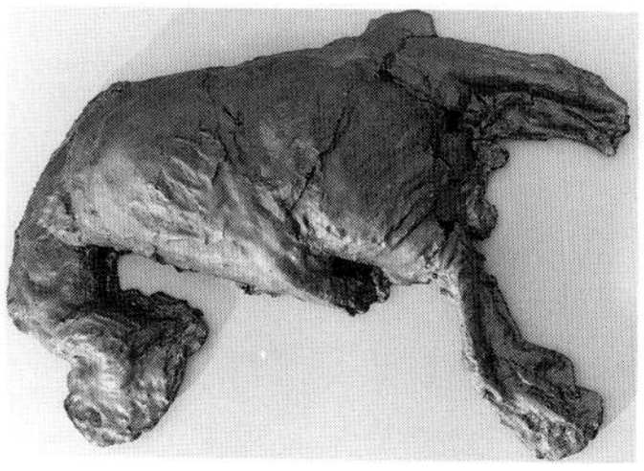

GEORGE SEGAL
American, born 1924

Chicken, 1965
from *7 Objects in a Box*
plaster with pigments
4⅛ × 18⅝ × 15¼″
10.5 × 47.3 × 38.8 cm

Gift of Lenore and Allan Sindler
76.254

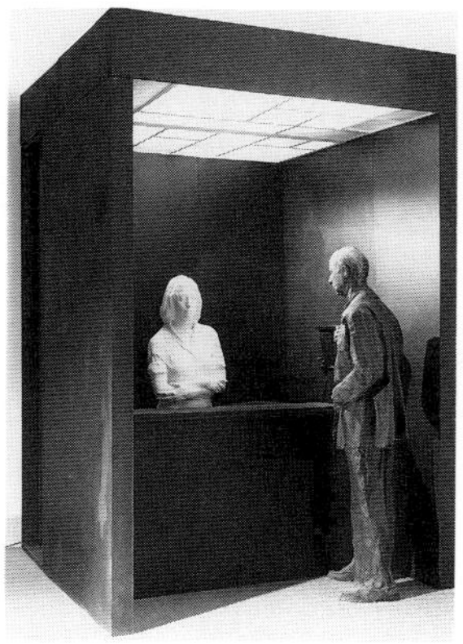

GEORGE SEGAL
American, born 1924

Hot Dog Stand, 1978
plaster and wood with acrylic, Plexiglas, stainless steel, and electrical apparatus
108¼ × 72¼ × 81½″
275.0 × 182.9 × 207.0 cm

T. B. Walker Foundation Fund and Clinton Walker Fund Purchase
79.118 A–F

DAVID SHAPIRO
American, born 1944

A Child's Pornography, 1973
acrylic on canvas
54 × 40″
137.2 × 101.6 cm

Gift of Mrs. Paul L. Wattis
76.98

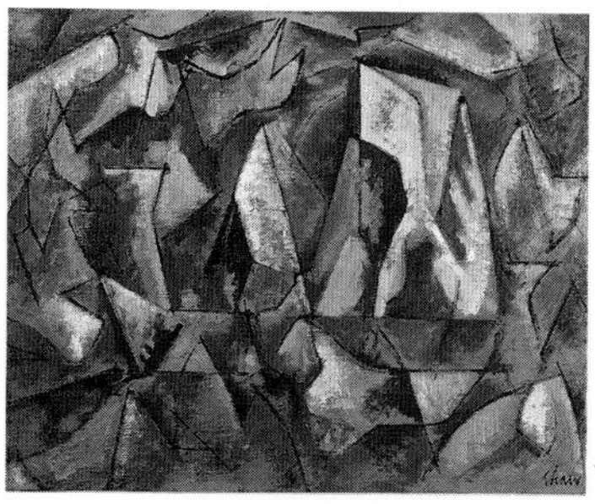

CHARLES SHAW
American, 1892–1974

Space Forms, 1952
oil on canvasboard
24⅞ × 29⅞″
63.2 × 75.9 cm

Gift of W. W. Crocker
52.4005

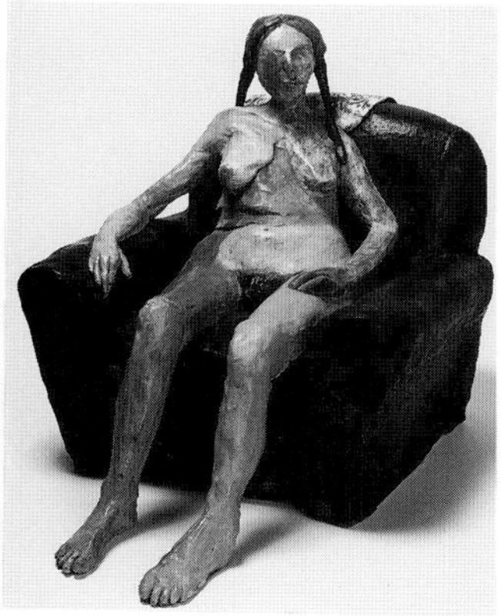

RICHARD SHAW
American, born 1941

Untitled, 1965
acrylic on gessoed earthenware clay
10⅜ × 11 × 16½″
26.3 × 28 × 41.9 cm

Gift of Wade and Eleanor Dickinson
82.157

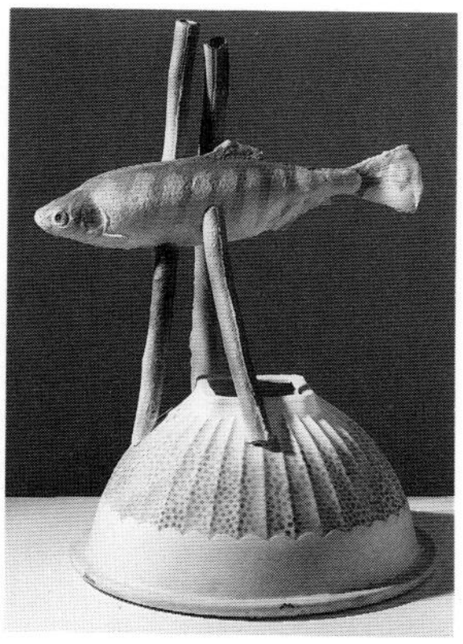

RICHARD SHAW
American, born 1941

Fishjar #2, 1973
porcelain with underglaze
13½ × 10 × 9⅛″
34.3 × 25.4 × 23.0 cm

Gift of Mrs. Creighton Peet
77.13

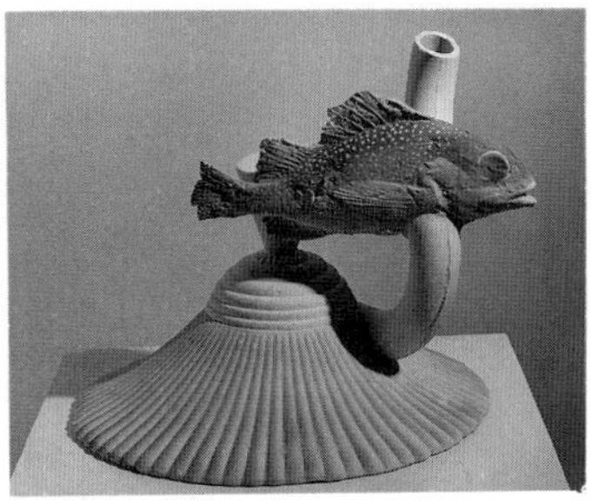

RICHARD SHAW
American, born 1941

Teapot, 1973
porcelain, glazes, and underglazes
$8\frac{7}{8} \times 11 \times 10\frac{1}{8}''$
$22.5 \times 27.9 \times 25.7$ cm

In memory of Alma Walker, given by her friends
73.47

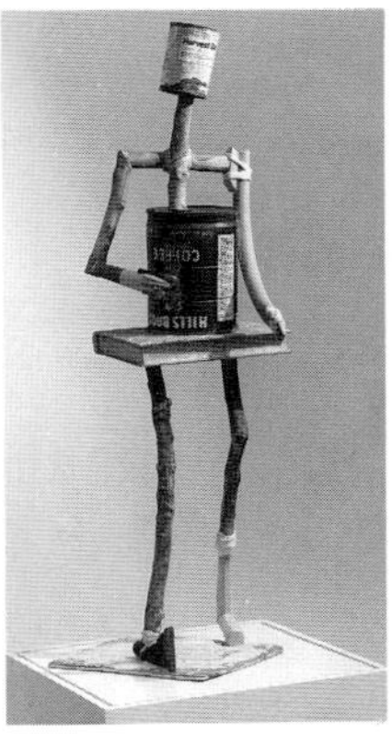

RICHARD SHAW
American, born 1941

Melodious Double Stops, 1980
porcelain with decal overglaze
$38\frac{3}{4} \times 12 \times 14''$
$98.4 \times 30.5 \times 35.6$ cm

Purchased with matching funds from the National Endowment for the Arts and Frank O. Hamilton, Byron Meyer, and Mrs. Peter Schlesinger
80.168

See colorplate, p. 225

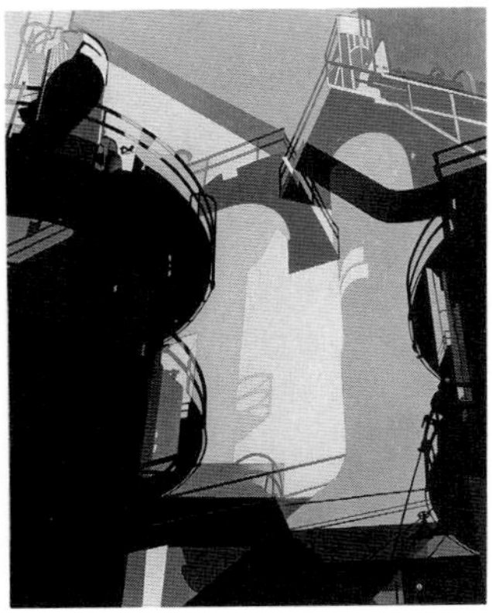

CHARLES SHEELER
American, 1883–1965

Aerial Gyrations, 1953
oil on canvas
$23\frac{5}{8} \times 18\frac{5}{8}''$
60.0×47.3 cm

Mrs. Manfred Bransten Special Fund Purchase
74.78

See colorplate, p. 135

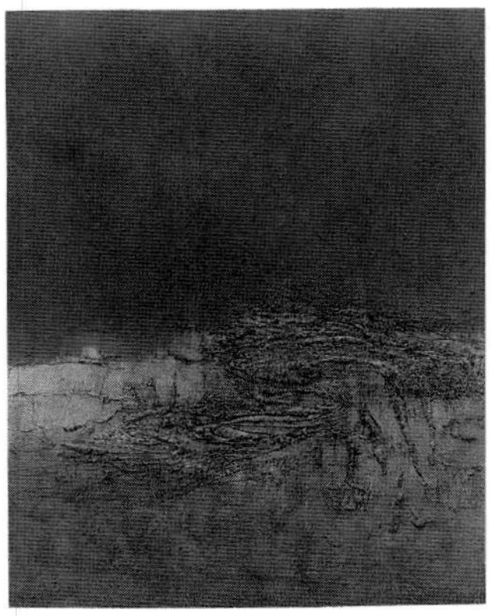

LOUIS SIEGRIEST
American, born 1899

Stormy Sky, 1965
oil and sand on Masonite
$60\frac{1}{4} \times 48\frac{1}{8}''$
153.0×122.2 cm

Members' Accessions Fund Purchase
66.2

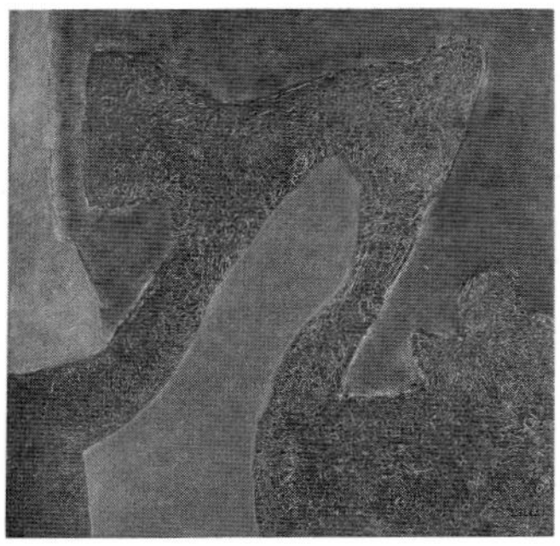

THOMAS SILLS
American, born 1914

South, 1970
acrylic on canvas
$49 \times 50''$
124.5×127.0 cm

Gift of Annie McMurray
72.27

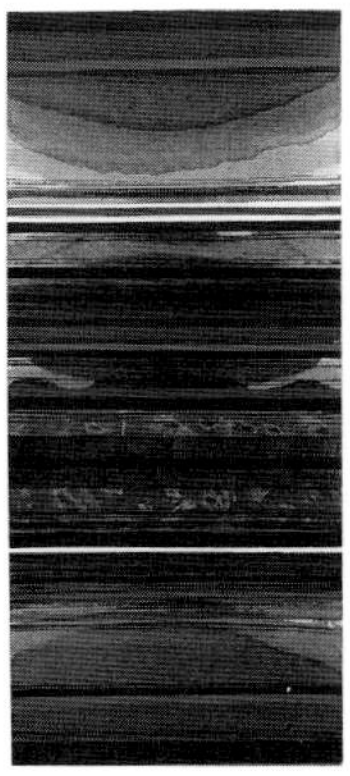

DAVID SIMPSON
American, born 1928

No. 11 Wind Stripes, 1962
oil on canvas
$51\frac{1}{8} \times 22\frac{3}{4}''$
129.9×57.8 cm

Gift of Richard Faralla in memory of John Humphrey
81.199

DAVID SIMPSON
American, born 1928

Spectre, 1962
oil on canvas
$95\frac{7}{8} \times 37\frac{1}{2}''$
243.5×75.3 cm

Anonymous gift through the American Federation of Arts
63.11

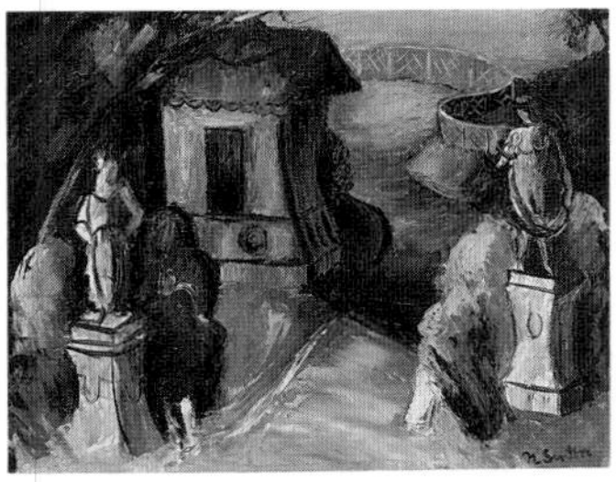

NELL SINTON
American, born 1910

Sutro Heights, 1947
oil on canvas
$18\frac{1}{8} \times 24''$
46.0×61.0 cm

Albert M. Bender Collection
Acquired through a bequest of Albert M. Bender
47.1985

NELL SINTON
American, born 1910

Heart of the Yellow Rose, 1957
oil on canvas
60¼ × 48″
153.0 × 121.9 cm

Gift of Albert E. Schlesinger
57.1253

NELL SINTON
American, born 1910

Legend of Reckendorf, 1971
acrylic on canvas
72⅛ × 108¼″
183.2 × 275.0 cm

Anonymous gift
72.28

DAVID ALFARO SIQUEIROS
Mexican, 1898–1974

Penitentiary (Penitenciaria), 1930
oil on canvas
32⅛ × 20½″
81.4 × 52.1 cm

Gift of Brayton Wilbur
50.6070

DIANE SLOAN
American, born 1940

Carapace #7, 1974
oil on canvas
72 × 57⅛″
182.9 × 145.1 cm

Gift of Mr. and Mrs. Jan Stussy
75.97

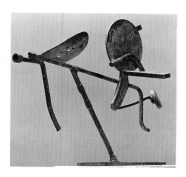

DAVID SMITH
American, 1906–1965

Noon Sun, 1959
steel
25⅞ × 17½ × 36⅛″
65.7 × 44.4 × 91.7 cm

Gift of Mr. and Mrs. William M.
Roth
63.23

GRANT SMITH
American, born 1939

An American Dream, 1974
makestone plaster, fiberglass, wood,
Masonite, aluminum, mirror, and
felt with oil enamel
42¼ × 33 × 20″
107.3 × 83.8 × 50.8 cm

Gift of the artist
80.351 A–E

HASSEL SMITH
American, born 1915

Brandenberg Barbecue, 1952
oil on canvas
69¼ × 53⅞″
175.9 × 136.8 cm

Gift of Irving Blum
73.44

HASSEL SMITH
American, born 1915

Untitled, 1953
oil on canvas
50⅜ × 45¼″
128.0 × 115.0 cm

Gift of Mr. and Mrs. William M.
Roth
73.23

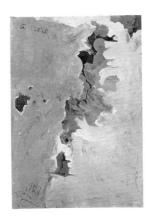

HASSEL SMITH
American, born 1915

A Rose, 1959
oil on canvas
69⅞ × 48″
177.5 × 121.9 cm

Gift of Mrs. Nancy Hills
67.54

HASSEL SMITH
American, born 1915

Hello Galveston! Goodbye France!, 1960
oil on canvas
68⅛ × 69¼″
173.0 × 175.9 cm

Gift of Robert Meyerhoff
83.245

HASSEL SMITH
American, born 1915

Untitled, 1960
oil on canvas
69½ × 68″
176.6 × 172.7 cm

Anonymous gift through the
American Federation of Arts
61.4484

HASSEL SMITH
American, born 1915

Untitled, 1960
oil on canvas
48 × 68″
121.9 × 172.7 cm

Gift of Edwin Janss
78.142

HASSEL SMITH
American, born 1915

2 to the Moon, 1961
oil on canvas
67⅞ × 67⅞″
172.4 × 172.4 cm

Gift of Mr. and Mrs. William C.
Janss
78.206

See colorplate, p. 193

HASSEL SMITH
American, born 1915

Untitled, 1961
oil on canvas
30 × 33⅛″
76.2 × 84.1 cm

Gift of Robert B. Howard
63.15

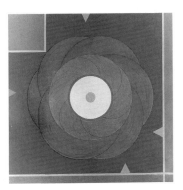

HASSEL SMITH
American, born 1915

Cosmic Funk (with Apologies to Lonnie Liston Smith), 1975–76
acrylic on canvas
68 × 67⅞″
172.7 × 172.4 cm

Acquired through the aid of a gift of
the Hamilton-Wells Collection
82.318

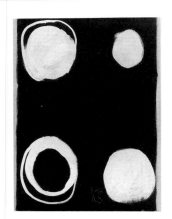

KIMBER SMITH
American, 1922–1981

Untitled, 1961
oil on canvas
39⅜ × 31⅞″
100.0 × 81.0 cm

Gift of Sam Francis
75.147

TONY SMITH
American, 1912–1980

Spitball, 1961
marble
11⅝ × 14½ × 15¼"
29.6 × 36.8 × 38.7 cm

Purchase
71.41

TONY SMITH
American, 1912–1980

Throwback, 1976–79
aluminum with oil enamel   2/3
79⅝ × 194¼ × 105½"
202.3 × 493.4 × 267.9 cm

William L. Gerstle Collection
William L. Gerstle Fund Purchase
80.48

VIC SMITH
American, born 1929

Mumonkan VIII, 1964
acrylic on canvas
61⅞ × 63¾"
157.2 × 161.9 cm

Gift of Comara Gallery, Los Angeles
67.16

WALTER SNELGROVE
American, born 1924

Winslow, 1963
oil on canvas
69½ × 62⅛"
176.5 × 157.7 cm

Gift of Mr. and Mrs. Clarence Postley
78.213

DOUGLAS SNOW
American, born 1927

Desert Landscape, 1967
acrylic with sand aggregates
60 × 39⅜"
152.4 × 100.0 cm

Anonymous gift
68.59

RAPHAEL SOYER
American, born Russia 1899

Nude in Profile, 1949
oil on canvas
40¼ × 36⅛"
102.2 × 91.8 cm

Gift of Ann Hatch
76.25

NILES SPENCER
American, 1893–1952

The Desk, 1948
oil on canvas
24¼ × 32⅜"
61.6 × 82.3 cm

Gift of the Women's Board
59.2669

EUGENE SPIRO
American, born Germany,
1874–1972

The Conqueror No. 2
(Le Conquérant No. 2), 1948
oil on canvas
18 × 15"
45.7 × 38.1 cm

Gift of M. Jean Louis
Forme-Becherat
50.6033

RALPH STACKPOLE
American, 1885–1973·

Fleishhacker Children, n.d.
marble
41 × 23 × 18½"
104.1 × 58.4 × 47.0 cm

Gift of Mr. and Mrs. Mortimer
Fleishhacker
40.5857

RALPH STACKPOLE
American, 1885–1973

Nude Resting, n.d.
bronze
4⅞ × 11⅛ × 5½"
12.4 × 28.3 × 14.0 cm

William L. Gerstle Collection
Gift of William L. Gerstle
41.3137

ALBERT STADLER
American, born 1923

Oasis, 1967
oil and acrylic on canvas
60⅜ × 56⅝"
153.4 × 143.8 cm

Gift of Mr. and Mrs. C. David
Robinson
70.54

FRANÇOIS STAHLY
French, born 1911

Untitled, n.d.
bronze 3/6
4⅞ × 2⅝ × 2⅞"
12.4 × 6.7 × 7.3 cm

Gift of Stanley H. Sinton, Jr.
74.65

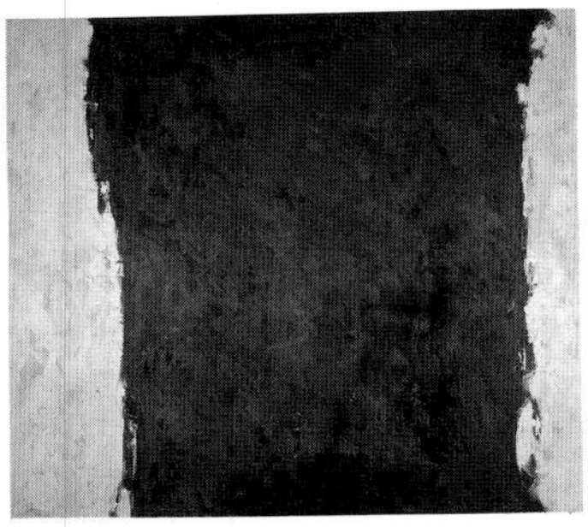

PAUL STAIGER
American, born 1941

Santa Cruz, 1974
acrylic on canvas
60⅛ × 89½"
152.7 × 227.3 cm

T. B. Walker Foundation Fund
Purchase
75.8

THEODORE STAMOS
American, born 1922

Ahab I for R.H., 1959
oil on canvas
70 × 80"
177.8 × 203.2 cm

Gift of the Women's Board and the
Arts Fund, Inc.
60.4177

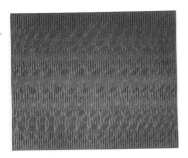

JULIAN STANCZAK
American, born Poland 1928

Color Variance 1 + 2, 1967
polymer tempera on canvas
62 × 76¼"
157.5 × 193.7 cm

William L. Gerstle Collection
William L. Gerstle Fund Purchase
69.8

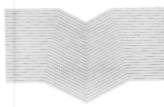

FRANK STELLA
American, born 1936

Adelante, 1964
from the Running V Series
metallic powder in polymer emulsion on canvas
96¼ × 165½"
244.5 × 420.4 cm

T. B. Walker Foundation Fund
Purchase
68.53

See colorplate, p. 215

FRANK STELLA
American, born 1936

Wolfeboro I, 1966
alkyd and epoxy on canvas
160⅜ × 99¾"
408.0 × 253.4 cm

Gift of Robert A. Rowan
78.54

FRANK STELLA
American, born 1936

Khurasan Gate (Variation) I
1969
from the Protractor Series
polymer and fluorescent polymer on
canvas
96¼ × 285½"
244.5 × 725.0 cm

Gift of Mr. and Mrs. Frederick R.
Weisman
78.193

See colorplate, p. 217

FRANK STELLA
American, born 1936

Bechhofen, 1972
wood
97 × 103 × 8"
246.4 × 262.6 × 20.3 cm

Gift of Mr. and Mrs. Hamilton
Robinson, Jr.
79.331 A–B

FRANK STELLA
American, born 1936

Rzochow III, 1973
acrylic, canvas, and cotton felt on
corrugated cardboard
107 × 95⅜ × 4½"
271.8 × 242.9 × 11.4 cm

Gift of Rita and Toby Schreiber
77.268

JOSEPH STELLA
American, born Italy, 1877–1946

Bridge, 1936
oil on canvas
50⅛ × 30⅛"
127.3 × 76.5 cm

WPA Federal Arts Project Allocation
to the San Francisco Museum of Art
3760.43

See colorplate, p. 133

GARY STEPHAN
American, born 1942

Untitled, 1970
polyvinyl chloride and pigment
43½ × 78½"
110.5 × 199.4 cm

Gift of Daniel Weinberg
78.194

MAURICE STERNE
American, born Latvia, 1877–1957

Woman Praying, 1912
oil on board
23⅛ × 14⅞"
58.7 × 37.8 cm

Albert M. Bender Collection
Gift of Albert M. Bender
38.63

MAURICE STERNE
American, born Latvia, 1877–1957

Untitled, n.d.
oil on paper mounted on cardboard
24 × 26⅜"
61.0 × 67.0 cm

Gift of Blanche C. Matthias
78.72

MAY STEVENS
American, born 1924

Mysteries and Politics, 1978
acrylic on canvas
78 × 142″
198.1 × 360.7 cm

Gift of Mr. and Mrs. Anthony Grippa
83.248

NORMAN STIEGELMEYER
American, born 1937

Altar of the Black Totems, 1969
acrylic on canvas
86 × 66½″
218.4 × 168.9 cm

Purchase
73.26

CLYFFORD STILL
American, 1904–1980

Untitled, 1934
oil on canvas
57⅝ × 31⅝″
146.4 × 80.3 cm
(Ph-323)

Gift of the artist
75.14

CLYFFORD STILL
American, 1904–1980

Untitled, 1936
oil on burlap
24⅞ × 16⅞″
63.2 × 42.9 cm
(Ph-436)

Gift of the artist
75.15

CLYFFORD STILL
American, 1904–1980

1936–7-No. 2, 1936–37
oil on canvas
63⅝ × 33⅛″
161.6 × 84.1 cm
(Ph-591)

Gift of the artist
75.16

CLYFFORD STILL
American, 1904–1980

Untitled, 1937
oil on canvas
42⅞ × 30¾″
108.9 × 78.1 cm
(Ph-164)

Gift of the artist
75.17

CLYFFORD STILL
American, 1904–1980

1938-N-No. 1, 1938
oil on canvas
30⅞ × 25¼″
78.6 × 64.0 cm
(Ph-206)

Gift of the artist
75.18

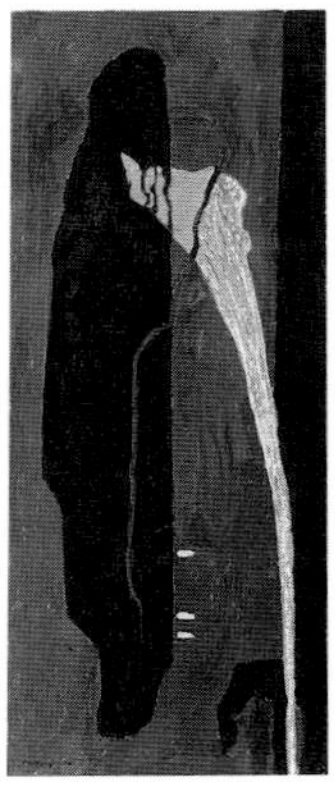

CLYFFORD STILL
American, 1904–1980

1941-R, 1941
oil on denim
58⅛ × 25⅝″
147.6 × 65.1 cm
(Ph-169)

Gift of the artist
75.19

CLYFFORD STILL
American, 1904–1980

Untitled, 1942
oil on denim
57½ × 26½″
146.1 × 67.3 cm
(Ph-298)

Gift of the artist
75.20

CLYFFORD STILL
American, 1904–1980

1943-J, 1943
oil on canvas
69⅛ × 32¾″
175.4 × 83.1 cm
(Ph-198)

Gift of the artist
75.21

CLYFFORD STILL
American, 1904–1980

1944-G, 1944
oil on canvas
68¼ × 31⅝″
173.4 × 80.3 cm
(Ph-204)

Gift of the artist
75.22

CLYFFORD STILL
American, 1904–1980

1945-H, 1945
oil on canvas
90⅜ × 68¾″
229.6 × 174.6 cm
(Ph-135)

Gift of the artist
75.23

CLYFFORD STILL
American, 1904–1980

Untitled
(formerly *Self-Portrait*), 1945
oil on canvas
70⅞ × 42″
180.1 × 106.7 cm
(Ph-233)

Gift of Peggy Guggenheim
47.1238

See colorplate, p. 151

CLYFFORD STILL
American, 1904–1980

1947-H-No.3, 1947
oil on canvas
91 × 57¼″
231.2 × 145.4 cm
(Ph-446)

Gift of the artist
75.26

CLYFFORD STILL
American, 1904–1980

1947-S, 1947
oil on canvas
84⅝ × 71⅝″
215.0 × 181.9 cm
(Ph-371)

Gift of the artist
75.25

CLYFFORD STILL
American, 1904–1980

Untitled, 1947
oil on canvas
70 × 39½″
177.8 × 100.3 cm
(Ph-123)

Gift of the artist
75.24

CLYFFORD STILL
American, 1904–1980

Untitled, 1948
oil on canvas
52 × 43¼″
132.1 × 109.7 cm
(Ph-128)

Gift of the artist
75.27

CLYFFORD STILL
American, 1904–1980

1950-K-No. 1, 1950
oil on canvas
108⅛ × 86⅛″
274.6 × 218.8 cm
(Ph-379)

Gift of the artist
75.28

CLYFFORD STILL
American, 1904–1980

Untitled, 1951
oil on canvas
82 × 68¾″
208.3 × 174.6 cm
(Ph-58)

Gift of the artist
75.29

CLYFFORD STILL
American, 1904–1980

Untitled, 1951–52
oil on canvas
113⅜ × 156″
288.0 × 396.2 cm
(Ph-968)

Gift of the artist
75.30

See colorplate, p. 154

CLYFFORD STILL
American, 1904–1980

1952-A, 1952
oil on canvas
118⅛ × 106⅛″
300.1 × 269.5 cm
(Ph-585)

Gift of the artist
75.31

CLYFFORD STILL
American, 1904–1980

Untitled, 1952
oil on canvas
60½ × 48″
153.7 × 121.9 cm
(Ph-84)

Gift of the artist
75.32

CLYFFORD STILL
American, 1904–1980

Untitled, 1954
oil on canvas
115 × 103⅞″
292.1 × 263.8 cm
(Ph-969)

Gift of the artist
75.33

CLYFFORD STILL
American, 1904–1980

1956-D, 1956
oil on canvas
114½ × 160″
290.8 × 406.4 cm
(Ph-245)

Gift of the artist
75.34

CLYFFORD STILL
American, 1904–1980

Untitled, 1957
oil on canvas
113¼ × 148″
287.7 × 375.9 cm
(Ph-971)

Gift of the artist
75.35

CLYFFORD STILL
American, 1904–1980

Untitled, 1959
oil on canvas
114½ × 103¾″
290.8 × 263.5 cm
(Ph-966)

Gift of the artist
75.37

CLYFFORD STILL
American, 1904–1980

Untitled, 1959
oil on canvas
115⅛ × 104¾″
292.4 × 266.0 cm
(Ph-973)

Gift of the artist
75.36

CLYFFORD STILL
American, 1904–1980

Untitled, 1960
oil on canvas
113⅛ × 155⅞″
287.3 × 395.9 cm
(Ph-174)

Gift of Mr. and Mrs. Harry W.
Anderson
74.19

See colorplate, p. 155

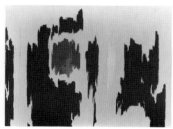

CLYFFORD STILL
American, 1904–1980

Untitled, 1962
oil on canvas
113 × 152⅛″
287.0 × 386.4 cm
(Ph-261)

Gift of the artist
75.38

CLYFFORD STILL
American, 1904–1980

Untitled, 1971
oil on canvas
93⅜ × 155″
237.9 × 393.7 cm
(Ph-795)

Gift of the artist
75.39

CLYFFORD STILL
American, 1904–1980

Untitled, 1974
oil on canvas
111⅞ × 174⅛″
284.2 × 442.3 cm
(Ph-919)

Gift of the artist
75.41

CLYFFORD STILL
American, 1904–1980

Untitled, 1974
oil on canvas
114¼ × 170½″
290.2 × 433.1 cm
(Ph-920)

Gift of the artist
75.40

379

JOHN STORRS
American, 1885–1956

***Study in Form (Architectural
Form)***, ca. 1923
stone
19½ × 3⅛ × 3¼″
49.6 × 8.0 × 8.3 cm

Purchased through a gift of Julian
and Jean Aberbach
81.3

See colorplate, p. 131

TAL STREETER
American, born 1934

The Bed, 1963
steel with enamel
30 × 54 × 42⅜″
76.2 × 137.2 × 107.6 cm

Gift of the artist
68.60

CHARLES STRONG
American, born 1938

Poland, 1981
from the series Heroes and Heroines
acrylic and charcoal on canvas
60 × 84¼″
152.4 × 214.0 cm

Gift of David B. Devine
81.247

CHARLES STRONG
American, born 1938

***Safe Passage
(Raoul Wallenberg)***, 1981
from the series Heroes and
Heroines
acrylic on canvas
103 × 79½″
261.6 × 201.9 cm

Gift of David B. Devine
82.65

JACK STUCK
American, born 1925

Pastorale—Hollywood, 1962
oil on canvas
72¼ × 86″
183.5 × 218.4 cm

Gift of Mr. and Mrs. Gene Lexen
68.19

ANTONIO SUAREZ
Spanish, born 1923

No. 3, 1960
oil and aluminum paint on canvas
26 × 32¼″
66.0 × 81.9 cm

Gift of Dr. and Mrs. Melvin B.
Black
71.35

KUMI SUGAI
Japanese, born 1919

Hunter (Kariudo), 1958
oil on canvas
39⅜ × 32″
100.0 × 81.3 cm

Gift of Keith Wellin
71.80

KUMI SUGAI
Japanese, born 1919

Afternoon (Gogo), 1959
oil on canvas
51⅛ × 38¼″
129.7 × 97.2 cm

Gift of Jacob Delman
71.79

JAMES SURLS
American, born 1943

*Being with the Sword and the
Needle*, 1981
oak and rattan
74 × 105 × 80″
188.0 × 266.7 × 203.2 cm

Gift of Mr. and Mrs. Carter P. Thacher
82.2

LEOPOLD SURVAGE
French, born Russia, 1879–1968

La Côte d'Azur, n.d.
oil on canvas
16⅛ × 13″
41.0 × 33.0 cm

Bequest of Blanche C. Matthias
83.54

YOSHIYASU SUSUKA
Japanese, born 1947

Wave Byobu with Kimono, 1978
photographic silkscreen on canvas;
photographic silkscreen on silk
89 × 168 × 96″
226.1 × 426.7 × 243.8 cm

Gift of Soker-Kaseman Gallery, San
Francisco
80.431 A–B

RUFINO TAMAYO
Mexican, born 1899

The Window, 1932
oil on canvas
19¾ × 23⅝″
50.2 × 60.0 cm

Gift of Howard Putzel
35.3399

RUFINO TAMAYO
Mexican, born 1899

The Lovers, 1943
oil on canvas
34¼ × 44¼″
87.0 × 112.4 cm

Purchased with the aid of funds
from W. W. Crocker
45.1571

YVES TANGUY
French, 1900-1955

Second Thoughts
(Arrières-pensées), 1939
oil on canvas
36⅛ × 29¼″
91.7 × 74.3 cm

William L. Gerstle Collection
William L. Gerstle Fund Purchase
52.4155

See colorplate, p. 115

FREDERICK TAUBES
American, born Poland, 1900–1981

William L. Gerstle, 1942
oil on canvas
36⅛ × 30″
91.8 × 76.2 cm

William L. Gerstle Collection
Gift of William L. Gerstle
42.5549

SAM TCHAKALIAN
American, born China 1929

Prescription, 1959
oil and paper on canvas
69⅛ × 68¾″
175.6 × 173.7 cm

Gift of the Hamilton-Wells
Collection
69.100

SAM TCHAKALIAN
American, born China 1929

Pink Lady, 1960
oil and paper on canvas
71½ × 70⅝″
181.6 × 179.4 cm

Gift of Mr. and Mrs. L. James
Newman
67.88

SAM TCHAKALIAN
American, born China 1929

Orange Juice, 1966
oil on canvas
76¼ × 97⅛″
193.7 × 246.7 cm

Beatrice Judd Ryan Bequest Fund
Purchase
67.57

SAM TCHAKALIAN
American, born China 1929

Green Ball, 1967
oil on canvas
76 × 80″
193.0 × 203.2 cm

Anonymous gift
77.196

SAM TCHAKALIAN
American, born China 1929

Cartoon, 1975
oil on canvas
48 × 240″
121.9 × 609.6 cm

Gift of John B. and Jane K. Stuppin
81.152

JORGE TEIXIDOR
Spanish, born 1941

Untitled, 1979
oil on linen
33⅝ × 33⅜″
85.4 × 84.8 cm

Gift of Mr. and Mrs. James Harwood
82.410

WAYNE THIEBAUD
American, born 1920

Display Cakes, 1963
oil on canvas
28 × 38″
71.0 × 96.5 cm

Mrs. Manfred Bransten Special
Fund Purchase
73.52

See colorplate, p. 227

JOHN TIMIRIASIEFF
American

Steep Ravine, 1937
oil on canvas
14⅛ × 18⅛″
35.9 × 46.0 cm

Gift of Michele and Mercury Bell
82.411

MARK TOBEY
American, 1890–1976

Cubist Vertical, 1943
gouache on cardboard mounted
on panel
17⅞ × 5⅞″
45.4 × 14.9 cm

Purchase
83.64

MARK TOBEY
American, 1890–1976

Written over the Plains, 1950
tempera on Masonite
30⅛ × 40″
76.5 × 101.7 cm

Gift of Mr. and Mrs. Ferdinand C.
Smith
51.3169

See colorplate, p. 145

MICHAEL TODD
American, born 1935

Daimaru IV, 1976
mild steel
137½ × 154 × 53″
349.3 × 391.2 × 134.6 cm

Gift of Mrs. Paul L. Wattis
82.3

HELEN TORR
American, 1886–1967

Windows and a Door, n.d.
oil on copper, mounted on board
15½ × 20½″
39.4 × 52.1 cm

T. B. Walker Foundation Fund
Purchase
80.341

JOAQUIN TORRES-GARCIA
Uruguayan, 1874–1949

Two Figures, 1930
oil on canvas
28¾ × 23¾″
73.0 × 60.3 cm

Gift of Roman Fresnedo Siri through
Adolfo J. Sasco
43.4376

JOAQUIN TORRES-GARCIA
Uruguayan, 1874–1949

Constructivist Painting No. 8
1938
gouache on paperboard
31⅝ × 19½″
80.5 × 49.5 cm

Purchased through the aid of a gift
of Willard Durham
50.3013

See colorplate, p. 85

GARNER TULLIS
American, born 1939

Number Sixteen, 1971
glass
21⅜ × 21½″
54.9 × 54.6 cm

Gift of Ruth Braunstein
71.77

RICHARD TUTTLE
American, born 1941

W-Shaped Yellow Canvas, 1967
canvas with dye
53¼ × 60⅜″
135.3 × 154.0 cm

Gift of Rena Bransten
73.15

JACK TWORKOV
American, born Poland, 1900–1982

Script II, 1963
oil on canvas
80 × 69″
203.2 × 175.3 cm

Purchased with matching funds from
the National Endowment for the
Arts and the Mr. and Mrs. Harry W.
Anderson Fund and the Evelyn and
Walter Haas, Jr. Fund
80.166

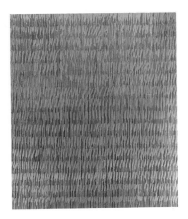

JACK TWORKOV
American, born Poland, 1900–1982

Idling III, 1970
oil on canvas
80 × 70″
203.2 × 177.8 cm

Gift of the artist
80.98

CHRIS UNTERSEHER
American, born 1943

Repainting for the 1934 Season
1975
porcelain with underglaze and
lithographic decal
11¾ × 15½ × 2¼″
29.8 × 39.4 × 5.7 cm

Purchased with the aid of funds
from the National Endowment
for the Arts
79.247 A–C

BUMPEI USUI
Japanese, born 1898

Hall Table, 1936
oil on canvas
24 × 19¾″
61.0 × 50.2 cm

WPA Federal Arts Project Allocation
to the San Francisco Museum of Art
3765.43

MAURICE UTRILLO
French, 1883–1955

The Petit Palais
(Le Petit Palais), 1922
oil on canvas
19⅜ × 25½″
49.2 × 64.8 cm

Purchase
38.121

BOAZ VAADIA
Israeli, born 1951

Untitled, 1977
bluestone, wood, leather, and fur
42 × 84 × 24″
106.7 × 213.4 × 61.0 cm

Gift of Schlomo Schwartz
83.250

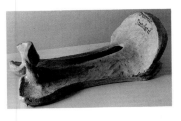

VAEA (MARX)
American, born Tahiti 1929

American Standard, 1971
stoneware with slip glaze
7 × 13 × 23″
17.8 × 33.0 × 58.4 cm

Anonymous gift
72.72

VAEA (MARX)
American, born Tahiti 1929

Saddle, 1971
stoneware with glaze
14½ × 16½ × 12⅛″
36.9 × 41.9 × 31.5 cm

Gift of Michele and Mercury Bell
82.412

LAURENCE VAIL
American, born France, 1891–1968

Rust and Dust, 1947
seashells, cloth with embroidery,
chain, buttons, metal clamps, compass, rhinestone pin, metal wire,
metal, metallic glitter, brush, canvas, lace, elastic, nails, screw, glass
beads, seed pearls, and keys
9⅜ × 12¼ × 10⅜″
23.8 × 31.1 × 26.4 cm

Gift of Peggy Guggenheim
67.53

RICHARD VAN BUREN
American, born 1937

Solos and Duets, 1972
resin, fiberglass, and pigments
63¼ × 70¼ × 6″
160.7 × 178.4 × 15.2 cm

Gift of Paula Cooper
77.95

JEAN VARDA
American, born Greece 1893

Abstraction, n.d.
watercolor, cardboard, newsprint,
and paper on board
21⅜ × 25⅝″
54.3 × 65.1 cm

Gift of Herman Flax
45.1297

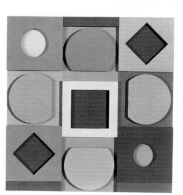

VICTOR VASARELY
French, born Hungary 1908

Granat, 1967
wood with enamel 26/50
12½ × 11¾ × ½″
31.8 × 29.8 × 1.3 cm

Gift of Byron Meyer
78.195

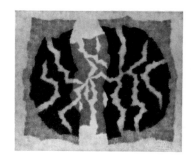

JOSEPH VASICA
American, born Austria 1921

***Broken Paths into a Split
Labyrinth***, 1972
oil on canvas
38⅛ × 45″
96.8 × 114.3 cm

Gift of Cyril Magnin
72.73

ESTEBAN VICENTE
Spanish, born 1906

Untitled, 1964
oil on canvas
48 × 66″
121.9 × 167.6 cm

Gift of Mr. and Mrs. Esteban
Vicente
66.15

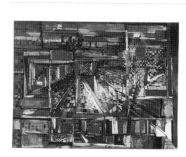

MARIA ELENA VIEIRA DA SILVA
Portuguese, born 1908

The Invisible Stroller
(Le Promeneur invisible), 1951
oil on canvas
52 × 66⅜″
132.1 × 168.6 cm

Gift of Mr. and Mrs. Wellington S.
Henderson
54.3275

MICHAEL VON MEYER
American, born Russia 1894

Untitled (***Head of a Man***), 1935
terra-cotta
8½ × 6 × 7⅛″
21.6 × 15.2 × 18.1 cm

Albert M. Bender Collection
Gift of Albert M. Bender
35.4542

PETER VOULKOS
American, born 1924

Sevillanas, 1959
stoneware with iron slip and
clear glaze
56¾ × 27¼ × 20″
144.1 × 69.2 × 50.8 cm

Albert M. Bender Collection
Albert M. Bender Bequest Fund
Purchase
64.9

See colorplate, p. 205

385

PETER VOULKOS
American, born 1924

Untitled, 1962
stoneware with glaze
25¼ × 9⅞ × 11⅛"
64.1 × 25.0 × 28.3 cm

Gift of Win Ng
81.238

PETER VOULKOS
American, born 1924

Hiro II, 1967
bronze
96 × 328 × 84"
243.8 × 833.1 × 213.4 cm

T. B. Walker Foundation Fund
Purchase and anonymous gift
71.66

PETER VOULKOS
American, born 1924

Anada, 1968
stoneware with iron slip and
clear glaze
34⅜ × 11½" diam.
87.3 × 29.2 cm

Gift of Mrs. Edgar Sinton
69.34

PETER VOULKOS
American, born 1924

Ceramic Drawing, 1973
stoneware and porcelain with glaze
17½ diam. × 3¾"
44.5 × 8.6 cm

Gift of Dr. and Mrs. David T. Wise
83.251

PETER VOULKOS
American, born 1924

Blue Line, 1977
stoneware with porcelain
34⅜ × 14⅝" diam.
87.3 × 37.2 cm

Gift of the Hamilton-Wells Collection
78.42

PETER VOULKOS
American, born 1924

Ceramic Drawing, 1978
stoneware with porcelain
22 diam. × 4⅜"
55.9 × 11.1 cm

Gift of the Hamilton-Wells
Collection
78.41

VREDAPARIS
American, born 1928

The Family, 1964
bronze with aluminum surface 1/1
48⅜ × 60⅜ × 37⅛"
122.9 × 153.4 × 94.3 cm

Gift of Mr. and Mrs. Eric Berger
80.192 A–E

GERALD WALBURG
American, born 1936

Opposing Soft Loops, 1966-67
Cor-ten steel
41½ × 155½ × 34⅛"
105.4 × 395.0 × 86.7 cm

Gift of Mr. and Mrs. Walter A.
Haas, Jr.
69.18

386

ANDY WARHOL
American, born 1928

A Set of Six Self-Portraits, 1967
oil and silkscreen on canvas
each 22½ × 22½″
57.2 × 57.2 cm

Gift of Michael D. Abrams
78.196 A–F

ANDY WARHOL
American, born 1928

Two Portraits of Paul Anka, 1976
acrylic on canvas
A: 40 × 40″
    101.6 × 101.6 cm
B: 40 × 40⅛″
    101.6 × 101.9 cm

Gift of Mr. and Mrs. Paul Anka
79.316 A–B

JULIUS WASSERSTEIN
American, born 1924

Shadows and Etc., 1961
oil on canvas
41⅜ × 32½″
105.1 × 82.6 cm

Anonymous gift
81.92

JULIUS WASSERSTEIN
American, born 1924

Paintscape Country #4, 1962
oil on canvas
72⅜ × 64⅜″
183.8 × 163.5 cm

Gerda Dorfner Memorial Fund
Purchase
69.46

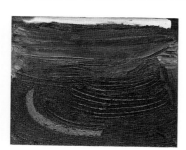

JULIUS WASSERSTEIN
American, born 1924

Paintscape Country #13, 1962
oil on canvas
29½ × 38⅛″
74.9 × 96.8 cm

Gift of Mr. and Mrs. Moses Lasky
63.1

JULIUS WASSERSTEIN
American, born 1924

From Rembrandt's Helmet, 1972
acrylic on canvas
69¾ × 60⅞″
177.2 × 154.6 cm

Gift of the Women's Board in
memory of Norma Lincoln
74.66

JULIUS WASSERSTEIN
American, born 1924

Untitled, 1978
acrylic on canvas
61 × 73¾″
155.0 × 187.3 cm

Gift of Elise Stern Haas
79.228

JAMES WEEKS
American, born 1922

Untitled, 1953
oil on canvas
78 × 96½″
198.2 × 245.1 cm

Gift of William M. Roth
73.24

JAMES WEEKS
American, born 1922

*Looking West from Spanish Fort—
Baker Beach #3*, 1962
oil on canvas
48 × 49⅝"
121.9 × 126.0 cm

Gift of the Women's Board
62.4522

NEIL WELLIVER
American, born 1929

Megunticook, 1980
oil on canvas
96⅜ × 120½"
244.8 × 306.1 cm

Gift of J. Gary Shansby
83.252

MASON WELLS
American, born 1906

Seville, 1964
oil and acrylic on canvas
109⅞ × 60"
279.0 × 152.4 cm

Gift of Frank O. Hamilton
77.96

MASON WELLS
American, born 1906

Red Rectangle and Verticals, 1965
acrylic polymer on canvas
49¾ × 59⅞"
126.4 × 152.1 cm

Anonymous gift
69.54

H. C. WESTERMANN
American, 1922–1981

Bullseye, 1963
glass, ink on mirror, and wood
13⅜ × 13¼ × 2⅝"
34.0 × 33.7 × 6.7 cm

Purchase
83.152

H. C. WESTERMANN
American, 1922–1981

Secrets, 1964
American walnut and brass
6¾ × 11 × 8½"
17.2 × 28.0 × 21.6 cm

Purchase
77.193

HAROLD WESTON
American, 1894–1972

Green Hat, 1927
oil on canvas
19⅞ × 25⅝"
50.5 × 65.1 cm

Gift of the Ladies' Auxiliary of the
Palace of Fine Arts
39.129

WHANKI
see KIM WHANKI

388

JOSEPH WHITE
American, born 1938

Winter 1967, 1967
oil on canvas
51⅜ × 113¼″
130.5 × 287.7 cm

Anonymous gift
69.103 A–B

WILLIAM T. WILEY
American, born 1937

Untitled, 1962
oil on canvas
68¼ × 76″
173.4 × 193.0 cm

Gift of the Women's Board
63.22

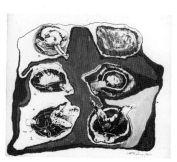

WILLIAM T. WILEY
American, born 1937

Untitled, 1962
oil on canvas mounted on panel
12¼ × 14″
31.2 × 35.6 cm

Gift of Dr. Samuel West
68.65

WILLIAM T. WILEY
American, born 1937

Untitled, 1962
oil on canvas
15½ × 19″
39.4 × 48.3 cm

Gift of Dr. Samuel West
68.67

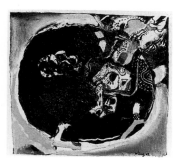

WILLIAM T. WILEY
American, born 1937

Untitled, 1962
oil on canvas
11⅛ × 12⅝″
28.3 × 32.1 cm

Gift of Dr. Samuel West
68.64

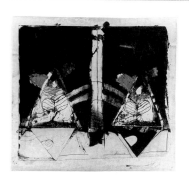

WILLIAM T. WILEY
American, born 1937

Untitled, 1962
oil on paper mounted on panel
12¾ × 13½″
32.4 × 34.3 cm

Gift of Dr. Samuel West
68.66

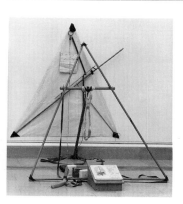

WILLIAM T. WILEY
American, born 1937

Ship's Log, 1969
cotton webbing, latex rubber, salt
licks, leather, plastic, wood, canvas,
lead wire, nautical and assorted
hardware, and ink and watercolor
on paper
82 × 78 × 54″
208.3 × 198.1 × 137.2 cm

William L. Gerstle Collection
William L. Gerstle Fund Purchase
70.37 A–L

See colorplate, p. 223

WILLIAM T. WILEY
American, born 1937

Tools and Trade, 1978
colored pencil and felt-tip pen ink
on canvas
77½ × 87⅛″
196.8 × 221.3 cm

Gift of Mr. and Mrs. William C.
Janss
81.248

ULFERT WILKE
American, born Germany 1907

Music to Be Seen, Anchorage
1967
oil on canvas
48 × 48⅛"
121.9 × 122.2 cm

William L. Gerstle Collection
William L. Gerstle Fund Purchase
68.51

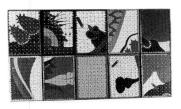

FRANKLIN WILLIAMS
American, born 1940

Untitled, 1968–69
cloth, paint, and thread on ten
paperboard boxes
each 36¾ × 26⅜ × 8⅝"
93.4 × 67.0 × 21.9 cm

Gift of Jim and Judy Newman
74.105.1–.10

FRANKLIN WILLIAMS
American, born 1940

Soul Cultivate, 1975
acrylic on paper on canvas with
vinyl
66⅜ × 59¼"
169.2 × 150.5 cm

Mrs. Manfred Bransten Fund
Purchase
76.38

CHRISTOPHER WILMARTH
American, born 1943

New, 1968
plywood and glass
95½ × 23½ × 24⅜"
242.6 × 59.7 × 61.9 cm

Gift of Mr. and Mrs. Richard
Dirickson, Jr.
82.415 A–C

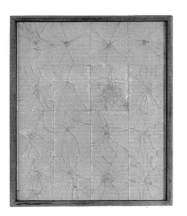

CHRISTOPHER WILMARTH
American, born 1943

Glass Drawing, 1969
glass and wood
13 × 10⅞ × 1¾"
33.0 × 27.6 × 4.5 cm

Gift of Carlos Villa
72.55

CHRISTOPHER WILMARTH
American, born 1943

Long Beginnings for My Brother
1974
steel and glass
30 × 60 × 5¼"
76.2 × 152.4 × 13.4 cm

Gift of Mr. and Mrs. C. David
Robinson
77.276 A–C

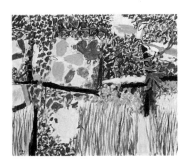

BRYAN WILSON
American, born 1927

Scrub Jays, 1957
oil on canvas
59⅞ × 71¾"
152.1 × 102.3 cm

Gift of the Women's Board
59.5124

BRYAN WILSON
American, born 1927

Yellow-Billed Magpies, 1957
oil on canvas
73 × 47⅛"
185.4 × 119.7 cm

Bequest of Jacqueline Marie Onslow
Ford
82.52

ED WILSON
American, born 1925

Seven Seals of Silence, 1966
bronze 1/1
A: *The Invisible*
 10⅝ × 13¼ × 1⅛″
 26.9 × 33.6 × 2.9 cm
B: *The Maimed and the Ignorant*
 (two parts)
 5½ × 8 × 1⅛″
 13.9 × 20.3 × 2.9 cm
 7¾ × 8¼ × 1⅛″
 20.0 × 20.9 × 2.9 cm

C: *The Conformists*
 12½ × 13 × 1¼″
 31.7 × 33.0 × 3.2 cm
D: *The Uninspired*
 14⅛ × 10¼ × 1¼″
 35.8 × 26.0 × 3.2 cm
E: *The Rejected* (two parts)
 10⅜ × 5 × 1¼″
 26.3 × 12.7 × 3.2 cm
 8⅝ × 11⅞ × 1″
 21.9 × 30.1 × 2.5 cm

F: *The Depraved*
 12¾ × 11⅝ × 1¼″
 32.7 × 29.5 × 3.2 cm
G: *The Dead* (two parts)
 11⅛ × 9½ × ⅞″
 28.2 × 24.1 × 2.2 cm
 2⅜ × 8⅝ × ⅜″
 6.0 × 21.9 × 1.0 cm

Gift of Lenore and Allan Sindler
77.4 A–G

JACKIE WINSOR
American, born 1941

#1 Rope, 1976
wood and hemp
42 × 42 × 42″
106.7 × 106.7 × 106.7 cm

Purchased with the aid of funds
from the National Endowment for
the Arts and the New Future Fund
Drive
77.73

FRITZ WINTER
German, born 1905

GS-34, 1934
oil on paper mounted on Masonite
43 × 30″
109.2 × 76.2 cm

Gift of Dr. George Sugarman
64.74

FRITZ WINTER
German, born 1905

GS-31, n.d.
oil and sand on canvas
28 × 19⅛″
71.1 × 48.6 cm

Gift of Dr. George Sugarman
64.71

ISAAC WITKIN
American, born South Africa 1936

Mabalel, 1974
steel
108 × 225½ × 140½″
274.3 × 572.8 × 356.9 cm

Gift of Mr. and Mrs. William C.
Janss
80.352 A–C

EMERSON WOELFFER
American, born 1914

90 Degrees, 1955
oil on canvas
34¼ × 31½″
87.0 × 80.3 cm

Gift of Mr. and Mrs. Paul Kantor
70.35

PAUL WONNER
American, born 1920

The Newspaper, 1960
oil on canvas
47⅜ × 54½″
120.3 × 138.4 cm

Gift of the Hamilton-Wells Collection
69.104

PAUL WONNER
American, born 1920

Dutch Still Life with Lemon Tart and Engagement Calendar, 1979
acrylic on canvas
47¾ × 96"
121.3 × 243.9 cm

Charles H. Land Family Foundation
Fund Purchase
80.81 A–B

PAUL WONNER
American, born 1920

Landscape, n.d.
oil on canvas
58⅛ × 60"
147.6 × 152.4 cm

Gift of Mr. and Mrs. Lloyd S.
Ackerman
55.6898

KAZUO YAGI
Japanese, 1918–1979

Queen, 1964
black stoneware
7 × 10½ × 10½"
17.8 × 26.7 × 26.7 cm

Gift of Mrs. Ferdinand C. Smith
65.11

MANOUCHER YEKTAI
American, born Persia 1922

Tomato Plant, 1959
oil on canvas
42 × 32"
106.7 × 81.3 cm

Gift of Louis Honig
76.193

JACK YOUNGERMAN
American, born 1926

June Blue, 1969
acrylic on canvas
65⅛ × 52¼"
165.4 × 132.7 cm

Gift of Mr. and Mrs. Philip M.
Stern
80.99

JACK ZAJAC
American, born 1929

Fallen Warrior 2, ca. late 1950s
oil on canvas
39⅛ × 58¾"
99.4 × 149.2 cm

Gift of Ned Pearlstein
81.202

NORMAN ZAMMITT
American, born Canada 1931

Blue Burning, 1982
acrylic on canvas
84 × 168½"
213.4 × 428.0 cm

Gift of Judge and Mrs. William J.
Lasarow
82.417

ZAO WOU-KI
Chinese, born 1920

Chinese Scene
(Scène chinoise), 1951
oil on canvas
12¾ × 15¾"
32.4 × 40.0 cm

Gift of Larry Aldrich
58.1896

JOSEPH ZARITSKY
Israeli, born Russia 1891

Towards the Light, 1965
oil on canvas
28⅝ × 35¼"
72.7 × 89.5 cm

Gift of Mr. and Mrs. Richard Swig
and Mr. and Mrs. Richard Dinner
69.44

PETER ZECHER
American, born 1945

Thing 5, Black Heart, 1968
wood, aluminum, and fiberglass
46 × 16¾ × 17¼"
116.9 × 42.6 × 43.8 cm

Anonymous gift
70.12

PETER ZECHER
American, born 1945

Steel Sculpture I, 1981
mild steel with zinc
70 × 21 × 17"
177.8 × 53.3 × 43.2 cm

Gift of James Corcoran Gallery,
Inc., Los Angeles
82.418

WILFRID ZOGBAUM
American, 1915–1965

II, 1962
oil on metal with stone
69 × 37 × 26"
175.3 × 94.0 × 66.1 cm

Gift of friends of the artist
64.1 A–D

WILLIAM ZORACH
American, born Lithuania, 1887–1966

Dahlov (The Artist's Daughter)
1921
bronze ed. 6
6⅞ × 1½ × 1½"
17.5 × 3.8 × 3.8 cm

Gift of Mr. and Mrs. Louis Honig
76.194

WILLIAM ZORACH
American, born Lithuania, 1887–1966

Father and Son, 1939–42
bronze ed. 6
10 × 12 × 6"
25.4 × 30.5 × 15.2 cm

Gift of A. A. Ehresmann
64.60

Index

Page numbers in italics refer to colorplate illustrations.
Numbers following the indication "ck" refer to the pages of the Checklist on which the artist's work appears. Since the Checklist itself is organized in index fashion, the individual works of art have not been listed again below; works of art are listed in this Index only if they are discussed or mentioned elsewhere in the book.

Abbott, Berenice, 24, 130
Abstract Expressionism, 27, 28, 146, 148, 150, 156, 160, 168, 170, 176, 184, 186, 190, 192, 194, 196, 200, 204, 206, 208, 210, 212, 214, 218, 220, 222, 226, 228, 230, 232
Académie Julian, Paris, 38, 50
Académie Matisse, Paris, 35
Action Sculpture, 230
Acton, Arlo, 23, ck 261
Acuña, Luis Alberto, ck 261
Adams, Ansel, 19, 21, 23, 24, 26, 28
Adams, Robert, 28
Adler, Jankel, ck 261
Admiral, Virginia, ck 261
African art, 17, 40, 52, 70
Akawie, Thomas, ck 261
Albers, Anni, 27, 194
Albers, Josef, 27, 90, 92, 94, 194, 244, ck 261–63; Foundation, 27
    Free Studies, 90, 92
    Growing, 22, 90, *91*, 244
    Homage to the Square Series, 27, 92, 94
    Study for Homage to the Square, 94, *95*, 244
    Tenayuca, 92, *93*, 244
    Tenayuca Dark, 92, 244
    Treble Clef Series, 92
Albright Art Gallery, Buffalo, N.Y., 248
Alexander, Peter, ck 263
Alfi, Zmira, ck 263
Alfred, State University of New York at, 208
Allan, William, ck 263–64
Altoon, John, 24, 28, 210, 212, ck 264
American Scene painting, 162
Anderson, David, ck 264
Anderson, Mr. and Mrs. Harry W., 153
Anderson, Jeremy, 23, 192, ck 264–65
Anderson Galleries, New York, 248
Anguiano, Raoul, ck 265
Appel, Karel, 23, ck 265
    Waiting for Us, 23
Archipenko, Alexander, 52, ck 265
architecture: Beaux-Arts, 14, 15; California, 25
Armer, Ruth, ck 265–66
Armory Show. SEE *International Exhibition of Modern Art*
Arneson, Robert, 24, 224, 228, 258, ck 266
    California Artist, 28, 234, *235*, 258
    Call Girl, 234
    Smorgy Bob, 234
Arnoldi, Charles, ck 266
Arp, Jean (Hans), 28, 84, 102–3, 106, 158, 218, 245–46, ck 266–67
    According to the Laws of Chance, 103
    Concrétion humaine sans coupe. SEE *Human Concretion without Oval Bowl*
    Head and Leaf; Head and Vase, 102, 103, *104*, 106, 245
    Head and Navel. SEE *Head and Leaf; Head and Vase*
    Human Concretion Series, 106
    Human Concretion without Oval Bowl, 106, *107*, 246
    Objects Arranged According to

the Laws of Chance III; Symmetrical Configuration, 102, 103, *105*, 106, 245–46
    Objets placés selon les lois du hasard III; Configuration symétrique. SEE *Objects Arranged According to the Laws of Chance III*
    Tête et feuille; Tête et vase. SEE *Head and Leaf; Head and Vase*
arte metafisica, 96, 114
Artigas, Joseph Llorens, 110
Art Nouveau, 46, 50, 102
Art of This Century, gallery, New York, 21, 148, 150, 152
Artschwager, Richard, ck 267
Art Students League, New York, 122, 132, 148, 194
Asawa, Ruth, ck 267
assemblage, 28, 29, 119, 202, 222, 224, 232
Ault, George, ck 267
Autio, Rudy, 204
automatism, 108, 148, 156, 164
Avery, Milton, 162, 253, ck 267–68
    Clear Cut Landscape, 22, 162, *163*, 253

Baber, Alice, ck 268
Bäckström, Holger. SEE Beck & Jung
Baer, Jo, ck 268
Bailey, Clayton, ck 268
Baldwin, Russell, ck 268
Ball, Hugo, 102
Balla, Giacomo, 14
Ballaine, Jerrold, 23, ck 268
Baltimore Museum of Art, Cone Collection, 40
Banks, Ellen, ck 268
Bannard, Walter Darby, ck 269
Barbizon School, 16
Barcelona: Academia de Bellas Artes, 84; Escola d'Arte de Gali, 108
Barela, Patrocinio, ck 269
Barletta, Joel, ck 269
Barnes, Matthew, ck 269
Baroque art, 148
Barth, Carl, ck 270
Barth, Jack, ck 270
Barye, Antoine-Louis, 38
Basel, Kunstmuseum, 241
Bauhaus, 27, 73, 86, 88, 90, 92, 94, 100
Baxter, John, ck 270
Bay Area, art of, 14, 16, 21, 22, 23, 24, 25, 27, 34, 152, 166, 184, 188, 190, 200, 222, 228, 230, 232
Bayer, Herbert, ck 270
Beat generation, 119, 234
Beauvoir, Simone de, 116
Beaux-Arts architecture, 14, 15
Bechtle, Robert, ck 271
Beck & Jung, ck 271
Beckmann, Max, 17, 76, 78, 188, 242–43, ck 271
    Blick auf den Tiergarten mit weissen Kugeln, 243
    Departure, 78
    Frau bei der Toilette mit roten und weissen Lilien. SEE *Woman at Her Toilette, with Red and White Lilies*
    Landscape, Cannes, 76, 77, 78, 242–43
    Landschaft, Cannes. SEE *Landscape, Cannes*

    Woman at Her Toilette, with Red and White Lilies, 78, 79, 243
Bell, Larry, 27, 210, 257, ck 271
    Untitled (1969), 210, *211*, 257
Bement, Alon, 122
Bender, Albert M., 16, 19, 21, 138, 140, 250
Benglis, Lynda, ck 271
Bengston, Billy Al, 204, 208, 210, 212, ck 271–72
Benjamin, Karl, ck 272
Bennett, Edward H., 130
Benton, Fletcher, 23, ck 272–73
Benton, Thomas Hart, 148
Berkeley, University of California. SEE California, University of
Berlandina, Jane, ck 273
Berman, Eugene, ck 273
Berman, Wallace, 119, 200, ck 273
Bernheim-Jeune, Galerie, Paris, 132, 238
Bernstein, James, 30
Berthot, Jake, ck 273
Bertoia, Harry, ck 274
Best, David, ck 274
Bevilaqua (Pignatelli), 38
Beziers, Musée des Beaux-Arts, 239
Bigenwald, Leo, ck 274
Bing, Ilse, 28
biomorphism, 102, 106, 110, 114, 146, 148, 150, 164, 166, 190, 232
Bischoff, Elmer, 28, 184, 186, 188; 192, 228, 230, 254–55, ck 274
    Orange Sweater, 184, *185*, 254–55
Bishop, James, ck 274
Blackburn, Ed, ck 274
Black Mountain College, N.C., 90, 92, 194, 204
Blakelock, Ralph, ck 275
Blaue Reiter, exhibition, 242. SEE ALSO Blue Rider
Blaue Vier. SEE Blue Four
Blue Four, 17, 73
Blue Rider, 68, 72, 98
Blume, Peter, 17, ck 275
Blumenfeld, Erwin, 28
Blunk, J. B., ck 275
Boccioni, Umberto, 14, 96, 130, 132
Bohan, Ruth, 248
Bolomey, Roger, ck 275
Bolotowsky, Ilya, 24, ck 275
Bombois, Camille, ck 275
Bonnard, Pierre, 14, 23, ck 275
Bosch, Hieronymus, 18
Bottini, David, ck 276
Boucher, François, 16
Boucher, Jean, attributed to, ck 276
Bouguereau, Adolphe, 38
Bourke-White, Margaret, 130
Bourdelle, Antoine, 38
Bowers, Cheryl O., ck 276
Bowman, Geoffrey, ck 276
Bowman, Richard, ck 276
Boyle, Keith, ck 276
Brady, Robert, ck 277
Brancusi, Constantin, 52, 102, 103, 106, 239, ck 277
    Blonde Negress, 22, 52, *53*, 239
    Blonde Negress I, 239
    Blonde Negress II, 239
    Negresse blonde. SEE *Blonde Negress*
    White Negress, 52, 239
    White Negress I, 239
    White Negress II, 239

Braque, Georges, 22, 46, 50, 54, 56, 58, 146, 160, 238, 239–40, ck 277
  Gueridon, 54, *55*, 239–40
  Vase, Palette, and Mandolin, 56, *57*, 240
Bray, Archie, Foundation, 204, 230
Bremer, Anne, ck 278
Breschi, Karen, ck 278
Breton, André, 112, 114, 148, 246
Bridge, The, 70, 72
Brigante, Nick, ck 278
Briggs, Ernest, 190, 192, ck 278–79
Broderson, Morris, ck 279
Brook, Alexander, ck 279
Brooklyn Museum, 248; School of Art, 202
Brooks, James, 168
Brown, Arthur, Jr., 15
Brown, Joan, 230, ck 279
Brown, Theophilus, ck 280
Bruce, Edward, ck 280
Brücke. SEE Bridge, The
Buck, John, ck 280
Bufano, Beniamino, ck 280–82
Bullitt, William, 248
Bullock, Wynn, 24, 28
Burri, Alberto, ck 282
Butterfield, Deborah, ck 282

Cage, John, 194, 206
Cahill, Holger, 132, 248
Calcagno, Lawrence, ck 282
Calder, Alexander, 23, ck 283
  Four Big Dots, 23
California, southern, art of, 17, 27
California, University of, 14; Berkeley, 16, 160, 166, 184; Davis, 224, 234; Los Angeles, 22, 24, 25, 182
California architecture, 25
California College of Arts and Crafts, Oakland, 188, 204, 230
California Historical Society, 19
California Palace of the Legion of Honor, San Francisco, 15, 20
California School of Fine Arts. SEE San Francisco Art Institute
Callahan, Harry, 21, 24
Callahan, Kenneth, ck 283
Callery, Mary, ck 283
Camacho, Cristiano, ck 283
Cameron, Julia Margaret, 21
Carnegie Institute, Pittsburgh, 17
Carnwath, Squeak, ck 284
Caro, Anthony, ck 284
Carrà, Carlo, 14, 17, 132
Carsman, Jon, ck 284
Casanova, Aldo John, ck 284
Cavalli, Guy John, ck 284
ceramic sculpture, 24, 28, 204, 206, 208, 224, 234
Cercle et Carré. SEE Circle and Square
Cerni, Vicente Aguilera, 241
Cerrito, Fanny, 119, 247
Cézanne, Paul, 16, 18, 22, 32, 38, 46, 54, 66, 108, 126, 134, 146, 160, 178, 236
Chagall, Marc, 23, ck 284
Chamberlin, Wesley, ck 284
Chase, Ronald, ck 285
Chase, William Merritt, 128, 134
Cheney, Warren, ck 285
Chevreul, Michel Eugène, 66
Chicago, Art Institute of, 22, 122
Chicago, Judy (née Gerowitz), 25, ck 285
  The Dinner Party, 25

children's art, 18, 98
de Chirico, Giorgio, 17, 96, 112, 144, 168, 170, 176, 244–45, ck 285
  Contrariétés du penseur. SEE *Vexations of the Thinker*
  Vexations of the Thinker; Inconsistencies of the Thinker, 96, *97*, 244–45
Chouinard Art Institute, Los Angeles, 160, 206, 210
Christian Science, 247
Christo, 26, 28
  Running Fence, 28
Chryssa, ck 285
Cimabue, 140
Cincinnati Art Museum, 92
Circle and Square, 84
Clark, Larry, 28
Clavé, Antoni, ck 286
Cleveland Institute of Art, 220
CoBrA, 23
Coen, Arnaldo, ck 286
Cohen, George M., ck 286
Coke, Van Deren, 25–26, 28
Coldwell, Ardath, ck 286
Colescott, Robert, ck 286
Collectors Forum, 26
(Collins), Jess, 22, 23, 24, ck 286
Colorado, University of, Boulder, 202
Color Field painting, 27, 94, 150
Columbia University, New York, 156
Conner, Bruce, 22, 24, 28, 119, 200, 202, 224, 230, 256, ck 286–87
  Looking Glass, 29, 202, *203*, 256
Constructivism, 26, 73, 82, 84, 86, 92, 100
Corbett, Edward, 228, ck 287–88
Corbusier, Le. SEE Jeanneret, Charles-Edouard
Cordellis, Alex, 18
Corinth, Lovis, 76
Cornell, Joseph, 28, 118–19, 247, ck 288
  Pink Palace Series, 247
  Untitled (*Pink Palace*), 118–19, *120*, 247
  Untitled (*Window Façade*), 118, 119, *121*, 247
  Window Façade Series, 119, 247
Costanzo, Tony, ck 288
Cravath, Ruth, ck 289
Crawford, Allan, ck 289
Crawford, Ralston, ck 289
Crevel, René, 98
Crocker, Helen. SEE Russell, Mrs. Henry Potter
Crocker, Mrs. W. H., collection of, 16
Crocker, William W., 16, 22
Croisé, Professor, 38
Cross, Henri-Edmond, 32
Cruz-Diez, Carlos, ck 289
Cubism, 17, 50, 54, 56, 58, 64, 68, 80, 82, 92, 96, 98, 102, 108, 119, 126, 130, 134, 136, 140, 146, 148, 150, 158, 160, 178, 184, 226; Analytic, 48, 50, 54, 56, 58, 64; Synthetic, 50, 54, 56, 58, 64, 136, 146, 184, 186
Culler, George D., 22, 23
Cuneo, Rinaldo, ck 289
Cunningham, Imogen, 21, 23
Cunningham, Merce, 194
Cyrsky, Frank, ck 289

Dada, 18, 102, 103, 112, 118, 222; neo-Dada, 224, 234
Dali, Salvador, 17, 96, 112, 114, 118, 246, ck 289
  Enigma of My Desire: My Mother, My Mother, My Mother, 112
  Oedipus Complex, 112, *113*, 246
Darricarrère, Henriette, 40, 238
Dasburg, Andrew Michael, ck 290
Daumier, Honoré, 18, 48
Davie, Alan, ck 290
Davis, Claudia, 15
Davis, Gene, 23, 24, ck 290
Davis, Jerrold, ck 290
Davis, Ronald, ck 290–91
Davis, Stuart, 21, 136, 249, ck 291
  Deuce, 136, *137*, 249
  Eggbeater Series, 136
Davis, University of California. SEE California, University of
Dean, Nat, ck 291
Deem, George, ck 291
DeFeo, Jay, 200, 230, 256, ck 291
  Deathrose, 200
  Incision, 200, *201*, 256
  Rose, 200, 256
  White Rose, 200
De Forest, Roy, 23, 27, 228, 234, 258, ck 292
  Country Dog Gentlemen, 228, *229*, 258
Degas, Edgar, 14, 16, 42
de Kooning, Willem, 28, 158, 168, 188, 214, 226, 252, ck 292
  Woman, 158, *159*, 252
  Woman I, 158
Delacroix, Eugène, 19, 60, 76
  Women of Algiers, 60
DeLap, Tony, ck 293
Delaunay, Robert, 68, 160, 216, 242
Derain, André, 23, 32, 44, 46, 238, ck 293
  Landscape, 44, *45*, 238
Des Moines Art Center, 26
Despiau, Charles, ck 293
Deutsch, Boris, ck 293
de Young, M. H., Memorial Museum, San Francisco, 15
Diao, David, ck 293
Diebenkorn, Richard, 27, 178, 180, 182, 184, 188, 190, 192, 226, 254, ck 294
  Berkeley #57, 178, *179*, 180, 182, 254
  Berkeley Series, 178
  Cityscape I, 180, *181*, 254
  Landscape I. SEE *Cityscape I*
  Ocean Park #54, 182, *183*, 254
  Ocean Park Series, 182
Dill, Laddie John, ck 294
Dine, Jim, 26, 198, ck 295
Disney, Walt, Studios, Hollywood, 224
di Suvero, Mark, ck 295
Dix, Robert, ck 295
Doesburg, Theo van, 82, 84, 243, ck 295
  Contre composition simultanée. SEE *Simultaneous Counter Composition*
  Simultaneous Counter Composition, 82, *83*, 243
Dongen, Kees van, 42, 238, ck 295
  Black Chemise, 23, 42, *43*, 238
  Chemise noire. SEE *Black Chemise*
Dove, Arthur, 22, 119, 122, 126, 247–48, ck 295

Silver Ball No. 2, 126, *127*, 247–48
Dow, Arthur Wesley, 122
Downing, Thomas, ck 295
Du Casse, Ralph, ck 295–96
Duchamp, Marcel, 18, 118, ck 296
Dudley, Donald, ck 296
Dufy, Raoul, 46
Dunlop, Ian, 236
Dunn, Alfred, ck 296
Dürer, Albrecht, 16, 18
Dusenbery, Walter, ck 296
Dutch art, 16
Dzamonja, Duan (Susan), ck 297
Dzubas, Friedel, ck 297

Eastern art, 122, 142, 144
Eckmann, Inge-Lise, 30
Ecole Communale de la Ville, Paris, 38
Ecole des Beaux-Arts, Paris, 50
Eddy, Arthur Jerome, 122
Edlich, Stephen, ck 297
Edmondson, William, ck 297
Edstrom, David, ck 297
Edwards, John Paul, 23
Egyptian art, 230
Eilshemius, Louis Michel, ck 297
Ekks, Redd, ck 297
Elderfield, John, 238, 239
Elementarism, 82
Elisofon, Elin, ck 298
Elsen, Albert, 40, 236, 238, 241
Engel, Irma, ck 298
Epstein, Jacob, ck 298
Ernst, Jimmy, ck 298
Ernst, Max, 114, 118, 148, ck 298
  The Numerous Family, 21
Evans, Walker, 130
Existentialism, 116
Expressionism, 26, 68, 70, 72, 78, 158, 206

f/64, 23
Falkenstein, Claire, ck 299
Fanfani, Amintore, ck 299
Fangor, Wojcjech, ck 299
Faralla, Richard, 23, ck 299–300
Farrow, Al, ck 300
Fauvism, 17, 28, 32, 34, 42, 44, 46, 54, 64, 70, 72, 108, 126, 160
Feininger, Lyonel, 17, 20, 73, ck 300
Feitelson, Lorser, 17, ck 300
Fenollosa, Ernest, 122
Fernie, John C., ck 300
Ferren, John, 19, ck 300–301
Ferus Gallery, Los Angeles, 190, 210, 212
Fesenmaier, Helene, ck 301
Fisher, Doris and Donald, Fund, 28
Flemming, Amy, ck 301
Foley, Suzanne, 23, 24, 25
folk art, 52
Fontana, Lucio, ck 301
Forner, Raquel, ck 301
Fort Worth Art Museum, 24
Fourest, Georges, 239
Fox, Terry, ck 301
Fragonard, Jean-Honoré, 16
Frances, Esteban, 246
Francis, Sam, 166, 253, ck 301
  Red and Pink, 166, *167*, 253
Francisco, Richard, ck 302
Franck, Frederick, ck 302
Frank, Robert, 28

Frankenthaler, Helen, 24, ck 302
Fraser, James Earle, 66
French, Stephen, ck 302
Freud, Sigmund, 112, 148
Frey, Viola, ck 302
Fried, Howard, ck 302
Friesz, Othon, 46, 238–39, ck 302
  Landscape (The Eagle's Beak, La
    Ciotat), 46, 47, 238–39
  Paysage (Le Bec-de-l'Aigle, La
    Ciotat). SEE Landscape (The
    Eagle's Beak, La Ciotat)
Frimkess, Michael, 204
Fuller, Loie, 118
Futurism, 14, 17, 68, 82, 96, 126,
  130, 132

Galerie 23, Paris, 84
Gallagher, Dennis, ck 303
Gallatin, Albert Eugene, ck 303
Garbell, ck 303
Gaudier-Brzeska, Henri, 130
Gauguin, Paul, 16, 44, 70, 136
Gauthier, Maximilien, 239
Gaw, William A., ck 303–4
Gechtoff, Sonia, ck 304
Geis, William, ck 304
Geist, Sidney, 239
Genn, Nancy, ck 305
German art, 16
Gerstle, William L., 16, 21
Giacometti, Alberto, 18, 116, 188,
  246–47, ck 305
  Annette VII, 116, 117, 246–47
Giacometti, Mme Alberto (Annette),
  116, 247
Giacometti, Diego, 116
Gibb, H. Phelan, ck 305
Gil, Mathew, ck 305
Gilhooly, David, 24, ck 305
Gimblett, Max, ck 305
Ginnever, Charles, ck 306
Giotto, 140
Giry, Marcel, 238, 239
Godwin, Judith, ck 306
Gogh, Vincent van, 16, 44, 76, 108,
  136, 236
Gogol, Nikolai, 176
Goings, Ralph, ck 306
Golden Gate International Exposition,
  18
González, Julio, 28, 62, 240–41,
  ck 307
  Grande Faucille. SEE Large
    Sickle
  Large Sickle, 241
  Mask "My," 62, 63, 240–41
  Masque "My." SEE Mask "My"
  Petite Faucille (Femme debout).
    SEE Small Sickle (Woman Stand-
    ing)
  Small Sickle (Woman Standing),
    62, 63, 241
Goodnough, Robert, ck 307
Göpel, Barbara, 243
Gorder, Clayton, ck 307
Gordin, Sidney, ck 307
Gordon, Donald E., 238
Gorky, Arshile, 20, 146, 158, 166,
  168, 190, 250–51, ck 308
  Enigmatic Combat, 21, 146,
    147, 250–51
  Nighttime series, 146
Gottlieb, Adolph, 162, 214, ck 308
Goya, Francisco, 18
Grafton Galleries, London, 236

Graham, Robert, ck 308
Grand-Palais, Paris, 44
Grant, Art, ck 308
Grant, James, ck 308–9
Graves, Morris, 142, 250, ck 309
  Bird Maddened by the Sound of
    Machinery in the Air, 142, 143,
    250
  Bird Maddened by the War, 250
  Bird Maddened by the War Fol-
    lowing St. Elmo's Fire, 250
Greco, El, 48
Greek art, 32, 106, 230
Greeley, Charles, ck 309
Green, George, ck 309
Greene, Stephen, 214, ck 309
Gropius, Walter, 86
Grosz, George, 19
Guggenheim, Peggy, 21, 148, 150,
  153
Guggenheim, Solomon R., Museum,
  New York, 23, 26, 80, 247
Guglielmi, O. Louis, ck 309
Guston, Philip, 24, 27, 168, 170,
  176, 253–54, ck 309–10
  Actor, 170
  Back View, 176, 177, 254
  For M., 168, 169, 253
  Painter, 170
  Red Sea; The Swell; Blue Light,
    170, 171–73, 253–54
  Traveller, 170
  White Painting I, 168
Guston, Mrs. Philip (Musa), 168

Haas, Elise S., Conservation Labora-
  tory, 29–30
Haas, Evelyn and Walter, Jr., Fund,
  28
Haas, Mrs. Walter, 22
Hack, Howard, ck 310–11
Hague, Raoul, ck 311
Hamada, 204
Hamilton, Frank, ck 311
Hanafusa, Hisao, ck 312
Hanson, Jo, ck 312
Hard Edge painting, 94
Hare, David, ck 312
Harnett, William, 224
Harris, Paul, ck 312
Hartley, Marsden, 20, 122, ck 312
Hassam, Childe, 14
Hausenstein, Wilhelm, 243
Hayter, Stanley William, ck 312–13
Heckel, Erich, 70
Hedrick, Wally, 200, 230, ck 313
Held, Al, 23, ck 313
Hélion, Jean, ck 313
Henderson, Gilbert, ck 313
Henderson, Mel, ck 313
Hennessy, Richard, ck 313
Henri, Robert, 66, 128, 136
Herms, George, 200, 224, ck 314
Hidai, Nankoku, ck 314
Hilger, Charles, ck 314
Hinz, Randal, ck 314
Hirsch, Joseph, ck 314
Hofer, Karl, ck 314
Hofmann, Hans, 16, 21, 28, 158,
  160, 214, 252–53, ck 314–15
  Table—Version II, 160, 161,
    252–53
Holland, Tom, 24, ck 315
Holman, Arthur, ck 315–16
Hopkins, Budd, ck 316
Hopkins, Charles Benjamin, ck 316

Hopkins, Gerard Manley, 166
Hopkins, Henry, 24–25, 26, 27, 252
Hopkins, Mark, 14; Institute of Art,
  San Francisco, 14
Hopper, Edward, 26, 128, 226, 248,
  ck 316
  Bridle Path, 128, 129, 248
Hord, Donal, ck 316
Horiuchi, Paul, ck 316
Howard, Charles, ck 316
Howard, Robert B., ck 317
Hoyer, T. A., ck 317
Hudson, Robert, 24, 224, 228, 232,
  258, ck 317–18
  Out of the Blue, 232, 233, 258
Hulten, K. G. Pontus, 23
Humphrey, John, 23, 24, 26
Humphrey, Ralph, ck 318
Hunt, Bryan, ck 318
Hutton, Peter, ck 318

Illustrated London News, 236
Impressionism, 14, 16, 42, 46, 54,
  64, 66, 76, 108, 128; American,
  162
Indiana, Robert, ck 318
Ingres, Jean-Auguste Dominique, 158
Inokuma, Genichiro, ck 318
International Exhibition of Modern
  Art (Armory Show), New York, 134,
  136
Ireland, David, ck 318
Irvine Foundation, 25
Irwin, Robert, 27, 210, 212, 257, ck
  319
  Untitled (1968), 212, 213, 257
Izu, David, ck 319

Jackson, Oliver, ck 319
Jacobsen, Rodger, ck 319
Jaffe, Shirley, ck 319
Janis, Sidney and Harriet, Collection,
  exhibition of, 23
Janss, Mr. and Mrs. William C., 28
Jawlensky, Alexej, 17, 18, 22, 72–73,
  242, ck 319
  Constructivist Heads, series, 73
  Frauenkopf. SEE Woman's Head
  Head: Red Light, 73, 75, 242
  Kopf: Rotes Licht. SEE Head:
    Red Light
  Woman's Head, 72, 74, 242
Jeanneret, Charles-Edouard (Le
  Corbusier), 64, 84
Jefferson, Jack, ck 320
Jenkins, Paul, ck 320
Jensen, Alfred, ck 320
Jepson Institute, Los Angeles, 212
Jess. SEE (Collins), Jess
Jianou, Ionel, 239
Johns, Jasper, 28, 119, 196, 198,
  214, 220, 255–56, ck 320–21
  By the Sea, 196
  Device Circle, 196
  Diver, 196
  Land's End, 196, 197, 255–56
  Periscope (Hart Crane), 196
Johns Hopkins University, Baltimore,
  34
Johnson, Buffie, ck 321
Johnson, Daniel La Rue, ck 321
Johnson, Sargent, ck 321–22
Jones, David, ck 322
Jonson, Raymond, ck 322

Joseph, Richard, ck 323
Josten, Werner E., collection, 239
Judd, Donald, 220, ck 323
Jung, Carl, 148

Kahlo, Frida (Frieda), 138, 249, ck
  323
  Frieda and Diego Rivera, 138, 139,
    249
Kallman, Edith, ck 323
Kaltenbach, Steven, ck 323
Kandinsky, Vasily, 17, 22, 52, 68,
  72, 73, 80, 88, 90, 98, 102, 122,
  126, 244, ck 324
  Bräunlich. SEE Brownish
  Brownish, 21, 88, 89, 244
Kanemitsu, Matsumi, ck 324
Kantor, Paul, Gallery, Beverly Hills,
  184
Katano, Marc, ck 324
Katzman, Louise, 26
Kauffman, Craig, 210, 212, ck 324
Kaufman, Donald, ck 324–25
Keck, Caroline, 29
Keck, Sheldon, 29
Kelly, Ellsworth, 24, 218, 257, ck
  325
  Red White, 218, 219, 257
Kelly, James, ck 325
Kent, Adaline, ck 325–26
Kepes, Gyorgy, ck 326
Kerkam, Earl, ck 326
Kerr, Leslie, ck 326
Kesting, Edmund, 28
Kienholz, Edward, 22, 119, ck
  326–27
Kim Whanki, ck 327
Kirchner, Ernst Ludwig, 70, ck 327
Kirk, Jerome, ck 327
Klee, Paul, 17, 18, 22, 23, 73, 90,
  94, 98, 100, 102, 103, 245, ck
  327
  Fast getroffen. SEE Nearly Hit
  Nearly Hit, 21, 100, 101, 245
  Red Suburb, 98, 99, 245
  Rotes Villenquartier. SEE Red Suburb
Klimenko, Mary Julia, 230
Kline, Franz, 168, ck 327–28
Knoop, Guitou, ck 328
Kohlmeyer, Ida, ck 328
Kokoschka, Oskar, 70
Konody, P. G., 236
Kos, Marlene, ck 328
Kos, Paul, ck 328
Kramer, Harry, ck 328
Krasnow, Peter, ck 328–29
Kriz, Vilem, 24
Kroll, Leon, ck 329
Krukowski, Lucian, ck 329
Kubin, Alfred, 68
Kuhlman, Walter, ck 329
Kupka, František, 80

Labaudt, Lucien, ck 329–30
Lachaise, Gaston, 24, ck 330
Land, Charles H., Family Foundation
  Fund, 28
Lane, John R., 249
Lankheit, Klaus, 242
Lanyon, Peter, ck 330
Lardera, Berto, ck 330
Lasky, Ruth and Moses, Fund, 28
Latin American art, 19, 20
Laurens, Henri, ck 330

Lavatelli, Carla, ck 331
Lavenson, Alma, 21
Lebrun, Rico, 226
Leck, Bart van der, 80
Léger, Fernand, ck 331
Lemmy, ck 331
Leper, S. Dewa Njoman, ck 331
Leslie, Alfred, 28, ck 331
Levin, Gail, 241
Levine, Jack, ck 331
Levine, Marilyn, ck 331
Levy, Harriet Lane, 16, 22
Levy, Isadore, ck 332
Levy, Julien, Gallery, New York, 118
Lewandowski, Edmund, ck 332
Lewis, Tom E., ck 332
LeWitt, Sol, 220, ck 332
Lhote, André, ck 332
Lichtenstein, Roy, 198
Lieber, Tom, ck 332
Liebermann, Max, 76
Light, Alvin, 24, ck 332
Linhares, Judith, ck 333
Lipchitz, Jacques, 50, 130, 239, ck 333
    Draped Woman, 50, *51*, 239
Lipofsky, Marvin, ck 333
Lipsky, Pat, ck 333
Ljungberg, Bo. SEE Beck & Jung
Lobdell, Frank, 152, 190, 192, 255, ck 333–34
    April, 23
    March 1954, 190, *191*, 255
Loberg, Robert, ck 334
Locks, Seymour, ck 334
Lockwood, Ward, ck 334
Loran, Earle, ck 334
Lord, James, 116
Los Angeles County Museum of Art, 25
Louie, Harry, ck 334
Louis, Morris, 27, ck 334
Louvre, Paris, 218
Lovet-Lorski, Boris, ck 334
Lozowick, Louis, 130
Luhan, Mabel Dodge, 124
Lundeberg, Helen, 17, ck 335

MacAgy, Douglas, 20, 152, 178, 186, 190, 192
MacAgy, Jermayne, 20, 22, 27
Macdonald-Wright, Stanton, 66
MacIver, Loren, ck 335
McChesney, Robert, ck 335
McCone, Michael, 24
McCracken, John, ck 335
McCrady, John, ck 335
McCray, James, 166
McLaughlin, John, ck 335
McMillan, Jerry, ck 335
Mack, Charlotte, 22
Macke, August, 68
Magritte, René, 96, 114, 118
Maillol, Aristide, ck 336
Malevich, Kasimir, 86
Mallory, Ronald, ck 336
Mangold, Robert, 28, 220, 257, ck 336
    Red X within X, 220, *221*, 257
Manguin, Henri, 22, 32, 38, ck 336
Man Ray, 18, 28
Mantegna, Andrea, 168
Manual Arts High School, Los Angeles, 168
Manzù, Giacomo, ck 337
Mapplethorpe, Robert, 28

Marc, Franz, 68, 80, 98, 241–42, ck 337
    Gebirge (Steiniger Weg/Landschaft). SEE *Mountains (Rocky Way/Land-scape)*
    Mountains (Rocky Way/Landscape), 68, *69*, 241–42
Marca-Relli, Corrado, 23, ck 337
Marien, Marcel, ck 337
Maril, Herman, ck 337
Marin, John, 22, 126, ck 337
Marini, Marino, ck 337
Marquet, Albert, 32, 38
Marsh, Reginald, 17
Martin, Agnes, 26, 27, ck 338
Martin, Fred, ck 338
Martins, Maria, ck 338
Martinson, Dorothy, 26
Mascherini, Marcello, ck 338
Mason, Alden, ck 338
Mason, John, 24, 204, 206, 224, 256, ck 338
    Untitled (*Monolith*), 206, *207*, 256
Masson, André, 114, 148, ck 339
Mastroianni, Umberto, ck 339
Matisse, Henri, 16, 17, 19, 22, 32, 34–35, 38, 40, 42, 44, 46, 60, 68, 72, 76, 78, 126, 134, 136, 160, 162, 178, 204, 216, 236–38, ck 339–41
    Femme aux yeux bleus. SEE *Girl with Green Eyes*
    Femme aux yeux verts. SEE *Girl with Green Eyes*
    Figure with a Scutari Tapestry, 238
    Fille aux yeux verts. SEE *Girl with Green Eyes*
    Girl with Green Eyes, 32, *33*, 35, 236
    Green Line, 72
    Grosse Tête. SEE *Henriette, II*
    Henriette, deuxième état. SEE *Henriette, II*
    Henriette, II, 40, *41*, 237–38
    Henriette, III, 40
    Jeune Femme aux yeux verts. SEE *Girl with Green Eyes*
    Lady with Green Eyes. SEE *Girl with Green Eyes*
    Luxe, calme, et volupté, 32
    Pink Blouse, 238
    Portrait of Michael Stein, 34, 35, *36*, 237
    Portrait of Sarah Stein, 34–35, *37*, 237
    Seated Nude, 40
    Serf. SEE *Slave*
    Slave, 32, 38, *39*, 237
    Still Life with a Greek Torso, 236
    Tiaré Series, 40
    Woman with Hat, 34
Matisse, Mme Henri (Amélie), 72
Matta (Roberto Sebastian Antonio Matta Echaurren), 246, ck 341
Mattox, Charles, ck 341
Maxim, David, ck 341
May, Wilbur D., 23
Maybeck, Bernard R., 14, 15
Meadows, Bernard, ck 341
medieval art, 14, 16, 76, 78
Mehring, Howard, ck 341
Melchert, James, 24, 224, ck 342
Mérida, Carlos, ck 342
Merrild, Knud, ck 342
Mesches, Arnold, ck 342
Metzinger, Jean, ck 342

Mexican art, 16, 17, 20, 138, 140
Meyer, Agnes E., 22
Meyer, Byron, 28
Meza, Guillermo, ck 343
Middlebrook, David, ck 343
Mills, Paul, 184
Mills College, Oakland, Calif., 19, 188
Minimalism, 206, 220
Miró, Joan, 17, 23, 108, 110, 114, 148, 158, 178, 204, 246, ck 343
    L'Aube parfumée par la pluie d'or. SEE *Dawn Perfumed by a Shower of Gold*
    Brown and White Oval. SEE *Painting*
    Constellations series, 110
    Dark Brown and White Oval. SEE *Painting*
    Dawn Perfumed by a Shower of Gold, 110, *111*, 246
    Painting, 108, *109*, 246
    Peinture. SEE *Painting*
Mitchell, Joan, 27, ck 343
Miyasaki, George, ck 343
Modernism, 42, 96, 122, 126, 130, 226
Modigliani, Amedeo, 52
Moholy-Nagy, László, 86, 90, 243–44, ck 343–44
    A IX, 86, *87*, 243–44
Mondrian, Piet, 52, 80, 82, 84, 94, 102, 243, ck 344
    Cathedral. SEE *Church Façade/Church at Domburg*
    Church Façade/Church at Domburg, 80, *81*, 243
    Composition, 80
    Pier and Ocean Series, 80
Monet, Claude, 14, 16, 19, ck 344
Monroe, Keith, ck 344
Monsen, Professor and Mrs. R. Joseph, collection, exhibition, 24
Montana State Univty, Bozeman, 204
Montenegro, Roberto, ck 344
Moore, Grace, 14
Moore, Henry, 22, ck 344
Morandi, Giorgio, 26
Moreau, Gustave, 38
Morehouse, William, ck 345
Morgan, Barbara, 21
Morley, Grace L. McCann, 15, 16–17, 18, 19, 20, 21, 22
Morris, Carl, ck 345
Moses, Ed, ck 345
Motherwell, Robert, 20, 118, 148, 150, 156, 252, ck 345–46
    Elegies series, 156
    Lyric Suite, 24
    Open Series, 24
    Wall Painting No. 10, 24, 156, *157*, 252
    Wall Painting with Stripes, 156, 252
Mullican, Lee, ck 346
Munch, Edvard, 188
Mundt, Ernest, ck 346
Mundt, Scott, ck 346
Mundy, Henry, ck 347
Munich: Academy, 68; Münchner Neue Sezession, 242
Münter, Gabriele, 68
Murray, Justin, ck 347
Museum of Modern Art, New York, 17, 18, 21, 22, 23, 25, 148, 158, 214

Nadelman, Elie, 52
Nagare, Masayuki, ck 347
Nagle, Ron, 224, ck 347
National Collection of Fine Arts. SEE Smithsonian Institution, National Museum of American Art
National Endowment for the Arts, 28, 30
Natkin, Robert, 23, ck 347–48
Nauman, Bruce, 26, ck 348
Nebraska, University of, Lincoln, 202
Neel, Alice, 226
Nelson, Art, ck 348
Neo-Classicism, 84
Neo-Impressionism, 32, 42, 44
Neo-Plasticism, 80, 82
Nepote, Alexander, ck 348
Neri, Manuel, 24, 230, 258, ck 348–49
    Mary and Julia, 230, *231*, 258
Neuberger, Roy R., Museum, State University of New York, Purchase, 244
Neubert, George, 26, 27
Newman, Barnett, 150, 162
New York School of Art, 128, 132
Nicholson, Ben, ck 349
Nicolle, Marcel, 44
Noguchi, Isamu, 26, ck 349
Noland, Kenneth, 27, ck 349
Nolde, Emil, 22
Nordfeldt, B. J. O., ck 349
Nordland, Gerald, 23, 24
Norman, Emile, ck 350
Norman, Irving, ck 350
Novalis, 102

Oakland Art Museum, 184
Odza, Theodore, ck 350
O'Hanlon, Richard, ck 350
Okada, Kenzo, ck 350
Okamura, Arthur, ck 350
O'Keeffe, Georgia, 22, 26, 122, 124, 126, 226, 247, ck 351
    Black Place I, 124, *125*, 247
    Black Place Series, 247
    Lake George, 122, *123*, 247
    Reflection Seascape. SEE *Lake George*
Oldenburg, Claes, 198, 256, ck 351
    Blue Legs, 198, *199*, 256
    The Store, 198
Olitski, Jules, ck 351
Oliveira, Nathan, 23, 24, 28, 188, 255, ck 352
    Adolescent by the Bed, 188, *189*, 255
Olodort, Michael, ck 352
O'Neal, Mary Lovelace, ck 352
Onslow Ford, Gordon, 23, ck 352
Op Art, 94
Oppenheim, Dennis, ck 352
Oppenheim, Meret, ck 353
Oriental art, 16
Orozco, José Clemente, 19, 140, 148, ck 353
Orphism, 66, 68
Otis Art Institute, Los Angeles, 186, 204, 206, 208, 212
Ozenfant, Amédée, 64, 241, ck 353
    Nature morte. SEE *Still Life*
    Still Life, 64, *65*, 241

Paalen, Wolfgang, ck 353
Pacific Northwest, art of, 142, 144
Palais de Légion d'Honneur, Paris, 15

Panama-Pacific International Exposition, 14; Palace of Fine Arts, 14, 15
Paris, Harold, ck 353
Park, David, 23, 166, 184, 186, 188, 192, 228, 255, ck 353–54
    Man in a T-Shirt, 186, *187*, 255
    Two Violinists, 186
    Woman in Red and White Robe, 186
Parker, Raymond, ck 354
Parke-Taylor, Michael, 238
Parthenon, Athens, 236
Patrick, Vernon, ck 354
Pattison, Abbott, ck 354
Pavia, Phillip, ck 354
Pearlstein, Philip, 226
Pearson, John, ck 355
Pechstein, Max, 28, 70, 242, ck 355
    Nelly, 70, *71*, 242
Pennsylvania Academy of the Fine Arts, Philadelphia, 66
Pennuto, James, ck 355
Pereira, Irene Rice, ck 355
Perez, Vincent, ck 355
Perrault, Charles, 247
Peters, Michael, ck 355
Pennsylvania, University of, Institute of Contemporary Art, Pittsburgh, 25
Petersen, Roland, ck 355
Peterson, Clifford R., 23
Peterson, Margaret, ck 356
Peto, John, 224
Pettibone, Richard, ck 356
Pettoruti, Emilio, ck 356
Philadelphia School of Art, 23
Phillips Academy, Andover, 214
Phillips, Helen, ck 356
Piazzoni, Gottardo F., ck 356–57
Picasso, Pablo, 16, 17, 18, 22, 42, 48, 50, 58, 60, 62, 108, 140, 146, 148, 158, 160, 162, 168, 184, 186, 190, 204, 239, 240, ck 357
    Cruche fleurie. SEE *Jug of Flowers*
    Demoiselles d'Avignon, 54, 58
    Femmes d'Alger, E. SEE *Women of Algiers, E*
    Guernica, 18, 48, 58, 62
    Jug of Flowers, 21, 58, *59*, 240
    Scène de rue. SEE *Street Scene*
    Street Scene, 48, *49*, 239
    Women of Algiers, E, 23, 60, *61*, 240
Piero della Francesca, 76, 134, 168, 170
Pissarro, Camille, 16
Pistoletto, Michelangelo, ck 357
Pointillism, 32
Pollock, Jackson, 20, 148, 150, 158, 168, 214, 251, ck 358
    Guardians of the Secret, 21, 148, *149*, 251
Polos, Theodore C., ck 358
Pompili, Lucian Octavius, ck 358
Pop Art, 194, 224, 234
Posada, José Guadalupe, 140
Posey, Ernest, ck 358
Post-Impressionism, 14, 44, 108, 136
Potts, Don, ck 358
Pratchenko, Paul, ck 358
Precisionism, 26, 126, 130, 134
Prestini, James, ck 359
Prestopino, Gregorio, ck 359
Price, Kenneth, 28, 204, 208, 210, 256–57, ck 359–60

Happy Curios Series, 208
    L. Red, 208, *209*, 256–57
Princeton University, N.J., 214
Provenzano, Sam, ck 360
Purism, 64
Purrmann, Hans, 35
Puvis de Chavannes, Pierre, 16, 84

Quirt, Walter, ck 360

Raciti, Cherie, ck 360
Raffael, Joseph, ck 360
Ramos, Mel, ck 360
Ramos-Martinez, Alfredo, ck 360
Raphael, Joseph, ck 361
Rasmussen, Robert. SEE Ekks, Redd
Rauh, Fritz, ck 361
Rauschenberg, Robert, 25, 119, 194, 196, 198, 255, ck 361
    Bed, 194
    black paintings, series, 194
    Collection, 194, *195*, 255
    red paintings, series, 194
    Untitled. SEE *Collection*
    white paintings, series, 194
Rayonism, 17
Realism, 226
Redon, Odilon, ck 361
Reed, Paul, ck 361
Regionalism, 148
Reich, Don, ck 362
Reichman, Fred, ck 362
Reid, Dorothy, ck 362
Reifenberg, Benno, 243
Reineking, James, ck 362
Reinhardt, Ad, ck 362
Rembrandt van Rijn, 16
Remington, Deborah, ck 362
Renaissance art, 16, 96, 106, 114, 134, 140, 148
Renfrow, Gregg, ck 363
Renoir, Pierre-Auguste, 16, 22
Resnick, Milton, ck 363
Reynal, Jeanne, 21
Richardson, Sam, 23, ck 363
Richier, Germaine, ck 363
Richmond Professional Institute, Va., 150
Rickey, George, 244, ck 363
Rippon, Tom, ck 363
Rivera, Diego, 16, 17, 19, 21, 26, 50, 138, 140, 148, 249–50, ck 364
    Flower Carrier, 19, 140, *141*, 249–50
    Flower Vendor. SEE *Flower Carrier*
    Landscape, 21
Rivera, José de, ck 364
Robus, Hugo, ck 364
Roche, Marcel, ck 364
Rockere, Herbert, ck 364
Rockwell, Tony, 30
Rococo art, 16
Rodin, Auguste, 38, 116, 130
Roeber, Philip, ck 364
Roeder, Emy, ck 365
Roeder, Lloyd La Page, 248
Roloff, John, ck 365
Romanticism, 19, 50, 60, 68, 148
Rood, Ogden, 66
Root, John W., 130
Rosen, James, ck 365

Rosenberg, Harold, 156
Rosenblum, Robert, 214
Rosenquist, James, 198
Roszak, Theodore, 21
Rothko, Mark, 20, 148, 150, 162, 164, 166, 186, 192, 214, 253, ck 365
    Slow Swirl at the Edge of the Sea, 21, 253
    Untitled (1960), 164, *165*, 253
Rouault, Georges, 22, 38, 76, ck 365
Rousseau, Henri, attributed to, ck 365
Rowell, Margit, 241
Ruben, Richards, ck 366
Rudd, Eric, ck 366
Ruscha, Edward, 26, 210
Russell, Mrs. Henry Potter, 16
Russell, Madeleine Haas, Fund, 28
Russell, Morgan, 66, 241, ck 366
    Four-Part Synchromy No. 7, 241
    Synchromy No. 3, 66, *67*, 241
Russo-Byzantine art, 72
Ryder, Albert Pinkham, 148

Saar, Betye, ck 367
Saccaro, John, ck 367
Safer, John, ck 367
Sage, Kay, 246
Salon d'Automne, Paris: 1905, 32, 34, 44, 46; 1906, 46
Salon des Indépendants, Paris, 32
Samaras, Lucas, 26, ck 367
Sandback, Fred, ck 367
Sander, Ludwig, 28, ck 367
San Francisco: City Hall, 15; Civic Auditorium, 15; Civic Center, 14, 18; Lincoln Park, 15; Musical Association of, 15; School of Design, 14; War Memorial Veterans' Building, 14, 15, 20, 29
San Francisco Art Association, 14–15, 16, 18, 20
San Francisco Art Institute, 16, 19, 20, 138, 140, 152, 166, 178, 184, 187, 188, 190, 192, 200, 222, 224, 228, 230, 232
San Francisco Bay Bridge, 20
San Francisco Chronicle, 21
San Francisco Institute of Art, 14
San Francisco Museum of Art. SEE San Francisco Museum of Modern Art
San Francisco Museum of Modern Art:
    Modern Art Council, 28
    photography collection, 19, 20, 22, 23, 24, 28
    Women's Board, 16, 21, 22, 23, 24
San Francisco Museum of Modern Art exhibitions: *America 1976*, 25; *Ansel Adams: Recollected Moments*, 24; *Art of Assemblage*, 22; *Arts of San Francisco*, 23; *Avant-Garde Photography in Germany: 1919–1939*, 26, 28; *Beyond Color*, 26; *Carnegie International, 1934/ 1935*, 17; *Ceramic Sculpture: Six Artists*, 26; *Collectors, Collecting, Collection: American Abstract Art since 1945*, 25; *Cubism and Abstract Art*, 17; *A Decade of Ceramic Art: 1962–1972*, 24; *Dove,

Arthur*, retrospective, 22; *Expressionism: A German Intuition, 1905–1920*, 26; *Fabricated to Be Photographed*, 25; *Facets of the Collection*, 26; *Fantastic Art, Dada, Surrealism*, 18; *Fifty-fifth Annual Exhibition of the San Francisco Art Association*, 16; *From the Collection of Professor and Mrs. R. Joseph Monsen*, 24; *Henri Matisse*, 21; *The Human Condition: SFMMA Biennial III*, 26; *Images of America: Precisionist Painting and Modern Photography*, 26; *Just Yesterday*, 23; *Kandinsky, Vasily*, retrospective, 22; *Kandinsky in Munich: 1896– 1914*, 26; *Klee, Paul*, retrospective, 23; *The Machine as Seen at the End of the Mechanical Age*, 23; *The Markers*, 26; *Masters of Photography*, 21; *New Photographers*, 21; *Nolde, Emil*, retrospective, 22; *The Nude in Photography*, 26; *On Looking Back: Bay Area 1945– 1960*, 23; *Painting and Sculpture in California: The Modern Era*, 25; *Peter Voulkos: Bronze Sculpture*, 24; *Photography in California: 1945– 1980*, 26; *Photography's Response to Constructivism*, 25; *Picasso: Forty Years of His Art*, 18; *Poets of the Cities: New York and San Francisco*, 25; *Precisionist View in American Art*, 22; *Recent Color*, 26; *Resource/Reservoir*, 27; *Resource/ Response*, 27; *Richard Diebenkorn: Paintings from the Ocean Park Series*, 24; *Sawdust and Spangles*, 20; *Sidney and Harriet Janis Collection*, 23; *Space/Time/Sound— 1970s: A Decade in the Bay Area*, 25; *Twenty American Artists*, 26; *20 American Artists: Sculpture 1982*, 26; *Twombly, Cy*, retrospective, 25; *Unitary Forms: Minimal Sculpture by Carl Andre, Don Judd, John McCracken, Tony Smith*, 23; *View of California Architecture: 1960– 1970*, 25; *Weegee*, 26; *The "Wild Beasts": Fauvism and Its Affinities*, 25; *Years of Ferment: Twentieth-Century Art 1886–1914*, 22
San Francisco Public Library, 19
San Francisco Society of Artists, 14
San Francisco State College, 228
San Francisco Stock Exchange, 16, 138, 140, 186
São Paulo: Museu de Arte Moderna, 239; *III Bienal*, 21
Sapien, Darryl, ck 367
Sargent, John Singer, ck 367
Sarkisian, Paul, ck 368
Sartre, Jean-Paul, 116
Saunders, Raymond, ck 368
Sazegar, Morteza, ck 368
Scanavino, Emilio, ck 368
Schapiro, Meyer, 156
Scheyer, Galka, 17, 18
Schiele, Egon, 70
Schmidt-Rottluff, Karl, 70
Schnier, Jacques, ck 368
Schongauer, Martin, 16
Schorer, Mark, 184
Schumacher, Emile, ck 368
Schwartz, Robert, ck 369
Schwitters, Kurt, 194

Scotti, Ernesto, ck 369
Searles, Edward F., 14
Searles, Mary Francis, Gallery, San Francisco, 14
Segal, George, 25, 28, ck 369
Seitz, William, 214
Seuphor, Michel, 84
Severini, Gino, 17, 132
Shapazian, Robert, 28
Shapiro, David, ck 369
Shaw, Charles, ck 369
Shaw, Richard, 24, 224, 232, 258, ck 369–70
   Melodious Double Stops, 224, 225, 257
Sheeler, Charles, 130, 134, 248–49, ck 370
   Aerial Gyrations, 134, *135*, 248–49
Sheets, Millard, 17
Siegriest, Louis, ck 370
Signac, Paul, 32
Signorelli, Luca, 76
Sills, Thomas, ck 370
Simpson, David, ck 370
Sinton, Nell, ck 370–71
Siqueiros, David Alfaro, 19, 140, 148, ck 371
Siskind, Aaron, 21, 24
Six, The, Gallery, San Francisco, 230
Sloan, Diane, ck 371
Sloan, John, 17
Smith, David, 62, ck 371
Smith, Mrs. Ferdinand C., 28
Smith, Grant, ck 371
Smith, Hassel, 28, 152, 186, 190, 192, 228, 255, ck 371–72
   2 to the Moon, 192, *193*, 255
Smith, Kimber, ck 372
Smith, Leon Polk, 23
Smith, Tony, 26, ck 373
   Tau, 26
Smith, Vic, ck 373
Smithsonian Institution, National Museum of American Art, Washington, D.C., 25
Snelgrove, Walter, ck 373
Snow, Douglas, ck 373
Société Anonyme, New York, 248
Soldner, Paul, 204
Sommer, Frederick, 21
Southern California, University of, Los Angeles, 208
South Seas art, 70
Soutine, Chaim, 158
Soyer, Raphael, 17, ck 373
Spear, Athena Tacha, 239
Spencer, Niles, 23, ck 373
   The Desk, 23
Spiro, Eugene, ck 373
Spohn, Clay, 166, 192
Spokane University, Wash., 150
Spreckels, Mr. and Mrs. Adolph, 15
Stackpole, Ralph, 20, 186, ck 374
Stadler, Albert, ck 374
Stahly, François, ck 374
Staiger, Paul, ck 374
Stamos, Theodore, 23, ck 374
Stanczak, Julian, ck 374
Stanford University, 19, 178
Starr, Sandra Leonard, 247
Stauffacher, Frank, 21
Stein, Gertrude, 34
Stein, Leo, 34
Stein, Michael, 16, 17, 34; portrait of, by Matisse, 34, 35, *36*

Stein, Sarah (née Samuels), 16, 17, 34–35; portrait of, by Matisse, 34–35, *37*
Steinlen, Théophile, 48
Stella, Frank, 27, 214, 216, 220, 257, ck 374–75
   Adelante, 24, 214, *215*, 257
   Aluminum Series, 214
   Benjamin Moore Series, 214
   Black Paintings, 214
   Copper Series, 214
   Irregular Polygon Series, 216
   Khurasan Gate (Variation) I, 216, *217*, 257
   Moroccan Series, 216
   Protractor Series, 216, 257
   Running V Series, 214, 216, 257
Stella, Joseph, 119, 130, 132, 248, ck 375
   Bridge, 132, *133*, 248
   New York Interpreted, 132
Stephan, Gary, ck 375
Sterne, Maurice, ck 375
Stevens, May, ck 376
Stiegelmeyer, Norman, ck 376
Stieglitz, Alfred, 22, 122, 124, 126
Stijl, De, 80, 82, 94
Still, Clyfford, 25, 27, 148, 150, 152–53, 166, 186, 190, 192, 222, 230, 251–52, ck 376–79
   Self-Portrait. SEE Untitled (1945)
   Untitled (1945), 21, 150, *151*, 250–51
   Untitled (1951–52), 152–53, *154*, 252
   Untitled (1960), 152–53, *155*, 252
Stoppenbach, Richard, 238
Storrs, John, 28, 130, 248, ck 380
   Forms in Space series, 130
   Studies in Architectural Form series, 130
   Study in Form (Architectural Form), 130, *131*, 248
   Study in Form I, 248
   Study in Form II, 248
   Study in Form III, 248
Strand, Paul, 21, 27, 28, 126
Streeter, Tal, ck 380
Strong, Charles, ck 380
Stuck, Jack, ck 380
Sturm, Der, gallery, Berlin, 242
Suarez, Antonio, ck 380
Sugai, Kumi, ck 380
Sullivan, Louis, 130
Supers, James, ck 381
Surrealism, 17, 18, 22, 58, 84, 96, 98, 102, 108, 110, 112, 114, 116, 118, 146, 148, 150, 156, 158, 164, 166, 222; Abstract Surrealism, 17; Post-Surrealism, 17
Survage, Leopold, ck 381
Susuka, Yoshiyasu, ck 381
Swift, Henry, Collection, 23
Symbolism, 38
Synchromism, 66

Tabard, Maurice, 28
Tamayo, Rufino, ck 381
Tanguy, Yves, 17, 19, 96, 114, 118, 246, ck 381

Arrières-pensées. SEE *Second Thoughts*
   Second Thoughts, 114, *115*, 246
Tato (Guglielmo Sansoni), 28
Taubes, Frederick, ck 381
Tchakalian, Sam, ck 381–82
Teixidor, Jorge, ck 382
Teske, Edmund, 24
Thannhauser, Moderne Galerie, Munich, 242
Theosophy, 52, 80
Thiebaud, Wayne, 24, 226, 258, ck 382
   Display Cakes, 226, *227*, 258
Timiriasieff, John, ck 382
Tobey, Mark, 142, 144, 250, ck 382–83
   Written over the Plains, 144, *145*, 250
Todd, Michael, ck 383
Toronto, Art Gallery of, 248
Torr, Helen, ck 383
Torres-García, Joaquín, 84, 243, ck 383
   Constructivist Painting No. 8, 84, *85*, 243
Toulouse-Lautrec, Henri de, 42, 48
Traphagen Commercial Textile Studio, New York, 119
Treasure Island, San Francisco, 18
Troyes, Musée d'Art Moderne de la Ville de, 239
Tsujimoto, Karen, 26
Tudor, David, 194
Tullis, Garner, ck 383
Tuttle, Richard, ck 383
Twachtman, John, 14
Twombly, Cy, 25
"291," gallery, New York, 122, 126
Tworkov, Jack, ck 383–84

Umbo (Otto Umbehr), 28
United Nations, 20
United States, Department of the Interior, 25
Unterseher, Chris, ck 384
Urbana, University of Illinois, 178
Usui, Bumpei, ck 384
Utrillo, Maurice, ck 384

Vaadia, Boaz, ck 384
Vaea (Marx), ck 384
Vail, Laurence, ck 384
Van Buren, Richard, ck 385
Van Dyke, Willard, 23
Vantongerloo, George, 84
Varda, Jean, ck 385
Vasarely, Victor, ck 385
Vasica, Joseph, ck 385
Velázquez, Diego Rodriguez de Silva y, 48
Vicente, Esteban, ck 385
Vieira da Silva, Maria Elena, ck 385
Villon, Jacques, 28
Virginia, University of, Charlottesville, 122
Vlaminck, Maurice, 32, 44
Von Meyer, Michael, ck 385
Vorticism, 130
Voulkos, Peter, 24, 204, 206, 208, 224, 230, 256, ck 385–86
   Sevillanas, 204, *205*, 256
Vredaparis, ck 386
Vuillard, Edouard, 14

Walburg, Gerald, ck 386
Walker, T. B., Foundation Fund, 23, 24, 28
Walker Art Center, Minneapolis, 22, 25
Walter, Mrs. Caroline, 250
Warhol, Andy, 28, 198
Washington [D.C.] Gallery of Modern Art, 23
Washington State College, Pullman, 27, 150
Wasserstein, Julius, ck 387
Wattis, Mrs. Paul L., Fund, 28
Weber, Max, 17, 130
Weeks, James, 23, ck 387–88
Weiler, Clemens, 242
Welliver, Neil, ck 388
Wells, Mason, ck 388
Westermann, H. C., ck 388
Weston, Brett, 20, 21, 23
Weston, Edward, 20, 21, 22, 23, 24, 28
Weston, Harold, ck 388
Whanki. SEE Kim Whanki
Whistler, James McNeill, 14, 16
White, Joseph, ck 389
White, Minor, 21
Whitney Museum of American Art, New York, 26, 241
Wiley, William T., 23, 24, 28, 222, 228, 234, 258, ck 389
   Ship's Log, 222, *223*, 258
Wilke, Ulfert, ck 390
Williams, Franklin, ck 390
Wilmarth, Christopher, ck 390
Wilson, Bryan, ck 390
Wilson, Ed, ck 391
Winsor, Jackie, ck 391
Winter, Fritz, ck 391
Withers, Josephine, 241
Witkin, Isaac, 28, ck 391
Witkin, Joel-Peter, 28
Woelffer, Emerson, ck 391
Wolfe, Bertram, 250
Wonner, Paul, 28, ck 391–92
Worth, Don, 24
Wotruba, Fritz, 204
WPA (Works Progress Administration) Federal Arts Project, 132, 168, 248

Yagi, Kazuo, ck 392
Yale University, New Haven, 94, 198, 220
Yektai, Manoucher, ck 392
Youngerman, Jack, ck 392

Zajac, Jack, ck 392
Zammitt, Norman, ck 392
Zao Wou-ki, ck 392
Zaritsky, Joseph, ck 393
Zecher, Peter, ck 393
Zen, 142, 144, 204
Zogbaum, Wilfrid, ck 393
Zorach, William, ck 393

Index of Donors

This index also includes individuals in whose honor or memory works of art have been donated.

Aberbach, Julian and Jean, 130, 248, 318, 380

Abrams, Michael D., 387

Ackerman, Mrs. Lloyd S. SEE Louise S. Ackerman

Ackerman, Lloyd S., Jr., Memorial Fund, 334

Ackerman, Lloyd Stuart, Memorial, 342

Ackerman, Louise S., 76, 242, 271, 280, 392

Albers, Anni, 94, 194, 244, 262, 263

Albers, Josef, Foundation, 27, 94, 244, 262, 263

Aldrich, Larry, 392

Alfi, Zmira, 263

Alon, Gene, 261

American Art Foundation, 210, 257, 271, 328, 365

American Federation of Arts, 264, 286, 334, 370, 372

Anderson, Mr. and Mrs. Harry W., 11, 152, 153, 186, 194, 196, 252, 255, 263, 272, 311, 321, 354, 361, 368, 379; Fund, 383

Anglim, Philip, 333

Anka, Mr. and Mrs. Paul, 387

Arensberg, Mr. and Mrs. Walter C., 342

Argentine Republic, 301

Armer, Ruth, in memory of, 269

Arts Fund, Inc., 374

Baldwin, Russell, 268

Bank of America, 347

Baredor Foundation, 353

Barnes, Matthew, Trust, 269

Barney, Arthur W., Bequest Fund, 263, 289

Barnlund, Dean, 272

Bass, Bill, 306

Baum, Alvin H., Jr., 358

Baxter, Mrs. F. K., 270

Baxter, Frances, 270

Baxter, John, in memory of, 299

Bell, Michele and Mercury, 358, 382, 384

Bender, Albert M., 10, 16, 19, 21, 118, 138, 140, 247, 249, 250, 266, 273, 275, 278, 281, 282, 285, 288, 289, 290, 293, 303, 304, 314, 317, 321, 322, 323, 326, 328, 329, 330, 342, 344, 349, 356, 357, 360, 361, 364, 368, 375, 385; Bequest Fund, 100, 148, 204, 245, 251, 256, 313, 327, 331, 358, 364, 385; Bequest of, 280, 281, 282, 289, 297, 298, 322, 353, 361, 370; Fund, 365; in memory of, 298; Memorial Fund, 269

Berger, Mr. and Mrs. Eric, 386

Bergeron, Victor, 280

Berggruen, John, 269, 273, 290; Gallery, San Francisco, 304

Bernell, Dr. William, 284

Bienstock, Anne and Peter, 333

Birge, Priscilla, 312

Black, Dr. and Mrs. Melvin B., 380

Bliss, Mildred B., 340

Blum, Irving, 287, 291, 304, 366, 371

Bocour, Leonard, 316

Boone, Charles, 308

Boone, Elizabeth Sharpe, in memory of, 308

Bourne, Agnes C. and William C., 276, 318

Bourne, Agnes Cowles, 230, 258, 349

Bowers, Cheryl O., 276

Bransten, Ellen Hart, in memory of, 270, 290, 294, 343

Bransten, John, 326

Bransten, Mr. and Mrs. John, 341

Bransten, Joseph M., 11, 108, 246, 269, 270, 290, 320, 343; Bequest of, 178, 254, 294

Bransten, Mr. and Mrs. Joseph M., 277

Bransten, Mrs. Joseph M., 293

Bransten, Mrs. Manfred, Fund, 390; Special Fund, 134, 226, 248, 258, 286, 370, 382

Bransten, Rena, 11, 264, 267, 268, 270, 313, 319, 324, 383

Braunstein, Ruth, 383

Breschi, Karen, 278

Brigante, Nick, 278

Bruehl, Anton, 284

Bufano, Marian, 280

Bullock, Benbow and Jean, 289

Bush, Pamela Djerassi, in memory of, 305

Campbell, Charles, 346

Caplan, Arthur L., 354

Carnwath, Squeak, 284

Castelli, Leo, 288

Cheronis, Dion, 366

Chicago, Judy (née Gerowitz), 285

Chidester, Mrs. Drew, 265, 300

Clark, Mr. and Mrs. Hervey Parke, 339

Coburn, Maurine Church, 298

Cohen, Arthur J., Jr., in memory of, 342

Cole, David, 345, 361

Comara Gallery, Los Angeles, 373

Conkey, Dr. Austin, 295

Conkey, Evelyn Blunt, in memory of, 274

Conkey, Floyd Douglas, in memory of, 274

Cooper, Paula, 385

Corbett, Rosamond Walling, 288

Corcoran, James, 288; Gallery, Inc., Los Angeles, 393

Cox, E. Morris, 62, 240, 241, 307

Cox, Mr. and Mrs. E. Morris, 11, 352

Cox, Margaret Storke, from the collection of, 307

Crocker, Gertrude Hopkins, Memorial Fund, 284

Crocker, Templeton, 316; Fund, 96, 245, 285

Crocker, William H. and Ethel W., Family Fund, 170, 253, 310

Crocker, William W., 10, 16, 22, 54, 56, 58, 239, 240, 277, 283, 312, 340, 344, 357, 365, 369, 381; Memorial Fund, 330

Cummings, Nathan, 34, 237, 340

Curry, Roy and Helga, 358

Dailey, Gardner, 357

Daniels, Mr. and Mrs. Alfred H., 271

David-Weill, Pierre, 328

De Forest, Roy and Gloria, 280

deGooyer, Kirk, 332

Delman, Jacob, 380

Devine, Mr. and Mrs. David B., 314

Devine, David B., 320, 380

Diao, David, 293

Dickenman, Dr. Robert C., 276

Dickinson, Wade and Eleanor, 369

Dinner, Mr. and Mrs. Richard, 393

Dirickson, Mr. and Mrs. Richard, Jr., 390

Djerassi, Carl, and Norma Djerassi Art Trust, 305

Doll, Mr. and Mrs. H. G., 328

Dorfner, Gerda, Memorial Fund, 387

Dreifus, Mr. and Mrs. Charles, Jr., 270

Dreifus, Donna B., in memory of, 270

Droll, Donald, 274

Dudley, Sharon, 296

Durham, Willard, 84, 243, 383

Ehresmann, A. A., 350, 393

Eisenhardt, Roy and Elizabeth, 306

Ekman, Dr. Paul, 348

Elisofon, Elin, 298

Elkus, Mr. and Mrs. Charles, 349

Engelhart, Mr. and Mrs. Forrest, 281, 300, 301

Escobosa, Hector, in memory of, 294

Estler, William, 279

Factor, Betty and Monte, 326

Fairman, Derek M., 276, 362

Fanfani, Mr. and Mrs. Amintore, 299

Faralla, Richard, 265, 299, 370

Feigen, Richard L., 288

Feigen, Mr. and Mrs. Richard L., 325

Feinberg, Joy E., Berkeley, 336

Feitelson, Lorser and Helen Lundeberg Feitelson Arts Foundation, Los Angeles, 300

Fenton, Dr. and Mrs. Robert, 297, 309

Ferren, Roy, 301

Field, Mr. and Mrs. Leonard S., 299

Fielder, Dr. William R., 341

Fielder, Dr. and Mrs. William R., 308, 314, 315, 318, 323

First Savings and Loan Association, San Francisco, 362

Fisher, Doris and Donald, 261; Purchase Fund, 28, 324

Flax, Herman, 346, 385

Fleishhacker, Mr. and Mrs. Mortimer, 374

Ford Foundation, 302

Forme-Becherat, Jean Louis, 373

Foster Goldstrom Fine Arts, 341

Fountain, Wil and Marilyn, 265

Francis, Sam, 319, 320, 343, 372

Freeman, Betty, 168, 253, 310

Freeman, Richard B., 296

Friends of the Museum, 68, 241, 320, 323, 337

Fromowitz, Dr. Arthur, 363

Frumkin, Allan, 278

Fuller Goldeen Gallery, San Francisco, 284

Furay, Michael, 350

Gardner, Dr. and Mrs. Richard, 348
Gardner, Dr. and Mrs. W. William, 287
Gaskin, William, 269
Gelfman, Eva, 365
Gersh, Mrs. Philip, 266
Gerstle, William L., 10, 16, 21, 88, 118, 244, 247, 280, 288, 324, 325, 329, 332, 374, 381; Fund, 24, 106, 114, 188, 222, 246, 255, 258, 263, 266, 267, 275, 276, 279, 290, 305, 317, 319, 326, 343, 348, 349, 350, 352, 362, 373, 374, 381, 389, 390
Gianelloni, Marjorie, 285, 316
Gianelloni, Mrs. V. J. SEE Marjorie Gianelloni
Goldberg, Arthur A., 318
Goldberg, Mr. and Mrs. Arthur A., 368
Goldman, Mr. and Mrs. Richard N., 92, 244, 262
Goodman, Wally, 273
Grant, Art, 308
Grippa, Mr. and Mrs. Anthony, 376
Grisanti, Don Albert, 305
Gross, Zora, 358
Guggenheim, Peggy, 10, 21, 82, 148, 150, 153, 164, 243, 251, 253, 261, 267, 295, 298, 355, 357, 365, 377, 384
Gump's, Inc., 325
Guston, Philip, 27, 176, 254, 309, 310

Haas, Elise Stern, 5, 11, 22, 29–30, 34, 52, 237, 239, 277, 281, 296, 298, 314, 340, 347, 368, 387
Haas, Evelyn and Walter, Jr., Fund, 28, 102, 208, 245, 256, 266, 359, 364, 383. SEE ALSO Mr. and Mrs. Walter A. Haas, Jr.
Haas, Peter, Jr., 288
Haas, Mr. and Mrs. Robert D., 306
Haas, Mrs. Walter. SEE Elise Stern Haas
Haas, Mr. and Mrs. Walter A., 10, 337
Haas, Mrs. Walter A. SEE Elise Stern Haas
Haas, Mr. and Mrs. Walter A., Jr., 386. SEE ALSO Evelyn and Walter Haas, Jr., Fund
Haas, Mrs. Walter A., Jr., 11
Haas, Mr. and Mrs. Walter J., 306
Hack, Mr. and Mrs. Paul W., 310, 311
Hague, William E., 306
Hamilton, Frank O., 224, 258, 370, 388
Hamilton-Wells Collection, 11, 228, 258, 269, 273, 280, 290, 292, 296, 307, 313, 314, 334, 348, 351, 372, 381, 386, 391
Harwood, Mr. and Mrs. James, 382
Hatch, Ann, 373
Hayakawa, S. I., 344
Heller, Alfred E., 279, 328
Heller, Mrs. E. S., 136, 249, 291, 293
Hellyer, Sally, 342. SEE ALSO Sally Lilienthal
Henderson, Mr. and Mrs. Wellington S., 50, 166, 239, 253, 333, 385

Henderson, Mrs. Wellington S., 296, 301
Henkin, Dr. William A., 324
Hermes, Louis A., 277
Herrmann, Carlo, 331
Heuvel, Jan Stein vanden, 305
Hidai, Nankoku, 314
Hilger, Charles, 314
Hills, Mrs. Nancy, 372
Holas, Raymond, 268
Honig, Louis, 392
Honig, Mr. and Mrs. Louis, 116, 246, 305, 336, 346, 347, 363, 393
Honig, Miriam, 264
Honig, Victor, 352
Horelick, Jules, 324, 337
Howard, Robert B., 264, 267, 279, 287, 292, 308, 317, 325, 349, 362, 372
Hume, Jaquelin H., 368
Hume, Mrs. Jaquelin H., 286
Humphrey, John, in honor of, 271, 333; in memory of, 370

Jackson, Martha, Gallery, New York, 297
Janss, Edwin, 292, 345, 357, 372
Janss, Mr. and Mrs. William C., 11, 28, 160, 192, 252, 255, 262, 272, 276, 283, 291, 292, 315, 320, 321, 327, 331, 336, 338, 372, 389, 391
Jaretzki, Mr. and Mrs. Alfred, Jr., 261
Jenkins, Paul, 336
Jones, Mr. and Mrs. John Lowell, 297
Joseph, Dr. and Mrs. Harold, 313

Kallman, Edith, 323
Kanemitsu, Shizumi Patia, 324
Kantor, Paul, 354
Kantor, Mr. and Mrs. Paul, 391
Karnebeek, J. D. van, 302
Keesling, Mary and Frank, 333
Keesling, Mary Heath, 287, 296, 348
Kim, Mrs. Whanki, 327
Kinkead, Angela and Robin, 320
Kirk, E. Bruce, 326
Klokke, Helen, 300, 335
Kluger, David, 268
Knechtges, Harlan J., in memory of, 341
Krasnow, Peter, 328, 329
Krasnow, Mr. and Mrs. Robert, 368

Labaudt, Lucien, 64, 241, 329, 353
Ladies Auxiliary of the Palace of Fine Arts, 388
Land, Charles H., Family Foundation Fund, 11, 28, 294, 392
Lannan, J. Patrick, 350
Larsson, Raymond, 326
Lasarow, Judge and Mrs. William J., 392
Lasky, Mr. and Mrs. Moses, 279, 297, 298, 304, 316, 338, 387
Lasky, Ruth and Moses, Fund, 28
Lauter, Mr. and Mrs. Robert S., 354
Lederman, Mrs. E. D., 265, 322
Lejwa, Dr. and Mrs. Arthur, 339

L'Esperance, Dr. and Mrs. Francis, 323
Levine, Mr. and Mrs. Jay J., 309
Levy, Harriet Lane, 10, 16, 22, 32, 38, 40, 44, 48, 236, 237, 238, 239, 293, 297, 305, 336, 339, 340, 341, 357
Lexen, Mr. and Mrs. Gene, 380
Lilienthal, Sally, 261, 334, 358, 363, 367. SEE ALSO Sally Hellyer
Lincoln, Norma, in memory of, 387
Lockwood, Clyde Bonebrake, 334
Long, Mr. and Mrs. Meredith, 282
Lorenz, Richard, 367
Louie, Lenore M., 334
Lowell, Dr. A. G. B., 289
Lucas, James, 358

MacAgy, Jermayne, 20, 22, 27, 278, 294, 312
McCann, Robert E., 279
McCulloch, Mr. and Mrs. David, 308
McMurray, Annie, 370
Mack, Charlotte, 10, 22, 72, 90, 122, 124, 242, 244, 247, 261, 293, 299, 319, 344, 351, 356
Magnin, Cyril, 267, 385
Matthias, Blanche C., 375; Bequest of, 381
May, Wilbur D., 10, 23, 42, 60, 110, 238, 240, 246, 275, 284, 293, 295, 327, 343, 357
Melzac, Vincent, 295
Members' Accessions Fund, 263, 268, 272, 322, 337, 338, 370
Membership Activities Board, 325, 350
Meyer, Agnes E., 22, 52, 239, 277
Meyer, Byron, 28, 224, 258, 338, 363, 370, 385; Fund, 232, 258, 318
Meyerhoff, Robert, 372
Modern Art Council, 11, 28, 202, 234, 256, 258, 266, 273, 287, 352
Moholy-Nagy, Sibyl, 86, 243, 343
Moore, Kristin, 264
Morley, Grace L. McCann, in honor of, 325
Mundt, Scott, 346

Nash, Ruth, Fund, 347
National Endowment for the Arts, 28, 30, 224, 258, 274, 283, 286, 288, 291, 295, 301, 302, 304, 311, 313, 320, 323, 331, 333, 351, 352, 360, 362, 363, 370, 383, 384, 391
Neilsen, Anna, 271
Neuberger, Mr. and Mrs. Roy R., 267
New Future Fund Drive, 283, 286, 288, 291, 301, 304, 313, 333, 360, 362, 391
Newman, Jim and Judy. SEE Mr. and Mrs. L. James Newman
Newman, Mr. and Mrs. L. James, 324, 327, 363, 382, 390
Ng, Win, 296, 302, 303, 311, 369, 386
Nichols, Mrs. W. Floyd, 303

Nordland, Gerald, friends of, 182, 254, 294
Nouri, Mr. and Mrs. Edmond, 367

Onslow Ford, Jacqueline Marie, 341, 352, 390
Owings, Mr. and Mrs. Nathaniel, 282

Paag, Jan T., 271
Paine, Mr. and Mrs. Stephen D., 263
Pearlstein, Ned C., 272, 392
Peet, Mrs. Creighton, 369
Petersen, Roland, 348, 355
Pflueger, Milton T., 327
Pflueger, Timothy L., in memory of, 327
Phoenix Gallery/Editions, San Francisco, 355
Picher, William S., 273
Poindexter, Mr. and Mrs. George, 348, 368
Poindexter, Mrs. George, 313
Postley, Mr. and Mrs. Clarence, 373
Putzel, Howard, 381

Quay Ceramics Gallery, San Francisco, 354

Rabinowitz, Martin J., 297
Rabow, Alexandre, in memory of, 336, 362
Rabow, Rose, 362
Ramer, Dr. Barry, 289
Ramer, Dr. Cyril, 289
Reynal, Jeanne, 10, 21, 146, 250, 308, 312
Rivera, Diego, friends of, 364
Robinson, Mr. and Mrs. C. David, 266, 269, 284, 307, 374, 390
Robinson, Mr. and Mrs. Hamilton, Jr., 301, 375
Robinson, Steven L., 315
Rockere, Herbert, 364
Roos, Dr. and Mrs. Allan, 303, 366
Rosa, Rene di, 302, 318
Rosa, Mr. and Mrs. Rene di, 300
Rosenberg, James N., 297
Rosener, Margaret H., in honor of, 346
Ross, Mr. and Mrs. C. George, 275
Ross, Charles, 294
Roth, William M., 304, 364, 387
Roth, Mr. and Mrs. William M., 118, 247, 288, 290, 299, 325, 330, 337, 350, 371
Rowan, Robert A., 307, 375
Ruben, Richards, 366
Rubin, Lawrence, 351
Rudd, Irving G., 366
Rushing, Mr. and Mrs. Herbert, 313
Russack, Suzanne and Neil, 335
Russell, Helen Crocker, Family Fund, 170, 253, 310; friends of, 156, 252, 345; in honor of, 330; Memorial Fund, 302, 320, 332, 347, 353, 360. SEE ALSO Mrs. Henry Potter Russell

Russell, Mrs. Henry Potter, 10, 337, 364; Bequest of, 340, 344, 361, 365, 366
Russell, Mr. and Mrs. Leon, 331
Russell, Madeleine Haas, 92, 244, 262, 318, 333; Fund, 28
Ryan, Beatrice Judd, Bequest Fund, 382

Salz, Mr. and Mrs. Ansley K., 330, 348, 367
Salz, Mrs. Ansley K., 265, 356
San Francisco Women Artists, 342
Sarkis, George, 309
Sasco, Adolfo J., 383
Saveri, Guido, 285
Saveri, Richard, 285
Sawyer, Dr. William C., 268, 284, 286, 307, 319, 328
Schaefer-Simmern, Dr. Henry, 270; students of, 365
Schlesinger, Albert E., 371
Schlesinger, Mr. and Mrs. Peter, 273
Schlesinger, Mrs. Peter, 224, 258, 370
Schley, Grant Barney, in memory of, 281
Schley, Lisbeth Backer, in memory of, 281
Schmidt, Dorothy and Paul, 312
Schorer, Mr. and Mrs. Mark, 184, 254, 274
Schreiber, Rita and Toby, 272, 375
Schroll, Maud Hill, 334
Schulthess, Amalia Loew de, 336
Schulthess, Hans G. M. de, 336
Schwartz, Robert G., 311
Schwartz, Schlomo, 384
Security Pacific National Bank, 367
Sedgwick, Edith, in memory of, 305
Selz, Peter, 366
Seymour, Dr. and Mrs. Robert, 338
Shansby, J. Gary, 388
Shapazian, Robert, 28
Shirley, Virginia, 359, 360
Silva, Larry J., 276
Sindler, Lenore and Allan, 369, 391
Sinton, Mr. and Mrs. Edgar, 353, 355
Sinton, Mrs. Edgar. SEE Marian W. Sinton
Sinton, Marian W., 11, 46, 78, 238, 243, 266, 271, 302, 331, 353, 355, 386
Sinton, Nell, 286, 291
Sinton, Stanley H., Jr., 374
Siri, Roman Fresnedo, 383
Slaughter, Betty and Glen, 360
Sloss, Mrs. Leon, 342; Fund, 349
Smith, Mr. and Mrs. Ferdinand C., 144, 250, 383

Smith, Mrs. Ferdinand C., 10, 304, 392; Fund, 28, 170, 253, 310, 345, 348, 354. SEE ALSO Margery Hoffman Smith Trust
Smith, Grant, 371
Smith, Margery Hoffman, Trust, 305. SEE ALSO Mrs. Ferdinand C. Smith
Smith Andersen Gallery, Palo Alto, 314
Soap Box Derby Fund, 274, 283, 286, 288, 291, 301, 302, 304, 313, 331, 333, 343, 360, 362, 363
Society for the Encouragement of Contemporary Art, 200, 256, 291, 298, 341
Soker-Kaseman Gallery, San Francisco, 381
Speigl, Dr. Ralph, 276
Staempfli Gallery, New York, 309, 329
Stern, Lucie, Trust Fund, 263
Stern, Mr. and Mrs. Philip M., 392
Stern, Rosalie M., Bequest Fund, 126, 247, 295
Stern, Mrs. Sigmund, in memory of, 293
Still, Clyfford, 11, 27, 152, 252, 376–79
Streeter, Tal, 380
Strong, Charles, 320
Stuart, David, 334
Stulsaft, Morris, 362
Stuppin, John B. and Jane K., 382
Stussy, Mr. and Mrs. Jan, 371
Sugarman, Dr. George, 391
Sullivan, Mr. and Mrs. Jerd, 367
Swift, Henry, 23
Swig, Mr. and Mrs. Richard, 393

Taylor, Mr. and Mrs. Archibald, 312
Thacher, Mr. and Mrs. Carter P., 381
Tirana, Bardyl Rifat, 288
Tirana, Turhan W., 288
Todd, Kathryn and Michael, 294
Trousdale, Paul, 355
Turko, Harry, 283
Tworkov, Jack, 384
Tyler, Mrs. B. Langdon, 303

Van Liew, Mary Birdsall, 270
Vicente, Mr. and Mrs. Esteban, 385
Victor, Dr. and Mrs. Ralph, 275
Villa, Carlos, 390
Voulkos, Peter, 326, 366

Walker, Alma, friends of, 370
Walker, Mr. and Mrs. Brooks, 317
Walker, Clinton, Fund, 324, 369

Walker, Mr. and Mrs. George C., 346
Walker, Margaret K., in memory of, 314, 338; Memorial Fund, 295
Walker, Peter, 296
Walker, T. B., Foundation, 10–11; Foundation Fund, 23, 24, 28, 212, 214, 218, 220, 257, 264, 265, 271, 274, 275, 283, 308, 309, 319, 325, 328, 332, 335, 336, 337, 369, 374, 383, 386
Walter, Caroline, in memory of, 364
Warner Communications Inc., 352
Wattis, Paul L., Special Fund, 170, 253, 274, 277, 279, 298, 310
Wattis, Mrs. Paul L., 11, 369, 383; Fund, 28
Weinberg, Daniel, 263, 375
Weisel, Thomas W., 291, 349
Weisman, Frederick, Company, 272, 361
Weisman, Mr. and Mrs. Frederick R., 216, 257, 375
Weisman, Marcia, 272
Wellin, Keith, 380
West, Dr. Samuel A., 317, 389
Whalen, Pearl Joseph, in memory of, 264
Wilbur, Brayton, 371; in memory of, 294
Wilstein, Denise, 312
Wirtz, Stephen and Connie, 343
Wise, Dr. and Mrs. David T., 386
Wolf, Dr. Barbara de, 301
Women's Board, 11, 16, 21, 22, 23, 24, 28, 68, 162, 206, 241, 253, 256, 261, 264, 268, 274, 287, 290, 292, 293, 294, 295, 299, 302, 315, 317, 319, 325, 329, 330, 332, 333, 337, 338, 345, 350, 352, 353, 354, 363, 373, 374, 387, 388, 389, 390
Woodsum, Channing J., 268
Woodsum, Judith L., 268
WPA Federal Arts Project Allocation, 132, 248, 269, 286, 309, 314, 316, 317, 331, 335, 347, 359, 360, 375, 384
Wright, Mr. and Mrs. Bagley, 287, 352

Yabroff, Samuel, 356

Zeitlin, Jacob, 321
Zellerbach, J. D., in memory of, 294
Zellerbach, Harold, 286
Zlotnick, Diana, 285, 321, 352, 356
Zogbaum, Wilfrid, friends of, 393
Zorthian, Seyburn, 276

Photo Credits

All color photographs were taken by Don Myer except the following:
Rudi Bender: pp. 151, 154, 155
Ben Blackwell: pp. 203, 223
eeva-inkeri, Courtesy Allan Frumkin Gallery, New York: p. 233
Phillip Galgiani: pp. 123, 131, 135, 143
Douglas M. Parker, Courtesy Daniel Weinberg Gallery, Los Angeles: p. 221
Rafael Salazar: p. 141
Joe Samberg: pp. 183, 217
Joe Schopplein: pp. 36, 37, 59

The black and white photographs reproduced in the Checklist were taken primarily by Phillip Galgiani, Don Myer, and Joe Schopplein. Additional photographs were supplied by: Courtesy Gallery Paule Anglim, San Francisco; Jim Ball; Rudi Bender; Ben Blackwell; eeva-inkeri; M. Lee Fatheree; Dwain Faubion; Courtesy Flow/Ace Gallery, Venice, California; Roger Gass; Courtesy Grapestake Gallery, San Francisco; William Hawken; Paul Klein; Scott McCue; Courtesy Quay Gallery, San Francisco; Joe Samberg; Courtesy William Sawyer Gallery, San Francisco; Robert Shankar; Steven Sloman; Courtesy Stanford University, California